Lincoln & Darwin

LINCOLN & DARWIN

Shared Visions of Race, Science, and Religion

James Lander

Southern Illinois University Press
Carbondale and Edwardsville

13 12 11 10   4 3 2 1

Library of Congress Cataloging-in-Publication Data
Lander, James.
Lincoln and Darwin : shared visions of race, science, and
religion / James Lander.
      p. cm.
Includes bibliographical references and index.
ISBN-13: 978-0-8093-2990-8 (cloth : alk. paper)
ISBN-10: 0-8093-2990-5 (cloth : alk. paper)
ISBN-13: 978-0-8093-8586-7 (ebook)
ISBN-10: 0-8093-8586-4 (ebook)
1. Lincoln, Abraham, 1809–1865—Philosophy. 2. Lincoln,
Abraham, 1809–1865—Religion. 3. Darwin, Charles, 1809–
1882—Philosophy. 4. Darwin, Charles, 1809–1882—Religion.
5. Presidents—United States—Biography. 6. Naturalists—Great
Britain—Biography. I. Title.
E457.2.L226 2010
973.7092—dc22   2009041678

Printed on recycled paper. ♻
The paper used in this publication meets the minimum
requirements of American National Standard for Information Sciences—Permanence of Paper for Printed Library
Materials, ANSI z39.48-1992. ∞

For Sarah, who has been so patient and encouraging

And on this day, that is also the bicentennial of Charles Darwin's birth, it's worth a moment to pause and renew that commitment to science and innovation and discovery that Lincoln understood so well.
—President Barack Obama, addressing the Abraham Lincoln Association, in Springfield, Illinois, on 12 February 2009

You must allow me to thank you heartily for the very great pleasure which it has in many ways given us. I always thought well of the negroes, from the little which I have seen of them; and I have been delighted to have my vague impressions confirmed, and their character and mental powers so ably discussed.
—Charles Darwin to former Union general Thomas Wentworth Higginson, praising his book *Life with a Black Regiment*, 27 February 1873

Contents

Illustrations gallery follows page 96

Preface

This study of certain mutual interests of Abraham Lincoln and Charles Darwin argues that they had surprisingly similar values, purposes, and approaches. It is not a dual biography, although it does trace the somewhat parallel development of the two men and their perspectives mainly in chronological order—except in the introduction, which uses a particular point in their lives to bring forward the subtitled themes regarding the mid-nineteenth-century collision between science and abolitionism. Lincoln and Darwin had no family link, did not share a common profession, were not rivals, came from very different backgrounds, and never met or even visited each other's country. They did not directly influence each other's views, yet they shared certain ideas that actually set them apart from most of their contemporaries. Of course, some contemporaries—and predecessors—did endorse ideas similar to theirs, providing a "common context" that must not be ignored.[1] However, Lincoln and Darwin were not running with the pack but were ahead of it, and they managed to draw it along a path it might not otherwise have chosen (or at least not so soon). When we recognize that Lincoln and Darwin were both leading society toward greater freedom of thought and a greater acceptance of human equality, we begin to understand the debt we owe them.

Lincoln and Darwin could not have been more "contemporary," having been born on the same day, a link significant only for an astrologer, which I am not. My interest in each man had separate origins: the first biography I can remember reading as a boy was of Lincoln, and my fascination with him has never ceased, while my curiosity about Darwin developed only a dozen years ago.

In 2005, a study collated surveys in thirty-four countries where people were asked to respond "true," "false," or "not sure" to the statement "Human beings, as we know them, developed from earlier species of animals." Of those surveyed in the United States, 39 percent answered "false," and the only country with a larger percentage was Turkey (51 percent).[2] Turkey was the only Muslim country in this study, but it was included in a later study of six Muslim countries that indicated that most were even less accepting of human evolution than Turkey, "one of the most educated and secular of Muslim countries."[3] For a quarter of a century, I have taught in an international school in Britain where half of my (highly affluent) students come from America and another large group from Islamic countries. A significant minority of students from these two groups has been raised to accept a religious rather than a scientific view of the origins of mankind, and a few have been openly hostile toward Darwin—while knowing little about him. While endeavoring to learn more about Darwin and about creationism, I increasingly became aware that certain values and interests of

Darwin overlapped those of Lincoln, and this awareness in turn made me wish to examine Lincoln in a new light.

I began serious research about 2001, thinking I might easily produce a small book in time to cash in on the 2009 bicentenary of their births. However, relevant material proved far more abundant than I had expected, partly thanks to the digitization of Lincoln's and Darwin's writings. In the spring of 2008, as I was completing my rough draft, David R. Contosta published *Rebel Giants: The Revolutionary Lives of Abraham Lincoln and Charles Darwin*, which, ultimately, did not explore the topics that interested me and only strengthened my feeling that a brief dual biography was not the best approach to these men and their ideas. Another study, Adam Gopnik's *Angels and Ages: A Short Book about Darwin, Lincoln, and Modern Life*, appeared just before the 2009 bicentenary, but the main focus of this brief work was on the two men's literary qualities. Dozens of other books about Lincoln or Darwin individually appeared at this same time, and two works particularly overlapped my own interests. Darwin scholars Adrian Desmond and James Moore produced an excellent book-length treatment of the influence of Darwin's abolitionism, *Darwin's Sacred Cause: Race, Slavery, and the Quest for Human Origins*.[4] And Jason Emerson's brief but well-researched *Lincoln the Inventor* touches on some issues that appear in this book.

When comparing any two men from roughly the same period who lived in radically different and rapidly changing environments, a good "Darwinian" would note divergent adaptations that might prove instructive. However, in the present case, the test is certainly skewed by the fact that Lincoln and Darwin were not "any two men" but extraordinary figures of the nineteenth century whose impact continues to the present day. Excellent biographies exist for each—all the less reason for a dual biography. It is frequently remarked that in America, annually, only Jesus has more books published about him than Abraham Lincoln; while Darwin has the rare distinction among scientists of never becoming obsolete: his texts are still *in print* a century and a half after he wrote them, and Darwinism shows no signs of being eclipsed by some new "ism." Measured by any standard of greatness—even down to having one's bearded face on one's national currency—the iconic status of Lincoln and Darwin is confirmed. Yet the fact that they achieved their greatness in very different professions has distracted us from an important point regarding similarities of character that helped to fashion those achievements.

Lincoln, the self-educated lawyer, the brilliant statesman, the Great Emancipator, was also fascinated by science, something rarely mentioned by biographers because he seemingly achieved nothing in that field—except the distinction of being the only president to have obtained a U.S. patent. Before Emerson's recent work, the book that came closest to elaborating Lincoln's scientific interests was Robert V. Bruce's *Lincoln and the Tools of War*, although this excellent work, now half a century old, concentrates mainly on Lincoln's concerns (as commander-in-chief during the Civil War) regarding innovative armaments. Darwin, the brilliant theorist who was also imaginative in experimentation and masterful at marshalling evidence, was probably not fully aware himself of how much his research was driven by his deep-seated loathing of slavery, as Desmond and Moore have shown. I try to carry further the story of how Darwin's abolitionism influenced his relationships with other naturalists and his treatment of issues and evidence that arose specifically out of the conflict in America over slavery.

The general public knows little about Darwin's hatred of slavery and less about Lincoln's scientific interests, yet an understanding of these can offer new perspectives on the choices and decisions of these men. The abhorrence felt by Lincoln and Darwin toward the rise of what eventually came to be known as "scientific racism" fueled their opposition to two proponents of that view: Lincoln's great political foe Stephen A. Douglas and Darwin's most influential rival (and America's best-known scientist in the mid-nineteenth century), Louis Agassiz.

Although shaped by vastly different environments, Lincoln and Darwin developed similar views on the clash between rationality and religion, views alien to the mass of their contemporaries. However, both took deliberate steps to avoid causing unnecessary offense, and by the time of their deaths, Lincoln was viewed with quasi-religious awe and Darwin with something close to reverence.

I believe that many people, especially in America, who are inclined to reject natural selection and even to demonize Charles Darwin probably at the same time revere Abraham Lincoln. They might dismiss my view that significant parallels exist in the thoughts and values of the two men, yet I would like to convince such people that if they admire Lincoln's intelligence and humanity in fighting the greatest evil of his time, they should also admire Darwin for similar reasons. And if they would denigrate Darwin's rationalism and materialism as reflecting an unwholesome rejection of religious beliefs, then they are in for a shock when they look more closely at Lincoln's attitude toward conventional religion. In a nutshell, if one of these men is great, then so is the other and for similar reasons.

The controversies surrounding these two giants of the nineteenth century are not fading. The recent bicentenary celebrations dwarfed those of a century ago, when some old men still survived who could speak of their personal acquaintance with Lincoln or Darwin. And a few of those who commemorated that first centenary may even have been old enough to recall that half a century earlier, neither Lincoln nor Darwin had yet—at the age of fifty—achieved enough to make anyone think either one was destined for greatness.

Acknowledgments

For answering questions or providing valuable source material, I am deeply grateful to Adrian Desmond, Allen C. Guelzo, James Moore, and especially Wayne C. Temple, who sent several important items, particularly a copy of "Herndon's Auction List." Christoph Irmscher provided access to his transcriptions of the Howe-Agassiz correspondence and was kind enough to read early chapters and offer encouragement.

For their generous assistance, I thank the staffs at the British Library and the Wellcome Library in London; Anna Smith, picture researcher at the Wellcome Trust; Adam Perkins of the Department of Manuscripts and University Archives, University Library, Cambridge University; Lynn Miller, Wedgwood Museum Trust, Stoke-on-Trent; Jon M. Williams, Andrew W. Mellon Curator of Prints and Photographs, Hagley Museum and Library in Wilmington, Delaware; Janice F. Goldblum, National Academies archivist, Washington, D.C.; Mary M. Huth, manuscripts librarian, University of Rochester; Lisa Marine, Wisconsin Historical Society, Madison; and Alex Rankin of the Howard Gottlieb Archival Research Center, Boston University.

My research would have been practically impossible but for the availability of four recent and ongoing digitization projects: *The Collected Works of Abraham Lincoln*, edited by Roy P. Basler, Marion Dolores Pratt, and Lloyd A. Dunlap and sponsored by Abraham Lincoln Association; *Abraham Lincoln Papers at the Library of Congress*; *Darwin Correspondence Project*, sponsored by the University of Cambridge and published by the university in *Correspondence of Charles Darwin*, edited by Frederick Burkhardt and Sydney Smith; and John van Wyhe's excellent *Complete Work of Charles Darwin Online*.

For particular assistance, I am most grateful to my son, George Lander, to Jonathan Cheng of the London School of Economics, and to Caroline Troein of Bryn Mawr.

I owe special thanks to my colleagues Perrin Tingley, John Smalley, Jonathan Kendall, and Karl Christiansen.

My editor at Southern Illinois University Press, Sylvia Frank Rodrigue, has been outstanding in her encouragement, wisdom, and high expectations, and Barb Martin, editorial, design, and production manager, has been particularly helpful and efficient. I also benefitted from the excellent suggestions made by three anonymous reviewers.

For her patience, diligence, and useful suggestions made while reading the entire text, my wife, Sarah, is owed a great debt that will require a very long time to pay off.

Despite all this help, I have no doubt managed to retain some errors of fact or judgment, for which I am solely responsible.

Lincoln & Darwin

Introduction

A man reaching his fiftieth year is more certain than he was at forty that he now possesses more past than future. After weighing his half century of achievements against the narrowing prospect of attaining any more, he might accept that his unfulfilled dreams will remain so and narrow his interests to the comforts of family and friends. Abraham Lincoln and Charles Darwin, upon reaching the age of fifty, each understood that following his own demise and that of surviving family and friends, he would be largely forgotten. It was a fate both men fought against, and, as it happened, within two years both achieved lasting fame. One published the results of two decades of the most far-reaching and contentious scientific research; the other was elected to the highest office in a country that then fell into civil war. Each met great opposition and overcame it to leave a mark still visible and highly controversial a century and a half later.

Charles Darwin on his fiftieth birthday, 12 February 1859, was not with his wife and seven children at their charming home in the Kent village of Downe but was fifty miles away, in Moor Park, Surrey, undergoing a "water cure" at Dr. Edward Lane's hydrotherapy establishment.[1] Ill health had plagued Darwin for years, so the fear of impending death was nothing new. He had long since arranged that what he considered his most important work might yet be given to the world in some form in the event of his early demise. For over twenty years, he had delayed publishing his particular theory—that species came into existence not through God's creative power but through the transmutation of previously existing species by means of natural selection. He knew this would cause great controversy, yet it was not fear of this that made Darwin delay but his keen desire to marshal substantial evidence to support his theory, a process requiring vast reading, consultation with specialists, and even experimentation.[2]

Eight months earlier, in June 1858, that slow effort of gathering and organizing data was suddenly accelerated as ambition—a desire for a certain type of immortality—overwhelmed him. Darwin was thunderstruck to learn that fellow naturalist Alfred Russel Wallace, living on the other side of the globe, had reached conclusions quite similar to his own regarding the mutability of species. Without doing any injustice to his colleague, Darwin was now determined to bring forth his theory, and he was laboring to produce a book, not as large as the multivolume work he had already begun writing yet more extensive than the earlier sketches shown only to a select few.

Until mid-August 1858, death and illness in his family kept Darwin from his work, but during the following six months, the intensive effort to produce a single-volume "abstract" affected his own health so severely that he was too ill to attend the February meeting of the Geological Society that awarded him the much-coveted Wollaston Medal for his many past contributions to geological science. So Darwin was at Moor Park on his fiftieth birthday, the single record of which is a brief letter to his cousin William Darwin Fox, a country parson with a passion for natural history who had trained at Cambridge back when Darwin was there thinking he, too, might become a clergyman.

> I have been extra bad of late, with the old severe vomiting rather often & much distressing swimming of the head; I have been here a week & shall stay another & it has already done me good. . . . My abstract is the cause, I believe, of the main part of the ills to which my flesh is heir to; but I have only two or more chapters & to correct all, & then I shall be a comparatively free man. I have had the great satisfaction of converting Hooker & I believe Huxley & I think Lyell is much staggered.[3]

The abstract was, of course, *The Origin of Species by Means of Natural Selection*, and Darwin was struggling to reduce his mass of evidence to a single five-hundred-page volume. Had Wallace not forced his hand, he might well have taken several more years to finish his multivolume study. Instead, he spent his fiftieth birthday regretting that he was ill, away from his family, and still two chapters short of completing a lesser work.

After rushing to boil down two decades' research, Darwin suddenly found it difficult to compose the book's ending. A month after his birthday and back at home, Darwin noted in his journal "finished last chapter." A fortnight later, the last chapter was "not even fully written out," and after another two months, he had "now written half." Four days later, Darwin finished—and immediately suffered a physical collapse that sent him back to Moor Park for another week's water cure before he could begin checking proofs.[4]

Despite, or because of, that agonized effort, the last paragraph of *The Origin* achieved an eloquence rivaling some of Abraham Lincoln's finest speeches:

> It is interesting to contemplate an entangled bank, clothed with many plants of many kinds, with birds singing on the bushes, with various insects flitting about, and with worms crawling through the damp earth, and to reflect that these elaborately constructed forms, so different from each other, and depen-

dent on each other in so complex a manner, have all been produced by laws acting around us. These laws, taken in the largest sense, being Growth with Reproduction; inheritance which is almost implied by reproduction; Variability from the indirect and direct action of the external conditions of life, and from use and disuse; a Ratio of Increase so high as to lead to a Struggle for Life, and as a consequence to Natural Selection, entailing Divergence of Character and the Extinction of less-improved forms. Thus, from the war of nature, from famine and death, the most exalted object which we are capable of conceiving, namely, the production of the higher animals, directly follows. There is grandeur in this view of life, with its several powers, having been originally breathed into a few forms or into one; and that, whilst this planet has gone cycling on according to the fixed law of gravity, from so simple a beginning endless forms most beautiful and most wonderful have been, and are being, evolved.[5]

That last word, "evolved," is the closest Darwin came in *The Origin* to using the term most often associated with his name, "evolution," a word not then possessing its modern meaning. Darwin instead used terms such as "development" or "transmutation" for the broad notion of changing species and phrases like "descent with modification" and "natural selection" to describe the mechanism of that change.[6] Darwin discussed how species *change*, not how—from nothing—the *first species* came into existence or whether "species" would then be plural or singular. Darwin equivocated, saying vaguely, with a biblical echo, that "life" was in some way "originally breathed into a few forms or into one."

Darwin endeavored to leave God out of the discussion. He was pursuing scientific truth, not trying to assist those who attacked the majority's belief that God had designed the universe. Yet, he also hoped the weight of his evidence might protect him against that majority's wrath. Darwin's purpose was to show how natural selection worked, not how it began or how it, in one sense, ended: with man. The book contained only two references to man, one frequently quoted, the other not (but discussed further below). The former is on the third page from the end, after Darwin had filled over four hundred pages discussing a myriad of *other* species: "In the distant future I see open fields for far more important researches. . . . Light will be thrown on the origin of man and his history."

Avoiding natural selection's beginning and ending did not prevent those concepts from seizing the popular imagination, causing great controversies that swirl to the present day. Yet Darwin left out God and man for separate reasons. Logically, although God might have created natural selection, he was not necessary to its ongoing operation. Darwin saw no way to collect data about God's creative activity, and the issue was fraught with other difficulties, social, familial, and personal. Regarding man, Darwin's premise was that natural selection applied to him if it applied at all; and there was more information on man than any other species—yet, when still working on his multivolume study (and before they knew of each other's theories), Darwin told Wallace in December 1857, "You ask whether I shall discuss 'man.' I think I shall avoid [the] whole subject, as so surrounded with prejudices; though I fully admit that it is the highest & most interesting problem for the naturalist."[7]

Although *The Origin* gave no direct account of man, everyone assumed it did: "man-descended-from-apes" was the theme of most reviews and subsequent debates. Darwin eventually produced two books that did focus on man, and throughout Darwin's earlier research the subject of man was always as important as his beloved beetles, the tortoises, mockingbirds, and barnacles. However, Darwin never mused on "man's fate" or asked, "Why are we here?" Even the more objective question, "Who are we?" became a matter of taxonomy: "*What* are we?" One important version of that question—one that motivated much of Darwin's research—had been made famous by Darwin's grandfathers before he was born. It involved the image of a black slave, kneeling and in chains, around whom was inscribed the question "Am I not a man and a brother?"

Darwin's family was committed to the abolition of slavery, and his scientific work became his contribution. Although Darwin deliberately challenged explanations of the natural world he found untenable, he also mounted an attack on the growing body of opinion, both popular and scientific, that theorized that slavery was somehow "natural" because, after all, black Africans were clearly not like "us." In *The Origin*, Darwin implies and in later works argues explicitly that man is part of the animal kingdom, and just as men share ancestors with other species, the human races have a common ancestor—though it was not Adam as many others in the antislavery movement were inclined to believe.[8]

The Origin did not discuss "negroes" or any particular human racial group; however, Darwin's second (and less frequently quoted) reference to "man" is this: "I may add that some little light can apparently be thrown on the origin of . . . the differences between the races of man, which are so strongly marked [and caused] chiefly through sexual selection of a particular kind." He hastened to add, "But without here entering on copious details my reasoning would appear frivolous." Darwin thus hinted at his deep concern with the common ancestry of human racial groups.[9]

Those details were later presented in *Descent of Man*, yet the topic was just below the surface in *The Origin*. In the book's full title, *On the Origin of Species by Means of Natural Selection, or the Preservation of Favoured Races in the Struggle for Life*, "races," of course, was another way of saying "varieties," applicable to plants and animals as well as man. For many of Darwin's contemporaries, the phrase "favoured races" might conjure images not only of man but particularly of white men; however, Darwin had bitter experience of the way natives in Latin America, New Zealand, and Australia suffered at the hands of more "civilised" races, and he had no wish to justify any exploitative colonial practices and was revolted by arguments that slavery was somehow "natural." For this reason, Darwin was greatly disturbed when he saw with his own eyes for the first time an example of animal behavior that suggested slavery might in some sense be "natural."

During an earlier sojourn at Moor Park in April 1858, when Darwin was supposed to be resting and reading novels, his habit of observation caused him during one of his walks to notice a rare type of ant, *Formica sanguinea* (or *rufescens*) the "slave-making" ant, and its "slave" *Formica nigra*. For over a decade, the cruel habits of these "African" ants had appeared in naturalist literature and had even been used to "justify" human behavior, before entomologist Frederick Smith first discovered such ants in England itself in 1854. It was to Smith that Darwin had recently sent enquiries, but now seeing these particular ants himself caused Darwin to mention them in letters, record his observations and experiments, and use this information in the massive work he was then still writing. A year later, when reducing this work to create *The Origin*, Darwin actually expanded his account of the slave-making ant.[10]

According to biographer Janet Browne, Darwin's "understanding of these biological relationships was probably influenced by his former colonial experiences. Recalling the horrors he encountered in South America, he regarded the red ants' behavior as enslavement rather than any comparable social structure such as symbiosis or co-operation." By writing "slavery" rather than "symbiosis," Darwin simply used the terms employed by earlier naturalists, yet Browne is certainly right that Darwin "felt very uncomfortable providing biological parallels for human practices he found abhorrent."[11] Darwin admitted approaching the subject "in a sceptical frame of mind, as any one may well be excused for doubting the truth of so extraordinary and odious an instinct as that of making slaves." He began humbly enough—"By what steps the instinct of *F. sanguinea* originated I will not pretend to conjecture"—but then *did* conjecture that natural selection could explain such an "odious" instinct. Various species of ants feed off the pupae of other species of ant; some develop the useful modification of stealing and storing those pupae; as a next step, some might discover their looted pupae hatching before they had been eaten and put the hatched alien ant to work just like every other ant in the colony; from there it could be a short step to stealing pupae precisely for the future labor rather than for nutrition.

Darwin concluded, "I can see no difficulty in natural selection increasing and modifying the [slave-making] instinct—*always supposing each modification to be of use to the species*—until an ant was formed as abjectly dependent on its slaves as is the *Formica rufescens*" (emphasis added).[12] Here is the implied contrast between ant slave-making and human slavery: one species of ant enslaved a different species of ant, but man enslaved other men, so human slavery is not something of use *to the whole species*. Moreover, in no other case did Darwin declare that a modification made a species "abjectly dependent," but perhaps the phrase reflected his low opinion of plantation owners. In any case, Darwin dismissed any idea that this animal behavior might somehow justify human slavery as "natural."

Although *The Origin* made no direct reference to human slavery and only brief references to man and human races, all three subjects frequently appeared in Darwin's early notebooks made between 1837 and 1840.[13] Fourteen years before writing *The Origin*, Darwin had published vivid expressions of his loathing for human slavery. As Darwin spent his fiftieth birthday at Moor Park trying to finish off the last chapters of *The Origin* and wandering around the familiar grounds, the slave-making ants he had first seen there a year earlier were still on his mind.[14]

Darwin is far less famous than Lincoln for his abhorrence of "slave-making." The Great Emancipator terminated the foulest evil in the American states although half of them had previously permitted slavery, including Lincoln's native state. He once said that he had always felt that if slavery was not evil, nothing was evil, yet his early political career had not been focused on slavery. However, in his fiftieth year, Lincoln was aware that over the previous five years, his various political campaigns had been entirely devoted to that issue.

To preserve national unity, compromises at every political crossroads since the onset of the War of Independence had allowed the continued existence of slavery, which in the 1850s had become the defining political topic. The Republican Party had recently arisen to address the issue ignored by the older parties, and Lincoln had raised himself up from his origins in frontier poverty to become the leader of the Republican Party in his adopted state of Illinois. Through an extraordinary process of self-education, Lincoln had turned himself into a successful lawyer and politician, serving four terms in the Illinois state legislature before spending one term in the U.S. House of Representatives. Twice in the last three years, 1856 and 1858, Lincoln had tried to win a seat in the U.S. Senate, and he reached his half century three months after his second defeat. Although his recent campaign debates with the victor, Stephen A. Douglas, had brought Lincoln much acclaim even beyond Illinois' borders, shortly after that defeat Lincoln wrote to a friend, "Though I now sink out of view, and shall be forgotten, I believe I have made some marks which will tell for the cause of civil liberty long after I am gone"—a consoling thought clearly outweighed by disappointment.[15]

Having failed twice to win a U.S. Senate seat, Lincoln also saw no prospect of winning Illinois' governorship and had no desire to return either to the state legislature or the House of Representatives. The 1860 presidential election was less than two years away, but the Democrats would almost certainly nominate the man who had just beaten Lincoln, and plenty of Republican officeholders back east had greater claims to the party's nomination than the prairie lawyer. The next senatorial election in Illinois was three years away, but the incumbent was a friend Lincoln had helped to elect, while Douglas's seat—unless Douglas was elected president in the meantime—was now safe until 1864. Lincoln was justified in thinking he himself might be all but forgotten by then. A month after his latest defeat, Lincoln wrote to another friend "merely to let you know that I am neither dead nor dying."[16]

Lincoln might have felt tempted to accept that his political career was over and that he should now devote himself to his legal practice and to his wife, Mary, and their three sons. Resuming legal work would restore depleted funds and take Lincoln's mind off his lack of political prospects. Some historians have even perceived an attempted career shift, from lawyer/politician to lawyer/lecturer. The lyceums, young men's clubs, and debating societies provided a ready market for touring lecturers who offered information along with entertainment. Lincoln admired lecturers, possessed broad interests, enjoyed research, and was a highly experienced public speaker with a notorious sense of humor. However, Lincoln only dipped his toe, rather than plunged, into the lecture circuit, beginning in April 1858, a few months before his last senate race—not, therefore, a result of his defeat. It was hardly a new career, lasting only two years (until Lincoln became preoccupied with his presidential bid) and consisting of delivering pretty much the same lecture on five or six occasions, two of them near his fiftieth birthday. Lecturing helped keep Lincoln's name before the public, but his lecture did not greatly impress many who heard it at the time, and few scholars, until recently, have seen much value in it. However, it was about a topic that Darwin, had he for some reason travelled four thousand miles to be in the audience, would have been able to appreciate—even amid the muddle of examples, political asides, and jokes. Lincoln's subject was the nature of man.[17]

We know exactly where Charles Darwin was on that shared birthday, but we have no record of Lincoln's activity. It was formerly thought that Lincoln spent part of that day on a forty-mile train journey home after delivering his lecture the previous evening in Jacksonville, Illinois, but Wayne C. Temple's research demonstrates that that lecture took place a week earlier, and it was delivered again just over a week later, this time in Lincoln's hometown, the Illinois capital, Springfield.[18] The very first delivery had occurred ten months earlier, and the last would take place fourteen months later. Only the last couple of deliveries drew large audiences because of Lincoln's rising political status. Three weeks after presenting his lecture for the last time—and in no way because of it—Lincoln was nominated for the presidency. Friendly newspapers gave glowing reports of the lecture (or chided readers for meager attendances), while others shared the view of one listener who wrote, "I think people generally were disappointed in his lecture as it was on no particular subject and not well connected," adding that if Lincoln had stuck to politics, "he would have done justice to his subject."[19] Lincoln's law partner and later biographer, William Herndon, wrote that the lecture "was a lifeless thing . . . no spirit and no life. The whole thing was a kind of farce and injured Mr. L.'s reputation as a man of sense among his friends and enemies."[20] Shortly before the last delivery, Lincoln himself wrote, "I am not a professional lecturer. Have never got up but one lecture; and that I think, a rather poor one."[21] He left a manuscript of the lecture with other loose papers in the care of his wife's cousin before departing for the White House, where he later said, "When I get out of this place I'll finish it up and get my friend [Noah] B[rooks] to print it somewhere."[22]

Death intervened, and the manuscript was divided between two private collections and later published as two separate lectures. Thus mangled, considered nonpolitical, and doing little for Lincoln's reputation anyway, the lecture was ignored until recent decades when scholars began to explore the material, especially after Temple demonstrated that the two lectures were really one.[23]

The manuscript's division probably resulted from the fact that one half *seems* different from the other.[24] Temple suggested that Lincoln wrote it in sections because his legal practice interrupted. Perhaps Lincoln simply rewrote parts: a newspaper account of the lecture's first delivery mentioned topics not in the existing text and ignored others that are. The lecture's second delivery—shortly before his fiftieth birthday—came ten months after the first and also three months after his second senatorial defeat, so he had plenty of spare time for revision.

The lecture, variously titled as "Inventions," "Inventions and Discoveries," and "Discoveries and Inventions," seems to have several themes, most of them ostensibly nonpolitical. Much in the lecture would have interested, or at least amused, Lincoln's contemporary Charles Darwin. Just as Lincoln would have been fascinated to learn of this English gentleman's abhorrence of slavery, Darwin would have been surprised by this frontiersman's curious fascination with science and technology. Probably few who attended the lectures on "Inventions" knew that the speaker had actually taken out a U.S. patent a decade earlier.[25]

Although the lecture had gained Lincoln no obvious financial or political benefit from his unimpressed audiences, he was probably not joking when he later said he planned to "finish" the piece someday. Historian Jason Emerson recently discovered that Lincoln's son Robert knew of a copy of the lecture that his father had carefully written out in a blank book bound with a black cover, and this version may have included some material mentioned in contemporary newspaper accounts but not appearing in the existing fragments.[26] Lincoln may indeed have had future publication in mind—for a lecture that, until recently, was largely dismissed by historians. So what made Lincoln compose this lecture in the first place?

In 1855, Lincoln was riding the Eighth Circuit with two other lawyers, all taking turns reading aloud a lecture entitled "The Necessity, the Reality, and the Promise of the Progress of the Human Race," which George Bancroft had delivered to the New York Historical Society a year earlier. One of the lawyers, Henry D. Whitney, reported that Lincoln informed them "that he had for some time been contemplating the writing of a lecture on *man*; he said he proposed to review man from his earliest primeval state to his present high development, and he detailed at length the views and opinions he designed to incorporate in his lecture" (original emphasis).[27]

At some time Lincoln acquired a copy of Bancroft's lecture.[28] However, Lincoln did not seek to "imitate" Bancroft, as Garry Wills suggests, but rather to refute Bancroft's emphases.[29] Whitney's account indicated that Lincoln had *already* thought a great deal on "man and his progress" and discussed how *he* would approach it—differently from Bancroft.

Other accounts of the origins of Lincoln's lecture do not mention Bancroft. Noah Brooks, a journalist and friend, recalled Lincoln saying in 1865 that his lecture "was not defined, but his purpose was to analyze inventions and discoveries—'to get at the bottom of things'—and to show when, where, how, and why such things were invented or discovered; and, so far as possible, to find where the first mention is made of some of our common things," showing "at least in a fanciful way, that all the modern inventions were known centuries ago."[30] A third source, the wife of Lincoln's fellow lawyer and political ally Norman Judd, said Lincoln and a friend once discussed "the relative age of the discovery and use of the precious metals [after which] he went to the Bible to satisfy himself and became so interested in his researches that he made memoranda of the different discoveries and inventions." Lincoln became "convinced . . . that the subject would interest others, and he therefore prepared and delivered his lecture on The Age of Different Inventions."[31]

That the lecture possibly started off as one thing and became several others perhaps explains its lack of coherence—or even a straightforward title. Mrs. Judd's reference to "precious metals" rings true, for Lincoln had a particular interest in geology (discussed later), and the lecture actually began with the line, "All creation is a mine, and every man, a miner."[32]

Man, Lincoln declared, has had to "dig out his destiny," a characteristic distinguishing him from the animal kingdom. "Man is not the only animal who labors; but he is the only one who *improves* his workmanship." Darwin might have been impressed when Lincoln, giving several examples of industrious but nonimproving animals, mentioned ants! Lincoln went on to say that man improves his workmanship through "discoveries and inventions." While Lincoln could admire many points in Bancroft's lecture (especially the stress on the unity of mankind), Bancroft's examples of human workmanship were rather parochial—though fitting the occasion of the fiftieth anniversary of the New York Historical Society, for Bancroft had emphasized inventions of the last half century (especially contributions by such NYHS members as Robert Fulton). Although Lincoln sought the *origins* of inventions—not Fulton's steamboat but the earliest use of steam power—he actually explored the very concept of invention and what it says about man. Unlike Bancroft, who depicted God as aiding man in his progress, Lincoln subtly argued that God had little to do with it.[33]

Without being offensively explicit, Lincoln depicted Adam not as "falling" from a blessed and perfect condition but as a backward savage. He gently made Adam the butt of several jokes. Adam "seems not to have been a very observing man," taking a long time to notice "the obvious fact" that he was naked. Also, after making a serious point about the communication of ideas, Lincoln said Adam used speech "even before the creation of Eve. He gave names to the animals while she was still a bone in his side; and he broke out quite volubly when she first stood before him, the best present of his maker." Having conjured that titillating image, Lincoln next declared that the world's first invention, the "fig-leaf apron," should be credited to Eve rather than Adam, who perhaps did "no more than to stand by and thread the needle" (the last phrase being sometimes used as slang for sexual intercourse). Lincoln could not resist piling on two more jokes: "That proceeding may be reckoned as the mother of all 'Sewing societies'; and the first and most perfect 'world's fair': all inventions and all inventors then in the world being on the spot."[34]

The jests were mild, and Lincoln neutralized any sacrilege by larding the first half of his lecture with authoritative quotations from Scripture. When listing the earliest evidence for the first inventions—clothing, spinning, weaving, iron, transportation by animal and by boat, agriculture, wind power, water mills, and steam power—Lincoln cited biblical evidence, chapter and verse, no less than thirty-seven times. Darwin, who would soon be adding "by the Creator" to the concluding paragraph of *The Origin*, was in no position to throw stones about such lip service to popular piety—although this may be one reason why the free-thinking Herndon considered Lincoln's lecture such a failure. But Herndon was less likely than Darwin to comprehend Lincoln's cautiously camouflaged point.

One audience member, apparently familiar with Lincoln's courtroom tactics, wrote that the lecture's two halves "forcibly reminded us of his legal argument, wherein he first states the facts in a clear and simple manner, and then reasons from those facts backward and forward to cause and effect."[35] A fellow lawyer once asserted that Lincoln "stated the case of his adversary better and more forcibly than his opponent could state it himself . . . [then] he presented his own case."[36]

After apparently paying homage to the Bible, Lincoln undermined its useful-ness for explaining human development. Without blatancy, Lincoln suggested that man had not fallen but risen and not through divine assistance but through a gradual improvement brought about by man's own effort along with a degree of unexplained contingency—chance. For Lincoln's curious mind, the Bible simply left too much unexplained, a point he made humorously: "We can scarcely con-ceive the possibility of making much of anything else, without the use of iron tools. Indeed, an iron *hammer* must have been very much needed to make the *first* iron hammer with. A *stone* probably served as a substitute. How could the 'gopher wood' for the Ark, have been gotten out without an axe? It seems to me an axe, or a miracle, was indispensable."[37]

Clearly, Lincoln was not relying on miracles any more than primitive man relied on divine assistance to invent a boat: "The sight of a crow standing on a piece of drift-wood floating down the swollen current of a creek or river, might well enough suggest the specific idea to a savage." Similarly, when Lincoln allowed that "it would appear that speech was not an invention of man, but rather the direct gift of his Creator," he immediately equivocated: "But whether Divine gift, or invention, it is still plain that if a mode of communication had been left to invention, *speech* must have been the first."[38]

Darwin and Lincoln lived a century before the development of scientific dating techniques, but Darwin, like most geologists of his time, already rejected the estimate (extrapolated from the Bible) that creation took place six thousand years ago. Many thoughtful people still assumed that however old the Earth might be, mankind's history was only six thousand years old. As discussed later, Lincoln understood that the Earth was far older than the biblical chronology, but the first part of his lecture seems to nod to the traditional chronology with regard to mankind. Whether or not he accepted that chronology, he let his audience think he did. He also seemed to concede the Bible's scrupulous accuracy when he said that although some "profane [i.e., nonreligious] authors" think spinning and weaving originated in Egypt, "this is not contradicted, or made improbable, by anything in the Bible," because the patriarch Abraham's mention of "thread" did not occur till after his sojourn in Egypt. Of course, this "concession" was again typical of Lincoln's courtroom technique, for it established that the "profane authors" were right that Egyptians, not God's chosen people, invented cloth making.[39]

Thus, Lincoln laid out the Bible's (and Bancroft's) version of man's early development in a way that suggested one could not use "God's will" to explain what made man advance further than animals (as Adam did) or what made some men advance further than others. The second half of the lecture offered Lincoln's own explanation, scarcely mentioning the Bible.

The opening discussion of the second half seems out of place—probable evidence of rewriting and of Lincoln's inability to avoid a bit of politicking. Between a slight reference to unexploited steam power near the end of the first half and a more extensive discussion of its utilization in the second half, Lincoln inserted a long and sarcastic digression on "Young America." Although Lincoln attempted a tie-in ("Is he not the inventor and owner of the present, and sole hope of the future?"), his audience would have understood that Lincoln was launching an attack on the Democratic Party in general and on Lincoln's political foe Douglas in particular.[40] Before long, Lincoln worked his way back to his main topic by borrowing a phrase that the "Young America" faction within the Democratic Party had formerly used against its rivals—"Old Fogy"—and applying it to "the first of all fogies, father Adam," who *"according to his chance"* was "quite as much of a man" as his descendants. Lincoln then argued that all the advances since Adam's time were the "result of *Discoveries, Inventions*, and *Improvements*. These in turn, are the result of *observation, reflection* and *experiment*," by which man built on "all he has learned from others" (original emphases).[41]

Learning from others was enormously facilitated by the inventions of "phonetic writing" and later printing. Writing was not divinely given to men, for which reason its development has been uneven among them: "That it was difficult of conception and execution, is apparent . . . [since] so many tribes of men have come down from Adam's time to ours without ever having possessed it."[42]

To writing and printing, Lincoln then added two more "inventions and discoveries" that were "of peculiar value on account of their great efficiency in facilitating all other inventions and discoveries": the discovery of America in 1492 (arguing, "a new country is most favorable—almost necessary—to the emancipation of thought") and the introduction of the first patent laws in 1624 (which "added the fuel of *interest* to the *fire* of genius, in the discovery and production of new and useful things").[43]

There the manuscript abruptly ended, leaving the lecturer perhaps to ad-lib some peroration. But there also seems to be a strange insertion between Lincoln's first reference to America's discovery and the patent laws and his actual discussion of them: "Though not apposite to my present purpose, it is but justice to the fruitfulness of that period, to mention two other important events—the Lutheran Reformation in 1517, and, still earlier, the invention of negroes, or, of the present mode of using them, in 1434." Listing the Reformation among inventions "of peculiar value" probably pleased Lincoln's Protestant audience—unless they thought about why he was calling their religion an "invention" and pairing it with another that was worthy of condemnation, slavery. Lincoln gave no further explanation for bringing up either topic (the larger significance of "the invention of negroes" is discussed later).[44]

In his lecture, Lincoln used the word "race" three times, always referring to the entire "human race." He spoke of different "tribes of men," some characterized as "savages." But while he agreed with Bancroft's view that "every man is in substance equal to his fellow man," Lincoln accepted that men have developed differently: not because God made them different or bestowed "inventions" on some but not others but exactly because inventions and discoveries were made by men, giving some advantages over others.[45]

Just as Darwin's phrase "favoured races" did not mean some blessing by God but rather a higher level of development, so Lincoln argued that it is to the invention of writing, for example, that "we owe everything which distinguishes us from savages." Although the institution of slavery had stimulated a degree of "fruitfulness" (or profit) at least for some, slavery, like writing, was an invention. Moreover, its modern version was based on another invention: negro inferiority. Lincoln saw nothing natural, innate, or divinely ordained to justify making blacks into slaves. As Lincoln could read in the *Encyclopaedia Americana* (which he possessed and cited elsewhere in the lecture), Africans' bondage to Europeans was "invented" in 1434, when a Portuguese captain kidnapped some Africans and sold them to some Moorish families in southern Spain. Unlike slaves in antiquity, these were not debtors, war captives, or even time-indentured laborers. Six years later, the captain repeated the effort, broadened the market, and found others who wished to join in or compete.[46]

Dr. Francis Lieber, who later as president of Columbia College conferred on President Lincoln an honorary doctorate of laws, edited the *Encyclopaedia*. His article on "slavery" called it "the greatest bar to civilization" and added the "melancholy reflection" that Europeans reestablished slavery in their colonies in modern times after ending it at home in the Middle Ages. Moreover, this "atrocity at which nature revolts . . . could never have reached the height it did, if the color of the slave had not given rise to the idea of his being by nature a degraded being." But Lieber touched on more than mere color, declaring in the article entitled "Negro" that the shape of the cranium allowed "less space for the brain than in some other varieties" of man. However, Lieber asserted, "The opinion formerly maintained, that they were of an inferior variety of animals, would not now find an advocate, or a convert, even in the ignorance or the worst passions of the whites."[47]

By the time he gave his lecture, Lincoln knew that that last assertion was out of date, for in the twenty-seven years since Lieber wrote it, there had indeed arisen serious advocates of the idea that blacks were if not "an inferior variety of animal" then at best an inferior variety of human, one created separately from Adam and on an inferior model. Important men of science were now effectively endorsing the prejudices of those who had some interest or need to view blacks as subhumans. It was a view that neither Lincoln nor Darwin ever accepted. Lincoln's lecture may have been stimulated by Bancroft's—as Darwin needed the catalyst provided by Wallace to produce *The Origin*—but Lincoln and Darwin also had a larger purpose: to address the incorrect thinking (whether based on religious dogma or weak science) used by some humans to justify enslaving others.

For Lincoln, slavery was wrong because, like it or not, it violated the principle that "all men are created equal." For Darwin, a special creation of mankind (or, worse, of separate groups of men) was wrong because, like it or not, the principle of natural selection applied equally to men and animals. Both principles faced considerable opposition—and still do because neither is subject to mathematical proof, and many people have an interest in treating others as inferiors. Yet, the principles advocated by Lincoln and Darwin have come to be accepted generally, advancing our understanding of man's place in relation to the rest of mankind and to the universe. For crystallizing these views and acting upon them, both Lincoln and Darwin have earned their iconic status as men who not only were products of their times but actually changed their world. Such enduring fame had been quite inconceivable during their first fifty years.

Origins and Education

braham Lincoln was named after his paternal grandfather. His maternal
grandfather's name is unknown, and probably Lincoln's mother, Nancy
Hanks, never knew it herself. Lincoln once confided that his mother "was
the daughter of a nobleman," that is, a Virginia planter. This is unconfirmed but
not unlikely.[1] The elder Abraham died twenty-three years before his namesake
was born: Lincoln's own father, Thomas, was only eight years old when he saw
his father killed by Indians in Kentucky. The youngest of three sons, Thomas
inherited nothing and lived a hard-working life up to and after his marriage to
the illegitimate Nancy Hanks. Abraham Lincoln, like his older sister, Sarah, was
born into frontier poverty and raised by illiterate parents.

Although both of Charles Darwin's grandfathers died before he was born, at
least he knew their names, as did thousands of other people in the late eighteenth
century. Erasmus Darwin was a highly respected doctor, an accomplished poet
and writer, a religious skeptic, and a "natural philosopher" (as "scientists" were
then called) who once authored a book, *Zoonomia*, which featured a clear belief
that the species of the world were the result not of a single creation but of some
evolutionary development. Erasmus was a close friend of Josiah Wedgwood,
the prosperous potter, technological innovator, and reform-minded Unitarian.
Erasmus arranged for his son Robert to marry Wedgwood's daughter Susannah
in 1796. Her £25,000 inheritance added to the wealth coming in from Robert's
successful medical practice in Shrewsbury. Thus, both of Charles's parents descended from intelligent and affluent men who were religious dissenters, and his
earliest memories were of an imposing five-bay, two-and-a-half-storied house,
The Mount, overlooking the Severn River on the edge of Shrewsbury, where he,
his older brother, and his four sisters were all born. Until he married and set up
his own household, Darwin knew no other home than The Mount.

Lincoln had no memory of his birthplace in Kentucky, being only two when
his family left the one-room cabin to rot and moved to better soil ten miles
away. When Lincoln was seven, his family moved again, this time ninety miles

northwest, out of Kentucky, across the Ohio River, and into Indiana. The North-west Ordinance of 1787, parts of which did not apply south of the Ohio River, meant that land in Indiana was properly surveyed, and slavery was prohibited, so Thomas Lincoln no longer had to argue with wealthier men's clever lawyers or compete with their slave labor.

Thomas's motivation was not self-interest alone: he was a religious man and believed that slavery was wrong. His son later wrote, "I am naturally anti-slavery. If slavery is not wrong, nothing is wrong. I can not remember when I did not so think, and feel."[2] Darwin, too, came from antislavery stock, with both grandfathers and an aunt active on abolitionist committees.

Abraham Lincoln was raised close to nature, living in unbroken forest, shooting wild turkey through the chinks in the cabin wall, and using an axe almost every day till he was twenty-three. For Charles Darwin, nature was landscaped, conquered by roads and canals, tamed in the greenhouse and orchard and pigeon cot, and read about in his father's vast library. Darwin became fascinated with the natural world, which for Lincoln had always meant grinding labor and something to escape.

When their mothers died, Darwin and Lincoln were, respectively, eight and a half and nine years old. Charles had little memory of the event. His mother was fifty-two and had been an invalid for years, so Charles was mainly looked after by his older sisters before and after their mother's death. Abraham's mother was about thirty-five when she died suddenly, leaving a gaping hole in the vulnerable family. The tragedy would have been far more damaging if his father had not swiftly remarried to a widow with three children who expanded and stabilized the family. Abraham's stepmother proved wonderfully affectionate. Nevertheless, he idealized his "angel mother" and once said, "All that I am or ever hope to be I get from my mother, God bless her."[3] This may be an irrational appraisal of his mother's possible influence, the real message being that Lincoln felt he had inherited no characteristics from his father.

Darwin's whole career revolved around issues of inheritance and "nature versus nurture," yet he never suggested that he had inherited anything from either parent (except considerable wealth). Once, describing his early "taste for natural history," he wrote, "The passion for collecting . . . was very strong in me, and was clearly innate." In the manuscript, the word "innate" replaced "inherent," which had been illogical since he also wrote, "None of my sisters or brother ever had this taste."[4] Darwin saw his own development as being unusual and largely inexplicable. He declared that his "passion for collecting" set him apart, but it was hardly a unique activity for a boy of his era and class, especially one whose mother had raised fancy pigeons, whose father had a fine library well stocked with tomes on natural history, and whose elder brother showed an early interest in science. Yet, the word "innate" subtly excluded any necessary influence from his parents. In his autobiography, Darwin went to great lengths to depict and praise his father's professional skill, extraordinary memory, "powers of observation and his sympathy" yet added, ambiguously, "I do not think that I gained much from him intellectually, but his example ought to have been of much moral service to all his children."[5]

Tales exist—almost certainly untrue—that Abraham Lincoln himself was not actually Thomas's son. Such rumors surfaced during Lincoln's presidency, but whether Lincoln was a source or gave them any credence is unknown.[6] One can empathize with the attitude, hardly unique, "This cannot possibly be my real father!" Lincoln grew unusually tall and lanky, unlike his stocky, five-foot-nine-inch father, which may have added to the other anomaly: the son far outstripping his father's intellect.

Although it is unlikely that Lincoln doubted his father's paternity, he may have believed he inherited fewer qualities from his father than from the anonymous aristocrat who fathered Nancy Hanks. Lincoln later attained a reputation for great powers of sympathy, yet he showed little for his father when he mentioned in an autobiographical sketch that his father "never did more in the way of writing than to bunglingly sign his own name."[7] The harsh adverb would not have been used on his "angel mother"—who could not write her name even bunglingly.

Looking back on their childhoods, Lincoln and Darwin saw themselves, with differing degrees of justification, as self-created through self-education. Indeed, their educational experiences, though radically different, caused tensions with their fathers. Lincoln's expected him to become, like father and grandfather, useful on the farm, which required no schooling; Darwin's father expected his son to follow his father and grandfather into the medical profession. Both fathers were dissatisfied by their sons' education: in Darwin's case because he seemed to gain too little from it and in Lincoln's because he gained too much.

Darwin was tutored by his sister Caroline before the age of eight, then had twelve years of formal education, including two years of medical studies in Edinburgh and three years at Cambridge University—all of which Darwin described disparagingly in his later autobiography. His school's classical curriculum "as a means of education to me was simply a blank," and his verdict on himself was worse: "I believe that I was considered by all my masters and by my father as a very ordinary boy, rather below the common standard in intellect." Yet, Darwin did develop a deep love of reading, partly thanks to the positive example of his older brother, Erasmus. Charles "used to sit for hours reading the historical plays of Shakespeare" as well as Byron, Scott, and Thomson's *Seasons*. He felt "intense satisfaction" in Euclid's proofs and "a wish to travel in remote countries" after reading a book entitled *The Wonders of the World*. Erasmus led him into collecting minerals and insects, drying plants, and experimenting in chemistry, an activity sufficiently odd to earn Darwin the nickname "Gas" among his fellow students. White's *Selborne* sparked an interest in the habits of birds, though he also developed a "zeal" for shooting them.[8] Lincoln, as far as we know, collected nothing and hated hunting, although, almost of necessity, he was a good shot.

Although young "Gas" thought his chemistry experiments with his brother were the best part of his education, he was once "publicly rebuked by the head-master" for wasting his time "over such useless subjects," and to his "deep mor-tification" his father once said, "You care for nothing but shooting, dogs and rat-catching, and you will be a disgrace to yourself and all your family." Since Charles "was doing no good at school," his father sent him at an earlier age than usual to Edinburgh, where Erasmus was already studying medicine. The lectures, except those on chemistry, "were intolerably dull," and when Charles attended two operations (in the days before anesthesia), "I rushed away before they were completed. Nor did I ever attend again." Darwin effectively abandoned medical studies, regretting only that he never practiced dissection, which "would have been invaluable for all my future work." Around this period, Charles also "be-came convinced" that his property inheritance from his father would obviate the need to earn a living, which news "was sufficient to check any strenuous effort to learn medicine."[9]

However, Darwin still enjoyed studying natural science. This was not, like medicine, a respectable profession but mainly an eccentric avocation for gentle-men, often country vicars not obliged to spend much time saving souls. It was actually Darwin's father who "proposed that I should become a clergyman." Sent to Cambridge, he attended only a few compulsory lectures and found the mathematics instruction "repugnant." Darwin later recalled that his time at Cambridge was "worse than wasted" and that his passion for shooting led him into "a sporting set, including some dissipated low-minded young men." Darwin was fairly amazed when his exam results earned him a pass degree.[10]

"But no pursuit at Cambridge was followed with nearly so much eagerness or gave me so much pleasure as collecting beetles." A friend's joke that one day Darwin would be a Fellow of the Royal Society seemed "preposterous" to him. And yet, just as he had attached himself in Edinburgh to a mentor, the sponge expert Robert Grant, Darwin in Cambridge became a devoted acolyte of some of the leading naturalists of the day, the clergymen/geologists J. S. Henslow, William Whewell, and Adam Sedgwick. Darwin attended their lectures and soirées and joined field trips that provided practical experience in geology: "Looking back, I infer that there must have been something in me a little superior to the com-mon run of youths, otherwise the above-mentioned men, so much older than me and higher in academical position, would never have allowed me to associate with them. Certainly I was not aware of any such superiority." These men raised Darwin's self-esteem and offered a model, as did his cousin William Darwin Fox, a devoted naturalist who had just obtained a curacy. After his examinations, Darwin accompanied Sedgwick to Wales on a geological tour that made him yearn for more. He planned an excursion to Tenerife, a Canary Island, having recently read Alexander von Humboldt's *Personal Narrative*, which, along with John Frederick William Herschel's *Introduction to the Study of Natural Philosophy*, "stirred up in me a burning zeal to add even the most humble contribution to the noble structure of Natural Science."[11]

Darwin's formal education ended when he was twenty-one, but his self-education—his real education—had begun when he was a child assisting Erasmus's chemistry experiments and expanded in stages, always accompanied by intense and wide-ranging reading. In addition to works on science, his interest in poetry continued for many years, yet eventually waned in middle age, while "books on history, biographies and travels . . . interest me as much as they ever did." He kept up with scientific journals, perused the *Times* regularly, and found fiction "a wonderful relief and pleasure." Darwin's leisure reading overlapped his scientific interests: he "happened to read for amusement" Malthus's *Essay on Population*, which greatly influenced his work.[12]

From various sources, one could compile a list of works read by Darwin that would number in the thousands. We have far less evidence regarding what Lincoln read.[13] His autobiographical sketches, legal work, and correspondence mention few books, and his speeches do not cite sources even though they were often based on wide research. Early poverty developed in him the habit of borrowing and reading books rather than buying and displaying them, but he did eventually have a small private library. Much of it was kept at the law office and was intermingled with the much larger collection owned by his bookish law partner, William Herndon. Both Lincoln and Darwin were passionate readers, and if Darwin ultimately read more, it is mainly because he had no need to earn a living and lived longer. While their purposes and opportunities differed greatly, both read far more widely than one might guess, and they read (or, in Lincoln's case, at least had access to) a large number of the same books, which brought Lincoln and Darwin into surprisingly close contact with each other's mental development. Books also helped them to escape their presumed destinies, on the one hand, that of a Shropshire doctor or provincial vicar with a penchant for entomology and, on the other, that of an Illinois farmer or carpenter.

Darwin shared Lincoln's love of Shakespeare, Milton, Gray, and Byron but never mentioned Robert Burns, whom Lincoln adored. A fortnight before his own fiftieth birthday, Lincoln attended a dinner celebrating Burns's centenary. Lincoln "could very nearly quote all of Burns' Poems from memory. . . . He had acquired the Scotch accent and could render Burns perfectly"—though possibly with a Hoosier twang.[14] Darwin, who met people in Edinburgh who had known Burns, may have found Burns's dialect writing unpalatable and felt little "auld lang syne" for Edinburgh. He could not share Lincoln's close identification with Burns's background of poverty, his satirical view of religion, and even his habit of always walking around with a book in one hand. Long before Darwin began to theorize himself out of orthodoxy, Lincoln had already become a religious skeptic partly because of Burns, who, as one early acquaintance said, "helped Lincoln to be an infidel I think—at least he found in Burns a like thinker & feeler."[15]

That Lincoln loved reading Burns or any poet is less surprising than that he was able to read at all. His parents and stepmother were basically illiterate, subscription schools cost money, schooling must have seemed a luxury for others to enjoy, and Abe experienced only a few months of it. He later wrote that "what he has in the way of education, he has picked up."[16] Probably many acquaintances had a similar education, which then languished through disuse. Darwin's environment overflowed with affluent and well-educated people, but in Lincoln's boyhood Indiana, "If a straggler supposed to understand latin, happened to so-journ in the neighborhood, he was looked upon as a wizzard." Darwin met nothing but high expectations at home, at school, in university; but in Pigeon Creek, wrote Lincoln, there was "absolutely nothing to excite ambition for education."[17]

By the time Darwin wrote about his education in his *Autobiography* in 1876, he was a world-famous scientist who could deprecate his neglect of the opportunities offered by his formal education and even believe his achievements came *in spite of* that education. When Lincoln wrote in December 1859 of his own education, he was consciously positioning himself as a possible presidential candidate, playing down any hint of intellectualism that might dampen popularity. There is no doubt that Lincoln was actually proud of his hard-won attainments.[18]

"He was the learned boy among us unlearned folks," according to a classmate.[19] Lincoln's ability and eagerness set him apart, and apparently from an early date, he saw education as the means to set himself free. But the path was strewn with obstacles. As one neighbor put it, Lincoln "was a constant, and I may say stubborn reader."[20] His father sometimes had to "slash" him to do his chores. "Lazy" is the word frequently used by contemporaries who shared Thomas Lincoln's inability to accept that his son had ambitions beyond farming. Because his family and neighbors were unaccustomed to seeing anyone in the *act* of reading, they found Lincoln's habits memorable. "He read setting, lying down & walking in the street"; he read while the plow horse caught its breath; cocked on a haystack; astraddle a woodpile; while others went to a dance; between customers in the post office; under a tree; up a tree. Most often, the descriptions include "lying down": on a trundle bed while rocking a cradle with his foot; flat on his back on a cellar door; usually stretching his six-foot-four-inch frame on the floor.[21] All this was odd to his "unlearned" neighbors—and even to us who love reading but do not live in a cabin crowded with children and devoid of sofas and good lighting.

Reading is largely a solitary activity, but Lincoln was always a sociable character who rubbed along well with his family (except for his father) and was never viewed as an upstart or a snob by his neighbors. He was happy to read aloud to those who couldn't and explained things patiently without showing off, though correcting his father on occasion earned him a slap. As a teenager, he wrote documents for illiterate adults, perhaps even assisting his "bungling" father.

Darwin, like his father and grandfathers, possessed a library. His books were often heavily annotated, and he developed the habit of cutting through the spine of particularly thick books so he could read half at a time. In contrast, there are few examples of marginalia by Lincoln, and mutilating such sacred items was unimaginable. Living in frontier communities with illiterate parents meant a dearth of books in Lincoln's home. During his brief periods of schooling, his teachers used the simplest textbooks, but young Abe's self-education was greatly aided by his stepmother, Sarah, who, though illiterate, at least appreciated learning and brought from her deceased first husband's house not only a *King James Bible* but also, perhaps, Bunyan's *Pilgrims Progress*, Aesop's *Fables*, Defoe's *Robinson Crusoe*, and *Sinbad the Sailor*. In the forests of Indiana, Lincoln's first glimpse of Western civilization came through William Scott's *Lessons in Elocution* with its excerpts from Shakespeare, Homer, Virgil, Milton, Dryden, *The Spectator*, Pope, Hume, and Dr. Johnson. While loving poetry, Lincoln never shared Darwin's pleasure in reading novels: Lincoln said that he "never read an entire novel" in his life, having once commenced but never finished *Ivanhoe*; however, a friend testified that Lincoln read at least one whole novel, Nathaniel B. Tucker's *George Balcombe* (1836). If little of Lincoln's reading was fictional, *all* of his reading was for pleasure while also being purposeful. Lincoln read William Grimshaw's *History of the United States* (all forty-nine years of it), Mason Locke Weems's *Life of Washington*, and David Ramsay's biographies of George Washington and Benjamin Franklin—all providing heroes to emulate.[22] Someone loaned Lincoln *The Revised Statutes of Indiana*, which also contained the *Constitution* and the *Northwest Ordinance*. One piece of campaign literature in 1860, perhaps for the propaganda value, mentioned that Lincoln had read Captain James Riley's popular *Authentic Narrative of the Loss of the American Brig "Commerce"* (1817), recounting the author's experience as a white slave in North Africa.[23]

When Lincoln left his father's house to live in New Salem, Illinois, his self-education moved up a gear. Having measured the gap between his spoken English and literary English, he worked intensely to master the rules laid down in Kirkham's *Grammar* and after a relatively short time told a friend, "Bill, if that is what they call a science, I'll subdue another."[24] When Lincoln became a postmaster, newspaper subscribers found their latest issues well thumbed, and customers who struggled with the alphabet appreciated Lincoln's fondness for reading aloud. When not in the post office, he was often by the bank of the Sangamo River with his friend Jack Kelso, a curiously cultured hunter and fisherman, who may have introduced Lincoln to Burns's poetry. They spent hours discussing Shakespeare while Kelso fished and Lincoln didn't. But Lincoln's interests ranged well beyond newspapers and poetry. According to a friend, after grammar, Lincoln studied

Arithmetic, then Natural philosophy, Astronomy & Chemistry, then Surveying, and Law, In the mean time read history & other books, the news papers of
the day, in fact any and all books from which he could derive information or
knowledge.... [Lincoln would] alternately, entertain and amuse the company
by witticisms jokes &c, and study his lessons. He never appeared to be a hard
student as he seamed to Master his studies with little effort, until he commenced the study of the Law, in that he became wholly engrossed.[25]

To turn himself into a surveyor, Lincoln read Flint's *System of Geometry
and Trigonometry* and Gibson's *Treatise on Practical Surveying*.[26] By the age of
twenty-one, he was perhaps already contemplating a career in law as he worked
through Blackstone's *Commentaries* with the help of a pocket dictionary and
Murray's *English Grammar*, and it was his habit "after reading or studying Murray or Blackstone for two or three hours, to take up Burns' poems, which he
read . . . with that hilarity which usually was so peculiar to him."[27] Later friends
in Springfield loaned him law books, and he could research his cases in the
State Supreme Court library.[28] Later still, as a congressman in Washington, D.C.,
Lincoln was deemed a "bookworm" because he spent so much time in the old
Congressional Library, from which he later borrowed books on military science
during his presidency.[29]

Lincoln's interest in geology is discussed later along with the scientific interests of Herndon, his law partner, but for now note that Lincoln, like Darwin,
had a special regard for Euclid whose work (as he told a campaign biographer) he
"studied and nearly mastered . . . since he was a member of Congress."[30] Lincoln
also read the eighteenth-century natural theologian William Paley, whose work
greatly influenced Darwin.[31]

The horizons of both men were broadened not only by books but also by
the direct effect of travel. While Darwin's youthful voyaging was more extensive
and famously life changing, Lincoln's traveling at a slightly younger age was
also important to his development. Lincoln never shared Herndon's great interest in botany, and we have no evidence that either of them ever read Darwin's
wonderful account of his experiences as a naturalist in *The Voyage of the Beagle*.
Had Lincoln read it, he would have discovered that the book raised issues about
slavery that might well have set Lincoln reminiscing about his own experiences
voyaging down the Mississippi River.

Voyages and the Experience of Slavery

In the spring of 1828, nineteen-year-old Lincoln made the first of two journeys by flatboat down the Ohio and Mississippi rivers, and about the time when the second one ended, Darwin embarked on a voyage that carried him around the globe. Lincoln's travels lasted a few months while Darwin's trip was supposed to finish in two years but lasted five. Lincoln's purpose was to transport farm produce as frontier settlers had done since moving west of the Appalachian Mountains. Lincoln's father had made the same journey and after selling off his produce downstream (and breaking up his flatboat to sell as firewood) had returned home on foot, but Abe was able to make his return trips by that wonder of the age, the steamboat. Darwin's purpose was anything but commercial—indeed, his father had to pay his expenses. Having recently graduated from Cambridge University, Darwin sought to delay becoming a clergyman by pursuing his interests in natural science. A plan to explore the Canary Islands with some friends fell through, but Professor J. S. Henslow arranged for Darwin to be invited aboard HMS *Beagle* for its projected two-year voyage charting the coast of South America. Captain Robert FitzRoy needed a "gentleman" to serve as his companion, but it was understood that Darwin could also pursue his naturalist's interests, although a naturalist had already been assigned to the mission.

Before Lincoln's second river journey, he and three companions had to build the flatboat themselves. It was eighteen by eighty feet and made to carry themselves, sacks of corn, barrel pork, and a small herd of hogs on their twelve-hundred-mile journey. HMS *Beagle* was only ten feet longer and six feet wider than Lincoln's flatboat. There were no live hogs, but salt pork featured prominently among the victuals. There were also the normal supplies and spares for a long-distance voyage, ten cannon and ammunition, seven additional boats carried onboard or on davits, an array of scientific equipment, and a sixty-five-man crew with nine "supernumeraries," Darwin among them. His quarters were in the ten-by-eleven-foot chart room in which he could not stand upright and had to sleep in a hammock above the four-by-six-foot chart table that competed for space with Darwin's personal belongings, his naturalist's accoutrements, and the ship's mizzen mast, poking up through the decks.

FitzRoy's obsessive surveying lengthened both the voyage and Darwin's opportunities to explore the Cape Verde Islands, Brazil's rain forest, the pampas, the Andes, and later Tahiti, New Zealand, and Australia, not to mention the Galapagos Islands. "The voyage of the *Beagle*," Darwin wrote four decades later, "has been by far the most important event in my life and has determined my whole career."[1] With hindsight, one can see that Darwin's voyage merely confirmed the course he had vaguely set for himself. He had never longed to be a doctor or a clergyman, and science was no longer a hobby. The specimens Darwin regularly sent to Cambridge fascinated the scientific community while his letters to Henslow were read to scientific bodies and printed for private distribution even before Darwin returned. Less than a month after that, the twenty-six-year-old was proposed as a Fellow of the Royal Geological Society.

As Darwin now turned his back on any career other than science (and never stepped aboard another ship), Lincoln decided there was more to life than being a farmer, carpenter, or even a river man. Circumnavigating the globe is quite unlike floating down and steaming up the Mississippi, yet the most significant difference is that Darwin was traveling away from civilization and Lincoln toward it. The Englishman left behind his managed countryside and highly stratified society to experience tropical forests, deserts, mountain ranges, and primitive peoples. Upon first seeing tropical vegetation, Darwin wrote in his diary, "It has been for me a glorious day, like giving to a blind man eyes," and his first walk in a rain forest was practically a religious experience: "The mind is a chaos of delight."[2] To Lincoln, a forest meant being handed an axe and told to start clearing. Trees were meant to be sawed in a mill that rivers were meant to power. The novelties Lincoln experienced on his voyage were social: towns and cities, especially New Orleans, "by far the largest city the two country boys had ever seen, with imposing buildings, busy shops, and incessant traffic. Here they heard French spoken as readily as English." Historian David Herbert Donald thus expressed what Lincoln never did: "perhaps it was too overwhelming."[3] Although Darwin was well read on natural history, his voyage brought him an essential experience of the vast diversity of species and varieties in the natural world. Likewise, although Lincoln's reading had opened worlds beyond the Ohio valley, seeing the diverse cities and peoples of the lower Mississippi must have been illuminating to a frontiersman.

Lincoln's later autobiographical sketch devoted four sentences to his first flatboat trip and ten to the second, though half of those were taken up with an irresistible yarn about someone's idea of sewing up the eyes of the live hogs so they would be easier to drive onto the flatboat; it didn't work.[4] He also later joked that during the first stage of one journey, the Sangamo River meandered so severely that he camped in the same place three nights in a row.[5] Other contemporaries later added some details to these stories, but none of this can compare with the classic travel narrative produced by Darwin, commonly known as *The Voyage of the Beagle*. The book contained a solid diet of factual and scientific information supplemented with lively opinions, all drawn from the extensive diaries, notebooks, and letters he wrote during his travels.

One common experience upon which both these two young travelers commented was slavery. Although both had already gained various impressions of human bondage, these were broadened during their voyages, probably more so in Darwin's case.

Among Lincoln's four sentences (in third person) about his first flatboat trip to New Orleans, he mentioned that "one night they were attacked by seven negroes with intent to kill and rob them. They were hurt some in the melee, but succeeded in driving the negroes from the boat, and then 'cut cable' 'weighed anchor' and left." Contemporaries later corroborated, or elaborated, parts of this story: "Abe told me so—saw the scar myself," and "Abe fought the Negroes . . . pretended to have guns . . . the Negroes had hickory clubs—my husband said 'Lincoln get the guns and Shoot'—the Negroes took alarm and left."[6]

The story of seeing a slave auction in New Orleans during the second trip is even more dramatic if less reliable. According to Herndon's interview notes, John Hanks, Lincoln's cousin and fellow flatboatman, said, "We saw Negroes Chained—maltreated—whipt & scourged. Lincoln saw it—his heart bled—Said nothing much . . . was thoughtful & abstracted—I can say knowingly that it was on this trip that he formed his opinions of slavery."[7] Hanks had not actually gone all the way to New Orleans and later suggested he heard the story from the third crew member, John Johnston, who had.[8] Nevertheless, the story appeared in Herndon's biography, with the embellishment of Lincoln saying to his fellows, "By God, boys, let's get away from this. If ever I get a chance to hit that thing [slavery], I'll hit it hard." Herndon assured readers that he had "also heard Mr. Lincoln refer to it himself."[9]

Until the age of seven, Lincoln lived in a slave state, where he probably saw slaves marched along the road in chains. After his family crossed the Ohio River, he saw slaves brought across to labor temporarily on land where slavery was supposedly forbidden. The sight of shackled slaves being transported by steamboat "was a continual torment to me; and I see something like it every time I touch the Ohio, or any other slave-border."[10] Even in supposedly free Indiana and Illinois, slavery was a familiar presence, and the only *novelties* Lincoln could report from his travels were being personally attacked by blacks and sickened by the sight of an actual auction.

Darwin's family was as strongly antislavery as Lincoln's, but before the *Beagle* voyage, Darwin had no immediate experience of slavery. Less than two months into the trip and shortly after reaching the first slave country Darwin ever visited, Brazil, he quarreled severely with Captain FitzRoy, who "defended and praised slavery, which I abominated." According to Darwin, FitzRoy mentioned that "he had just visited a great slave-owner, who had called up many of his slaves and asked them whether they were happy, and whether they wished to be free, and all answered 'No.' I then asked him, perhaps with a sneer, whether he thought that the answers of slaves in the presence of their master was worth anything. This made him excessively angry."[11] Darwin was later gratified when a visiting Royal Navy captain recounted the story of a slave who was very well treated by his master yet said, "If I could but see my father & my two sisters once again, I should be happy. I can never forget them." Darwin commented archly in his diary, "Such was the expression of one of these people, who are ranked by the polished savages in England as hardly their brethren, even in God's eyes."[12]

Like Lincoln, Darwin also learned something of the desperation of fugitive slaves. He heard that a group were contriving "to eke out a subsistence" in mountains near Rio de Janeiro when a party of soldiers found them. "One old woman, . . . sooner than again be led into slavery, dashed herself to pieces from the summit of the mountain." Darwin added with bitter irony, "In a Roman matron this would have been called the noble love of freedom: in a poor negress it is mere brutal obstinacy." And the notion of slave auctions also shocked Darwin. While staying on a hacienda,

> I was very nearly being an eye-witness to one of those atrocious acts which can only take place in a slave country. Owing to a quarrel and a law-suit, the owner was on the point of taking all the women and children from the male slaves, and selling them separately at the public auction at Rio. Interest, and not any feeling of compassion, prevented this act. I do not believe the inhumanity of separating thirty families, who had lived together for many years, even occurred to the owner. Yet I will pledge myself, that in humanity and good feeling he was superior to the common run of men.

Darwin often indicated how much his own impressions differed from the perceptions of other whites. He was also interested by the slaves' self-perceptions, as he mentioned in "one very trifling anecdote, which at the time struck me more forcibly than any story of cruelty." While trying to make himself understood by a black ferryman, Darwin gesticulated overmuch, and the black, expecting to be hit, dropped his hands to his sides: "I shall never forget my feelings of surprise, disgust, and shame, at seeing a great powerful man afraid even to ward off a blow, directed, as he thought, at his face. This man had been trained to a degradation lower than the slavery of the most helpless animal."[13]

Lincoln and Darwin, while still young men, both had reactions against slavery that were as admirable as they were untypical. Slavery had been widespread for centuries, was taken for granted by most people, and was thought by many to be sanctioned by the Bible. Writing in his *Beagle* diary, Darwin came close to prophesying about an unknown flatboatman in Illinois: "As far as my testimony goes, every individual who has the glory of having exerted himself on the subject of slavery, may rely on it his labours are exerted against miseries perhaps even greater than he imagines."[14]

The Declaration of Independence proclaims that "all men are created equal," and although Jefferson and many others who signed his composition were slaveowners, it is an important fact—which Lincoln highlighted later in his career—that they viewed slavery as an evil, somehow imposed on America by the British, and now destined for extinction as British rule ended. Many northern states began to abolish slavery through various methods and time scales and assumed the southern states would soon follow, although it was acknowledged that they faced a more complex set of problems. Recognition of that shared conviction and those divergent situations made it easier to tolerate compromises on any *national* issues relating to slavery on the assumption that such expedients were temporary.

The first national compromise was the 1787 law forbidding slavery in the western lands north of the Ohio River but not south of it—one reason why many small farmers such as the Lincolns later moved north of the river. In that same year, the founders drafting the Constitution thrashed out a set of compromises that they viewed as necessary, temporary, and embarrassing (for which reason they avoided the words "slave" or "slavery"). The Fifth Amendment, protecting property from federal encroachment, effectively guaranteed that the power to abolish slavery would remain as it had been, solely with the individual states.

That year, 1787, also marked two important developments in Britain's antislavery evolution. American independence removed two-thirds of the slaves over whom Britain had previously had jurisdiction, but the Atlantic slave trade itself was still a vast part of the British economy. Recognizing that abolishing the slave trade was the first step toward ending slavery itself, antislavery leaders such as Granville Sharp and Thomas Clarkson founded the Society for Effecting the Abolition of the African Slave Trade. Darwin's grandfather Josiah Wedgwood was the committee member who designed the famous medallion bearing the motto, "Am I not a man and a brother?" He sent some examples to the president of the Abolition Society in America, Benjamin Franklin, to show that abolition "is daily more and more taking the possession of men's minds on this side of the Atlantic as well as with you."[15] Darwin's other grandfather, Erasmus Darwin, described the image in verse:

> The Slave in chains, on supplicating knee,
> Spreads his wide arms, and lifts his eyes to Thee;
> With hunger pale, with wounds and toil oppress'd,
> "Are we not brethren?"—Sorrow chokes the rest.[16]

Also in 1787, Sharp was instrumental in establishing the Sierra Leone Company, which was perceived as a parallel effort: to colonize freed blacks back to

Africa. While slaves were scattered throughout various parts of the United States, principally in the south, most British-owned slaves lived in the West Indies, four thousand miles from Britain. About fourteen thousand slaves or freedmen resided in England, and in 1787, the first ships began implementing their repatriation to Africa. Although some black leaders who preferred to remain permanently in Britain withdrew their support for a project that suffered great difficulties, most people viewed colonization not as futile or racist but as the most obvious redress for the original crime of kidnapping Africans—although this remedy was not applied where most British-owned slaves resided, in the West Indies.[17]

The American Constitution had provided that the federal government could end the slave trade after a twenty-year moratorium, and many expected slavery to die out in the United States shortly after the slave trade's scheduled ending in 1808. British abolitionists could look forward to no such date, but after years of political activism—and with the Americans about to cease being consumers or competitive suppliers—the antislavery forces finally obtained Parliamentary approval to outlaw the British slave trade in March 1807.

Despite legal prohibitions, an illicit trade may have brought into America as many as 250,000 slaves between 1808 and 1860, but the growth in slave numbers was mainly the result of natural increase. The slave population grew by half a million in the decade before 1830, when the total stood at two million.[18] This growth would not have occurred without an increased demand. Late-eighteenth-century British inventions helped mechanize the process of producing cotton cloth, and the American invention of the cotton gin in 1793 reduced costs for producing the particular species of cotton that was easiest to grow. The Industrial Revolution in Britain stimulated the growth of King Cotton in the American south.

Private emancipations decreased as the dollar value of slaves rose and as southern legislatures worried that the presence of freed slaves might undermine the slave system. To address this problem, some prominent citizens, mostly southerners, organized in 1817 the American Colonization Society (ACS) to promote the repatriation of blacks to Africa, imitating the Sierra Leone Company.[19] This project soon spread to nonslave states as well but overall had a far greater task and far less success than the British effort. The ACS ultimately failed, yet Lincoln became and long remained a supporter of colonization.

Eventually both the British and American antislavery organizers realized that ending the slave trade had not killed off slavery. Further actions were required, but there was disagreement about how gradual these steps should be. After British antislavery activists formed the Society for the Mitigation and Gradual Abolition of Slavery in 1823, Sarah Wedgwood, daughter of Josiah and the aunt of the teenage Charles Darwin (and of his later wife), was involved in protests that led to the removal of the word "gradual" from the organization's title, although it continued an essentially gradualist approach.[20] Gradualism was even more strongly challenged in America by William Lloyd Garrison, who in his abolitionist newspaper, the *Liberator*, made it abundantly clear that he would have nothing to do with gradualism, compensation schemes, or constitutional impediments. Although many American abolitionists later distanced themselves from Garrison's radical "immediatism," the gradualist middle ground was eroded not only by the greater activism of the immediatists but also by the stiffening resistance of slaveowners to any type of change.[21]

In 1831 two unsuccessful slave revolts in Jamaica and Virginia highlighted the difference in the British and American situations. The Jamaican revolt hastened Parliament's passage of the Abolition of Slavery Act in 1833, which ordered the end of slavery on 1 August 1834. Yet, the measure was gradualist: only children under six were immediately freed; older slaves became "apprentices" for up to six years, working three-quarters of the time for their owners; and the owners themselves (but not the slaves) were compensated by the British tax-payer to the tune of £20,000,000, or about £37 per slave.[22] Darwin cheered from aboard the *Beagle*, "What a proud thing for England, if she is the first European nation which utterly abolishes it."[23] Meanwhile in Virginia, the unsuccessful Nat Turner uprising in 1831 influenced a month-long debate in the Virginia legislature about slavery's future. The legislators voted by seventy-three to fifty-eight to continue slavery.[24] Had that important state revived the former trend of state-by-state abolition, patient hope might have been restored. Instead, while Britain was abolishing slavery on all British soil, in America it was increasingly difficult to see how slavery would, or even could, end. "How well I remember thinking," Darwin later wrote, "that Slavery would flourish for centuries in your Southern States."[25]

While Darwin, departing from Brazil, sighed, "I thank God, I shall never again visit a slave country," and his Aunt Sarah fretted as abolition proceeded too gradually, American abolitionists like Garrison adhered to immediatism, causing many other Americans, such as the clerk devouring newspapers in New Salem, Illinois, to see nothing but danger in their approach.[26] The former expectation that slavery would wither away was crushed by its increasing profits and the growing costs, potentially, of compensation or repatriation. Yet, white Americans were loath to accept that such an evil institution must continue solely for economic reasons. With no simple solution in sight, many people resolved the tension by either looking the other way or looking at slavery in a new way: as something *not* evil. Toward this end, efforts were made to depict slaves as something less than human and more like cattle—an endeavor against which both Lincoln and Darwin later fought.

The Racial Background, Personal Encounters, and Turning Points in 1837

Why blacks were so "suitable" for slavery was a question for which there was no obvious answer. Lincoln's line about "the invention of negroes" opposed the view that slavery was natural for blacks or divinely planned. But opposition is not refutation. Today, we are still in the process of learning about race, but in the 1830s, this process was in its early stages, with ideas multiplying and diverging just as Lincoln and Darwin embarked on careers that, separately, helped to shape the debate.

The Great Chain of Being had developed from ancient and medieval concepts as a system of classification, or taxonomy, that grouped together plants and animals possessing a collection of similar features. But the metaphor of a chain allowed too many contrary interpretations: unity and relationship, multiplicity and difference, hierarchy, not to mention the purpose of the chain maker and whether he manufactured it all at once or over time. If chain links were grouped into distinct families, one suddenly had several chains, either destroying the metaphor or sending one in search of missing links. In any case, a chain implied permanence, and individual links were not expected to multiply or divide.

As European plants and animals were studied more closely thanks to the microscope and overseas exploration, it became difficult to keep even broad classes separate: even plants and animals overlapped with "zoophytes." Worse, the sacred distinction between animals and men came under assault. European explorers encountered *widely* different types of men: not just black men in Africa but also Indians, Orientals, Malays, Lapps, and Hottentots, among others; and newly discovered animals—orangutans and chimpanzees—seemed uncomfortably similar to humans.[1] Alexander Pope expressed it darkly, "[Man] hangs between; in doubt to act, or rest: / In doubt to deem himself a God, or Beast."[2] It was one thing to be *between* God and animals, perhaps even part angel; it was something else to be partly a brute. Mankind seemed no longer a link but a set of links, with some men more brutish than others.

Establishing how many groups of men existed proved difficult. In 1684, the Frenchman François Bernier came up with four, but sometimes six, categories of mankind. Richard Bradley (1721) said five; David Hume (1748) four or five; Carl Linnaeus (1758) had four; Oliver Goldsmith (1774) six; and Johann Friedrich Blumenbach (1775) four and later (1781) five, after which five was fairly standard.[3] With multiplicity came ranking, for even the great Linnaeus's characterizations were usually value laden, so that whites (or Europeans or Caucasians) came out best. More difficult than description was explanation: how did humans come to be so varied? The Bible, as usual, allowed contrary interpretations: one view—later called "monogenism"—holds that variations must have arisen *after* God's single creation of Adam and Eve, while the other—"polygenism"—proposes that the variations resulted from separate divine creations implied elsewhere in Scripture.[4] On one level, polygenism simplified matters: human races were not only different but designedly so. However, polygenists then diverged over whether God had expressed this racial distinction through some mark on Cain or on Ham or on some earlier pre-Adamite creation or on some separate creations in regions unknown to the Hebrews. Monogenists were spared that debate yet were burdened with explaining how Adam's descendants diverged. Climatic differences or degenerative diseases were often cited to explain variations in color and just as often refuted. Some said that men started out white and then degenerated; others that the original color of man was "tawny" with changes spreading in either direction from there. Few suggested an essentially black origin (the more common view today).[5] Because color seemed an awkward measure of variation, "facial angle" was regularly employed after the 1770s. When distinguishing between humans and animals, many placed blacks outside of the human species, while those who insisted that all races of men were members of the same species found it necessary to repeat the view frequently in the face of disbelief.[6] But the very concept of a species had become a problem even though by the 1750s Linnaeus had extended to animals and men the principle John Ray had used back in 1682 to define a plant species: a set of individuals who reproduce new individuals similar to themselves.

By this definition, blacks' ability to breed with (for example) whites and produce fertile offspring indicated they were members of the same human species. Yet, some refused to believe this, and even Linnaeus was troubled by alleged examples of fertile offspring successfully bred from separate species. It was mooted that blacks were not fully human because they were themselves hybrid products of some early intercourse between men and apes. Tales of man/ape couplings had multiple (and somewhat contradictory) purposes, supposedly explaining how blacks came into existence and why they are so "bestial," and usually involving a male ape breeding with an unwilling (or sometimes willing) black female—which nonsensically made blacks progenitors of their own hybridity. Nevertheless, the garbled theory was deemed at least possible by such men as Linnaeus, the influential French naturalist Le Comte de Buffon, Lord Monboddo, Thomas Jefferson, Dr. Benjamin Rush, and Dr. Charles White.[7]

Some observers connected physical variations with mental capabilities. Those who agreed that blacks were mentally deficient might dispute whether this resulted from historical deprivations (the ravages of slavery) or simply being inferior by nature, the former being remediable, the latter not. David Hume declared that blacks were "naturally inferior to whites" and that blacks enslaved in the colonies showed none of the "symptoms of ingenuity" evident in even the "most rude and barbarous of whites."[8] In 1812, Georges Cuvier, the French Aristotle, deemed Africans "the most degraded of human races, whose form approaches that of the beast and whose intelligence is nowhere great enough to arrive at regular government."[9]

By the 1830s, the Great Chain of Being had become a collapsed cat's cradle, with no agreed definition for "species," "man," or "race" and with contradictory explanations for the causes and future outcomes of perceived racial differences. Today, despite DNA evidence that the genetic difference among human races is negligible, many people still take for granted that biological difference implies intellectual inferiority in certain races; and in the early nineteenth century, whatever philosophers or scientists had to say, the vast majority of people held that view. Lincoln and Darwin were raised in a world in which European superiority seemed proved, not by physical but by social data: comparative technology, social organization, and imperial control. It is not amazing that both men were affected by this view, but it is surprising how much they rejected it. Both gave an early demonstration of this at about the age of twenty-three.

For a generation, the U.S. government's policy toward the Indian tribes east of the Mississippi had been to move as many of them west of the river as could be bribed, threatened, or tricked into going. But the Sauk and Fox tribes soon regretted their decision to cooperate, and their leader, Black Hawk, led two thousand of them back into Illinois. The state governor called for militia to drive them out, and Lincoln joined Sangamon County's company. Militiamen chose their own officers, and Lincoln's unit elected him—a man they had known less than a year. It was, Lincoln recalled in 1859, "a success which gave me more pleasure than any I have had since."[10] Lincoln's company never saw any action, but having nothing better to do and needing the money, he reenlisted twice, until honorably discharged.

Popular with his men, Lincoln demonstrated real ability as a leader and made friends later important to his career. In an era when politicians boasted of any military exploits, Lincoln forever cracked jokes about fighting no Indians but having "a good many bloody struggles with the musquetoes."[11] Lincoln was only once in serious danger—from his own men.

An old Indian wandered into the militia's camp, and though he carried a certificate of good character from American authorities, some of Lincoln's men prepared to shoot the man, saying, "We have come out to fight the Indian and by God we intend to do so."[12] Lincoln had no reason to like Indians. They had killed his grandfather "by stealth," and he evidently had no qualms about fighting Indians or about the removal policy. Every frontiersman knew these wars involved atrocities on both sides. Lincoln's men had already seen another militia unit's casualties: "horribly mangled—heads cut off—heart taken out—& disfigured in every way"; and "strong men wept" over mutilated civilians. The militiamen's blood was up, and killing this old Indian was, to them, different from killing a white man. But in the end this popular captain placed himself between his men and the Indian and reportedly said, "Men, this must not be done. He must not be shot and killed by us."[13]

Unlike a commissioned officer in the regulars, an elected captain of short-term militia could expect arguments: "The Indian is a damned spy"—before, it had been enough that he was an Indian. Then some fool suggested Lincoln lacked guts. "If any man thinks I am a coward let him test it," said the young captain. Assuming he meant a wrestling match—and they had admired his prowess in plenty of those—they grumbled about his advantage in strength and size. "Choose your weapons then," he replied, showing he would risk serious harm to himself or to his opponent—and all for the sake of a savage that most of Lincoln's men, like most of his contemporaries, barely considered a human being. The militiamen calmed down, and the old Indian was spared.

About three months after Lincoln's discharge, Darwin had his first opportunity to learn how Europeans in Latin America treated the native populations. While collecting specimens in the interior, he heard stories about the frontier war between whites and Indians: "The Indians torture all their prisoners & the Spaniards shoot theirs."[14] One "very intelligent" soldier recounted how in the most recent campaign more than a hundred Indians, men, women, and children, were taken or killed—"for the soldiers sabre every man" while "all the women who appear to be above twenty years old are massacred in cold blood." When Darwin exclaimed that this seemed "inhuman," the soldier replied, "Why, what can be done? They breed so!" Darwin rightly called this a "war of extermination" and related tales of the Indians' desperate courage. When three Indian prisoners were killed one after the other for refusing to betray information, the last said, "Fire, I am a man and can die!" Darwin added, "Not one syllable would they breathe to injure the united cause of their country!"[15]

Part of FitzRoy's purpose on this voyage was to return to Tierra del Fuego three natives who had been taken to England three years earlier and schooled in English and Christian ways. Darwin, having lived with these "civilised" natives for several months, was shocked when he first saw Fuegians in their original habitat: "These poor wretches were stunted in their growth, their hideous faces bedaubed with white paint, their skins filthy and greasy, their hair entangled, their voices discordant, and their gestures violent. Viewing such men, one can hardly make oneself believe that they are fellow-creatures, and inhabitants of the same world."[16] And yet, Darwin believed in their essential humanity and attributed the differences between the "civilised" and the "savage" to social development rather than to any specific racial differences. On first seeing the Fuegians, "the reflection at once rushed into my mind—such were our ancestors."[17] Darwin also pondered how the physical environment might influence development. After observing that the Fuegians' numbers were not decreasing, Darwin explained, "Nature by making habit omnipotent, and its effects hereditary, has fitted the Fuegian to the climate and the productions of his miserable country. . . . I believe, in this extreme part of South America, man exists in a lower state of improvement than in any other part of the world."[18]

Back in his Edinburgh days, Darwin had been privately tutored in taxidermy by a black freedman, John Edmonston, who had been trained by the eccentric English naturalist Charles Waterton. Darwin called Edmonston "very pleasant and intelligent."[19] Becoming acquainted with FitzRoy's "civilised" Fuegians aboard the *Beagle*, Darwin was "incessantly struck . . . how similar their minds were to ours."[20] At the first landfall, the Cape Verde Islands, Darwin enthused that he had never seen anyone "more intelligent than the Negros, especially the Negro or Mulatto children," who showed curiosity and perception about his silver pencil case and percussion gun.[21] Darwin seemed to expect his readers to doubt his descriptions of positive qualities in nonwhites.

Comparing FitzRoy's "civilised" Fuegians and the original article, Darwin saw the effects of social conditioning. The precivilized Fuegians' lack of private property "must for a long time retard their civilisation," whereas in Tahiti, where missionaries had "inculcated the value of property," the natives "now fully understand the value of money, and prefer it to old clothes or other articles." Revealing some conditioning of his own values, Darwin noted, "It requires little habit to make a dark skin more pleasing and natural to the eye of an European than his own colour." Darwin was quite willing to reject other observers' views, as when he wrote that the Australian aborigines "appeared far from being such utterly degraded beings as they have usually been represented." Sometimes he praised the work of missionaries, sometimes not, but always asserted that groups can make forward or retrograde steps: "It is a pleasant thing to see the aborigines advanced to the same degree of civilisation, however low that may be, which their white conquerors have attained." But he noted that while the Fuegians had had little contact with Europeans, the number of Australian aborigines "is rapidly decreasing," and the same was happening to the Indians of Patagonia. Like Lincoln during the Black Hawk War, Darwin hovered above other men's racial prejudices: "The varieties of man seem to act on each other in the same way as different species of animals—the stronger always extirpating the weaker"—thus differentiating men as "varieties" not "different species."[22]

As the *Beagle* neared home Darwin wrote in his diary the same thought that had struck him when he first saw the wild Fuegians: "One's mind hurries back over past centuries: could our progenitors be such as these?"[23]

While Darwin encountered different human varieties by traveling overseas, Lincoln could observe "aliens" by staying in America, the land of immigrants. In the 1830s, the population was swelled by over half a million immigrants—four times as many immigrants as in the previous decade, while in the following decade the number nearly trebled. Along with Englishmen following in the footsteps of Lincoln's English forebears, increasing numbers came from Germany and Ireland. And while European immigrants were pushing aside Native Americans, they were also dragging in Africans in chains. The social, economic, and political issues that ensued from all this mixing of people were of importance to political leaders—and Lincoln became one when he managed to win a seat in the state legislature shortly after his service in the militia.

Some Americans, unhappy that politicians had not stemmed this flow, joined the anti-immigrant American Party, better known as the Know-Nothings—a nickname reflecting either secretiveness or embarrassment about the party's discriminatory basis. If such a party could establish itself in a nation comprising immigrants' descendants and could rant about foreign tongues and religion in a country that had always absorbed foreign speakers and was the only one on Earth to have religious tolerance written into its Constitution, then one can imagine how exercised that nation could become about men of other races.

Lincoln expressed the link between antialien feeling and antiblack feeling when explaining in 1855 why he could never be a Know-Nothing:

> How could I be? How can any one who abhors the oppression of negroes, be in favor of degrading classes of white people? Our progress in degeneracy appears to me to be pretty rapid. As a nation, we began by declaring that *"all men are created equal."* We now practically read it "all men are created equal, *except negroes."* When the Know-Nothings get control, it will read "all men are created equal, except negroes, *and foreigners, and catholics."*[24]

When the *Beagle* returned to England in 1836, Darwin discovered that antislavery agitation in Britain continued because immediatists like his Aunt Sarah were fighting the gradualist legislation that had established an "apprentice" system intended to keep adult blacks in forced labor for another six years. While that campaign continued in Britain, in America, twenty-eight-year-old Abraham Lincoln—now, in 1837, a lawmaker himself—took his first public position on the issue of slavery.

As abolitionist activity expanded both in Britain and America, proslavery elements in America's southern states grew increasingly angry. Their legislatures appealed to northern colleagues to denounce abolitionism, and the Illinois legislature found itself debating a lengthy resolution to that effect. On the national stage, Henry Clay regularly denounced abolitionists for endangering the Union, and Lincoln allegedly once said of his political hero, "I never had an opinion upon the subject of slavery in my life that I did not get from him."[25] Yet, in 1837, Lincoln reacted to abolitionism in a significantly different way.

The antiabolitionism resolution before the legislature maintained "that the right of property in slaves is sacred" under the federal Constitution, adding that "the General Government cannot abolish slavery in the District of Columbia, against the consent of the citizens of said District without a manifest breach of good faith."[26] The upper house approved the resolution unanimously. In the lower house, the voice vote proceeded alphabetically all the way to the *L*s before anyone voted nay. After that, only five more colleagues joined Abraham Lincoln's vote against the seventy-seven-vote majority.

No political advantage was to be gained by opposing the resolution or in submitting a written "protest" some weeks later to explain his negative vote. Most of Lincoln's fellow Whigs had voted for the resolution, and only one, Dan Stone (a native of Vermont), cosigned the "protest" that stated that he and Lincoln

> believe that the institution of slavery is founded on both injustice and bad policy; but that the promulgation of abolition doctrines tends rather to increase than to abate its evils; . . . that Congress . . . has no power, under the constitution, to interfere with the institution of slavery in the different States; . . . that the Congress has the power . . . to abolish slavery in the District of Columbia; but that power ought not to be exercised unless at the request of the people of said District.[27]

"The kernel of the whole event," as historian William Lee Miller rightly stresses, "is that Lincoln and Stone did, and the assembly did not, say plainly that slavery is unjust." Some have suggested that Lincoln and Stone delayed their "protest" until other issues were settled, but a "more striking point," as Miller puts it, is "that they issued any written 'protest' at all."[28]

The apparent disharmony in condemning slavery as immoral *and* abolitionists as harmful is resolved by understanding Lincoln's concept of how slavery might best be ended. "Like many of his contemporaries," comments biographer David Herbert Donald, "Lincoln viewed slavery as an institution that would die out if it was confined to the areas where it already existed."[29] Although Lincoln himself did not record that particular view until 1845 and a decade later began to doubt the possibility of a "peaceful extinction of slavery," presumably in 1837 he *did* believe slavery was destined to die a "natural death"—exactly what abolitionists had stopped believing.[30] Their evidence was the growth of King Cotton, the increasing number of slaves despite the cessation of the slave trade, and the fight over Missouri's admission in 1820, which demonstrated southern leaders' reluctance to accept any geographical limit to the spread of slavery. But in 1837, none of this had yet convinced Lincoln that the abolitionists were right.

Lincoln had plenty of straws to grasp at. The British were debating whether to accelerate their abolition process, and their navy was actively suppressing the Atlantic slave trade. In the last two decades, emancipation had either begun or been completed in a dozen other countries. Mexico abolished slavery in 1829—a major reason why American slaveowners living in Texas had revolted against Mexican rule and were now seeking (to the horror of abolitionists) admission to the United States as a slave state. The Virginia legislature nearly voted for abolition and might yet do so. In 1832, Clay had secured a form of federal funding for the American Colonization Society. Lincoln might even have taken heart from the desperation of southern efforts to shield slavery from abolitionist propaganda by preventing the distribution of antislavery writings in the mails, by imposing a "gag rule" in Congress to counter a massive petition campaign, and, of course, by appealing to northern legislatures for antiabolitionist resolutions.

The two-month gap between Lincoln's negative vote and his protest may not signify a delay as much as a reaction to a new provocation. John C. Calhoun, the south's most eminent voice, speaking on 6 February in favor of extending the "gag rule," startled the Senate by urging that slavery "is beyond the jurisdiction of Congress" and that "Abolition and the Union cannot coexist." More shocking was Calhoun's *rejection* of the notion that slavery was evil: "far otherwise; I hold it to be a good, as it has thus far proved itself to be to both [races]."[31] Whether or not Calhoun's speech influenced Lincoln and Stone, it was on this key point that they drew a moral line that others refused to draw and Calhoun was willing to cross.

In the same month as Lincoln's "protest," there occurred in London a "moment more than any other in Darwin's life" that, according to biographer Janet Browne, "deserves to be called a turning point." Darwin had recently received important information from ornithologist John Gould regarding specimens brought back on the *Beagle*. Darwin scribbled in a notebook, "The same relation that common ostrich bears to Petisse, extinct guanaco to recent: in former case position, in latter time." In essence, this means that since two types of South American "ostriches" could be shown to be two different species, this geographical difference might somehow relate to the chronological difference between extinct South American mammals and existing ones. Here was evidence that species were not immutable but could somehow change. Darwin now realized, as Browne points out, that "[Charles] Lyell's general principles linking past with present could be applied to the biological world as much as to the geological."[32]

Six years earlier, Darwin had boarded the *Beagle* without planning to test any theory about species, yet early in the voyage, he found evidence to support someone else's theory about geology.[33] In preparation for the voyage, J. S. Henslow advised him to study the recently published first volume of Lyell's *Principles of Geology* but "on no account to accept the views therein advocated." Darwin ignored the latter advice and instead became a disciple—for long the only one—of Lyell's theories. "I am proud to remember," Darwin wrote in old age, "that the first place . . . which I geologised, convinced me of the infinite superiority of Lyell's views over those advocated by any other work known to me."[34]

Lyell's theory, dubbed "uniformitarianism," maintains that geological evidence did not fit the Christian story of a creation of the Earth followed (as most geologists then believed) by a gradual cooling of the Earth's core, after which the planet was stable. Instead, according to science historian Martin J. S. Rudwick, Lyell argues that landmasses are continually rising and falling according to pressure from internal molten rock while rain, rivers, and glaciers cause erosion and sedimentation and that these present-day processes are "fully representative of those that have acted in the past, not only in *kind* but also in *degree*." There is no beginning or end in Lyell's "system," because "the overall pattern of earth history has been steady-state or cyclic, and not directional at all."[35] Along with this cycle of new land being made and old land destroyed, Lyell accepts that there were "new species arising and old ones becoming extinct in a gradual 'birth' and 'death' of species. . . . [H]e found causes for species extinctions in disturbances to the fine balance of interspecific competition, disturbances initiated by climate, land and sea changes," but because Lyell rejects the transmutation of species, "he left unexplained how new species were 'created.'"[36] According to Rudwick, because the fossil evidence was then so limited, "Lyell has no great difficulty in arguing here that the apparent progress in the rank of organic life is an illusion, owing simply to the differentially selective preservation of terrestrial and aquatic animals." Lyell recognizes no progression from simpler to more complex organisms, thus rejecting the radical thinking of Jean-Baptiste Lamarck and of Darwin's own grandfather Erasmus Darwin. Lyell felt that his nonbiblical view of geology actually supports a biblical view of organic life: only God created species which were "immutable," and if the fossil record suggests that new species sometimes appeared, then these result from subsequent phases of *new* creation, the creation of man being the greatest of these and of an entirely different order. Although fossil evidence suggests man first appeared in geologically recent times, Lyell argues that this is not evidence of "a progressive system." "Lyell maintains this inconsistent position," according to Rudwick, "because he makes a sharp separation between man's physical and mental characteristics: man's evident superiority is due to his power of reason, particularly his power of *improvable* reason, which is precisely the feature that distinguishes him from other animals" (original emphasis).[37]

Although Darwin felt that Lyell's ideas liberated science—or at least geology—from dependence on the Bible to understand nature, he would later address Lyell's inconsistency in applying uniformitarianism to both geology and organic life—but not to man. Eventually, Darwin employed Lyell's gradual elevation and subsidence of landmasses as part of an explanation for changes in organisms: changes that were "uniform" in their law-like causes but "progressive" in their long-term effects. As Darwin later said in a different context, he eventually "out-lyelled Lyell" by applying an important aspect of uniformitarianism to all species.[38]

Yet all that was in the future. During the *Beagle*'s voyage, Darwin was overwhelmed by the tremendous variability he found in plant, animal, and most intriguingly, in human life, all seeming at first glance to conflict with uniformitarianism. Observing how Australian marsupials were so similar and yet so different from analogous species on other continents, Darwin jested in his diary, "An unbeliever in everything beyond his own reason might exclaim 'Surely two distinct Creators must have been [at] work.'" But after puzzlement at God's failure to come up with a more uniform blueprint, Darwin found reassurance when he saw how an Australian lion-ant caught its prey in the same intricate way that European lion-ants do: "Now what would the disbeliever say to this? Would any two workmen ever hit on so beautiful, so simple & yet so artificial a contrivance? It cannot be thought so.—The same hand has surely worked throughout the universe."[39]

During the last weeks of the voyage, Darwin began to reflect more deeply on the variations noticed among similar animal groups in the separate Galapagos Islands and among similar yet differentiated foxes in East and West Falkland islands, noting that "the zoology of Archipelagoes will be well worth examining; for such facts would undermine the stability of Species."[40] Six months later and back in England, the specialists' reports on the specimens he had brought back made Darwin think his wild speculation about the mutability of species might be valid.

In March 1837, Darwin received confirmation that the Galapagos mockingbirds differed not only from any other known species but also from each other, depending on which island they inhabited.[41] These diversities, not just of variants but also of species, were also apparently true of the tortoises, and now there was further corroboration regarding Galapagos iguanas. And the evidence was not only from the islands. Gould, who declared the mockingbirds separate species, saw a similar diversity between Darwin's specimens (some fossil) of South American ostriches. Darwin now saw a pattern of distribution that was not confined only to islands or determined solely by geography but also related to the patterns of extinctions found in geologists' fossil discoveries.

This was the turning point at which Darwin embraced the concept of transmutation advocated by his own grandfather Erasmus and Lamarck, even though their explanations for how transmutation worked seemed utterly insufficient. Unfortunately, Darwin could not openly discuss the issue with colleagues because transmutation was tarred by the Lamarckian brush, and the religious implications were severe.

Groping for some explanation of how transmutation actually occurred, Darwin found "a theory by which to work" in the following year.[42] When, two decades later, Darwin published a theory regarding transmutation of species, he avoided any discussion of the human species: it would take another dozen years before he published on that. And yet, from the start, mankind was on Darwin's mind and particularly the issues of race and slavery, as his notebook jottings from 1838 demonstrate. Early in that year, as Parliament was finally ending slavery on British soil, Darwin scrawled, "Animals—whom we have made our slaves we do not like to consider our equals.—Do not slaveholders wish to make the black man other kind?"[43] In May, Darwin showed that he disagreed not just with slaveholders but with most of his own race:

> Has not the white man, who has debased his nature by making slave of his fellow Black, often wished to consider him as other animal.—it is the way of mankind & I believe those who soar above such prejudices yet have justly exalted nature of man—like to think his origin godlike, at least every nation has done so as yet.[44]

In August 1838, Darwin jotted in a notebook "origin of man now proved."[45]

Both Darwin and Lincoln considered slavery immoral and recognized that any notion that blacks were not fully human helped to delay abolition. Lincoln supported efforts to circumvent the majority's bigotry or apathy (rather than attack it head on) by advocating policies of gradual change and, later, colonization. Darwin would not only assert that men were all of one species: he also sought to prove it. Darwin needed to convince an opposition of elite scientists, many of them his mentors, while Lincoln had to win votes among the prejudiced masses from which he himself had sprung.

Bigotry and bad science were obstacles to an enlightened view of races and their relationships, but another obstacle was religion. And soon, both Lincoln and Darwin had to make crucial choices about the way to present their own evolving religious views.

Religious Reformation

he literature about Lincoln's and Darwin's religious opinions is vast because those beliefs in differing ways posed a challenge in their own time and for subsequent generations. Darwin's work has greatly influenced the Western world's view of divine purpose, and Lincoln's amalgam of unorthodoxy and religiosity remains a puzzle. Since both men had reasons to be deliberately ambiguous about personal views that not only influenced public opinion but also changed over time, the evidence is controversial and needs plenty of context—therefore, the topic must be discussed at more than one stage in each life.

England had an established church, but both of Darwin's parents came from a nonconforming tradition. In the United States, there was no established church but a mass of competing denominations, particularly on the barely settled frontier. Britain exhibited more religious toleration than most countries, yet religious dissenters still faced practical disadvantages and even civil disabilities. No such inequalities existed in America, though extralegal forms of prejudice could have similar effects. During Darwin's childhood, his comfortably middle-class family actually leaned away from mild dissent and toward loose conformity. Lincoln's formative years were passed in places like Pigeon Creek, where the "meeting house" still smelled of freshly cut timber and the preachers were often itinerants, or New Salem, where there was no real church at all.

Having lost their mothers at an early age, Lincoln and Darwin felt the influence of their fathers' religious views, to which they reacted quite differently. Darwin's father had turned against his own father's radical deism, keeping his views to himself and having his children baptized in Shrewsbury's Anglican church—although, in the Wedgwood tradition, their mother led them to the town's Unitarian chapel on Sundays. After her death, the family attended the Anglican church. For Dr. Darwin, the issue was social rather than theological, appearances mattering more than doctrine. Lincoln's family lived amid the fluctuations of denominational splits and evangelical competition. His parents were married by a Methodist preacher but joined local Baptist congregations.

However different the English and American religious environments, children generally adopted their parents' religious choices, a pattern followed by young Charles and his siblings and also by young Abe's sister—but not by Abe.

Up to his early twenties, Darwin barely gave a thought to religious matters and certainly did not question the literal truth of the Bible. Although he spent morning chapel cribbing Virgil, when running late to class he prayed for God's assistance to avoid a beating.[1] Lincoln, on the other hand, seems to have looked askance at religious practices from a remarkably early age. There is no obvious explanation, but it may reflect Lincoln's intellectual precociousness and antipathy toward his father.

Lincoln's father and stepmother were formally accepted into the Pigeon Creek Baptist Church when Lincoln was fourteen; his older sister joined three years later; and when the family left the area, the twenty-one-year-old Abe had still not joined. He attended services, enjoyed reading the Bible, and (as his affectionate stepmother later recalled) "would hear sermons preached—come home—take the children out—get on a stump or log and almost repeat it word for word." Another source put it differently: ten-year-old Abe's mimicry of the "style & tone of the old baptist preachers" interfered with chores until his father "would come and make him quit—send him to work."[2] While his father may have been less concerned about blasphemy than work-shyness, Abe may have begun to link his father's lack of ambition to his religious piety.

After his family moved to Illinois in 1830, Lincoln was helping to clear a neighbor's land when Peter Cartwright, a well-known Methodist circuit rider then running for governor, came by. The neighbor recalled that Lincoln, "awkward and very shabbily dressed," argued with Cartwright, who "laid down his doctrines in a way which undoubtedly seemed to Lincoln a little too dogmatical." The neighbor admired how Lincoln "met the great preacher in his arguments, and the extensive acquaintance he showed with the politics of the State—in fact he quite beat him in the argument."[3] It may have been on political rather than religious points that the uneducated Lincoln, barely twenty-one, scored against an experienced orator, but his later encounters with the famous evangelist were decidedly about religion.

While the lanky farmhand was sparring with a preacher, Charles Darwin was at Cambridge supposedly preparing for the Church. Darwin was not averse to becoming a country clergyman with leisure for natural history pursuits, and yet "I had scruples about declaring my belief in all the dogmas of the Church of England." This was putting the point mildly, considering his Unitarian antecedents, but becoming a clergyman—even obtaining a degree at Cambridge—required acceptance of the Thirty-Nine Articles. "Accordingly I read with care Pearson on the Creeds and a few other books on divinity; and as I did not then in the least doubt the strict and literal truth of every word in the Bible, I soon persuaded myself that our Creed must be fully accepted."[4]

At Cambridge, Darwin preferred "beetling" to theology, but a useful overlap was found in the writings of William Paley, some of which were required texts. Darwin admired the "clear language" of Paley's *Moral Philosophy*, the "logic . . . of his *Natural Theology*," and "could have written out the whole of the *Evidences [of Christianity]* with perfect correctness." Paley considered nature so full of design that there had to be a designer: his famous analogy was of a pocket watch found by the wayside that proved the existence of a watchmaker. According to historian John Hedley Brooke, there are two main interpretations of Darwin's embrace of natural theology in his youth. One view is that he "found God *in* nature rather than deduced God's existence *from* it" (original emphases), as when during his first walk in a Brazilian rain forest, he felt moved by nature. The other view is that Darwin narrowed the scope of natural theology by taking the view that God's designs were to be seen "in providential combinations of laws rather than in specific organic structures."[5] But whether nature revealed God as the creator of laws or as the author of repeated interventions, Paley provided Darwin with a theology that was logically organized and buttressed by nature, and this helped make conventional religion acceptable to Darwin. Still, Darwin was concerned that when the time came for ordination, he might not be able to answer yes when some bishop asked if he felt "inwardly moved by the holy spirit."[6] He overcame his scruples sufficiently to take his degree in 1831 and then found opportunities to delay ordination until the voyage of the *Beagle* eventually shelved the whole idea.

As Darwin set off on his life-changing trip, Lincoln returned from his second journey down the Mississippi River and settled in New Salem, Illinois, where later reports from acquaintances suggest Lincoln was developing highly unorthodox views, influenced by the skeptical writings of Voltaire, Thomas Paine, Constantin-François Volney, and Robert Burns. Calvinist predestination and eternal punishment for all but the "elect" were satirized in Burns's poem "Holy Willie's Prayer," which Lincoln quoted so fondly that a friend said, "That was L[incoln's] religion."[7] Doubting that God would inflict eternal damnation was the mildest part of Lincoln's unorthodoxy. More shocking was that Lincoln followed Paine in rejecting the Bible's literal truth and Jesus's divinity.[8]

Lincoln and Darwin were in their early twenties when the former, just entering politics, became most extreme in his infidelity, while the latter, circumnavigating the globe, reached the high-water mark in his orthodoxy. Darwin's "firm conviction of the existence of God, and of the immortality of the soul" was heightened while experiencing "the grandeur of a Brazilian forest." Darwin's faith withstood the corrosive influence of hard-nosed seamen, who once "heartily laughed" at him "for quoting the Bible as an unanswerable authority on some point of morality."[9] Others recollected that Darwin attended Protestant religious services wherever possible and felt "shock" when a shipmate "openly avowed disbelief in the flood."[10]

Meanwhile, in New Salem, it was Lincoln who caused "shock" around the cracker barrel in Sam Hill's store by expounding on the fallibility of scripture and the lack of evidence for Jesus's incarnation and resurrection and by writing two pieces on religion in 1834, one of which was probably destroyed at the time, while the other was only identified in 1994. Lincoln had boarded and worked at Hill's store, which was his campaign headquarters when he ran for the state legislature. One candidate, who had defeated Lincoln in 1832 but was defeated by him in 1834, was Cartwright, the politically ambitious Methodist preacher. Cartwright had previously defended in a newspaper his opinion that more Methodists should be appointed locally as teachers in the growing "common school" movement. Lincoln wrote a scathing reply, accusing Cartwright of all manner of hypocrisy and adding, "I believe the people in this country are in some degree priest ridden." The letter, paid for as an advertisement, was not signed by Lincoln but by Sam Hill, who had his own reasons for disliking Cartwright but lacked the ability to write such a piece. Whether or not Lincoln wrote it as a favor for Hill, Hill signed it as a favor for—or to protect—Lincoln.[11]

Evidence strongly suggests that, also in 1834, Lincoln wrote a "book" (more likely some folded sheets) on "infidelity" that attacked "the divinity of Christ—special inspiration—revelation &c." Apparently, Lincoln showed it to Hill, who promptly threw it in a red-hot stove to save Lincoln's reputation. Some voters in the recent election had been reluctant to back Lincoln because he was said to be a "deist" or an "infidel," and certain friends realized that he must stop. The matter was generally hushed up: over three decades later, former acquaintances were reluctant to discuss it, and one who was away from New Salem at the time claimed that he never learned anything of it on his return.[12] But many years after Lincoln's death, it was reported that Hill's wife had once asked Lincoln, "Do you really believe there isn't any future state?" and he allegedly replied, "Mrs. Hill, I'm afraid there isn't. It isn't a pleasant thing to think that when we die that is the last of us."[13]

Albert Taylor Bledsoe, a fellow Kentuckian transplanted to Illinois and close friend of Lincoln in the 1840s, later felt Lincoln had deliberately disguised his attitude toward religion. After West Point and a stint in the Episcopalian ministry, Bledsoe turned to law, practicing in Springfield from 1839 to 1848. Bledsoe was one of the few men who had known Lincoln well—sometimes having an office adjoining Lincoln's and living in the same boardinghouse for a while—yet later came to despise him. After Lincoln's death, Bledsoe wrote a review of the biography by Ward Hill Lamon, who had employed William H. Herndon's evidence about Lincoln's early years as an "infidel." "From our various conversations," Bledsoe commented bitterly, ". . . we had supposed that we had some adequate idea of his religious sentiments, but Colonel Lamon's work has dispelled this illusion." While Lincoln never pretended to believe "in the being of God, or in a moral government of the world, much less in the truth of Christianity . . . he always seemed to deplore his want of faith as a very great infelicity, from which he would be glad to be delivered; and all this was uttered with an air of such apparent modesty, that his gloom . . . awakened in our minds no other feeling than one of deep compassion."[14] That compassion clearly dissipated after Bledsoe read Lamon's biography.

Lincoln's religious views were submerged sufficiently so that in 1836 he received more votes than any other candidate in his district. Spending more time in Springfield to attend the legislature and study law, Lincoln became a political ally and friend of Ninian W. Edwards, leader of the Springfield's loftiest social set. Edwards gave Lincoln a present, *The Works of William Paley*, perhaps thinking Lincoln's faith in God's existence needed shoring up.[15] Paley's "natural theology" may have succeeded, just as it had earlier bolstered Darwin. Yet Lincoln did not entirely stop criticizing Christian orthodoxy and scriptural authority, and he apparently began to use "nature" in his arguments.

Early in 1837, shortly after Lincoln settled in Springfield as a partner in John T. Stuart's law firm, he wrote (ungrammatically) to a friend, "I've never been to church yet, nor probably shall not be soon. I stay away because I am conscious I should not know how to behave myself."[16] Lincoln avoided church but not religious debate. The law office was next door to the court clerk's office, and one clerk, James H. Matheny—nine years Lincoln's junior but later a groomsman at his wedding—recounted to Herndon that:

> Lincoln used to talk Infidelity in the Clerks office. . . . Lincoln attacked the Bible & New Testament on two grounds—1st From the inherent or apparent contradiction under its lids & 2ndly from the grounds of Reason—sometimes he ridiculed the Bible & New Testament—sometimes seemed to scoff [at] it. . . . Sometimes Lincoln bordered on absolute Atheism: he went far that way & often shocked me. I was then a young man & believed what my good mother told me. . . . Lincoln would come into the clerk's office where I and . . . others were writing or staying; & would bring the Bible with him—read a chapter— argue against it.[17]

Significantly, Matheny's very next phrase is: "Lincoln then had a smattering of Geology if I recollect it." Lincoln was now using "expert testimony," employing not just reason but also science against revelation. Allen C. Guelzo argues that Lincoln probably read Charles Lyell's *Principles of Geology*, but he might also have read the American edition of Robert Bakewell's *Introduction to Geology* (1813), or William Maclure's *Observations on the Geology of the United States of America* (1817) or even the 1804 translation of *A View of the Soil and Climate of the United States*, by Volney, the French deist whose skeptical *Ruins* supposedly influenced Lincoln's religious thinking.[18] In addition to reading, Lincoln's surveying job may have sparked his interest in geology, and certainly, he was later acquainted with at least three geologists in Illinois.

While Lincoln may have brought geology into religious debates, Darwin probed the subject deeply during the *Beagle* voyage, just as his faint interest in a church career waned.[19] After the voyage, as Darwin groped for some mechanism to explain transmutation, he read widely and sought information from colleagues without sharing with them his scientifically unorthodox notions. After reading Lyell's latest thinking in the fifth edition of the *Principles*, published in 1837, Darwin wrote in the margin, next to Lyell's argument that variation in species can only go so far before it must stop: "If this were true, adios theory."[20]

Wary of revealing his theorizing to his colleagues, Darwin poured his thoughts into a series of notebooks. He expressed his frustration that religious feeling tolerated new laws discovered by astronomers and geologists but balked at "fixed laws of generation" because they touched mankind too closely.[21] "Why is thought being a secretion of the brain, more wonderful than gravity a property of matter? It is our arrogance . . . our admiration of ourselves."[22] Increasingly seeing evidence for those "fixed laws" in the *Beagle* specimens, Darwin gradually abandoned some conventional religious beliefs. Darwin spent hours conversing with the free-thinking intellectuals who made up the London coterie in which his brother Erasmus moved. "During these two years," he later wrote, "I was led to think much about religion. . . . I had gradually come by this time, to see that the Old Testament from its manifestly false history of the world, . . . was no more to be trusted than the sacred books of the Hindoos, or the beliefs of any barbarian."[23]

Darwin did not suddenly lose faith. Not "until a considerably later period" of his life did he think much "about the existence of a personal God." Perceiving that the New Testament contradicted the Old, he wondered if God made "a [new] revelation to the Hindoos," would he let them retain their earlier beliefs? "This appeared to me utterly incredible." Darwin believed that the New Testament did not have to be discarded with the Old; however: "The clearest evidence would be required to make any sane man believe in the [Christian] miracles; . . . the men at that time were ignorant and credulous to a degree almost incomprehensible by us; . . . the Gospels cannot be proved to have been written simultaneously with the events . . . they differ in [too] many important details . . . to be admitted as the usual inaccuracies of eye-witnesses." While claiming no "novelty" in these "reflections," Darwin "gradually came to disbelieve in Christianity as a divine revelation." His "complete" disbelief in orthodox Christianity developed so slowly as to cause "no distress, [and] . . . I have never since doubted even for a single second that my conclusion was correct." Far from distressed, Darwin felt relief. The teaching that "men who do not believe, and this would include my Father, Brother and almost all my best friends, will be everlastingly punished" he called "a damnable doctrine."[24] This was the same criticism that Lincoln found so agreeable in Burns's "Holy Willie's Prayer." Like Lincoln, Darwin avoided throwing out the baby with the bath water—the moral with the miraculous—for, while writing of one "damnable doctrine," he also used the words "beautiful" and "perfection" to describe "the morality of the New Testament."

Darwin apparently discussed religion with his father in 1838, at the same time that the subject of marriage arose. His father advised Darwin "to conceal carefully my doubts, for he said that he had known extreme misery thus caused with married persons. Things went on pretty well until the wife or husband became out of health, and then some women suffered miserably by doubting about the salvation of their husbands, thus making them likewise to suffer."[25]

Dr. Darwin sought to preserve his son's future happiness in marriage, just as Hill hoped to secure Lincoln's political prospects by throwing his "book on Infidelity" into the red-hot stove. Lincoln gradually became less blatant about his views, while Darwin, though already circumspect, presently failed to follow his father's advice.

Darwin may have couched his religious views in the best possible terms when he proposed to his cousin Emma Wedgwood in 1838. Ten days after he had returned to London to prepare the house for his future wife, Emma wrote to him, mostly with family news but adding a long expression of her "fear that our opinions on the most important subject should differ widely. . . . My reason tells me that honest & conscientious doubts cannot be a sin, but I feel it would be a painful void between us. . . . I should dread the feeling that you were concealing your opinions from the fear of giving me pain." She asked Charles as "a favour" to read a passage from the Gospel of John.[26]

Lincoln's marriage courtship was far more complicated, but after one broken engagement, Lincoln finally married Mary Todd, whose intellectual attainments, social graces, and political connections far exceeded those of most of the women he had encountered previously. Although Mary did not inform her sister and brother-in-law of her plan to marry Lincoln until a few hours before the ceremony, and Lincoln did not tell his "best man" until late in the afternoon, the wedding, on the evening of 4 November 1842, was not an impulsive move: Lincoln had obtained the license, booked a clergyman, and had the wedding ring engraved: "Love is eternal." The two weddings were barely sacramental events. The Darwins' Anglican ceremony was modified to respect Unitarian sentiment, the attendance was small, and within two hours the newlyweds were eating sandwiches on a train for London. The Lincolns' suddenly announced wedding was conducted in Mary's sister's house by a minister of the Episcopalian church that Lincoln did not attend and that Mary abandoned for another a decade later. The Darwins' first child was born eleven months after their marriage, but when the boy was baptized, there were no godparents because Charles and Emma objected to "religious proxies." Lincoln's first child came along almost exactly nine months after Lincoln's marriage, and apparently only the last of their four sons was baptized.[27]

Despite marital disharmonies—not only more public in the Lincolns' case but also probably more exaggerated by contemporary notice—both marriages, begun in some trepidation, successfully lasted "until death us do part," with none of the partners ever being unfaithful. "Infidelity" was a problem only in the religious sense. Mary Lincoln was superficial in her religious sensibilities and probably felt satisfied that her husband, though not an orthodox Christian, was a truly good and moral being. He was careful—at least by the time she met him—not to disturb other peoples' religious feelings, although Mary had difficulty getting Lincoln to attend church. Compared with Mary Lincoln, Emma Darwin was far more devout, despite coming from a Unitarian tradition. Her husband—the erstwhile trainee for a country parsonage—had by the time of their marriage developed ideas that would shake the Christian world and create a painful wound in their marriage.

Sometime after Lincoln used geology in arguing against scripture in 1837, he became more wary about discussing religion at all. In October, Lincoln wrote a letter to a newspaper expressing concern that a political opponent had asked one of Lincoln's friends if "he ever heard Lincoln say he was a deist."[28] His friend Matheny reported that as Lincoln "grew older he grew more discreet—didn't talk much before strangers about his religion."[29] The change must have been fairly swift, for by 1838 or 1839, when Herndon came into the circle of Matheny and Lincoln, he apparently never heard about the "book on Infidelity" even though Herndon himself was a freethinker.[30] Lincoln now kept to himself views that might alienate clients, voters, and members of the Edwards circle with whom he increasingly socialized. Any rumors of Lincoln's unorthodoxy failed to prevent his reelection to the legislature in 1838 and 1840.

In January 1841, Lincoln was depressed after his first engagement with Mary Todd broke down, so he stayed for a month with Joshua Speed, his closest friend for the last three years but recently returned to his (and Lincoln's) native state, Kentucky. A skeptic himself, Speed knew as much as anyone about Lincoln's religious views, but when Herndon later sought his opinion, Speed wrote cautiously, "I think that when I first knew Mr L he was skeptical as to the great truths of the Christian Religion. I think that after he was elected President, he sought to become a believer—and to make the Bible a preceptor to his faith and a guide for his conduct."[31] Speed offered one story to Herndon (and alluded to it in two later letters) that cast a pious light on Lincoln's religious views. Speed's mother had presented the "moody & hypochondriac" Lincoln with a Bible, advising him to read it and "adopt its precepts and pray for its promises." Later, as president, Lincoln sent Mrs. Speed a photograph with an inscription recalling that gift.[32]

After returning from Kentucky, Lincoln wrote to Speed's sister in Louisville, recounting the surprisingly cheerful behavior of a group of slaves being transported in chains on the same steamboat that carried Lincoln. He added the pious comment, "How true it is that 'God tempers the wind to the shorn lamb,' or in other words, that He renders the worst of human conditions tolerable, while He permits the best, to be nothing better than tolerable. . . . Tell your mother that . . . I intend to read [the Bible] regularly when I return home. I doubt not that it is really, as she says, the best cure for the 'Blues' could one but take it according to the truth."[33]

Those sentences epitomize Lincoln's self-presentation regarding religion. An avid reader of the Bible, Lincoln knew that his ability to quote scripture with great appropriateness always impressed listeners. However, Lincoln qualified Mrs. Speed's suggestion that the Bible was a cure for melancholy by adding "could one but take it according to the truth"—the difficulty being that he did *not* take much of it as true. To say so bluntly would offend; not to say it at all would be hypocritical. The balancing bar that kept him from falling off that tightrope was his use of language: if his Bible-quoting, his use of scriptural analogies, and his carefully phrased allusions to himself made people feel comfortable about his religious views, that was fine with Lincoln.

Darwin also became more careful about how he presented his interlinked religious and scientific views. Although some were discussed with his father and possibly his brother's progressive friends in London, Darwin remained cautious toward his scientific colleagues.[34] It was his own reading of Malthus's *Essay on the Principle of Population*—which stated that as human populations grow faster than resources, some of the population will always fail in the competition to survive—that gave Darwin a "theory by which to work." He called his theory "natural selection" in contrast to the artificial selection applied by men in the breeding of plants and animals. Although the idea needed much filling out, Darwin felt he had identified a mechanism for transmutation excelling (if not entirely supplanting) Lamarck's "acquired characteristics." This success occurred shortly before he married Emma, and some aspects disturbed her.

After the newlyweds were living under the same roof in London, Emma was reluctant to discuss religion face-to-face and wrote her husband another letter. She couched her feelings in terms that might appeal to his scientific sensibilities, expressing concern that his absorption in "following up yr own discoveries" might prevent him giving "attention to both sides of the question." She connected Erasmus's influence with Charles's loss of "some of that dread & fear which the feeling of doubting first gives & which I do not think an unreasonable or super-stitious feeling." Darwin's response is unknown. He could not stop his research or the conclusions to which it led, as Emma must have realized. Darwin folded up the letter and at some point wrote on the outside "When I am dead know that many times I have kissed & cryed over this."[35]

When Joshua Speed wrote to thank Lincoln for helping him through a crisis regarding Speed's upcoming marriage, Lincoln's reply suggested that, however skeptical both men were, they could accept the notion of a Supreme Being who is in control—although perhaps Lincoln worried that Speed would not believe he was being sincere. "I am not sure there was any merit, with me, in the part I took in your difficulty; I was drawn to it as by fate; if I would, I could not have done less than I did. . . . I always was superstitious; and as part of my superstition, I believe God made me one of the instruments of bringing your Fanny and you together, which union, I have no doubt He had fore-ordained." After reassuring Speed that his marriage was, as it were, made in heaven, Lincoln applied the concept to himself: "Whatever he designs, he will do for *me* yet. 'Stand *still* and see the salvation of the Lord' is my text just now."[36]

Either Lincoln retained some predestinarian aspect of his parents' religion despite, like Darwin, rejecting all Christian orthodoxy or he simply determined for himself that, logically, an omnipotent and omniscient God might well direct events according to His own plan, however unknowable. Lincoln had scraped his religion down to this essence, and the (admittedly ambiguous) evidence does not compellingly suggest that he ever abandoned this position or developed it further. Referring to his religion as "my superstition" was perhaps meant to reassure Speed that Lincoln was not abandoning rationalism and had circumscribed this bit of "faith."

Much has been written of Lincoln's fatalism, determinism, and belief in "the doctrine of necessity."[37] Of course, reconciling such a view with free will and moral responsibility is an age-old problem, and balance is harder to achieve than simple vacillation. In Lincoln's case, the conflict was intense. He seemed to believe in an all-knowing Creator who can direct events, but he had also freed himself from his own most obvious destiny by laboring hard to raise himself up through education and experience. As historian William Lee Miller expresses it, "We might say that his own life, which would be shot through with choices that made a difference, would disprove his own youthful theory [of necessity]."[38] Lincoln's dilemma came from recognizing that he was exceptionally able, ambitious, and successful—without ever discovering what made him so.

The scientifically minded Lincoln tried but failed to put everything down to reason. In a speech in 1842, Lincoln could declare, "Happy day, when, all appetites controlled, all passions subdued, all matters subjected, *mind*, all conquering *mind*, shall live and move the monarch of the world," yet eight months later, he could ask his newly married best friend: "Are you now, in *feeling* as well as *judgement*, glad you are married as you are? From any body but me, this would be an impudent question not to be tolerated; but I know you will pardon it in me."[39] Lincoln was "impatient to know" Speed's answer because such feeble evidence as another man's feelings about his married state might help Lincoln decide whether to propose again to Mary Todd. Thus did Lincoln juggle emotion and reason just as he juggled fatalism and free will.

In the middle of 1842, Darwin found time, amid numerous projects, to write out a thirty-five-page sketch of his transmutation theory. Employing the phrase "natural selection" for the first time, Darwin laid out his basic argument, beginning with the "unnatural selection" of domestication of animals by men, bringing in the struggle for resources derived from Malthus, carefully noting the numerous potential objections to his theory but holding back the detailed evidence building up in his notebooks. Man as a selector (domestication) was contrasted with nature as a selector (natural selection), but the effect of selection on humans themselves was studiously avoided, even though the subject had featured prominently in Darwin's notebooks for the last four years. Not only was the topic too emotive but also Darwin accepted that God might still be deemed the instigator of natural selection as a primary law, something that "should exalt our notion of the power of the omniscient Creator."[40] With his theory on paper and no clear plan for its future, Darwin returned to other publishing tasks and continual note taking.

At the same time, the ambitious Lincoln, while becoming a successful lawyer, planned his next political move as his fourth term in the legislature drew to a close. He began maneuvering in 1842 for a party nomination for a congressional seat and found himself the victim of a whispering campaign. Accusations that his upmarket marriage made him "the candidate of pride, wealth, and aristocratic family distinction" were patently absurd, but Lincoln was worried by "the strangest combination of church influence against me . . . it was every where contended that no Christian ought to go for me, because I belonged to no church, was suspected of being a deist."[41]

When he failed to get the nomination—for reasons relating more to party seniority than religion—Lincoln cleverly pushed through a resolution effectively creating a "succession" so his turn would come in the election after next. Lincoln settled back, concentrated on the law, and waited for the congressional election of 1846 to roll around. If Lincoln thought that by saying nothing offensive about religion during the interval he could bury the religious issue by 1846, he was wrong.

In 1843, a year after writing out the first sketch of his theory, Darwin briefly overcame his reluctance to mention it to any of his scientific colleagues. When zoologist George Waterhouse sought Darwin's advice about problems he and every other naturalist had with taxonomy, Darwin knew the problem was in the very endeavor "to discover the laws according to which the Creator has willed to produce organized beings . . . [which] means just nothing. According to my opinion, (which I give everyone leave to hoot at . . .) classification consists of grouping beings according to their actual relationship, i.e. their consanguinity, or descent from common stocks." After revealing a bit more about "linking all, say the Mammals, into one great, quite indivisible group," Darwin pulled back: "But it is no use my going on this way." The seed fell on stony ground: Waterhouse's eventual publication attacked any notion that groups of animals "blend perceptibly into each other."[42]

Six months later, Darwin tried again, this time with Joseph Dalton Hooker, eight years his junior, an admirer of *The Voyage of the Beagle,* and recently returned from a similar voyage. Hooker was a fine botanist whose father supervised the Royal Botanic Gardens at Kew. In the midst of a growing and mutually admiring correspondence, Darwin suddenly confided in Hooker, explaining the circumstances that led to the "very presumptuous work" he had been engaged in for seven years, before breaking the news: "At last gleams of light have come, & I am almost convinced (quite contrary to opinion I started with) that species are not (it is almost like confessing a murder) immutable." After disclaiming any connection with "Lamarck nonsense," Darwin added, "I think I have found out (here's presumption) the simple way by which species become exquisitely adapted to various ends. . . . You will now groan & think to yourself on what a man have I been wasting my time in writing to. I should five years ago, have thought so."[43]

Darwin waited several agonizing days for Hooker's reaction, which proved positive, though measured.[44] Hooker's intelligent questions evinced no shock about religious implications but rather a willingness to help. Emboldened, Darwin soon revised his first sketch, producing one over two hundred pages long, perhaps intending someday to show it to Hooker. Again, Darwin left out the risky—and at this stage unnecessary—issues of God the designer and the origin of man. In Hooker, Darwin had found a confidant and a wise critic who became a lifelong friend.

In that same year, 1844, Lincoln also gained the closest thing to a protégé that he ever had, although his relationship with Herndon was never as close as Darwin's with Hooker. Billy Herndon, born in 1818 (a year after Hooker), had met Lincoln when he first came to Sangamon County. Herndon's father was in the legislature with Lincoln, and from about 1838 Herndon worked and boarded at Speed's store, where Lincoln also then lived. Herndon was a bright young man but had left Illinois College without a degree. He married in 1840, decided to study law, and became a clerk in the office of Logan and Lincoln. Sometime late in 1844, Lincoln, who was amicably ending his partnership with Stephen T. Logan, bounded up the stairs to the office and asked Billy if he wanted to become his legal partner. An amazed Herndon said yes, and the papers were drawn up.

Scholars have speculated about why Lincoln chose Herndon, and there must have been speculation at the time, to which Herndon gave his own answer: "I don't know and no one else does."[45] To add a new suggestion to all the others: although Lincoln did not need technical legal information from Herndon and was not in the habit of speculating out loud with anyone, Herndon could be useful to Lincoln in one particular way. One of Herndon's peculiarities was that, even more than Lincoln, he was mad about reading, especially scientific works. At college, Herndon "acquired an unmanageable appetite for books." An exuberant Springfield bookseller reportedly said that in the 1850s, "Mr. Herndon read every year more new books in history, pedagogy, medicine, theology, and general literature, than all the teachers, doctors, and ministers in Springfield put together."[46] In 1866, an eastern journalist deemed Herndon's one of the best private libraries in the west. Although a portion of it—a thousand books, many of which may have been owned by Lincoln—was put up for auction by an impoverished Herndon in 1873, he still possessed (or, less likely, reacquired) enough books to fill the walls of a sixteen-feet-by-sixteen-feet room in 1879.[47] Many of whatever books Herndon and Lincoln separately owned were, after 1844, adorning the shelves and tables of the office of Lincoln and Herndon, and many more were added over the next seventeen years until Lincoln's final departure for Washington. "I had an excellent private library," Herndon later recalled, "probably the best in the city for admired books. To this library Mr. Lincoln had, as a matter of course, full and free access at all times." Herndon then gave the following sample: "Locke, Kant, Fichte, Lewes; Sir William Hamilton's *Discussions on Philosophy*; Spencer's *First Principles*, Social Statics, etc.; Buckle's *History of Civilization*, and Lecky's *History of Rationalism*; . . . the works of Paine, Parker, Emerson and Strauss; Gregg's Creed of Christendom, *McNaught on Inspiration*, Volney's *Ruins*, Feuerbach's *Essence of Christianity*, and other works on Infidelity." Herndon offered this particular sample to demonstrate Lincoln's access to progressive and infidel literature, adding, "Mr. Lincoln read some of these works."[48]

Neither this list nor Herndon's 1873 Auction List specify which works Lincoln actually read.[49] Separate evidence suggests Lincoln had read Paine and Volney in his youth, and a reliable source indicates that Lincoln admired and was possibly influenced by some writings of the transcendentalist, liberal theologian, and antislavery activist Theodore Parker. (Herndon idolized Parker and corresponded with him for six years until Parker's death in 1860.)[50] There is no independent evidence that Lincoln ever read any of the other works listed above. However, a contemporary wrote that at the end of an office day, Lincoln would remark, "Billy, what book have you worth while to take home tonight?" and another source related that Lincoln "would stretch himself on the office cot, aweary of his toil, and say, 'Now, Billy, tell me about the books;' and Herndon would discourse by the hour, ranging over history, literature, philosophy, and science."[51]

Whether Lincoln experienced these works directly or only vicariously, records show that Darwin had read most of these authors and knew several personally. In 1850, Lyell brought back from a trip to America some of Parker's writings— probably antislavery pamphlets—for which Darwin thanked him.[52] The other writers listed above either wrote for or were reviewed in the *Westminster Review*, and through his brother, Darwin was familiar with the "Westminster circle." The *Review* itself is one of several English periodicals to which Herndon apparently subscribed.[53] It is unknown whether Herndon purchased Darwin's *Voyage of the Beagle*, but the auction list shows that he possessed a copy of *The Origin of Species*.

In his later biography of Lincoln, Herndon was contradictory and haughty about Lincoln's reading habits, writing that Lincoln "read less and thought more than any man in his sphere in America. No man can put his finger on any great book written in the last or present century that he read thoroughly"; and that Lincoln "often quoted" the Bible and Shakespeare but "never read either one through." Herndon expressed frustration that Lincoln's interests differed from his own, and although Lincoln probably enjoyed Herndon's efforts to act as a mentor on some subjects, Herndon never felt he had much effect. After mentioning a few works on slavery that both he and Lincoln read, Herndon added, "After reading them we would discuss the questions they touched upon and the idea they suggested, from our different points of view. I was never conscious of having made much of an impression on Mr. Lincoln, nor do I believe I ever changed his views."[54]

One book Herndon owned and Lincoln certainly read also had a significant impact on Darwin. *Vestiges of the Natural History of Creation* was first published anonymously in London in 1844 by the Edinburgh writer and publisher Robert Chambers. Obviously influenced by Lyell and many other scientific writers, Chambers rejected special creations and instead argued for a progressive "development" that involved not only plants and animals but also geology (cutting across Lyell's view) and, indeed, the entire cosmos. No area escaped Chambers's analysis, from astronomy to zoology, and he included man as developing according to "natural laws" originally laid down by the Creator. Chambers was a good writer whose cheerful and elegant explanations of the latest arcane research made *Vestiges* a publishing phenomenon. Herndon seems to have owned an 1853 edition.[55]

According to Herndon's two slightly differing accounts, James W. Keyes, a tailor in Springfield, either gave or loaned Lincoln the book "which interested him so much that he read it through." The book's "doctrine of development or evolution . . . interested him greatly, and he was deeply impressed with the notion of the so-called 'universal law'—evolution." (The term "evolution" was probably not yet in common usage whenever Herndon and Lincoln discussed "development.") According to Herndon, after reading the book Lincoln "did not extend greatly his researches," although Lincoln "subsequently read the sixth edition of this work, which I loaned him." Herndon believed that "by continued thinking in a single channel [Lincoln] seemed to grow into a warm advocate of the new doctrine." In Herndon's view, this was Lincoln's only "investigation into the realm of philosophy. . . . 'There are no accidents,' he said one day, 'in my philosophy.'"[56]

When collecting materials for a biography of Lincoln, Herndon obtained from Keyes a statement that, while never mentioning *Vestiges*, discussed only one topic, Lincoln's religious beliefs: "Mr Lincoln . . . believed in a Creator of all things, who had neither beginning nor end, who possessing all power and wisdom, established a principal, in Obedience to which, Worlds move and are upheld, and animal and vegetable life came into existence. A reason he gave for his belief was, that in view of the Order and harmony of all nature which all beheld, it would have been More miraculous to have Come about by chance, than to have been created and arranged by some great thinking power." All this accorded with what Lincoln had read in *Vestiges* and before that in Paley's work on natural theology. However, Keyes continued, regarding "Christian theory," Lincoln "said that it had better be taken for granted—for by the test of reason all might become Infidels on that subject, for evidence of Christ's divinity came to us in a somewhat doubtful shape." Lincoln did not "express any preference" for one denomination over another and allowed that Christianity was "ingenious . . . and perhaps was calculated to do good."[57] Regarding *Vestiges*'s possible influence on Lincoln, Herndon later wrote:

> Mr. Lincoln had always denied special creation, but from his want of educa-
> tion he did not know just what to believe. He adopted the progressive and
> development theory as taught more or less directly in that work. He despised
> speculation, especially in the metaphysical world. He was purely a practical
> man. . . . He held that reason drew her references as to law, etc., from observa-
> tions, experience and reflection on the facts and phenomena of Nature. . . . He
> was a materialist in his philosophy.[58]

Lincoln may have "despised speculation" partly because it kept getting him in trouble politically. As noted earlier, suspicions in the "religious community" helped deny him a nomination in 1842, and in 1846, when Lincoln did gain the nomination, he discovered that his Democratic opponent—his old rival Reverend Cartwright—was willing to use rumors about "infidelity" against him. However, the sixty-two-year-old Methodist preacher found himself repeatedly outfoxed on the stump by the thirty-seven-year-old Lincoln, who at one point boldly attended one of Cartwright's revival meetings. The preacher shouted from the platform, "If you are not going to repent and go to Heaven, Mr. Lincoln, where are you going?" Lincoln replied that he was, in fact, going to Congress.[59] But shortly before elec-tion day, Lincoln heard that Cartwright was "whispering the charge of infidelity against me."[60] Lincoln felt it necessary to respond with a handbill "To the Vot-ers of the Seventh Congressional District."[61] This handbill, first discovered and published in 1942, was so ambiguously worded that it has been cited by scholars arguing for and against the view that Lincoln had grown more religious by 1846.[62] Neither a straightforward confession of faith nor a comprehensive denial of the charge of infidelity, this text demonstrates Lincoln's "damage limitation" tech-nique of stating carefully worded truths from which incorrect inferences could easily be drawn. In the text below, some of those potentially false inferences or disguised facts are inserted within brackets.

FELLOW CITIZENS:

A charge having got into circulation in some of the neighborhoods of this District, in substance that I am an open scoffer at Christianity, I have by the advice of some friends concluded to notice the subject in this form. That I am not a member of any Christian Church, is true; but I have never denied the truth of the Scriptures [although denying whatever seemed false]; and I have never spoken with intentional disrespect of religion in general, or of any denomination of Christians in particular [although questioning Christianity in general]. It is true that in early life [although "no longer"] I was inclined to believe in what I understand is called the "Doctrine of Necessity"—that is, that the human mind is impelled to action, or held in rest by some power, over which the mind itself has no control; and I have sometimes (with one, two or three, but never publicly) tried to maintain this opinion in argument [as if merely a debating point]. The habit of arguing thus however, I have, entirely left off for more than five years [as if no longer believing it]. And I add here, I have always understood this same opinion to be held by several of the Christian denominations [as if, despite previous denials, it was not a problem, anyway]. The foregoing is the whole truth, briefly stated, in relation to myself, upon this subject.

I do not think I could myself, be brought to support a man for office, whom I knew to be an open enemy of, and scoffer at, religion [his own "scoffing" having been in private]. Leaving the higher matter of eternal consequences, between him and his Maker [as if he believed in some future punishment], I still do not think any man has the right thus to insult the feelings, and injure the morals, of the community in which he may live. If, then, I was guilty of such conduct, I should blame no man who should condemn me for it; but I do blame those, whoever they may be [i.e., Cartwright], who falsely put such a charge in circulation against me.

July 31, 1846. A. LINCOLN.

In a letter written to an editor a fortnight later, Lincoln not only named Cartwright but also counterintuitively defined "false accusation" as making "an assertion without knowing whether it is true or false, the accidental truth of the assertion" being no justification. Standing on this thin ice, Lincoln could "aver, that he, Cartwright, never heard me utter a word in any way indicating my opinions on religious matters, in his life."[63]

At this point, only two facts were important: Lincoln had not committed to paper any statement about his religious views that could be proven untrue; and between writing the handbill and the letter, Lincoln had defeated Cartwright by an unprecedented majority in the district and a two-to-one margin in Springfield. Whatever his Maker might decide about Lincoln's "eternal consequences," the voters were indeed sending him to Washington, D.C.

Whether Lincoln read *Vestiges* before or (more likely) after the 1846 election, it had no direct effect on his contretemps with Cartwright, except that the "determinism" found in Chambers's work meshed with the "doctrine of necessity" that Lincoln to some degree accepted. For Charles Darwin, deeply engaged in his own investigation of "development," *Vestiges* had much more impact.

When *Vestiges* first appeared in London in October 1844, Darwin had only recently written the longer sketch of his theory, showing it to no one, not even Hooker, while nevertheless making arrangements for its publication "in the event of my sudden death."[64] Emma was eventually allowed to read it and even made some corrections in style—writing "a great assumption" in the margin beside Darwin's effort to explain the evolution of the eye.[65] The next time Darwin was in London, he found that the popular *Vestiges* was unobtainable, so he skimmed a copy in the British Museum.[66] "The writing & arrangement are certainly admirable," Darwin wrote to Hooker, "but his geology strikes me as bad, & his zoology far worse."[67] While joining the intelligentsia in trying to guess the author, Darwin was "much flattered and unflattered" when this "strange unphilosophical, but capitally-written book" was even attributed to him.[68] Chambers would not admit authorship, but Darwin and Hooker suspected him, especially after Darwin received a presentation copy from the publisher shortly after he and Chambers first met at a British Association meeting in 1847. Chambers had delivered a paper on marine terraces, citing some of Darwin's work, and while the audience responded negatively, Darwin offered support.[69]

On his own copy of *Vestiges*, Darwin made extensive notes, mainly about problems to avoid. The circular system of classification was all wrong, and Chambers's use of terms like "higher" and "lower" would be spurned in favor of phrases like "more complicated."[70] Darwin saw that *Vestiges*'s effort to appease religious sensibilities (by taking "it for granted . . . that God created animated beings, as well as the terraqueous theatre of their being") did not prevent pious venom being added to the legitimate criticisms of the book's scientific flaws.[71] When Darwin's former professor Adam Sedgwick wrote a withering review, Darwin "read it with fear & trembling," as he reported to Lyell, "but was well pleased to find, that I had not overlooked any of the arguments, though I had put them to myself feebly as milk & water."[72] He later scribbled on his copy of Sedgwick's review, "The publication of the *Vestiges* brought out all that could be said against the theory excellently if not too vehemently."[73]

Vestiges's reception reenforced Darwin's instinct to make sure his facts were plentiful and accurate, to stick to biology and zoology, and to avoid theological issues, which meant postponing the subject of man because natural selection could be supported just as well with evidence from other species. Before springing his theory on fellow scientists—however much popular opinion was softened by *Vestiges*—Darwin must endeavor to bring more naturalists of stature onto his side. And also he decided he must develop his skills as a specialist, something he had never really done, relying on other naturalists—and now Hooker—for detailed work. In a recent letter, Hooker had criticized a French naturalist who endlessly theorized when he did "not know what it is to be a specific naturalist," and Darwin felt stung: "How painfully (to me) true is your remark that no one has hardly a right to examine the question of species who has not minutely examined many."[74]

In 1846, while Lincoln was making arrangements before departing for Congress, Darwin finished various publishing chores, including a new edition of the *Voyage of the Beagle,* so he could settle down to the serious and *specialist* study of a particular family of creatures, barnacles. Darwin thought this research would require only a year or two. Lincoln was hoping that in that amount of time he might be able to launch a long-term career in Washington, climbing the greasy pole of national politics. Both men's expectations proved wrong.

Career Preparations and Rivals, 1845–49

Before embarking on his study of barnacles, Darwin decided to revise his part of FitzRoy's *Beagle* publications, issuing it separately as *The Voyage of the Beagle*. This new edition would reach a wider public for whom Darwin served up a few small hors d'oeuvres of natural selection. For example, regarding the Galapagos material, he added, "Seeing this gradation and diversity of structure in one small, intimately related group of birds, one might really fancy that from an original paucity of birds in this archipelago, one species had been taken and modified for different ends."[1]

Something else crept into the last chapter, completed in August 1845, just after Darwin read Charles Lyell's new book about his recent travels in the United States. Annoyed by Lyell's suggestions that slaves were treated benignly by their masters, Darwin wrote to Lyell, praising his book generously but adding tersely, "Your slave discussion disturbed me much; but as you would care no more for my opinion on this head than for the ashes of this letter, I will say nothing except that it gave me some sleepless, most uncomfortable hours."[2] To Lyell's accommodating reply, Darwin responded that he wished "the same feelings had been apparent in your published discussion."

> But I will not write on this subject, I should perhaps annoy you, and most certainly myself. I have exhaled myself with a paragraph or two in my Journal on the sin of Brazilian slavery; you perhaps will think that it is in answer to you; but such is not the case. I have remarked on nothing which I did not hear on the coast of South America. My few sentences, however, are merely an explosion of feeling. How could you relate so placidly that atrocious sentiment [of a planter quoted by Lyell] about separating children from their parents; and in the next page speak of being distressed at the whites not having prospered; I assure you the contrast made me exclaim out. But I have broken my intention, and so no more on this odious deadly subject.[3]

That Darwin could use this harsh tone when addressing Lyell—to whom he had actually dedicated his new volume—demonstrates the depth of his feeling, as do the book's "few sentences" that begin "I thank God, I shall never again visit a slave-country" and continued for over a page with descriptions of several horrors he had witnessed in Latin America: the sound of moaning coming from a house where he suspected a slave was being tortured, an old lady who kept thumbscrews for that purpose, staying in a house where a "young mulatto" was beaten "and persecuted enough to break the spirit of the lowest animal," a six- or seven-year-old boy struck with a horsewhip while his father trembled, a negro afraid to ward off a blow. Darwin also reviled those who thought any cheerfulness in a slave proved that slavery is "a tolerable evil" or who believed slaves can speak truthfully about their condition in front of their masters. He was infuriated that slave owners "profess to love their neighbours as themselves, . . . believe in God, and pray that his Will be done on earth!" He acknowledged the guilt of the British "and our American descendants, with their boastful cry of liberty" but was consoled that Britons "at least have made a greater sacrifice, than ever made by any nation, to expiate our sin."[4] The presentation copy of *The Voyage* reached Lyell just before he departed for a second tour of the United States, where he found that Americans' feelings on the issue of slavery had moved closer to an explosion than three years before.

Darwin apparently chose barnacles for his specialist study partly because of Louis Agassiz, one of the few contemporaries of whom it can be said that his influence was felt both by Darwin, whom he met in 1840, and by Lincoln, who must have known Agassiz's work long before the naturalist visited the White House for a significant conversation in 1865. Born in Switzerland in 1807 and initially trained as a doctor, Agassiz moved into natural history, studying under such great pioneers as Alexander von Humboldt and Georges Cuvier. While mastering geology and zoology, Agassiz became most renowned as an ichthyologist, yet Darwin first noticed him because of his startling theory that glaciers and moving ice sheets could better account for the transportation of "erratic boulders" than the action of giant icebergs drifting in ancient seas, the Lyellian view adopted by Darwin. Agassiz also asserted that the "parallel roads" at Glen Roy in Scotland were not, as Darwin had argued in 1839, "marine beaches" but the result of glacial action creating lakes. In 1840, Darwin sent him a copy of his *Journal and Remarks* in which he had criticized some of Agassiz's work on glaciers, although the accompanying letter said diplomatically that "your work on Glaciers . . . has filled me with admiration. As I have briefly treated of the boulders of S. America in the accompanying volume I thought you possibly might like to possess a copy; and sending it you, is the only means I have of expressing the regret I feel at the manner in which I have alluded to (although probably the fact is unknown and quite indifferent to you) your most valuable labours on the action of Glaciers."[5]

While the opinions of other geologists wavered on the topic, Darwin had difficulty accepting that Agassiz might be right. In 1843, Darwin wrote about his Glen Roy theory being "for a time knocked on the head by Agassiz's ice-work—but it is now reviving again."[6] In the following year, Darwin mentioned to Joseph Dalton Hooker—who had only recently read Darwin's view that species could change—that "Agassiz has lately brought the strongest arguments in favour of immutability."[7] As late as 1846, after exclaiming to a colleague that "Agassiz or Buckland . . . will sneer" at his efforts to obtain fresh data about Glen Roy, Darwin himself sneered that "there never was a more futile theory" than Agassiz's glacier lake.[8] A few days later at a conference in Southampton, Darwin heard a presentation by Agassiz in which he suggested that "a monograph on the Cirripedia [barnacles] was a pressing desideratum in Zoology." That at least is how Darwin later recounted Agassiz's words in two letters, one to Agassiz himself: "your sentence . . . much helped to decide me."[9] Darwin had a long-standing interest in marine invertebrates, and some specimens from the *Beagle* voyage had never been written up properly.[10] A year had passed since Hooker's remark made Darwin consider studying in depth a particular species, and now Agassiz's statement provided a peculiar stimulus.[11]

Agassiz's fame was ascending rapidly. Already an honorary member of scientific societies in France and America, in Britain he received further memberships and the Geological Society's Wollaston Medal. His brilliance and charm won many supporters, including Lyell, who helped arrange for Agassiz to deliver lectures at the Lowell Institute in Boston. There Agassiz achieved stunning success, accepted a Harvard professorship, married into a Boston Brahmin family, and eventually became not only a citizen but also America's most famous scientist in the mid-nineteenth century.[12]

Still smarting over Glen Roy, Darwin now labored to gain his own reputation as an expert on a particular species—one that Agassiz had already admitted was outside his own expertise.

The America that Agassiz entered in 1846 was increasingly convulsed by the issue of slavery, and Lincoln had seen one painful result—when his hero Henry Clay lost the presidential election in 1844. Lincoln had labored in the previous presidential election in 1840 and was elated when William Henry Harrison, the Whig candidate, won and equally deflated when Harrison died of pneumonia after a single month in office. John Tyler, the first vice president to fill a suddenly vacated office, was actually a Democrat, and the Whigs floundered. Lincoln was then delighted when the Whigs nominated Clay in 1844 and crushed when Clay was narrowly defeated by the Democrat James Polk. Clay might have won if some Whigs had not abandoned the party because, like the Democratic Party, it had avoided the issue of slavery. As first happened in 1840, those wishing to protest against slavery voted for the new Liberty Party, which won few votes outside of New York but enough in 1844 to prevent Clay from winning that state's crucial electoral votes.

Lincoln complained about those who thus helped the Democrats regain control of the presidency, but blaming abolitionists was pointless: the Whigs needed to achieve something that would help them retain the growing antislavery vote.[13] Lincoln himself would work on this before the end of his term in Washington, D.C. However, Lincoln's initial effort upon first arriving in December 1847 was an attempt to surpass the reputation of his main political rival. Just as Darwin had begun and would long continue a scientific duel with Louis Agassiz, so Lincoln had, a dozen years earlier, found his great political opponent in Stephen A. Douglas.

Douglas was four years younger than Lincoln and a foot shorter. "The Little Giant" had origins in Vermont almost as humble as Lincoln's, and he settled in Illinois only a year or two after Lincoln. At twenty-one, Douglas passed the bar and was practicing law in 1834 when Lincoln first met him. Douglas was bright, ambitious, and belonged to Illinois' dominant Democratic Party, which steadily raised him to the office of public prosecutor, then to the state legislature as its youngest member, then to the Land Office as Registrar, and eventually to the House of Representatives in Washington—four years before Lincoln got there. Occasionally, in court cases and in the state legislature, the two men were on the same side, but usually they were opponents. Lincoln pulled out all the stops to ensure that his law partner, John T. Stuart, defeated Douglas in a congressional race, during which Lincoln wrote to a fellow Whig: "We have adopted it as part of our policy here, to never speak of Douglass at all. Isn't that the best mode of treating so small a matter?"[14]

In January 1838, Lincoln made a high-flown speech in Springfield in which he never mentioned Douglas by name yet alluded to him as possessing extraordinary and dangerous ambition, like "an Alexander, a Caesar, or a Napoleon . . . a man possessed of the loftiest genius, coupled with ambition sufficient to push it to its utmost stretch."[15] Suspiciously similar attacks on Douglas appeared around this time in letters probably written by Lincoln to the *Sangamo Journal*.[16] "Lincoln despised Douglas," said one contemporary, while another declared that Lincoln "always admitted that Douglass was a wonderfully great political leader and with a good cause to advocate he thought he would be invincible."[17] Lincoln rarely thought Douglas advocated for a good cause, but he could see in Douglas many of his own virtues and ambitions. It grated that Douglas did less to hide his ambition yet seemed to fulfill it more easily. After performing poorly in a debate with Douglas around this time, Lincoln was "conscious of his failure," said a witness who "never saw any man so much distressed."[18] The Christmas season of goodwill found little expression in Lincoln's descriptions of Douglas: "not now worth talking about," he wrote on 23 December 1839, and in a speech three days later, he declared that Douglas was "deserving of the world's contempt."[19]

When Douglas went to Congress in 1843, he quickly established a reputation for excellent speaking and clever compromise that brought him swift reelection. Douglas supported Polk's expansionist line, helped bring about the long-delayed annexation of Texas, and leapt to defend Polk against attacks by the likes of John Quincy Adams, who suggested (correctly) that the president had deliberately inflamed a border dispute in order to cause the Mexican-American War, by which Polk intended to add to the United States what later became New Mexico, Arizona, Nevada, and California.

When Lincoln finally made it to Washington, he showed none of the reserve expected from a freshman congressman. Trying to make a name for himself quickly, Lincoln attacked the legality of the war's origin with better arguments than those already made by Adams and refuted by Douglas. In well-researched speeches, Lincoln analyzed Polk's prewar maneuvers and asked Polk to name the "spot" (in relation to the disputed boundary line) where in April 1846, as Polk had claimed, innocent Americans had been viciously attacked by Mexican troops. But a year and a half had passed, and because Douglas had recently been elected to the Senate, he was not present in the House in December 1847 to rise to Lincoln's bait, and everyone else simply ignored him. The only name he made for himself was coined by opponents: "Spotty Lincoln."

During his second year in Washington, Lincoln tried to achieve something worthwhile by drafting an ambitious measure regarding the highly politicized topic of slavery in Washington, D.C. Like many representatives in Washington, Lincoln was pained that the country's largest slave traders had their warehouse—which Lincoln termed "a sort of Negro livery-stable"—within sight of the Capitol. Also, he may have been present on the evening when three hired slave-catchers invaded his boardinghouse to arrest a black waiter who had been allowed to work to save up the money his master demanded for the purchase of his freedom—until the master changed his mind.[20] Since Washington, D.C., was not a state, and slavery was not protected by "states' rights," it had long been the point of conflict between abolitionists and their opponents. Lincoln sought a *rational* compromise consistent with the principles he had expressed on this very issue in his first "protest" against slavery in 1837.

Lincoln's plan involved freeing all children born to slave mothers after 1850; allowing federal officials to retain slaves as personal servants; allowing owners to remove their slaves from D.C. or receive federal payments for the full value of slaves they freed; once the District was "free," putting in place "active and efficient means" for arresting and returning any fugitive slaves who came into the District; and allowing a majority of free white male citizens in D.C. to accept or reject the plan in a referendum.[21]

Lincoln worked quietly to rally support from all sides, but when the proposal became public, the support vanished. Abolitionists, with their moral rather than practical viewpoint, objected to compensation for slave owners—though that had helped British emancipation to succeed sixteen years earlier. Also, many abolitionists were actively engaged in helping fugitives, so they considered Lincoln's move to establish in Washington (where none existed) a system for returning fugitives a retrograde step. Southerners, meanwhile, had for years fought any move by Congress to interfere with slavery where it existed, especially in Washington, and failed to appreciate that Lincoln's plan bent over backwards to appease them. John C. Calhoun himself dismissed the plan as misguided and dangerous to southern rights.

"Abandoned by my former backers and having little personal influence," Lincoln later said, "I dropped the matter knowing that it was useless to prosecute the business at that time."[22] Lincoln was doubly disappointed by his colleagues' lack of compromise and his own failure to achieve something of lasting value. Lincoln's plan would have emancipated few if any slaves, yet it could have marked an important turning point, restarting the momentum of emancipation and countering the expansion of slavery. It could have established, at initial low cost, the principle of compensation, which might have reduced "north versus south" antagonism by having everyone share the cost of eliminating an evil from which the whole country had economically profited. It could have shown the federal government using the power it did possess but with due regard for local opinion—exactly what Lincoln had advocated in 1837.

In view of Lincoln's later attacks on Douglas's policies, Lincoln's regard for "local opinion" is somewhat ironic. In the recent presidential election, the Democrats had advocated a policy of local consent called "popular sovereignty": allowing the citizens of a territory to decide whether a state seeking admission to the Union should prohibit slavery. However, the principle had actually been proposed even earlier during the final debate on the admission of Texas—by then congressman Stephen A. Douglas.[23] A year after Lincoln left Washington and during the storm of controversy that resulted in the Compromise of 1850, it was Douglas who played the key role in applying "pop. sov." to the territories recently taken from Mexico. While both Lincoln and Douglas preferred to let local people rather than the federal government choose whether slavery should be prohibited, the crucial difference between them is that Lincoln had proposed using "local consent" to end slavery in a place already possessing it, while Douglas applied "pop. sov." to allow slavery into territories where it did not yet exist under law. Since August 1846, Congress had been deadlocked over the Wilmot Proviso, which sought a federal prohibition against slavery in any new territory that might be gained from Mexico; Lincoln supported the proviso, while Douglas pushed "pop. sov." as an alternative, one much preferred by the southern states.

Lincoln finally left Washington in March 1849, having failed to achieve enough to escape the system he himself had helped to create whereby the prominent Whigs in his district took turns seeking a two-year term. Lincoln now tried and failed to obtain the position of General Land Office Commissioner, which would have trumped Douglas's former state-level position and would politically counterbalance Douglas's current chairmanship of the Senate Committee on Territories. When news arrived that he had not obtained the position, Lincoln laid down in depression for an hour or so and later said, "I hardly ever felt so bad at any failure in my life."[24] He turned down a dead-end governorship of Oregon territory and considered a return to the state legislature too retrograde. So, without political office, Lincoln was back to practicing law and hoping for some unforeseeable opportunity.

By March 1849, Lincoln's career in national politics had apparently come to an end after only two years. Meanwhile, Darwin was realizing that his study of barnacles, supposedly requiring only a year or two, would take considerably longer. An early discovery made the whole project seem more useful to his theory of natural selection than expected, so Darwin decided he must compare the Beagle's barnacle specimens with those that colleagues all over the world might dredge up for him (sometimes literally). Then he added fossil specimens. A less thrilling discovery was that the numerous body parts for each barnacle needed to be individually classified, a job done under a microscope with needles and minute tweezers. Preparing separate slides for further examination proved unimaginably slow work, delayed further by grave health problems.[25]

Darwin revealed his early exultation to Hooker, the only naturalist who had yet seen Darwin's 231-page sketch on natural selection. Without utterly rejecting Darwin's theory, Hooker still doubted that new species could be derived from previous ones, pointing out numerous problems and offering intelligent criticisms, all greatly appreciated by Darwin. Briefly but hyperbolically, Darwin explained the importance of his current discoveries:

> I should never have made this out, had not my species theory convinced me, that an hermaphrodite species must pass into a bisexual species by insensibly small stages, & here we have it, for the male organs in the hermaphrodite are already beginning to fail, & independent males ready formed. But I can hardly explain what I mean, & you will perhaps wish my Barnacles & Species theory al Diabolo together. But I don't care what you say, my species theory is all gospel.[26]

But in mid-March 1849, Darwin had to leave his barnacles behind temporarily and travel to Malvern to undergo three months of cold showers in an effort to restore his collapsing health.

There has been growing interest in the way the illnesses of famous people might have influenced their behavior and possibly history. Although Lincoln has not escaped the attention of armchair diagnosticians, they have been speculatively poking at a patient who was essentially so healthy that he could tolerate surprisingly well the stresses of a presidency that would have broken most men. On the other hand, "Darwin's medical history," as medical historians Roy Porter and G. S. Rousseau write, "has been, and remains, one of the 'source of the Nile' mysteries of nineteenth-century scholarship."[27] Entire books have been shaped by, or even devoted to, Darwin's malaise.[28] Although his mysterious malady undoubtedly affected both the pace and direction of his research, a discussion of Darwin's personal health—or that of Lincoln—is tangential to this work. Rather than survey how the present world has applied science to their biographies, the more relevant task is to probe how they applied science to their world, especially to the subjects of man and God.

Mortality, Invention, and Geology

Like many contemporaries, Darwin and Lincoln suffered tragic losses of family members to the ravages of disease; however, they had less capacity than many contemporaries to find solace in religion, and the deaths may indeed have contributed to their loss of faith. Before reaching their teens, Darwin and Lincoln had lost their mothers, and a few years later, Lincoln's only full sister, Sarah, also died. Darwin was in his late thirties and Lincoln in his early forties when their fathers passed away. Far more painful was the tragic loss of children. Darwin's third child, Mary, died less than a month after her birth in 1842. Emma Darwin wrote, "Our pain is nothing to what it would have been if she had lived longer and suffered more."[1] That proved all too true for both families a few years later. Lincoln's second son, Edward, was sickly from an early age and died in February 1850 of pulmonary tuberculosis at the age of three.[2] A little over a year later, Darwin's second child, ten-year-old Annie, also died, probably of tuberculosis, after a long illness.[3]

Eddie's death affected Mary Lincoln deeply, contributing to her decision to move from the Episcopal church favored by her Edwards in-laws to the Presbyterian church, where she had many friends. But three years after Eddie's death, Mary wrote to a friend, "I grieve to say that even at this day I do not feel sufficiently submissive to our loss."[4] Emma used similar words in a letter written the day after Annie's death: "I hope I shall be able to attain some feeling of submission to the will of Heaven."[5] The following day, Charles wrote to his brother, "Poor Emma is well bodily & firm, but feels bitterly & God knows we can neither see on any side a gleam of comfort."[6] There is no evidence that Emma's religious beliefs or practice were altered, though she may have come closer to understanding the harsh view Darwin expressed a few years later about "the clumsy, wasteful, blundering low & horridly cruel works of nature!"[7]

Lincoln's reaction to Eddie's death was muted. "We miss him very much," he wrote to his stepbrother. Mary later asserted that Eddie's death directed her husband's heart "toward religion."[8] The Presbyterian minister who performed

Eddie's funeral service, Reverend James Smith, soon became a family friend, and within two years, Mary underwent formal examination to join his church. Lincoln now rented a pew and when not on the circuit or campaigning often accompanied Mary to Sunday services. Lincoln could find much to admire in Reverend Smith, a former deist converted at a camp meeting in Indiana, who in 1843 published a massive tome entitled *The Christian's Defense, Containing a Fair Statement, and Impartial Examination of the Leading Objections Urged by Infidels against the Antiquity, Genuineness, Credibility, and Inspiration of the Holy Scripture*. Lincoln saw the book before 1850 and later possessed a copy. Smith delivered sensible sermons, took an interest in education and temperance, and was a member of the Illinois State Colonization Society, which Lincoln also supported.[9]

Smith's influence on Lincoln is much disputed, but there is no evidence that Lincoln changed his mind about the main doctrines of Christianity.[10] Unlike his wife, Lincoln avoided formal membership of any church, although liberally supporting his wife's and other Springfield churches. Although "one could argue logically that an ambitious politician or statesman might utter religious platitudes in public to sway voters," this was not, according to historian Wayne C. Temple, the case with Lincoln, who "professed his belief in God" on many occasions both public and private.[11] Nevertheless, Lincoln did not mind if more frequent church attendance not only pleased his society-conscious wife (who joined the First Presbyterian simultaneously with three of her best friends) but also helped submerge old rumors about his own deism.

If Lincoln attended church more after Eddie died, Darwin's attendance apparently decreased after Annie's death. He continued to support the village church and was on friendly terms with its vicar, but on Sundays, after accompanying his family to the lych-gate, Darwin reportedly became accustomed to remaining outside or going for a walk.[12] Yet, this decline in Darwin's church attendance, like the increase in Lincoln's, may have resulted from such mundane concerns as Lincoln's desire to promote a more conventional image and Darwin's fear of being embarrassed by his turbulent digestive system.

Darwin's ill health drove him to try out the latest medical technology (Dr. Gully's Water Cure) in 1849, the same year in which Lincoln made a serious effort to contribute something of his own to the history of technology—though he did not refer to it in his lecture on "Discoveries and Inventions" a decade later.

Most Lincoln biographies mention the oddity that he is the only president ever to obtain a U.S. patent and perhaps briefly link this to his wider interest in technology.[13] But far more significant than the fact that Lincoln obtained a patent is his very idea of becoming an inventor.

In September 1848, as Lincoln and Mary were returning to Springfield after his first session in Washington, they watched from aboard a river steamboat as the crew of another steamboat that had run aground labored to get free of the sandbar by lightening the vessel and shoving loose planks and empty barrels under the hull.[14] Lincoln knew from his flatboating days the complications of shifting sandbars and variable drafts. He had begun his political career campaigning for improvements in river navigation and knew that New Salem had expired partly because the Sangamo River was too difficult for steamboats. Now Lincoln reasoned laterally: when it is not possible to dredge or widen rivers or to provide alternatives such as canals or railroads (the latter having barely reached Illinois by then), perhaps steamboats themselves could be fitted with a device to create additional buoyancy as needed.

The problem of turning a clever idea into a practical reality intrigued Lincoln. Before returning to Washington for the second session, Lincoln constructed a model of his invention, hardly difficult for a carpenter's son who had formerly built an entire flatboat. Lincoln used a neighbor's carpentry shop and, according to Herndon's acerbic account, spent a good deal of time in the law office whittling on the model and explaining "its merits and the revolution it was destined to work in steamboat navigation."[15]

Lincoln carried his model back to Washington and engaged a patent agent to phrase the patent application properly and a draughtsman to prepare the necessary drawings of his "new and improved manner of combining adjustable buoyant air chambers with a steam boat or other vessel for the purpose of enabling their draught of water to be readily lessened to enable them to pass over bars, or through shallow water, without discharging their cargoes." On 22 May 1849, Lincoln was issued Patent Number 6,469.[16]

To bring the invention to life would have required commercial and manufacturing contacts, capital, and some entrepreneurial spirit, but Lincoln was busy trying to recoup his finances and support his family from the fees he split with Herndon. Perhaps Lincoln dreamed that some entrepreneur would take up his idea, manufacturing the product under a license giving Lincoln a percentage of worldwide sales: the "fuel of interest" Lincoln later mentioned in his lecture "Inventions." However, the dream remained a dream. At some point, Lincoln gave friends in Springfield a demonstration of how his invention worked, using a large horse trough for the trial.[17] After that, nothing more was heard of the invention until *Scientific American* mentioned it as a curiosity shortly after Lincoln became president-elect.[18]

Herndon later quipped that Lincoln was as bad at making inventions as he was at lecturing about them, yet his invention was not absurd: later, certain dredging machines and modern submarines employed something similar.[19] But his timing was poor, for he addressed a problem already being solved by better dredging, improved port facilities, and expanding canal and railroad systems. Twenty years earlier, when steamships were still new and railroads practically nonexistent, Lincoln's "adjustable buoyant air chambers" might have improved river transportation and even saved New Salem. Yet the facts that Lincoln's invention failed to meet expectations but succeeded in making him unique among presidents are less significant than Lincoln's ability to imagine himself achieving success through the same superior intelligence that raised him from a field hand to riverboatman, clerk, militia captain, surveyor, lay theologian, lawyer, propagandist, and legislator. In his fortieth year, Lincoln added "inventor" at the very time when, unfortunately, he had to subtract "legislator." He would not, it seemed, feed his family by making inventions or laws but by being a successful lawyer.

The very railroad system that made Lincoln's invention obsolete created legal problems and litigation that provided a major source of Lincoln's income.[20] Railroads also improved Lincoln's home life as he could now return home from the circuit on weekends. Railway development also greatly affected Darwin's work. His troublesome internal organs made travel unappealing, except to some spa, but the railways helped information to flow in a way not matched again until the invention of the Internet. Railways and steamships caused a huge expansion in national and international postal systems, and Darwin was able during his barnacle research to collect information and specimens from other naturalists in a manner inconceivable a generation earlier.

Because Darwin immersed himself for eight years in barnacle studies, an observer might have considered that to be his major contribution to science: the complete classification of a major infraclass (Cirripedia) of crustaceans. One of Darwin's children growing up during these years remarked while visiting a neighbor's house, "Then where does *he* do his barnacles?"[21] But "doing" his barnacles was secondary to Darwin's life's work. The crustaceans posed classification problems that Darwin now realized he could solve through his still-secret theory of species "modification through descent." Also, Darwin was earning a respectable reputation as a precise observer, dissecting, describing, and publishing. Louis Agassiz, famed for his vast knowledge of natural science while also a world authority on fish, had never thoroughly mastered a class as vast as the barnacles. He had beaten Darwin in geology, but now Darwin challenged Agassiz on his own ground (or water).

The financial success of the law practice allowed Herndon to expand his intellectual horizons with further book purchases and journal subscriptions, resources Lincoln could exploit as well. A noted "book-worm" in the Library of Congress, after returning from his brief stint in Washington, Lincoln thirsted for knowledge with new zeal. Herndon commented, "Lincoln from 1849 to 1855 became a hard student and read much, studied Euclid and some mathematical books, read much in the political world."[22] The scattered evidence of Lincoln's research during this period suggests little of it was literary, most was political but a great deal was scientific.

When Herndon later asked one of Lincoln's closest acquaintances "whether Mr. Lincoln was given to abstract speculation," Joseph Gillespie replied, "He wanted something solid to rest upon, hence his bias for mathematics and physical sciences." Gillespie recounted Lincoln's theorizing—"even before he had read the philosophical explanation"—that a musket ball fired horizontally and one dropped vertically would hit the ground at the same time. "He was fond of astronomy but I can't call to mind any reference of his to geology. He doubtless had read and thought of the subject but it did not engage his attention to the degree that astronomy and mechanical science did."[23] In contrast, Lincoln's former law partner John T. Stuart told an inquirer in 1860, "I consider [him] a man of very general and varied Knowledge—Has made Geology and other Sciences especial Study."[24] Another Lincoln associate, David Davis, according to Herndon's notes, believed that Lincoln read "no histories, novels, biographies &c," but that "his mind struggled to arrive at moral & physical-mathematical demonstration . . . had a good mechanical mind and knowledge . . . studied Euclid . . . the exact sciences."[25]

Herndon himself was interested in natural science, taking his children for carriage rides into the countryside "to teach them botany, geology, and ornithology." One nephew never "saw a botany book that knew more about plants"; and in 1867, Herndon knowledgably described regional geology to a journalist, adding, "We had no need of Agassiz out here to tell us what things meant."[26] Although Herndon at times despaired of his student, he approved of Lincoln's fascination with *Vestiges* and illustrated Lincoln's interest in science with this recollection:

> Sometime about 1855 I went into a bookshop in this city and saw a book, a small one, entitled, called, I think, *The Annual of Science*. I looked over it casually and liked it and bought it. I took the book to Lincoln and H.'s Office. Lincoln was in, reading a newspaper of value; he said me: "Well, Billy, you have got a new book, which is good, I suppose. What is it? Let me see it." He took the book in his hand, looked over the pages, read the title, introductions, and probably the first chapter, and saw at a glance the purpose and object of the book, which were as follows: to record, teach, and fully explain the *failures* and *successes* of experiments of all philosophies and scientists, everywhere, including chemistry, mechanics, etc. He instantly rose up and said that he must buy the whole set, started out and got them. On returning to the office he said: "I have wanted such a book for years because I sometimes make experiments and have thoughts about the physical world that I do not know to be true or false. I may, by this book, correct my errors and save time and expense."[27]

The Annual of Scientific Discovery: or, Year Book of Facts in Science and Art, Exhibiting the Most Important Discoveries and Improvements in Mechanics, Astronomy, Geology, Zoology was edited from 1850 to 1866 by David Ames Wells, a former student of Agassiz who was later appointed chairman of the National Revenue Commission by Lincoln.[28]

Herndon's later auction list included a wide range of scientific works, most presumably purchased by Herndon. "When I heard of a good work, I ordered it, English, French or German, if the two latter were translated," he related. He imported books from London including works by "English scientists, all of which I devoured with relish. . . . I kept abreast of the spirit of the age. . . . I was of a progressive turn of mind and tried to get Lincoln in the same channel of thought." No doubt some of Herndon's purchases were too speculative for Lincoln's liking, for he "would snatch one up and peruse it for a while, but he soon threw it down with the suggestion that it was entirely too heavy for an ordinary mind to digest."[29] Yet, many of the books that Herndon later auctioned must have appealed to an inventor and may have been Lincoln's own purchases, such as the Reverend J. Blakely's *Theology of Inventions* (1856) and John Beckman's two-volume *History of Inventions, Discoveries and Origins* (1846), a *History of Wonderful Inventions* (1849), and *Patent Office Reports* (ten nonconsecutive volumes beginning in 1847 and none dating from after Lincoln's departure from Springfield in 1861). Among the many natural history books are several major works on geology, and those published before 1861 include: W. R. Johnson, *On the Use of Anthracite in the Manufacture of Iron* (1841), Charles Lyell, *Manual of Elementary Geology* (probably sixth edition, New York, 1857), Hugh Miller, *Footprints of the Creator* (1849) and *Popular Geology* (1859), Robert Dale Owen, *Key to the Geology of the Globe* (1857), David Page, *Introductory Textbook of Geology* (perhaps the 1854 edition), and Edward Hitchcock, *Religion of Geology and Its Connected Sciences* (1851) and *Religious Truth Illustrated from Science* (1857).[30] Several of these authors were British and their works well known to Darwin.

Lincoln's interest in geology, begun before 1837, was nourished not only by *Vestiges* and Wells's *Annual* but also by Lincoln's service in the early 1850s on the state Board of Canal Commissioners.[31] Canal building and search for iron and coal had spurred the development of state-funded geological surveys early in the nineteenth century, and by the 1840s, over twenty states had established them.[32] Illinois tardily established its own geological survey in 1851 and appointed a medical doctor, J. G. Norwood, as the first state geologist. By the end of 1853, Norwood and two assistants had collected vast numbers of minerals and fossils, and the collection resided temporarily in various locations in Springfield.[33] There was tension between legislators and geologists over whether the latter should be seeking fossils to aid the classification of strata rather than simply reporting on mineral resources and also over politics. One of Norwood's assistants, Amos H. Worthen, ran unsuccessfully as a Whig for the state legislature in 1854, after which the legislature's Democrat majority drove him from his assistant's position. Worthen then worked for the nation's foremost geologist, James Hall of the New York Geological Survey, who was so pleased with Worthen's fossil collecting that he named ten newly discovered species after him. When the Republicans gained control of Illinois in 1858, they replaced Norwood with the politically correct Worthen.[34] Hall had written a recommendation for Worthen and had encouraged scientists Agassiz, James Dwight Dana, and Edward Hitchcock to do the same. Yet Hall hedged his bet by also supporting another candidate, Joseph Henry McChesney. About thirty years old and an early graduate of the progressive (and strongly antislavery) Oberlin College in Ohio, McChesney had become "the owner of another large and unstudied collection of fossils" that Hall was eager to obtain. Hall wrote to McChesney that whenever McChesney became state geologist in Illinois, Hall would be pleased to have the chance to describe his fossils.[35] But McChesney had to settle for a position under Worthen.

Three months after Worthen's appointment, Lincoln received a letter from geologist Richard P. Stevens in New York City, apparently an old Republican acquaintance from Danville, Illinois. "I see our friend McChesney has taken the Northern part of your state as his appropriate field. It is sincerely to be wished that the new head of your survey will give the State a good report and contribute to popularize the Science of Geology among the people."[36] Stevens, like McChesney, eventually published a string of new fossil discoveries, and McChesney apparently worked with Hall in Albany for a while. During the 1860 presidential election, McChesney campaigned for Lincoln, and later McChesney benefited from his friendship with the president, who in 1862 effectively gave the geologist a grand opportunity to study in Europe by appointing him U.S. consul in Newcastle upon Tyne.[37]

The only documents connecting Worthen with Lincoln relate to a debt-collection suit in which Lincoln represented the geologist when Worthen was still running a dry-goods business in Warsaw, Illinois, in 1841. However, after November 1859, Worthen owned a house five lots north of Lincoln's, and his geological collection was for a while in a building just around the corner from the law office.[38] Lincoln probably would not have been surprised that Worthen once complained about meager appropriations from the legislature, blaming "fossilized members of the Senate who are members of orthodox churches, and are afraid of the infidel tendencies of Geology."[39]

Lincoln once demonstrated his interest in geology in an undated fragment stimulated by a visit to Niagara Falls, New York, in 1857.[40] The meditative piece, though ending mid-sentence, demonstrates Lincoln's scientific cast of mind and deserves to be read in full:

> Niagara-Falls! By what mysterious power is it that millions and millions, are drawn from all parts of the world, to gaze upon Niagara Falls? There is no mystery about the thing itself. Every effect is just such as any intelligent man knowing the causes, would anticipate, without [seeing] it. If the water moving onward in a great river, reaches a point where there is a perpendicular jog, of a hundred feet in descent, in the bottom of the river,—it is plain the water will have a violent and continuous plunge at that point. It is also plain the water, thus plunging, will foam, and roar, and send up a mist, continuously, in which last, during sunshine, there will be perpetual rain-bows. The mere physical

of Niagara Falls is only this. Yet this is really a very small part of that world's wonder. It's power to excite reflection, and emotion, is it's great charm. The geologist will demonstrate that the plunge, or fall, was once at Lake Ontario, and has worn it's way back to it's present position; he will ascertain how *fast* it is wearing now, and so get a basis for determining how *long* it has been wearing back from Lake Ontario, and finally demonstrate by it that this world is at least fourteen thousand years old. A philosopher of a slightly different turn will say Niagara Falls is only the lip of the basin out of which pours all the surplus water which rains down on two or three hundred thousand square miles of the earth's surface. He will estim[ate with] approximate accuracy, that five hundred thousand [to]ns of water, falls with it's full weight, a distance of a hundred feet each minute—thus exerting a force equal to the lifting of the same weight, through the same space, in the same time. And then the further reflection comes that this vast amount of water, constantly pouring *down*, is supplied by an equal amount constantly *lifted up*, by the sun; and still he says, "If this much is lifted up, for *this one* space of two or three hundred thousand square miles, an equal amount must be lifted for every other equal space, and he is overwhelmed in the contemplation of the vast power the sun is constantly exerting in quiet, noiseless operation of lifting water *up* to be rained *down* again.

But still there is more. It calls up the indefinite past. When Columbus first sought this continent—when Christ suffered on the cross—when Moses led Israel through the Red-Sea—nay, even, when Adam first came from the hand of his Maker—then as now, Niagara was roaring here. The eyes of that species of extinct giants, whose bones fill the mounds of America, have gazed on Niagara, as ours do now. Contemporary with the whole race of men, and older than the first man, Niagara is strong, and fresh to-day as ten thousand years ago. The Mammoth and Mastadon—now so long dead, that fragments of their monstrous bones, alone testify, that they ever lived, have gazed on Niagara. In that long—long time, never still for a single moment. Never dried, never froze, never slept, never rested, [*sic*].[41]

Later, in his lecture on "Inventions," Lincoln mentioned the traditional dating for creation of about six thousand years ago, but in this earlier piece, "the world is at least fourteen thousand years old" and Niagara "older than the first man." Lincoln connected this revised geological chronology with both scripture and paleontology, but what was Lincoln's source for that date?

For decades geologists had hoped the falls' rate of erosion might somehow serve as a giant clock to give the age of the Earth. One calculation in 1790 suggested the falls had been receding for 55,440 years.[42] In 1830, Lyell cited a recent article asserting that the falls had been excavating the ravine for "nearly 10,000 years," but he cautiously added that "the retrograde movement" probably varied greatly at different times.[43] Lyell visited the falls in 1841 accompanied by Hall, and their findings were separately published by Hall in 1843 and Lyell in 1845.[44] In 1842, "Mr. Hall, by Governor Seward's direction, caused a trigonometric survey to be made of the fall," though a few years would have to pass before any data would be able "to throw some true light upon this subject."[45] Hall wrote in 1843 that the estimates of the age of the falls have "alarmed those who would consider [the Earth] still youthful in years," yet added that "we may regard the problem as undecided with respect to time . . . [and] impossible to calculate accurately."[46] Both Hall and Lyell noted the discovery near the falls of mastodon bones, mentioned in Lincoln's fragment.[47] Lyell later abandoned (without explanation) his earlier estimate of the recession rate and suggested that "35,000 years would have been required for the retreat," though he still stressed that there was no reason to "assume that the [rate of] retrograde movement had been uniform" over time.[48]

An 1851 souvenir guidebook to the falls avoids any reference to dating but includes a pious outburst: "What a scene for an atheist to look upon, and then deny the existence of an all powerful Creator! . . . Dwell on it, stranger . . . and acknowledge yourself an atom, a mere atom in nature, for that you are, and no more."[49] That alone might have been enough to elicit Lincoln's rationalist meditation. In 1857, the year Lincoln probably visited the falls, a new guidebook cited Lyell's recession rate of "a foot every year" but avoided doing the sums.[50]

Even without guidebooks, Lincoln could have gained relevant information from his neighbor the state geologist Worthen, or from his friend McChesney, both of whom had previously worked for Hall or perhaps from his other geological friend Stevens, by then resident in New York. Lincoln might even have learned about Niagara from a Republican colleague with whom he had campaigned in the past, William H. Seward, Hall's employer when governor of New York, later Lincoln's main rival within the Republican Party, and, later still, his trusted Secretary of State.

The trigonometric points that Hall installed (at Seward's behest) in 1842 have indeed demonstrated that the erosion rate is highly variable (which, ironically, has made Niagara Falls a favorite source of "evidence" for modern-day "creationists"!). Geologists have since worked out from other evidence that the Niagara River could not have begun flowing until the recession of the last ice age, about twelve thousand years ago. So, whatever source Lincoln found for his dating, it was a surprisingly good one.

Herndon enjoyed describing his conversation with Lincoln in 1858, just after Herndon's first visit to Niagara Falls:

> The recollection of the gigantic and awe-inspiring scene stimulated my exuberant powers to the highest pitch. After well-nigh exhausting myself in the effort I turned to Lincoln for his opinion. "What," I inquired, "made the deepest impression on you when you stood in the presence of the great natural

wonder?" I shall never forget his answer, because it in a very characteristic way illustrated how he looked at everything. "The thing that struck me most forcibly when I saw the Falls," he responded, "was, where in the world did all that water come from?"[51]

Occasionally deflating Herndon was one of Lincoln's simple pleasures, but Herndon might have been more impressed if he had known that Lincoln had already composed that fragment that mingled his rationalism (and serious consideration of where all that water came from) with a conventionally poetic awe. Herndon would have approved Lincoln's opinion that the falls were "Contemporary with the whole race of men" because it asserted mankind's unity as well as its antiquity. However, that inclusive view was increasingly coming under assault by science, and Lincoln, in addition to his own interest, was probably up-to-date with the scientific debate about race for the simple reason that Herndon was certain to be.

Scientific Racism

In 1845, after Darwin had included in the new edition of *The Voyage of the Beagle* a heart-felt cry against slavery, he set out on a month-long jaunt northward during which he read Alexander von Humboldt's latest work, volume 1 of *Cosmos*, which included this agreeable sentiment.

> While we maintain the unity of the human species, we at the same time repel the depressing assumption of superior and inferior races of men. There are nations more susceptible of cultivation, more highly civilized, more ennobled by mental cultivation than others, but none in themselves nobler than others. All are in like degree designed for freedom.[1]

"He is indeed a wonderful man," Darwin wrote of Humboldt in a letter to Charles Lyell, then on his second tour of America. Darwin also mentioned a recent visit to the Dean of Manchester, William Herbert, a considerable expert who "gave me much curious information" about hybrids. Darwin further entertained Lyell with a description of a visit with Charles Waterton, an eccentric Roman Catholic aristocrat but brilliant naturalist: "an amusing strange fellow; at our early dinner, our party consisted of two Catholic priests & two Mulattresses! He is past 60 years old & the day before run down & caught, a Leveret in a turnip field."[2]

Waterton had authored *Wanderings in South America, the North-west of the United States, and the Antilles*, rarely out of print since first published in 1825. This had an obvious appeal to Darwin, who also had another connection with Waterton. While in British Guyana, Waterton trained former slave John Edmonston in taxidermy, which Edmonston in turn taught Darwin when he was a medical student in Edinburgh.[3] Edmonston's former master had three daughters with his mulatto wife, and Waterton married one in 1829 when she was seventeen. Tragically, she died in childbirth the following year, but her infant boy survived to be raised by Waterton with the help of his sister and his wife's sisters—the "two Mulattresses" mentioned by Darwin.

Darwin no doubt remembered well Waterton's assertion published a few years earlier that "the man under Afric's burning zone, and he from the frozen regions of the North, have both come from the same stem. Their difference in colour and in feature may be traced to this: viz., that the first has had too much, and the second too little sun."[4] Waterton's family offered living evidence about "hybridity." In the same letter mentioning Waterton, Darwin told Lyell about an author who maintained he had never known two mulattoes to have offspring. "Can you obtain any comparative information on the crosses between Indian & Europæans & Negros & Europæans?" Darwin asked.[5] Based on Lyell's inquiries among American friends, Darwin later reported that mulatto families that intermarried for several generations "continued on an average as fertile as either pure whites or pure blacks."[6]

At that time, a belief in the unity of the human species was shared not only by Darwin, Waterton, and Humboldt but also by Humboldt's protégé Louis Agassiz, who wrote in 1845: "Here is revealed anew the superiority of the human genre and its greater independence in nature. Whereas the animals are distinct species in the different zoological provinces to which they appertain, man, despite the diversity of his races, constitutes one and the same species over all the surface of the globe." However, Agassiz soon abandoned this view.[7] Logically, it was inconsistent to suggest that God created different species of animals in all those "different zoological provinces" but *not* (according to traditional monogenist teaching) different species of man. Yet, logic probably had less to do with Agassiz's reversal than the fact that shortly after arriving in America to make a lecture tour, Agassiz underwent a bizarre conversion, not on the road to Damascus but in "the city of brotherly love," Philadelphia.

In December 1846, Agassiz wrote a long letter to his mother recounting his first two months' experiences in America. A portion of this letter was excluded when later published by Agassiz's widow but was restored in 1981 by Stephen Jay Gould, the brilliant Harvard paleontologist whose office was in a museum built by Agassiz:

> It was in Philadelphia that I first found myself in prolonged contact with Negroes; all the domestics in my hotel were men of color. I can scarcely express to you the painful impression that I received, especially since the feeling that they inspired in me is contrary to all our ideas about the confraternity of the human type (genre) and the unique origin of our species. But truth before all. Nevertheless, I experienced pity at the sight of this degraded and degenerate race, and their lot inspired compassion in me in thinking that they were really men. Nonetheless, it is impossible for me to repress the feeling that they are not of the same blood as us. In seeing their black faces with their thick lips and grimacing teeth, the wool on their head, their bent knees, their elongated hands, I could not take my eyes off their face in order to tell them to stay far away. And when they advanced that hideous hand towards my plate in order

to serve me, I wished I were able to depart in order to eat a piece of bread else-where, rather than dine with such service. What unhappiness for the white race—to have tied their existence so closely with that of Negroes in certain countries! God preserve us from such a contact.[8]

This experience helped Agassiz to resolve the earlier paradox—that all creatures seem to have been created in distinct and differing zones except (according to Genesis) humans—and it also suited his taxonomic approach, that of an extreme "splitter" continually "discovering" new species. According to Gould, Agassiz "once named three genera of fossil fishes from isolated teeth that a later paleon-tologist found in the variable dentition of a single individual."[9] But this change in his view of the species of man from "unity" to "plurality" (or from monogen-ism to polygenism) was immediately reinforced when Agassiz met Dr. Samuel G. Morton in Philadelphia and saw his "unique collection of human skulls," as Agassiz informed his mother. "Imagine a series of six hundred skulls, mostly Indian, of all the tribes who now inhabit or formerly inhabited America. Nothing like it exists elsewhere. This collection alone is worth a journey to America."[10]

Agassiz was delighted when Morton gave him "a copy of his great illustrated work" (presumably *Crania Americana*) in which measurements of cranial capac-ity were used to rank different races, with Caucasians having greatest capacity, Negroes the least, and Mongolians, Malays, and American Indians in between in descending order. Morton's measuring system has since been entirely discred-ited, but his data then suited Agassiz's new convictions. Because Agassiz's trip to America soon turned into permanent residence, and because, as Gould expresses it, "No man did more to establish and enhance the prestige of American biol-ogy during the nineteenth century," the fact that this scholar from Switzerland embraced polygenism partly explains why the latter came to be viewed as an "American" theory. The other reason is that many more American naturalists also adopted this view, especially southerners.[11]

Prior to his arrival in America, Agassiz had apparently never seen blacks or slavery. Darwin, in contrast, virtually inherited an abhorrence of slavery, enjoyed a positive relationship with the first black he encountered, John Edmonston, and was intrigued rather than disturbed by his contacts with other races during the *Beagle* voyage. Darwin's research was partly driven by his desire to demonstrate that blacks and whites belonged to the same human species.

Lincoln did not initially approach race from a scientific standpoint, but his experience of blacks and slavery went far more deeply. As a child in a slave state, a young man traveling by flatboat or steamboat, a lawyer handling cases involv-ing slavery, and a guest on two slaveholding plantations in Kentucky (Joshua Speed's and Lincoln's in-laws'), Lincoln encountered the institution frequently. The 1840 census listed 115 African Americans living in Springfield, 4.5 percent of the town's population. Although Illinois outlawed slavery, six of those blacks were listed as "slaves," three of them owned by friends of Lincoln, including his later brother-in-law Ninian Edwards. Most of Springfield's blacks were free, although the census listed many as "indentured." Most free blacks worked in menial jobs, but some were self-employed, and Lincoln used one of Springfield's two black barbers. Before Lincoln left Springfield in 1861, at least twenty-one blacks were living within three blocks of Lincoln's home. "By twentieth century standards," one scholar writes, "the Lincolns lived in an integrated neighborhood."[12]

Lincoln later learned about scientific thinking on the subject of race, but his main interest in blacks was political, while men like Darwin and Agassiz endeavored, however unsuccessfully, to keep scientific objectivity above any personal interest. Agassiz had no desire to defend slavery or attack biblical authority, but his views made him see human species and races differently from the Genesis view of unity. Combining the patterns he saw in the geographical distribution of vast numbers of species with his notions of the massively destructive power of glaciers, Agassiz concluded that God's creation was more complex than the Hebrews who wrote the Bible could understand. An omnipotent God could cause more than one creation, and an inscrutable God had no need to explain why. Separate creations fit the evidence better than the Eden story, and Agassiz always said that science provided better testimony than scripture of "the plan of the Creator."[13]

Agassiz also concluded that a species moving outside the zone for which it was created (and that was created for it) might not prosper, and if it tried to breed with another species that, however similar, had been created separately in a different zone, the offspring might be weakened or even infertile. Abandoning Le Comte de Buffon's classic concept of "specific infertility" as the defining criteria for species, Agassiz decided that some interbreeding could occur without proving that two creatures are truly of the same species but that such interbreeding was essentially unnatural, against God's plan, and resulting in offspring so degraded that their survival as a hybrid would be short lived. These conclusions, Agassiz believed, reenforced the immutability of "real" species, now defined by their "primordial origins" in different locations. In short, by adopting multiple creations and a limited kind of interbreeding between species, Agassiz felt he had strengthened the arguments against transmutation.

Darwin was moving in the opposite direction. Creation, whether occurring in one place and time or several, was replaced with natural selection, a multitude of small, unplanned adaptations in millions of species over great swathes of time. This, of course, jettisoned the immutability of species, yet Buffon's specific infertility was as awkward for Darwin as it was for Agassiz, for opposite reasons. Agassiz had to depict hybridization as possible but ultimately impermanent. For Darwin, hybridization was not only possible but necessary to preserve and spread modifications (or variations) throughout a species. Darwin upheld specific infertility because his theory insisted that different races of men could all interbreed successfully since they were all actually of the same human species, but they were also variants, splitting from the same tree, identifiable but also potentially liable to further change. Whatever caused earlier "splittings" could cause later ones, and some variants might prove for social rather than biological reasons more successful in the struggle for survival than others. While Agassiz and others praised Morton's cranial research, Darwin found Morton's work "too credulous" when citing other researchers' evidence on hybridity. Darwin noted "a want of exactness in the manner Morton gives the facts." Morton was not "a safe man to quote from."[14]

As his barnacle project expanded, Darwin sought barnacles from Dr. Augustus A. Gould, a Boston physician, author of a major work on *Mollusca* in 1841, and recently coauthor of *The Principles of Zoology* with Louis Agassiz. Darwin had not applied to Agassiz, but Gould communicated some information to Agassiz that caused him to send additional barnacles for Darwin's study. About seven weeks after writing to Gould, Darwin sent to Agassiz a reply to a letter that has not survived. After first thanking Agassiz for the barnacles he and Gould were sending, Darwin said, "In your letter . . . you say you should like to hear what results I have arrived at; as far as the limits of a letter go, it will give me *real* pleasure to do so."[15]

After telling how Agassiz himself had inspired this barnacle research, Darwin summarized his findings but politely requested that Agassiz "not mention my present results" partly because they were tentative and "partly because I should like to have the satisfaction of publishing myself." Along with the suggestion that Agassiz might in some sense steal his material, a slight barb is also in Darwin's remark that he had made out the homologies of the barnacles "with certainty from dissection & not from analogies." After describing a plethora of variations in barnacle reproductive systems, Darwin suggested, "You will laugh at this account, but I assure you I would not presume to tell you anything, of which I was not *sure*, from repeated examinations of specimens taken at different periods & from different countries." Darwin subtly indicated that he had found far more variation among barnacles than any theory based on separate creations or limited geographical distribution could account for. Darwin postscripted: "I do not suppose I shall finish my Monograph for two or three years—my health allows me to work very little." This prediction—slightly more realistic than earlier ones—signaled Agassiz to await Darwin's publication before using his material in any public lectures.[16]

Nearly two years passed before Darwin wrote to Agassiz again, in June 1850, to thank him for the gift of his book *Lake Superior*, an account of Agassiz's first natural science "expedition" in the tradition of Waterton, Humboldt, and, indeed, Darwin. The book was filled with data that interested Darwin and theories he disliked about "the direct intervention of a Supreme Intelligence in the plan of Creation." Agassiz believed that except when otherwise transported by men, "animals must have originated where they live, and have remained precisely within the same limits since they were created. . . . [T]he order which prevails through creation is intentional."[17]

Darwin wrote a gracious note of thanks for "your most kind present of *Lake Superior*: I had heard of it, & had much wished to read it, but I confess that it was the very great honour of having in my possession a work with your autograph, as a presentation copy, that has given me such lively & sincere pleasure. I cordially thank you for it. I have begun to read it with uncommon interest, which I see will increase as I go on."[18] Although a biographer of Agassiz has quoted these lines to indicate Darwin's admiration, "uncommon interest" is not critical acclaim, and this letter must be set against one Darwin sent a week earlier to Lyell: "Agassiz has sent me his Lake Superior Book,—is not that an immense Honour!"[19] That this was meant to be ironic becomes evident from later statements by Darwin and his closest associates.

Darwin waited two months to read *Lake Superior* and then scored and annotated the text, pasting four pages of notes in the back of the volume.[20] Darwin's letter had also thanked Agassiz again for the barnacles "you & Dr. Gould were so good as to send me" but then commented that while one species appeared to be exclusive to America and another exclusive to Europe, the other three were found in both—contradicting Agassiz's thinking on geographical distribution. Darwin provided brief descriptions, "though I do not know whether you will care to hear about them." Darwin also said he had not yet examined the two specimens that "you sent me from Charlestown."[21] Darwin meant Charleston, South Carolina, where Agassiz had four months earlier addressed the American Association for the Advancement of Science (AAAS). Darwin had undoubtedly heard from Lyell about Agassiz's success as a popular lecturer in Boston and New York and during his first visit to South Carolina in 1847. These earlier lectures, reported in newspapers and later issued as a pamphlet, continued to develop the polygenist view of the races of man that Agassiz had adopted after his experiences in Philadelphia.[22] Although many northerners were reluctant to accept a view clashing with Genesis's account of a single creation and single family of man, many southerners welcomed the change. As Darwin suggested in a letter, "I wonder whether the queries [in recent publications] . . . about the specific distinctions of the races of man are a reflexion from Agassiz's Lectures in the U.S. in which he has been maintaining the doctrine of several species,—much, I daresay, to the comfort of the slave-holding Southerns."[23]

At the 1850 AAAS meeting in slaveholding Charleston, Agassiz for the first time presented to a scientific assembly his developed opinion that "viewed zoologically, the several races of men were well marked and distinct." Their geographical distribution indicated that "these races did not originate from a common centre, nor from a single pair," so the differences were both primordial and permanent.[24] Most of Agassiz's audience were familiar with Morton's work since Dr. Josiah Nott of Mobile, Alabama, who delivered a paper immediately before Agassiz, had been promoting Morton's polygenist view even before Agassiz adopted it. A scion of a prominent South Carolina family, Nott had earned his medical degree in Philadelphia, where he became familiar with Morton's work, and by 1843, Nott was publishing in books and learned journals his polygenist views on the demonstrable inferiority of negroes.[25] Nott was thrilled to have this European-trained Harvard professor on their side and told Morton, "With Agassiz in the war the battle is ours. This was an immense accession for we shall not only have his name, but the timid will come out from their hiding places."[26]

Because polygenists like Nott rejected the Genesis story of a single creation, many saw themselves as modern Galileos suffering persecution. These included George Robins Gliddon, a bumptious and unscholarly Egyptologist, and E. G. Squier, a more serious student of the antiquity of American Indians.[27] Both rejected the traditional dating of creation to 4004 B.C. as far too recent, and both supplied Morton with skulls that, based on Morton's dubious measurements, allowed them to agree that from the dawn of human history, the different races of men had remained unchanged and unchangeable. Although Agassiz had adopted similar views, by Nott's standard Agassiz was "timid" because he not only maintained that his observations of nature simply revealed "the plan of the Creator" but had also bothered to publish an article in the *Christian Examiner*, Boston's widely read Unitarian organ, to demonstrate that multiple creation did not contradict but merely supplemented the Genesis account.[28] This article was part of a publishing phenomenon, as this one scientific issue about the unity or plurality of man spilled out of the learned journals and received wider coverage exactly because of its religious and political implications.

While Morton and Nott had been publishing scholarly tomes or in serious journals (which even brought Nott to the attention of the visiting Lyell), Nott began spreading the polygenist gospel more widely through popular southern journals such as *De Bow's Review*.[29] Also, Nott's books were widely reviewed in both Whig and Democratic journals.[30] In one such journal, Squier published a long article, "American Ethnology," which includes a reference to Morton's view that "Negroes were numerous in Egypt, but their social position in ancient times was the same that it now is, that of servants and slaves."[31]

However, a major advocate of the "unity of man," Dr. John Bachman, opposed Nott and Agassiz. A native of New York who had moved to South Carolina for his health thirty-five years earlier, Bachman became a devoted southerner (and later a fervent secessionist), but he was also a Lutheran minister and an outstanding naturalist who considered polygenism both heretical and scientifically unsound. Darwin had met him in London twelve years earlier, when Darwin admiringly copied into his notebooks various ideas gained from the American. Bachman now published his views in the most respected scientific publication in the south, the *Charleston Medical Journal and Review*. Bachman attacked Morton's assertions on grounds partly religious but mainly based on his own expertise regarding geographical distribution of animals and issues of hybridity. Bachman and Morton began a lively exchange in the pages of the journal that lasted for months.[32]

Bachman's book *The Doctrine of the Unity of the Human Race Examined on the Principles of Science* appeared shortly after the Charleston meeting. It received a brief notice in the *American Journal of Science* and a long and negative review by Nott in *De Bow's Review.*[33] Various reviews in 1850 mentioned Charles Pickering's *Races of Man; and Their Geographical Distribution*, first printed in 1848 as one of a projected twenty-four volumes of reports of the U.S. Exploring Expedition that had sailed the Pacific Ocean in 1838–42 under the command of Charles Wilkes, USN. This American version of the *Beagle* voyage was funded by Congress, which, unfortunately, also supervised the publication of its specialist reports, five of which were never completed (including two volumes on ichthyology farmed out to Agassiz). The congressional committee controlling the project authorized print-runs of a mere one hundred or two hundred copies, and the committee chairman, Senator Benjamin Tappan of Ohio—brother of two of America's staunchest antislavery activists, Arthur Tappan and Lewis Tappan—particularly disapproved of an early draft of Pickering's anthropological report.[34] Wilkes had to arrange that "the parts of his paper on the races of man that you criticized and objected to" were altered so that "you could have no possible objection to its publication, now."[35]

During the voyage, Pickering wrote to his close associate Dr. Morton that although formerly believing there were only five races of men, he had now seen eight and expected to see more. If others wished to believe all the races belonged to one species, he was "content to let them have their way," but Pickering believed that the various races had "different origins, or, were originally placed in different countries," which was also Morton's view. Now, to gain Tappan's imprimatur, Pickering watered down his language, creating what one reader called "the oddest collection of fragments that was ever seen . . . amorphous as a fog, unstratified as a pudding, and heterogeneous as a low priced sausage."[36] The first commercial edition of Pickering's *Races of Man* was produced in 1850 in London by an editor who actually thought Pickering was arguing *for* the unity of the human species![37] A better-informed reviewer who compared Pickering's *Races of Man* not only with Bachman's recent *Doctrine of Unity of the Human Race* but also with a second journal article that Agassiz had published in the *Christian Examiner* regretted Pickering's "guarded style of expression," praised Bachman's "thoroughness of investigation . . . and triumphant establishment of [his] conclusions," and criticized "both the nature of . . . and the manner in which Prof. Agassiz has presented [his views] to the public. . . . We do not perceive that any new law has been established, or any new principle developed."[38]

Agassiz's first article in the *Christian Examiner* had sought to counter charges of irreligion, and the second denied subsequent charges of serving the interests of slave owners. But after disclaiming "any question involving political matters," he later asserted that it was "mock-philanthropy" to assume all races have the same abilities and that "human affairs with reference to the colored races" would be better if we understood "the real difference" rather than "treating them on terms of equality."[39] A third article in the *Christian Examiner* reduced all the issues to a single stark choice: either one accepts the evidence of geographical distribution and the "primordial" differences between human races as reflecting a divine plan or one accepts a single "Garden of Eden" creation but must then account for subsequent distributions and well-known variations by appealing to some natural law that allows for "development" (or transmutation) of species. He commented, "Recognition in the animal creation of specific [divine] thoughts excludes . . . the idea of a natural development from law, and acknowledges a personal, intelligent God."[40]

Agassiz's rejection of all "development" theories espoused by Lamarck, Erasmus Darwin, and "Mr. Vestiges" (and lurking in Charles Darwin's private sketches and notebooks) crystallized the issue. "I must confess," Lyell later wrote, "that Agassiz . . . drove me far over into Darwin's camp . . . for when he attributed the original of every race of man to an independent starting point . . . the miracles really became to me so much in the way of S. Antonio of Padua."[41]

Yet, the market for polygenism was strong. Nott had earlier assured Squier, "All the . . . articles I have written on niggerology have been eagerly sought for at the South, and in the present excited state of the political world, I think the thing will go well."[42] The excitement in the "political world," which had been building up before Lincoln left Washington in 1849, nearly broke up the United States in 1850. The territories acquired through the Mexican-American war raised the question of whether slavery might expand into these regions. The Wilmot Proviso, which Lincoln supported, had sought to prevent this extension of slavery but was stopped by southern opposition in the Senate. However, after the Gold Rush made it imperative to admit California into the union, the issue boiled over as Californians expressed their desire to enter as a free state. Southerners would not accept this without concessions on several other slavery-related issues, and during the protracted negotiations, there were serious calls in the south for secession if denied the right to extend slavery. Henry Clay came out of retirement, returned to the Senate, and in January 1850 proposed a series of compromises. Congress debated furiously but could not pass the "omnibus bill," and it was only in September that the compromise bills were finally steered one by one through Congress by the chairman of the committee on territories, Stephen A. Douglas.

Lincoln played down Douglas's role in the passage of the Compromise of 1850 and had already advised the Whig who was supposed to take his place in Congress to oppose any extension of slavery but not if secession proved a genuine threat, for "of all political objects the preservation of the Union stands number one."[43] There was much for Lincoln to dislike in the compromise's appeasement of the south. The problem of slavery in Washington, D.C., itself, on which Lincoln had labored in vain, was lamely "settled" by abolishing the slave trade there but not slavery itself. The new Fugitive Slave Act was a travesty, and, worst of all, the territories of New Mexico and Utah were opened to the possibility of slavery on the basis of popular sovereignty, whereby the citizens of a given territory rather than Congress could decide for or against slavery. The greatest champion of this policy was now Douglas. Lincoln, from his law office in Springfield, uttered no protest, but when eighty-three prominent Illinois Whigs and Democrats signed a call for a meeting of citizens to endorse the proposed compromise, Lincoln's and Herndon's names were not among them.[44]

Although numerous other countries far less democratic than the United States had recently abolished slavery, it might now continue indefinitely in America, nourished simultaneously by the compromise and the southern slave owners' newfound justification provided by the theory of separate creations. Despite raising some orthodox hackles, Louis Agassiz himself had cobbled together a compromise between the religious and scientific worldview. Slave owners had always found divine support in scripture, and now they could read "the plan of the Creator" in nature. As polygenism spread through the popular press, millions of Americans who were not slave owners also felt inclined to accept a scientific view that so conveniently reconciled their religious notions and racial prejudices. Darwin felt he had a better explanation for racial diversity that did not involve God; and Lincoln, in a later lecture, blamed man, not God, for "the invention of negroes."

Having read widely and also drawing on Herndon's even wider reading, Lincoln was more aware of these scientific debates than most Americans. In the 1850s, the strongly antislavery Herndon expanded his library with publications about slavery and quite a few on race.

> I was in correspondence with Sumner, Greeley, Phillips, and Garrison, and was thus thoroughly imbued with all the rancor drawn from such strong anti-slavery sources. . . . Every time a good speech on the great issue was made I sent for it. . . . Lincoln and I took such papers as the *Chicago Tribune, New York Tribune, Anti-Slavery Standard, Emancipator* and *National Era.* On the other side of the question we took the *Charleston Mercury* and the *Richmond Enquirer.* . . . I purchased all the leading histories of the slavery movement, and other works which treated on that subject.[45]

Herndon owned at least two books by Agassiz, both collections of popular lectures dating to the period after Lincoln had moved to the White House. But "Herndon's Auction List" also included Hugh Miller's *Footprints of the Creator,* first published in Britain in 1849 and strongly attacking the "development" theory as popularized in *The Vestiges.* Herndon probably owned the 1850 American edition that included a twenty-six-page "memoir" of Miller written by Agassiz, who proudly took credit for bringing this "successful combination of Christian doctrines with pure scientific truths" to the American public.[46]

The scientific debate waned somewhat after the Compromise of 1850 dampened political flames, and Morton's death in May 1851 ended his joust with Bachman in the *Charleston Medical Journal*. A hiatus occurred as the rumor that
Agassiz was writing a book about special creation proved false, and Nott, assisted
by George Gliddon, was for three years busy producing a book-length treatment
of polygenism based on Morton's notes.

Herndon bought a book published late in 1854 by George Fitzhugh and entitled *Sociology for the South; or, the Failure of Free Society*. According to Herndon, the book "defended and justified slavery in every conceivable way" and also
"aroused the ire of Lincoln more than most pro-slavery books."[47] Fitzhugh, a Vir-
ginian lawyer and social theorist, demonstrated a perverse shift in slave-owning
culture that no longer saw "the peculiar institution" as an embarrassment, or
expected it gradually to extinguish itself, or sought merely to protect slave states
from outside interference but instead hoped to expand a system that it proudly
defended. According to Fitzhugh, the negro "is but a grown up child, and must
be governed as a child, not as a lunatic or criminal. The master occupies towards
him the place of parent or guardian." He based his conclusions on "the course of
nature, the lessons of history, [and] the voice of experience."[48]

Although Fitzhugh later converted to "scientific racism," in *Sociology for the
South* he rejected the polygenism that enthralled so many fellow southerners,
"first, because it is at war with scripture, which teaches us that the whole human
race is descended from a common parentage; and, second, because it encourages
and incites brutal masters to treat negroes, not as weak, ignorant and dependent
brethren, but as wicked beasts, without the pale of humanity." In 1854, Fitzhugh
was still content to defend slavery as being part of the "higher law" of God, who
did not make blacks as "brutes" but as "weak" men and "instituted slavery from
the first, as he instituted marriage."[49] He specifically disparaged "the doctrine of
the 'Types of Mankind,'" which was actually the title of an influential 738-page
polygenist volume that had appeared earlier in 1854. Nearly a thousand people
subscribed to the first edition, and nine more editions appeared before 1871.[50] Darwin, who disliked it even more than Fitzhugh did, though for different reasons,
owned and cited the work, usually with distrust.[51] It does not appear in "Herndon's
Auction List," and whether Lincoln ever read the work or merely read about it,
he would have shared Darwin's distaste. *The Types of Mankind* was the work
Nott and Gliddon had been preparing for the last three years, using notes of the
late Dr. Morton, to whom they dedicated the volume. They also enhanced their
work by including a prefatory essay written by Harvard professor Louis Agassiz.[52]

The Types of Mankind *and the Kansas-Nebraska Act, 1854–55*

In the autumn of 1850, Charles Darwin, who earlier had thanked heaven he would never have to visit another slave country, wrote to his cousin that he sometimes speculated about emigrating, perhaps to Australia, "or what I fancy most, the middle States of N. America."[1] Darwin never left the British Isles again, but while he fantasized about moving to the American midwest, it appears that a resident of that area, Billy Herndon, was intellectually escaping in the opposite direction. Beginning in the early 1850s, Herndon expanded the law office's library with not only works on slavery but also a surprising number of British publications: collections of essays from the London *Times* and from the universities of Oxford, Cambridge, and Edinburgh and odd volumes of *Blackwood's*, *North British Review, Edinburgh Review, Chambers' Journal of Popular Literature, Arts and Sciences, Chambers' Papers for the People,* and *Chambers' Repository* (the last three coedited by Robert Chambers, anonymous author of *Vestiges*).[2]

Herndon also obtained forty-nine issues of the *Westminster Review*, from 1851 to 1868, which was edited during some of these years by the brilliant Marian Evans, later known as George Eliot. Before taking control of the *Westminster Review*, Eliot had translated David Friedrich Strauss's *Life of Christ* and Ludwig Feuerbach's *Essence of Christianity*, both possessed by Herndon. According to Eliot's 1851 prospectus, the *Westminster Review* stood for the "law of progress," maintaining "that the institutions of man, no less than the products of nature, are strong and durable in proportion as they are the results of gradual development."[3] Thomas Huxley became the journal's science reviewer in the early 1850s, though not at that time sharing Eliot's devotion to "development": he upset her by writing (in another journal) a scathing review of *Vestiges*'s latest edition.[4]

Darwin met Huxley in 1851, finding the young man as brilliant as he was acerbic. Although later becoming the greatest champion of Darwin's natural selection, Huxley's admiration for Darwin was already clear in 1854, when he wrote a brief notice (which Herndon might have read in Springfield): "Mr. Darwin's present work shows him to be as able an observer of nature on the small as on the large scale. It deals with the anatomy and metamorphoses of certain crustaceans, those well-known barnacles, in all their varieties."[5] After eight years' labor, Darwin had finally completed his study. Darwin considered using the material as a vehicle for introducing his theory of natural selection but decided the barnacles deserved their own place among specialist studies while his theory required broader comparative data.

The eight years of struggling to classify these amazingly variable barnacles had not only reenforced Darwin's conviction that natural selection was correct but also gained Darwin valuable contacts with naturalists worldwide, many struggling with classification problems in their own fields. As Huxley had noted, Darwin had proved his ability to specialize as well as theorize and was thrilled that the Royal Society cited his recent work when awarding him the Royal Medal for Natural Science in 1853. Darwin's closest colleague, Joseph Dalton Hooker, who was on the award committee, indicated the magnitude of the victory by pointing out, "I neither proposed you, nor seconded you, nor voted for you."[6]

Darwin was now better positioned to bring his theory before a world better prepared to receive it. The thousands of new specimens discovered by recent British and American expeditions kept an increasingly professional body of naturalists busily "lumping" or "splitting" each other's particular varieties and species. And in the background, surviving continued insult and slowly gaining ground, was the development concept. The Lamarckian view simply would not die, and *Vestiges*, still selling widely ten years and ten editions since its first appearance, continued to spread the gospel, as did Herbert Spencer's work and the whole tone of the "Westminster set." Darwin knew it would take time to pull together his notes and work out the scheme for presenting the evidence as convincingly as possible: building half a bridge would not get him to his destination.

As Darwin finished up his barnacle work, Louis Agassiz was not far from his thoughts. When Charles Lyell passed on a copy of Agassiz's *Lake Superior*, Darwin reminded Lyell (with a dose of irony) that "the great man honoured me with a copy" earlier.[7] Darwin's view of Agassiz was probably echoed in what Hooker, Britain's greatest botanist, wrote to his American counterpart Asa Gray of Harvard at the beginning of 1854: "I have long been aware of Agassiz's heresies. His opinions are too extreme for respect and hence are mere prejudices. They are further contradicted by facts. Lyell and I have talked him over by the hour."[8]

Lyell, Hooker, and Darwin often shared their correspondence, and Hooker began showing Darwin some of his letters from Gray, starting with Gray's response to Hooker's condemnation of Agassiz. Darwin had once met the American when he was touring England in 1839, and now he thanked Hooker for passing along Gray's letter, adding, "how very pleasantly he writes."[9] One thing Gray so pleasantly describes is his decreasing respect for Agassiz. "It often does more harm than good" to combat Agassiz's views in public. "I confine myself to trying to show him that his own data do not at all necessitate the conclusions he sometimes draws from them."[10] Darwin, tongue firmly in cheek, commented to Hooker:

> I cannot quite understand why you & [Gray] think so strongly that it "does more harm than good to combat [Agassiz's] views." It is delightful to hear all that he says on Agassiz: How very singular it is that so *eminently* clever a man, with such *immense* knowledge on many branches of Natural History, should write such wonderful stuff & bosh as he does. Lyell told me that he was so delighted with one of his [Agassiz's] lectures on [i.e. against] progressive development &c &c, that he went to him afterwards & told him "it was so delightful, that he could not help all the time wishing it was true." I seldom see a Zoological paper from N. America, without observing the impress of Agassiz's doctrines,—another proof, by the way, of how great a man he is.

Huxley, in his recent review savaging *Vestiges*, called Agassiz "the great investigator . . . whose lively fancy has done at least as much harm to natural science as his genius has assisted its progress." Darwin praised the review but thought Huxley had been "rather hard on the poor author" of *Vestiges*: "But I am perhaps no fair judge for I am almost as unorthodox about species as *Vestiges* itself, though I hope not *quite* so unphilosophical." On Agassiz, Darwin added, "I am rather sorry you do not think more of Agassiz's embryological stages, for though I saw how excessively weak the evidence was, I was led to hope in its truth."[11] Agassiz's notion that the fossil sequence of the paleontological record somehow reflected the stages in the embryological development of the four main branches of the animal kingdom appealed to Darwin and had no direct relation to multiple creations.

After telling Hooker how Huxley had made "mincemeat with Agassiz's embryonic fish," Darwin mentioned that he would "begin to look over my old notes on species" as soon as he had finished sending "ten-thousand Barnacles" back to their donors. When Darwin returned specimens to Augustus Gould in Boston with effusive thanks, he asked Gould to forgive him for "sending in the same box the specimens which Prof. Agassiz was so kind as to send me, & a copy of my work for him.—When you next see Prof. Agassiz, will you be so good as to give him my cordial thanks & my kind & respectful remembrances."[12] So, only indirect thanks from the normally punctilious Darwin: there is no evidence of further communication between the two until 1858.

Darwin had been a collector, explorer, observer, describer, and dissectionist, and, at all times, a theorist, but now he became a serious experimenter and continued so for the rest of his life. His first experiments, begun in April 1855, concerned whether seeds might have been transported long distances without losing their ability to germinate.[13] The question—whether identical species could have arisen in separate continents *without* separate creation or transportation by humans—had interested Darwin since at least 1837.[14] Although Hooker dismissed Darwin's notion in both letters and published work, Darwin never yielded to Hooker's authority. In April 1855, Darwin informed Hooker, "I have begun my seed-salting experiments," which involved Darwin's entire family looking after dozens of jars filled with artificial seawater and various seeds.[15]

Darwin gloated over the successful results. "You are a good man," he told Hooker, "to confess that you expected the crop would be killed in a week, for this gives me a nice little triumph. The children at first were tremendously eager & asked me often 'whether I should beat Dr Hooker?'!!" Darwin removed the sting by adding: "If you knew some of the experiments (if they may be so called) which I am trying, you would have a good right to sneer for they are so *absurd* even in *my* opinion that I dare not tell you."[16] Hooker himself obtained some seeds washed up on the Azores Islands, planted them at Kew, and had the "unutterable mortification" of seeing them germinate. Darwin enjoyed Hooker's mock humiliation but stressed the real point: "It is the funniest thing in the world that you do not rejoice; for you have (& I never have) put in print that you do not believe in multiple creation, & therefore you surely should rejoice at every conceivable means of dispersal."[17]

The connection between these experiments and Agassiz's multiple creations is evident in a report Darwin submitted to the *Gardeners Chronicle*: "As such experiments might naturally appear childish to many, I may be permitted to premise that they have a direct bearing on a very interesting problem, which has lately, *especially in America*, attracted much attention, namely, whether the same organic being has been created at one point or on several on the face of our globe" (emphasis added).[18] Darwin posted a copy of that report to his new correspondent Asa Gray, whose response was the first letter in the Darwin-Gray correspondence to mention Agassiz. "I am most glad to be in conference with Hooker & yourself, on these matters, and I think we may, or rather *you* may, in a few years settle the question as to whether Agassiz's—or Hooker's views are correct: they are certainly widely different." Thanking Darwin for the paper on "your experiments on seeds exposed to sea-water," Gray said he would have it reprinted in the *American Journal of Science* "as a *nut* for Agassiz to crack."[19] Along with occasional references to Agassiz, the correspondence was for the moment filled with Darwin's questions about geographical distribution of plants, suggestions of future lines of research, and Gray's generous offers of further assistance.

When writing about Agassiz and nuts, Gray had presumably already read Agassiz's prefatory sketch in Joseph C. Nott and George R. Gliddon's *Types of Mankind*, which had been published over a year earlier. Gray and Darwin had still not mentioned the book in their correspondence, and Darwin had yet to read it. Certainly, he could guess its contents after reading various reviews, including one in the *Westminster Review* in July 1854. "Grant that the Negro is a distinct species," Huxley summed up ironically, "or even a metamorphosed orang, if you will, and what difference does it make to the social effect of [slavery]? [It] is an evil to society—because it degrades the man who practices it and increases the proclivity to crimes injurious to society in himself and others. And we are bound to put down the slaveholders for precisely [this] reason. . . . Ethnology had better perish as a science than be swamped by the accession to her ranks of the Legrees of the South."[20] Huxley knew *Uncle Tom's Cabin* but did not adore it as Emma and Charles Darwin did. Darwin probably tolerated Huxley's flippancy about blacks because Huxley's antislavery position was as solid as his dislike of multiple creationists.

Despite or because of Huxley's review, seventeen months passed before Darwin read *Types of Mankind* in December 1855, but he could have read Agassiz's preface when it was reprinted in October 1854 in a journal Darwin often read.[21] That he did so is suggested by his comment in November 1855, after thanking Lyell for passing along two pamphlets by John Bachman, probably those based on Bachman's four separate reviews of *Types of Mankind*—two of which were scathing about Agassiz's preface. "It is *most* useful to see what is said on all sides," Darwin told Lyell, "though I am surprised, from what I remember of Bachman, that he did not do the thing better, & that he deals in assertions, which I do not believe he can substantiate by a single fact."[22] A month later, Darwin himself finally read the *Types of Mankind*. Whether he had previously seen Agassiz's "Sketch" or not, Darwin now reacted with an outburst of negative marginal notes: "How false," "What forced reasoning!" "Primordial begs the question," and "Look at same race [native Americans] in United States & S. America." On a sheet of notes pinned to the last page, Darwin expressed in a nutshell how his view of human racial groupings differed from that of Agassiz, Nott, and Gliddon: "As mere naturalist, *excepting* from blending of races to certain extent, independently of crossing, I sh[oul]d look at races of man as deserving to be called distinct species, yet I consider as descended from common stock, so come back at common belief." Darwin's original emphasis points out that two factors—variations (or gradations) within racial groups and cross-breeding between them—already weaken the authors' view that human races are distinct species; but Darwin's new theory of descent from "common stock" actually aligns him somewhat with the earlier "common belief" (descent from Adam and Eve). The note continues, "only difference is name whether to be called species or variations."[23] For Darwin, there are in a sense no species, only degrees of variation, and the variation between human races is small—*how* small is what he would continue to research and then discuss in his two later books on man. In *On the Origin of Species*, Darwin would say only that his theory of natural selection as applied to animals might someday "throw light" on the origin of human beings. Ironically, Agassiz felt *his* theory of multiple creations did the same thing, as he stated in his preface for *Types of Mankind*:

[T]he geographical distribution of all the organized beings now existing upon the earth . . . cannot fail to throw light, at some future time, upon the very origin of the differences existing among men, since it shows that man's physical nature is modified by the same laws as that of animals, and that any general results obtained from the animal kingdom regarding the organic differences of its various types must also apply to man.[24]

Perhaps Darwin remembered Agassiz's supposed throwing of "light" when he used the same phrase four years later. But it was not a case of imitation being the highest form of flattery, for what Darwin felt was contempt. At the bottom of the last page of the preface, Darwin scribbled: "Oh proh pudor Agassiz!" (Oh for shame!)[25]

There is no evidence that Lincoln or Herndon ever read *Types of Mankind*, but they probably read Huxley's review in the law office's copy of the *Westminster Review* or other reviews such as those in *Putnam's Monthly Magazine*, a Whig organ (soon to become Republican). Notices in southern journals were often summarized in the *Charleston Mercury* and the *Richmond Enquirer*, which the two lawyers also received.[26] Although Lincoln would not disagree with *Types*'s antiscriptural position, these reviews showed that religious sentiment could help to limit the general acceptance of the polygenist view of human races. Lincoln could also see that when natural science veered into social science, problems arose. This was not Euclid, the proofs were not demonstrable, and the biology behind Dr. Samuel G. Morton's craniometry and Agassiz's multiple zones of creation, while impressing many, did not convince all serious reviewers. When even more controversial evidence was dragged in from philology, ethnology, and Egyptian archaeology, those eager to be convinced perceived concurrence, while others simply saw accumulations of logical flaws. Agassiz's contribution to *Types* raised some reviewers' estimation of multiple creation but tarnished others' opinions of Agassiz.

Convincing or not, the ideas promoted in *Types of Mankind* arose precisely when the debate about slavery in America was taking a new turn. In the past, whatever the difficulties in abolishing slavery where it existed, the actual *expansion* of slavery territorially was difficult for southerners to advocate because slavery was generally held to be "wrong"—morally, politically, or economically. But the ethical view usually relied on the notion that blacks were fellow human beings—a notion now under attack *intellectually* by those promoting separate creations and *politically* by those advocating separate decision making—that is, "pop. sov."

Lincoln could see that this new polygenist view was dangerous but also vulnerable to an attack—which Lincoln was about to launch for an entirely separate reason. However, Lincoln knew enough science to recognize his own limitations and, more important, those of his audience: rather than employing directly the terminology of geographical distribution or hybridity, one might better attack these new doctrines by appealing to religious sentiments and emphasizing the new doctrine's antitraditional and counterintuitive nature. This Lincoln would do by reminding his listeners of their trust in the Bible, in the Declaration of Independence, and in their own sense of rightness: not a very scientific approach yet ultimately grounded in the real world as a practical formula for political success.

The year 1854 was not so much a turning point for Lincoln or Darwin as simply the year each got back on track. Having finally completed his barnacle work, Darwin was perhaps partly spurred on by the rise of scientific racism, which may also have had some influence on Lincoln's thought and action.[27] But what energized Lincoln primarily was the passage of the Kansas-Nebraska Act in May 1854.

Senator Stephen A. Douglas's prime intention in introducing this bill was to improve his chances of winning the Democratic Party's presidential nomination. His strategy was to please the railroad interests in Illinois by promoting the "northern route" for the projected transcontinental railroad between the Pacific Ocean and Chicago without displeasing the southern wing of the party who preferred New Orleans as the eastern terminus. Ostensibly, Douglas's more noble purpose, as chairman of the Senate committee on territories, was to facilitate the country's development through the swift admission to statehood of the remaining territories in the northern half of the Louisiana Purchase.

Because the Missouri Compromise had prohibited slavery in those territories, southerners were likely to delay future admissions. Douglas thought he could break the logjam by applying popular sovereignty so local citizens rather than Congress could wrangle about whether to permit slavery in their new state constitutions. But southerners would support Douglas only if the compromise's prohibition was formally repealed. Douglas predicted correctly that this more radical step would cause a "hell of a storm" but thought he could ride it out, earning southern support by doing so.[28] The bill was introduced on 4 January 1854 and after bitter debate became law on 30 May.

The Kansas-Nebraska Act altered Lincoln's life, but the question is whether it simply created a vital political opportunity or actually angered Lincoln so much that he felt compelled to speak out against slavery in a new way. When Lincoln said in October 1854 that Douglas "should remember that he took us by surprise. . . . We were thunderstruck and stunned; and we reeled and fell in utter confusion," he was making a rhetorical point about unprepared forces swiftly rallying to oppose the act.[29] His later campaign biographies depict him as a man unexpectedly drawn into the fight, not a politician exploiting an opportunity: "I was losing interest in politics, when the repeal of the Missouri Compromise aroused me again"; "In 1854, his [legal] profession had almost superseded the thought of politics in his mind, when the repeal of the Missouri compromise aroused him as he had never been before."[30]

Lincoln's law partner and biographer, Herndon, echoed these professions of unexpected transformation but also recognized the political opportunism.

> Now, however, a live issue was presented to him. No one realized this sooner than he. . . . That man who thinks Lincoln calmly sat down and gathered his robes about him, waiting for the people to call him, has a very erroneous knowledge of Lincoln. He was always calculating, and always planning ahead. His ambition was a little engine that knew no rest.[31]

Historian William Lee Miller's analysis of Lincoln's actions in 1854 allows for political opportunism but repeatedly emphasizes that Lincoln "rose to the occasion" morally by beginning—and for the next six years continuing—to make with exceptional clarity the case that slavery was evil.[32] Although Miller accepts that Lincoln had always opposed slavery, he stresses that in 1854, Lincoln "dropped all the old Whig topics" and "concentrated only on slavery" by "stepping forward by his own initiative to join the great argument about his country's future."[33]

There are two problems with Miller's analysis. First, Lincoln "dropped all the old Whig topics," including those (according to Miller) "on which the Democrats were vulnerable," exactly because Lincoln was encouraging some Democrats to oppose Douglas and therefore was not looking for vulnerable points in Democratic policies generally but in Douglas particularly. Second, Miller himself notes that *two years before* the Kansas-Nebraska Act was proposed, Lincoln was "making the transition, by way of condemning those who denied . . . the application [of the statement 'all men are created equal']"; and Miller merely creates an illusion of innovation by suggesting that in 1852, Lincoln was "treating the Declaration only in its historical context" and did not until 1854 begin "using it as a moral norm for today."[34]

Lincoln was capable of considering the Declaration in its "historical context" and as a "moral norm" simultaneously and did so in 1852 in his eulogy of his hero Henry Clay. Lincoln emphasized the universal (and not merely historical) concept behind the Declaration's phrase "all men are created equal" by noting that Clay "did not perceive, that on a question of human right, the negroes were to be excepted from the human race." Lincoln asserted that

> a few, but an increasing number of men, . . . for the sake of perpetuating slavery, are beginning to assail and to ridicule . . . the declaration that "all men are created free and equal [*sic*]." So far as I have learned, the first American, of any note, to do or attempt this, was the late John C. Calhoun; and if I mistake not, it soon after found its way into some of the messages of the Governors of South Carolina.[35]

Lincoln was probably unaware that Calhoun had been directly influenced by the work of Morton and that one former governor of South Carolina, James H. Hammond, who was outspoken about negro inferiority, was a friendly correspondent of Nott. However, Lincoln quoted a letter sent "only last year" to a St. Louis, Missouri, newspaper by an "influential clergyman of Virginia" who said that the phrase "All men are born free and created equal" was unbiblical, invented by Voltaire, "baptized by Thomas Jefferson," exploited by "professional abolitionists," and merely a "coin in the political currency of our generation. I am sorry to say that I have never seen two men of whom it is true." Lincoln responded, "This sounds strangely in republican America. The like was not heard in the fresher days of the Republic." He then contrasted this clergyman's notions with a Clay quotation about "the benevolent efforts among free men, in behalf of the unhappy portion of our race doomed to bondage."[36] What Lincoln so strongly reacted against in this 1852 eulogy was the view that received so much attention after Agassiz and Nott addressed the American Association for the Advancement of Science (AAAS) conference in Charleston in 1850. Lincoln never referred to polygenism by that or any other technical term, and yet he did note that the idea of "saying all men were *not* created equal" sounded "strangely" indeed.

In short, intellectually and morally Lincoln had already been "aroused" *before* 1854, and the Kansas-Nebraska Act essentially provided a political opportunity because Lincoln recognized that Douglas had blundered, and Lincoln could now use a moral argument (based on the antipolygenist view that "all men are created equal") in order to create the political force that might stop his old rival in his tracks.[37]

Slavery's opponents had hitherto developed an array of somewhat ineffective ways to attack the "peculiar institution." Lincoln realized that the real value in concentrating on the Kansas-Nebraska Act was that one was then fighting for so little: the reversal of a repeal of a prohibition against slavery's expansion. It was a fight around which a Whig in Illinois might, for one time only, hope to rally support not only from other members of the dissolving Whig party and from the clamoring Free-Soilers, abolitionists, and Know-Nothings but even from temporarily disaffected members of Douglas's Democratic Party. That party throughout Lincoln's residence in Illinois had held a controlling majority everywhere except Sangamon County. To Lincoln's amazed delight, many of Douglas's fellow Democrats had suddenly split off as "anti-Nebraska Democrats."

Although Lincoln might have attacked the Democrats on various other issues, his tactic was *not* to raise issues around which Democrats could be rallied (and thus heal their split). Lincoln needed to win over at least some Democrats if he was ever to have a chance of being elected by the state legislature to sit in the Senate in Washington. The old rail-splitter now saw that Douglas's Kansas-Nebraska Act had handed him a wedge: he would now complete the split by promoting a policy to reverse not only the repeal of the Missouri Compromise but also the repeal of "the ancient faith," a phrase Lincoln used frequently over the next few years, which nicely rolled together the Declaration of Independence and traditional single creation of Genesis. It was the old-time religion and good

enough for Lincoln. He stressed the moral argument not because it was so difficult but because, to him, it was so obvious, and he sensed that most people,
despite their deep prejudices, shared at least the essence of his view. Douglas had
blundered by adopting two new and primarily southern views: slavery's right
to expand and the polygenist view that blacks were not fully men. Armed with
"the ancient faith," Lincoln could stand as popular champion against both views.

However, Lincoln's new weapon, sufficient for slaying such a doubleheaded
monster, also cut on both edges. If, ultimately, the Kansas-Nebraska Act was evil
because blacks were actually men and so on, then must we do more than merely
halt slavery's expansion? Must we force other states to free their slaves? Must
we grant those "fellow men," once freed, the right to settle in Illinois, to enjoy
equal protection under law, to serve on juries, to vote? "In fact," Miller points
out, "Douglas was going to beat him over the head with that."[38]

In 1854, both of Illinois' senators were Democrats. Douglas was not up for
reelection until 1858, but in early 1855, a newly elected state legislature would
decide whether to reelect James Shields, Douglas's colleague in the Senate, who
also supported the act.[39] If the upcoming statewide election altered the state
legislature from a Democratic majority to a working coalition of Whigs, Free-
Soilers, Know-Nothings, and Anti-Nebraska Democrats willing to vote against
Shields, then some Anti-Nebraska Democrat—or perhaps a Whig with broad
support—might be elected. It seemed Lincoln's only opportunity to move up
the political ladder.

Lincoln did not sit back and await events but began systematic research into
the historical background of the current issues, "nosing for weeks in the State
Library, pumping his brain and his imagination for points and arguments," as
one hostile newspaper put it.[40] Too often described by historians as a fatalist or
a believer in divine providence, Lincoln took full control and worked tirelessly
to influence the coming struggle.

Abraham Lincoln at age fifty.
Photograph taken 4 October 1859
in Chicago by Samuel M. Fassett.
Library of Congress.

Charles Darwin at
age fifty-one or fifty-
five. Photographed
in London by Maull
and Polyblank, at "age
fifty-one," according
to Karl Pearson; but
Darwin's son Francis
guessed (but could
never confirm) that the
photograph showed
Darwin about age fifty-
five. Reprinted from Pearson,
*The Life, Letters, and Labours of
Francis Galton*, 1:56.

Antislavery medallion designed and produced in the potteries of Darwin's grandfather Josiah Wedgwood, 1787.
Image courtesy of the Wedgwood Museum Trust, Barlaston, Staffordshire, England.

AM I NOT A MAN AND A BROTHER?

Sir Charles Lyell (1797–1875), geologist and mentor of Charles Darwin. Photographed in 1860s in London by John J. E. Mayall.
Wellcome Library, London.

Sir Joseph Dalton
Hooker (1817–1911),
botanist and
Darwin's closest
scientific confidant.
Photographed ca. 1855
in London by Maull
and Polyblank.
Wellcome Library, London.

William H. Herndon
(1818–91), Lincoln's
law partner and
bibliophile. From a
halftone reproduction,
probably ca. 1870, by
L. C. Handy Studios of
a now-lost photograph.
Reprinted from David Herbert
Donald, *Lincoln's Herndon:
A Biography* (New York: Knopf,
1948), facing p. 40.

Louis Agassiz (1807–73), America's leading scientist in the mid-nineteenth century and foremost opponent of Darwin's theories. Photograph taken ca. 1864 in Boston by Antoine Sonrel, who produced illustrations for many of Agassiz's publications.
Wellcome Library, London.

Stephen A. Douglas (1813–61), Lincoln's most prominent political opponent for over a quarter of a century. Photographed ca. 1858 in the Mathew Brady Studio. Library of Congress.

Thomas Huxley (1825–95) beside a blackboard on which he has drawn a gorilla's skull. "Darwin's bulldog," as Huxley was known, lacked Darwin's compassion for blacks. Photographed ca. 1858 by Cundall Downes and Company of London. Wellcome Library, London.

Asa Gray (1810–88), America's foremost botanist and collaborator with Darwin. Photographed ca. 1864 by John A. Whipple in Boston. Wisconsin Historical Society.

Alfred Russel Wallace (1823–1913), codiscoverer of natural selection, with whom Darwin maintained a warm relationship. Portrait taken in 1862 in Singapore, photographer unknown. Reprinted from James Marchant, ed., *Alfred Russel Wallace: Letters and Reminiscences* (London: Cassell, 1916), vol. 1, facing p. 36.

Rear Admiral John A. Dahlgren (1809–70), commander of the Washington Navy Yard and Lincoln's friend and closest adviser on military technology. Photographed standing by a Dahlgren gun on deck of the USS *Pawnee*, June 1865, in Charleston Harbor, S.C., probably by Mathew Brady's field staff. Library of Congress.

Lammot du Pont (1831–84) in 1856, five years before he carried out a secret mission in London at Lincoln's behest while pretending to be serving only the interests of his family's gunpowder-making company. Photographer unknown. Courtesy of Hagley Museum and Library, Wilmington, Delaware.

Albert Herter's imaginative 1924 depiction of the founding of the National Academy of Sciences in 1863. *Left to right*: Benjamin Peirce, Alexander Dallas Bache, Joseph Henry, Louis Agassiz, President Lincoln, Senator Henry Wilson, Admiral Charles Henry Davis, and Benjamin Apthorp Gould. Courtesy of the National Academy of Sciences.

Statue of Louis Agassiz at Stanford University, after falling from a height of thirty feet during San Francisco earthquake, 1906. Photographed by Frank Davey.
Courtesy of U.S. Geological Survey.

The Politics of Race

espite holding no political office, Lincoln managed to spearhead the campaign in Illinois against the Kansas-Nebraska Act prior to the statewide elections at the end of 1854. He nearly won the U.S. Senate race but was compelled, in order to prevent James Shields or another pro-Douglas Democrat from winning, to ask his supporters to shift their votes to an Anti-Nebraska Democrat. Lincoln then joined the new Republican Party and gained its nomination to challenge Stephen A. Douglas in his reelection bid in 1858, which drew national attention through the Lincoln-Douglas debates. Despite losing to Douglas in that race, Lincoln became the Republicans' choice to oppose Douglas in the presidential election in 1860. For our purposes, the fascinating details of these maneuvers, coalitions, and debates must largely be set aside to concentrate on why and how, over those six years, both Lincoln and Douglas referred in their speeches and debates to the issue of whether or not blacks were fully equal humans.

In his eulogy for Henry Clay in 1852, Lincoln had already shown awareness of recently arisen polygenism by stressing that blacks were not "to be excepted from the human race." However, Douglas, like many of his political allies, may have felt encouraged to believe that their policies were bolstered by the new "science."

When John C. Calhoun declared on the floor of the Senate in 1837 that slavery was a "positive good," he offered no "scientific" evidence about race, but later he supported similar statements with evidence from the 1840 census indicating that free blacks in the north suffered more from mental disorders than slaves in the south. Although the census figures were soon shown to be entirely wrong, Calhoun ignored this and was later delighted to receive cranial information from Dr. Samuel Morton and archeological information from George Gliddon, all indicating that blacks had been created separately from whites as an inferior model of man.[1]

When Calhoun died in 1850, other politicians carried the polygenist torch. Not only was South Carolinian James H. Hammond linked to Josiah Nott but

Alexander H. Stephens, Robert Toombs, and Robert B. Rhett were three more "leading southern politicians who adopted the argument from science in their defense of the slave system."[2] Some version of the polygenist view was accepted by most Democrats and many Whigs, north and south.

Douglas was greatly interested in science but has never been shown to be directly linked closely to polygenist scientists. He was certainly as aware as Lincoln of the new anthropology, which may help to explain a shift in Douglas's approach to slavery. In 1848 (two years before the main launch of the polygenist debate), Douglas had reacted fairly negatively to Calhoun's views: "In the North it is not expected that we should take the position that slavery is a positive good—a positive blessing. . . . We say to you of the South, if slavery be a blessing, it is your blessing; if it be a curse, it is your curse; enjoy it, on you rest all the responsibility."[3] But according to historian Harry V. Jaffa, the reason why, after 1848, "Douglas never again spoke so openly of the vicious tendency of the Southern 'positive good' school" was that he came to believe that "practical measures directed toward the containment of slavery could succeed only if they did *not* involve the abstract question of the intrinsic good or evil of slavery."[4] Although Jaffa is correct, a further explanation for this change of view is that sometime after 1850, Douglas came to accept the polygenist view that blacks are inferior by nature and somehow had to be controlled by whites.

Biographers of Douglas have overlooked one direct connection between Douglas and one propagandist for polygenism. Dr. John H. Van Evrie, a New York physician, publisher, strong Democrat, and vehement racist, wrote in 1864 that "ten years ago," he had published a pamphlet that "first promulgated to the world the simple, obvious, every day, but momentous truth, that so called slavery was the normal condition of the Negro."[5] The pamphlet, entitled *Negroes and Negro "Slavery": The First an Inferior Race; the Latter Its Normal Condition*, was published in several editions in 1853 and 1854 and was later expanded into a book in 1861.[6] Van Evrie has been dismissed as a "perpetually indignant" figure on the fringe who "did not influence the tide of battle" within the scientific community's debate, and he himself admitted that his pamphlet's "profound impression" was not based on its "originality or profundity" but rather on its "novelty" in showing that a "truth so obvious" had been "so long thrust out of sight by the mental dictation of the enemies of American institutions." However, Van Evrie may well have achieved his stated desire to influence politicians rather than scientists.[7]

When Van Evrie wrote to Calhoun in 1846 to condemn the "sickly sentimentality" that made some New Yorkers advocate granting suffrage to blacks, he made no scientific argument. But by the time his pamphlet appeared in 1853, Van Evrie had clearly adopted polygenism: "[the negro] is not a black white man, or a man merely with a black skin, but a different and inferior species of man." He quoted the most extreme statistics from Morton's skewed cranial measurements, borrowed Nott's notion that "the Mulatto, or Hybrid of the fourth generation, is as sterile as the mule," and complained that Agassiz did not "rise above the prejudices of Boston" and more "boldly grapple" with the absolute diversity of different human species.[8]

The pamphlet's second edition carried endorsements from southern spokesmen including Secretary of War Jefferson Davis and publisher J. D. B. De Bow, and a decade later, Van Evrie described how he had tried to bring his ideas to the attention of other politicians, though "some of the most intellectual men then in Congress, hesitated to accept the doctrine announced." Specifically, Stephens of Georgia (a Whig colleague when Lincoln was in Congress) was mentioned as a reluctant convert. Van Evrie also recounted, "Some few Northern men, then in Congress, assented to the new doctrine in *private*, but declined the responsibility of standing by the truth in *public*, and the late Senator Douglas distributed a considerable number of copies among his constituents, under the *frank of* Mr. Slidell."[9]

If this self-serving account is true, it provides an important insight into Douglas's attitudes: reluctant to appear to be personally influenced by scientific speculation, yet basically agreeing with polygenists and using Van Evrie's pamphlet to influence constituents. Van Evrie admired Douglas so much that during the Civil War, when publishing a Copperhead newspaper, the *New York Day Book* (later *New York Caucasian*), he printed immediately below the banner: "'I hold that this Government was made on the WHITE BASIS, by WHITE MEN, for the benefit of WHITE MEN and THEIR POSTERITY FOREVER' S. A. Douglas"—words from the first great Lincoln-Douglas debate in 1858.

During the seven months between the introduction of the Kansas-Nebraska bill early in 1854 and Douglas's return to Illinois to defend the act, there were heated discussions in Congress that Lincoln, reading about them in Springfield, noted for future reference. However, only occasionally did those congressional discussions raise the issue of black and white equality, in contrast with the prominence it received in exchanges between Lincoln and Douglas over the next six years. Various members of Congress opposed the bill's provision for extending slavery, and some condemned slavery as counter to God's creation of all men as descendants of Adam and to the Declaration of Independence's principle that "all men are created equal."[10] Douglas moved slightly closer to a scientific argument when he opened the formal debate by saying he disliked "the system of legislation on our part, by which a geographical line, in violation of the laws of nature, and climate, and soil, and of the laws of God, should be run to establish institutions for a people"—the language of Agassiz's "geographical zones."[11]

A clearer reference to scientific racism came in the speeches of Senator John Pettit of Indiana, who spoke of "the principle that two races distinct in their organization, in the volume and amount of intellect, of mind, of brain, different in the rapidity of the coursing of the blood through their veins, cannot live and enjoy equality together." By saying that these arrangements all resulted from "the stern decree of the Almighty himself," Pettit accepted Agassiz's reconciliation of religion and polygenism. And Pettit parroted Van Evrie's line when he added, "Look to any point in history, ancient or modern, and you will find the same truth developed. . . . Where one race is inferior to the other, it is necessarily subservient, and it is only a question of extent as to whether they shall be slaves fully or slaves partially." Turning to a point raised earlier by others—and mentioned many times later by Lincoln—Pettit said:

> It is alleged that all men are created equal, and the Declaration of Independence is referred to, to sustain that position. However unpopular, or however displeasing it may be to the mass of my fellow-citizens, I am constrained to dissent from any such position or dogma. It is not true in fact; it is not true in law; it is not true physically, mentally, or morally that all men are created equal. . . . I hold it to be a self-evident lie. . . . Tell me, sir, that the slave in the South . . . with but little over one half the volume of brain that attaches to the northern European race, is his equal, and you tell me what is physically a falsehood.

Having brought cranial measurement into the debate, Pettit also elaborated Douglas's argument that "the climate, the latitude, the soil, the heat, and cold—shall determine the line of demarkation where slavery may or may not go." Finally, Pettit quoted the sort of statistics that Nott had used to create a false impression about the decline of black population in the northern states and its increase in southern states: "Thus speak the statistics . . . so far as philanthropy, kindness, and humanity to the black himself is concerned, he would be better off in slavery than out of it."[12]

The following day Charles Sumner of Massachusetts responded forcefully that no one had the right to hold "in bondage their fellow-men, only 'guilty of a skin not colored like their own.'" When Pettit came under further attacks, he countered, "It is utterly false that men are, either mentally, morally, physically, or politically, created equal, whatever ought to have been their condition. But blame the Almighty, not me."[13]

Reading these congressional debates, Lincoln must have noted that while Douglas avoided discussions of race and concentrated on political principles, other politicians referred to the question of racial equality. When the opportunity arose, Lincoln would bring that issue to the fore.

Among Lincoln's writings from this period are important undated fragments probably intended to crystalllize thoughts before speeches or debates. The beginning of one fragment is lost but obviously asserted that slavery is wrong,

> made so plain by our good Father in Heaven, that all *feel* and *understand* it, even down to brutes and creeping insects. . . . So plain, that the most dumb and stupid slave that ever toiled for a master, does constantly *know* that he

is wronged. So plain that no one, high or low, ever does mistake it, except in a plainly *selfish* way; for although volume upon volume is written to prove slavery a very good thing, we never hear of the man who wishes to take the good of it, *by being a slave himself*. . . . *Most governments* have been based [on the idea that] . . . some men are too *ignorant*, and *vicious*, to share in government. Possibly so, said we; and, by your system, you would always keep them ignorant, and vicious. We proposed to give *all* a chance; and we expected the weak to grow stronger, the ignorant, wiser; and all better, and happier together [original emphasis].[14]

Lincoln referred not to separate creations of races but to God creating in all of humanity (and even in animals) an innate understanding that slavery is wrong. The issue of race was muted. The slave was not described as black; some slaves were "dumb and stupid" (meaning others were not); and that condition was not inherent since slaves might become "stronger" and "wiser"—exactly the possibility that *Types of Mankind* denied. Race provided no justification for slavery, and no one had ever chosen that "positive good" for himself.

Lincoln first spoke against the Kansas-Nebraska Act in August 1854 but the first speech for which we have a fairly complete summary took place in Bloomington, Illinois, on 26 September. Douglas had just returned to Illinois to try to heal the breach within his own party before Whigs could exploit it in the state elections. He encountered some angry audiences but was a masterful speaker, confident he could restore party unity. When Douglas was to speak in Bloomington, Lincoln asked to share the rostrum. Douglas understandably refused, but Lincoln simply announced that he would address the pressing issues later that evening.[15]

Like many of Lincoln's major speeches, this one contained ample evidence of research into the history of attempts to limit the expansion of slavery and the nature and intent of earlier compromises. Lincoln made only two rather subtle references to the racial issue: chiding Douglas (who was present) for calling "the new party *Black Republicans*" in order to "pander to prejudice," and mentioning "the famous Georgia Pen, in Washington, where negroes were bought and sold within sight of the National Capitol," which was "offensive" to "all good men, Southerners as well as Northerners."[16]

On 4 October, following a Douglas oration in Springfield, Lincoln delivered, according to William Lee Miller, "the first great speech of his life."[17] Comparing the repeal of the Missouri Compromise to tearing down a fence that had kept cattle and hogs out of a field, Lincoln asked if anyone could think slave owners would stay out any more than the animals would: "*Even the hogs would know better*—Much more *men*, who are a higher order of the animal world." That humorous remark was echoed more seriously later: "It is said that the slaveholder has the same right to take his negroes to Kansas that a freeman has to take his hogs or his horses. This would be true if negroes were property in the same sense that hogs and horses are. But is this the case? It is notoriously not so." Lincoln offered evidence that even "southern men do not treat their negroes as they do their horses." Four hundred thousand negroes in the United States were "free": "Can you find *two million dollars worth* of any other kind of property running about without an owner?" The masters who freed these negroes clearly believed they had "mind, feeling, souls, family affections, hopes, joys, sorrows—something that made them more than *hogs or horses.*" Lincoln pointed out that the overseas trade in slaves but not in any other commodity was "classed with piracy and murder" and that "the Southern people, the Slaveholders themselves, spurn the domestic slave dealer, refuse to associate with him, or let their families associate with his family."[18]

A few days later, Lincoln followed Douglas in giving a speech in Peoria, Illinois.[19] He improved several points made earlier at Springfield but also raised new points, partly in response to Douglas's efforts to depict Lincoln as an abolitionist wishing to free blacks in the south so they could flood into Illinois and demand absolute equality on all levels. Just as Lincoln's whole argument depended on "the ancient faith" in all men being created equal, Douglas's position depended on the belief in race superiority that allowed white men to enslave black men or to keep them out of their states. Laying out his views cautiously, Lincoln asked whether when slaves are freed, we should then

> make them politically and socially, our equals? My own feelings will not admit of this; and if mine would, we well know that those of the great mass of white people will not. Whether this feeling accords with justice and sound judgment, is not the sole question, if indeed, it is any part of it. A universal feeling, whether well or ill-founded, can not be safely disregarded. We cannot, then, make them equals.[20]

This passage is a favorite for those wishing to portray Lincoln as a straightforward nineteenth-century racist, though many scholars have emphasized how carefully Lincoln worded his statements, so that his listeners might hear rather more than he was saying.[21] First, equality is qualified as political or social, not biological or intellectual. Second, the issue is not whether slaves *are* "our equals" inherently, primordially or by divine will, but whether we can "*make*" them equals. Lincoln says his "*feelings* will not admit of this," not that his *reason* demands or forbids it. Indeed, he contrasts "feelings" on one side and "justice and sound judgment" on the other. And, having said his "feelings will not admit of this," he immediately allows the possibility: "if mine would." As a politician, he cannot *safely disregard* "a universal feeling," but he does not say that feeling is correct or that he agrees with it—rather, it might be "ill-founded."[22]

In another part of the speech, Lincoln dismissed as "a *palliation*—a *lullaby*" the notion that climate could prevent slavery from moving into Kansas, pointing out that five existing states as far north as Kansas already contained over eight hundred thousand slaves: "It is not climate, then, that will keep slavery out of these territories." Lincoln further developed his view that most people, even southerners, found it difficult to treat blacks as animals. He reworked a point about "hogs" and ended up discussing what Darwin would later call a "social instinct" but Lincoln called "human sympathies":

> [W]hile you thus require me to deny the humanity of the negro, I wish to ask whether you of the south yourselves, have ever been willing to do as much? . . . The great majority, south as well as north, have human sympathies, of which they can no more divest themselves than they can of their sensibility to physical pain. These sympathies in the bosoms of the southern people, manifest in many ways, their sense of the wrong of slavery, and their consciousness that, after all, there is humanity in the negro.

For evidence, Lincoln again noted that southerners and northerners together had legislated that participation in the Atlantic slave trade was a capital crime: "The practice was no more than bringing wild negroes from Africa. . . . But you never thought of hanging men for catching and selling wild horses, wild buffaloes or wild bears." Also, Lincoln pointed out that "something" caused even slave owners to ostracize domestic slave dealers and to free a surprising amount of slave "property." Asking "What is that SOMETHING?" Lincoln answered, "In all these cases it is your sense of justice, and human sympathy, continually telling you, that the poor negro has some natural right to himself—that those who deny it, and make mere merchandise of him, deserve kickings, contempt and death."[23]

Lincoln then tied this issue of negro humanity to what others considered the central issue—the extension of popular sovereignty:

> The doctrine of self government is right . . . but it has no just application, as here attempted. Or perhaps I should rather say that whether it has such just application depends upon whether a negro is *not* or *is* a man. If he is *not* a man, why in that case, he who *is* a man may, as a matter of self-government, do just as he pleases with him. But if the negro *is* a man, is it not to that extent, a total destruction of self-government, to say that he too shall not govern *himself*? When the white man governs himself that is self-government; but when he governs himself, and also governs *another* man, that is *more* than self-government—that is despotism. If the negro is a *man*, why then my ancient faith teaches me that "all men are created equal"; and that there can be no moral right in connection with one man's making a slave of another.[24]

Having returned to the Declaration of Independence, Lincoln pointed out, "When Pettit . . . called the Declaration of Independence 'a self-evident lie' he only did what consistency and candor require all other Nebraska men to do." Lincoln said Douglas had stated "that he always considered this government was made for the white people and not for the negroes. Why, in point of mere fact, I think so too." With the phrase "mere fact," Lincoln distanced himself from Douglas's actual pleasure in the fact. Lincoln argued that Douglas's "great mistake" is that he "has no very vivid impression that the negro is a human; and consequently has no idea that there can be any moral question in legislating about him." Lincoln then contrasted Douglas's lack of human sympathy with the "totally different view" taken by "the great mass of people": "They consider slavery a great moral wrong; and their feeling against it, is not evanescent, but eternal. It lies at the very foundation of their sense of justice . . . and, I think, no statesman can safely disregard it." From the brief reports of Lincoln's next major speech at Chicago on 27 October, it appears that Pettit's "self-evident lie" came in for another drubbing as much as Douglas.[25]

When the state elections took place, Douglas's Democrats lost their majority in the state legislature to the mixed multitude of the Whigs, Free-Soilers, Know-Nothings and Anti-Nebraska Democrats. Lincoln worked feverishly to get this body to fuse in order to elect him rather than a Douglas supporter to the U.S. Senate. However, in the end, Lincoln could only keep Douglas's candidate out by telling the large minority of legislators who supported him to shift their votes to an Anti-Nebraska Democrat, Lyman Trumbull. It was a bitter disappointment but also "a great consolation," said Lincoln about Douglas's forces, "to see them worse whipped than I am."[26] Lincoln knew Douglas's own senate seat would be in contention in 1858, and as the anti-Douglas forces in Illinois gradually merged into the new party developing among antislavery forces in other northern states, Lincoln, though holding no office, managed to make himself leader of this Republican Party in Illinois.

More than his personal defeat, other recent developments caused Lincoln to abandon his former belief that there would someday be a "peaceful extinction of slavery." Citing the Kentucky legislature's failure in 1849 to initiate a gradual emancipation, "together with a thousand other signs," including that the Declaration's concept of equality was now called "a self-evident lie," Lincoln wrote in a letter, "The Autocrat of all the Russias will resign his crown, and proclaim his subjects free republicans sooner than will our American masters voluntarily give up their slaves." A few days later, Lincoln replied to a letter from his old confidant Joshua Speed.[27] Lincoln first pointed out that their views were not as different as Speed had apparently suggested: "You know I dislike slavery; and you fully admit the abstract wrong of it. . . . I do oppose the extension of slavery, . . . [and] if for this you and I must differ, differ we must." Lincoln reminded Speed of a steamboat journey they made in 1841: "You may remember, as I well do, that . . . there were, on board, ten or a dozen slaves, shackled together with irons. That sight was a continual torment to me; and I see something like it every time I touch the Ohio, or any other slave-border."[28] Lincoln stressed the "abstract wrong" by emphasizing that he could not think of slaves as simply another form of property and closed with a seething statement (quoted earlier in a different context):

> Our progress in degeneracy appears to me to be pretty rapid. As a nation, we began by declaring that "*all men are created equal.*" We now practically read it "all men are created equal, *except negroes.*" When the Know-Nothings get control, it will read "all men are created equal, except negroes, *and foreigners, and catholics.*" When it comes to this I should prefer emigrating to some country where they make no pretence of loving liberty—to Russia, for instance, where despotism can be taken pure, and without the base alloy of hypocracy [*sic*].

Mentioned in both letters was Russia, the mascot for autocracy as America was for democracy. Both nations had antiquated systems of unfree labor that rivaled each other for odiousness, though Russia lacked the "justification" of enslaving a different race. Lincoln had formerly assumed that the southern states would eventually follow the example not of Russia but of the northern states, Britain, and numerous other countries. However, that assumption, based on continued agreement that slavery was an evil since blacks were men, was being eroded by polygenism.

Having previously read and loathed George Fitzhugh's *Sociology for the South*, Lincoln may not have been aware that an editorial appearing in the *Richmond Enquirer* on 15 December 1855 was written by Fitzhugh. Although he had not yet adopted the polygenism of Nott, Gliddon, and Agassiz, Fitzhugh now defended slavery by declaring it had nothing to do with race but, as a labor system, was simply "good" per se: "While it is far more obvious that negroes should be slaves than whites . . . principle of slavery is itself right and does not depend on difference of complexion."

Lincoln decided this "rather rank doctrine," as he called it, might be turned to good use. He and Herndon hatched a plan to arrange for part of the editorial to be republished in a local newspaper that supposedly supported the Know-Nothing Party but was actually funded by Democrats hoping to split the anti-Democrat vote. The plan worked: the editorial was republished, the newspaper was "almost ruined," and Lincoln "joined in the popular denunciation, expressing great astonishment that such a sentiment could find lodgment in any paper in Illinois."[29] In at least two other speeches delivered in 1856, Lincoln referred to the new doctrine in the Richmond *Enquirer*, and some of Lincoln's undated notes for a speech show he planned to read out and ridicule a newspaper clipping (perhaps the same one) from the Richmond *Enquirer* and two more from the New York *Day-Book*—Van Evrie's racist newspaper.[30]

In May 1856, Lincoln gave what is known as the "Lost Speech," a supposedly impromptu but actually well-planned address delivered so stirringly that the journalists present all stopped taking notes as the emotion and cheering distracted them. A brief newspaper summary and a version made forty years later by one witness who said he had taken notes are the only records. Lincoln, though asked, never produced a written version for campaign purposes: he may have been quietly pleased that some of his more extreme remarks thus remained off the record. Yet, he had no way of knowing that no reporter would take down his words, which, in any case, were well received by an intelligent audience, and he made similar remarks in subsequent speeches.

The single newspaper summary suggested that Lincoln declared, "The sentiment in favor of white slavery now prevailed in all the slave state papers, except those of Kentucky, Tennessee and Missouri and Maryland."[31] The line nearest to this in the reconstructed version is: "And if the safeguards to liberty are broken down, as is now attempted, when they have made things of all the free negroes, how long, think you, before they will begin to make things of poor white men?"[32]

If Lincoln was wrong to suggest that it was widely held in the south or by men like Stephen A. Douglas that slavery could be extended to white people, he nevertheless made the point that the slavocracy was morally bankrupt, that the Declaration's "all men" was ironically being taken literally, and that the only racial distinction that applied was skin color. In a similar vein, in the same (reconstructed) speech Lincoln supposedly said, "The whole country will turn out to help hang the [horse]thief; but if a man but a shade or two darker than I am is himself stolen, the same crowd will hang one who aids in restoring him to liberty. Such are the inconsistencies of slavery, where a horse is more sacred than a man."[33]

This issue of color was raised in another undated fragment of Lincoln's writing:

> You say A. is white, and B. is black . . . the lighter, having the right to enslave the darker? . . . By this rule, you are to be slave to the first man you meet, with a fairer skin than your own. . . . You mean the whites are *intellectually* the superiors of the blacks, and, therefore have the right to enslave them? Take care again. By this rule, you are to be slave to the first man you meet, with an intellect superior to your own.[34]

William Lee Miller has suggested Lincoln may have been influenced by a similar argument in Francis Wayland's *Elements of Moral Science*, but Wayland did not mention "color," and Lincoln might as easily have been thinking of an 1849 letter written by Henry Clay, who also ridiculed the "principle of subjugation, founded upon intellectual superiority."[35] Lincoln later quoted this letter in a speech in 1858, while campaigning not merely to promote the Republican Party but to take over personally Douglas's seat in the U.S. Senate.[36]

Campaigning, 1856–58

In late summer of 1856, as Lincoln made speeches throughout Illinois supporting the new Republican Party, a zoologist at Yale University received a letter
from an English colleague. "We are all here now much interested in American
politics—You will think us very impertinent, when I say how fervently we wish
you in the North to be free." James Dwight Dana, an expert on crustaceans who
had assisted Darwin's studies, probably deciphered Darwin's allusion to a catchy
campaign slogan of John C. Frémont, the antislavery Republican candidate in the
1856 presidential election: "Free Soil, Free Labor, Free Speech, Free Men, and Frémont." But when a slice of the northern vote went to the anti-immigrant Know-
Nothing Party, the Democrats managed to elect James Buchanan, who would
make no move against slavery. Thus, the north failed to elect a candidate "for
freedom," no doubt upsetting Darwin and Dana and quite infuriating Lincoln.[1]

Everything else in the letter was science, including Darwin's reference to
Louis Agassiz's unwillingness to learn from his errors: he "seems to me to retreat a step & take up a new position with a front so bold as to be admirable in a
soldier." Darwin cautiously mentioned that he was "becoming, indeed I should
say have become, sceptical on the permanent immutability of species: I groan
when I make such a confession, for I shall have little sympathy from those, whose
sympathy I alone value." The latter group apparently did not include Agassiz,
who, "if he ever honours me by reading my work, will throw a boulder at me."
Darwin let Dana know that his sympathy was valued and that he was in good
company: "It may sound presumptuous, but I think I have to a certain extent
staggered even Lyell."[2]

For several months, Charles Lyell had been urging Darwin to publish his
theory, and as early as 1854, Lyell told a colleague about something "which will
figure in C. Darwin's book on species."[3] But while Darwin was distracted by his
experiments with seed dispersal and then pigeon breeding, Lyell grew impatient,
having just read an article by Alfred Russel Wallace that seemed to have ideas

similar to those about which Darwin was so coy.[4] Lyell himself began a new journal—on species, starting with notes about Wallace's article.[5]

Wallace's careful efforts to avoid offending religious sensibilities caused Darwin to fail to see the real significance in Wallace's early article, annotating it with comments such as "It seems all creation to him . . . put generation for creation & I quite agree." Lyell visited Darwin, saw the experiments, chatted about transmutation, probably discussed Wallace's article, and pressed Darwin to "publish some small fragment of your data, *pigeons* if you please & so out with the theory & let it take date—& be cited—& understood." Perhaps as encouragement, Lyell added, "The multiple creation of Agassiz will one day rank with spontaneous generation." Lyell had also heard that Darwin met with Joseph Dalton Hooker, Thomas Huxley, and Thomas Wollaston and "made light of all species & grew more & more unorthodox."[6] Darwin was intensifying his effort to build a consensus for transmutation, discovering how much interested colleagues would and would not accept. Lincoln was not the only one forging an alliance.

Darwin now began to write in earnest, and by July 1856 he had opted for a "big book . . . as complete as my present materials allow."[7] The first two chapters on variation under domestication were completed by autumn, but questions kept popping up, so Darwin continued consulting experts far and wide. He confessed to Hooker that each struggle to explain some odd distribution of plant species "drives me to despair . . . & not being able to do so gives in my eyes the multiple creationists an awful triumph." If a single case of multiple creation "could be proved, I should be smashed."[8] When one fellow naturalist, S. P. Woodward, who had provided useful information to Darwin for months, praised Agassiz for protecting "our ancestors" by doing "battle with the transmutationists," the correspondence ended after Darwin mentioned in his reply, "I do not see that I shall have to beg any further favours."[9] Likewise, some queries about fish that might have gone to Agassiz went instead to Dana, who (like zoologist John Gould before him) sometimes reported the replies he received after forwarding the questions to Agassiz.[10]

Meanwhile, Darwin let Dana know that he was "getting M.S. ready for press" but doubted he would publish "for a couple of years." As his "big book" grew bigger, Darwin constantly sought information from Asa Gray, who was forced by Darwin's questions to rethink his own ideas. Together, they developed a statistical approach to plant distribution, and in September 1857, Darwin paid Gray the compliment of sending him a four-page enclosure laying out his basic theory. "I think it can be shown," Darwin explained in the accompanying letter, "that there is such an unerring power at work, or *Natural Selection* (the title of my Book), which selects exclusively for the good of each organic being."[11]

Saying that anything selects "for the good" had religious implications, yet Darwin tried awkwardly to depersonify natural selection. Contrasting it with multiple creations, Darwin wrote, "What a jump it is from a well marked variety, produced by natural cause, to a species produced by the separate act of the Hand of God." Still, Darwin broke off the thought: "But I am running on foolishly." The two friends might disagree on whether the "unerring power at work" was caused by "the Hand of God," but both rejected Agassiz's multiple creations.[12] Their alliance was sealed with humor at Agassiz's expense, for a quotation from Agassiz (picked up from Lyell) became a joking catch-phrase between Darwin and Gray: "Nature never lies!"[13] With Huxley, Darwin was more frank: "I have always suspected Agassiz of superficiality & wretched reasoning powers; but I think such men do immense good in their way. See how he stirred up all Europe about Glaciers."[14]

Neither Darwin nor any of his correspondents immediately mentioned that in 1857, Agassiz contributed to another Nott and Gliddon publication even less scientific than *The Types* and entitled *Indigenous Races of the Earth*. In a three-page letter included in the preface, Agassiz concentrated on making two points about one species—man. First, citing recent work by Richard Owen identifying three distinct species of monkeys, Agassiz argued that if such similar anthropoids were nevertheless different species, the same was true of the different races of men. Agassiz then strayed even further beyond his expertise by arguing that those who suggested that mankind's common origin was demonstrated by the philological evidence of a common ancient language were simply wrong.[15] Gray sent Darwin an amusing account of how Agassiz ("foolish man") asserted that languages do not "derive from other languages any more than species derive from other species" and then failed to get the joke when Gray agreed that the statement was "perfectly logical."[16]

In 1858, Darwin wrote to Agassiz for the first time in eight years and for the same reason as last: to thank him for a presentation copy, in this case, of the first parts of his *Contributions to the Natural History of the United States of America*. The volumes were impressively lavish, as was Darwin's praise for Agassiz's generosity (though not for any of his particular findings): "I thank you most truly for this magnificent present; & feel much flattered & gratified by this mark of your esteem. I have eagerly turned over the pages & plainly see that there will be much of the highest interest to me." Part 1, entitled *Essay on Classification*, bore directly on the main issue underlying Darwin's own half-finished book, which would never accept that classifications had to be "grounded firmly on the concept of the immutability of species" and were merely "translations, in human language, of the thoughts of the Creator."[17]

Darwin asked Huxley's opinion of "Agassiz's *Contributions*—not that I have yet begun to read it," but within a few weeks, he did read it and eventually annotated it and wrote an abstract. Darwin told Gray, "I am disappointed: I cannot realise his rules on the value of the higher groups, & all his prophetic &c &c types." Nearly a year later, agreeing with Huxley's view, Darwin wrote that the *Essay on Classification* "is all utterly impracticable rubbish, about his grades

&c &c. But, alas, when you read, what I have written on this subject, you will be just as savage with me."[18]

By that time, Darwin was no longer working on the massive *Natural Selection*, which probably would have taken him at least until 1861 to finish. Suddenly, Darwin felt the need to produce an "abstract" of that larger, unfinished work, to go into print as *Origin of Species*.

It is a familiar if complex story how the arrival at Down House in June 1858 of another essay by Wallace, sent to Darwin with a request that he perhaps show it to Lyell, caused Darwin to abandon his plan for a multivolume work and instead publish a single volume—which would be the only work Darwin ever produced without full source references (750 having already accumulated in *Natural Selection*, now set aside). The story has four key points. First, Darwin now saw what he had missed in Wallace's earlier article: that Wallace had somehow reached the same conclusions about transmutation that he had. Second, Darwin faced an ethical dilemma not only about losing priority to Wallace but also about having their theory born prematurely, without the substantiation Darwin was halfway to producing. Third, Darwin had to deal with this dilemma just as severe illness was raging through his own household, and an infant son was dying. Finally, the entire episode demonstrated the strong personal and professional support that Darwin had won from Lyell and Hooker, who came magnificently to his rescue, while the final result did justice to Wallace, who also became a stalwart ally.

Wallace's essay, along with extracts from Darwin's "sketch" and a copy of the enclosure sent to Gray in 1857, was read before the Linnaean Society meeting on 1 July and published in the society's journal, establishing Darwin's priority and the fact that his theory had remained consistent. The reaction of the Linnaean Society members was relatively subdued because the men doing the reading, Lyell and Hooker, had the highest reputations yet could hardly be questioned on work that was not their own. Of the actual authors, one was still in the Malay Archipelago and the other was that day attending his infant son's funeral. Darwin tried for a while to proceed with *Natural Selection* but soon decided to postpone that work and get something into print that was more coherent than the pieces now published. By October, Darwin was certain the "abstract" of *Natural Selection* would have to be "a small volume . . . published separately."[19]

The announcement at the Linnaean Society had more impact in America, galvanizing Gray to launch a frontal assault on Agassiz, with whom Gray was losing patience. He complained to Hooker about the damage Agassiz caused "by associating himself with Gliddon and Nott, and by his views on human species . . . always writing and talking ad populum—fond of addressing himself to an incompetent tribunal."[20] Now that Darwin's (and Wallace's) theory was in the public domain, Gray felt he could employ Darwin's ideas without robbing him of any future credit. According to his biographer, "Gray's whole spirit quickened at the thought of bringing Agassiz to bay with Darwin's tools."[21]

In December 1858, Gray presented to a meeting of the Cambridge Scientific Club an informal outline of his new view about the distribution of plants in eastern North America and eastern Asia. Only two men in the room fully understood that Gray was undermining everything Agassiz had recently published, yet Gray reported that Agassiz "took it very well indeed." Agassiz was preoccupied by dealings with wealthy philanthropists, legislators, lawyers, bankers, and architects as he labored to realize his cherished dream, a Museum of Comparative Zoology, which probably seemed more important than quibbling about plant statistics.[22]

Before the next confrontation, Gray asked a colleague to come up from New York so he could watch Gray "knock out the underpinning of Agassiz's theories about species and [turn] . . . some of Agassiz's own guns against him." Gray's presentation depicted Agassiz's basic view as offering "no *scientific* explanation of the present distribution of species over the globe" and merely "affirming, that as things now are, so they were at the beginning." He then described "the idea of the descent of all similar or conspecific individuals from a common stock." Agassiz defended his own theories as being "founded on observation of the animal kingdom": multiple creations better explained the distribution of flora than extensive migrations or climatic changes. "What rubbish Agassiz talks," Darwin told Hooker after reading of these proceedings.[23]

While Gray promoted Darwin's views in America even before they were known to be Darwin's and American scientists began to take sides, Darwin was still writing the abstract he hoped would prove convincing. "Last chapter, but one," he told Wallace in January 1859, "hard enough with my poor health," which was about to force him to take a few days' hydrotherapeutic rest at Moor Park, where he spent his fiftieth birthday. Had it not been for the sudden appearance of Wallace's essay, Darwin acknowledged, "I almost think that Lyell would have proved right & I should never have completed my larger work." He added sincerely, "I owe indirectly much to you."[24] Lincoln could have written the same line to the man who had recently brought him nationwide fame, temporarily at least, in what are now the most famous debates in American history.

After failing to win a U.S. Senate seat in 1855, Lincoln campaigned for Frémont in the 1856 presidential race, only to see him lose. As dramatic developments—bloodshed in Kansas, the Supreme Court's intervention, and Douglas's break with President Buchanan—provided Democrats and Republicans with ammunition, Lincoln and Douglas essentially continued the debate begun in 1854, though it grew more heated when the confrontation became head-to-head in 1858.

Democratic newspapers in Illinois never ceased to connect Lincoln with radical abolitionists, declaring that Lincoln's "niggerism has as dark a hue as that of Garrison or Fred Douglass"; that a Lincoln speech was "prosy and dull in the extreme—all about 'freedom,' 'liberty' and 'niggers'"; and that Lincoln was "the depot master of the underground railroad."[25] Nevertheless, Lincoln's stature within the Republican Party steadily increased while Douglas's position within the Democratic Party grew awkward. The rivals' speeches, and later their formal debates, dealt with wide-ranging issues (as well as mutual misrepresentations), yet the actual discussion of race, while never overtly scientific, was at the heart of the matter.

Douglas's position was both helped and hurt by the Supreme Court's *Dred Scott* decision in March 1857. Most of the Court's members were southerners, who now chose to address issues relating to slavery, apparently hoping to settle some of them peacefully—in contrast to the growing violence in Kansas and even on the floor of Congress. The decision seemed to support Douglas by overturning the Missouri Compromise's prohibition of slavery north of the 36° 30′ line as unconstitutional. This was only the second time in its history that the federal Supreme Court had overturned a federal law—which Douglas's Kansas-Nebraska Act had effectively nullified already by allowing popular sovereignty to determine whether slavery could be prohibited or not. While Douglas took comfort from the *Dred Scott* decision, Lincoln and others argued that the court's decision could be interpreted as *undermining* popular sovereignty: if *Congress* could not constitutionally prevent a citizen from taking his property (slaves) into a federal territory, how could a mere *territorial* government do so?

Chief Justice Roger B. Taney, writing the majority opinion, went beyond the call of duty—and, indeed, beyond the rational judicial arguments for which he was normally acclaimed—in order to express a view on negro racial inferiority. Taney argued that Dred Scott could not bring a suit because, despite being born in the United States, he was not a citizen: not because of his slave status (the issue of the suit) but because he was a descendant of Africans who "were not intended to be included, under the word 'citizens' in the Constitution . . . on the contrary, they were at that time considered as a subordinate and inferior class of beings who had been subjugated by the dominant race, and, whether emancipated or not, . . . had no rights or privileges but such as those who held the power and the Government might choose to grant them." Taney specified that if the phrase "all men are created equal" had been intended to "embrace" negroes, then the signers of the Declaration of Independence would have been "utterly and flagrantly inconsistent with the principles they asserted" and "would have deserved and received universal rebuke and reprobation."[26]

Forty years earlier as a young lawyer, Taney had defended a Baltimore minister accused of stirring up insurrection among slaves and had argued that his client's only sin was to quote the Declaration of Independence and insist "on the principles contained in that venerated instrument [by which] every friend of humanity will seek to lighten the galling chain of slavery."[27] Taney's change of heart was possibly a severe reaction against the threat of abolitionism, but his language in the *Dred Scott* decision also echoed the polygenist view of the "primordial" nature of Africans: "The unhappy black race were separated from the white by indelible marks, and laws long before established, and were never thought of or spoken of except as property."[28]

Douglas, in a speech in Springfield, Illinois, in June 1857, endorsed Taney's view, adding that the signers of the Declaration were only asserting that a "British subject, born on American soil was equal to a British subject born in England.... They did not mean the negroes and Indians—they did not say we white men and negroes were born equal." He also agreed that negroes belonged to an inferior race incapable of self-government but went much further by adding supposedly historical and scientific assertions about "the sad and melancholy results of the mixture of the races" in Spanish and French colonies. Although no term as esoteric as specific infertility passed Douglas's lips, he echoed the polygenist view that a "great natural law . . . declares that amalgamation between superior and inferior races brings their posterity down to the lower level of the inferior, but never elevates them to the high level of the superior race. . . . Amalgamation is degradation, demoralization, disease and death."[29]

Two weeks later, Lincoln, now the leading spokesman for Illinois Republicans, used the same location to reply to Douglas. He paraphrased Taney's assertion that "the public estimate of the black man is more favorable *now* than it was in the days of the Revolution," countering that "as a whole, in this country, the change between then and now is decidedly the other way; and their ultimate destiny has never appeared so hopeless as in the last three or four years." Citing new limitations on emancipation and prohibitions against the free black person, Lincoln declared, "All the powers of earth seem rapidly combining against him. Mammon is after him; ambition follows, and philosophy follows, and the Theology of the day is fast joining the cry." As "philosophy" was then the usual term for "science," Lincoln was referring to the rise of polygenism.[30]

Regarding Douglas's assertion that amalgamation caused dire physical and moral degradation, Lincoln conceded only that there was a "natural disgust in the minds of nearly all white people, to the idea of an indiscriminate amalgamation of the white and black races." Lincoln did not say he shared this disgust but charged Douglas with wishing "to appropriate the benefit of this disgust to himself." Lincoln then mocked Douglas's argument that Republicans insisted "that the Declaration of Independence includes ALL men, black as well as white . . . only because they want to vote, and eat, and sleep, and marry with negroes!" He called it a "counterfeit logic which concludes that, because I do not want a black woman for a *slave* I must necessarily want her for a *wife*. I need not have her for either, I can just leave her alone." Lincoln added an important distinction he would repeat many times: "In some respects she certainly is not my equal; but in her natural right to eat the bread she earns with her own hands without asking leave of any one else, she is my equal, and the equal of all others." Lincoln argued that the Declaration's signers "intended to include *all* men, but they did not intend to declare all men equal *in all respects,* [such as] color, size, intellect, moral developments, or social capacity." Lincoln mocked Douglas's view, "The English, Irish and Scotch, along with white Americans, were included to be sure, but the French, Germans and other white people of the world are all gone to pot along with the Judge's inferior races."[31]

Using statistics from the 1850 census, Lincoln ridiculed Douglas's horror "at the thought of the mixing [of] blood by the white and black races." Of 405,751 mulattoes in the United States, "very few" were "the offspring of whites and *free* blacks."[32] While some mulattoes were born in or had fled to the north, the 348,874 mulattoes in the slave states were "all of home production." Lincoln's statistics appealed to reason rather than prejudice and suggested the mulatto population was growing despite Douglas's polygenist image of languishing hybrids. Lincoln did not use Douglas's pejorative term "mongrel," and while an abolitionist might have charged that mulattoes were frequently the result of rape, Lincoln mocked the slave owners' tendency to euphemism by saying mulattoes resulted from "home production." The statistics did not absolutely prove that treating blacks more like equals reduced "amalgamation," but the overall effect was a novel argument for treating blacks as fellow humans: "These statistics show that slavery is the greatest source of amalgamation; and next to it, not the elevation, but the degeneration of the free blacks. Yet Judge Douglas dreads the slightest restraints on the spread of slavery, and the slightest human recognition of the negro, as tending horribly to amalgamation."[33]

Douglas continually urged Democrats to endorse his and Taney's racist position. One Illinois county duly denounced any effort to place "negroes on an equality with white men," rejecting the "claim that the declaration of Independence asserts that white men and negroes were created equal by the Almighty," while a friendly newspaper reported Douglas saying that "Black Republicans . . . will allow the blacks to push us from our sidewalk and elbow us out of car seats *and stink us out of our places of worship.*" Lincoln recorded both incidents for possible later use as some Republicans began to argue that Douglas was not so bad after all, since he had broken with President Buchanan over Kansas.[34] To keep the anti-Douglas forces unified, Lincoln emphasized that Douglas remained content to see slavery spread.

With his famous "House Divided" speech, Lincoln accepted the Republican nomination to challenge Douglas for his senate seat. Boldly laying out the most pressing issues around which to rally the party, Lincoln stressed that Douglas gave no sign of disapproving of slavery itself. However, Lincoln did not raise any purely racial issues and offered none of the usual arguments for the view that "all men are created equal" or against the propaganda about amalgamation. It was Douglas who resurrected these matters when replying to Lincoln's "House Divided" speech in Chicago on 9 July 1858.[35]

Ignoring Lincoln's political and constitutional arguments against the *Dred Scott* decision, Douglas declared that Lincoln "thinks it wrong because it deprives the negro of the privileges, immunities and rights of citizenship, which pertain, according to that decision, only to the white man. I am free to say to you that in my opinion this government of ours is founded on the white basis. It was made by the white man, for the benefit of the white man, to be administered by white men, in such manner as they should determine." While allowing that the "inferior" races "should be permitted to enjoy . . . all the rights, privileges and immunities which he is capable of exercising consistent with the safety of society," Douglas repeated that amalgamation only resulted in "degeneration, demoralization, and degradation below the capacity for self-government."[36]

The following evening Lincoln again made light of Douglas's fear of amalgamation. "The Judge regales us with the terrible enormities that take place by the mixture of races; that the inferior race bears the superior down," said Lincoln, before turning to Douglas. "Why, Judge, if we do not let them get together in the Territories they won't mix there." Near the end of his speech, Lincoln pressed his case with a reference—almost unique for Lincoln—to Jesus: "The Savior, I suppose, did not expect that any human creature could be perfect as the Father in Heaven; but He said, 'As your Father in Heaven is perfect, be ye also perfect.' He set that up as a standard, and he who did most towards reaching that standard, attained the highest degree of moral perfection. So I say in relation to the principle that all men are created equal, let it be as nearly reached as we can."[37]

In another undated fragment written around this time, Lincoln was contemptuous of religious figures, such as the Reverend Frederick A. Ross, author of *Slavery Ordained of God* (1857), who claim to find a clear answer in the Bible to a question such as "'Is it the Will of God that Sambo shall remain a slave, or be set free?' The Almighty gives no audible answer to the question, and his revelation—the Bible—gives none—or, at most, none but such as admits of a squabble, as to its meaning. No one thinks of asking Sambo's opinion on it. So, at last, it comes to this, that *Dr. Ross* is to decide the question."[38]

Lincoln had also suggested in his Chicago speech that the debate over race missed the real point. "Let us discard all this quibbling about this man and the other man—this race and that race and the other race being inferior, and therefore they must be placed in an inferior position . . . [and] once more stand up declaring that all men are created equal." But a week later in Springfield, Douglas plunged further, "I am not only opposed to negro equality, but I am opposed to Indian equality. I am opposed to putting the coolies, now importing into this country, on an equality with us, or putting the Chinese or any inferior race on an equality with us." He also caricatured Lincoln's scriptural argument, saying Lincoln thinks "that the Almighty made the negro equal to the white man" and "that the negro is his brother." Douglas denied "that the negro is any kin of mine at all. And here is the difference between us."[39]

On the same day, Lincoln replied that his views "may be misrepresented, but cannot be misunderstood. . . . [Blacks] are not our equal in color; but . . . they are equal in their right to 'life, liberty and the pursuit of happiness.'" He again appealed to religious sentiment: "In pointing out that more has been given you, you can not be justified in taking away the little which has been given him. All I ask for the negro is that if you do not like him, let him alone. If God gave him but little, that little let him enjoy." Again, by saying "you" and "if" Lincoln avoided endorsing opinions he might not share while specifying no actual inferiority.[40]

Later, in Lewistown, Illinois, Lincoln again connected religion with the sign-ers' description of the Creator's action: "Yes, gentlemen, to *all* His creatures, to the whole great family of man. In their enlightened belief, nothing stamped with the Divine image and likeness was sent into the world to be trodden on, and degraded, and imbruted by its fellows. They grasped not only the whole race of man then living, but they reached forward and seized upon the farthest posterity." Lincoln's "imbruted" expresses the same idea found in notes (probably written to prepare for the formal debates with Douglas that began on 21 August) accusing Douglas of "moulding public sentiment to a perfect accordance with his own [views] . . . that negroes are not men."[41]

As the first formal debate got under way in the town of Ottawa, Illinois, Douglas pulled out all the stops, linking Lincoln's name (as he had done before) to that of the well-known African American abolitionist Frederick Douglass, referring always to the "Black Republican" or "Abolition" Party, and working on his audience's prejudice by asking, "Do you desire to turn this beautiful State into a free negro colony, ('no, no,') in order that when Missouri abolishes slavery she can send one hundred thousand emancipated slaves into Illinois, to become citizens and voters, on an equality with yourselves? ('Never')." Douglas also com-bined religion with a natural-law argument—the first time he employed this so fully—that might have come straight from Nott, Gliddon, Fitzhugh, or Van Evrie: if "the Almighty ever intended the negro to be the equal of the white man, . . . he has been a long time demonstrating the fact. For thousands of years the negro has been a race upon the earth, and during all that time, in all latitudes and climates, wherever he has wandered or been taken, he has been inferior to the race which he has there met."[42]

Lincoln replied carefully, clarifying his position by quoting at length (as he did repeatedly over the next few weeks) from his own Peoria speech of 1854. He, too, stressed "nature" but in the form of "natural rights":

> I have no purpose to introduce political and social equality between the white and the black races. There is a physical difference between the two, which in my judgment will probably forever forbid their living together upon the footing of perfect equality, and inasmuch as it becomes a necessity that there must be a difference, I, as well as Judge Douglas, am in favor of the race to which I belong, having the superior position. I have never said anything to the contrary, but I hold that notwithstanding all this, there is no reason in the world why the

negro is not entitled to all the natural rights enumerated in the Declaration of Independence, the right to life, liberty and the pursuit of happiness.

Although acknowledging that there was "a physical difference" between the races that "will probably" prevent "perfect equality" on a practical basis and make inequality a social "necessity," Lincoln neither praised nor condemned that situation. So that his prejudiced audience need not view him as a hopeless idealist, he said he was "in favor" of having his race hold "the superior position." This might upset radical abolitionists, but Lincoln measured what his audience could accept and what he himself could live with. Crucially, he again made that statement conditional ("inasmuch as it becomes a necessity").[43]

In the second debate, in Freeport, Illinois, Douglas went further by associating Lincoln with Douglass through a dubious story of having recently seen in Freeport "a carriage, and a magnificent one it was, drive up and take a position on the outside of the crowd; a beautiful young lady was sitting on the box-seat, whilst Fred Douglass and her mother reclined inside, and the owner of the carriage acted as driver. I saw this in your own town." According to one account, someone in the crowd shouted, "What of it?" Douglas was pleased to expand:

If you, Black Republicans, think that the negro ought to be on a social equality with your wives and daughters, and ride in a carriage with your wife, whilst you drive the team, you have perfect right to do so. I am told that one of Fred Douglass's kinsmen, another rich black negro, is now traveling in this part of the State making speeches for his friend Lincoln as the champion of black men.

Again someone shouted, "What have you to say against it?" Douglas replied, "All I have to say . . . is, that those of you who believe that the negro is your equal and ought to be on an equality with you socially, politically, and legally, have a right to entertain those opinions, and of course will vote for Mr. Lincoln." Lincoln ignored all this, perhaps to concentrate on more substantial issues or because he saw the crowd was already with him.[44]

Between the second and third debates, Lincoln made several other speeches and dealt with the race issue by simply quoting from his Peoria speech of 1854. At Carlinville, Illinois, however, he introduced some lateral thinking: that to deny blacks "natural rights" in America was somehow wrong since "no sane man will attempt to deny that the African upon his own soil has all the natural rights that [the Declaration] vouchsafes to all mankind." At Edwardsville, Illinois, Lincoln again referred to the Democrats' effort at "dehumanizing the negro."[45]

In the third debate in Jonesboro, Illinois, both men repeated their stock arguments, but Douglas's list of "inferior races" now included "the Fejee, the Malay, or any other inferior and degraded race," again suggesting familiarity with polygenist literature. Since Douglas continued to raise the amalgamation issue, Lincoln again resorted to ridicule in the fourth debate in Charleston, Illinois. After repeating the point that the white man holds "the superior position" (but not saying "is su-perior"), Lincoln jested, "I am now in my fiftieth year, and I certainly never have had a black woman for either a slave or a wife. So it seems to me quite possible for us to get along without making either slaves or wives of negroes." He added that he had never seen "a man, woman or child who was in favor of producing a perfect equality, social and political, between negroes and white men" with one excep-tion "and that is the case of Judge Douglas's old friend Col. Richard M. Johnson. [Laughter.]" Johnson, who died in 1850, was a Kentuckian, former Democratic vice president, and bachelor known for having two daughters by a slave he treated as his wife. Having won that laughter, Lincoln turned his sights back to Douglas:

> I have never had the least apprehension that I or my friends would marry negroes if there was no law to keep them from it, but as Judge Douglas and his friends seem to be in great apprehension that they might, if there were no law to keep them from it, I give him the most solemn pledge that I will to the very last stand by the law of this State, which forbids the marrying of white people with negroes.

Lincoln added that since only the state legislature could change that law, "I pro-pose as the best means to prevent it that the Judge be kept at home and placed in the State Legislature to fight the measure." Douglas sought revenge by mentioning Douglass four times, describing him as "Lincoln's ally," no doubt because a few weeks earlier, "the negro" had made a widely reported speech ridiculing Douglas and praising Lincoln. Punning on the similarity of their surnames, Frederick Douglass had said, "Once I thought he was about to make the name respectable, but now I despair of him, and must do the best I can for it myself. I now leave him in the hands of Mr. Lincoln." This was the first time the abolitionist mentioned Lincoln, quoting approvingly from Lincoln's "House Divided" speech.[46]

In the fifth debate in Galesburg, Illinois, Douglas quoted Lincoln's earlier appeal to "discard all this quibbling" about race and then asserted, "This Chicago doctrine of Lincoln's—declaring that the negro and the white man are made equal by the Declaration of Independence and by Divine Providence—is a mon-strous heresy." Lincoln countered this vehemently (and somewhat incautiously) by arguing that Douglas was the "heretic":

> I believe the entire records of the world, from the date of the Declaration of Independence up to within three years ago, may be searched in vain for one single affirmation, from one single man, that the negro was not included in the Declaration of Independence. I think I may defy Judge Douglas to show that he ever said so, that Washington ever said so, that any President ever said so, that any member of Congress ever said so, or that any living man upon the whole earth ever said so, until the necessities of the present policy of the Democratic party, in regard to slavery, had to invent that affirmation.

Repeating that Douglas saw no distinction between the ownership of blacks and "of horses and every other sort of property," Lincoln pointed out that Jefferson once said regarding slavery that "he trembled for his country when he remembered that God was just," and he offered to pay Douglas "the highest premium in my power . . . if he will show that he, in all his life, ever uttered a sentiment at all akin to that of Jefferson."[47]

The sixth debate at Quincy, Illinois, raised nothing new about race, although Douglas quoted various statements by Lincoln on "negro equality" to depict them as contradictory—which was easily done, given Lincoln's tendency to word his statements so the audience could read into them more than he actually said. But when Douglas suggested Lincoln was afraid to declare in the more proslavery south of Illinois the same views that he professed in the more antislavery north, Lincoln pointed out that all his views and Douglas's were in print all over the state.[48]

In the last debate in Alton, Illinois, all the set pieces were brought out for their final performance, although Lincoln labored to explain away a problem that arose from his assertion at Galesburg that until three years ago, no one had ever said, "The negro was not included in the Declaration of Independence." A letter to a newspaper asserted that Henry Clay had done just that, so Lincoln now quoted extensively from Clay's speeches, splitting some hairs unconvincingly. Lincoln argued that, formerly, some politicians had said that the statement "all men are created equal" was simply untrue (for even among whites inequalities existed), but now some politicians—perhaps espousing polygenism—were declaring that the statement *was* true for all members of the white race but not for negroes because they were not fully men and therefore lacked the capacity for self-government. Lincoln thus got himself out of a hole by continuing to characterize Douglas's view as a recent break with "the old faith."[49]

Despite his tremendous fight over a period of four months, Lincoln learned a few weeks later that the state legislature was still controlled by the Democrats, enough of whom were sufficiently loyal to reelect Douglas to his Senate seat in January 1859. Lincoln was disappointed, yet in letters to friends, he took consolation in a battle well fought, and this is consistent with another fragment of writing that must date roughly to this period. He admitted that "the honors of official station" were appealing, "yet I have never failed—do not now fail—to remember that in the republican cause there is a higher aim than that of mere office." And he reminded himself that it took "a hundred years" for British reformers to end their slave trade while arguing against the "stealthy 'don't care' opponents; the 'dollar and cent opponents'; the 'inferior race opponents'; and the 'religion and good order opponents.'" And "school-boys know that Wilberforce and Granville Sharp helped that cause forward; but who can now name a single man who labored to retard it?"[50]

Although defeated in a second Senate race, Lincoln did not give up the struggle. He was soon back in the thick of the fight against the Democrats, the slavocracy, and Stephen A. Douglas, while the Republican Party sought a candidate who could beat Douglas in the presidential election of 1860. Lincoln undoubtedly wanted to be that candidate but knew the likelihood of his nomination was minute.

For a brief spell, Lincoln gave the appearance of simply returning to his family and law practice and to a new activity, lecturing. But his only lecture did not go down particularly well, possibly because his message about man's ability to control his own destiny was somewhat lost amid the jokes, the playfulness with the Bible masked as orthodoxy, and the indirect references to Douglas. Only one important line about race slipped in: Lincoln's mocking reference to "the invention of negroes, or, of the present mode of using them, in 1434." Negroes had existed before the fifteenth century and so had slavery, but it was not until then that slavery was somehow justified by race. And what Lincoln had been mulling over even before 1854 was a more recently invented notion about "the negro": that civilized nineteenth-century men should continue this barbaric fifteenth-century practice of slavery because some authorities had recently decided that negroes were not only different or alien but also incapable of looking after themselves since they had been created separately from white men and as an inferior lot. It was a notion that tried to make slavery seem "good," when Lincoln had always known—and suspected everybody else knew, deep down—that slavery was always evil.

Publications and Crocodiles, 1859–60

y the time he turned fifty in February 1859, Charles Darwin had been working on his abstract for seven months and thought it nearly finished. Yet
another eight months passed before Darwin signed off the corrected proofs.
Immediately, on 2 October, the exhausted Darwin escaped to another water-cure
establishment, this time in Yorkshire, to await the 22 November publication date
for *On the Origin of Species by Means of Natural Selection*.

Darwin had deliberately left man out of *The Origin* for reasons explained
over a decade later, in the introduction to *The Descent of Man*:

> During many years I collected notes on the origin or descent of man, without
> any intention of publishing on the subject, but rather with the determina-
> tion not to publish, as I thought that I should thus only add to the prejudices
> against my views. It seemed to me sufficient to indicate in the first edition
> of my "Origin of Species," that by this work "light would be thrown on the
> origin of man and his history," and this implies that man must be included
> with other organic beings in any general conclusion respecting his manner of
> appearance on this earth.[1]

Darwin's notebooks confirm how long and how intensely he had "collected notes"
on man, only to set them aside so that the data employed to demonstrate natural
selection would not include the shocking idea that man had not been directly
created in God's image. However, the subject of mankind's origins simply refused
to be postponed.

Charles Lyell had been keeping his own notebooks on species since 1855,
but in 1859, just after reading the proof sheets for *The Origin*, he began writing
Darwin long letters in which the topic of man kept recurring.[2] Lyell suggested it
was "impossible that intellectual powers of a species should be much improved
by the continued natural selection of the most intellectual individuals." Darwin
countered that intellectual powers could be as important for the welfare of an
individual as "corporeal structure," therefore "the most intellectual individuals of

a species" could be "continually selected." He added that the "effects of inherited mental exercise" might also assist certain individuals—an example of Lamarckian "acquired characteristics" that Darwin never completely abandoned. Although Darwin needed to ponder this further, for the moment he was content to allow that the different human races might vary not only in skin color and hair texture but also, theoretically, in intellect, whether resulting from long-standing or recently acquired inheritance. However acquired, a differential in intellect might help explain the devastation he witnessed when the *Beagle* carried him to Brazil, Australia, and South Africa, where whites were destroying nonwhite populations: "I look at this process as now going on with the races of man; the less intellectual races being exterminated. But there is not space to discuss this point." In another response to Lyell, Darwin wrote, "The Races of Man offer great difficulty. . . . I do not think the doctrine . . . of Agassiz that there are several species of man, helps *us* in the least," but he again broke off: "Much too long a subject for letter."[3]

A few days later, he sent a letter to Agassiz to accompany a gift copy of *The Origin*. Darwin's publisher was sending presentation copies to nearly a hundred of Darwin's friends and colleagues, and early in November, Darwin began posting separate notes to announce the gift and, in some cases, to cushion its landing. The note written to Agassiz on 11 November was more terse than most:

> I have ventured to send you, a copy of my Book (as yet only an abstract) on the origin of species. As the conclusions at which I have arrived on several points differ so widely from yours, I have thought (should you at any time read my volume) that you might think that I had sent it to you out of a spirit of defiance or bravado; but I assure you that I act under a wholly different frame of mind. I hope that you will at least give me credit, however erroneous you may think my conclusion, for having earnestly endeavoured to arrive at the truth.[4]

No reply is recorded, and some time passed before Darwin heard—indirectly—of Agassiz's reaction to the book itself, but in the meantime, and even before the book was on general sale, Darwin began to receive comments from others, including reviewers, who had received gift copies. The *Athenaeum*'s reviewer, jumping feet first into the issue Darwin had avoided, asked, "If a monkey has become a man, what may not man become?"[5] Darwin disliked "the manner in which [the reviewer] drags in immortality, & sets the Priests at me & leaves me to their mercies. . . . He would on no account burn me; but he will get the wood ready & tell the black beasts how to catch me."[6] Equally unpleasant was a letter from Darwin's old mess mate Admiral Robert FitzRoy: "*I*, at least, *cannot* find anything 'ennobling' in the thought of being a descendant of even the *most* ancient *Ape*."[7] Likewise Darwin received a scathing letter from his old Cambridge professor Adam Sedgwick, who impishly referred to himself as a "son of a monkey."[8]

Fortunately, there were many more encouraging letters of support and admiration, such as those sent by a London-based naturalist Darwin had long respected, William B. Carpenter.[9] Darwin was even more pleased when Carpenter published two highly favorable reviews.[10] Carpenter, who was strongly antislavery, did not hesitate to note *The Origin*'s implications for the study of man: "Orthodoxy (on this side of the Atlantic at least) is decidedly in favour of the abolition of the two-and-twenty species into which man has been divided by some zoologists."[11]

Darwin frequently commented to close associates about the number of scientists who seemed to be accepting that natural selection resolved many questions while raising many more. Clergyman, author, and amateur naturalist Charles Kingsley sent Darwin such words of praise that Darwin asked permission to quote them in the next edition. This was soon underway as Darwin's publisher wrote that the first edition of 1,250 copies had sold out on the first day, and he wished to print 3,000 more.[12] Darwin insisted on a few changes, including this on page 481: "A celebrated author and divine [Kingsley] has written to me that 'he has gradually learnt to see that it is just as noble a conception of the Deity to believe that He created a few original forms capable of self-development into other and needful forms, as to believe that He required a fresh act of creation to supply the voids caused by the action of His laws.'" Darwin also inserted three words in the final sentence of the book: "There is a grandeur in this view of life, with its several powers, having been originally breathed *by the Creator* into a few forms or into one." Likewise, Darwin added at the front of the book an epigraph by eighteenth-century divine Joseph Butler, author of *Analogy of Religion, Natural, and Revealed* (1736), a highly rational and influential effort to show that morality and religion are essential components of nature and common life: "The only distinct meaning of the word 'natural' is *stated*, *fixed*, or *settled*; since what is natural as much requires and presupposes an intelligent agent to render it so, *i.e.*, to effect it continually or at stated times, as what is supernatural or miraculous does to effect it for once." Darwin was signaling that natural selection could be considered a secondary cause, the primary still being God. Interestingly, a journalist friend of Lincoln's listed "Butler's Analogy of Religion" as the first of three "philosophical books" that he knew Lincoln particularly liked.[13] Arguably, Lincoln could accept more of Butler's views than Darwin could.

While Darwin was seeing the first two editions of *The Origin* through publication, Abraham Lincoln was engaged in his only venture into the world of book publishing—although nearly half of his book was essentially produced by Stephen A. Douglas, for it was a collection of their speeches and debates, mostly during the 1858 Senate campaign. If one subtracted Douglas's half as well as the parts where both speakers repeated or quoted the same arguments in subsequent debates, the core of Lincoln's argumentation would fill about a fifth of the volume's length. While Darwin was boiling his work down to an "abstract," Lincoln was compiling a work that was hugely repetitious: yet, that was part of the message.

He wanted a larger public to know that, despite Douglas's allegations, both men had been consistent in their views from start to finish. If Douglas, as seemed likely, was soon to run for the presidency, Lincoln wanted it known that Douglas had not modified his views simply because he had got himself in trouble with the Buchanan administration and with the more radical of southern leaders. Lincoln made clear that Douglas remained the only politician in America who had not declared that slavery was either a good or a bad thing.

Although Lincoln lost the Senate election, he had weakened Douglas's position generally and repulsed his worst attacks on the Republican Party. Lincoln decided also that other Republican leaders—William H. Seward, Salmon P. Chase, and Edward Bates, for example—were putting forward the party's message in ways that were not always the most helpful to the *national* party. It took Lincoln over a year to get his book before the public, during which time Lincoln increasingly received invitations to speak in other states on behalf of Republican candidates and principles. The purpose of the book evolved from helping the party generally to improving his own growing chances of becoming his party's nominee for the 1860 presidential election—an unlikely prospect when he started the work. Even during the debates, Lincoln had compiled a "scrapbook" of newspaper accounts and later filled gaps with further newspaper reports, "being desirous," he told a friend, "of preserving in some permanent form the late joint discussions." A month later, the issue was no longer merely preservation: "There is some probability that my Scrap-book will be reprinted."[14]

Lincoln managed successfully to avoid the appearance of self-promotion, to create a text that did not falsify his own or Douglas's original statements, and to prevent anyone, especially Douglas, gaining a veto over any aspect of the book. Modern analysis indicates that Lincoln did indeed make only "small verbal corrections"—as he described them when predictably accused of being unfair to Douglas.[15] Fortunately, a group of Ohio Republicans decided Lincoln had the potential to lead the party rather better than Chase, Ohio's ambitious governor, and rather publicly arranged for the debates to be printed in Cincinnati. However, Lincoln actively ensured that neither the Ohioans nor Douglas gained any editorial control over the project.[16]

Various delays meant that *The Political Debates between Hon. Abraham Lincoln and Hon. Stephen A. Douglas in the Celebrated Campaign of 1858 in Illinois* did not go on sale until May 1860, but the publishers later claimed thirty thousand were sold—which, at that point, was several times more than *On the Origin of Species*.[17] Sales were helped by the fact that Lincoln had by then become the Republican Party's candidate for the 1860 presidential election, expecting to challenge the Democratic Party's presumed nominee, Stephen A. Douglas.

The Ohioans who backed the publication had been impressed not only by the 1858 debates but also by speeches Lincoln gave in Ohio, Indiana, Iowa, Wisconsin, and

Kansas prior to local elections in the fall of 1859. The speeches mostly covered familiar ground, but Lincoln raised new points in response to a speech Douglas delivered in November 1858, shortly after the Illinois campaign. Trying to shore up support in the south, Douglas said in Memphis:

> If old Joshua R. Giddings [a noted abolitionist] should raise a colony in Ohio and settle down in Louisiana, he would be the strongest advocate of slavery in the whole South; he would find when he got there his opinion would be very much modified; he would find on those sugar plantations it was not a question between the white man and the negro, but between the negro and the crocodile. He would say that between the negro and the crocodile, he took the side of the negro. But, between the negro and the white man, he would go for the white man.[18]

Douglas's point, amid the jesting, was that environment determined interests that determined values, slavery being "natural" in the southern climate and (less explicitly) the negro being "natural" for slavery. More than nine months passed before Lincoln found the suitable occasion to respond, when Ohio Republicans invited him in September 1859 to visit in order to counter the effect of Douglas's campaigning in their state. By the time Lincoln arrived in Columbus, Douglas had already spoken there a week earlier, using the crocodile story again: "In Ohio it is a question only between the white man and the negro. [laughter.] But if you go further South you will find that it is a question between the negro and the crocodile. [Renewed laughter.]"[19]

In a long speech, Lincoln mentioned Douglas's crocodile story three times in order to caricature the amorality of Douglas's position.

> [T]here is no wrong in slavery, and whoever wants it has a right to have it, is a matter of dollars and cents, a sort of question as to how they shall deal with brutes, that between us and the negro here there is no sort of question, but that at the South the question is between the negro and the crocodile. That is all. It is a mere matter of policy; there is a perfect right according to interest to do just as you please.

Lincoln again charged Douglas with undermining traditional views.

> [T]here has been a *change* . . . and a very significant change it is, being no less than changing the negro, in your estimation, from the rank of a man to that of a brute. They are taking him down, and placing him, when spoken of, among reptiles and crocodiles, as Judge Douglas himself expresses it. . . . [He is] blowing out the moral lights around us; teaching that the negro is no longer a man but a brute; that the Declaration has nothing to do with him; that he ranks with the crocodile and the reptile. . . . [T]here is now going on among you a steady process of debauching public opinion on this subject.[20]

Lincoln repeated this attack the following day in Cincinnati, adding that Douglas "did not make that declaration accidentally at Memphis. He made it a great
many times in the canvass in Illinois last year, (though I don't know that it was
reported in any of his speeches there,) but he frequently made it. . . . It is, then,
a deliberate way of expressing himself upon that subject."[21] Lincoln's memory
may be better than our records, but there is no evidence—and it is unlikely—that
Douglas mentioned crocodiles during the Illinois campaigns. Lincoln also drew
some doubtful inferences: "that if you do not enslave the negro you are wronging
the white man in some way or other, and that whoever is opposed to the negro
being enslaved is in some way or other against the white man. Is not that a false-
hood?" Lincoln argued that there was no "necessary conflict between the white
man and the negro," that "there is room enough for us all to be free," and that
Douglas was actually making "a sort of proposition in proportion, which may
be stated thus: As the negro is to the white man, so is the crocodile as a beast or
reptile, so the white man may rightfully treat the negro as a beast or a reptile."
Lincoln apparently repeated this point in speeches in Indiana and Wisconsin,
adding: "These are Douglas' sentiments. The man who expresses such sentiments
as these can see no moral wrong in slavery."[22]

Building on the political momentum of his successful tour in Ohio and Indiana,
Lincoln was pleased to accept an invitation to speak in February 1860 at the Cooper Institute in New York City. In his address, Lincoln focused almost entirely on
the issue of federal power relating to the extension of slavery into federal territories. Backed up by solid research, Lincoln proved that the views of the founding
fathers differed from those of Senator Douglas and Chief Justice Roger B. Taney.
But underlying this issue, Lincoln said, was the fact that Republicans considered
slavery an evil while their opponents considered it a good. All else flowed from
this. Significantly, Lincoln did not explain *why* slavery was evil, apparently seeing
no need to tell this particular audience that blacks were human beings.[23] During a subsequent tour of New England, Lincoln returned to the usual themes.
Only newspaper summaries exist for most of these speeches, but when Lincoln
spoke in Hartford, he employed for the first and last time the phrase "natural
theology" while playfully inverting William Paley's "design argument" to prove
not God's existence but slavery's evil: "I think that if anything can be proved
by natural theology, it is that slavery is morally wrong. God gave man a mouth
to receive bread, hands to feed it, and his hand has a right to carry bread to his
mouth without controversy." Lincoln thus acknowledged the question of whether
God had or had not ordained that the different races of men were "equal," but he
ridiculed those (such as Douglas) who thought "that the Almighty has drawn a
line across the country, south of which the land is always to be cultivated by slave
labor; when the question is between the white man and the nigger, they go in for

the white man; when it is between the nigger and the crocodile, they take sides with the nigger." Lincoln's use of "nigger" further disparaged Douglas's attitude.[24]

Everyone understood the battle between Lincoln and Douglas to be about slavery, but it was actually about mankind. When Douglas first tried out his crocodile story on a Memphis audience in November 1858, he was stressing the negro's superiority to a reptile and inferiority to a white man. Lincoln argued in the September 1859 that there was no "necessary conflict between the white man and the negro," because both were men. Three months later, when *On the Origin of Species* arrived from England, racial conflict was not ostensibly the topic of the book, which instead described how conflict, or at least competition, might occur both between and within rather mutable but nonhuman species. And although the book did not even discuss mankind, everyone understood that it somehow had great bearing both on human origins and diversification.

More Debates and New Reviews

The first copies of *On the Origin of Species* sent to America went mostly to New England during the winter of 1859–60. Harvard's Asa Gray had already employed Darwin's theory in tense debates with Louis Agassiz and had reported to Joseph Dalton Hooker that Agassiz "was worried a great deal." Twenty years later, he remembered Agassiz exhorting him privately: "Gray, we must stop this."[1] Agassiz had escaped briefly to Europe in June 1859 to purchase materials for his new museum, pick up the Cross of the Legion of Honor in Paris, and dine in London with old friends such as Richard Owen and Sir Charles Lyell.[2] His visit left no trace in the correspondence of Darwin, then checking proofs of *The Origin*. Agassiz was back in Boston by the fall and probably received his copy just before Christmas 1859, as did Gray.

Agassiz's reading of *The Origin* was slowed as he heavily annotated his presentation copy, still preserved in Harvard's Museum of Comparative Zoology. Gray read Darwin's book between Christmas and New Year and praised it to Hooker with great emphasis before adding that Agassiz "says it is *poor—very poor*!! (entre nous). The fact is he growls over it, like a well cudgelled dog,—is very much annoyed by it—to our great delight." Expecting Agassiz to write a review, Gray began working on one himself: "And really it is no easy job. . . . I doubt if I shall please you altogether. I know I shall not please Agassiz at all."[3]

Darwin entered the new year in a fine mood and penned another ironic statement to Gray: "That great man Agassiz, when he comes to reason seems to me as great in taking a wrong view as he is great in observing & classifying."[4] The first edition of *The Origin* had already garnered some good reviews and converted a few fence-sitters, a second edition was about to appear, and Darwin was delighted that Lyell, whose authority with the public far exceeded his own, was now planning to include "a grand discussion" on the origins of man in the next edition of *Principles of Geology*.[5]

Soon Gray informed Darwin that Agassiz "has been helping the circulation of your book by denouncing it as *atheistical* in a public lecture! I suspect, also, he means to attack it in the *Atlantic Monthly*. The book annoys him; and I suppose the contrast I run between his theories and yours will annoy him still more." Gray discovered that Agassiz was also attacking Darwin and Gray in classroom lectures, remarking on the "laziness" of "those naturalists who adopt some pleasing but false theory like that of Darwin instead of investigating the difficult point of Science." An infuriated Gray wrote a few days later to Francis Boott (his and Darwin's mutual friend in London) that he wanted "to stop Agassiz's mouth with his own words, and to show up his loose way of putting things. He is a sort of demagogue, and always talks to the rabble." Darwin asked Hooker to preserve part of one of Gray's letter that was "rich about Agassiz" and informed his publisher that he was pleased by the "excitement my Book has made amongst Naturalists in U. States," repeating Gray's point that Agassiz's denunciations made "a fine advertisement!"[6]

Suddenly, Darwin was shocked to learn from Gray that in *The Origin* he had wrongly attributed to Agassiz a moderately embarrassing statement about having difficulty in distinguishing different types of embryos.[7] Agassiz denied he had ever said it, Gray hoped Darwin could provide a reference, and Darwin had to admit he had confused Agassiz with Karl Von Baer. Darwin's explanation to Gray unattractively combined remorse with self-defense: "I have shamefully blundered. . . . Please forward enclosed to Agassiz & read if you think worthwhile. I wrote all latter part of volume from memory, & it is a blessing more blunders have not yet been detected: but the state of my health left me no choice: I felt on the point of quite breaking down." The enclosure—presumably an apology—is not recorded or mentioned elsewhere in Darwin's or Agassiz's correspondence, unless there is some connection with Darwin's statement to Gray two months later that a Harvard chemistry professor visiting England "brought me direct from Agassiz all sorts of very civil speeches. What can this mean? I hope to God A. is a sincere man; I had always fancied that he was so." Darwin prefaced this, "I shall be very curious to see Agassiz's remarks" in the anticipated review.[8]

Darwin described Gray's review for the *American Journal of Science* as "*admirable*; by far the best which I have read." He added needlessly, "By the way if Agassiz writes anything on [the] subject, I hope you will tell me."[9] The strengthening alliance between Darwin and Gray was obvious to Boott, who perceptively commented to Darwin that Gray "does not grapple with your hypothesis, . . . nor do I see how he could, in the wish he had to oppose Agassiz."[10] The Gray-Darwin alliance could not be put at risk; differences between them were submerged. When Gray maintained in publications and in correspondence that there was some divine planning in the universe that Darwin's natural selection in no way undermined, Darwin did not wrangle, considering Gray's assertion useful against charges of atheism: "I have been interested by your theological remarks in the Review, but I must reconsider them." He wrote of "an uncomfortable puzzle . . . quite beyond the scope of the human intellect" and shielded himself with the fact that Gottfried Leibniz had attacked Sir Isaac Newton's law of gravity as "'subversive of all Natural Religion'!!" To Lyell, Darwin wrote, "How splendidly Asa Gray is fighting the battle," while to Hooker, he expressed amusement, "Agassiz pities me much at being so deluded."[11]

Although William H. Herndon probably purchased his copy of *The Origin* soon after it appeared at the end of 1859, Lincoln had little free time and probably less inclination to read such a work. Lincoln's secretary John Hay later wrote that Lincoln "made no attempt to keep pace with the ordinary literature of the day, [although] sometimes he read a scientific work with keen appreciation, but he pursued no systematic course."[12] It appears that Herndon believed Lincoln never read *The Origin*. Once, after mentioning works by various authors including Darwin, Herndon wrote, "Lincoln read some parts of these books and reviews. I admit he read none of them thoroughly at a sitting; he would read by snatches, a little here and there now and then." Lincoln was "a firm believer in the theory of development," said Herndon, but "as presented in *The Vestiges of Creation*."[13] On whether Lincoln changed his views about religion after becoming president, Herndon wrote, "There is no evidence of this, especially as to the extent of the change, nor which way. Did he go toward the force and matter theory of the universe, toward [Herbert] Spencer and Darwin?"[14] The very question shows Herndon had little idea what Lincoln might have thought of Spencer or Darwin. Herndon deeply admired Spencer, carefully annotating and indexing his 1855 London edition of *Principles of Psychology*, but if Herndon ever discussed Spencer or Darwin with his law partner, it was probably a fairly one-sided conversation.[15] Even if Lincoln never read *The Origin*, he could not have avoided the numerous reviews that appeared in several publications to which he had access. Indeed, no one with any interest in science could have been unaware of Darwin's general views—if only because they were so strongly opposed by America's best-known scientist, Louis Agassiz.

In the late spring of 1860, Darwin thanked Alfred Russel Wallace for his generous praise of *The Origin* and mentioned his delight that Lyell "this autumn will publish on Geological History of Man." "One thing I see most plainly," Darwin told Hooker, "that without Lyell, yours, Huxley & Carpenter's aid my book would have been a mere flash in the pan."[16] These expressions of modesty by Darwin, although sincere, also served to bind colleagues more closely to him. While Lincoln was busy garnering support as he launched his campaign for the Republican presidential nomination, Darwin was letting others campaign on his behalf through favorable reviews, arranging foreign editions and translations, and defending Darwin's views at scientific conferences. Gray performed most of those tasks in America, but Darwin was also ably defended when the British Association for the Advancement of Science met in Oxford in June 1860.[17] Darwin chose not to attend, partly because of his own and his eldest daughter's ill health and mainly because the discussions, like so many of the reviews, were bound to concentrate on man's descent from earlier forms, the topic Darwin hoped Lyell would soon be treating authoritatively. For Darwin, any indignity from being descended through an unplanned process from some hairy primate was vastly outweighed by the social value of demonstrating the equality among men logically implied by that common origin. However, Darwin knew that his critics were interested not only in whether man was "created" once or several times in different places but also in whether God had any hand in it at all—a subject even more carefully avoided in *The Origin.*

The main event at Oxford occurred at a session opened by a native of Liverpool but now professor of chemistry in New York, John William Draper.[18] Draper was known for his denunciations of organized religion, and the title announced for his address, "On the Intellectual Development of Europe, Considered with Reference to the Views of Mr. Darwin," caused rumors that either Bishop Samuel Wilberforce or Owen would use Draper's presentation as an excuse to launch an attack on Darwin's views. Wilberforce did exactly that, alluding at some point to earlier remarks by Thomas Huxley and asking whether "it was through his grandfather or grandmother that he claimed descent from a monkey." The actual wording of the question is as uncertain as the wording of Huxley's famous reply: "If I would rather have a miserable ape for a grandfather or a man highly endowed by nature and possessed of great means and influence, and yet who employs those faculties for the mere purpose of introducing ridicule into a grave scientific discussion—I unhesitatingly affirm my preference for the ape."[19]

Almost as startling as this exchange was the interjection at its end by an admiral who rose to his feet with a Bible in his hand. Robert FitzRoy, Darwin's old companion from the *Beagle*, attended the conference to make a report on meteorology but stayed to hear the discussion of Darwin's theories. He exclaimed to a departing audience paying little attention that he was sorry he had ever given Darwin the opportunity to collect evidence for his "shocking theory." J. S. Henslow, Darwin's old Cambridge mentor, who had chaired the session, mentioned this to Darwin, who replied, "I did not hear of poor FitzRoy with the Bible at the Geographical Section—I think his mind is often on Verge of insanity."[20]

"I really think his mind has deteriorated within a few years," Gray wrote to Hooker—not about FitzRoy but about Agassiz and as some explanation why by the end of March 1860 he still had not published his review of *The Origin.* "I do not wonder that he hesitates to commit himself to print."[21] When Agassiz's review finally appeared in the *American Journal of Science* in July, it was in the form of a ten-page "digression" from a two-page discussion of jellyfish that was to appear in the third volume of Agassiz's *Contributions to the Natural History of the United States*, then "in press." The tone and language were unscholarly verging on the ungentlemanly, declaring that "the arguments presented by Darwin in favor of a universal derivation from one primary form . . . have not made the slightest impression on my mind, nor modified in any way the views I have already propounded." Agassiz dismissed Darwin's work with phrases such as "unsupported by fact," "ingenious circumlocution," "illogical deductions and misrepresentations," "he overlooks," "he ought to know," "has failed to establish a connection," "he does not even seem correctly to understand," "futile," and "remote from the truth." Agassiz's conclusion was unsurprising apart from the moralizing point in the final clause: "I shall therefore consider the transmutation theory as a scientific mistake, untrue in its facts, unscientific in its methods, and mischievous in its tendency."[22]

Defending Darwin's theory in the July and August issues of *Atlantic Monthly*, Gray picked up on Agassiz's last remark by writing that "several features of [Darwin's] theory have an uncanny look. They may prove to be innocent: but their first aspect is suspicious, and high authorities pronounce the whole thing to be positively mischievous."[23] Gray was skilled at defending Darwin's views without appearing partisan—and, indeed, without mentioning his disagreement with Darwin about God's possible role. But it was exactly because Gray argued that natural selection was not incompatible with "design" that he was able to minimize the science versus religion dispute—in contrast to Darwin's "bull-dog" in England, Huxley, who reveled in baiting bishops. Rather boldly, Gray also raised the controversial topic of man. While Agassiz's review had avoided the issue (and any reminders of his own views about negroes), Gray was the first to suggest that natural selection actually resolved the debate between what he termed "uni-humanitarians" and "multi-humanitarians."

> Indeed, when we consider the endless disputes of naturalists and ethnologists over the human races, as to whether they belong to one species or to more, and if to more, whether to three, or five, or fifty, we can hardly help fancying that both may be right,—or rather, that the uni-humanitarians would have been right several thousand years ago, and the multi-humanitarians will be a few thousand years later; while at present the safe thing to say is, that, probably, there is some truth on both sides.[24]

Gray skirted around the problem that man's "common ancestor" was no longer Adam by first looking to the future and offering the appealing prospect that the present species of man might make further progress. Gray's discussion of human origins had less appeal.

> It is only the backward glance, the gaze up the long vista of the past, that reveals anything alarming. Here the lines converge as they recede into the geological ages, and point to conclusions which, upon the theory, are inevitable, but by no means welcome. The first step backwards makes the Negro and the Hottentot our blood-relations—not that reason or Scripture objects to that, though

pride may. The next suggests a closer association of our ancestors of the olden time with "our poor relations" of the quadrumanous family than we like to acknowledge.[25]

Gray's *Atlantic Monthly* review is very likely the source that brought Lincoln closest to *The Origin*, assuming he probably never read the book himself. And just now, since political tradition prevented the Republican nominee from hitting the campaign trail personally, Lincoln perhaps had leisure to scan the *Atlantic Monthly*. Having once said we should "discard all this quibbling" about races while simultaneously parrying Douglas's pseudoscientific attacks on the inferiority of black people, Lincoln could appreciate Gray's use of ambiguous language that left it to the reader to work out how equal or unequal this made whites and blacks. After undermining Agassiz's notion of separate primordial creations, Gray went no further than to say, "It is practically very difficult, perhaps impossible, to draw a clear line between races and species. Witness the human races, for instance." We know from Lincoln's fragment about Niagara Falls that he accepted that the Earth's history was much longer than the traditional six thousand years, so he would have been interested by Gray's assertion that the Earth has, indeed, been around long enough for the slow processes of natural selection to have taken place. Assuming Lincoln was at least aware of Agassiz's opposition to Darwin's views, he could have admired Gray's clever defense of those views by using his opponent's own testimony: "Agassiz tells us that the same species of polyps which are now building coral walls around the present peninsula of Florida actually made that peninsula, and have been building there for centuries which must be reckoned by thousands."[26]

While preserving the religious concept of design, Gray admitted that natural selection jettisoned the traditional date and manner of the Biblical creation, a point expressed less elegantly by Josiah Nott to fellow polygenist E. G. Squier in August 1860: "I have been well enough to skim Darwin's book—the man is clearly crazy, but it is a capital dig into the parsons—it stirs up Creation & much good comes out [of] such thorough discussion."[27]

In his references to early man, Gray employed information beyond his own botanical expertise, such as the man-made flint tools found beside the bones of animals now extinct. Lyell was investigating exactly this evidence for inclusion in his study of early man—for which Darwin was waiting impatiently. "I expect your Book on Geological History of man will with a vengeance be a bomb-shell," he told Lyell at the end of July. "*I hope it will not be very long delayed.*"[28]

To Huxley, Darwin described Agassiz's review as a "weak metaphysical & theological attack on the *Origin*" and to Lyell as "not good at all. . . . Asa Gray tells me that a very clever friend has been almost converted to our side by this Review." Darwin told Gray he was "surprised that Agassiz did not succeed in writing something better. How absurd that logical quibble: 'if species do not exist how can they vary?' As if anyone doubted their temporary existence." The review seemed "hardly worth a detailed answer (even if I could do it, & I much doubt whether I possess your skill in picking out salient points & driving a nail into them)."[29]

Darwin arranged to have Gray's *Atlantic* articles republished in Boston and London as a pamphlet entitled *Natural Selection Not Inconsistent with Natural Theology. A Free Examination of Darwin's Treatise on the Origin of Species, and of Its American Reviewers*. Although doing this mainly to deflect religious criticism, Darwin was also promulgating Gray's discussion of the origins of man, the topic on which he himself was delaying any publication while hoping that Lyell would soon be publishing his work.

Darwin and Lyell exchanged ideas on man's origins during the summer and fall of 1860, with Darwin clarifying that the human races are "certainly descended from single parent" and "infinitely closer" to each other "than to any ape"; that it was "probable that the races of man were less numerous & less divergent formerly than now"; and that perhaps one or more among the races of man had already "become extinct," such as "some lower & more aberrant race, even than the Hottentot"—whose existence Darwin had good reason to fear might soon end. Darwin concurred with Lyell that the "White man is 'improving off the face of the earth' even races nearly his equals." He pointed out that "Agassiz & Co. think the Negro & Caucasian are now distinct species," yet whether the polygenists would have called them different species when they were formerly "less distinct" is essentially a "vain discussion" since they do not accept that species change anyway.[30] This last point suggests Darwin found Gray's argument—that natural selection reconciled monogenist and polygenist views—less than convincing; however, Gray's view would later prove more relevant than Darwin's when polygenists discovered they could co-opt natural selection to serve their own purposes by, in effect, replacing "multiple creations" with "multiple variations" as the explanation for the inequality between races.

Meanwhile, Darwin was pleased that, along with Lyell and Gray, Henslow was also investigating whether the discoveries of flint tools really provided evidence of men existing at the same time as now extinct animals. Meanwhile, Huxley was continuing to argue against Owen's sharp distinction between man and other primates by coming up with concepts such as a "pithecoid pedigree" for mankind that in no way lowered "the great and princely dignity of perfect manhood." However, Lyell then broke the news that his "work on antiquity of Man is entirely suspended" while he produce new editions of his two standard works on geology, though he promised these would include "nearly all I can say on the subject."[31] Darwin would have to be patient.

Lincoln also had to allow others to campaign on his behalf while he avoided issuing any statement that might be interpreted as some divergence from the party platform. Meanwhile, southern Democrats had splintered their party by refusing to acknowledge Stephen A. Douglas's nomination and backing instead a second Democrat, John C. Breckenridge. Realizing he could not now win the election, Douglas could nevertheless weaken his foes so that the party might later reunite under his leadership before the next election in 1864. He might also limit Lincoln's electoral success in the north, yet, knowing Lincoln was almost certain to win, Douglas did his best to dissuade southern legislators from carrying out their threat to secede from the Union if a "Black Republican" was elected president. Douglas broke with tradition and toured the whole country, giving speeches with a grace that came from serving his country and not worrying that Lincoln might turn up for some debate.

Cooling his heels in Springfield, Lincoln probably read in the *New York Times* that Douglas, while pretending not to be politicking, tarried for a few days in August in Newport, Rhode Island, coinciding with the fourteenth annual meeting of the American Association for the Advancement of Science (AAAS). "Prof. Agassiz's address on Methods in Zoology, . . . had the first place on today's programme," wrote the *Times* reporter. "The hall . . . accordingly was excessively crowded with visitors, among whom [was] Senator Douglas." Reading on, Lincoln could learn that "Prof. Agassiz's address, however, was quite brief; nor did he touch any of the grand theories of Life—only in a single sentence skirting along the verges of the great Darwin problem."[32] On the previous day, while discussing someone's ethnological paper, Agassiz "threw out some linguistic observations—the same as occur in his communication to Nott and Gliddon's *Indigenous Races*—which proved him far from being as strong on philosophy as he is on fossils."[33] The *Times* reporter also accused the AAAS of "either cowardice or incompetence [because] the great Darwin question . . . [was] purposely and pointedly ignored."[34]

The AAAS, like the nation, was suffering from internal tensions, some sectional, some personal, but both sometimes overlapping on "the Darwin question." Few southern scientists attended this year's meeting, yet they held the balance between larger factions and found themselves controlling the association's higher offices.[35] Senator Douglas knew all about such maneuverings and the risks of compromising with southerners. If Lincoln's election triggered secession, Douglas knew the Republicans would have difficulty achieving compromise and that Lincoln would not let the Union fall apart without a fight.

The fear of an upcoming war heightened interest in the presentation on "modern warfare" by Captain Edward B. Hunt of the Coastal Survey. The *Times* reporter called Hunt's paper "an exceedingly pleasant *mélange* . . . not so severely scientific in character as most of the papers read." The captain told his audience, "War is the applied science of destructive projectiles, and the philosophy of military material depends on scientific application. . . . Warlike science needs to be progressive." Hunt spoke of "the steam-gun" of the future, the need for chemical production (rather than importation) of niter (or "saltpeter"), replacing smooth-bores with rifled handguns and artillery, asphyxiating shells, balloon telegraphic observatories, and much more.[36] In the audience, Douglas may have mused that his opponent back in Springfield would probably read the newspaper account of Hunt's martial presentation with the grim interest of a one-time inventor and soon-to-be commander-in-chief.

Two months later, Lincoln won the presidential election, taking a majority of the electoral votes while winning only 39 percent of the popular vote: in ten southern states where the Republican party did not exist, Lincoln's name was not listed on the ballots. During the following four months, as several southern states seceded and as lame-duck President James Buchanan said he could do nothing about it, Lincoln kept silent, still lacking power to act and feeling that more words might simply exacerbate raw feelings. Although few southerners could vote for the Republicans, more than half voted for the "pro-union" candidates, Douglas and John Bell, rather than for the "secessionist" Breckenridge.[37] Lincoln was not being as irrational as his biographer David Herbert Donald has suggested by believing "that Unionists were in a majority throughout the South and that, given time for tempers to cool, they would be able to defeat the secessionist conspirators."[38]

If that rational hope proved wrong, Lincoln might need to consider the suggestions contained in the paper by Captain Hunt, who would never attend another AAAS conference. The next one was scheduled to meet in Nashville in April 1861, but the war's outbreak prevented it.

Designers and Inventors

Whatever else Lincoln may have seen in the newspapers, about two weeks after his election he certainly read about a speech "recently delivered (I think) before the Georgia Legislature, or its assembled members. If you have revised it, as is probable, I shall be much obliged if you will send me a copy."[1] Lincoln first met the speech's author, Alexander H. Stephens, twelve years earlier when they served as fellow Whigs in Congress. Back then, Lincoln wrote, "Mr. Stephens of Georgia, a little, slim, pale-faced, consumptive man . . . has just concluded the very best speech, of an hour's length, I ever heard." Even Stephen A. Douglas was happy to urge the audience during the 1858 debates to "read the speeches of that giant in intellect, Alexander H. Stephens, of Georgia."[2]

Now, with Lincoln elected president and several southern states already seceded from the union, Lincoln was impressed that on 14 November 1860, Stephens spoke during a stormy debate in Savannah about whether to secede, arguing impressively against secession—which few southern leaders of Stephens's stature had been doing lately. He asserted that constitutional checks should prevent Lincoln from restricting the extension of slavery, and if they did not, then Stephens himself would advocate secession: but he wanted the Republicans, not Georgia, to make the first wrong move.[3]

Lincoln would grasp at any unionist straw in the south, yet he was wary, probably recognizing what Stephens had left out of *this* address but had included in a speech delivered over a year earlier upon his retirement from Congress. In that 1859 speech, Stephens maintained, "African Slavery with us rests upon principles that can never be successfully assailed by reason or argument. . . . The world is grown wiser, and upon no subject more rapidly than that of the proper status of the negro. In my judgment there are more thinking men at the North now who look upon our system of Slavery as right, socially, morally and politically, than there were even at the South thirty years ago." Stephens admitted that "nearly all" of the founding fathers "were against" slavery, but "it was a question which they did not, and perhaps could not thoroughly understand at that time." According to

Stephens, the ancient Greeks' slave system failed because they enslaved people of their own race, but Americans had avoided this error and increasingly recognized that "subordination is the normal condition of the negro. This great truth, that such was the normal condition of any race, was not recognized in [the ancients'] theories." Going further into natural history, Stephens declared, "'Order is nature's first law'; [and] with it come gradation and subordination [as seen] in the vegetable and animal kingdoms, ranging . . . from the hugest monsters of life . . . to the smallest *animalcule*. . . . We see similar distinctions and gradations in the races of men—from the highest to the lowest type." Stephens concluded that it was folly to "attempt to make things equal which God in his wisdom has made unequal."⁴

Stephens had actually used a phrase echoing the subtitle of John H. Van Evrie's 1853 pamphlet, *Negroes and Negro "Slavery": The First an Inferior Race; the Latter Its Normal Condition.* This lends credence to Van Evrie's later claim that he once presented Stephens with a copy of the pamphlet, converting him into the "most complete exponent and advocate of the new doctrine among all the public men of the day."⁵ Although Van Evrie's claim of directly influencing both Stephen A. Douglas and Alexander Stephens was unknown to Lincoln, he recognized that the same views, based on the new scientific racism, were offered by both men, if more thoughtfully by Stephens. Yet, Stephens's more recent speech against secession made no reference to race, and possibly Lincoln hoped Stephens had modified his views. When Stephens replied briefly to Lincoln's request for a copy of that speech, he confirmed that the press accounts were substantially correct and closed sympathetically: "No man ever had heavier or greater responsibilities resting upon him than you have in this present momentous crisis."⁶

Lincoln wrote back that he fully appreciated the present peril but said the people of the south had no reason to fear "that a Republican administration would *directly, or indirectly*, interfere with their slaves, or with them, about their slaves." Lincoln knew this assurance meant nothing: Stephens's argument for delaying secession was to allow southerners to oppose the one policy on which Lincoln could not yield—halting the expansion of slavery. But Lincoln went straight to the more essential difficulty: "You think slavery is *right* and ought to be extended; while we think it is *wrong* and ought to be restricted. That I suppose is the rub. It certainly is the only substantial difference between us."⁷

Stephens's reply also sought the essence: "The [Republican Party's] leading object . . . [has been] to put the institutions of nearly half the States under the ban of public opinion and national condemnation. . . . We at the South do think African slavery, as it exists with us, both morally and politically right. This opinion is founded upon the inferiority of the black race." Stephens freely admitted that since the writing of the Constitution, "the changes have been mainly to our side"—exactly Lincoln's point during his debates with Douglas—but also stressed that the union could not be saved by use of force. He could recommend no specific course of action except to suggest Lincoln should say something to modify the threat posed by his party's stated policy. Alluding to scripture, Stephens wrote, "A word 'fitly spoken' by you now would indeed be like 'apples of gold in pictures of silver.'"[8]

There was no further correspondence, yet that scriptural passage goaded Lincoln to write a memorandum as if in reply. In this fragment, Lincoln argued that "there is something back of these," and "that something is the principle of 'Liberty to all'" as stated in the Declaration of Independence. There was no need to make some statement now that might placate the south because "the assertion of that *principle*, at *that time*, was *the* word, *'fitly spoken'* which has proved an 'apple of gold' to us."[9]

Both men had boiled the conflict down to the "inferiority of the black race" versus "liberty to all," and Lincoln would not consider that "all" could exclude blacks.

As the excitement over *The Origin* began to abate, Darwin returned to writing the first volume of his "big book," though he made little progress because of ill health and a sideline into the study of orchids. Meanwhile, he told Charles Lyell he feared "your volume on Geolog. Hist. of Man will slip through your fingers."[10] Darwin continued reading and thinking about man, was delighted to receive a gift copy of Jean Louis Armand de Quatrefages de Bréau's *L'Unité de l'Espèce Humaine* (1861), asked Lyell to help him obtain an 1850 pamphlet by Samuel G. Morton attacking John Bachman on issues of hybridity, and told Leonard Horner, outgoing president of the Geological Society, that he had learned a great deal from his recent address (which in part dealt with "Evidence of the early existence of the human race") even though Darwin "thought that I had read up pretty well on the antiquity of man."[11]

Darwin's correspondence with Asa Gray slackened after the intense exchanges during *The Origin*'s publication, but also political events proved a distraction for Gray, and their differences over religion were becoming more visible. Although content that Gray's writings seemed to reconcile natural selection with "natural theology," Darwin was grieved "to say that I cannot honestly go as far as you do about Design. I am conscious that I am in an utterly hopeless muddle. I cannot think that the world, as we see it, is the result of chance; & yet I cannot look at each separate thing as the result of Design." Pressed to clarify his objections, Darwin balked, "I have no real objection, nor any real foundation, nor any clear view. As I before said I flounder hopelessly in the mud."[12]

While both Lincoln and Darwin had long since abandoned conventional Christianity, Lincoln was more content with the probability of design. Darwin did not like to see the world as "the result of chance" but allowed that we might see it wrongly in any case. He saw no evidence of a designer or any need to argue the point. For Lincoln, perhaps the most significant, yet bizarre, evidence of a designer, or perhaps of Providence, was the fact of his own life. By normal processes, someone of his origins should not have become the occupant of the White House. Lincoln knew how greatly his development had been the result of his own effort and will, and yet, as he now struggled with a crisis that had made him the sixteenth president of the thirty-three United States and threatened to reduce that number by eleven, Lincoln seemed almost eager to see evidence of Providence—some intended purpose—behind the threatened conflict. When confronting certain developments that were intrinsically inexplicable, Lincoln was at least willing to imagine some supernatural explanation, while Darwin was more insistent that at bottom there was some natural explanation. For all his much-vaunted rationalism, Lincoln still had a capacity, and perhaps a need, for the spiritual. And although Darwin took cover behind Gray's theistic essays, supportive quotations from the Reverend Charles Kingsley, and the Butler epigraph that asserted God's agency in the natural as well as the supernatural, he had little capacity for belief in the supernatural and less need.

About June 1861, Emma Darwin wrote a letter to Charles, the third and apparently last time she used this mode to express her mixed feelings of love for him and spiritual pain at his inability to see a role for God. While she felt "in my inmost heart your admirable qualities & feelings," she also expressed her hope "that you might direct them upwards, as well as to one who values them above every thing in the world." Around this time, Darwin told his friend Gray, "I have been led to think more on this subject [of design] of late, & grieve to say that I come to differ more from you [as a result of] studying lately domestic variations & seeing what an enormous field of undesigned variability there is ready for natural selection to appropriate for any purpose useful to each creature."[13]

Darwin closed that letter on a different topic: "But I suppose you are all too overwhelmed with public affairs to care for science. I never knew the newspapers so profoundly interesting." This was not the first time Darwin's correspondence revealed his concern about the political crisis developing in America, and several of Gray's letters from this time that have failed to survive may have made some reference to Lincoln's election or other political issues. Darwin showed his interest in a postscript: "Have you read Olmsted *Journey in the Back Country*; what a remarkably interesting Book."[14]

Frederick Law Olmsted, a New Englander who traveled extensively in the south, wrote perceptive accounts of his journeys. Darwin had already admired two that appeared in 1856 and 1857.[15] The book mentioned in Darwin's postscript was published in 1860 and also provided "an admirably lively picture of man & Slavery in the S. States," as Darwin wrote when he recommended *Journey in the Back Country* (twice) to Joseph Dalton Hooker.[16] One of Darwin's sons remembered his father "talking with horror of his sleepless nights when he could not keep out of his mind some incidents from Olmsted's [book, which] he had lately been reading." Similarly, another son recalled, "The remembrance of screams, or other sounds heard in Brazil, when he was powerless to interfere with what he believed to be the torture of a slave, haunted him for years, especially at night."[17]

In early 1861, as the secession crisis developed prior to Lincoln's inauguration, Darwin wrote to Gray, "I fear that the state of the U. States must stop all interest in everything not political." Gray had recently asked a fellow scientist in Charleston if there were no union men in South Carolina; "I answer none" was the reply.[18]

Lincoln's hopes that pro-union sentiment would eventually push aside the secessionist hotheads were fading as his inauguration approached in March and as Stephens was sworn in as Vice-President of the Confederacy on the very day that Lincoln began his slow train journey to Washington, D.C. Lincoln's farewell to his friends in Springfield struck a deeply religious note: "I go to assume a task more difficult than that which devolved upon General Washington. Unless the great God who assisted him, shall be with and aid me, I must fail. But if the same omniscient mind, and Almighty arm that directed and protected him, shall guide and support me, I shall not fail, I shall succeed. Let us all pray that the God of our fathers may not forsake us now."[19]

Similar sentiments were addressed to audiences all along the roundabout route to the nation's capital. On inauguration day, soldiers lined the streets, and riflemen watched from the rooftops as the president-elect proceeded to the swearing in. His inaugural address offered no concessions on fundamental issues but echoed Stephens's argument that the Republican administration had no authority to interfere with slavery where it already existed. He also paraphrased what he had told Stephens: "One section of our country believes slavery is *right*, and ought to be extended, while the other believes it is *wrong*, and ought not to be extended."[20] He did not attempt to explain the basis for those beliefs: whether one considered slavery right or wrong was largely determined by received tradition and economic interest, and scientific racism gave only a veneer of intellectual justification to preexisting attitudes.

Stephens had advised Lincoln that the union could not be maintained by force, and for the same tactical reason that made Stephens delay his support for secession, Lincoln declared he would not launch the first attack. The south would have to strike the first blow, as he knew eventually it would when the federal government, no longer led by the insipid Buchanan, stopped yielding to southern demands for control of federal installations in their states.

Despite southern claims to the contrary, Lincoln knew that the south actually lacked the "just cause" their grandfathers had when they seceded from the British Empire. Instead of basing the Confederate system on liberty, even the most brilliant of southern leaders made the mistake of basing the Confederacy on the doctrine of negro inferiority. Two weeks after Lincoln's inauguration, Stephens delivered what became known as the Cornerstone Speech, which echoed ideas found in Van Evrie's writings and in Stephens's retirement speech two years earlier.

Our new government is founded upon [and] its cornerstone rests upon the great truth, that the negro is not equal to the white man; that slavery—subordination to the superior race—is his natural and normal condition. This, our new government, is the first, in the history of the world, based upon this great physical, philosophical, and moral truth. This truth has been slow in the process of its development, like all other truths in the various departments of science. It has been so even amongst us. Many who hear me, perhaps, can recollect well, that this truth was not generally admitted, even within their day.

Just as Lincoln in his inaugural called for "a firm reliance on Him, who has never yet forsaken this favored land," so Stephens urged that the slave system was "in conformity with the ordinance of the Creator. It is not for us to inquire into the wisdom of his ordinances, or to question them. For his own purposes, he has made one race to differ from another."[21]

The issue dividing the country could not be resolved through theology or politics, let alone anthropology. Yet, other sciences would be crucial in the coming struggle for survival, since the fittest would be those whose leaders were best able to adopt the latest military technology.

A month after Lincoln's election, *Scientific American* included a piece entitled "The President Elect's Mode of Buoying Vessels. Patented May 22, 1849": "The merits of this invention we are not disposed to discuss; but we hope the author of it will have better success in presiding as Chief Magistrate over the people of the entire Union than he has had as an inventor in introducing his invention upon the western waters, for which it was specially designed." The editors included a large image of the model in the Patent Office and a copy of the patent itself. They also acknowledged that "among our readers there are thousands of mechanics who would devise a better apparatus for buoying steamboats over bars, but how many of them would be able to compete successfully in the race for the Presidency?"[22]

Unfortunately, this was exactly the moment when the secession crisis boiled over, and Lincoln's success as chief magistrate would be measured by his ability to quell what he always referred to as a "rebellion." Lincoln now had to apply his rational brain to finding a way to save the union. "The tug has to come," he told Lyman Trumbull back in December, "& better now, than any time hereafter."[23] That ruled out two options preferred by many, perhaps most, Americans. One was letting the Confederates go, saying good riddance, and possibly expecting they would return when they realized their folly. The other was, as so often in the past, to cobble together another compromise—but this meant concessions Lincoln could not make without betraying those who had voted for the Republican platform. That left only the resort to force, which courted disaster since the eight slave states then still remaining in the union expected Republicans to make concessions. Lincoln was hoping some of those states would rally to the union if the rebels attacked it before being themselves assaulted by the federal government. A rebel attack might also increase northern support for armed conflict, which is why Lincoln handled the issue of Fort Sumter so carefully, maneuvering the South Carolinians into becoming the aggressors when they began the bombardment on 12 April 1861.

As war became a reality, four more slave states joined the Confederacy and greatly strengthened it by increasing the overall population from five million to nine million. The greatest loss was Virginia, which chose secession after Stephens made a long speech before the legislature: "The enemies of our institutions . . . set out with the assumption that the races are equal; that the negro is equal to the white man. If their premises were correct, their conclusions would be legitimate. But their premises being false, their conclusions are false also."[24] Although President Lincoln was devastated that Confederate territory across the Potomac River was now visible from the windows of the White House, he was relieved that for the moment Delaware, Kentucky, Maryland, and Missouri—the Border States—remained in the union, and that the north responded enthusiastically when Lincoln called for seventy-five thousand volunteers for ninety days' service.

Lincoln intended to avoid the error of George III, who had repeatedly committed too few troops and too late when attempting to suppress the colonial rebellion. It was assumed that the Confederacy would have far more difficulty than the north in recruiting, supplying, and transporting an army. The south's population was less than half of the north's, and nearly half of the Confederacy's people were slaves. Only a quarter of the free population were themselves slave owners, and Lincoln still hoped there were unionists among the less "aristocratic" classes. Transporting men and supplies to defend specific points would be difficult for the south's underdeveloped railroad system, and its industrial base was almost nonexistent. Although the rebels had been able to seize arms and ships at several federal installations, the largest stockpiles of small arms were in the north along with the industries to make new ones. Northerners hoped for a quick victory, but evidently the president and his advisers were also planning for a longer struggle.

Lincoln's call for seventy-five thousand troops on three-month enlistment did not mean he seriously thought that number and period would prove sufficient. While some bandied slogans about one Yankee being worth ten rebels, or vice versa, Lincoln accepted that "exceptional advantages on one side are counterbalanced by exceptional advantages on the other. We must make up our minds that man for man the soldier from the South will be a match for the soldier from the North and *vice versa*." When Congress assembled in early July, Lincoln requested support for an army of four hundred thousand men, and Congress immediately raised this to five hundred thousand.[25]

That Lincoln thought the war might not end swiftly is also indicated by his effort to bring about technological improvements in the union's weaponry that some experts, including General James W. Ripley, the head of the Army's

Ordnance Department, thought unnecessary and even reckless, since there were already large stockpiles of arms. The loss of uniformity and interchangeability in types of ammunition might complicate supply issues, and the war might be over before new designs could be fully tested and manufactured. Lincoln increasingly ignored this sensible view—with tremendous long-term benefits for the union cause—partly because of his own peculiar fascination with science and inventions.

Lincoln's interest in science and technology remained a fixture throughout his life. A young legal colleague recalled seeing Lincoln distracted in 1856 by an exhibition of a "self-raking reaping machine." Lincoln "examined it with much interest" before "explaining, in the fewest words but with great clearness, how power and motion were communicated to the different appliances, especially to the sickle, the revolving rake, and the reel. His faculty for comprehending and understanding machinery I afterward saw exemplified when I heard him argue a patent case."[26]

Lincoln might have read the article about the Illinois State Agricultural Society's "Trials of Reapers" in his 1855 volume of the *Annual of Scientific Discovery*. In a different trial earlier that year, Lincoln learned a great deal about reapers when some high-priced Ohio patent lawyers retained him to assist as a local attorney in a patent-infringement case between two Illinois reaper manufacturers. When the case was transferred to Cincinnati, the specialist lawyers dispensed with Lincoln's services, but he had already visited the factory and "spent half a day examining and studying Manny's Machine."[27]

In March 1857, a young telegrapher in Pekin, Illinois, noticed Lincoln staring at the telegrapher's key and receiver. Answering Lincoln's questions about various intricacies, the telegrapher found him "already well furnished with knowledge of collateral facts and natural phenomena; and . . . he comprehended quite readily the operation of the telegraph, [even though the] wires had been extended west of the Alleghany Mountains only five or six years."[28]

In September 1859, Lincoln addressed the Wisconsin State Agricultural Society, and despite jokingly calling himself "in some sort a politician, and in no sort a farmer," he discussed agriculture in familiar terms while also stressing the need for exploiting "recent discovery, or invention." He cited Patent Office reports on crop yields per acre; advocated "deeper plowing, analysis of soils, experiments with manures, and varieties of seeds, observance of seasons, and the like"; and judged that "the soil has never been pushed up to one-half of its capacity." He gave an almost Euclidean analysis of the potential for "the successful application of *steam power*," arguing that any "steam plow" must be "so contrived as to apply the larger proportion of its power to the cutting and turning the soil, and the smallest, to the moving itself over the field," while suggesting that currently, with horse-drawn reapers, "fully nine-tenths of the power is expended by the animal in carrying himself and dragging the machine over the field." Lincoln spoke of the "profitable enjoyment" of studying problems connected with "drain-ing, droughts, and irrigation[,] . . . saving crops, pests of crops, diseases of crops, and what will prevent or cure them—implements, utensils, and machines, their relative merits, and [how] to improve them." He mentioned the assistance to be gained from botany, chemistry, and "the mechanical branches of Natural Phi-losophy . . . especially in reference to implements and machinery."[29]

Now, less than a month after his inauguration and shortly before Fort Sumter, Lincoln displayed keen interest in the testing and production of weapons when he paid the first of many visits to the Washington Navy Yard.[30] Fascinated by the steam hammers, blast furnace, hydrostatic press, pyrotechnical laboratory, rolling mill, foundries, and all the boring, turning, and planing machinery, Lincoln was equally pleased by the enthusiasm of Captain John A. Dahlgren, who had served at the yard since 1847 and was shortly to replace the previous commander who had deserted to the Confederacy.

For three months after Fort Sumter, while others still hoped for a short war, Lincoln became interested in new types of weapons that might help to shorten a long war. He was aware that Jefferson Davis, President of the Confederacy, knew a great deal about military technology, since the 1855 volume of *Annual of Scientific Discovery* had given a detailed account of a report to Congress by then Secretary of War Davis about the latest European advances in weapons technology, emphasizing the "superiority of the grooved or rifle barrel and elon-gated ball" over the smooth-bore musket with its round ball and noting that the difficulties of loading rifles compared with smooth-bores was overcome by replacing the old muzzleloaders with breechloaders. The *Annual* also reported that in the following year, Davis's department found a practicable way to turn old musket barrels into rifled barrels: "it is not improbable that all now on hand at the Springfield [Massachusetts] Armory—some 255,000—will ultimately receive that improvement."[31]

Lincoln could assume that Davis was now applying his experience to the task of securing—under even more adverse conditions than Lincoln faced—the best weapons available for Confederate troops. Lincoln's problem was that, in fact, few of those old muskets had been converted to rifles, and Ordnance Chief Ripley was busy distributing existing weapons into the hands of the tens of thousands of fresh recruits. Governors and commanders who were contribut-ing troops to the cause often demanded that their men receive the few superior weapons in the armories. New York state sent an agent to Britain to purchase nineteen thousand Enfield rifles, and General Ripley at first supported the idea of purchasing a hundred thousand arms in Europe, but the Secretary of War Simon Cameron opposed, mainly to avoid spending money abroad rather than at home.[32] This proved a great blunder, because the South, with fewer options, had no such qualms about foreign purchases.

If Ripley and Cameron had been less obstructive, Lincoln might not have interfered, but pressure came not only from recruits clamoring for modern rifles as a matter, literally, of life and death but also from a flood of letters and visits by inventors and manufacturers, both genuine and would-be, and all offering some new killing device that would save the union. Lincoln's private secretaries, who sifted the piles of post and passed to the president only those that could not be immediately discarded or redirected, allowed a disproportionate number of the letters from inventors through the screen, knowing Lincoln relished them.[33]

Lincoln was most interested in the designs for rifling both small arms and artillery, new breechloaders, "repeating" systems that allowed more rapid fire, and the corresponding new types of projectiles. Before the end of April, Lincoln endorsed a letter from the vice-president in favor of placing a large order for rifled cannon. On 16 May, Lincoln and Secretary of State William H. Seward inspected the Ordnance Office at Dahlgren's Navy Yard, and in the same month, Dahlgren hinted to Lincoln that if the war lasted any considerable time, there could be problems about maintaining supplies of niter (saltpeter) for gunpowder production. Early in June, Lincoln watched a demonstration of an early machine gun, which he dubbed "the coffee mill gun." He praised it to Dahlgren and recommended it to Ripley as "worth the attention of the Government." He was less impressed with a "centrifugal gun" meant to be powered by steam. The prototype Lincoln tested was hand cranked and so inaccurate that the target had to be quite close, causing the balls flying out of the machine to bounce back among the shins of the bystanders, which, according to his secretary John Hay sent Lincoln into "peals of Homeric laughter."[34]

The next day, Lincoln was introduced to some of that potential military technology Captain Edward B. Hunt had mentioned at the Newport AAAS meeting. The head of the Smithsonian, Joseph Henry, brought a young balloonist named Thaddeus Lowe to the White House. A few days later, Lowe was floating over it in the *Enterprise* and sending telegraph messages to demonstrate the balloon's usefulness for reconnaissance. Lincoln gave Lowe a letter of introduction to the highest officer in the Army, General Winfield Scott, who managed temporarily to sideline the project.[35]

Later in the month, Lincoln dragged Cameron and Ripley along to watch experiments with rifled cannon at the arsenal in Washington, and at least twice around this time, Lincoln went out to an empty field near the White House to test some weapons himself. He usually took along an ex-soldier and messenger named Mullikin from the Ordnance Office, but once when a clerk told him that Mullikin was unavailable, Lincoln made do with the clerk. Lincoln was keen that day to try out the new Spencer repeating rifles that Dahlgren had already tested to great satisfaction. Lincoln thought he had a better idea about the design of the gun sight and whittled one out of wood. The clerk placed a paper target on a large woodpile, and Lincoln fired seven rounds in rapid order, reloaded and fired another seven, hitting the target nearly every time.[36]

Lincoln carried out a similar test on two breech-loading rifles, and this time his shooting partner was his third secretary, William O. Stoddard, who fired a single-shot weapon while Lincoln tried out a new repeater. Stoddard proved a good shot, and Lincoln laughed, "I declare, you are beating me!" Some soldiers heard the unauthorized gunfire and came running up shouting, "Stop that firing!" They had not come very close before they recognized the tall marksman and beat a retreat. "Well," Lincoln remarked, "they might have stayed and seen the shooting."[37]

Lincoln had testing times not only with the weapons but also with their inventors, although, according to secretary Hay, they "were more a source of amusement than annoyance."[38] One brought a rocket to Lincoln's office and seemed surprised when as he struck a match, his president ducked behind a desk. "Mr. Lincoln," said the inventor, "you make a better President, I guess, than you would a soldier." Lincoln's sense of self-preservation was usually less attuned. "On my arrival at the White House," recalled another inventor, "I was ushered immediately into the reception room, with my repeating rifle in my hand, and there I found the President."[39] If Lincoln showed little fear that any of his inventive visitors were deliberately dangerous, he had less confidence in their devices. Bullet-proof steel vests to protect the troops were brought to Lincoln in such profusion that he sifted out the really hopeless ones by offering to let the inventor wear his own device in a test. One such vest was described by its inventor as a "cuirass," an archaism that moved Lincoln to pun: "Well, the inventor must be a queer ass to think a man could lug that thing on a march in a hot sun." One might have thought nothing could be more absurd than the gun with two diverging barrels to be used by cross-eyed men who, according to its cross-eyed inventor, "could march down the river and clear out both banks at once," but Lincoln only laughed, "There's about as much in it as there is in some of the other plans they want me to take."[40]

According to Hay, "Lincoln had a quick comprehension of mechanical principles, and often detected a flaw in an invention which the contriver had overlooked."[41] Nevertheless, General Ripley simply could not take Lincoln seriously and complained to the Secretary of War in June 1861 of "the great evil" of "the vast variety of the new inventions, each having, of course, its advocates, insisting on the superiority of his favorite arm over all others and urging its adoption by the Government." Ripley said all this was "very injurious to the efficiency of troops," and the solution was to refuse to purchase "new and untried arms" and to adhere to the "rule of uniformity of arms for all troops of the same kind."[42]

So far Lincoln had shown interest, curiosity and open-mindedness, but he had often bowed to the authority of military chiefs. After the Union defeat at

Bull Run on 21 July 1861, Lincoln showed less deference and more insistence on the importance of new technology.

Darwin's best source of information about the American Civil War came from letters that American colleagues sent to him or to Lyell and Hooker. The colleagues were mainly New Englanders since Darwin had no regular contact with any southern scientists and might doubt their opinions anyway. The same applied to Agassiz, who otherwise might have made a useful observer, being a nonnative resident in New England but also very familiar with the south. Even Darwin's most frequent and admired correspondent, Gray, wrote at best only once every three weeks, the least time required for a letter sent across the Atlantic to fetch a reply. Darwin's daily dose of war news came from the *Times* of London.

Darwin was an avid reader of the *Times*, which proved aggravating since, after initially taking a position Darwin could approve, the newspaper was blatantly pro-South for most of the war. A contemporary wrote in 1865 that the *Times*'s "errors were of a class which, besides the ordinary measure of human fallibility, implies a total misconception of the conditions of the struggle," while a more recent study concluded, "*The Times* made a fool of itself over the American Civil War."[43] President Lincoln showed considerable respect when William Howard Russell, the newspaper's star foreign correspondent, was first introduced to him.[44] "The London *Times* is one of the greatest powers in the world," said Lincoln. "In fact, I don't know anything which has much more power, except perhaps the Mississippi. I am glad to know you as its minister." Further cajoleries from the president left Russell "agreeably impressed with his shrewdness, humour, and natural sagacity," and the following day, he was invited to attend the first state dinner in Lincoln's White House, the other guests being cabinet members and their families.[45]

Shortly after this, Russell began touring the country, starting in the south. His reports were objective, sometimes complimentary, yet never disguised his hatred of slavery or his amazement at the way it warped southern society. Russell's dispatches took nearly a fortnight to reach Darwin's breakfast table and another to rebound across the Atlantic to the White House.[46] So Darwin and (some days later) Lincoln would both have memories stirred by Russell's description of a negro being auctioned in Alabama, which deeply affected Russell despite his declaration that he was "neither a sentimentalist nor Black Republican, nor negro worshipper." His closing line showed his contempt for polygenism: "There was no sophistry which could persuade me the man was not a man—he was, indeed, by no means my brother, but assuredly he was a fellow creature." Two weeks later, Russell wrote in his diary about southern "gentlemen . . . who indulge in ingenious hypotheses to comfort the consciences of the anthropo-proprietors. The negro skull won't hold as many ounces of shot as the white man. Potent proof that the white man has a right to sell and to own the creature!"[47]

Lincoln could only be pleased while Russell filed such reports for British readers, although Darwin possessed his "own foreign correspondent." Because Gray's letters were also greatly valued for their scientific content and were passed among Darwin, Hooker, Lyell, and Francis Boott, many went missing, and none have survived that Darwin saw between July 1860 and August 1861, during which time Darwin wrote at least seventeen letters to Gray.

Hooker's letters to Gray entirely lacked the sympathy normally expressed by Darwin, and Gray was often annoyed by reports in or reprinted from British newspapers.[48] Writing to Darwin on 6 May 1861, Gray must have expressed some displeasure about the lack of British support among other things, and Darwin's belated reply apparently responded point by point but also made clear what he considered the most vital issue.

> But I suppose you are all too overwhelmed with public affairs to care for science. I never knew the newspapers so profoundly interesting. N. America does not do England justice: I have not seen or heard of a soul who is not with the North. Some few, & I am one, even wish to God, though at the loss of millions of lives, that the North would proclaim a crusade against Slavery. In the long run, a million horrid deaths would be amply repaid in the cause of humanity. What wonderful times we live in. Massachusetts seems to show noble enthusiasm. Great God how I should like to see that greatest curse on Earth Slavery abolished.[49]

Five days after Darwin first raised the issue of slavery—before Gray even received that letter—Gray, too, mentioned slavery for the first time, in a touchy letter to Hooker: "I am no *abolitionist*, but if the rebels & scoundrels persevere, I go for carrying the war so far as to liberate every negro, tho' what we are to do with this population I see not." Hooker, perhaps unimpressed that Gray seemed to view emancipation as an expedient rather than a moral imperative, condescendingly sought to terminate the discussion: "I think the less said the sooner mended about the war & your *slightly animated!* description of John Bull's opinions & notions. A nation at war is no longer in its senses; however just the cause."[50]

To another fellow naturalist in America less pro-Union than himself, Gray wrote, "Peace is not worth having till the rebellion, based on a plot formed years ago, is put down. . . . If you think me belligerent, I am nothing to Agassiz."[51] Biographer Edward Lurie comments that Agassiz "advocated the Union cause with an uncompromising patriotism," citing his very public application for American citizenship and his letters to friends in England "chiding them for the policy of their country toward the United States"—very like Gray in that regard.[52] This was commendable considering Agassiz's previously close relations with southern colleagues, but he had more important ties with the influential, wealthy, and solidly pro-Union Bostonians who lavishly funded his museum. Moreover, Agassiz was part of a clique of leading scientists who jokingly nicknamed themselves the

"Lazzaroni" (lepers in Naples, i.e., outcasts) and included high-ranking government officials and military officers such as Alexander Dallas Bache of the Coastal Survey and Captain Charles Henry Davis of the Nautical Almanac office. Yet, Agassiz's patriotism dampened when it conflicted with his professional activities. After catching a student reading a newspaper in the museum, Agassiz threatened to ban such publications from the building, and another student recorded in his diary how cross Agassiz became when the same student joined the army: "If they knew in Boston how greedy Prof is of our time . . . and actually unpatriotic, it would kill the museum."[53] Obviously, Gray must not have known any of this when he praised Agassiz's support for the war.

Darwin wrote that he sympathized with Gray's insistence that the war was necessary: "After carefully reading Olmsted's last Book I never doubted the North would conquer the South." Yet, Darwin had other doubts: "But then what is to follow? From Olmsted & Russell's letters in *Times*, I cannot believe that the South would ever have fellow-feeling enough with the North to allow of government in common. Could the North endure a Southern President?"[54] Darwin could see that bitterness was an obstacle to re-union—without quite grasping the lesson of Lincoln's election: that the south had lost its controlling influence on presidential elections.

Correspondent Russell, although glad to condemn slavery, was also impressed by the growing evidence that the Confederacy was determined—and possibly able—to maintain its independence, while his editors back in London were increasingly confident about expressing their pro-Confederate opinion—infuriating Gray—that the divided United States could never be rejoined.[55] While Gray was willing, if the rebels "persevered," to see slaves freed, Darwin saw no point in the war if it did not end slavery. "The whole affair is a great misfortune in the progress of the World," Darwin told Gray, "but I should not regret it so much, if I could persuade myself that Slavery would be annihilated. But your president does not even mention the word in his Address." Clearly, Darwin had read carefully the reports of Lincoln's address to the special session of Congress on 4 July and was disappointed—as were American abolitionists—that Lincoln made no reference to slavery.[56] And yet, it was understandable that Lincoln, to avoid George III's mistakes, did not wish to broaden the conflict beyond the illegality of secession or undermine the Unionists of the Border States by taking any precipitous action against slavery.

Whether Darwin grasped this intellectually, on gut level he was dissatisfied. "I sometimes wish the contest to grow so desperate, that the north would be led to declare freedom as a diversion against the Enemy," he told Gray, anticipating events. Darwin was also correct that ending slavery might itself cause long-term trauma: "In 50 or 100 years your posterity would bless the act." Darwin could not know how prescient he was on both points. "But Heaven knows why I trouble you with my speculations; I ought to stick to Orchids."

Darwin wrote these speculations on the very day Lincoln's invasion force was defeated at Bull Run, extinguishing hope that the war would end quickly. Russell of the *Times* described the defeat in an unsparing report that, when it bounced back to America, angered Northerners intensely. As one historian expresses it, "Unhappily Russell's dispatches were unendurable mostly because they appeared in *The Times*."[57]

Lincoln had more to worry about than Russell's dispatches. As he now prepared for a long war, the potential military usefulness of new weapons grew in his estimation. The most useful innovations were exactly those that could only be developed on a large scale, in a reasonable time, at minimal cost, and with the expectation of inflicting the greatest damage on the enemy. The inventor in Lincoln now went back over some of the weapons projects that military "experts" had so far resisted. And he also began to consider a highly dangerous weapon that might easily backfire. Yet Lincoln was still eighteen months away from implementing the idea that already exercised the minds of most abolitionists, including one in England: to "declare freedom as a diversion against the enemy."

Inventions for a Long War

A fter the debacle at Bull Run in July 1861, Lincoln placed General George McClellan in charge of reorganizing the swelling army of volunteers, but he also pursued more vigorously the development of new weapons of war. Four days after Bull Run, Thaddeus Lowe, the balloonist recommended by Professor Joseph Henry, informed Lincoln that although he had just returned from making an important reconnaissance of rebel forces following the battle, the army still had not commissioned him to develop a useful balloon service. Lincoln wrote a note for Lowe on 25 July: "Will Lieut. Gen. Scott please see Professor Lowe once more about his balloon?" The president may even have escorted Lowe to see the general. Soon Lowe obtained a government contract to develop an "air corps" of seven balloons, which performed valuable service in several battles in 1862. By 1863, Lowe gave up the effort when the army failed to commission or fund him properly.[1]

To help Lincoln conquer not only the air but also the sea, in September 1861 Brutus de Villeroi, an immigrant inventor in Philadelphia, described in a long letter his experiments with a submarine whose crew could remain submerged for up to three hours while also sallying through an airlock to carry out reconnaissance or plant explosives on the keels of enemy ships. Lincoln personally endorsed the letter to the Navy Department, whose officials ordered a larger model for testing. Just over a year later and after numerous delays, one test of the *Alligator* took place in the presence of President Lincoln, Assistant Secretary of the Navy Gustavus V. Fox, General Benjamin F. Butler, and Professor Eben Horsford, the last of whom actually descended in the vessel and remained submerged for over an hour. All were described as being "perfectly satisfied." Although Lincoln apparently recommended another submarine proposal to navy experts early in 1862, they decided the air supply was insufficient and the probable speed too slow. In April 1862, Villeroi grew so disgusted over the treatment of his project that he washed his hands of the whole business, and a year later, the *Alligator* sank in a heavy gale while under tow.[2]

Another tragedy connected with underwater technology was the death in October 1863 of one of the best scientists in the navy, Captain Edward B. Hunt, who had delivered many papers before the A A A S, including the one on future military technology read in the presence of Stephen A. Douglas. Hunt had argued for the development of numerous weapons, including asphyxiating shells, and while testing an artillery battery that could be fired underwater, Hunt was suffocated by escaping gases and killed by falling into the hold of the test vessel.[3] Hunt's brother was a former governor of New York, so Lincoln would certainly have heard of this loss to science, and another who probably mourned that loss was Charles Darwin. Two months before Hunt's death, Darwin had received from him a scientific paper arguing that Florida's coral reefs were at least 5.4 million years old.[4]

Hunt had also advocated the "steam gun," and early in September 1861, some politically influential Bostonians endorsed a design for one, which they sent first to General James W. Ripley and then, when he showed no interest, to the president. Impressed or not, Lincoln knew better than to offend the project's distinguished backers and asked the engineer in chief of the navy to examine the proposal. When he declared the concept unfeasible, Lincoln let the matter drop.[5]

Returning to more conventional weapons, Lincoln scrutinized a breech-loading cannon in September 1861 and ordered twenty into service by November. On 5 September, Lincoln endorsed a deal belatedly arranged by Secretary of War Simon Cameron for the overseas purchase of a hundred thousand rifled muskets with percussion-cap firing: the guns were surplus weapons of European governments modernizing their arsenals with breechloaders. Two days later, Lincoln interviewed a Philadelphia merchant about arranging further European purchases.[6]

On the evening of 15 September, Captain John A. Dahlgren took Lincoln to watch tests of an "electro-mercury light" recently developed by a British chemist. Dahlgren was interested in its potential for signaling or illumination for night fighting.[7] Lincoln also made almost daily rounds of the military camps surrounding Washington to see how the equipping and training of the Army of the Potomac progressed. On 20 September, the New York Times reported that "the President, Secretaries Cameron and Seward, the Prince de Joinville and suite, Private Secretary Nicolay, Gen. McClellan and Staff, Gen. Mansfield and Staff, and a large number of ladies and gentlemen" attended a review of Colonel Hiram Berdan's regiment of sharpshooters: "Something like four hundred shots were fired at a distance of 630 yards."[8]

Berdan, a New York engineer whose avocation was rifle marksmanship, had recruited this specialist corps of skirmishers by advertising for men skilled with fine weapons and promising to outfit them with the single-shot Sharps rifle, a breechloader that had been on the market since the mid-1850s. Unfortunately, General Ripley refused to purchase the new weapons and instead issued old Springfield muskets. At the very least, Lincoln must have collaborated in arranging the high-profile visit by this prestigious delegation, which was a deliberate coup. Lincoln himself fired a few rounds, commenting, "Boys, this reminds me of old-time shooting!"—which brought a cheer from the troops. Lincoln told the colonel to come see him the following day so he could write out an order for the breechloaders. After various further delays and a near-mutiny by the troops themselves, eventually the unit was properly equipped and went on to kill more Confederates than any other regiment in the Union army.[9]

In the month of October alone, Lincoln observed the ascension of another balloonist on the fourth, personally inspected a new design for a gun carriage on the fifth (dropping it when other experts pointed out shortcomings), directed General Ripley to order twenty-five thousand Marsh breechloaders on the fourteenth, again walked out to Treasury Park with an inventor to test his new type of bullet on the twenty-fifth, and on the twenty-sixth invited General McClellan to join him and a group of military and scientific men for a demonstration of a battery of repeating guns on wheels—and when McClellan was unable to attend, Lincoln went without him and took the responsibility by the end of the day to order ten batteries at $1,300 apiece.[10]

In November, an inventor from New Hampshire, failing to interest General Ripley in his new breech-loading cannon, arranged an audience with Lincoln, who spent nearly an hour going over the plans. Promising to arrange a test if the inventor's state governor would endorse him, Lincoln soon received the letter and endorsed it with a request that the War Department send someone to New Hampshire to test the weapon. However, General Ripley found ways to delay the inspection and then bury the report, so nothing came of Lincoln's intervention. Shortly afterward, Lincoln managed to get McClellan to express a desire for more machine guns, so in December, Lincoln ordered Ripley to purchase fifty of them; and a week later, again by Lincoln's direct intervention, Ripley finally ordered ten thousand Spencer repeating rifles.[11]

Apart from whittling a temporary gun sight, Lincoln played no role in actually designing new weapons. However, the perception that he valued new technology encouraged inventors to bring forward their ideas despite General Ripley's obstructive reputation. Most new regiments were provided with better weapons than they would otherwise have had simply because Lincoln overruled objections to the purchases abroad.[12] Lincoln's personal attention to inventors and growing resistance to the opinions of his chief of ordnance and his secretary of war meant that by the end of 1861, thirty-seven thousand American-made breech-loading rifles, single-shot or repeating and using both paper and metallic cartridges, were on order. According to historian James M. McPherson, "These guns turned out to be the best shoulder weapons of the war. The carbines gave Union cavalry a significant advantage in the last fifteen months of the war. Infantry regiments armed with the Spencer rifles gained a fearsome reputation among enemy units." What Robert V. Bruce, the best authority on Lincoln's interest in weapons, says of the entire period of the war was actually true by the end of the first year: "During the Civil War, the nearest thing to a research and development agency was the President himself."[13]

Various people, whether inspired or appalled by Lincoln's efforts and Ripley's stubbornness, hoped to place research and development on a more professional level. At the end of 1861, Secretary of the Navy Gideon Welles wrote out instructions for a "Naval Examining Board" that would make recommendations about inventions on the basis that money could not "be applied to any experimental purpose but only for objects of undoubted utility." This board, though somewhat a failure in itself, marked an important preliminary step in the development of science in America.[14] Welles, already pressured by Congress about costs and corrupt contractors, was disturbed about the time Dahlgren spent dealing with increasingly hare-brained inventors. Also, the U.S. Navy seemed particularly backward at that moment because of two simultaneous and related crises, both involving a new technology in which Lincoln took a particular interest: ironclads.

Another of George III's blunders that Lincoln tried to avoid was allowing the colonial rebels to obtain vital supplies of arms from abroad. Both the North and the South knew that international trade was a crucial issue: Lincoln's navy must close or blockade Southern ports, and the South must prevent such an effort from succeeding. The Confederacy was fortunate that its Secretary of Navy, Stephen R. Mallory, a Floridian who previously chaired the Senate's naval affairs committee, recognized immediately that the South lacked the resources to challenge the Union navy in any conventional way.

Exactly when President Lincoln first learned that the Confederate navy was building an ironclad warship is unknown, but neither the technology nor the South's wish to build such a vessel was any surprise. Despite his patent for a device to aid navigation, Lincoln knew even less about naval armaments than he did about land armaments, which was still a great deal more than most people. Although Lincoln allegedly joked once, "I do think I knew the difference between the bow of a ship and her stern, and I don't believe Secretary Welles did," he admired the administrative ability of Welles, who had some prior experience of the Navy Department, if less than the Confederacy's Mallory.[15] Moreover, Welles was a Connecticut Yankee who had been a canny journalist—and soon he had an important scoop for Lincoln. On 8 May, only three weeks after Confederate forces seized the naval yard in Norfolk, Virginia, Mallory had written to the Confederate Congress urging the immediate construction of an ironclad that he believed could destroy the Union's wooden fleet. Somehow, this document came into Welles's possession.[16]

As a congressman, Lincoln had once sponsored a petition from a Baltimore inventor who since 1814 had been seeking support for a steam warship with sloping armored sides, but nothing came of it at the time.[17] Early in 1861, *Scientific*

American regretted that "the Secretary of the Navy has not paid attention" to the fact that while the United States did not have "a single first class war steamer," the French and British were building "iron-cased war wolves."[18] A month later, *Harper's Weekly* offered an illustrated account of the first ocean-going ironclad warships built by the French and British in 1859 and 1860, respectively. In the same week, Captain Dahlgren urged the Senate Committee on Naval Affairs to order the "the construction of some *armored* Gun Boats" as well as "at least the one heavy frigate [which] may cost 1¾ to 2 millions which is the estimated expense of the English Plated-frigate [HMS] *Warrior*, just launched." Dahlgren urged haste: it would take at least two years "to get a ship ready for service."[19] Dahlgren probably expressed these views to Lincoln when, a few months later, he became the new president's favorite weapons adviser.

In the month following Mallory's letter, further information reached Welles regarding the Confederates' efforts to raise a ship, the USS *Merrimack*, which had been only half-destroyed when retreating federals abandoned Norfolk, Virginia, to the rebels. Eventually this ship (rechristened CSS *Virginia* but still known in most histories as the *Merrimack*) was to be rebuilt above the waterline with sloping sides covered with iron plates—a process slowed by the Confederates' relative lack of iron foundries.

Meanwhile, early in the summer of 1861, Lincoln had already met with James B. Eads, an engineer and inventor from St. Louis, Missouri, who had ideas for an ironclad vessel to help the Union campaign along the Mississippi River. Eads brought a model to the president, "and they sat down together and discussed Western steamboats and flatboats and gun-boats, and they turned the thing inside out," wrote Lincoln's secretary William O. Stoddard. "It is the first model of a 'tin-clad' gunboat, . . . and the President has had more to do than most men are aware of with the beginnings of the Mississippi flotilla."[20] Eads had previously met obstructions as Welles sought to shift responsibility for river operations to the War Department, but some time after showing Lincoln his model, Eads signed a contract with the navy to build eight ironclad gunboats for use in the river war in the west.[21] Two years later, Eads sent Lincoln a photograph of the USS *St. Louis*, which Eads's accompanying letter called "the first armored vessel against which the *fire of a hostile battery* was directed on this continent; and . . . the first iron clad that *ever engaged* a *naval force in the world*" (original emphasis). Eads presented the picture, "assured that your identification with the interesting incidents of her history would make it acceptable."[22]

Reacting to Mallory's effort to clad the *Merrimack* with iron, Welles and assistant secretary Fox consulted with various department heads about building ironclads. "All were skeptical," according to Welles's biographer, so Welles decided to wait until Congress met in July, when he drafted a bill to approve not only an "ironclad board" to examine designs but also appropriations for constructing three experimental vessels.[23] Both houses approved, and Lincoln signed the bill on 4 August 1861. It is inconceivable that Welles arranged all this without Lincoln's prior approval.

To lobby the bill through committee, Welles had employed an old Connecticut friend, businessman Cornelius S. Bushnell, who now submitted one of the seventeen design proposals examined by the Ironclad Board. After the board criticized it, Bushnell contacted naval engineer John Ericsson, who showed him a model of an iron-hulled vessel he had designed five years earlier. Bushnell perceived the design's great virtues and began promoting it instead of his own. Bushnell's lobbyist instincts drove him along an indirect route back to the Ironclad Board via Welles, two New York iron contractors, Secretary of State William H. Seward, and President Lincoln.[24] Ericsson also wrote to Lincoln, assuring him he could construct a "vessel for the destruction of the rebel fleet at Norfolk," although it is not certain Lincoln ever saw this letter.[25] Bushnell himself explained Ericsson's proposal to Lincoln, who "was at once greatly pleased with the simplicity of the plan" and probably learned also that Ericsson's differences in the past with the Navy Department might cause prejudice against him and his revolutionary design. Backed up by information from Ericsson and the iron manufacturers, Bushnell was confident the vessel could be built within ninety days, far less time than other designs required. Lincoln knew that time was becoming precious as intelligence filtered in regarding the Confederates' progress with converting the *Merrimack*. According to Bushnell, the president "agreed to accompany us to the Navy Department . . . the following day, and aid us as best he could."[26]

Lincoln was not competent to judge any technical issues but probably feared the experts' reluctance to take a reasonable risk on something so radical. Bushnell recalled that the president "was on hand promptly at 11 o'clock" at the meeting, where all present "were surprised at the novelty of the plan." Some advised trying it; others ridiculed it. The conference ended with Lincoln's remark, "All I have to say is what the girl said when she put her foot into the stocking, 'It strikes me there's something in it.'" Lincoln avoided any pretense of expertise or any sign of giving an order, but his evident interest meant Ericsson's design could not be easily dismissed.[27]

Eventually, approval was given, and the USS *Monitor*'s delivery was contracted for no later than 12 January 1862, whereupon it was to head for Norfolk to sink what little there was of a Confederate fleet there and, in particular, to finish the job only half done before: the destruction of the *Merrimack*, which Northern experts assumed would still be in dry dock.[28] When the Confederates proved more efficient than expected, it was not only the rebel ironclad that demonstrated that the U.S. Navy was woefully behind times. Six weeks before the *Monitor* was scheduled for completion, a more severe threat arose—and not from the South but from Britain.

When Gray did not reply for over a month to his letter of 21 July, Darwin may have feared he had complained too stridently about Lincoln's inaction regarding slavery. The reply did finally arrive in mid-September, and Darwin was pleased not only by Gray's still friendly tone but even more by his reference to the respected head of the Smithsonian, Joseph Henry. In an earlier letter, Darwin had been unable to resist mentioning that John Stuart Mill had praised the inductive logic of *The Origin*, and Gray now responded, "What you say of *Mill* well accords with what Prof. Henry of Smithsonian Inst. says of your investigations, your method, &c, and he is the best judge of the logic of investigation I know of."[29]

Gray's letter, of which only one page survives, must have reflected on events following Bull Run. Darwin replied at length, addressing numerous points presumably brought up by Gray's "very long & interesting letter, political & scientific."

> I agree with much of what you say & I hope to God we English are utterly wrong in doubting (1) whether the N. can conquer the S. (2) whether the N. has many friends in the South & (3) whether your noble men of Massachusetts are right in transferring your own good feelings to the men of Washington. Again I say I hope to God we are wrong in doubting on these points. It is number (3) which alone causes England not to be enthusiastic with you. What it may be in Lancashire I know not, but in S. England cotton has nothing whatever to do with our doubts. If abolition does follow with your victory, the whole world will look brighter in my eyes & in many eyes. It would be a great gain even to stop the spread of Slavery into the Territories: if that be possible without abolition, which I should have doubted. You ought not to wonder so much at England's coldness, when you recollect at the commencement of the war how many propositions were made to get things back to the old state with the old line of Latitude. But enough of this: all I can say is that Massachusetts & the adjoining States have the full sympathy of every good man whom I see; & this sympathy would be extended to whole Federal states, if we could be persuaded that your feelings were at all common to them. But enough of this. It is out of my line, though I read every word of news & formerly well studied Olmsted.[30]

Hoping to God that "we English are utterly wrong," Darwin deferred to Gray's more direct understanding, while also expressing disagreement and the depth of his interest. Darwin was right that, were the war to end tomorrow, the Southern states could return to the Union with slavery still intact. Having thought about it seriously, Darwin wondered if a return to the status quo ante bellum would mean the Republicans could even achieve their narrower goal of preventing the extension of slavery.

Gray's letter apparently alluded to the notion widespread in America that Britain was likely to support Southern independence in order to gain unfettered access to the cotton crop so vital to the wealth of Lancashire mill owners. While Darwin admitted uncertainty about attitudes in Lancashire, he felt confident that

England in general was not motivated by greed. Confederates certainly hoped the British would be driven by their hunger for cotton into recognizing their country and opening direct trade, with profits from cotton sales used to purchase arms for the rebel armies. Lincoln was probably as aware as most Southerners that during the American Revolution, the colonists' ability to purchase French arms had been crucial to the Revolution's success—and that Robert E. Lee's great-uncle Arthur Lee had been the colonies' first agent for negotiating arms deals with Pierre-Augustin Beaumarchais.[31]

Lincoln's method for interdicting Confederate trade has received much criticism, which originated during cabinet infighting over which policy to follow. Those whose advice Lincoln did not heed (especially Welles) later contended that Lincoln had made a grave mistake.[32] In fact, Lincoln's approach to the problem was calculating and subtle.

First, Lincoln collected data by asking Welles "what amount of Naval force you could at once place at the control of the Revenue service. And also, whether at some distance of time you could so place an additional force; and how much? and at what time."[33] Determining that there were far too few ships for any *effective* control in the *near* future, Lincoln saw that his two main options could not be differentiated solely on the basis of likely effectiveness. Congress could pass laws closing Southern ports, but the Confederates would not obey them, and Lincoln had too few ships to implement the laws. Alternatively, Lincoln as commander-in-chief could declare a blockade, but that was internationally recognized as act of war that would technically elevate to the status of "foreign enemy" the people Lincoln always maintained were U.S. citizens in rebellion—and he also lacked the force to effect an offshore blockade. Through Secretary of State Seward, Lincoln obtained the opinion of the British ambassador, Lord Lyons, that Britain was more likely to respect an international blockade than any domestic legislation (as required for a port closure) that failed to acknowledge that an actual war existed.[34]

"The President said we could not afford to have two wars on our hands at once," Welles recalled, but the navy secretary remained bitter about this decision for years, blaming Seward and arguing that the Proclamation of a Blockade on 19 April was the main cause for Britain's decision, three days after learning of the blockade, to issue a Proclamation of Neutrality that acknowledged the Confederacy as a "belligerent" and might be the first step toward full diplomatic recognition.[35] But Welles was wrong, and Lincoln and Seward were right: avoiding war with Britain outweighed all issues of trade, the status of the conflict as "war" or "insurrection," the legitimacy of the Confederacy, and even the risk of foreign recognition of the Confederacy.

Lincoln's carefully worded blockade proclamation "deemed it advisable to set on foot a blockade of the ports within the States aforesaid, in pursuance of the laws of the United States and of the law of nations in such case provided."[36] "To set on foot" was a quiet admission that the blockade could not immediately be "effective." The cleverness of this move is that the proclamation gave the appearance of strong action but would not reduce the flow of cotton for a long time, thus postponing the moment when Britain would feel the stress of a cotton shortage. Lincoln was aware that as that stress grew, the British cabinet would feel more inclined to make some intervention, either to reopen trade with the South by force or at least demand a right to intervene as a mediator. Lincoln wanted neither and was buying crucial time.

Congressman Thaddeus Stevens chided Lincoln for issuing a proclamation under international law that in effect recognized the Confederacy. "I don't know anything about the law of nations," Lincoln replied. "I'm a good enough lawyer in a western law court, but we don't practice the law of nations up there, and I supposed Seward knew all about it, and I left it to him. But it's done now and can't be helped, so we must get along as well as we can."[37] This combination of self-deprecation, shifting blame or credit to Seward, avoiding a genuine explanation, and joking at the expense of the humorless Stevens, is pure Lincoln. What remains unknown is whether Lincoln's intelligent analysis foresaw either of two actions by the Confederate government that followed closely upon the blockade decision. One was Jefferson Davis's announcement that he would issue letters of marque so that the virtually nonexistent Confederate navy could be supplemented with privateers. Lincoln promptly responded that the so-called privateers would be considered pirates, liable to hanging. The news of the blockade, the privateers, and Lincoln's promise to hang them reached London together and only shortly after the news of Fort Sumter arrived. The British government had to consider its position in view of what was now an actual war. The privateer issue alone was sufficient to force the decision that, as historian Stuart Anderson explains, "since only a belligerent could legally send privateers to sea, Great Britain either had to recognize the South as a belligerent or treat Southern privateers as pirates."[38] Consequently, on 13 May, the British government was forced, more by Davis than Lincoln, to issue the Queen's Proclamation of Neutrality acknowledging the belligerent status of both sides.

Many Americans—including Asa Gray—were offended that the British government had gone so far. What Lincoln and Seward feared and Davis hoped was that the British might take the next step and fully recognize the Confederate government, receiving its envoys publicly and according them diplomatic status. But the British had done what they had to do and went no further, for the moment.

The second action by the Confederates was intended to hasten the involvement of Britain and France. Grasping that Lincoln's "set-on-foot" blockade would not in the short term impede cotton exportation, the Confederates decided to impede it themselves: the sooner the Europeans felt the pinch, the sooner they would take steps to break the blockade. By August, cotton merchants in the major Southern ports, prohibited from exporting their goods, were refusing to receive further consignments from the interior. Thus, it was the South rather than the North that created the shortage of cotton in the mills in Europe. The South had blundered into a step it would hugely regret and struggle to reverse a few months later.[39]

The men of Lancashire had little reason to blame Lincoln for the shortage of cotton when it finally occurred. And as Darwin had told Gray—before that shortage had yet developed—"cotton has nothing whatever to do with our doubts."

The Trent *Affair: A Chemistry Problem*

Asa Gray's letter dated 9 November 1861 dealt mainly with botanical matters but closed with optimistic hopes about Captain Samuel F. du Pont's naval expedition to capture Port Royal on the coast of South Carolina. At the time, Gray could not know that the expedition had already proved successful or that on the previous day an entirely separate naval action would have results that were potentially disastrous. Darwin's reply on 11 December began (after thanks for previous letters): "What a thing it is, that when you receive this we may be at war, & we two be bound, as good patriots, to hate each other, though I shall find this hating you very hard work."[1]

On 27 November, the day after Gray's letter had arrived, the London newspapers broke the news of "The *Trent* Affair"—which brought Britain and America closer to war than they had been since the Queen's Proclamation in May had recognized the South as a "belligerent."[2] Darwin could soon learn all the background in the *Times*. Following the Queen's Proclamation, the three Confederate envoys then in Europe hoped they would soon be accorded full diplomatic recognition and could begin coordinating plans with Britain for formal trade agreements and a speedy breaking of Lincoln's blockade. When none of that happened, the Confederate government replaced the failed envoys with two possessing greater status and experience, James M. Mason and John Slidell.

These were prestige appointments and well publicized. Word leaked—or was planted—that the new envoys would run the blockade from Charleston, South Carolina, aboard a Confederate warship, CSS *Nashville*, but for various reasons, they used other vessels. Eventually, the envoys reached Havana, where they planned to depart on the next British packet on 7 November.

While Mason and Slidell were privately entertained by the diplomatic corps in Cuba, a U.S. warship, the *San Jacinto*, arrived off the coast. Ordered to return from a station on the African coast in order to participate in the attack on Port Royal (about which Asa Gray had boasted to Darwin), the *San Jacinto*'s captain, Charles Wilkes, on reaching Cuba, heard about the hunt for the envoys and eventually discovered not only the date of their planned departure but also which vessel they would use, the *Trent*. Gray and Darwin probably recognized Wilkes's name when it appeared in the newspapers, for he had formerly commanded an American version of the *Beagle* voyage, the United States Exploration Expedition.

Wilkes waylaid the *Trent* in international waters and sent a boarding party to search for Confederate dispatches (which, as "contraband," would give Wilkes legal justification, he hoped). No dispatches were found (though they were there), but the two envoys and their secretaries were removed from the *Trent* before it was allowed to continue its voyage to Britain. By 15 November, Wilkes had conveyed the captives to the United States, but the British government, although aware that the U.S. Navy had hoped to capture the envoys, did not learn of their seizure from a British vessel until 27 November.

"How curious it is," Darwin continued in his 11 December letter to Gray, "to see two countries, just like two angry & silly men, taking so opposite a view of the same transaction! So far as I can see we rest entirely on Wilkes' acting as Judge." Darwin had obviously read his *Times* carefully. One passenger from the *Trent* reported that the officer commanding the boarding party had been heard to say that Wilkes was not acting under any specific orders, but the British newspapers emphasized that, according to the British government, Wilkes had not followed the correct procedure: to make any seizures from a neutral ship, he should have taken the vessel as a "prize" to some port where a court could decide the fate of the ship, its crew, passengers, cargo, and mails. Wilkes had instead acted as his own judge, probably concluding that procedures mattered less than capturing Mason and Slidell with minimal inconvenience to the *Trent*'s other passengers.

The news caused a storm in Britain. An emergency cabinet meeting determined that Wilkes had violated international law, and on 30 November, a letter was drafted and sent to the British ambassador in Washington for presentation to the American government. Up until 2 December, the *Times* had dismissed the report that Wilkes was not acting under orders and blamed the warmongering Secretary of State William H. Seward for causing this crisis. The contents of the official letter were not yet published, but judging from the reports that the British government had ordered ten thousand troops to be sent to Canada, Darwin guessed correctly that the letter was an ultimatum that the United States either release the envoys or accept war.

It would probably take a month before Britain would know the American response to the ultimatum, but there was naturally hope that Wilkes's superiors had by now recognized his blunder and released the envoys. Darwin held off replying to Gray's letter.

On 4 December, Darwin could read in the *Times* William Howard Russell's dispatch (written on 19 November) describing the jubilation that swept through America at the news of the envoys' capture.[3] In another dispatch printed on 10 December, Russell described the hysterical joy caused by this Union "victory" in the face of so many Union defeats. Two traitors had been captured, the British Lion's tail had been twisted, and Wilkes was the hero of the hour. Russell interviewed various foreign dignitaries and American officials who believed Wilkes's action violated international law, but he also saw "so much violence of spirit among the lower orders of the people . . . saturated with pride and vanity" that if Lincoln's government attempted "any honorable concession," such as releasing the prisoners, it "would prove fatal to its authors."

When young Henry Adams, the secretary and also son of the American ambassador in London, read Russell's dispatches, he wrote to his brother in America, exclaiming, "Good God, what's got into you all? What in Hell do you mean by deserting now the great principles of our fathers . . . ? You're mad, all of you."[4] Two days earlier, Darwin's similar distress caused a temporary loss of the sympathy:

> I fear there is no shadow of doubt we shall fight, if the two Southern rogues are not given up. And what a wretched thing it will be, if we fight on side of slavery. No doubt it will be said we fight to get cotton; but I fully believe that this has not entered into the motive in the least. Well, thank Heaven we private individuals, have nothing to do with so awful a responsibility. Again how curious it is that you seem to think that you can conquer the south; & I never meet a soul, even those who would most wish it, who thinks it possible, that is to conquer & retain it. I do not suppose the mass of people in your country will believe it; but I feel sure if we do go to war, it will be with the utmost reluctance by all classes, ministers of government & all. Time will show, & it is no use writing or thinking about it.[5]

Darwin could then put the matter aside and turn to the science that bonded himself and Gray, but Lincoln had no such option and had already spent nearly a month "thinking about it." When news of Wilkes's action reached Lincoln on 16 November, he made no snap decision about how to proceed. Congress was not in session, there was no sudden emergency cabinet meeting, and Russell of the *Times* recorded "reticence" at both the State Department and the British legation—while American lawyers rummaged for arguments to justify Wilkes.[6]

Sources of varying reliability reported that Lincoln immediately recognized that Wilkes was in the wrong and the envoys would have to be released.[7] That view, however, was opposed by a later and semi-official view largely accepted by historians: that Lincoln's cabinet had to talk a reluctant president into handing back the envoys.

Lincoln the lawyer probably soon discovered that international law on such matters was thoroughly muddled.[8] Considering this low degree of legal certainty and high degree of popular joy, Lincoln would have been foolish to release the envoys sooner rather than later, after the euphoria had begun to subside. Perhaps as lawyers began to quibble, the legality of Wilkes's move would become less widely assumed in America; or the British, remembering their own past sins, might not press a claim that, apart from upholding some dubious legal principle, would gain them nothing but two extra Confederate emissaries. Possibly, the British would appreciate Wilkes's sea-dog spirit, or his courtesy in letting the *Trent* finish her voyage, or that, prior to the incident, he had been patrolling the African coast alongside British squadrons trying to suppress the Atlantic slave trade. Lincoln's best course was to wait for the British response while saying nothing that might make it even more unpopular to hand over Mason and Slidell should that become necessary. If the worst happened and Britain made angry demands, Lincoln had to avoid the appearance of kowtowing while he weighed the risk of war.

Lincoln knew that the Royal Navy already possessed iron-hulled warships, such as HMS *Warrior*, while the U.S. Navy would not have even one until January, if Ericsson kept to schedule. The Royal Navy had the capability to bombard American ports more or less with impunity and to turn Lincoln's blockade of the South into Britain's blockade of the North. Yet, it seemed unlikely that Britain would resort to violence merely to maintain an uncertain maritime principle and liberate two unsavory slave owners. Lincoln soon discovered, however, that the British had other options.

Seven months earlier, Captain John A. Dahlgren had suggested to Lincoln that if the war was not brief, there could be a problem maintaining an adequate supply of niter.[9] In May 1861, Captain du Pont had learned from his cousin Henry du Pont that the family's gunpowder company—the largest supplier to the Union army—possessed only six months' supply of niter, imported from British India. Speculators in Boston and New York were buying up stocks hoping for large profits as prices rose. This information was passed along until the army, possessing 3.8 million pounds of niter accumulated during the Mexican-American War, decided there was no cause for alarm (even though that degradable material was a dozen years old), and the matter was dropped.[10]

Bull Run changed everything: the price of niter began increasing rapidly in October, and this time, Captain du Pont raised the issue with Assistant Secretary of the Navy Gustavus V. Fox, a close adviser of the president.[11] Fox conferred with Lincoln, and action was taken far above the level of ordnance chiefs. Henry du Pont was summoned for a meeting on 30 October with both Secretary of the War Simon Cameron and Seward. They decided to send Lammot du Pont, Henry's thirty-year-old nephew, to London urgently to purchase vast quantities of niter, avoiding suspicions (and higher prices) by pretending not to be purchasing for the U.S. government.[12] Seward now became Lammot's high-level minder and no doubt kept Lincoln fully informed. Within two days, Lammot had a passport, and he arrived in London on 17 November. This was ten days before London learned about the seizure of Mason and Slidell, by which time Americans had already been celebrating for twelve days.[13]

While Southerners joyfully assumed the "*Trent* Affair" would at last bring Britain into the war, Bostonians held a public banquet on 28 November to honor Captain Wilkes, and Lincoln could read the *New York Times*' paraphrase of Wilkes's speech asserting the legality of his action by declaring that "bearers of dispatches were the very embodiment of contraband."[14] Lincoln no doubt dismissed Wilkes's wishful thinking and felt appalled by Wilkes's naive description of the South as a "belligerent"—exactly what Lincoln's government formally denied. Lincoln probably enjoyed the rest of the article even less, for it quoted two prominent Massachusetts judges proclaiming that international law was on America's side—which Lincoln knew was doubtful at best. Later that day, Lincoln held a previously scheduled cabinet meeting, but what had not been scheduled were the two letters sent out the following day, 30 November, by Seward and Secretary of the Navy Gideon Welles.[15]

During the previous fortnight, while others wined and dined the heroic Wilkes, Lincoln had made no public comment, Welles had given no official reaction to Wilkes's behavior, and Seward had offered no explanation to the British government. Now, while Lincoln remained mute, Welles sent Wilkes a congratulatory letter (swiftly leaked to the press) praising the officer's "intelligence, ability, decision, and firmness" and declaring that his conduct "has the emphatic approval of this department" but adding a firm warning to Wilkes that his action "must not be permitted to constitute a precedent hereafter for [handling British] infraction of neutral obligations."[16]

The letter sounded nothing like an attempt to appease Britain, yet the British cabinet might note that "department" approval was not government approval and that the ambiguous "warning" at least implied there had been no prior authorization for Wilkes's action—the very point also conveyed to the British through a letter Seward now sent to his ambassador in London. When that official message reached London two weeks later, it caused great relief. But, of course, the day that Seward wrote his official letter, 30 November, was the same day the British government had dispatched to Washington its letter, expressing the hope that Wilkes had acted without authorization but nevertheless containing an ultimatum: whether or not Wilkes acted alone, if the envoys were not released now, it would mean war.

While those two letters were passing each other on the Atlantic, Lincoln faced the problem that Congress would reassemble on 2 December. He was obliged to submit a written address about current affairs, and senators and congressmen might exacerbate the situation in their rush to place their praise for Wilkes on the record, especially when they saw that the president's wide-ranging address made absolutely no reference to the *Trent* Affair. But instead of a free-for-all of representatives outdoing each other's panegyrics, with Democrats leading the way in order to flush out the mysteriously silent president, one Republican congressman immediately proposed a moderately worded joint resolution (which, avoiding any reference to "seizure," "envoys," "contraband," "belligerents," or "international law," might have been describing an arrest on some American street), and another Republican congressman immediately suggested an appalling amendment—giving Wilkes a gold medal and calling Mason and Slidell "ambassadors." This amendment became the sole focus of debate before it was cheerfully voted down and the original resolution swiftly approved. Lincoln's possible role is suggested by the fact that the original proposer was Owen Lovejoy, later described by Lincoln as "the best friend I had in Congress," while the ludicrous amendment was moved by Sidney Edgerton, subsequently appointed by Lincoln to a judgeship in Idaho and later the governorship of Montana Territory. In the senate two days later, Republican Senator John P. Hale moved that the proposal for the joint resolution be referred to the Committee on Naval Affairs, which he chaired. The resolution did not reemerge until February, when it was "postponed indefinitely."[17]

On the day Hale buried the resolution in committee, 13 December, American newspapers contained the first information from British newspapers about London's reaction to the seizure of Mason and Slidell, which was basically furious. But Seward and Lincoln would be particularly worried by a financial report reprinted from the London *Times* of 28 November: the news of the "aggression" produced "an indescribable effect" on the London Exchange, "the market for saltpetre had been singularly affected by some recent transactions" by buyers acting for the federal government, and it was "now assumed to be likely" that the British Government would immediately prohibit the export "of such contraband of war"—perhaps including the large quantities of rifles that hitherto had been shipped to the United States under the designation "hardware."[18]

Lincoln now knew that the incensed British, without threatening war, a diplomatic rupture, or recognition of the Confederacy, could exert enormous pressure on the United States by simply preventing the departure of all that niter that Lammot du Pont had been sent to purchase.[19] It was unpleasant to contemplate the political damage to Lincoln if he was forced to release Mason and Slidell simply because the British had such control over the world's supply of niter. The hope that Lammot du Pont had already shipped his purchases before the embargo was implemented was soon dashed: immediately after the prohibition began on 30 November, Lammot must have sent a message to his uncle Henry du Pont, who informed Seward on 13 December.[20]

Lincoln and Seward recognized that unless the British lifted the prohibition, the Union could not defeat the South, let alone fight the British. They would have to comply with almost any demand the British made regarding Mason and Slidell. The hope remained that the British cabinet might swiftly lift the embargo when—any day now—it learned officially via Ambassador Adams that Wilkes's action had been unauthorized. But within two more days, further press reports made clear that the British had sent some sort of ultimatum and also that they had been further enraged when they received the reports of the celebrations for Wilkes. The *New York Times* reported on England's preparations for war: a large vessel being loaded with Armstrong guns, eighty thousand Enfield rifles and ammunition, and ten thousand troops to be sent to Canada. The same newspaper also carried a British press report: "The export of saltpetre and warlike stores was formally prohibited. It was stated that one ship with a cargo of saltpetre for America has been stopped, and that the relanding of warlike stores, already shipped, had been required."[21]

The challenge now was how to make the best of this dire situation and avoid the appearance that Lincoln's government lacked courage and unity of purpose—never easy with the touchy and ambitious egos in the administration. Cabinet members, the newspapers, and the people all needed time to be acclimated to an eventual decision without being entirely informed about its necessity. Fortunately, the month-old ecstasy about Wilkes was subsiding, while the stark threat of war with Britain was sobering.

Lincoln's old friend Senator Orville Hickman Browning was visiting him on 15 December when "Mr. Seward came in with dispatches stating that the British cabinet had decided that the arrest of Mason and Slidell was a violation of international law, and that we must apologize and restore them to the protections of the British flag." These "dispatches" were not yet official, and Browning believed the British would not do "so foolish a thing," yet he told Lincoln and Seward that if Britain "is determined to force a war upon us why so be it. We will fight her to the death."[22] Lincoln or Seward were not likely to say anything about the niter situation in front of Browning, who made no mention of it in his diary. Indeed, far from rebuking Browning's rash talk, Seward echoed it the next evening at a social event to which the London *Times* correspondent had been invited. Russell found Seward "in very good humour," pointing out to "all who were inclined to listen how terrible the effects of a war would be if Great Britain forced it on the United States. 'We will wrap the whole world in flames!' he exclaimed. 'No power so remote that she will not feel the fire of our battle and be burned by our conflagration.'" Russell was naturally alarmed—until someone told him, "That's all bugaboo talk. When Seward talks that way he means to break down. He is most dangerous and obstinate when he pretends to agree a good deal with you." The following evening, Seward found some excuse to invite Russell to dinner, where "Mr. Seward was in the best spirits, and told one or two rather long, but very pleasant, stories"—a contrast Russell considered "not intelligible."[23]

Seward was good humored because the month-long uncertainty was now over. He and Lincoln knew they had no options, and, ironically, Britain's serious threat of war made everything easier than it would have been if the British had simply trumpeted the niter prohibition. Caving in to the British so they might lift the prohibition would give the administration's opponents reason to denounce not only its incompetence in not securing adequate niter supplies in advance but also its vulnerability should Britain yank this particular leash again in the future. But the actual threat of war—which could be depicted as British opportunism during America's national crisis—simply made the British appear unreasonably belligerent and Lincoln's appeasement seem serenely sensible. Besides, a war with Britain would kill any chance of defeating the Southern rebels—and all for the sake of keeping one pair of them behind bars.

Those who at first reacted like Browning, blustering defiantly while thinking the British were bluffing, calmed down as it became clear that the British seemed prepared to resort to arms to uphold a principle. Of course, Lincoln and Seward knew that Britain had no need either to bluff or to resort to arms. By 19 December, Seward learned from Britain's ambassador, Lord Lyons, that the newspaper reports were largely accurate about his government's demands, that the government wished to avoid conflict and to believe Wilkes had acted without instructions and against traditional U.S. policy, and that he, Lyons, was privately instructed to divulge the ultimatum's contents a few days before giving official notification, allowing Seward more time to respond than the official seven-day deadline.[24]

Seward's phony blustering in front of Russell on 16 December was the beginning of a campaign to shape the public impression of the administration's decision making in order to minimize the potentially disastrous political effects of the inevitable release of the two envoys.

On 18 December, Lincoln and Seward visited the Navy Yard, whose commandant, Dahlgren, having "never seen the President or Mr. Seward more quiet or grave," understood the cause: "The British affair seems to weigh on them." While Dahlgren's visitors were tight-lipped, their message was being spread by others. On the same day, John W. Forney, a journalist close to Lincoln and called "Lincoln's dog" by the president's opponents, editorialized in his *Philadelphia Press* that war with Britain would be a disaster and that Mason and Slidell should be released. "We must yield every feeling of pride to maintain our existence."[25] The following day, the *New York Times* reported that at the previous day's cabinet meeting, it was agreed that the government "has no right to give new life to the rebellion by entering upon another and vaster quarrel, which at the same time would increase tenfold the burden upon the people of the North," while the *New York Evening Post* (whose editor, William Cullen Bryant, was a staunch supporter of Lincoln) ran an item mentioning casually that the nation's stocks of niter were "sufficient for all emergencies."[26] Seward and Lincoln, who probably supplied that information, knew otherwise. At some point, Seward must have asked Captain Dahlgren whether niter could be obtained from non-British sources, though he probably knew what the reply would be and had perhaps even received it long before 26 December when Dahlgren put the discouraging information in a letter.[27] Meanwhile, Lincoln and Seward exploited Lord Lyons's willingness to delay the formal presentation of the ultimatum so they could prepare the ground. It was probably no accident that the announcement of the envoys' release eventually fell in the week between Christmas and New Year.

On 21 December, Russell of the *Times* recorded in his diary a story related by "an old Treasury official the other day." Lincoln reportedly exclaimed, "I would sooner die than give them up!" The reply was, "Mr. President, your death would be a great loss, but the destruction of the United States would be a still more deplorable event."[28] Thus, with no reference to the facts that Wilkes acted improperly and that the niter embargo tied their hands, Lincoln and Seward were presenting the problem as a stark choice between permanent destruction of the old Union and temporary humiliation for a proud president reluctant to cave in.

On the same day, Senator Browning recorded a conversation with Lincoln, who said that "he feared trouble" with the British.[29] Lincoln told Browning he had already drafted a reply to the British demand for a swift apology and surrender of Mason and Slidell. He then read to Browning a draft letter to Lord Lyons proposing some third-party arbitration—which may at one time have made sense as a delaying tactic but no longer.[30] Nevertheless, Browning could now tell anyone who asked that the situation was grim but the president was dealing with it rationally: no rash defiance but also no backing down. Again, there was no mention of niter.

The idea of arbitration may have been proposed to Lincoln by Charles Sumner, chairman of the Senate Foreign Relations Committee, who had seen the president "almost daily and most intimately ever since the 'Trent' question has been under discussion." Sumner's own views on the *Trent* Affair were undergoing change. According to an early biographer, "sympathizing strongly with the American feeling that Captain Wilkes had won a great triumph . . . , [Sumner] was at first desirous of upholding him; but whether through the influence of Seward and Lincoln, or by reason of his own research . . . he speedily saw that this position was untenable."[31]

The day after showing the arbitration proposal to Browning, Lincoln told Sumner, "There will be no war unless England is bent upon having one." Before the crisis was resolved, Sumner wrote privately to a friend, "The President himself will apply his own mind carefully to every word of the answer, so that it will be essentially his; and he hopes for peace," and that although Sumner had earlier proposed arbitration to Lincoln, "in her present mood England will not arbitrate. . . . Seward is tranquil and confident." But after the crisis, Sumner explained to his British friend, the opposition politician John Bright, that "it was necessary that the case be decided at once. Its pendency caused a paralysis upon all our naval and military movements against the rebellion, which gave us a foretaste of the certain effect of a British war." Sumner's term "paralysis" may reflect some understanding that gunpowder could not be wasted until the British reopened the niter supply line—which would certainly not happen if war actually broke out with Britain. Whatever Lincoln told him, Sumner had—by his own account written on 24 December—already discussed with Lincoln the fact that a war with England would have the Royal Navy "sponging" American ships off the ocean and blockading Northern ports and the British government recognizing, trading with, and soon allying with the South.[32]

Meanwhile, Lincoln and Seward finally stopped stalling Lyons and accepted the formal presentation of the British government's demands on 23 December—probably a week since the two men had been fully apprised of them. Lyons's immediate report to his superiors included some remarkable perceptions:

> You will perhaps be surprised to find Mr. Seward on the side of peace.... He sees himself in a very painful dilemma. But he knows his countrymen[:] ... if he can convince them that there is a real danger of war, they may forgive him for the humiliation of yielding to England, while it would be fatal to him to be the author of a disastrous foreign war.

Lyons added that while he could not predict how Seward would eventually act, Seward wished to avoid letting "the President and Cabinet throw the whole burden on his shoulders."[33]

Many members of Congress were now dispersing for the Christmas holiday, and whatever Lincoln decided upon during their absence would become slightly old news by the time they reassembled. The problem was that no cabinet member wished to be isolated from the rest or to bear "the whole burden"—including Lincoln. He especially did not wish to give the ambitious Secretary of Treasury Salmon P. Chase an opportunity later to accuse him of ill judgment, or ignoring cabinet advice, or simply ignoring Chase's advice. It was entirely in Lincoln's interest, therefore, to continue the charade that he himself was being forced by others—almost against his will and certainly against his inclination—to hand over Mason and Slidell.

Also on 23 December, Lincoln held various conferences with Seward, Welles, Chase, and Sumner. Seward could show a letter received two days earlier from Ambassador Adams, indicating that Britain was fully prepared, however reluctantly, to go to war, which was confirmed by Sumner's letters from two sympathetic British politicians. The following day, a letter from the American ambassador in Paris emphasized French support for the British position.[34]

On Christmas Day, Lincoln convened a cabinet meeting that lasted four hours. At the end, it was decided to meet again the following day. This holdover gave the appearance that Lincoln was undecided, which is not credible. Seward led the discussion, and there is no reason to think he differed with Lincoln on essentials. Neither appears to have brought up the subjects of arbitration or niter.

Little credence should be given to an account written half a century later by Seward's son and secretary, Frederick Seward, who was not present at the two conversations between Lincoln and Seward that he recounted. Both conversations occurred after the other cabinet members had left the room and, as Seward must have described them to his son, depicted Lincoln still hoping to find a way to avoid surrendering the envoys and Seward still laboring to convince him there was no alternative.[35] Whether Seward misled his son or his son simply remembered the tale Seward was spinning for everyone, it is inconceivable that either Lincoln or Seward doubted the necessity of surrendering Mason and Slidell. It is more likely that Seward and Lincoln thought they could more easily bring the other cabinet members on board if they were allowed to believe their support was necessary to move the president in the right direction.

Welles wrote a decade later that Seward started out by taking "high and untenable ground" but then inexplicably "lost heart and courage, and [became] provokingly submissive to British exactions." Welles also suggested that Seward then joined Lincoln and Postmaster General Montgomery Blair in wishing to release the two envoys. Attorney General Edward Bates, whose diary provides the best firsthand account of the 25–26 December cabinet meetings, summarized Seward's argument that surrendering Mason and Slidell was the only way to avoid war. At some point, Sumner was invited in to read out letters recently received from two British members of Parliament, urging the release of Mason and Slidell.[36] No source indicates who invited Sumner, but Lincoln, who often conferred with Sumner, is more likely than Seward, who saw Sumner as something of a rival. Still, since everyone feared Congress's eventual reaction, having the Foreign Relations Committee chairman on board made sense; and his letters from British friends served Seward's purposes.[37]

Sumner left the 25 December meeting confident that "the immediate pending question will be settled," and that evening Lincoln told Browning that the cabinet had agreed not to divulge anything—"and there would be no war with England."[38] If Sumner and Lincoln were both expressing confidence that war would be avoided, then they, like Seward and Blair and probably Bates, accepted that the prisoners would have to be released. *Why, then, was there any need for another meeting on 26 December?* Perhaps further effort was needed to bring Chase on board so he could not later claim to have stood by the people and justice and so on while the rest of the cabinet trembled when the British Lion growled.

Seward's daughter Fanny recorded in her diary on 26 December that "this morning Father read his wise & beautiful dispatch to England." Whether this was the final twenty-six-page version delivered the following day to Lord Lyons is unknown, but the scene suggests Seward was confident of Lincoln's approval. Fanny's next sentence reads: "sec. Chase called & he read it to him."[39] Perhaps this helped to enlist Chase's assistance in overcoming any argument for delay, knowing the dire effect the crisis was having on Chase's ability to raise loans to fund the war. Possibly, Seward mentioned to Chase, ingenuously or not, the subject of Lincoln's earlier thoughts on arbitration or promoted the view (which he certainly promoted later) that Lincoln was still trying to avoid releasing Mason and Slidell. Seward's best approach would be to appeal to Chase's ego, as if only Chase's voice could change stubborn minds in the cabinet to support the necessary step—with Lincoln depicted as the main recalcitrant.

Whether his private meeting with Seward made the difference, Chase wrote a long passage into his diary, ostensibly after the first cabinet meeting on Christmas Day but probably after the final meeting the next day. It was a justification for the step he may have refused to take at the previous session. The entry supposedly recorded his "remarks" to the cabinet, yet it had the tone of a pronouncement.

> But we cannot afford delays. While the matter hangs in uncertainty the public mind will remain disquieted, our commerce will suffer serious harm, our action against the rebels must be greatly hindered, and the restoration of our prosperity . . . must be delayed. Better, then, to make now the sacrifice of feeling involved in the surrender of these rebels than even avoid it by the delays which explanations must occasion. I give my adhesion, therefore to the conclusion at which the secretary of state has arrived.[40]

At the cabinet meeting on 26 December, unanimous agreement was reached. Bates recorded in his diary no individual's arguments but an apparent summing up: "the necessity of the case," war with England meant abandoning all hope of suppressing the rebellion, Britain's maritime superiority "would sweep us from all the southern waters," trade will be ruined, the treasury will be bankrupt. It was probably Chase who raised those last two points. Bates concluded his record, "There was great reluctance on the part of some of the members of the cabinet— and even the President himself—to acknowledge these obvious truths; but all yielded to the necessity, and unanimously concurred in Mr. Seward's letter."[41]

Missing from every account of the cabinet discussions is the subject that must have weighed heavily with Lincoln and Seward: the niter embargo. Historian Arthur D. Chandler made a fascinating argument over fifty years ago that the niter shortage played some role in these deliberations, and more-recent works support this view.[42]

After his niter-purchasing mission had been halted by the British prohibition, young Lammot du Pont caught a ship for America on 7 December. Evidence suggests he spent Christmas Day at his home in Delaware, but the next day he was certainly in Washington writing a letter addressed to Seward, presumably at Seward's request. The letter summarized Lammot's activities of the past few weeks and was endorsed as received by the State Department the same day, 26 December.[43]

Chandler argued that since Seward himself already knew the details, the letter was written "in order to give the Cabinet first hand information on the nitre purchases and the embargo" and to give Seward "an effective means of bringing Lincoln and most of the Cabinet to his more pacific way of thinking." But this is unlikely since no one recorded any cabinet discussion of niter, and more recent studies have suggested that Lammot met with Seward during some interval between sessions of that day's decisive cabinet meeting and may not have written the letter until *after* the decision had already been agreed in cabinet.[44] Moreover, since Lammot sailed from England on 7 December, he should have reached America long before Christmas. A confidential agent on a vital government mission would not head home, even for Christmas, without first reporting to the man who sent him, Secretary Seward. There is indirect evidence that at whatever point Lammot met with Seward, Lammot also met with Lincoln, for Lammot's aunt later recounted that her nephew "never saw two more worn down, haggard, worried-looking men."[45] Having probably reported to Washington some days earlier, when Lammot came to the capital on 26 December, it was not to provide new information but to receive fresh instructions.

Cabinet unity had been achieved, but the niter problem remained. Perhaps it was in order to maintain the fiction that Lammot's purchases were not for the government that his 26 December letter included a request that the secretary of state instruct Ambassador Adams in London to do what he could toward having the embargo lifted. Before that day ended, Seward not only handed Lord Lyons his formal twenty-six-page reply to the British demands but also gave Lammot a letter to carry to Ambassador Adams, instructing him to take action "for the relief of E. I. du Pont de Nemours and Co." regarding the niter shipment.[46]

The news of the cabinet decision hit the newspapers, and instead of uproar, there was a general sigh of relief from press, people, and even Congress. Mason and Slidell were quietly put on board a ship on New Year's Day—the same day that Lammot du Pont began another voyage to London. On 13 January 1862, Lammot wrote back that the niter embargo would probably be lifted within a week, and indeed it was on the eighteenth. The first of the reloaded ships sailed on 2 February, arriving a fortnight later. So few people were informed of the operation that even Chief of Ordnance General James W. Ripley said he knew no more about the shipments than what he read in the newspapers.[47]

The resolution of the *Trent* Affair was played out on a very public stage but far behind the scenes only a handful of people—Lincoln, Seward, the du Ponts, Dahlgren, and, perhaps, the British cabinet—knew that the outcome was largely determined by niter. Although the supply had been resumed, Lincoln understood that until some alternative source was found, the United States remained vulnerable. On the same day that Seward gave the formal letter to Lord Lyons, Lincoln delivered an order (rather than his accustomed request) to General Ripley to purchase ten thousand Spencer repeating rifles—which might yet be needed for a war on two fronts unless a solution was found for Lincoln's chemical problem.[48]

Less than a month after the *Trent* Affair seemed to be over, Lincoln was arranging congressional approval for a reorganization that placed Dahlgren in complete charge of research and development at the Navy Yard, with an assistant to handle administrative duties.[49] Dahlgren realized that the supply of niter was still a major concern. The spring and summer campaigns in 1862 brought the Union more defeats than victories and used up much of the niter brought from England in February. Most of what remained was under the army's control, while the navy needed more as blockade duties increased and a new threat developed from Confederate warships built in British shipyards—which might yet lead to war with Britain. Dahlgren made new arrangements: Henry du Pont was to make further indirect purchases in London and Calcutta; Welles was asked to approve the construction of storage facilities; a U.S. naval officer was sent to Yokohama in July to send back samples of possible Japanese sources of niter; and on 27 July, advertisements appeared in newspapers requesting bids from companies for domestic sources of niter.[50]

On 7 August, Seward and Secretary of War Edwin M. Stanton accompanied Lincoln to the Navy Yard to observe Dahlgren's tests of a new "Rafael" machine gun that, despite using standard paper cartridges, could fire forty shots in twenty seconds, and it would be surprising if the event did not stimulate a discussion of the long-term problem of the supply of niter.[51] About a week later, a possible solution arose when Lincoln received a visit from an old acquaintance from Springfield.[52] Isaac R. Diller had briefly served as consul in Germany where he met chemist Heinrich Hochstätter, who had developed a gunpowder that relied on a chlorate instead of niter. Now acting as an agent, Diller wanted the secret formula to be tested in a way that would not negate future patent rights. Lincoln understood the motivation and sent Diller—carrying notes from the president—to Dahlgren and also to David P. Holloway, the commissioner at the Patent Office, who was asked to allow Dr. Charles M. Wetherill, the only chemist employed by the federal government, to work with Diller.[53] On 21 August, the day after contacting Holloway, Lincoln vaguely requested that Welles "afford all facilities" to Diller and Wetherill "for some chemical experiments which they desire to make privately under my direction."[54]

Preliminary tests showed promising results.[55] A detailed contract drafted in December included a long list of questions, apparently Lincoln's, that had to be satisfactorily answered through full-scale testing before Lincoln would "advise" (having no authority to promise) the payment of the huge sum of $150,000. A week later, when Dahlgren was summoned to the White House to discuss something else, the president showed him yet another letter from an inventor of some new gunpowder. Lincoln said he had already burned a bit of the sample that had been sent and thought it left too much residue. "Now, I'll show you," said Lincoln, conducting a mini-experiment by placing some powder on a sheet of paper and touching it with a live coal picked from the fireplace with tongs. After the flash and smoke, Lincoln glanced at the paper and said, "There is too much left there."[56]

Eventually, Welles learned "something . . . in regard to the great secret of this man Dillon." If unclear about Diller's name, Welles was precise about the

$150,000 that figured in "a written promise" from the president, about which he was informed after he apparently cornered Dahlgren on the subject on 22 February. In his diary, Welles ranted, as he no doubt had to Dahlgren, that "the President had no authority for it," "no appropriation," and he "could not divert sums." Welles blamed Dahlgren as an example of "subordinates, flattered by [Lincoln's] notice" who should not be "encouraging the President in these well-intentioned but irregular proceedings." In self-defense, Dahlgren suggested his efforts to restrain the president were "impotent" since Lincoln "has a propensity to engage in matter of this kind, and is liable to be constantly imposed upon by sharpers and adventurers." Welles noted, "Finding the heads of Departments opposed to these schemes, the President goes often behind them," and Dahlgren apparently provided his own "written promise" that neither he nor Welles was responsible for this deal with "Dillon."[57]

After various delays, Lincoln arranged in April that Dr. Wetherill (who in the meantime had become an employee of the Department of Agriculture) should be seconded for a month along with an assistant to do unspecified work in Philadelphia. In May, Lincoln called for Dahlgren and Ripley to share the costs of the experiments, and in July, he wrote directly to their chiefs to pay further bills "as former ones have been paid."[58] The new powder passed an important trial in mid-June, though a question remained whether the powder "preserves its properties after graining"—converting the powder into a more stable form for transport and controlled rate of burn.[59] But by October, it was found that the powder could only be grained if its formula was altered, which then made it too unstable for safe storage.

When Diller implored Lincoln for additional funding, Lincoln returned his calling card with a note, "I am sorry, but I fear I shall have to drop this powder business."[60] The project was partly superseded by Dahlgren's success, in cooperation with Henry du Pont, in finding by the end of 1862 some domestic manufacturers who could produce a substitute for niter made out of sodium nitrate (available in America but most easily mined in Chile) and potash. Initially, the price seemed prohibitive, but Dahlgren was determined to end dependence on British sources, and the prices eventually equalized as production of the substitute increased, and the price of niter from India rose. Chile then, and until World War I, replaced India as the primary source of saltpeter.[61]

Although Lincoln's pet project had failed, his unstinting support for Dahlgren had paid off, and one major result was that by the beginning of 1863, it was impossible for Britain to threaten the United States with a chemistry problem of which few were aware but which Lincoln had understood and helped to solve.

Delegation and Control

"Will the evidence that this mail carries satisfy the English that we want to live in peace with them?" Asa Gray wrote to Darwin on New Year's Eve 1861, knowing that the ship conveying his letter would also carry the news that James Mason and John Slidell were to be released. Gray acknowledged that some intemperate remarks in Darwin's last letter were "very natural" but also defended American actions, asserting that the Lincoln administration had "promptly conceded" and was "cheerfully" releasing the envoys: Gray was not one of the very few who knew the actual explanation, which was left out of William H. Seward's letter to the British foreign minister. Gray declared that America "must be strong to be secure and respected—Natural selection quickly crushes out weak nations" and was prescient on the issue dearest to Darwin. "As to slavery, the course of things is getting to meet your views. . . . [I]f the [Southerners] give up now they may save their institution in their own States to have the chance of abolishing it themselves in the only safe and easy way, with time and the gradual competition of white labor. But obstinate resistance will surely bring on wide sweeping manumission." Closing with New Year's greetings, Gray urged Darwin, "Keep up your lively sympathies with those who have very severe trials to undergo and sacrifices to make for what they deem the cause of right, honor, & future safety."[1]

Darwin had been disappointed for months that Lincoln had apparently done nothing to strike at slavery and then failed to disavow immediately the actions of Captain Charles Wilkes. He was miffed that Gray's letter, written the moment the crisis passed, still blamed the British for being too sympathetic to the South and "peremptory" in issuing demands to the North. Gray's letter arrived at a bad time, while the Darwin household was plagued by influenza: "What misery there is in this life," Darwin wrote to Joseph Dalton Hooker. Out of sorts, Darwin did not reply immediately but sent Gray's letter to Hooker with the extraordinarily sour comment: "Asa Gray is evidently sore about England: he does not say much; nor do I; but I have hitherto been able to write with some sympathy; now I must be silent; for I look at the people as a nation of unmitigated blackguards."[2]

Although that was Hooker's standard view, he was surprised by Darwin's fit of anti-Americanism. Eventually, Darwin felt able to send Gray a letter that mixed cordiality with grit. After various pleasantries and botanical business, Darwin grasped the nettle. "Now for a few words on politics; but they shall be few, for we shall no longer agree." After detailing his disgust over the *Trent* Affair—especially the Boston dinner in Wilkes's honor, which "quite turned my stomach"—Darwin concluded, "It is well to make a clean breast of it at once; & I have begun to think whether it would not be well for the peace of the world, if you were split up into two or three nations." With that off his chest, Darwin added that he could not "bear the thought of the Slave-holders being triumphant" or of a permanent frontier between North and South "with armies, fortifications, & custom-houses without end with your retrograde tariff. Bad man, as you will think me, I shall always think of you with affection. Here is an insult! I shall always think of you as an Englishman."[3]

It was a frank letter, tempered so as not to kill a friendship if charm could save it. Darwin must have felt relief at Gray's genial reply: "As I have not given you up notwithstanding your very shocking principles and prejudices against *design in nature*, so we shall try to abide your *longitudinarian* defection"—an injoke about different attitudes resulting from different geographical origins. Gray agreed that the Boston banquet was all "bosh" but said it was odd that Darwin of all people should "fail to appreciate that it is simply a struggle for existence on our part, and that men will persist in thinking their existence of some consequence to themselves." Darwin's next letter showed his own feelings were still raw: "It is really almost a pleasure to receive stabs from so smooth, polished & sharp a dagger as your pen. . . . The Millennium must come before nations love each other, but try & do not hate me." Gray responded cheerfully, "Yes, I will promise not to *hate* you: quite the contrary!" and signed himself "Your cordial friend and true Yankee."[4]

As Darwin entered one of his worst phases of ill health, his research seemed to have lost direction. The two decades of preparation for a vast work on natural selection had been followed by two years of intense effort to produce and promote *On the Origin of Species*. After that, Darwin at first planned to write up his vast collection of notes on natural selection in a three-part project: a volume on variation among the relatively knowable domesticated animals and plants, followed by a study of the harder-to-measure variations among wild animals and plants, and concluding with the application of these analogies to the examination of the more difficult and controversial question of how only slight variations and modifications could have separated man from the rest of the animal world.

Although Darwin planned to demonstrate his theory's validity *before* applying it to man, most of his admirers and critics had prematurely connected the dots. But Darwin tried to stick to his original plan, expecting the subject of man's origins to be dealt with soon by other sympathetic colleagues. He was pleased that Thomas Huxley, Charles Lyell, and John Lubbock, a young biologist and Darwin's neighbor, were all investigating human origins or development and presumably applying natural selection to the subject. Darwin was content to let them bear the brunt of any new controversy while further experiments and data collection sidetracked his own larger study.

After barnacles and seed experiments, it was pigeons, primulas, and orchids: all useful studies, testing ideas about sexual selection and resulting in several papers and another book. At the start of 1862, Darwin was delighted when his publisher said his volume on orchids would probably appear about the same time as Lyell's study of human antiquity.[5] But the orchid book came out in four months, leaving the anxious Darwin to wait nearly a year before Lyell went to press.

As he waited, Darwin enjoyed Huxley's long-running scrape with Richard Owen, who argued that the human brain is utterly distinguishable from those of even the closest primates because it possessed a structure called a *hippocampus minor*, while Huxley insisted that this was simply another feature that, in fact, men shared with apes. Huxley also gave a series of lectures called "The Relation of Man to the Rest of the Animal Kingdom" to an attentive audience of largely working-class men. After one particularly full house, Huxley told his wife, "By next Friday evening they will all be convinced that they are monkeys."[6] Owen also gave a lecture, printed in the *Athenaeum* and entitled "The Gorilla and the Negro." Since his main purpose was to draw a rigid line between animals and men, Owen might have simply compared "Gorilla and Man," but Owen held that although the negro is indeed a man (being blessed with a *hippocampus minor*), he is also the "lowest variety of human race," inferior anatomically and mentally when compared with "Europeans." So, Owen's disparaging point was that *even* a negro is different from a gorilla! Huxley responded with a brief letter to the *Athenaeum*—printed under the title "Man and the Apes"—asserting simply that gorillas also have the *hippocampus minor* and never mentioning negroes. Owen sought to continue the debate, but Huxley protested, "Life is too short to occupy oneself with the slaying of the slain more than once."[7] Darwin told Huxley that his letter was "very well done, but almost too civil" and praised it to Hooker in a letter that also expressed admiration for Lyell's "capital work" investigating the flint tools fashioned by early men and found in preglacial geological levels in France: "The case gets more & more complicated. All, however, tends to greater & greater antiquity of man."[8]

Meanwhile, Huxley grew more assertive about man's origins, informing Darwin that during a lecture in Edinburgh, he made a "distinct statement that I believe Man & the apes to have come from one stock." Darwin was delighted that Huxley planned to publish his lectures soon. Between them, Huxley and Lyell might now apply evidence from geology, archeology, paleontology, and comparative anatomy to show that the races of man had a common origin, pushed back in time in a manner that would allow for that origin and later variations (races) to be explained by natural selection. While Lyell and Huxley worked on the problem from new directions, Darwin continued to seek less controversial evidence—from primulas and orchids—to demonstrate the viability of his theory, but he praised Gray for perceiving that the orchid book "was a 'flank movement' on the enemy."[9]

Flanking actions did not distract Darwin from the developing battle regarding human origins and unity. Corresponding with Charles Kingsley on the "grand & awful question of the genealogy of man," Darwin declared that compared with his initial reaction on first seeing the natives of Tierra del Fuego, he had no difficulty with his "present belief that an incomparably more remote ancestor was a hairy beast." And looking at it from the other side, Darwin added, "Monkeys have downright good hearts, at least sometimes, as I could show, if I had space. I have long attended to this subject, & have materials for a curious essay on Human expression, & a little on the relation in mind of man to the lower animals." Yet, though continually gathering materials, Darwin held back from publishing. "How I should be abused if I were to publish such an essay!" he told Kingsley. He was still hoping Lyell would soon produce something "on the relations of men & other animals; but I do not know what his recent intentions are."[10]

Huxley, meanwhile, lectured "On Fossil Remains of Man," arguing that it was necessary to "extend by long epochs the most liberal estimate that has yet been made of the antiquity of Man." Darwin doled out more praise and was delighted when Huxley told him the lecture would be written up "as a chapter of my forthcoming *Evidence as to Man's Place in Nature*."[11] Hooker, seeing an early draft, told Darwin the book was "an amusing as well as clever book on Monkey Man. It will be a great success," and Darwin replied that he heartily hoped "Huxley's book will be very successful. . . . he will be well abused." Darwin also told Lyell that he "heartily hoped" Lyell's book would be out in October, though "I fancy Huxley will be out sooner."[12] Unfortunately for the eager Darwin, neither book appeared until early in 1863.

In the meantime, Darwin's anxiety about the bloodletting in America had been temporarily eased in April 1862. "The North seems going on grandly victorious," he wrote Gray, "& thank God there is distinct ground broken on the Slavery question; but we stupid English cannot yet believe that you will ever be a single Union again."[13]

The Northern victories to which Darwin alluded were mainly in the west, though there was also the success in March at Hampton Roads, Virginia, when the Confederate ironclad, the former USS *Merrimack*, now renamed the CSS *Virginia*, was forced to halt its attack on the Union's wooden fleet after destroying two ships and damaging several others. It was stopped by the arrival of the USS *Monitor*, with its entirely metal hull of a revolutionary design by John Ericsson. The ships fought each other to a standstill, but the *Merrimack* retreated to its haven, never to fight again while ships of the *Monitor* design would soon be produced in large numbers, helping to capture Confederate coastal positions and tighten the blockade. Without Lincoln's personal involvement, the *Monitor* might never have been built. He also played a role—less subtle and perhaps less effective—in the land victories that had taken place between January and April.

Especially after the *Trent* affair, Lincoln was mindful that the threat of some foreign intervention increased as time passed without clear indications that the North was capable of victory. Although Lincoln cultivated the image of a delegator who left affairs in the hands of those more capable, over the winter he lost patience with his generals. He had previously commanded nothing larger than a company of Illinois militia, yet all his life, Lincoln had accomplished what he was not supposed to be able to achieve, and now, having survived for the moment the threat of an additional war with Britain, Lincoln wanted victories that would allay that threat and crush the rebellion. He moved beyond testing weapons to reading military science, giving "himself, night and day, to the study of the military situation," according to his secretaries and later biographers John G. Nicolay and John Hay. "He read a large number of strategical works, . . . held long conferences with eminent generals and admirals, and astonished them by the extent of his special knowledge and the keen intelligence of his questions."[14]

Early in 1862, Lincoln borrowed from the Library of Congress a copy of *Elements of Military Art and Science* (1846) by Henry W. Halleck. Later nicknamed (not always kindly) "Old Brains," Halleck was currently Lincoln's fourth-highest-ranking general. Six months later, Lincoln made him general-in-chief of all the armies, at which point Halleck proved he was good with administration and offering advice but not with decision making. From Halleck's *Elements*, Lincoln may have learned a fair amount of military science—or that military science did not amount to much.[15]

At present, Halleck was one of several army and naval officers passing the buck rather than arranging for the speedy delivery of a flotilla of craft specially designed to carry mortars so huge they could not really be transported by land, though they proved decisive in reducing Confederate strongholds along rivers and estuaries. On 10 January, Lincoln began firing telegrams in several directions, and when no one acted, he went to the Navy Bureau of Ordnance and told Lieutenant Henry Wise to "put it through. . . . Now I am going to devote a part of every day to these mortars and I won't leave off until it fairly rains bombs." By the end of the month, Wise wrote that the president "is evidently a practical man, understands precisely what he wants, and is not turned aside when he has his work before him."[16]

In January, while promoting Captain John A. Dahlgren at the Navy's Ordnance Office, Lincoln decided he must get rid of General James W. Ripley, the army's chief of ordnance (which proved difficult), but he did succeed in replacing

Simon Cameron as secretary of war with Edwin M. Stanton—a man who six years earlier had grievously insulted Lincoln during a patent trial in Cincinnati, Ohio, but also a man Lincoln believed, rightly as it turned out, could do the job. By the end of January, Lincoln and Stanton composed the "President's General War Order No 1," calling for "a general movement" of all the land and naval forces of the Union "against the insurgent forces," to commence on 22 February, George Washington's birthday. Although this has been characterized as "little more than high-flown persiflage" and "less an order . . . than a distress signal," it indicated, according to historian James M. McPherson, that "Lincoln grasped sooner than many of his generals the strategic concept of 'concentration in time.'"[17] To two of his doubtful generals, Don C. Buell and Halleck, Lincoln tried to explain his

> general idea of this war to be that we have the *greater* numbers, and the enemy has the *greater* facility of concentrating forces upon points of collision; that we must fail, unless we can find some way of making *our* advantage an over-match for *his*; and that this can only be done by menacing him with superior forces at *different* points, at the *same* time; so that we can safely attack, one, or both, if he makes no change; and if he *weakens* one to *strengthen* the other, forbear to attack the strengthened one, but seize, and hold the weakened one, gaining so much.[18]

Probably realizing that that particular order was unlikely to accomplish much, Lincoln soon issued "Special War Order No. 1" on 1 February. This was a specific plan for attacking a Confederate army at Manassas Junction, Virginia. General George McClellan, commander of the Army of the Potomac, argued in favor of his own plan: to send a Union army down Chesapeake Bay to land on the coast fifty miles east of Richmond, Virginia, in order to attack the Confederate capital from an "undefended" approach. Lincoln tried to build a case, sending McClellan specific questions, comparing the two plans' expenditures of time and money, the certainty and value of any victory, the likelihood of breaking the line of the enemy's communications or exposing Washington, D.C., to danger, and the provision of a line of retreat, if needed. McClellan never provided answers but only excuses about the conditions of roads and the size of the enemy's force between Washington and Richmond—estimates McClellan constantly exaggerated.[19]

Lincoln now made a desperate effort to outflank his own general by putting both plans to a council of McClellan's senior divisional commanders—a poor idea because most knew their careers depended more on their senior commander than on a likely one-term president. When his plan was voted down, Lincoln pressed McClellan at least to plan an operation to push the Confederates farther away from Washington before setting off on his Peninsula Campaign. McClellan ordered the construction of special boats to be floated up the Potomac River for a crossing near Harpers Ferry, Virginia. After much delay and cost, the operation was launched on 27 February but was "a damned fizzle," in Stanton's words, for the boats proved to be a few inches too wide to get through the locks on the river. "I am no engineer," a furious Lincoln told McClellan's chief of staff, "but it seems to me that if I wished to know whether a boat would go through a hole or a lock, common sense would teach me to go and measure it!"[20]

As March arrived and McClellan still showed no sign of movement, Lincoln took advice from other generals, read up on the Napoleonic "corps system," and then informed McClellan that he was going to reorganize the army into five corps and personally select their commanders. McClellan was incensed but still would not move. Lincoln made desperate efforts to replace McClellan, but the only candidate possibly acceptable to McClellan's staff, General Ethan Allen Hitchcock, refused to command the army in the field.

In April, McClellan finally began his Peninsula Campaign, proceeding with extreme caution. Lincoln was frustrated that McClellan did not take the opportunity once the army was in the vicinity of the naval base at Norfolk to capture the city and destroy the *Merrimack*. Lincoln decided to get closer to the action and took Chase and Stanton with him on a naval vessel. Stationed outside Norfolk in case the *Merrimack* attempted another foray was the *Monitor*. Lincoln paid an emotional visit to the vessel he had done so much to bring into existence. He then summoned several officers to help formulate a plan for capturing Norfolk. In some accounts, Lincoln actually walked along a moonlit beach in Confederate territory to see if it was suitable for an amphibious landing. The next day, Lincoln's plan was implemented, and he soon heard the satisfying explosion as the *Merrimack* was blown up.[21]

McClellan's slow advance toward Richmond ended badly as he was forced to retreat to Harrison's Landing near the end of June. Lincoln now had to determine whether McClellan should continue his ill-conceived Peninsula Campaign or withdraw the army to protect Washington from threats by Stonewall Jackson.

"It is surprising to me that you should have strength of mind to care for science, amidst the awful events daily occurring in your country," Darwin wrote gloomily to Gray in mid-June, assuming the failure in the peninsula was sapping Gray's optimism as it had Darwin's. "I daily look at the *Times* with almost as much interest as an American could do. When will peace come: it is dreadful to think of the desolation of large parts of your magnificent country; & all the speechless misery suffered by many."[22]

Gray admitted that prospects were "looking badly enough" and that "McClellan has clearly been over matched." Darwin avoided the subject in his next few letters, but Gray recurred to the martial topic at the end of July: "The South force us at length to do what it would have been more humane to have done from the first,—i.e. to act with vigor,—not to say *rigor*." Three more letters crossed before Darwin responded briefly in August: "Affairs seem to be getting with you more

& more terrible. What will the end be? It seems to us here far more fearful, than it apparently does to you."[23]

It would have interested Darwin that when Lincoln visited McClellan's peninsula headquarters early in August to consider the next course of action, his decision turned partly on an issue of natural science. Of McClellan's five corps commanders, three agreed with McClellan that the campaign should continue, but Lincoln was more convinced by another general who argued that the defeated army's morale was worsened by the area's malarial swamps causing illness that could soon reduce the army's manpower—he estimated by 20 percent. He recommended withdrawal, at least while summer lasted. Lincoln recognized that this West Point graduate, former member of General Winfield Scott's staff, and recently a successful corps commander, probably knew something about disease because his father was a prominent Massachusetts physician—who had named his son after a famous English doctor. General Erasmus Darwin Keyes's diagnosis of Lincoln was also perceptive: "There was not one of his most trusted warlike counsellors in the beginning of the war that equaled him in military sagacity."[24]

Lincoln ordered McClellan to return most of his force to the Washington area, where Lincoln casually arranged to place the troops under the command of General John Pope.

In April 1862, when Darwin thanked God "there is distinct ground broken on the Slavery question," he was reacting to several developments.[25] Between 6 March and 10 April, Congress passed legislation forbidding the military to return fugitive slaves forcibly to their rebel masters, abolished slavery within Washington, D.C., and approved a resolution supporting compensated emancipation (although it was a diluted version of what Lincoln had requested).

If Darwin thanked God rather than Abraham Lincoln, he was not alone because many Americans considered Lincoln too conservative with regard to slavery. Lincoln himself had to consider the majority, who still opposed any abolitionist action that might make it more difficult for the Southern states to return to the Union or more likely that blacks would move into Northern states. Most historians agree Lincoln walked this tightrope well, taking rational steps forward when it was politically possible and militarily useful to do so. But one of Lincoln's major policies regarding blacks has divided historians, many considering the rational Lincoln to have acted somewhat irrationally. The policy was colonization of blacks, either back to Africa or to the Caribbean or out west—basically out of the way of white people.

The British colony of Sierra Leone, which was begun in 1787 as a place to send blacks liberated during the American War of Independence (who otherwise might have remained in Canada or London), had also become a refuge for slaves liberated from slave ships by the Royal Navy. Darwin's Wedgwood relatives donated more than £70 in 1824 to support the colony, and his later professors in Cambridge, Henslow, and Whewell, made subscriptions of a guinea each.[26] Britain made no concerted effort to return to Africa the blacks emancipated in the British West Indies, four thousand miles from London. Even Britons as sensitized as Darwin could only imagine how twenty-six million white Americans felt about living in a country alongside four and a half million present or former slaves. Whether a white man can consider a black to be "a man and a brother" while also believing he must live elsewhere is a dilemma Darwin never had to confront.

The Rationality of Colonization

The literature on Lincoln and colonization is vast because the subject is peculiarly emotive. Scholars debate how far Lincoln raised himself above the average racism of his time and how early he took particular steps to fight slavery, but most agree that Lincoln was generally on the right side, moved in the right direction, and was ahead of the public opinion he helped to shape. But the policy of black colonization, even apart from Lincoln's involvement, is today viewed as "bad" practically and morally. Since it did not work, many conclude it could not work and that intelligent people should have recognized this at the time. As a moral issue, black colonization is glibly linked to the twentieth-century horrors of eugenics, "final solutions," *Lebensraum*, and "ethnic cleansing." To suggest colonization was anything but bad seems (however illogically) to imply that millions of African Americans today somehow have less right to be United States citizens than their white compatriots and that we might have avoided the racial integration to which we now aspire. Historians believing colonization to be doubly wrong—unable to achieve what it should not have attempted—struggle to explain why such an intelligent and good man as Abraham Lincoln supported it.

Historian Michael Vorenberg concisely states the logical extremes of possible explanations: "Those who tend to see Lincoln as a racist usually assume that he never gave up the idea of deporting all free blacks, while those who believe in Lincoln as a racial egalitarian typically assert that his racial views matured as he realized that colonization could not work and that he came to believe that blacks had a legitimate claim to remaining in the United States." Leaning toward the second view, Vorenberg argues that Lincoln never demonstrated real devotion to colonization for its own sake but found it politically useful, discarding it when it no longer served. Historian Gabor Boritt largely agrees, emphasizing "the contradiction and ambivalence [that] were the hallmarks of Lincoln's support for colonization." However, neither view—that Lincoln supported colonization as an ad hoc "political calculation" or as a "defense mechanism that psychologists call avoidance"—allows that he might have considered it a good idea per se.[1] Both historians perceived intellectual faltering, with Vorenberg suggesting Lincoln fused emancipation and colonization "even more tightly together in his mind, making it nearly impossible for him to believe that one could exist without the other" and with Gabor Boritt using a range of phrases suggesting Lincoln acted irrationally.[2] David Herbert Donald writes that colonization "was entirely rational—and wholly impracticable" yet emphasizes Lincoln's pursuit of a "fantasy."[3]

Colonization becomes a test of whether Lincoln based his policy choices on evidence and logic or genuinely failed to see the faults in colonization until he later "matured." I support the less-popular view that colonization *in the middle of the nineteenth century* had far more about it that was "good" than "bad" and that intelligent people like Lincoln were rational to support it as a feasible way to fight slavery and give justice to freedmen—and to reject it when circumstances radically changed.[4] Indeed, Lincoln may have hoped at one stage that increasing tolerance of blacks by the white majority might make colonization unnecessary, but ultimately his perception of the scale of white prejudice kept the policy alive.

One could construct long lists of prominent nineteenth-century Americans—white and black, North and South—who believed colonization offered justice to the Africans being returned homeward and would hasten the end of slavery or who denounced colonization as inhumane, impractical, and effectively proslavery. Several prominent abolitionists moved from the first view to the second. Some members of the new Republican Party opposed colonization, while many others considered it part of the party platform even before Lincoln gained the White House.[5]

Modern immigration patterns have created many multiracial societies, but in the early nineteenth century, most immigration involved Europeans going to the Americas, South Africa, New Zealand, and Australia, where, as Darwin witnessed during the *Beagle* voyage, they preferred some form of extermination of indigenous populations to any version of integration. Native Americans found themselves sharing their regions with immigrating Europeans and enslaved Africans. Whites constantly pushed the Indians aside, and there was no reason to imagine that the blacks, if ever freed, would be treated any better. Indeed, the very "success" of the U.S. government's "Indian removals" made moving blacks back to Africa seem feasible. Europeans came to America from racially homogeneous societies, and their descendants saw that nearly all countries comprised a single race. Removing Indians and blacks was a way toward greater homogeneity for Anglo-Americans—who had enough difficulty coping with Germans and Catholics.

Opponents of slavery could salve their consciences that colonization somehow addressed the problem when constitutional and economic factors barred other action. They could imagine Christianized blacks being returned to convert the Dark Continent or—more absurdly—that black colonists would spread whatever blessings of democracy they had come to admire while laboring in America.

Some Republicans promoted schemes to colonize freed slaves into tropical areas in the Western Hemisphere, reducing transport costs, providing access to new resources (perhaps cotton grown by paid labor), extending American influence, perhaps countering British influence in the isthmus where someday a canal might be built. Opponents of colonization dismissed all this but rarely on the grounds that colonization itself was not feasible.

The most obvious reason for supporting colonization then is rarely mentioned today: simple justice. Blacks had been brought to America against their will, transported in the worst conceivable conditions, with millions dying along the way from disease or desperate suicide. Such crimes could have no redress, but at least the surviving remnant could, in theory, be restored to their homeland. Of course, the practical difficulty increased over time as the "remnant" steadily increased, despite the slave trade's abolition in 1808.

Most whites assumed black slaves *wanted* to leave America. The colonization movement began shortly after the slave trade ceased, when most blacks were considered "Africans" even though more and more were American born with no direct memory, or even a parent's stories, of African life. Only slave owners defending their treatment of blacks ever argued that conditions in Africa could be worse than being enslaved in the south or subjected to gross indignities and civil disabilities throughout the north. Finally, polygenists such as Louis Agassiz had recently pronounced that blacks were separately created in Africa by God, designed for some "tropical" environment that was only approximated in a few southern states, and were otherwise doomed to ultimate extinction according to natural laws. Science seemed to confirm what recent history indicated globally: that differing races simply could not live together, and one must be destroyed, enslaved, or removed by the other.

No white person, north or south, would trade places with a black, and most dismissed those articulate blacks who denounced colonization, such as Frederick Douglass, as a tiny, untypical faction—which in many respects they were. The slaves' contribution to America's great prosperity was acknowledged less than as the contribution of dumb cattle, and few whites perceived that a growing number of blacks were unwilling to leave the homeland they had helped create. (Later, most whites were amazed when thousands of African Americans showed themselves willing to stay among their oppressors and even to don uniforms and fight for the freedom that America was meant to represent.)

Some whites who recognized that blacks might not willingly depart argued for forced deportation. There were many such within the Republican Party and even inside Lincoln's cabinet, but Lincoln himself always maintained that colonization must be voluntary. Forced deportation would involve a larger bureaucracy and targets more difficult to meet, as well as personal anguish, while a voluntary program allowed for a more flexible system that might take on a life of its own. Opponents of colonization might prove unable to dissuade those wishing to leave, while those arguing for forced deportation might feel differently later about neighbors who made a conscious choice to remain. In terms of improving race relations, different "benefits" might come from achieving complete colonization or merely advocating a partial colonization.

Ethical issues aside, large-scale colonization was never going to be easy and grew more difficult over time. Changing circumstances could make it seem less worth the costs, and during certain phases in his presidency, Lincoln curtailed his promotion of the policy. None of that makes his long-standing support for colonization an irrational act.

Scholars, including those quoted earlier, tend to suggest that Lincoln's interest in colonization was first evident in 1852, when he delivered the eulogy for Henry Clay and praised the concept of "restoring a captive people to their long-lost father-land."[6] But Clay had supported the American Colonization Society (ACS) from its founding in 1816, and it is not surprising that Lincoln and many colleagues showed an interest long before 1852. Charles R. Matheny (whose son was later Lincoln's "best man") and John T. Stuart (whose law practice Lincoln joined in 1837) were, respectively, president and vice-president of the Sangamon County Colonization Society, organized in August 1833 in Springfield as an auxiliary to the Illinois State Colonization Society (ISCS). Stuart and Dan Stone (the state legislator who cosigned Lincoln's 1837 protest against slavery) participated in a lyceum debate in 1833 on whether the national government should "appropriate funds from the treasury in aid of the Colonization society." In 1839, Porter Clay, Henry's brother and an ACS agent, delivered a lecture in Springfield, and Reverend Charles Dresser (who later performed the service at Lincoln's wedding) presided over a first annual meeting of the revived local organization. Stuart, Dr. John Todd (Mary's uncle), and other Whig supporters were on the governing committee. By then, the ISCS had about 150 members, twenty of whom paid an annual donation of $10 each to help fund the transport and settlement in Africa of twelve emancipated slaves.[7]

Lincoln possibly numbered among those 150 members and was presumably among the four hundred guests who attended a 3 January 1845 party at the home of his brother-in-law Ninian Edwards, apparently following a meeting held in the state house to re-form the ISCS. Lincoln's friend Orville Browning was elected vice-president of the new board of managers arranged for copies of the ACS journal, *The African Repository*, to be "sent gratuitously to every Clergyman in the State, who is willing to receive it."[8]

The first annual report of the ISCS included a statement that was later quoted by an ACS leader during a visit to London in 1849 when he gave testimony before a select committee of the House of Lords. It included statistics comparing the costs of purchasing four thousand miles of the West African coastline (an ACS aspiration to close down the illegal slave trade) with the costs of maintaining naval squadrons from the United States and the United Kingdom.[9] Although there is no evidence Lincoln helped to produce these statistics, one can imagine his interest in learning how large sums appropriated for military purposes might have been better used more imaginatively to combat slavery—a point he would later make during the Civil War.

Congressman Lincoln presumably attended on 18 January 1848 the annual ACS meeting held in the House of Representatives and addressed by Henry Clay.[10] In April, while Lincoln was in Washington, a thirty-five-year-old African American in Springfield named Samuel S. Ball temporarily left his barbershop and his wife and six children in order to investigate conditions in the ACS's colony in Liberia. Upon returning, he made a favorable report to the Colored Baptist Association, and probably only the heavy expense prevented him from taking his family to Liberia. In 1851, Ball actually drafted a bill for the Illinois legislature proposing financial support for free blacks wishing to migrate to Liberia, but it never got out of committee. Ball died the following year of typhoid fever.[11]

Although Lincoln used Springfield's other black barber, he must have known Ball, probably read his report, and may have hoped his attitude was typical. However, Lincoln must also have known that other black neighbors opposed colonization, perhaps increasingly as time passed. He must have been moved in 1858 by the newspaper report of a statement produced by Springfield blacks who declared, "We have been unable to ascertain that any intelligent man of color either desires to remove to Africa, or requires aid for such an enterprise." Although obviously aimed against those still sharing Ball's views, this statement firmly asserted, "We have no desire to exchange the broad prairies, fertile soil, healthful climate and Christian civilization of Illinois, for the dangerous navigation of the wide ocean, the tangled forests, savage beasts, heathen people and miasmatic shores of Africa." Lincoln could hardly contest the peroration: "We take [the] Declaration as the Gospel of freedom; we believe in its great truth, 'that all men are created equal.'"[12]

Five years earlier, in 1853, it was advertised that Lincoln was going to talk on "Colonization" at the First Presbyterian Church, which Mary had recently joined and whose preacher, Reverend James Smith, was on the board of the ISCS. Five months later, Lincoln and Browning were scheduled to speak at the ISCS's annual meeting, but illness in the family prevented Lincoln.[13] But in October 1854, Lincoln made an important statement about colonization in his famous Peoria speech as he campaigned against Douglas's Kansas-Nebraska Act.

> If all earthly power were given me, I should not know what to do, as to the existing institution [of slavery]. My first impulse would be to free all the slaves, and send them to Liberia,—to their own native land. But a moment's reflection would convince me, that whatever of high hope, (as I think there is) there may be in this, in the long run, its sudden execution is impossible. If they were all landed there in a day, they would all perish in the next ten days; and there are

not surplus shipping and surplus money enough in the world to carry them there in many times ten days.[14]

This was Lincoln's courtroom style, conceding numerous points in order to win one, admitting short-term difficulties but allowing the "high hope" for colonization in some "long run." His rejection of less-likely alternatives ("keeping them among us as underlings?" or "make them politically and socially, our equals?") simply recognized his audience's feelings, which may or may not accord "with justice and sound judgement." He concluded with vague support for an equally long-run strategy, "gradual emancipation."

Lincoln was able to address the next ISCS meeting in January 1855, and fortunately notes survive, filling both sides of one page, that Lincoln probably wrote while planning this speech.[15] First, he listed eight dates, beginning with 1434 (when a Portuguese captain "seizes a few African lads"—the event he later linked to "the invention of negroes") and ending with 1776, which for Lincoln marked the close of the approved development of slavery. Before tracing the story of the disapproval of slavery, Lincoln paused to make the point that in 1776, "there were about 600,000 slaves in the colonies; and there are now in the U.S. about 3¼ millions"—highlighting that delay only made colonization more difficult.[16] Lincoln might have pointed out that the ACS's early plans had included colonizing high proportions of women of childbearing age to slow the growth of the problem.[17] Lincoln's notes then listed seven antislavery landmarks, from a protest by a Catholic priest in 1543, through those by Quakers before the Revolution and Congress's subsequent actions prohibiting slavery in the Northwest and outlawing the slave trade. He added, "1776–1800: Slavery abolished in all the northern states."

Next, Lincoln jotted down with emphasis: *"All the while*—Individual conscience at work." Moving from the individual to the collective, he noted, "1816— Colonization Society is organized." Then Lincoln divided the discussion into "direct objects" and "collateral objects," apparently distinguishing between actually *attaining* colonization and the possible benefits of simply working *toward* it. Of three "collateral" benefits, the first was the "suppression of the Slave trade," which continued despite being outlawed in 1808. Since then, an average of thirteen thousand to fifteen thousand Africans were smuggled into the United States annually, when the colonizationists' concept of buying up African coastline might have reduced that figure. The other two collateral benefits were "commerce" and "civilization and religion": broad canvases on which Lincoln might have painted pleasant images appealing to his audience's self-interest, sense of superiority, and religious zeal.[18]

Under "present prospects of success," Lincoln was likely to stress that if the federal government helped cover the costs of colonization, these could be spread over a century, not straining a budget that had shown annual surpluses in the

1850s as high as $15 million. Moreover, the government merely needed to get the ball rolling until enough blacks had become really successful in Liberia, experiencing genuine rights and prosperity, so that they might, like German and Irish immigrants, financially assist relatives to enjoy the same opportunity. Lincoln might have mentioned those Germans and Irish as being among the 600,000 immigrants to the United States in the decade before 1840 and 1.7 million in the decade during which he was speaking: all migrations involving no costs to a government that, on the other hand, had willingly spent close to $100 million in the 1830s to move 46,000 Indians west of the Mississippi River.[19]

For many historians, the starting and ending point in judging the viability of colonization is the single and oft-repeated fact that between 1820 and 1860, the ACS managed to send fewer than twelve thousand blacks to Liberia, as if no more blacks were willing to go. But the figure ignores colonists aided by separate state societies and the thirty thousand blacks who escaped to Canada in the antebellum period.[20] Hundreds of thousands of blacks had been brought to America in the seventeenth and eighteenth centuries, and large numbers had also left, many with British help during the Revolutionary War and the War of 1812.[21]

A large proportion of the ACS's limited funds went toward purchasing land in Africa, hiring vessels, and providing supplies, but between 1830 and 1850, Brazilian and Cuban slaveholders imported forty thousand new slaves every year, at an annual cost of $4 million, a sum the U.S. government could easily have supplied annually to transport forty thousand freedmen from America to Africa.[22] Even after the slave trade to America was outlawed, some Americans paid large sums to smuggle Africans across the Atlantic Ocean, and when they advocated reopening the slave trade, they did not worry—and their opponents had no fond hopes—that the costs or availability of transport would impede traffic in that direction.

Lincoln probably acknowledged that the ACS had made no headway against the sheer growth of the slave population, but he could also point out that the ACS, after seriously faltering in the mid-1830s under withering attacks from radical abolitionists, had become more active since 1850, as blacks felt increasing pressure from the Fugitive Slave Act and from the deepening intolerance fostered by scientific racism.By January 1857, Lincoln was elected one of the ISCS's eleven managers.[23] Five months later, while campaigning for Douglas's Senate seat, Lincoln used colonization to deflect Douglas's charge that by asserting that blacks were equally human, he was somehow encouraging amalgamation. At the end of a long speech, Lincoln stressed that "the separation of the races is the only perfect preventive of amalgamation." He admitted that colonization did not appear in the Republican Party platform but asserted that "a very large proportion" of Republicans were for it (though he knew many were dead against it) and that the party's opposition to the extension of slavery was also "favorable to that separation."

Such separation, if ever effected at all, must be effected by colonization; and no political party, as such, is now doing anything directly for colonization. . . . The enterprise is a difficult one; but "when there is a will there is a way;" and what colonization needs most is a hearty will. Will springs from the two elements of moral sense and self-interest. Let us be brought to believe it is morally right, and, at the same time, favorable to, or, at least, not against, our interest, to transfer the African to his native clime, and we shall find a way to do it, however great the task may be.[24]

There were sufficient qualifications here to avoid offending any Republicans who opposed colonization, whether they believed blacks should be accorded civil rights instead or simply thought colonization impractical. Lincoln obviously considered colonization more plausible than the idea that whites would grant blacks civil rights.

In the 1858 Lincoln-Douglas debates, Lincoln did no more than quote from that section of his earlier Peoria Speech, for he found better ways to parry Douglas's "amalgamation" swipe: besides, colonization had more vocal opponents among Republicans than among Democrats. Later, when Lincoln sought support outside of Illinois, there was little to be gained from mentioning colonization, and the issue was sidelined as Lincoln maneuvered to win the White House, becoming the first occupant who had deeply considered and favored colonization.

Lincoln's first presidential effort to promote colonization was the Chiriqui Project, although for a long time, this scheme had nothing to do with colonization. Ambrose W. Thompson owned a vast tract of land in Central America that he had nearly, but not quite, been able to sell to the Buchanan administration. According to Thompson, the land offered the perfect route for a new transisthmian railroad or even a canal, the perfect location for naval stations, and a perfect source of coal supplies for the navy. Thompson first wrote to Lincoln shortly after his inauguration, giving advice about saving the Union but not mentioning the Chiriqui land. It was a month later and to Secretary Gideon Welles that Thompson first mentioned his scheme, presumably emphasizing naval stations and coal.[25] Welles dismissed Thompson as a pure speculator, and there is no sign that Lincoln took any interest at this time, concentrating instead on defeating the rebel forces.

As the war lengthened, the problem of dealing with the vast number of slaves fleeing to Union lines gave Thompson a new angle to exploit. Sometime before August, he printed a pamphlet that added to the list of potential uses of the Chiriqui land "a home for the Negro Race, now in the United States, and the only true place for their colonization."[26] It was no coincidence that Congress had been debating, and on 6 August 1861 passed, the first Confiscation Act, which declared that masters who used slaves in the service of the Confederacy thereby forfeited their property rights in the slaves, thus legalizing what General Benjamin F. Butler and others had already done by refusing to return fugitives to owners they decided were rebels. Lincoln was not pleased with Congress's handling of this delicate topic and made known to Butler his ambiguous desire to be guided by this law in disloyal states while respecting all existing rights in all states.[27]

Lincoln asked his bother-in-law, Ninian Edwards, to investigate Thompson's Chiriqui proposals. The choice of Edwards probably had less to do with his former involvement in the ISCS than with the fact that he was unemployed and would presumably carry out this task diligently to earn a more permanent position.[28] However, Edwards's eventual eight-page report was too uncritical generally, and its single sentence about colonization added nothing to what was in the printed proposals.[29]

The day before Edwards submitted his report to Lincoln, Thompson tried to buy Welles's support by offering to supply coal at half the current price.[30] In like manner, Edwards's report emphasized the value of Chiriqui's coal by referring to an earlier report by government geologist Dr. John Evans "that the coal is inexhaustible in quantity, while the analysis of it by Dr. Charles T. Jackson—a well known geologist of Boston, proves its quality to be of the best kind, and highly desirable for steam purposes." This was based on Evans's *final* report to Congress (before Lincoln took office): his preliminary report had been doubtful enough to cause him to send a coal sample for analysis to Jackson, a suspiciously poor choice because Jackson was notoriously unstable and went mad a few years later.[31]

Thompson's pamphlet had boasted that according to "Dr. Evans, the Geologist, . . . the best Coal for Steam Navigation, exists at and near the Atlantic harbors of the Chiriqui Lagoon." Lincoln, knowing a good deal about geology, may have wondered whether it was "the best Coal" of all possible types or only in this region and whether the Chiriqui's other coal measures were far worse. Edwards had suggested the "immense saving" to the government if it utilized this new source for coal, but Lincoln probably knew that Thompson was not above bribing the impecunious Edwards.

At some point, the Chiriqui file included a two-page "Memorandum" criticizing both pamphlet and report and giving figures indicating Chiriqui coal would be more than twice as expensive as current sources, adding, "The anaylasis [*sic*] of a small portion of coal by a chemist for practical purposes is not sufficient. Its usefulness depends upon its being generally free from impurities. Has the quantity or quality of this coal been spoken of other than in general terms [?]"[32] Who requested or composed this memorandum is unknown. It may have been added to the file before Welles returned it to Lincoln with a frosty comment about not having "the time necessary to investigate the subject of the proposed Chiriqui contract." After a two-month gap in the documentary evidence, Lincoln sent Welles's letter to Interior Secretary Caleb Smith, asking whether the draft contract was legal "and ought to be made."[33]

The file expanded with various materials from Frank Blair Sr., a founder of the Republican Party, magnate in the Border State of Missouri, and father of Lincoln's postmaster general, Montgomery Blair. The elder Blair, who strongly believed in colonization, pushed Lincoln to close the deal. Blair suggested an associate with mining experience who could investigate the geological claims, adding that he could be accompanied to the Chiriqui lands by Thompson's son, an army officer who was willing "to open the mines immediately and provide coal for the Navy, at a dollar less per ton than the existing price now paid. This is certainly the best earnest that can be given in regard to this most essential matter."[34]

The senior Blair also sent to Lincoln a printed "Memorandum of Proposals" presumably produced by Thompson, incorporating suggestions from Blair.[35] Of nine items listed as benefits for the government, only one related to colonization, clarifying that five hundred thousand acres would be set aside for colonization "by free negroes who have been residents of the United States"; the Chiriqui Company would not charge for those acres as it would be grateful for the labor supply. However, three more items were handwritten in: the tenth ensuring that the company could not overcharge for transportation and subsistence costs of colonists; the eleventh giving the government an option to buy another five hundred thousand acres at $1.25 per acre; and the twelfth clarifying that the colonists would be paid "fair wages" while working first on railroad construction and then in mining and in erecting works useful for convenience or protection. These additions were farsighted, but the handwriting is not Lincoln's, and the ideas probably originated with the Blairs, who also prepared three draft letters for Lincoln to send out over his own name.[36] The first, addressed to Caleb Smith, made the politically astute suggestion that funds allocated in an 1819 law to send to Liberia Africans freed by the navy in anti-slave-trade operations be reapplied to pay for "some of the unoccupied lands of Central America" and "the removal of negroes from this country." The second was to order Welles to transport the mining expert and the younger Thompson to Chiriqui, and the third asked the secretary of war to expedite the younger Thompson's temporary secondment.[37] There is no evidence that Lincoln sent any such letters.

Lincoln passed the Chiriqui file to the secretary of the treasury. Although Salmon P. Chase's support would be helpful because he had strong links with radical Republicans who opposed colonization, Lincoln had good reasons other than colonization to ask the treasury head to review the file. Chase avoided taking a position and suggested waiting until Congress resumed in three weeks' time.[38]

At this point, the Chiriqui contract was on hold. Lincoln had given no sign of any interest in Chiriqui's alleged colonization potential: all the links to colonization were in the writings of the Blairs or of Thompson, who probably planted Ninian Edwards's slight reference to colonization. The Blairs were genuinely keen, but their effort to expedite matters and Chase's to stall both point to likely opposition in Congress when it resumed in early December. In the end, Lincoln may have agreed with Chase that it was better to involve Congress. And, of course, all through December, Lincoln was dealing with the *Trent* affair.

Lincoln's first public statement as president in favor of colonization came in his first annual message to Congress on 3 December 1861. To deal with the influx of refugee slaves, Lincoln suggested Congress appropriate funds for colonizing these people but also suggested these funds could also be used for blacks who were already free. Lincoln used the idea apparently suggested by the Blairs about reapplying the 1819 appropriation more broadly, and he argued that there was no constitutional obstacle to purchasing territory for colonies. Opposing forced deportation, Lincoln declared that "colored people already in the United States" might be eligible "so far as individuals may desire." Also, while many assumed blacks would emigrate to the established independent black republics, Liberia or Haiti, Lincoln broadened this to "some place, or places, in a climate congenial to them."[39]

As Congress got under way, Republicans more radical than Lincoln almost immediately proposed bills to abolish slavery outright—which had no chance of passage—while Lincoln expended great effort trying to convince Border State representatives to start the process of voluntary and gradual emancipation on a state level, offering compensation from federal funds for citizens who thus surrendered their "property." If just one state took the first step, other slave states still in the Union might do the same. Lincoln argued that federal compensation did not undermine any state's control over the decision whether or how to emancipate and that "gradual" systems need not be complete for thirty years—permitting slavery to exist into the 1890s, which sounds more incredible to us than it did to Americans who had doubted they would live to see slavery ended.

As mentioned in the last chapter, in March Congress passed a resolution offering federal compensation for voluntary emancipation of slaves, abolished slavery in Washington, D.C., and appropriated $1 million to compensate owners. Lincoln was bothered that this act lacked the element of local consent, and he would have preferred a Border State to take the lead on emancipation rather than the federal government. However, the act also appropriated $100,000 for the president to spend "to aid in the colonization" of "free persons of African descent now residing in said District." The maximum expenditure of $100 per colonist was sufficient for transport costs and some initial support. The law mentioned "Hayti or Liberia" but also any "other country beyond the limits of the United States." So Chiriqui was not ruled out.

Signing the bill into law, Lincoln informed Congress that despite other misgivings, he was "gratified that the two principles of compensation and colonization are both recognized and practically applied in the act."[40] He was also pleased that a new treaty with Britain committed the United States to give full support for the final suppression of the Atlantic slave trade, thus terminating the source of supply.[41] At the same time, Congress authorized diplomatic relations with Haiti and Liberia, a useful step for advancing colonization, although even colonization's opponents supported this sign of treating black nations as equals.

All this energized colonization efforts by Lincoln's administration. Various proposals to accept some colonists came in from foreign governments other than Haiti and Liberia, especially some Central American states. The Chiriqui project was resurrected, and on 22 April, Secretary Chase sent a solicitor's report Lincoln had requested on the Chiriqui contract's validity; the report was favorable and said the region was well suited for black colonists. Interior Secretary Smith wrote a few days later to Thompson asking the terms under which the Chiriqui Company would take on the job of colonizing freed blacks, and some effort was made to link the company with the New York Colonization Society.[42]

In May 1862, Smith responded to some presidential query by reporting that the Chiriqui contract offered "good coal at a cheap rate" and a chance to begin colonization, which in turn would give the United States "an influence as would most probably secure to us the absolute control of the country."[43] Smith also recommended that Lincoln appoint the Reverend James Mitchell to run the colonization program. Lincoln already knew and trusted Mitchell as a former colonization agent in Indiana. By 18 May, Mitchell sent Lincoln a copy of a twenty-eight-page circular about the need for colonization, printed at the Government Printing Office.[44]

Secretary of State William H. Seward also sent information to Lincoln, though it is unclear whether he was carrying out instructions or trying to convince Lincoln to abandon the Chiriqui plan. One note from Seward's office mentioned that Marcelino Hurtado, commissioner from New Grenada (the site of Chiriqui), was pleased to accept an invitation to dinner at the White House, and in a second note, dated the following day and presumably carried by Hurtado, Seward himself wrote that Hurtado "visits you for the purpose of imparting information which it is understood you desire, in regard to a certain region of that country."[45] Also, sometime prior to 28 May, someone—probably Seward and presumably with Lincoln's approval—gave to Lincoln's erstwhile scientific adviser Joseph Henry of the Smithsonian what Henry described as "an elaborated paper on the subject [of Chiriqui coal] from . . . the Interior Department in which all this testimony in favor of the existence of good coal was convincingly set forth." On 28 May, Henry wrote to Philadelphia geologist J. Peter Lesley, a coal expert, asking "on behalf of the President and the secretary of state" for a confidential opinion about the coal "in which Mr Thompson of your city is so much interested." Henry explained that the proposed Chiriqui contract involved coal "for the use of the navy in connection with a plan of establishing a colony of negroes." He added that he was "somewhat suspicious" and "must be true to myself and the government."[46]

Within two days, Lesley promised to look into the matter, but his eventual report apparently arrived after Henry himself wrote a preliminary one. Thompson learned about the consultation with Henry, who soon received "a direct offer from *St. Ambrose* of a share in the speculation if I would make a favorable report." Henry did no such thing, and his preliminary report "stated that from the age of the geological formation of the rocks of the Isthmus, of which there was sufficient evidence in the Smith[sonian] Inst[itute], there could be no real coal in that locality."[47] That report is not extant, and perhaps the attempted bribery caused Henry to wish it kept confidential. It is not clear whether the report reached Lincoln. If Seward was the recipient, he had no reason not to show it to Lincoln, and Henry might as easily have conveyed his opinions in one of his occasional meetings with Lincoln.

Meanwhile in July, Congress's Second Confiscation Act quintupled the appropriation for colonizing freedmen to $500,000. Although Lincoln was disturbed by aspects of the act—such as a tendency to assert federal power to emancipate slaves, which Lincoln feared would make rebel states even less likely to surrender—the law helpfully gave the president the authority to

> make provision for the transportation, colonization, and settlement, in some tropical country beyond the limits of the United States, of such persons of the African race, made free by the provisions of this act, as may be willing to emigrate, having first obtained the consent of the government of said country to their protection and settlement within the same, with all the rights and privileges of freemen.[48]

Shortly before signing this act, Lincoln revealed to Seward and Welles on 13 July that he was considering an executive action on emancipation, and a week later, he raised the matter with the whole cabinet. This was apparently the first time the whole cabinet discussed colonization, but the issue was sidelined by the more important topic of Lincoln's first draft of the Emancipation Proclamation.

In August, a new draft contract drawn up by the Interior Department proposed that the Chiriqui Company handle colonization but that no money be laid out for coal until a further inspection determined "the productiveness of the mines, and the value of the same for steam purposes."[49] This suggests Lincoln was indeed aware of Joseph Henry's negative stance in his preliminary report and did not ignore it as Henry later suggested.

On 14 August 1862, Lincoln held two meetings in the White House that both related to colonization, but the second of them has a wider importance that requires close inspection before continuing the story of Lincoln's colonization policy.

Colonization and Emancipation

n 14 August 1862, Lincoln met with William McLain, the ACS treasurer, and Joseph J. Roberts, the visiting president of Liberia. Both men gave Lincoln a glowing report about Liberia's condition and prospects. But transportation costs were probably inclining Lincoln toward a location where commercial shipping was expanding, as was the case with the Caribbean and Central America but not with Africa, a view expressed already in Caleb Smith's report of 9 May. Apparently, McLain and Roberts were both annoyed that Lincoln praised Liberia to their faces but then an hour later promoted Central America rather than Liberia in a landmark address on colonization.[1]

The address was historic partly because the audience was a small deputation of free African Americans brought to Lincoln by the Reverend James Mitchell: the first time a group of blacks were in the White House to meet with a president rather than to cook and clean for him. Knowing the event would cause some stir, Lincoln took care to avoid having falsehoods spread about how he treated and addressed his guests. No official text was preserved or released, but Lincoln's comments were hardly off-the-cuff, and it appears that the event was covered by a single Associated Press reporter—who no doubt behaved in order to obtain similar exclusives in future. His version is what appeared in all the newspapers and has come down to us.[2]

The reporter mentioned first that the "Committee of colored men" was introduced by Mitchell and that its chairman "remarked that they were there by invitation to hear what the Executive had to say to them"—so, not petitioners seeking favors. Lincoln began by mentioning Congress's appropriations to aid colonization to some country by "the people, or a portion of them, of African descent." The word "portion" accorded with Lincoln's notion of a voluntary colonization and caused Lincoln to raise the obvious question: why should *any* of them "leave this country?" His answer was aimed also at that larger audience for whom the reporter's pencil was scratching.

"You and we are different races. We have between us a broader difference than exists between almost any other two races," Lincoln said, expressing a common view of human races with which both Louis Agassiz and Charles Darwin could agree, if for different reasons. Far from ranking races according to abilities, Lincoln spoke only of the "difference" causing "disadvantages" that applied to both races: "Whether it is right or wrong I need not discuss, but this physical difference is a great disadvantage to us both, as I think your race suffer very greatly, many of them by living among us, while ours suffer from your presence." Discussing mutual "disadvantages" suggested a balance; explaining their real cause—racial intolerance by the white majority—would upset that balance. "In a word we suffer on each side. If this is admitted, it affords a reason at least why we should be separated," Lincoln said. The ethical, as well as practical, issue was not about race but about slavery:

> Your race are suffering, in my judgment, the greatest wrong inflicted on any people. But even when you cease to be slaves, you are yet far removed from being placed on an equality with the white race. You are cut off from many of the advantages which the other race enjoy. The aspiration of men is to enjoy equality with the best when free, but on this broad continent, not a single man of your race is made the equal of a single man of ours. Go where you are treated the best, and the ban is still upon you.
>
> I do not propose to discuss this, but to present it as a fact with which we have to deal. I cannot alter it if I would. It is a fact, about which we all think and feel alike, I and you.

Lincoln went on to note that the present war was one of the evils caused by having two races on one continent. He acknowledged that free blacks like themselves were not inclined "to go out of the country," but he suggested that actual slaves would hardly hesitate if colonization were the condition for obtaining freedom. In view of that connection between colonization and future emancipation, Lincoln argued that for the men before him to maintain they "have nothing to do with the idea of going to a foreign country . . . is (I speak in no unkind sense) an extremely selfish view of the case." He now urged his guests to "give a start" that "would open a wide door for many to be made free."[3]

Patronizing as much of this sounds to modern ears, in fact Lincoln avoided any expression of actual denigration on racial grounds. In arguing why free blacks should start the process, Lincoln stated that unfree blacks "whose intellects are clouded by Slavery" would provide "very poor materials to start with." No suggestion that blacks are *naturally* less intelligent; indeed, Lincoln said that the men before him were "intelligent colored men" as "capable of thinking" as any white man, unlike slaves "who have been systematically oppressed."[4]

Lincoln spoke of certain hardships as he mentioned Liberia and his recent chat with its president, but after explaining away some of Liberia's perceived disadvantages, Lincoln suggested blacks might prefer to colonize somewhere "within reach of the country of your nativity"—avoiding the phrase he dared not use: "your country." Lincoln revealed that he was thinking about Central America, which was nearer, "on a great line of travel," possessed natural resources, and was advantageous "especially because of the similarity of climate with your native land—thus being suited to your physical condition." That last phrase was superbly ambiguous. Most readers would probably infer that Lincoln was referring to Africa, though he never said so; in fact only once does a cognate word appear in the address, in an introductory phrase about people "of African descent." Most of the delegation before Lincoln were presumably "native" to the United States and indeed to southern states whose climate was at least more like that of Central America than that of New England or Illinois. But, again, Lincoln avoided direct reference to the fact that the members of the delegation were Americans. And his reference to being physiologically suited to a particular climate was vaguely acceptable to both polygenists and monogenists, whether they explained that harmony as resulting from God's design for creation, some degradation following creation, or some undesigned modification through natural selection.[5]

Lincoln continued his description of a potential colony: "The particular place I have in view is to be a great highway from the Atlantic or Caribbean Sea to the Pacific Ocean," which could certainly refer to the Chiriqui lands, not named. There was "evidence of very rich coal mines," Lincoln added, lawyer-like, not mentioning the counterevidence he knew about. "A certain amount of coal is valuable in any country," he continued, "and there may be more than enough for the wants of the country"—meaning the area being colonized (though perhaps Joseph Henry subsequently misinterpreted "the country" to mean the United States). "Why I attach so much importance to coal is, it will afford an opportunity to the inhabitants for immediate employment till they get ready to settle permanently in their homes." Lincoln said nothing about providing the navy with cheap coal, presumably because he understood the Chiriqui coal might only be good enough for the "wants" of the colony itself by creating some immediate, if short-term, employment. Lincoln repeated the point: "if something is started so that you can get your daily bread as soon as you reach there, it is a great advantage. Coal land is the best thing I know of with which to commence an enterprise."[6]

Knowing these men were aware of the Chiriqui scheme, Lincoln sought to allay understandable concerns. "We have been mistaken all our lives if we do not know whites as well as blacks look to their self-interest. . . . I shall, if I get a sufficient number of you engaged, have provisions made that you shall not be wronged." Lincoln was reassuringly frank: "I am not sure you will succeed. The Government may lose the money, but we cannot succeed unless we try; but we think, with care, we can succeed." Lincoln optimistically suggested that Central Americans "have no objections" to "your colored race" but also spoke vaguely of "protection"—causing some Central American diplomats, reading the next day's newspapers, to wonder how invasive U.S. "protection" might prove to be.[7]

Lincoln ended his address with a call to action, even if only on a small scale. "Could I get a hundred tolerably intelligent men, with their wives and children, to 'cut their own fodder,' so to speak? Can I have fifty? If I could find twenty-five able-bodied men, with a mixture of women and children, good things in the family relation, I think I could make a successful commencement." Lincoln was emphasizing that the delegation members need not feel overwhelmed by the task he was setting them.[8] "I want you to let me know whether this can be done or not. This is the practical part of my wish to see you." The AP reporter finished with, "The above is merely given as the substance of the President's remarks"—a disclaimer less important to the reporter than to Lincoln, who might deny any particular statement.[9]

Whether the men Lincoln addressed were able to arouse much interest for colonization among free blacks—and the evidence is mixed—Mitchell and Ambrose W. Thompson were having success with recruitment, and the latter soon informed Lincoln that he had enough would-be colonists to make a start as soon as a vessel could be made ready.[10] A week after Lincoln addressed the black deputation, Joseph Henry wrote to fellow scientist Alexander Dallas Bache, expressing his surprise that Lincoln "believed in the humbug coal mines of the Isthmus" and explaining the background to the preliminary report he had made earlier. He told Bache that he "afterwards"—sometime between early June and mid-August— "received a letter from Peter Lesley condemning the whole affair as a swindling speculation, and asserting that the general character of the material found in that region was an inferior kind of lignite." Henry then added, somewhat confusingly, "After having communicated these facts cautiously but clearly in my report, and much more fully to Mr. Seward privately I was much surprised to learn from a speech of the President that he still believed in the phantom."[11] Lincoln apparently did not see Lesley's report until *after* speaking to the black delegation, but he probably *had* seen Henry's preliminary report and at least heard more about Henry's final report through William H. Seward, which is why Lincoln's references to the coal were restrained—though so subtly that Henry missed the point.

Around this time, Lincoln appointed Kansas Senator Samuel C. Pomeroy as a higher-level colonization agent. Despite unsavory aspects in Pomeroy's personal history, he had some experience as a "colonizer" (in Kansas in 1854) and, more important, he was an associate of Salmon P. Chase, whose opposition to colonization might thus be partly neutralized. Pomeroy was to travel to Chiriqui with Thompson to ensure all was well before authorizing the allocation of certain funds to Thompson. Before 25 August, Pomeroy had printed up a pamphlet, publicized in some newspapers, urging free blacks to apply for the colonization adventure.[12]

At this point, Joseph Henry was approached again. On 5 September, he addressed a letter to Seward's son and secretary, Frederick, enclosing an extract of Lesley's report on the Chiriqui coal. The extract carries no date, and Henry's letter merely describes the author as a "gentleman who has been extensively engaged in geological surveys and has published a work of much merit on coal," adding that "the letter was received after I had written and presented my Report," which had been written "before I had time to fortify my opinion by reference to authorities and hence I spoke very cautiously." Further enquiry had "confirmed my assertion that the geological formation of the District is not that of the true coal measures but that of the tertiary deposit in which only *lignite* is found." He hoped no contract would be signed to purchase the Chiriqui land "until it has been thoroughly examined by persons of known capacity and integrity." He accepted that further examination might alter the situation, but previous reports had so far "failed to convince me."[13]

Henry's letter accompanying the extract was sent to Frederick Seward (signed "very truly your friend & servant"), which suggests his father, the secretary of state, was gathering ammunition to kill off the Chiriqui plan. While a senator, the elder Seward had participated in earlier debates about the contract, which perhaps made him doubt the earlier coal reports and Thompson's integrity. Now Seward was concerned that by late August the Chiriqui project was upsetting U.S. relations with Latin America.

Historian Michael Vorenberg suggests that Lincoln "seemed to be making some hasty and short-sighted decisions," as when "he touted the rich coal deposits of Chiriqui, but then chose to ignore Henry's dismal report." But Lincoln knew the coal's quality was controversial, and he was not going to be tied down either by Thompson's favorable reports or by negative ones brought in by Frederick Seward. Lincoln now ensured that Thompson would receive no money until Pomeroy took the responsibility to say the coal deposits were suitable. Thompson later said that Lincoln, who signed the contract on 11 September, wrote portions of it himself. The following day, Lincoln instructed Interior Secretary Smith to oversee the project and pay for it out of the funds Congress had appropriated two months earlier. Soon five hundred colonists were reported ready to embark, and on 15 September, Lincoln approved Pomeroy's request to be allowed to advance Thompson limited sums to cover immediate costs.[14]

Then the Chiriqui project once again stalled as Robert E. Lee caused a crisis by deciding to invade the North.

From the moment on 12 September when Lincoln learned that Lee had crossed the Potomac River into Maryland, he was eager for General George McClellan to trap and crush the Confederate forces.[15] McClellan managed to win the bloody Battle of Antietam on 17 September, but Lincoln ached for further news that Lee's army had been destroyed before it could recross the Potomac. The president was bitterly disappointed when McClellan failed in this, but Lincoln decided Antietam was enough of a victory to justify issuing the preliminary Emancipation Proclamation on 22 September.

Lincoln had discussed the concept with his cabinet in July, after several developments convinced Lincoln that he could and must take this step. The collapse of the Peninsula Campaign at the beginning of July renewed the risk of European intervention, recognizing the Confederacy. The passage of the Second Confiscation Act later in July suggested emancipation would receive more support than opposition in Congress. Lincoln was bitterly disappointed by the Border States' failure to create momentum for the most constitutional approach: gradual emancipation initiated by state governments, with compensation supplied by the federal government. And people who had never been abolitionists were calling for measures that would weaken the Confederates' grip on that enslaved labor force, whose exploitation helped sustain the South's military operations.[16]

The majority of the cabinet had supported the president's proposal, but Lincoln heeded Seward's advice that if the plan were announced then, just after McClellan had been out-generalled in the Peninsula Campaign, the emancipation of slaves might seem an act of desperation. Lincoln agreed to delay an announcement, which in any case risked driving some Border States into the Confederacy and some Union soldiers into dropping the weapons they had willingly carried for defending the Union but not for ending slavery. Now, in September, Lee's invasion raised the possibility that the war could suddenly end with a great Northern victory, removing the military justification for the Emancipation Proclamation and casting a different light on all issues connected with colonization. But Lee's eventual escape meant the war would continue, along with the problems of financing it, recruiting more troops, and somehow preventing foreign intervention. It was necessary to announce the proclamation, which would emancipate slaves only in rebel-held territory and would not go into effect until 1 January 1863, thus giving rebellious states three months to return to the Union if they wished to preserve slavery.

As Lincoln probably expected, no rebel politicians dared propose the destruction of the Confederacy in order to save slavery. But as the hundred days passed until the actual promulgation of the emancipation, Lincoln turned his attention back to colonization. In cabinet meetings on 24–26 September, some members were lukewarm in general while others called for forced deportations—which Lincoln always rejected. No doubt, many cabinet members doubted Thompson's claims about the quality of the coal, although Joseph Henry's recent report was not specifically mentioned in the accounts. A central concern was whether the colonization should be protected through specific treaties with the countries concerned or whether the colonists should simply emigrate as individuals. Gideon Welles pushed the latter approach and thought he had support from Secretary Seward, who expressed concern about the negative reactions from Latin American governments. Lincoln still considered treaties necessary, even though this would bring the issue before the Senate Foreign Relations Committee, whose chairman, Senator Charles Sumner, disliked colonization.[17]

On 27 September, Pomeroy addressed a meeting of blacks in Washington, but his language—like that in his 25 August pamphlet and, indeed, like Lincoln's address to the delegation of blacks in the White House—added to the uneasiness of Latin American diplomats. The U.S. government naturally desired to reassure colonists that they were not simply being dumped into some new form of slavery, yet Latin American governments, which had earlier welcomed the idea of colonists aiding agricultural development, increasingly protested against any notion of further land sales to or ongoing interference by their expansive northern neighbor. Seward sent out a circular on 30 September to representatives of various European powers—less likely than vulnerable Latin American states to feel threatened—to see if any of their colonies in the Western Hemisphere might welcome freed blacks, under terms protecting the colonists.[18]

Meanwhile, the government found a vessel to transport the first set of colonists ready to depart for Chiriqui, but on 7 October, according to Welles, the cabinet was reluctant "to press the subject of negro emigration to Chiriqui . . . against the wishes and remonstrances of the States of Central America." Later that day, Pomeroy was informed through the Department of the Interior that the operation was "temporarily suspended" by presidential order. Pomeroy was angry, later telling Lincoln's friend Orville Browning that over thirteen thousand free blacks had already formally applied for colonization—an assertion neither doubted at the time nor since disproved.[19]

The cabinet's unease was about Chiriqui and not about colonization itself, and Lincoln felt able to address the topic a few weeks later in his second annual message to Congress on 1 December. After noting the expressions of interest received from "many free Americans of African descent" as well as "other parties, at home and abroad—some from interested motives, others upon patriotic considerations, and still others influenced by philanthropic sentiments," Lincoln admitted that "several of the Spanish-American republics have protested against the sending of such colonies to their respective territories." Lincoln stressed that he still hoped to attain international agreements agreeable to the Senate, but at present, "Liberia and Hayti are, as yet, the only countries to which colonists of African descent from here, could go with certainty of being received and adopted as citizens." He regretted that blacks "contemplating colonization, do not seem so willing to migrate to those countries, as to some others, nor so willing as I think their interest demands. I believe, however, opinion among them, in this respect, is improving; and that, ere long, there will be an augmented, and considerable migration to both these countries, from the United States."[20]

While Lincoln still advocated a protected, financed, and voluntary form of colonization, he was preoccupied as the final signing of the Emancipation Proclamation approached. Near the end of his December message to Congress, Lincoln proposed three constitutional amendments: first, that states should receive compensation if they abolished slavery any time between the present and the year 1900; second, that all slaveholders who had not been disloyal but had lost slaves "by the chances of war" should receive compensation and that their slaves be declared forever free; and, third, that "Congress may appropriate money, and otherwise provide, for colonizing free colored persons, with their own consent, at any place or places without the United States." Such amendments, if ratified, would be harder to reverse than similar legislation, and they could add incentive for rebel states to surrender and for slave owners to accept emancipation, while also safeguarding freed blacks against forced deportation. Lincoln was planning for the time when he could no longer direct these policies, either because victory ended his use of "war powers" or because he failed to win reelection. He was trying to bind Congress to certain options.[21]

In discussing his third proposed amendment, Lincoln embarked on a curious argument. "I cannot make it better known than it already is, that I strongly favor colonization. And yet I wish to say there is an objection urged against free colored persons remaining in the country, which is largely imaginary, if not sometimes malicious." Lincoln argued that emancipating blacks did not make them more likely to take jobs away from whites or lower the value of labor, so these were not valid objections to letting freedmen remain in the United States, while any degree of colonization "even to a limited extent" made it "mathematically certain" that the wages of white labor would be "enhanced." Lincoln was acquainting the public with the idea that colonization need not be all or nothing: the country would benefit from any departures yet not suffer from any refusals to emigrate. There was no reason, Lincoln argued, to believe emancipated blacks would "swarm forth" and cover the north as well as the south; and, even if they did, Lincoln offered statistics showing that the average proportions of free blacks to whites that might result already existed in some areas without causing serious difficulties for either race.[22]

Lincoln's primary goal remained the restoration of the Union, but he now recognized that the most economic and least-bloody way to achieve that goal was through emancipation, achieved through constitutional means, allowing for individual state consent, offering a gradual rather than a sudden alteration in the condition of blacks, providing the lubrication of financial compensation, and offering colonization to any blacks desiring it. To those whites who strongly favored or opposed black colonization, he offered a funded program that was nevertheless voluntary as well as reassurances that no disasters would follow if colonization were only partial. Lincoln finished his recommendation by eloquently declaring:

> In *giving* freedom to the *slave*, we *assure* freedom to the *free*—honorable alike in what we give, and what we preserve. We shall nobly save, or meanly lose, the last best, hope of earth. Other means may succeed; this could not fail. The way is plain, peaceful, generous, just—a way which, if followed, the world will forever applaud, and God must forever bless.[23]

Lincoln had no delusions about the practicability of colonization, but its political value had been greater when abolition had seemed a more-remote possibility and intolerance of blacks had seemed to be growing. If Lincoln's sole interest in colonization had been political, now was the time—four weeks before he signed a document to free several million blacks in the South—to offer colonization as a panacea for racist America's worst fears. Yet, even while proposing that colonization be protected constitutionally for blacks who chose it, Lincoln was preparing white Americans for a future that could include black Americans. Also, Lincoln was planning but had not yet announced a development that could do more to make whites accept that blacks were their fellow human beings than any of his own arguments or statistics, or any pleas from radical abolitionists, or any religious doctrine that everyone was descended from Adam, or any scientific theories about mankind's common evolutionary heritage. Lincoln understood that the attitudes of white Americans—including himself—were about to be affected radically by the scarcely imaginable sight of blacks serving in uniform.

Lincoln had made no mention of it in the preliminary Emancipation Proclamation in September or in his message to Congress in December. Yet, in the final proclamation of 1 January, Lincoln declared that freed slaves "of suitable condition, will be received into the armed service of the United States to garrison forts, positions, stations, and other places, and to man vessels of all sorts in said service."[24] When Lincoln reached this important decision is unknown. Genuine difficulties with recruitment of white Northerners for the ongoing slaughter played a major role, as did the urgings of various idealists wishing to prove that blacks could and would fight for the freedom of their race.

Lincoln had previously had good reason to ignore calls for the arming of African Americans, which smacked of John Brown's 1859 attempt to foment a slave insurrection, alarming not only rebels but also Border State slaveholders. In July 1862, Congress had authorized the president to employ "as many persons of African descent as he may deem necessary and proper," specifying that they may be used for "any military or naval service for which they may be found competent," but Lincoln was used to Congress moving too precipitously on such delicate matters. However, Lincoln began to adapt his own thinking. Near the beginning August, Lincoln turned down an offer of "two colored regiments" from a deputation from Indiana, reportedly saying that "he was not prepared to go the length of enlisting negroes as soldiers" and "that to arm the negroes would turn 50,000 bayonets from the loyal Border States against us that were for us." However, by the end of August, Lincoln allowed Secretary of War Edwin M. Stanton to authorize a Union commander operating in the Carolinas to "arm, uniform, equip, and receive into the service" as many local volunteers "of African descent" as he saw fit.[25]

Lincoln was waiting for popular feeling to catch up with the lead offered by Congress's act in July. In September, he reportedly said, "If we were to arm [blacks], I fear that in a few weeks the arms would be in the hands of the rebels," which suggested lack of confidence in the suitability of former slaves for military service. Ten days before announcing the preliminary Emancipation Proclamation, Lincoln again mentioned his concern that fifty thousand white soldiers from the Border States might abandon the army (whether or not he armed blacks), yet he also expressed his hope that opinions were changing and that of those fifty thousand white soldiers: "I do not think they all would [leave the army]—not so many indeed as a year ago, or as six months ago—not so many to-day as yesterday. Every day increases their Union feeling."[26]

In November, Senator Sumner had given the president a pamphlet by George Livermore entitled *An Historical Research: Opinions of the Founders of the Republic on Negroes as Slaves, as Citizens, and as Soldiers*, which, Sumner reported, "interested President Lincoln much." Spurred by Congress's action, by positive reactions to the preliminary proclamation, or by Livermore's pamphlet, sometime between September and the last day of 1862 Lincoln added to the final Emancipation Proclamation his provision for black recruitment. When Lincoln signed the final draft of the Emancipation Proclamation, he sent the pen to Livermore. A North Carolina editor sneered that the circus owner P. T. Barnum, should have received the pen "which was employed to affix the name of Gorilla to the most infamous document that ever emanated from any civilized government." Browning recorded in his diary various opinions he heard at that time, including the view that the recruitment of blacks would cause a hundred thousand whites or more to leave the army. But Lincoln became increasingly assertive about the rightness of his decision. In March 1863, he wrote to the governor of Tennessee, "The colored population is the great *available* and yet *unavailed* of, force for restoring the Union. The bare sight of fifty thousand armed, and drilled black soldiers on the banks of the Mississippi, would end the rebellion at once."[27]

Lincoln soon felt encouraged—and hoped others would as well—by reports of large numbers of blacks enlisting and performing well. In April, he wrote to General David Hunter, glad "to see the accounts of your colored force" and that "the enemy are driving at them fiercely, as is to be expected. It is important to the enemy that such a force shall *not* take shape, and grow, and thrive, in the South; and in precisely the same proportion, it is important to us that it *shall*."[28] Black troops distinguished themselves in engagements in May in Louisiana, in June near Vicksburg, Mississippi, and in July near Charleston, South Carolina. By August, Lincoln trumpeted the black troops' patriotism in a letter he asked his long-time Republican colleague James C. Conkling to read to an important meeting in Springfield, addressing in particular those who opposed his policies. He stressed that some of the military commanders felt that using colored troops inflicted "the heaviest blow yet dealt to the rebellion" and that at least one victory could not have been achieved "but for the aid of black soldiers." His tone became more severe:

> You say you will not fight to free negroes. Some of them seem willing to fight for you. . . . [When the war is over], there will be some black men who can remember that, with silent tongue, and clenched teeth, and steady eye, and well-poised bayonet, they have helped mankind on to this great consummation; while, I fear, there will be some white ones, unable to forget that, with malignant heart, and deceitful speech, they have strove to hinder it.[29]

With that single vivid image of a determined black soldier, Lincoln broke completely with over a century of tradition, going back to Linnaeus, of classifying "negroes" as "indolent," "negligent," and "docile."

After closing down the Chiriqui scheme in October 1862, Lincoln had backed another project early in 1863 that actually sent some colonists to an island near Haiti, Ile á Vache, but this was so mismanaged by private contractors that the scheme had to be abandoned and the colonists rescued.[30] Although this was not the end of Lincoln's interest in colonization, its political use to promote emancipation was becoming obsolete, and there was hope that white intolerance of blacks would be lessened by the latter's splendid service in the army. Nearly a year after Lincoln praised that service in his Springfield letter, Congress voted on 2 July 1864 to rescind all the appropriations for colonization, and Lincoln made no objection. His secretary John Hay with that vote in mind wrote in his diary, "The President has sloughed of that idea of colonization"—though that may have been wishful thinking on Hay's part.[31]

In August 1863, one year after receiving a delegation of relatively unknown black leaders in the White House, Lincoln received the most famous black leader in America, Frederick Douglass. "There was not the slightest shadow of embarrassment from the first moment," Douglass later wrote. The president received him "just as you have seen one gentleman receive another. . . . In his company I was never in any way reminded of my humble origin, or of my unpopular color."[32] If blacks were to remain in the country, then they could only enjoy their new freedom if whites treated them as equals. For a century and a half, Lincoln has set millions of Americans an example they have found difficult to follow.

Societies

L ate in the summer of 1862, as Lincoln awaited the opportune moment to announce the preliminary Emancipation Proclamation, Darwin followed the war news in the London *Times* while also waiting expectantly for Thomas Huxley and Charles Lyell to publish their respective researches about man.[1] Darwin was growing impatient with the *Times*'s pro-Southern slant, but he could always find the Yankee view in Asa Gray's letters. On the very day the Emancipation Proclamation was first announced, 22 September, Gray was writing to Darwin about the war's slow progress: "We find it a far tougher job than we supposed. But we have no more notion of giving it up than—the English nation would have, under a similar case. For my part, I would fight till ⅓ of our property and half our men were destroyed before I would give up!—and I think that is the general opinion."[2]

Darwin first mentioned the preliminary proclamation in his next letter and was clearly not impressed. "If I could believe that your President's proclamation would have any effect, it would make a great alteration in my wishes. . . . But slavery seems to me to grow a more hopeless curse." Darwin also complained about the *Times*'s American correspondent (no longer William Howard Russell) who "has not a shade of feeling against slavery" while telling Gray it was incredible "that you all seem to believe that you can annex the South; whilst on this side of the Atlantic, it is the almost universal opinion that this is utterly impossible."[3]

In a subsequent letter, Gray said, "The President's Emancipation proclamation [was] working well on the whole. Our Courage does not fail, and I think will not. . . . You don't see, as you would if here—the total impossibility of coming to any terms of peace with the South, based on their independence. Before that can be they or *we* must be thoroughly beaten." At least they agreed about Lincoln's decision to dismiss General McClellan: Gray "rejoiced," and Darwin called it "great news."[4] Although saving his harshest remarks about "the Yankees" for Joseph Dalton Hooker, who was bound to agree, Darwin always saw the central issue as slavery, which "draws me one day one way & another day another way."

Responding to Hooker's attempt to use natural selection to explain why the Americans had so far failed "to develop any settled Govt. at all," Darwin said, "What a new idea of Struggle for existence being necessary to try & purge a government! I daresay it is very true." The huge casualties in the North's defeat at Fredericksburg, Virginia, on 13 December upset Darwin, and the day after the Emancipation Proclamation had been signed by Lincoln, Darwin commented to Gray, "When will peace come! But then Slavery, I know not what to wish." A few days later, Darwin passed one of Gray's letters to Hooker, commented with a note, "It is marvellous to see Asa Gray so cock-sure about the doom of Slavery."[5]

Darwin recognized that the proclamation only emancipated slaves in rebel-held territory and was not a constitutional amendment or even a law. "Well, your President has issued his fiat against Slavery—God grant it may have some effect," he wrote Gray. "I fear it is true that very many English do not now *really* care about Slavery; I heard some old sensible people saying here the same thing; & they accounted for it (& such a contrast it is to what I remember in my Boyhood) by the present generation never having seen or heard much about Slavery. . . . [The war] is a cruel evil to the whole world; I hope that you may prove right & good come out of it."[6]

Meanwhile, what seemed like good news soon turned sour for Darwin. "Hurrah," he said to Huxley, "the Monkey Book has come." This was Huxley's *Evidence as to Man's Place in Nature*, which Hooker decided was a "coarse-looking little book[:] not fit, as somebody said to me, for a gentleman's table." Darwin, however, told Huxley, "I have just finished with very great interest 'Man's Place.'" After further praise, Darwin asserted that he had "no criticisms; nor is it likely that I could have." Yet he did: Huxley "could have added some interesting matter on the character or disposition of the young Ourangs . . . [and] might have enlarged a little on the later embryological changes in man & on his rudimentary structure—tail as compared with tail of higher monkeys intermaxillary bone, false ribs & I daresay other points—such as muscles of ears &c &c." After tempering this with more praise, Darwin made reference to the recent publication of Lyell's long-awaited *Geological Evidences of the Antiquity of Man*: "I am fearfully disappointed at Lyell's excessive caution in expressing any judgment on Species or origin of man."[7]

Although Darwin had swiftly informed Gray that "Lyell's Book on Man . . . quotes you at end with gusto," Darwin was upset that although Lyell accepted "almost fully the modification of species by variation & selection," he seemed "afraid to say so. . . . The public may well say, if such a man dare not or will not speak out his mind, how can we who are ignorant, form even a guess on [the] subject." To Hooker, Darwin complained of Lyell's "timidity. . . . I wish to Heaven he had said not a word on [the] subject."[8]

The problem was not only that Lyell would not commit himself fully on natural selection but especially, as Adrian Desmond and James Moore suggest, that Lyell persisted in maintaining that divine intervention may be necessary to explain the "leap" to the higher forms of human intellect. "To say that such leaps constitute no interruption to the ordinary course of nature is more than we are warranted in affirming," said Lyell, before compounding the error (in Darwin's eyes) by implying that these "leaps" could become transmissible by inheritance, and therefore "we may possibly discern in such leaps the origin of the superiority of certain races of mankind."[9] That sentence, Darwin told Lyell frankly, "makes me groan. . . . [A]nyone might argue . . . that you were far from believing that man was descended from any animal." Lyell's views seemed to throw a lifeline to the devotees of Agassiz. A few days later, Darwin wrote to Lyell that he wished "that your state of belief could have permitted you to say boldly & distinctly out that species were not separately created."[10]

According to biographer Janet Browne, "Despite all their friendly connections, Darwin never really forgave [Lyell] for betraying his hopes." While Darwin found fault with Huxley's and Lyell's work, their reception by critics showed there were still dangers for those who appeared to undermine Genesis. The *Athenaeum* took aim: "Lyell's object is to make man old, Huxley's to degrade him."[11] Whether Darwin felt relief at not being the target or frustration that others had not done the subject justice, he did not rush in to place his own views before the public, yet his fascination continued.

In 1862, Dr. James Hunt, honorary secretary of the Ethnological Society of London (ESL), offered a paper "On Ethno-Climatology; or the Acclimatization of Man," presenting statistics to demonstrate that the various races of man were so distinct that they could not long survive outside the geographical zone where they had originated. Although Hunt did not cite Agassiz, who held a similar view, he did quote Dr. Josiah Nott of Mobile, Alabama. Criticized for being cavalier in his use of statistics, Hunt seceded from the ESL along with some others who had various grievances and formed the Anthropological Society of London (ASL). Hunt issued honorary memberships to many prominent researchers, including Darwin and Huxley, and began publishing the *Anthropological Review*. Although initially many supporters of Darwin contributed articles, they were unlikely to admire Hunt's introductory essay for the first volume. "Whether [Man] has risen from an ape or descended from a perfect man, . . . the Races of Europe have now much in their mental and moral nature which the races of Africa have not got." Hunt said it was ". . . a gross calumny . . . against the American School of Anthropology" to suggest "their interest in keeping up slavery induced the scientific men of that country to advocate a distinct origin for the African race."[12]

While Hunt made Nott an honorary foreign member of the new ASL, the *Anthropological Review* became a vehicle for polygenist writings, including a review attacking Lyell's *Antiquity of Man* for dealing with "theories of progression and development . . . [which have] nothing to do with the antiquity of man" and condemning Lyell for not referencing that "great national American work *The Types of Mankind*."[13] That review was written by "a jackal of Owen's by the name of C. Carter Blake," as Huxley described him after Blake also attacked Huxley's work. Huxley returned his "Diploma of Honorary Fellowship" and called Hunt's ASL a "nest of imposters." Other "Darwinians," like Edward B. Tylor, resigned their honorary memberships; George Rolleston called Hunt an "ignorant charlatan"; Alfred Russel Wallace referred to the ASL as "that *bête noire*." Hunt in turn described the ESL as "a sort of Darwinian club." To a foreign colleague, Darwin described himself as "not an active, only a honorary member of the [ASL]," but he often found articles in the *Review* worth reading.[14]

While some maintained joint memberships, generally the "Ethnologicals" were more inclined toward monogenism, the unity of man, and were leaning toward species-change through natural selection. The "Anthropologicals" tended toward polygenism and were, if not overtly proslavery, at least pro-Confederacy. Of course, many other Englishmen favored Southern independence, and any Southerners reading ASL publications would likely approve. The ASL was not bankrolled by the Confederacy, but Richmond did directly fund two members of its council, one of whom made occasional payments to two more members. That leader was a young man who had become the Confederacy's best propagandist in Europe, Henry Hotze.[15]

Born in Zürich in 1834, Hotze, while still a boy, immigrated to America—not many years after his fellow countryman Louis Agassiz.[16] Although their meeting is not recorded, it probably occurred when Agassiz visited Mobile, Alabama, in the spring of 1853. Dr. Josiah Nott then persuaded Agassiz to write his prefatory essay for *Types of Mankind* and in the following year persuaded young Hotze, then tutoring on a plantation near Mobile, to assist with another publication supporting scientific racism. Because, like Agassiz, Hotze had developed an affinity for the Southern states and a strong sense of the inferiority of blacks, he was willing to translate Arthur de Gobineau's recently published *Essai sur l'inégalité des Races Humaines*. Hotze (or Nott) reduced Gobineau's four volumes to one, omitting portions considered counterproductive for an American audience but adding a hundred-page "Analytical Introduction." The volume began with a dedication "to the Statesmen of America" and ended with an appendix by Nott on "the questions of unity or plurality of species." There is no sign that Lincoln, let alone Darwin, ever read the book. Nevertheless, Nott had managed, as he had with Agassiz's earlier preface, to give his racist doctrines a gloss of European support that impressed some reviewers.[17]

Hotze subsequently used his linguistic skills as secretary to the U.S. Minister to Brussels and later gained valuable experience working for the *Mobile Register*. When war broke out, Hotze served briefly in an Alabama regiment before coming to the attention of officials in Richmond, Virginia, who sent him to Europe to assist with funding Confederate agents and purchasing arms. Hotze then proposed a plan for improving the Confederacy's image in Europe and obtained a commission and a small budget. With ability, charm, and ample supplies of bourbon and cigars, Hotze placed pro-Southern articles in various London journals before starting his own weekly, *The Index*.[18]

Another Confederate agent in London who served on the Anthropological Society's council was Albert Taylor Bledsoe. Many members of the Anthropological Society knew Darwin personally, but Bledsoe was the only one who could say he had once been an intimate friend of Abraham Lincoln. Earlier (in chapter 4), we noted Bledsoe's disillusionment when he decided in 1873 that Lincoln had never been honest with him about his religious opinions when they had been friends in Springfield. But already, when Lincoln became president in 1861, Bledsoe had decided his old friend was criminally deluded to think he had any right to declare the secession a rebellion. When the war broke out, Bledsoe left the faculty of the University of Virginia and accepted from his old West Point colleague Jefferson Davis a commission in the Confederate army. Soon Davis made him an assistant secretary of war before sending him on a special mission to London late in 1862. Here Bledsoe did research for a two-volume work justifying the secession while also doing his best to promote the Southern cause by collaborating with Hotze, who developed a stable of journalists who wrote for *The Index* as well as other journals. Hotze made sure that important opinion-makers in London saw their work.[19]

The London *Times* needed little encouragement in becoming more pro-South, suggesting shortly after the Emancipation Proclamation that there was some validity to the biblical arguments for slavery, a common view in America but rarely expressed in England. It caused a storm in Darwin's house. "*The Times* is getting more detestable,—but that is too weak a word,—than ever," he moaned to Gray. "My good wife wishes to give it up; but I tell her that is a pitch of heroism, to which only a woman is equal." Hotze also played the religious card, printing an "Address of the Confederate Clergy to the World" in *The Index* and arranging for it to be stitched into a quarter of a million copies of popular British quarterlies. However, a backlash caused Hotze to shift from revelation to anthropology. In August 1863, Hotze reported his success to Richmond:

> A new scientific society composed of prominent names has been formed in London which has set itself the task of exposing the heresies that have gained currency in science and politics—of the equality of the races of men. The society is an offshoot or secession from the celebrated Ethnological Society. The president, in writing to offer me a seat in the council, said: "You should and must take a strong interest in our objects, for in us is your only hope that the negro's plan in nature will ever be scientifically ascertained and fearlessly explained."[20]

Hunt's phrase "the negro's plan in nature" echoed Huxley's *Evidence as to Man's Place in Nature*, and in August, Hunt delivered a paper to the British Association for the Advancement of Science on "The Negro's Place in Nature." Hunt subsequently boasted that "my statement of the simple facts was received with . . . loud hisses," but Hotze—on the ASL's governing council since July—soon printed it in *The Index*. Simulating fairness, Hotze also reprinted exchanges between Hunt and Huxley that had appeared in another new journal in which Huxley chastised Hunt for quoting the "nonsense" written by American Dr. John H. Van Evrie. Darwin must have been aware of all this and probably shared a colleague's view of Hunt: "I dare say the brute is paid by Confederates to lie as he does."[21]

During his feuds with the "Ethnologicals," Hunt occasionally invoked the name of Agassiz, but at that time, Agassiz was occupied with his own feuds in America, about which Darwin learned snippets from Agassiz's main opponent, Asa Gray.[22]

Above a marble fireplace in the National Academy of Sciences (NAS) in Washington, D.C., hangs a painting that depicts Abraham Lincoln signing the academy's charter on 3 March 1863. Lincoln is in the center among a group of scientists including Alexander Dallas Bache (head of the U.S. Coastal Survey and the academy's first president), Joseph Henry (Lincoln's friend and head of the Smithsonian), Admiral Charles Henry Davis (the highest-ranking scientist in the military forces), and Benjamin Apthorp Gould and Benjamin Peirce (both mathematicians at the Harvard Observatory and working for the Coastal Survey). Immediately to Lincoln's left is Senator Henry Wilson of Massachusetts, who secured Congress's approval for the charter, and in the privileged position on Lincoln's right is Louis Agassiz. It was not until 1924 that the artist Albert Herter was commissioned to depict the scene, which never actually took place.

By 1863, Lincoln was personally acquainted with half of these figures, but he had probably not yet met Agassiz, although in March 1862, Agassiz addressed a letter to him requesting federal support for Albert Bierstadt, a young artist planning an expedition to the far west. Agassiz sent the artist to his friend Senator Charles Sumner, along with a note asking Sumner to read the "few lines" Agassiz had written for Bierstadt to take to the president. "If you approve of it," Agassiz wrote, "please tell him how and when he can best present himself at the White House." The "few lines" are:

Dear Sir,

In these days of trial of the nation, every thing which manifests intellectual activity and life is important, especially in reference to the estimation in which we are to be held abroad. A party of artists and scientific men, headed by W. A. Bierstadt, prepare to go among the Rocky Mtns this summer, to paint and collect specimens. It has occurred to me that it would not be improper to make an appeal to you, in their behalf, asking the patronage of the country for an expedition which is altogether intended to advance our knowledge of a region thus far little visited.

With highest regard, Yours very truly, Louis Agassiz

The evidence suggests that Agassiz's letter never got beyond Sumner.[23] However, Agassiz employed the same argument—that in perilous times, it was good for the country to display its intellectual vitality—in February 1863 when he wrote to Wilson, Massachusetts's other senator, seeking his support for the creation of a National Academy of Sciences "as an evidence to go before the civilized world at large of the intellectual activity displayed even in these days of our public troubles . . . [which] would tell strongly in our favor, wherever learning is duly appreciated."[24]

A letter Agassiz wrote on the same day to Joseph Henry of the Smithsonian did not mention this lobbying with Wilson. Agassiz knew well that Henry opposed any effort to create such an academy at this time since Henry had discussed the issue a month earlier with Bache and Davis (who, along with Henry and some Harvard professors such as Agassiz, were members of the scientific clique called the "Lazzaroni," mentioned earlier). Henry, Bache, and Davis were all eager to see a more coordinated effort by scientists to help the war effort, but Henry's experience with the political establishment made him argue that Congress would neither support a body that might appear elitist nor adequately fund conferences and publications, that bitterness might arise between those scientists enrolled and those not, and that there was "great danger" that such a body's purposes of might be "perverted to the advancement of personal interest or to the support of the partizan politics."[25]

It was widely known that Agassiz longed to supplant the older American Association for the Advancement of Science (AAAS), which he considered too decentralized and unprofessional, with a European-style academy: setting the agenda for scientific research and education nationally, chartered and funded by the national government, with membership deemed a high honor.[26] True, the AAAS provided no scientific support for the war effort while President Lincoln dealt with inventors and tested weapons; nevertheless, three of the scientists depicted in the 1924 painting, Henry, Bache, and Davis, provided increasingly valuable service to the government. Henry had already offered advice on such matters as the balloon trials and the Chiriqui coal deposits, Bache headed a committee providing technical advice for the blockade system, and Davis had served on that committee as well as the Ironclad Board. Henry, believing Bache and Davis had accepted his arguments against pushing for an academy right now, worked with both men to propose a simpler commission to advise the government on scientific matters. The navy was more open to the proposal than the army, and by 11 February 1863, Secretary Gideon Welles had approved the Permanent Commission of the Navy Department, comprising Henry, Bache, and Davis.[27]

The commission first met on 20 February and over the next two and a half years evaluated three hundred proposals for inventions and devices. The commission did no research but provided far better expertise on technological matters than could be offered by the harried president—who in the previous month alone had involved himself with Diller's gunpowder, the gauge for the transcontinental railroad, an electric detonating system, and what John Dahlgren called "some inflammable humbug." Shortly before the commission's first meeting, Lincoln was still pushing the army and navy to cooperate more, requesting that Edwin M. Stanton and Welles "appoint an officer from each of your Departments, for the purpose of testing the incendiary shell, & incendiary fluid, of A. Berney, and reporting to me whether it would be proper to introduce the shell, or the fluid, in some other form, one or both, into the Military or Naval service." Meanwhile on 19 February, Lincoln arranged to raise Davis as well as Dahlgren to the rank of rear admiral.[28]

To Lincoln, the Permanent Commission may have seemed impressive; to Agassiz, it was a distraction. The day before Henry joined Davis and Bache for the first commission meeting, Agassiz met with Davis and Bache at the latter's house, without Henry but with two other Lazzaroni, Peirce and Gould, and with Agassiz's friend, Senator Wilson. Wilson had recently obtained for Agassiz a seat on the Smithsonian Board of Regents, Agassiz's ostensible reason for being in Washington at this time. The group meeting at Bache's house not only wrote a charter for the National Academy of Sciences but also drew up a list of the fifty "founding" members. Someone may have argued that this would avoid delay, and Agassiz was happy to pontificate on who would be on the list.[29]

By the following day, when Henry first heard about this meeting, Senator Wilson was already introducing the charter as a bill for Congress's approval. Henry later told Agassiz he had made no immediate fuss because he never believed the bill would *be* approved.[30] However, a certain amount of lobbying may even have targeted Lincoln, though the evidence, in a letter Davis wrote, is frustratingly ambiguous: "I am looking for Agassiz to come here and be introduced to Admiral Foote, and then to go with me to the Capitol to see Mr. Grimes about the Academy bill. I go to the President's once more, and I hope for the last time, this morning."[31] With or without Lincoln's support, Wilson arranged for the bill to reach its final vote on the session's last day, 3 March 1863, avoiding debate by saying the list of fifty names need not detain Congress and no appropriations were involved. Lincoln, busily signing last-minute bills until 11 P.M., made the National Academy of Sciences a legal entity before the day ended. Whether Lincoln was then aware of how the bill originated, he might easily have learned the background later from Dahlgren or even Henry himself.

Naturally, Henry and Gray found themselves listed among the fifty "incorporators." Henry magnanimously declared support for the new organization, while Gray wrote to him that the "list on the whole is good . . . my being in is the only thing that troubles me." Captain Dahlgren was the first to resign his membership for reasons unknown, and it was a blow to lose a technician so important in the military and so close to the president. When the American Academy of Arts and Sciences met in Boston in May and elected Gray president, Peirce claimed this was done by "opponents . . . to show their hatred" of the NAS.[32]

Gray's letters to Darwin and Hooker did not mention the NAS fuss directly but contained amusing phrases about hoping "to torment Agassiz delightfully" at some meeting in Boston, doubting Agassiz "will ever be of any more direct use in nat. history," mentioning that "Agassiz and his small clique" were working against Gray, and saying he would "tease Agassiz, if I could see him, only he is of late so cross and sore. He has been digging various pits for me, but has fallen himself into [them] . . . However, I am good-natured; and only laugh at him." Agassiz was also digging holes for Darwin by frenetically accumulating samples for his museum, even enlisting the services of the federal government through Davis, Bache, and Henry. His purpose was partly revealed to a friend with contacts in Europe: "Spain alone might give us the materials to solve the question of transmutation *versus* creation."[33]

When Gray felt Darwin needed distraction from his illness, he entertained him with tales of Agassiz's increasing isolation. "It is amusing to see how *worried* Agassiz is. . . . By the way, now that you are in for 'reading of the very lightest sort' let some one read to you Agassiz on *Glaciers* in the *Atlantic* Mag. for November. It will not strain your brain." Gray also thought little of Agassiz's latest book, *Methods of Study in Natural History*, which stated that one of his purposes was to record his "earnest protest against the transmutation theory." There was little to discuss when Agassiz presented a lightweight paper "On Individuality among Animals, with Reference to the Question of Varieties and Species" at the new NAS's first proper session in Washington in January 1864.[34]

Just over half of the fifty "incorporators" attended, fewer presented papers, and of the four papers concerning natural science, three were by Agassiz. Few natural scientists were then interested in the NAS, and Gray had yet to attend a meeting.[35] Secretary Salmon P. Chase hosted a reception for the academicians, outdone two nights later by Secretary William H. Seward's soirée on 7 January, which was also attended, according to Welles's diary, by "the Cabinet, heads of foreign missions, the learned gentlemen and the committees on foreign relations of the two houses" as well as "a goodly number of ladies, Agassiz, Silliman, Professors Story and Caswell, etc., etc." Welles would have noted if Lincoln had been present. The next day, 8 January, Seward sent a formal letter to assure the members of the academy "that, with the authority of the President, I shall be happy to avail myself of the assistance" offered by the academy.[36] The NAS members also received that day an invitation, at rather short notice, to a one o'clock White House reception of which there is no record except that it happened.[37] Assuming Agassiz was among the twenty-two members who answered that day's roll call and attended the brief reception, it is unlikely that Lincoln used the occasion to converse individually with him.

Another ambiguous report of a possible encounter between Lincoln and Agassiz comes from an acerbic entry in Count Adam von Gurowski's diary for 13 January 1864, the day after the final session of the NAS:

> The President, the Cabinet, and the dignitaries run after the lectures on the Glacial Period. That is the fashion. Oh! those men have already enough of a glacial period in their brains. What innocent sheep to listen to this old rehash, which an academician serves to them as being the latest and newest dish. How one class of dignitaries is humbugged by that other class, the dignitaries of a sham academy![38]

According to Henry, Agassiz had lingered in Washington after the NAS conference ended to give "a very interesting course of three lectures on the subject of glaciers" in the institute's lecture room, "crowded to overflowing every night."[39] Gurowski's splenetic reference to politicians chasing after a particular "academician" is not solid evidence that the president actually attended any particular lecture by Agassiz. Gurowski himself attended few, if any, and may have merely assumed (if his diary is to be taken literally) Lincoln's presence. When Lincoln undoubtedly held a conversation with Agassiz a year later, the president reportedly said that he had never met the scientist before. If true, it was not for want of opportunities.

Mill Workers and Freedmen

The American Civil War affected the global economy and the lives of the thousands of Britons with some connection to the economic, political, or social development of the United States. Few had more concerns and personal contacts than Darwin. Letters from Americans such as Asa Gray occasionally mentioned relatives or students wounded or killed in the war, and Darwin presumably knew that Thomas Huxley's sister had moved to Nashville, Tennessee, where her surgeon husband worked in Confederate hospitals, assisted by their fifteen-year-old son, a nephew Huxley had never seen. Darwin no doubt agreed with the view Huxley expressed to his sister in 1864 that "slavery means, for the white man, bad political economy; bad social morality; bad internal political organisation, and a bad influence upon free labour and freedom all over the world." However, Darwin could never have written, as Huxley did, that "I have not the smallest sentimental sympathy with the negro; don't believe in him at all, in short. . . . [It is] for the sake of the white man, therefore, for your children and grand-children, directly, and for mine, indirectly, I wish to see [slavery] ended."[1] Darwin possessed ample sympathy for "the negro," and his concerns about the war went beyond second-hand contact with combatants. In Britain, there were also casualties, many of them fatal: the victims of the Lancashire "Cotton Famine." Any newspaper reader knew of their deepening plight as the Union blockade of Southern ports became effective, but Darwin also had a personal link to a former mill owner, William Rathbone Greg.

In their student days in Edinburgh, Greg had been a notable freethinker in the Plinian Society, later gaining renown for an unorthodox book, *The Creed of Christendom* (1851), positively reviewed by George Eliot, admired by the "Westminster set," and purchased for the shelves of the Lincoln-Herndon law office. Greg's father had pioneered the cotton textile industry, founding a mill in 1784 that was one of the first to import large amounts of American cotton. W. R. Greg himself gave up direct interest in running the mills a decade before the American Civil War wrought havoc in the industry. Greg's son Percy Greg was one of the

London journalists that Henry Hotze paid out of his Confederate funds to write pro-South propaganda for *The Index*. Shortly after the war, W. R. Greg wrote an article criticizing bourgeois civilization for social measures that allowed weaker members of society to survive and overpopulate, and later still, in *The Descent of Man*, Darwin cited some of Greg's ideas without actually embracing them.[2] But back in 1862, Darwin on at least three occasions donated to a relief fund for the Lancashire cotton workers who were being crushed in a "struggle for survival" not of their own making, and, considering the attitudes W. R. Greg displayed then and later, it is unlikely that he felt as keenly as Darwin did about the victims of the Lancashire "cotton famine."[3]

"We are sorry that you suffer in England," Gray told Darwin, "but you must blame the rebels for it, not us, and your Manchester people should have looked earlier to India for cotton." Darwin was pleased to reply: "We in north England seem tiding over our difficulty far better than anyone ever ventured to hope. The subscriptions have been gigantic."[4] Darwin wrote that on the day after Lincoln signed the final draft of the Emancipation Proclamation. At the same time, America's ambassador in London sent to Washington a document received from the mayor of Manchester. A great crowd had assembled in the city's Free-Trade Hall on 31 December to welcome the New Year and also the new era that Lincoln's Emancipation Proclamation heralded. The lengthy "Address to the President," which the mayor forwarded, had been "agreed upon at a public meeting of the working men and others of this city" and includes the following heartfelt expressions:

> Since we have discerned . . . that the victory of the free North, in the war which has so sorely distressed us as well as afflicted you, will strike off the fetters of the slave, you have attracted our warm and earnest sympathy. We joyfully honor you, as the President, and the Congress with you, for many decisive steps toward practically exemplifying your belief in the words of your great founders: "All men are created free and equal."[5]

Lincoln was moved to make a formal yet emotional reply "To the working-men of Manchester," part of which reads:

> I know and deeply deplore the sufferings which the workingmen at Manchester and in all Europe are called to endure in this crisis. . . . Under these circumstances, I cannot but regard your decisive utterance upon the question as an instance of sublime Christian heroism which has not been surpassed in any age or in any country. . . . I hail this interchange of sentiment, therefore, as an augury that, whatever else may happen, whatever misfortune may befall your country or my own, the peace and friendship which now exist between the two nations will be, as it shall be my desire to make them, perpetual.[6]

Today, not far from Manchester's Free-Trade Hall stands a remarkable statue of Abraham Lincoln sculpted by Pennsylvanian George Grey Barnard, whose depiction of Lincoln's rough-hewn features and slouching stance caused much controversy. A later casting, commissioned as a gift to Britain during the First World War, ended up not in Parliament Square, London, as originally intended but in Manchester. On the plinth is inscribed a large excerpt from Lincoln's finely hewn letter to his working-class friends in Manchester, who suffered uncomplainingly to see slave labor ended.

Lincoln's decision to recruit blacks for military service led to investigations into the condition and capabilities of blacks that resulted in the accumulation of an exceptional body of anthropological data. Although Lincoln was not closely involved, Darwin certainly made use of some of this material, which had a long-lasting influence on anthropologists and sociologists. Three different bodies were involved in these investigations—the U.S. Sanitary Commission, the Provost-Marshal General's Bureau, and the American Freedmen's Inquiry Commission (AFIC)—all technically under the authority of the executive branch and overseen by Secretary Edwin M. Stanton, although the Sanitary Commission was actually a body of private citizens, and the AFIC worked closely with congressional committees.

Shortly after Fort Sumter, Lincoln received a proposal for the creation of a Sanitary Commission to offer medical and hygiene aid to troops beyond that provided by army medical services. On 13 June 1861, Lincoln signed into existence the commission whose membership included one of the nation's leading scientists, Alexander Dallas Bache of the Coastal Survey; Samuel Gridley Howe, a renowned Boston philanthropist and reformer; and Frederick Law Olmsted, whose books about the South had been so admired by Darwin and Herndon. As general secretary for the organization, Olmsted often liaised with the president.

Olmsted, who "had always been fascinated by statistics," instituted within the Sanitary Commission a Bureau of Vital Statistics to tabulate reports from the sanitary inspectors regarding mortality and sickness of volunteers. However, in September 1863, Olmsted resigned from the commission for several reasons, one possibly being a change in policy on the collection of statistics.[7]

According to a commission member, "early in 1863 a new class of examinations was undertaken . . . [to create] the most important contribution of observations ever made in furtherance of 'anthropology'" because the statistics could be used to compare white soldiers and the large number of "persons of African descent" now being enlisted in the army. This could provide far better data about human variation than Dr. Samuel G. Morton's six hundred mislabeled and mismeasured skulls gathering dust in Philadelphia. After Olmsted's departure, data collection was directed by Harvard astronomer and mathematician Benjamin Apthorp Gould, who initially reported—almost contemptuously—"No examinations of negro troops seem to have been made yet, and the importance of such inspections needs no comment."[8]

Gould, who had helped Louis Agassiz create the NAS a few months earlier, later reported that because he was working outside his field, he consulted with "friends whose pursuits are of an anthropological or physiological nature," listing Agassiz first among those who "aided with useful counsel."[9] Agassiz's influence can be seen throughout Gould's published report, but that report did not appear until 1869, so we will first examine another important wartime investigation of black people on which Agassiz also left a mark.

On 16 March 1863, Secretary of War Stanton commissioned a study that was not primarily anthropological but intended "to investigate the condition of the colored population" recently emancipated and to recommend "what measures will best contribute to their protection and improvement, so that they may defend and support themselves; and also, how they can be most usefully employed in the service of the Government for the suppression of the rebellion."[10] The American Freedman's Inquiry Commission comprised Robert Dale Owen of Indiana, Colonel James McKaye of New York, and Samuel Gridley Howe of Massachusetts. All were active abolitionists and may have been suggested to Stanton by Senator Charles Sumner, who had especially close links with fellow Bostonian Howe, a founder of the Republican Party, who also served with the Sanitary Commission.[11] Lincoln knew all three as well, and one historian has described McKaye as "Lincoln's eyes and ears concerning the Negro in the South."[12]

The three commissioners worked expeditiously, consulting widely and visiting the Carolinas, Florida, Louisiana, and even Canada for evidence about freedmen's conditions. Military men were interviewed about the loyalty, abilities, and needs of this transformed population. A preliminary report was issued within three months, and a final report eleven months later. These encouraged Stanton to proceed with black recruitment and also made recommendations that, according to historian John G. Sproat, later served as a "blueprint" for radical reconstruction.

After the preliminary report was published, Howe decided to consult with his friend Agassiz since the AFIC investigation "requires consideration of political, physiological, & ethnological principles" about which "I feel my own incompetency." Howe asked directly whether blacks and mulattoes, with no further additions from Africa, "will be a *persistent* race in this country," whether amalgamation was likely to become "more general" after abolition, and whether "the mulatto is *unfertile* [sic], bearing but few children, & those mainly lymphatic & scrofulous." If the black race was likely to grow, Howe suggested it would be futile to "resist it"; but if the "natural tendencies are to the diffusion, & final disappearance" of blacks, "then our policy should be modified accordingly."[13]

Agassiz replied in four letters dated 9, 10, 11, and 15 August, and his main themes were the gulf between the white and black races, the dire effects of amalgamation, and the policies needed to control both. He began with the declaration that if the black race was in decline, "a wise policy" would be to accelerate emigration and assist the decay. He mentioned both "the prevalent theory of the Unity of Mankind" and "the theory of a multiple origin of mankind," saying that whichever was true, some "races" are limited in their geographic range. However, he readily admitted that both Africans and Europeans had demonstrated they could flourish in America, and although blacks in the northern states would die out, those moving to "the warmer parts of our States" would flourish.[14]

With black numbers likely to increase, "the welfare of our own race" required that we avoid "the combination in one social organisation of two races more widely different from one another than all the other races." Agassiz felt blacks should be allowed "legal equality," but "social equality" was "a natural impossibility," according to evidence from antiquity as well as more recent European contacts with blacks in Africa. Agassiz conditionally prophesied, "With a free black population enjoying identical rights with the whites, [the Southern] States will sooner or later become Negro States with a comparatively small white population. This is inevitable . . . [under] the laws of nature." Rather than allow a black majority effectively to "extend the area of Africa," we should "do for the blacks all that humanity, the most active charity & the most disinterested Christian devotion may require of us . . . [without allowing] them to become an insuperable obstacle to our own progress." The principle underlying policy should be: "No man has a right to what he is unfit to use"—almost a quotation from Stephen A. Douglas's speeches.[15]

Agassiz referred dismissively to "contemporaries . . . who in their youth advocated the wildest plans for social reform. . . . All one-sided doctrines are doomed to disappointment . . . [and] there is no more one-sided doctrine concerning human nature, than the idea that all men are equal, in the sense of being equally capable of fostering human progeny & advancing civilization generally." Whether Agassiz had Lincoln in mind, he effectively reversed a famous statement Lincoln made eight months earlier: "But unless we are prudent now, we run simply the risk of losing our own liberties in the effort of securing to another race more than what it is now capable of maintaining."[16]

When later publishing these letters, Mrs. Agassiz omitted some of her husband's statements about amalgamation that might have offended Southern friends. For example, referring to the "production of half-breeds," Agassiz suggested that "the sense of abhorrence against slavery which has led to the agitation culminating in our civil war, has been chiefly and unconsciously fostered by the recognition of our own type in the offspring of Southern gentlemen, moving among us as negroes, which they are not." Agassiz argued that there should be different policies regarding "half-breeds" and "the pure black," aiding the latter toward "the fullest development of all its capabilities" while sparing no efforts "to check that [amalgamation] which is abhorrent to our better nature." Mrs. Agassiz also omitted her husband's rather prurient explanation for why this amalgamation—"abhorrent . . . unnatural . . . [and] most repugnant to my feelings"—nevertheless abounded in the South: he blamed "the family negress" for seeking the "advantages" gained by gratifying the "sexual desires . . . in the young men of the South," who then "gradually . . . seek more 'spicy partners,' as I have heard the full blacks called by fast young men."[17]

In his reply of 18 August, Howe asserted that he was no advocate of amalgamation but declared that it was slavery itself that had "impaired the purity and lowered the equality of the national blood." He accepted the distinction between "a vigorous black race" and "a feeble mulatto breed" and that some of both groups "have drifted northward, right in the teeth of thermal laws," so that they now dwell "where they would never live by natural election [sic]." With slavery's termination and thanks to "natural laws, . . . the colored population will disappear from the Northern and Middle States, if not from the Continent." In accepting the points pronounced by Agassiz, "it will be the duty of the statesman to favor by wise measures the operation of these laws, and the purification and elevation of the national blood."[18]

Although Howe agreed that "mulattoism is hybridism, . . . unnatural and undesirable," he added that "we should grant to every human being all the rights we claim for ourselves, and bear in mind the cases of individual excellence of colored people." In a postscript omitted by Mrs. Agassiz, Howe added rather optimistically, "Whatever may be the conclusion with regard to mulattoes, you will agree with me I trust in regard to the excellent qualities inherent in the Afric [sic] negroes."[19]

The final AFIC report quoted numerous witnesses by name but not Agassiz, even though several points made in the final chapter, "The Future in the United States of the African Race," were paraphrased from Agassiz's letters to Howe.[20] However, while repeating Agassiz's view that amalgamation was "a physical evil injurious to both" races and "ought to be discouraged by public opinion," the commission believed "it is beyond the legitimate reach of legislation." And while Agassiz's views were unchanged since 1850, the final report stressed, "The whites have changed, and are still rapidly changing, their opinion of the negro. And the negro, in his new condition as freedman, is himself, to some extent, a changed being. No one circumstance has tended so much to these results as the display of manhood in negro soldiers." The report ignored Agassiz's distinctions between legal and social rights and instead recommended strongly that the rebel states should be allowed back into the union *after* they changed their constitutions to secure "equal rights" for freedmen. It also went beyond the operation of the "natural laws" by urging the government to support the process of leasing to blacks in the insurrectionary districts properties that had been abandoned by rebels.[21]

Lincoln must have read the AFIC reports with great interest. He had already indicated a desire to see some confiscated lands made available to former slaves under Union protection in the Carolinas and Louisiana, and he personally wrote to Owen and McKaye a letter of introduction for an army chaplain who later became a leader in the Bureau of Refugees, Freedmen, and Abandoned Lands.[22] Lincoln also sent McKaye to Louisiana in February 1864 to investigate whether blacks might be granted the vote when Louisiana produced its new constitution before rejoining the Union. McKaye reportedly assured an assembly of blacks that the president was concerned for their welfare and had sent him "to inquire into their condition and to ascertain their wishes."[23] McKaye may have caused the military governor, General Nathaniel P. Banks, to express his new view in favor of "such extension of suffrage as will meet the demands of the age," and Lincoln suggested to Michael Hahn, the new governor-elect, that Louisiana might let "some of the colored people" have the vote, "for instance, the very intelligent and those who have fought valiantly in our ranks." McKaye also urged Sumner to treat the disposition of freedmen and of the abandoned lands together, a topic McKaye may have discussed with Lincoln after returning from the Carolinas in the summer of 1863.[24]

McKaye recounted a meeting during which he related to Lincoln (in dialect, which he thought would amuse Lincoln) a discussion he overheard among some recently liberated Carolina slaves who were concerned whether "Massa Linkum" knew of their plight and could guarantee their freedom. One elderly "praise leader" dismissed their fears:

> "Brederin," said he, "you don't know nosen' what you'se talkin' 'bout. Now, you just listen to me. Massa Linkum, he ebery whar. He know ebery ting." Then, solemnly looking up, he added: "He walk de earf like de Lord!" . . . Mr. Lincoln was very much affected by this account. He did not smile, as another might have done, but got up from his chair and walked in silence two or three times across the floor. As he resumed his seat, he said, very impressively, "It is a momentous thing to be the instrument, under Providence, of the liberation of a race!"[25]

The Emancipator, six months after signing the proclamation, was pleased that European governments were now less inclined to aid the South, abolitionists had modified their criticisms, no slave insurrections or mutinies by white soldiers had occurred, and the Union army was swelling with black recruits. The AFIC's final report was hopeful that attitudes of both blacks and whites were changing, and evidence of a change in whites' attitude—but also of the need for much more—was provided at the end of that year when Lincoln became the first president in over thirty years to be reelected in what proved to be the most racist election in American history.

Testing Hopes and Hoaxes

S ome time after learning that a black man had equated him with Jesus, Lincoln also learned of General Robert E. Lee's second coming—a second invasion of the North. It was a further desperate gamble by Lee, still hoping for some sort of "Saratoga," the colonial victory in 1777 that helped convince the French to support the Americans' War of Independence. But Lee failed at Gettysburg, Pennsylvania, in July 1863, and at the same moment Vicksburg, Mississippi, fell to General Ulysses S. Grant, finally opening the Mississippi River and splitting the Confederacy. The South should have surrendered soon after these major defeats; however, once again, Lee's army was allowed to escape back into Virginia, infuriating Lincoln even more than the similar blunder after Antietam. Lincoln wrote an angry letter to General George G. Meade and then wisely decided not to send it, but the next day, he apparently told a secretary, "If I had gone up there, I could have whipped them myself."[1]

Military strategy might be another science that Lincoln felt he could master, but he also recognized the unique complexity of war and had a government to run. A defeated general could be replaced; a defeated president would lose all authority. So Lincoln tested further generals, searching for a victor, until he decided, eight months after Vicksburg, to make Grant lieutenant general in charge of the entire war. Grant later passed the test by securing total victory.

The Union army itself tested and gradually disproved the Southern hypothesis that one rebel was worth two Yankees, and now African Americans—no longer born on some other continent—were being tested to see if they would enlist in sufficient numbers, fight as well as white men, and demoralize the South into submission while inspiring the North into tolerance.

Lincoln himself would soon face the test of reelection. He had not yielded to secession, or despaired after numerous military setbacks, or let financial or constitutional obstacles impede the struggle, or allowed the Confederacy to gain the foreign recognition that would have ensured its independence, but he had also failed after three years to crush the rebellion.

Lincoln knew there was a larger test than all of these and made it the central point of his Gettysburg Address. Lincoln concisely described how a great civil war was testing a nation that, unlike other nations, was itself an experiment. A government based on the principle that "all men are created equal" had been brought into existence, but could it "long endure"? Few nations had even tried the experiment: Britain had achieved a mixed constitution and equality before the law, but only a tiny fraction of Britons possessed the right to vote, while the French had more than once proclaimed *egalité* but were again ruled by an emperor. The American "proposition" of equality was a promise it had yet to keep while slavery stood in denial. Yet, the promise was there and was now in the process of being fulfilled—if the whole experiment was not ruined by disunion. Elites in Europe hoped the United States would fail, lest the experiment be extended. Lincoln knew it would be the world's loss, and not just America's, if government "of the people"—not of kings, nobles, or a dominant race—perished from the Earth.

Gettysburg and Vicksburg indicated that the hypothesis had not been disproven, yet. But democracy would undergo further tests and still does.

"You in London were daily awaiting & expecting the capture of Washington . . . [with] a good-deal of little-concealed joy," wrote Gray with unconcealed joy after events disproved the pessimistic prophecies that had appeared in British newspapers when Lee began his bold invasion. "Oh foolish people! When will you see that there is only one end to all this:—and that the North never dreams of any other,—the complete putting down of the rebellion . . . attended with the annihilation of slavery."[2] Darwin replied promptly:

> How profoundly interesting American news is. . . . Do not hate poor old England too much. Anyhow she is the mother of fine children all over the world. I declare no man could have tried to wish more sincerely for the north than I have done. My reason tells me that perhaps it would be best,—of course best if it would end Slavery, but I cannot pump up enthusiasm. The boasting of your newspapers & of your little men, & the abuse of England, and the treatment of the free coloured population, and the not freeing Maryland slaves stops all my enthusiasm. If all the States were like New England the case would be different. I find a man cannot hope by intention. You will think me a wretched outcast. Farewell & do not hate me much.[3]

Gray volleyed back, blaming the press on both sides of the Atlantic for stirring up ill feeling, before addressing Darwin's prime interest: "[S]ome day . . . you will see that I was a fairly good prophet.—that the South might have *delayed* the abolition of slavery by giving up early in the conflict, but that every month of continued resistance hastened and ensured the downfall of slavery. That is now *doomed*, and sure near to rapid death, quick in some places—slower in others, but sure." Acknowledging Darwin's concern not only for freedmen in the South but also for those still enslaved in the Border States and still abused elsewhere in the North, Gray responded with a less than brilliant prophecy: "Ill usage of *negroes*—who make such good soldiers—will soon be unheard of"—wishful thinking that may have been shared by Lincoln.[4]

"Homely, honest, ungainly Lincoln is the *representative man* of the country." Like Gray, growing numbers of Americans increasingly valued the determination and intelligence of the president, despite his supposed lack of certain graces.[5] Lincoln might be reelected in nine months—easily if the war could be won by then, less so if not. However, his Democratic opponents attacked Lincoln not only for his failure to win the war but also for the Emancipation Proclamation, which, according to the scaremongers, would lead to widespread amalgamation. With abolition nearly a dead issue, the Democrats ranted instead about "racial purity." And as if the word "amalgamation" had been devalued by overuse, a new word was coined and doled out freely by Democratic politicians and newspapers.

Miscegenation: The Theory of the Blending of the Races, Applied to the American White Man and Negro was the title of a pamphlet that appeared in New York shortly before Christmas 1863. The anonymous but skillful author appeared to be an abolitionist—though that term was becoming obsolete, and the author took for granted that slavery was doomed. He concentrated on arguing *against* the fear of amalgamation. While the AFIC reports assured readers that "thermal lines" would prevent freed blacks from moving northward and cause those in the North to move southward, *Miscegenation* provided a freshly coined word and an opposite spin for amalgamation: race mixing should not be feared but embraced.

Miscegenation declared that both science and religion proved that "all the tribes which inhabit the earth were originally derived from one type," extensively quoted such monogenist authorities as "Dr. John W. Draper of New York University" (a well-known Darwinian), and proclaimed the "physiological equality of the white and colored races." The anonymous author asserted that "mixed races are much superior, mentally, physically, and morally, to those pure or unmixed," so the admixture of the blood of blacks would actually improve American blood. A natural attraction between whites and blacks explained rape on plantations and why radical abolitionists tended to have fair hair. It was now, said the author, the Republican Party's duty to promote miscegenation.[6]

Gift copies of *Miscegenation* were posted—along with a respectful letter inviting their opinions—to prominent antislavery speakers and writers such as sisters Sarah Grimké and Angelina Grimké, Lucretia Mott, Wendell Phillips, Theodore D. Weld, and possibly New York *Tribune* editor Horace Greeley. Prominent Republicans such as William H. Seward and Charles Sumner also reportedly received complimentary copies.[7]

Some of the antislavery press favorably reviewed the pamphlet, and on 8 February, Darwin might have read a dispatch by the London *Times*'s New York correspondent that "the advanced spirits" of the Republican Party were promoting a new doctrine that the black was "in many important respects the superior of the whites," and if whites do not "amalgamate," they will die out in America. The correspondent dismissed *Miscegenation* as something "for the study of such Yankee girls as have exhausted the sensational novels," yet he perceptively suggested that the author's unctuous style "might almost make one suspect him of being a *mauvais farceur*."[8]

The Democratic press naturally used *Miscegenation* as a stick for beating Republicans. Samuel S. Cox, a rabid Democratic congressman, not unreasonably questioned the science behind *Miscegenation* but then went beyond the worst polygenist to assert that the "mulatto does not live; he does not recreate his kind; he is a monster," adding, contradictorily, that mulattoes "scarcely survive beyond one generation." Curiously, Cox also quoted from two or three letters that had been written by the antislavery recipients of gratis copies of *Miscegenation*. These letters—offering qualified praise and written in all innocence—had been sent, as recommended, to "The author of *Miscegenation*" at the publisher's address. Cox's access to them casts doubt on his denials of any knowledge of the authorship of the pamphlet. Shortly afterward, Dr. John H. Van Evrie attacked Cox for condemning "miscegenation" but not emancipation: "the mixing of blood follows the mixing of 'freedom.'"[9]

Journalists David Goodman Croly and George Wakeman of the Democratic organ the *New York World* are the actual authors of *Miscegenation*, a fact not revealed for decades.[10] The *World* cleverly delayed commenting until there was a bandwagon to board. Greeley's pro-Republican *Tribune* defensively suggested the discussion merited a more seriously scientific approach and two days later set an example by publishing a report from London about Thomas Huxley's recent lecture that had lacerated James Hunt's paper "On the Negro's Place in Nature" for its utter lack of scientific credibility.[11]

Having apparently read the *Times*'s account of *Miscegenation*, Huxley first dismissed "the fanatical abolitionists [who] do not scruple to affirm that the negro is the equal of the white man—nay, some go so far as to tell us that the American stock would be the better for the infusion of a little black blood." Hunt's paper, of course, took the entirely opposite view, and Huxley stormed, "Nothing, indeed, can surpass its scandalous absurdity, except the reasoning by which it is supported." After reading several quotations, Huxley concluded, "And this is put before the unsuspecting public, without comment or qualification, as the verdict of science touching 'The Negro's Place in Nature!'"[12]

Count Adam von Gurowski, the Washington insider and diarist, was evidently familiar with the scientific controversies. His *Diary* not only discusses "the newly-invented sacramental word . . . *miscegenation* . . . [that] agitates the press and some would-be savants in Congress" but also echoed Huxley by asserting that if the slaveholders' brains were "dissected, their *cerebella* would be found to have less convolutions than those of the negro." The count's little rant noted that "the newly made Academicians come not to the rescue of science! Poor souls, still entangled in Blumenbach, and under the leadership of an Agassiz, wailing against Darwin." Whether Darwin ever read *Miscegenation*, he would know all about it from numerous reviews, including a scathing one in Hunt's *Anthropological Review* and from the attention the subject received in the weekly journal that Huxley edited, the *Reader*.[13]

Back in New York, Van Evrie seized the moment to turn Hunt's *Negro's Place in Nature* into a pamphlet and also to publish a book, *Subgenation: The Theory of the Normal Relation of the Races; an Answer to "Miscegenation."* Supposedly anonymous, this was actually just a new edition of Van Evrie's 1861 diatribe, *Negroes and Negro "Slavery": The First an Inferior Race; the Latter Its Normal Condition*, updated with topical references to Lincoln's "Miscegenation Proclamation" and a quotation in which Agassiz supposedly demolished the "great luminary of the single race theory" James C. Prichard. Van Evrie, literally capitalizing on the debate while promoting a Democratic victory in the upcoming election, advertised the sale of printed cartoons such as "Miscegenation, or the Millennium of Abolitionism" and campaign pamphlets such as "The Miscegenation Record of the Republican Party." Another pamphlet, possibly unconnected to Van Evrie, appeared in September entitled "Miscegenation and the Republican Party" and includes excerpts from some of the letters that Croly and Wakeman, the authors of *Miscegenation*, had harvested from unsuspecting antislavery leaders.[14]

Lincoln had also received a copy of *Miscegenation* along with a polite letter asking permission to dedicate a new work, *Melaleukation*, to the president.[15] Other Republican officials who received copies of *Miscegenation* had made no response, and Senator Sumner reportedly suspected a hoax from the start. Lincoln was too canny to take the bait, and his only reported comment on the affair came months later when someone asked if he was in favor of miscegenation. Punning in several directions, Lincoln quipped, "That's a democratic mode of producing good Union men, & I don't propose to infringe on the patent."[16]

A well-informed New York correspondent for the London *Morning Herald* sent a dispatch late in October—when its information could not possibly bounce back to America before the election—exposing *Miscegenation* as a hoax. That he was probably in league with the authors is suggested by his respect for their anonymity and knowledge that a free copy had been sent to Lincoln who had so far proved himself "shrewd enough to say nothing on the unsavoury subject."[17]

The Democrats, shifting from defending slavery to advocating white supremacy, caricatured Lincoln as "Abraham Africanus I" and (with a nod to the evolution debate) "the original ourang-outang," while Lincoln's swarthy complexion was attributed to some African blood in his genealogy.[18] The political effect of all this was small. Lincoln picked up only a third of the votes cast in New York City but won the state overall and would still have been reelected without it.[19] The hoax merely indicated that ignorance about the nature of species and hybridity did not prevent anyone from hanging his preexisting views on whatever supposedly scientific evidence was at hand. Allegedly scientific discourse was still reflecting rather than supplanting prejudice. This demonstration of ignorance and racism failed to remove Lincoln from office, yet it may have dampened his hope that white Americans were steadily becoming more tolerant of black Americans.

On 12 April 1864, Darwin wrote to Agassiz for the first time since publishing *On the Origin of Species* nearly five years earlier. The present letter thanked Agassiz for sending his *Methods of Study in Natural History* "with some other publications," as Darwin vaguely expressed it. He found something positive to say, though not about the publication itself: "I thank you sincerely for the above present. I know well how strongly you are opposed to nearly everything I have written & it gratifies me deeply that you have not for this cause taken . . . a personal dislike to me." To the distinguished entomologist B. D. Walsh, Darwin confessed that he "only skimmed" Agassiz's *Methods* and "thought it a very poor Book." Darwin also told Walsh, who had written a paper calling Agassiz's review of *The Origin* an "absurdity," that he was "delighted at the manner in which you have bearded this lion in his den."[20]

When Asa Gray urged Darwin to "set [Alfred Russel] Wallace upon . . . *Methods of Study* (forsooth)," Darwin passed the comment verbatim to Wallace, adding, "So Asa Gray seems to think much of your powers of reviewing & I mention this as it assuredly is *laudari a laudato*." Darwin was always keen to praise Wallace, who was so modest about his own abilities, which Darwin rated highly. Their mutually respectful relationship had grown warmer since Wallace's return from Malaysia in 1862. To Darwin's invitation, Wallace immediately responded that Agassiz "seems so utterly wrong . . . that it would be a very long & wearisome task to answer him." Wallace mentioned being lately stimulated by reading Herbert Spencer, who "appears to me as far ahead of John Stuart Mill as J. S. M. is of the rest of the world, and I may add as Darwin is of Agassiz."[21]

Spencer's influence possibly contributed to Wallace's sudden interest in the topic so dear to Darwin and, more recently, to Charles Lyell and Huxley: the origins of man. In May 1864, while the miscegenation controversy flared on both sides of the Atlantic, Wallace sent to Darwin a paper on "The Origin of Human Races and the Antiquity of Man Deduced from the Theory of 'Natural Selection.'" He told Darwin that he wanted to explain "the vast mental & cranial differences between man & the apes combined with such small structural differences in other parts of the body" and "the diversity of human races combined with man's almost perfect stability of form during all historical epochs." Along the way, Wallace also developed the point made earlier by Gray: that monogenism and polygenism could be combined "by means of Mr. Darwin's celebrated theory of 'Natural Selection.'"[22] Wallace argued that the existing human races originated from a "single homogeneous race" inhabiting some tropical region and still lacking the faculty of speech or higher reason: yet, man had enough "reason" to give him advantages over other species, allowing him to multiply and spread to different environments. Through the process of "natural selection," those different environments caused infinitesimally small changes (over not thousands but millions of years) resulting in the "specific modifications which still distinguish the chief races of mankind." Those racial characteristics became fixed because *then* these races all developed that "higher reason" that allowed them to control their environment, which in turn prevented natural selection from causing any further changes in man's physical forms. However, natural selection *did* continue to act—and differentially—on the brain because a "hardier . . . more social race" developed in temperate zones while regions with a more "perennial supply of vegetable food"—thus reducing the need to "prepare for the rigours of winter"— prevented the development of "an indigenous inter-tropical civilisation."

Invoking the subtitle of *On the Origin of Species*, Wallace argued that the "great law of 'the preservation of favoured races in the struggle for life'" leads to the "inevitable extinction of all those low and mentally underdeveloped populations with which Europeans come in contact." Wallace listed Red Indians, Tasmanians, Australians and New Zealanders, who will eventually "die out"—not mentioning Africans even though the logic of his argument would include them. The difference between polygenists and monogenists, Wallace concluded, rested solely in the fact that polygenists defined man by his possession of "higher faculties," while monogenists emphasized "form and structure." Wallace implied that agreeing on some criteria might resolve some disputes and also looked forward to a time when the species of man would once again become a "homogeneous race" as the continuing effects of natural selection on intellect meant that eventually "no individual . . . will be inferior to the noblest specimens of existing humanity."[23] Wallace did not speculate whether this new homogeneity would result from making love or making war, that is, through miscegenation or extermination. Darwin was impressed. "The great leading idea is quite new to me, viz that during late ages the mind will have been modified more than the body; yet I had got as far as to see with you that the struggle between the races of man depended entirely on intellectual & *moral* qualities." However, "I am not sure that I go with you on all minor points. . . . I rather differ on the rank under classificatory point of view which you assign to man: I do not think any character simply in excess ought ever to be used for the higher divisions." Darwin felt that difference in intellect even between man and ape was one of degree rather than kind, and the degree was far less between races of man. Darwin preferred to look at non-mental variables: "With respect to the differences of race, a conjecture has occurred to me that much may be due to the correlation of complexion (& consequently Hair) with constitution. Assume that a dusky individual best escaped miasma & you will readily see what I mean." Darwin mentioned that he had persuaded the British army's medical department to send a survey to surgeons in the tropics to collect information on correlations between racial characteristics and resistance to disease—at the very time when the Sanitary Commission and military doctors in the United States were collecting anthropometric data from soldiers in the Union army. "I dare say I shall never get any returns," Darwin predicted correctly. Returning to the question of how human variations became long-lasting (though perhaps not permanent) races, Darwin thought intellect and morality less important than another factor. "I suspect that a sort of sexual selection has been the most powerful means of changing the races of man. I can shew that the different races have a widely different standard of beauty. Among savages the most powerful men will have the pick of the women & they will generally leave the most descendants."[24]

Sexual selection was extremely important to Darwin but too complex to describe in a letter. Just recovering from a prolonged period of illness, Darwin may have doubted he would ever have the energy and time to pursue this important work. And Wallace's approach, however faulty at present, was far closer to his own than Lyell's or Huxley's. Darwin suddenly tried to pass his work onto Wallace's shoulders: "I have collected a few notes on man but I do not suppose I shall ever use them. Do you intend to follow out your views, & if so would you like at some future time to have my few references & notes?"[25]

Wallace replied immediately, grateful for Darwin's "flattering remarks" and "critical observations" but skeptical about sexual selection and politely evading Darwin's offer: "I may possibly some day go a little more into this subject, & if I do will accept the kind offer of your notes." Wallace added that another writing project would occupy him for "a long time." After a fortnight, Darwin replied briefly, "merely to thank you & just to say that probably you are right on all the points you touch on except as I think about sexual selection which I will not give up." His offer was quietly shelved: "I doubt whether my notes would be of any use to you, & as far as I remember they are chiefly on sexual selection."[26]

Wallace and Darwin continued their stimulating correspondence and debated "sexual selection" for years, but after that summer of 1864, there was no further suggestion of direct collaboration. While Darwin could believe Wallace would do a better job than Huxley or Lyell in applying natural selection to man, another self-professed "Darwinian" felt he was doing exactly that. Karl Vogt was a distinguished botanist whose *Vorlesungen über den Menschen* (1863) had so enthusiastically espoused natural selection that he became known as the Darwin of Germany. However, the real Darwin was alarmed that Vogt's "Darwinism" seemed to support a form of polygenism by theorizing that at least three different types of ape evolved into as many types of man. Darwin did not, and did not wish to, believe this. The English translation of Vogt's work, *Lectures on Man*, was published in 1864 by the odious James Hunt of the ASL, and Darwin noted in the margin of his copy: "gives Agassiz blunders on first coming in of various classes."[27]

By the end of 1864, Darwin could see that Vogt, Huxley, and Lyell were far behind Wallace, but any lingering hope that Wallace would adopt his ideas more fully was dispelled when Wallace began to embrace a view that was simply anathema to Darwin—and also rejected as irrational by Lincoln. Wallace was about to become a believer in spiritualism, only three or four years after Mary Lincoln began holding séances in the White House.

Spiritual Forces

The belief in unseen forces controlling changes in the environment is the essence of primitive religion. The slow development of rationalism eroded its edges, replacing magic with logic. The pace of change accelerated: gravity was explained, and magnetism harnessed into electricity and eventually telegraphy. This, along with the Atlantic steam packets and improvements in printing processes, allowed any interesting development among one civilized people to become quickly known to all the rest. Mesmerism and hypnotism—still parlor games or lyceum demonstrations—seemed the next mysteries to be explained. By the mid-nineteenth century, these trends advanced a movement that was partly an extension of and partly a reaction against modern science. "Modern spiritualism" either negated science or represented its next step. The gullible were exploited, while the skeptical scrutinized "mediums" just as they would self-styled magicians, assuming any powers at work were natural and explicable. Lincoln and Darwin are alleged to have joined other skeptics investigating that quintessential spiritualist manifestation, the séance; however, the evidence that they fully participated is (appropriately) lacking in substance.

Modern spiritualism has no agreed starting point, though many say it began in upstate New York in 1848. One evangelist called this region "the burned over district" after concluding that the fires of Methodism, passing through earlier, left too few nonconverts to provide further "fuel." Actually, the "burning-over" cleared space for all sorts of new growths during the decades preceding the Civil War, including Shakers, Millerites, Mormons, Charles Grandison Finney's revivalism, and the first women's rights convention, held in Seneca Falls in 1848. Also in that year, two young daughters of John Fox of Hydesville, Margaret, thirteen, and Kate, eleven, began their association with a sort of "spiritual telegraph": the "knocks" and "raps" supposedly produced by departed spirits seeking to communicate with this world. News of the phenomena spread rapidly among neighbors and reached an older, married sister living in Rochester, who now came to help turn her siblings' gift into a career.[1]

From the start, the Fox sisters' noisy manifestations from the spirit world differed from the inspirations or revelations bestowed on palm readers and crystal-ball gazers. The rappings, knockings, and inexplicably moving objects brought about through the medium of the sisters were more open to public investigation and objective measurement than, say, the phrenological relationship between bumps on one's head and one's intellectual and moral qualities. The more open activities of the sisters allowed supporters to emphasize natural law rather than the supernatural, external facts rather than a state of mind, and an expanding knowledge rather than some revelation.[2] In any case, the sisters ignited a flame of interest in spiritualism and soon had many imitators, some bringing comfort to many who were bereaved but found little solace in orthodoxy, and others—more obviously charlatans—requiring payment in advance and working in darkened parlors.

The Fox sisters were repeatedly investigated. The "Rochester Rappers" gave demonstrations in New York City that won over Horace Greeley's New York *Tribune*, yet three distinguished doctors at the University of Buffalo reported in February 1851 that the knocks and raps were caused by toe-joint cracking. Other mediums were investigated in Pennsylvania when a prominent university chemist, Dr. Robert Hare, set out in 1853 to discredit them but ended up a convert. He published his results in 1855 but failed to convince his state legislature to fund further research and was howled down at a meeting of the AAAS in 1854. In that year, thirteen thousand citizens asked Congress to institute serious investigations, but the legislators generally laughed before tabling their petition.[3]

To promote such investigations—or to sell newspapers—the Boston *Courier* in 1857 offered a $500 reward to any medium who could satisfy a panel of Harvard scientists, including Louis Agassiz. Kate Fox, by then nineteen years old, was one of those investigated, but the manifestations were poor, and Agassiz was uncooperative: refusing to sit in the circle, moving about, making desultory remarks, and, when some knocks were heard, saying he would soon explain their cause, which he never did. Instead of a promised written report, the panel issued a verdict more moralistic than scientific: "That any connection with spiritualistic circles, so called, corrupts the morals and degrades the intellect. [The panel members] therefore deem it their solemn duty to warn the community against this contaminating influence, which surely tends to lessen the truth of man and the purity of women."[4]

Most mainstream clergymen, feeling usurped, adopted the same tone of disapproval but, like most politicians and scientists, were simply ignored as the number of believers swelled into the millions. Other mediums quickly rivaled the Fox sisters, of whom the most prominent, Kate, was hardly seen between

1861 and 1866 when she served as the private medium for a recently bereaved New York banker who managed to have many reunions with his late wife during four hundred séances with Kate. He was later instrumental in sending Kate to England where her impact was significant.

Abraham Lincoln could hardly escape the spiritualist phenomenon so long as he read newspapers and reviews.[5] There were frequent reports in his admired *Annual of Scientific Discovery*, whose editor, David Ames Wells, once signed a statement attesting the mediumship of D. D. Home, a young man who often appeared with Kate Fox both in America and later in England.[6] The senator who introduced the spiritualist petition to an amused Congress in 1854 was Lincoln's old political rival James Shields, who made it clear he thought spiritualism a "delusion." Lincoln's friend Orville Browning went to a spiritualist in Illinois in 1855, finding her talk "intolerable twaddle," and a clairvoyant apparently operated in Springfield in the 1850s.[7] William H. Herndon, whose interest in the metaphysical extended to the paranormal, had purchased for his library several books that related to spiritualism and had been published before Lincoln left for Washington. These included detailed accounts of the Fox sisters; three volumes by "the seer of Poughkeepsie," Andrew Jackson Davis; a British compendium on *Occult Sciences*; and an influential study by skeptic-turned-believer Robert Dale Owen—the Indiana politician later appointed to the American Freedmen's Inquiry Commission.[8] When Lincoln became president, spiritualists showered him with dozens of books and hundreds of letters.[9] He presided over a war that created hundreds of thousands of grieving relatives, an obvious market for clairvoyants who openly advertised in Washington newspapers. Among colleagues who may have embraced spiritualism were his commissioner of agriculture Isaac Newton, General Daniel Sickles, and Gideon Welles. Mrs. Welles, one of Mary Lincoln's few close friends, may have consulted a clairvoyant after her son died, perhaps influencing Mary to do the same after the death of eleven-year-old Willie in February 1862. Mary's black seamstress, Elizabeth Keckley, who sought out Washington's spiritualists after her only son was killed in the war, could also put Mary into contact with them.[10]

Mary certainly attended numerous séances during and after her Washington years, at least one and perhaps more occurring in the White House itself or in the Soldiers' Home where the Lincolns spent summer evenings. The most frequently cited source for Lincoln's own participation in a séance is unreliable, published by the medium Nettie Colburn (later Maynard) in 1891, after most who might have refuted her had died and a year before her own death.[11]

Lincoln almost certainly met Nettie herself, but the best evidence of this contradicts her account. Lincoln's friend Joshua Speed visited Washington and became acquainted with Nettie and her landlady, Mrs. Cosby, who prevailed on him to write them an introduction to the president. Speed wrote in a sly-dog tone, suggesting that "it will I am sure be some relief from the tedious round of office seekers to see two such agreeable ladies . . . both mediums & believers in spirits and . . . I am quite sure very choice spirits themselves. . . . Mrs Cosby says she is not a medium though I am quite sure she is or should be."[12] Whatever Speed expected Lincoln to read between these lines, they were written several months *after* Nettie, by her later account, had already performed in front of Lincoln at a séance in Georgetown in December 1862.

Mrs. Lincoln attended a séance at that place and period, according to Orville Browning: "Mrs. Lincoln told me she had been, the night before, with Old Isaac Newton, out to Georgetown, to see a Mrs. Laury, a spiritualist and she had made wonderful revelations to her about her little son Willy who died last winter, and also about things on the earth." The medium revealed that the cabinet "were all enemies of the President" and "would have to be dismissed."[13] Nettie Colburn is not mentioned, and if Mary had said that her husband had come along, Browning would have recorded it.

Whether Lincoln ever attended one of his wife's séances, he apparently took an interest in one of her mediums. Charles Colchester styled himself "Lord Colchester," being, he said, the illegitimate son of an English nobleman. He is mentioned in Nettie's book, but two sources more objective than Nettie's fail to sustain the conclusion that Lincoln was actually present at a Colchester séance.[14]

According to Lincoln's friend journalist Noah Brooks, Colchester came to Mary's notice while she was grieving over Willie. Mary told Brooks about Colchester's manifestations during one or more séances held at the Soldiers' Home, but Brooks declined her invitation to attend an "exhibition" of Colchester's powers at the White House. "Meanwhile," according to Brooks, he attended a Colchester séance at a private home in Washington, taking the opportunity to expose Colchester as a "swindler and a humbug" and threatening him with prison if he did not leave Washington immediately. How Brooks's account relates to two others written by astronomer Simon Newcomb is unclear since neither man specified dates, and only Brooks actually names Colchester.[15] Newcomb worked at Washington's Naval Observatory and was a colleague of the Smithsonian's director, Joseph Henry, about whom Newcomb later wrote a memoir. It was Henry's visceral dislike of spiritualism that had prevented Robert Hare from bringing the topic before the AAAS in 1854. Whenever spiritualists asked permission to use the Smithsonian's lecture room, Henry told them they must first "cause a table in my room, in open day, to rise into the air by a spiritual volition, without physical contact. . . . But in no case was this feat attempted in my presence." Newcomb's first anecdote stated that Henry "frequently" told the story about a spiritualist who "had held several séances with the President himself," while the later account only implied that Lincoln himself attended séances: "President Lincoln, . . . though not a believer in spiritualism, was from time to time deeply impressed by the extraordinary feats of spiritualistic performers, and naturally looked to Professor Henry for his views and advice on the subject. Quite early in his administration one of these men showed his wonderful powers to the President, who asked him to show Professor Henry his feats." Henry agreed to meet the spiritualist at the Smithsonian although Henry "generally avoided all contact with such men." When aural manifestations occurred, supposedly in different parts of the room, Henry declared that he did not know how the sounds were made but was certain they came not from the room but from the spiritualist's person. According to Newcomb's second anecdote, during a later train journey, Henry found himself conversing with an electrical instruments maker who, discovering he was addressing an expert, boasted of making for "spiritual mediums" the apparatus necessary for their "manifestations" and had, in fact, supplied the very man (still unnamed) that Henry had met at the Smithsonian.[16]

One assumes, though Newcomb did not say, that Henry reported this to Lincoln. Whether such information led to Brooks's confrontation with Colchester, both Brooks and Lincoln naturally aimed to protect Mary from charlatans, yet Lincoln probably did not wish to deprive his wife of any consolation she could find after Willie's death. As grief piled on grief, Mary continued to consult spiritualists, and the last photograph of Mary Lincoln was taken in 1872 by an exploitive "spirit photographer" in Boston who falsified a ghostly image of Lincoln resting his hands on her shoulders.[17] Lincoln, while still alive, sought no consolation in spiritualism but found distraction in the tremendous burden of his work. As a young man, Lincoln reportedly said he doubted there was any afterlife, and according to Dr. Phineas D. Gurley, whose church both he and Professor Henry attended in Washington, Lincoln expressed annoyance that people thought him interested in spiritualism: "A simple faith in God is good enough for me, and beyond that I do not concern myself very much."[18]

Lincoln's simple faith, which did not include dead people spiritually telegraphing the living, barely encompassed any communications between man and God. He invoked God's name in speeches and led the nation in a form of national prayer through proclamations—usually based on resolutions passed by earnest members of Congress. Lincoln sometimes requested prayers but also questioned their logic, especially since "the rebel soldiers are praying with a great deal more earnestness, I fear, than our own troops, and expecting God to favor their side," as Lincoln wrote in September 1862 in reply to a memorial from "Chicago Christians of all denominations" calling for the immediate emancipation of the slaves. Lincoln rather pointedly added that he received "opposite opinions and advice" from "religious men, who are equally certain that they represent the Divine will." He told these Chicago Christians—whose advice was no more helpful than that he constantly received from spiritualists—that he hoped "it will not be irreverent for me to say that if it is probable that God would reveal his will to others, on a point so connected with my duty, it might be supposed he would reveal it directly to me." Irreverent or not, Lincoln said, "It is my earnest desire to know the will of Providence in this matter. *And if I can learn what it is I will do it!*" (original emphasis). Then, Lincoln the empiricist described the only way forward: "I must study the plain physical facts of the case, ascertain what is possible and learn what appears to be wise and right."[19]

Lincoln showed no personal interest in spiritualism even though his own wife brought into the house what had become a national pastime. Spiritualism also became, like cotton and wheat, one of America's exports to Britain. Even the original "Rochester Rappers," the Fox sisters, made their way to London, to be investigated by scientists well known to Darwin. Indeed, spiritualism became a sore point between Darwin and a colleague he greatly admired.

During his twelve years in the tropics collecting specimens until 1862, Alfred Russel Wallace "heard occasionally of the strange phenomena said to be occurring in America and Europe under the general names of 'table-turning' and 'spirit-rapping.'" Having dabbled with mesmerism in his youth and now hearing of these new mysteries "which modern science ignored because it could not explain, I determined to seize the first opportunity on my return home to examine into these matters." Wallace later wrote that it was in July 1865 that he first witnessed "the phenomena of what is called Spiritualism, in the house of a friend—a sceptic, a man of science, and a lawyer, with none but members of his own family present."[20] Wallace began a serious and life-long study.

Darwin's first inkling probably came from Joseph Dalton Hooker in November: "Wallace has turned table turner I am told." Darwin wrote no reply as he was about to see Hooker in London, where he might also quiz Charles Lyell or Thomas Huxley about the rumor. In his next letter to Wallace, Darwin made no allusions and included more than his usual quota of praise for Wallace's latest scientific papers that not only "interested me, as everything that you write does" but also "will make many more converts among naturalists than long-winded books such as I shall write if I have strength." When Wallace next sent a letter five months later, he argued that Darwin should employ Spencer's phrase "survival of the fittest" in place of "natural selection," which implied too much "thought and direction" and was thus too easily misunderstood as "personifying Nature." Impressed by the argument, Darwin agreed to use Spencer's terminology in his next book. "Whether it will be rejected," Darwin joked, "must now depend on the 'survival of the fittest.'"[21]

Just weeks later, Wallace began publishing a series of articles entitled "The Scientific Aspect of the Supernatural" in an obscure journal. He also had a pamphlet printed for private distribution. One recipient, Huxley, responded, "I am neither shocked nor disposed to issue a commission of lunacy against you. It may be all true, for anything that I know to the contrary, but really I cannot get up interest in the subject." Darwin must have had difficulty believing that Wallace, having so recently and rationally warned against "personifying Nature," could be dabbling with spiritualism. The subject did not appear in their letters or, so it seems, in conversations over the next two years.[22]

Then in April 1869, Wallace forced the issue while reviewing new editions of two of Lyell's works. Wallace asserted that natural selection could explain most other developments but not that of human consciousness. The brain of "the lowest savages, such as Australians or the Andaman Islanders," was barely smaller or less complex than "that of the average members of our learned societies," yet the savages' actual "mental requirements" for their way of life "are very little above those of many animals." Natural selection should have provided the savage with a brain only slightly larger than an ape's, so why "was an organ developed far beyond the needs of its possessor?" Wallace concluded that "in the development of the human race, a Higher Intelligence has guided the same laws for nobler ends."[23]

Darwin could not abide such teleological arguments, whether Gray's insistence on "design" or Wallace's reliance on "a Higher Intelligence." He considered both essentially supernatural explanations that obstructed the search for genuine explanations. Forewarned by Wallace before the review appeared, Darwin worried, "I hope you have not murdered too completely your own and my child." After reading the review (and writing "No!" underlined three times in the margin beside the remarks on man), Darwin spluttered, "If you had not told me I should have thought that they had been added by someone else. As you expected, I differ grievously from you, and I am very sorry for it."[24]

Regarding "my 'unscientific' opinions as to Man," Wallace replied, "a few years back I should myself have looked at them as equally wild and uncalled for," but his views had been altered by the evidence he had seen of "forces and influences not yet recognised by science." Wallace listed three other men of science "who have all investigated the subject for years" and reached similar conclusions. He asked that Darwin suspend "judgment for a time till we exhibit some corroborative symptoms of insanity."[25]

It was bad enough that one of these three allies was Robert Chambers, the suspected author of *Vestiges*, but Darwin was annoyed further when Lyell, after receiving Darwin's lament about Wallace, blithely replied, "I rather hail Wallace's suggestion that there may be a Supreme Will and Power which may not abdicate its function of interference but may guide the forces and laws of Nature."[26]

"Modern spiritualism" had revolted Darwin ever since it crossed the Atlantic in the early 1850s. He once dismissed some hypothesis, saying it "makes me sick— it is like 'magnetism' turning a table."[27] Yet, while most of Darwin's colleagues shared his view, others, like Wallace, were showing interest. Dr. James M. Gully, Darwin's hydrotherapist, joined the Spiritual Athenaeum, a society founded in 1866 by the American medium D. D. Home, who had come to London a decade earlier. Francis Galton, anthropologist, later eugenicist, and Darwin's cousin, was by 1872 attending séances during which investigations of Home and Kate Fox were conducted by the eminent chemist and physicist William Crookes, with whom Wallace worked closely.[28]

Galton sent Darwin descriptions, assurances that Crookes was making a careful study, and even suggestions that his cousin take part in a séance himself: Darwin pleaded ill health.[29] When Lady Derby was "staggered" by an article by Crookes and insisted on an opinion, Darwin admitted being "much perplexed; . . . I cannot disbelieve Mr. Crooke's statement, nor can I believe in his result." Finding "consolation" in possible explanations of "nerve-force," Darwin hoped "that a number of men, such as Professor Stokes, will be induced to witness Mr. Crooke's experiments."[30]

Darwin's cousin and brother-in-law Hensleigh Wedgwood had recently begun attending séances with Wallace and later became vice president of the Society for Psychical Research. Eventually, he and Darwin's brother Erasmus coaxed Darwin to attend his first and last séance in January 1874 at "Ras's" house, next door to Wedgwood's London home. Erasmus, the arch skeptic Darwin had always respected, was either genuinely interested or simply playing host. He knew Charles was more likely to attend if Emma did, and both would be interested in meeting at least two of his guests, G. H. Lewes and George Eliot. Lewes dabbled in science and was a known critic of spiritualism, and the Darwins greatly admired Eliot's novels. Most of the other guests were close relatives, and Erasmus hired a medium and "spirit guide" for the occasion.[31]

Lewes refused to take seriously a medium who insisted on total darkness and, with George Eliot, left early, missing "the grand fun," as Darwin described it later to Hooker: "a medium . . . made the chairs, a flute, a bell, and candlestick, and fiery points jump about in my brother's dining room, in a manner that astounded every one, and took away all their breaths." Lewes and Eliot were not the only ones who missed all this: so did Darwin. He had found the room "so hot and tiring," he told Hooker, "that I went away before all these astounding miracles, or jugglery, took place." After escaping for some rest upstairs, "I came downstairs and saw all the chairs, etc., on the table, which had been lifted over the heads of those sitting round it." Admitting that it "passes my understanding . . . how the man could possibly do what was done," he clung to his own skepticism—despite a momentary lapse: "The Lord have mercy on us all, if we have to believe in such rubbish."[32]

Fortunately for Darwin, his wife, unlike Lincoln's, showed no enthusiasm for spiritualism beyond her orthodox belief in an afterlife. Emma spoke dismissively of her brother Hensleigh's "life among the spirits" but kept an open mind, unlike her husband who "quite made up his mind he *won't* believe it, he dislikes the thought of it so much." When asked if this was not a flaw in her husband's scientific method, Emma replied, "Yes, but he does not act up to his principles," adding, tongue in cheek, "Oh yes, he is a regular bigot."[33]

A few weeks later, another séance took place with the same medium, this time at Hensleigh's house and with Huxley present. Whatever happened did not undermine Hensleigh's conviction or weaken Huxley's disdain. Huxley sent Darwin a lengthy report more notable for sardonic humor than verifiable results, concluding, "Mr. Williams is a cheat and impostor." Darwin sighed, "Now to my mind an enormous weight of evidence would be requisite to make one believe in anything beyond mere trickery. . . . I am pleased to think that I declared to all my family, the day before yesterday, that the more I thought of all that I had heard happened . . . the more convinced I was it was all imposture."[34]

On this issue, Darwin was content to ignore some colleagues' serious investigations so long as other colleagues supported his view. He had not been so hidebound when studying transmutation, yet the common factor is that in order to overcome prejudice against species change, Darwin had to oppose all explanations not grounded on material or natural causes. He lacked incentive to investigate what he deemed trivial nonmaterialism: no spiritual force planned human racial diversity.

Wallace's supernatural explanation of human development had dismayed but also stimulated Darwin, who was "now writing and thinking much about Man." Wallace was delighted Darwin was "really going to bring out your book on Man." In 1858, Wallace had caused Darwin to start writing *On the Origin of Species*, mainly to establish his precedence. Now, eleven years later, Wallace's invocation of a "Higher Intelligence" was a kind of last straw for Darwin. Lyell's and Huxley's recent work on man was disappointing, while Vogt's and Wallace's seemed to hand victory to the special creationists of Agassiz's ilk. If Lyell could "hail" Wallace for allowing some "Supreme Will" to interfere with natural selection, then it might still be argued that God created men unequal.[35]

In January 1870, Wallace sent Darwin a volume of his collected essays including a revised version of "The Limits of Natural Selection as Applied to Man." Darwin heaped praise on most of the volume, "But I groan over Man—you write like a metamorphosed (in retrograde direction) naturalist, and you the author of the best paper that ever appeared in the *Anthropological Review!*"[36] Darwin now realized that the public might never see natural selection applied properly (as "sexual selection") to the issue of human races unless he did it himself.

Both Lincoln and Darwin instinctively turned to scientists (Joseph Henry and Thomas Huxley) to expose fraudulent mediums, even though they knew that other highly rational men—such as Robert Dale Owen and Alfred Russel Wallace—believed one could bring spiritualism under the umbrella of science. Lincoln and Darwin saw spiritualism as religious superstition having nothing to do with science and reason.

Wallace's argument that some "Higher Intelligence" influenced human evolution left Darwin unmoved, but Lincoln seemed to accept that God might play some role in the world, however remote and inscrutable. Lincoln once reportedly said, "Doesn't it strike you as queer that I, who couldn't cut the head off of a chicken, and who was sick at the sight of blood, should be cast into the middle of a great war, with blood flowing all about me . . . Doesn't it seem strange to you that I should be here?" Calling something "strange" and "queer" barely evokes divine influence, and yet at times, Lincoln seemed to accept even that: "It is a momentous thing to be the instrument, under Providence, of the liberation of a race!"[37]

Excellent scholars disagree about whether Lincoln's religious views changed during the Civil War. Lincoln's religious references were meant to rally people to a cause, while contemporaries' testimonies usually had some axe to grind, leaving scholars to take their pick. One source that at least can be said to have above-average value is Joshua Speed, Lincoln's intimate friend and a fellow skeptic from the 1830s. Speed saw Lincoln many times during the Civil War, and his brother was in the cabinet. Regarding Lincoln's possible religious transformation, Speed said in a lecture in the 1880s, "The only evidence I have of any change, was in the summer before he died." Speed entered a room and found Lincoln by a window reading the Bible. Speed said, "I am glad to see you so profitably engaged." "Yes," said Lincoln, "I am profitably engaged." "Well," said Speed, "If you have recovered from your skepticism, I am sorry to say I have not." Lincoln looked him in the face and, placing a hand on Speed's shoulder, said, "You are wrong Speed, take all of this book upon reason that you can, and the balance on faith, and you will live and die a happier and better man." Elsewhere in his lecture, Speed provided context for this "evidence." The same tension between "reason" and "faith" was present when, according to Speed, Lincoln "often said that the most ambitious man might live to see every hope fail; but no Christian could live to see his fail, because fulfillment could only come when life ended." And Speed said frankly that Lincoln "was cautious about expressing himself against public opinion when it did no good" and "very cautious never to give expression to any thought or sentiment that would grate harshly upon a Christian's ear."[38]

The horrendous strain of the war, which engraved itself on Lincoln's face, might indeed have influenced his religious views. Not referring specifically to religion, Lincoln's secretary John Hay wrote in 1890 that "it would be impossible to say when the change began; but he was in mind, body and nerves a very different man at the second inauguration from the one who had taken the oath in 1861."[39] In that brief but powerful Second Inaugural Address, Lincoln attempted, as the long war neared its end, to begin the healing by diminishing any sense of victory or defeat, dispelling self-righteousness and partisan blame, and, unexpectedly, undermining the view so prevalent around him: that God had obviously backed the North.

> Neither party expected for the war, the magnitude, or the duration, which it has already attained. Neither anticipated that the *cause* of the conflict [i.e., slavery] might cease with, or even before, the conflict itself should cease. Each

looked for an easier triumph, and a result less fundamental and astounding.
Both read the same Bible, and pray to the same God; and each invokes His aid
against the other. It may seem strange that any men should dare to ask a just
God's assistance in wringing their bread from the sweat of other men's faces;
but let us judge not that we be not judged.

That last sentence, echoing a line often used during his debates with Stephen A.
Douglas, also delivered a moral judgment—just before Lincoln quoted scripture
to say we should do no such thing. He continued, "The prayers of both could
not be answered; that of neither has been answered fully. The Almighty has His
own purposes." Thus, Lincoln again emphasized God's inscrutability—before
scrutinizing God's will and offering this interpretation:

> If we shall suppose that American Slavery is one of those offences which, in the
> providence of God, must needs come, but which, having continued through
> His appointed time, He now wills to remove, and that He gives to both North
> and South, this terrible war, as the woe due to those by whom the offence came,
> shall we discern therein any departure from those divine attributes which the
> believers in a Living God always ascribe to Him?

The numerous qualifications—"if we shall suppose" that events *might* accord
with the nature of God as "always" described by "believers"—suggest Lincoln
had not suddenly joining the latter. After doubting God had responded to either
side's prayers, he went on to equate prayers with something he could at least feel:
hope. The fact that the war still continued was better ascribed to divine will than
presidential incompetence.

> Fondly do we hope—fervently do we pray—that this mighty scourge of war
> may speedily pass away. Yet, if God wills that it continue, until all the wealth
> piled by the bond-man's two hundred and fifty years of unrequited toil shall
> be sunk, and until every drop of blood drawn with the lash, shall be paid by
> another drawn with the sword, as was said three thousand years ago, so still
> it must be said "the judgments of the Lord, are true and righteous altogether."

That God might be the source of justice does not remove the difficulty of discern-
ing his will. Lincoln had his own view of what was "right" to do and encouraged
his audience to hope this might be the same as God's view.

> With malice toward none; with charity for all; with firmness in the right, as
> God gives us to see the right, let us strive on to finish the work we are in; to
> bind up the nation's wounds; to care for him who shall have borne the battle,
> and for his widow, and his orphan—to do all which may achieve and cherish
> a just, and a lasting peace, among ourselves, and with all nations.[40]

Lincoln was addressing a shattered nation and trying to give meaning to
recent horrific events and purpose to an uncertain future; Darwin was merely

corresponding with thoughtful men, many of whom, like Gray, Lyell, and Wallace, still believed that God had some immanent role in nature. Lincoln made no pretense of certainty ("as God gives us to see"), and, conversely, Darwin avoided pure atheism by likewise confessing ignorance and relying, as Lincoln did, on hope. "I feel most deeply that the whole subject is too profound for the human intellect," Darwin told Gray in one of their exchanges about design. "A dog might as well speculate on the mind of Newton. Let each man hope & believe what he can."[41]

Meeting Agassiz

In January 1865, reelected but still drafting his Second Inaugural Address, Lincoln had what was apparently his first and last face-to-face conversation with America's most famous scientist, Louis Agassiz.[1] Noah Brooks, the president's journalist friend, was one of two witnesses to the interview in the White House and the only one to describe it, in three slightly different accounts.[2] When the nation's chief executive met the nation's foremost scientist, Lincoln was in a good mood, with imminent military victory making the burdens of office more bearable. The normally ebullient Agassiz, however, bore the signs of recent depression and physical illness caused, indirectly, by Darwin.

Agassiz maniacally added specimens to his Museum of Comparative Zoology, as if possessing more than any other institution in the world would give his scientific views greater authority. He spoke of soon-to-be-acquired evidence that would prove natural selection false and separate creation true, yet the piles of specimens catalogued by assistants were hardly utilized by their master, and the few works he published contained nothing new.[3] He rejected natural selection but without offering rigorous argument in peer-reviewed journals, while the rehashed content of his popular lectures was rehashed again for *Atlantic Monthly*.

In July 1864, *Atlantic Monthly* published Agassiz's recent lecture "The Ice-Period in America," in which he asserted, "The glacier was God's great plough; and when the ice vanished from the face of the land, it left it prepared for the hand of the husbandman." When others pointed to evidence that rich vegetation also *preceded* the Ice Age, Agassiz declared, "The soil we have now over the temperate zone is a grain-growing soil" intended for man, as part of God's "purpose." The entomologist, B. D. Walsh, asked Darwin, "Do any European authorities uphold him in these views?" Darwin replied, "All the younger good naturalists, whom I know think of Agassiz as you do . . . & *no* geologist now agrees with Agassiz."[4]

In America, Agassiz's standing remained high with the public, but the scientific community was steadily abandoning him. More and more of his students rebelled, and in August 1864, Agassiz suffered a particular humiliation at the second biennial National Academy of Sciences (NAS) session—the first that Asa Gray attended—when a new member was elected that Agassiz had specifically opposed. Agassiz was furious; the heated debate was later expunged from the minutes; and on the train back from New Haven, Agassiz spoke so offensively to Gray that he formally broke relations. When Agassiz attacked Joseph Henry for supporting Gray, Henry calmly tried to show Agassiz how he was wrong and also urged him "to first take care of your health. . . . It is lamentable . . . how much time, mental activity, and bodily strength have been expended among us . . . in personal altercations, which might have been devoted to the discovery of new truths."[5]

Agassiz remained unwell and irritable through the fall and winter, but when he attended the next NAS session in Washington on 3–7 January 1865, he seemed chastened by the memory of the previous meeting, and all went smoothly. Agassiz stayed on for a meeting of Smithsonian regents on 9 January, when a new chancellor was elected: Salmon P. Chase, who was no longer secretary of the treasury. To Chase's surprise, Lincoln accepted his fourth offer to resign in June 1864 but then secured Chase's appointment as chief justice of the Supreme Court, replacing the deceased Roger B. Taney—who had also preceded Chase as chancellor of the Smithsonian.[6]

While lingering in Washington, Agassiz may have begun planning his next project, a trip to Brazil. In a letter dated 22 March, he wrote that "a few weeks ago"—so, perhaps in January—he was pondering how best to recover "after all the fatigue of the two last years. . . . I felt that I must have new scenes to give me new life." Agassiz's "attention was turned to the natural history" of Brazil, whose emperor, Dom Pedro II, had already shown him "many marks of kindness," such as ordering his subjects to gather rare fish for the great scientist, who, at the outset of his career, had done pioneering work on Brazil's fishes. Agassiz's recent public lectures had theorized that South America should offer evidence of a worldwide glacial destruction of organic life that, as he later told students in a lecture during the voyage to Rio, would demonstrate that the transmutation theory was "wholly without foundation in facts" for such a destruction would sever any evolutionary link and require a special creation of new life forms.[7]

By coincidence, Washington was just then buzzing with news that the U.S. Navy, while capturing a Confederate raider, had violated Brazilian neutrality. "Every one says we must make rightful *amende* to Brazil," Gray wrote Darwin about this miniature "*Trent*" affair." Agassiz's old friend Senator Charles Sumner later appealed to him, "You are a naturalist; but you are a patriot also; . . . plead for our country, to the end that its rights may be understood," which Agassiz eventually did.[8]

Agassiz had visited Washington many times and perhaps even attended a White House reception but apparently had never before met the president individually. But now, he was brought to the White House by Samuel Hooper, a wealthy Boston businessman, a trustee for Agassiz's museum, and a Republican

Congressman then under consideration for Chase's vacated post. Perhaps, Hooper hoped Agassiz's fame and charm would somehow improve Hooper's chance of joining the cabinet, but Brooks's account implies that it was Lincoln's idea that he should meet Agassiz. With the war going well, the president may have felt he could indulge himself in other interests. In a recent statement to *Scientific American*, Lincoln promised to support the more practical aspects of science by doing "all in his power to encourage and to promote the progress of these arts by sanctioning all wise legislation in behalf of inventors."[9]

Agassiz's only "inventions," according to detractors, were his theories. What Lincoln knew about Agassiz or his detractors is impossible to gauge. Agassiz's widely known views on the human races had to be distasteful to Lincoln, who may have shared the disdain expressed by William H. Herndon in 1867 (quoted earlier): "We had no need of Agassiz out here to tell us what things meant."[10] Herndon was then referring to geology but certainly felt likewise about supernatural notions of special creation. Any of the three American Freedmen's Inquiry Commission (AFIC) commissioners could have told Lincoln about Agassiz's correspondence with Howe, and since, according to Gray, Henry admired Darwin's work, he may have explained to Lincoln the controversies dividing Darwin and Agassiz. Lincoln could also have learned from Henry about Agassiz's role in the sudden creation of the NAS, and the matter probably came up whenever Admiral John A. Dahlgren explained the reason (otherwise lost to history) why he was the first of the original fifty "incorporators" to resign from the academy back in May 1863.

Whoever instigated this meeting, the fourth person who was present, Noah Brooks, prefaced his earliest account with a revealing context:

> In his eagerness to acquire knowledge of common things [Lincoln] sometimes surprised his distinguished visitors by inquiries about matters that they were supposed to be acquainted with, and those who came to scrutinize went away with a vague sense of having been unconsciously pumped by the man whom they expected to pump. One Sunday evening last winter, while sitting alone with the President, the cards of Professor Agassiz and a friend were sent in.[11]

That preface hints at Lincoln's slyness as an interrogator, but another memory caused Brooks to preface his two later accounts of the interview differently—with an anecdote about Lincoln's reaction to the news just received that Edward Everett had died. Lincoln was somewhat acerbic about the man who had shared the platform at Gettysburg, mentioning his overrated oratorical style and fondness for "props." Of course, the news of Everett's death and the arrival of Agassiz were unconnected, and yet, Agassiz's style of lecturing was one of the conversation's topics that stuck in Brooks's memory.

Also in the later accounts, Brooks named Agassiz's friend and described the moment when the visitors' cards were brought to Lincoln: "'Agassiz!' exclaimed the president with great delight, 'I never met him yet, and Hooper promised to bring him up to-night.' I rose to go, when he said, 'Don't go, don't go. Sit down, and let us see what we can pick up that's new from this great man.'"[12] (Lincoln was perhaps being as ironic as Darwin when he, too, had described Agassiz as a "great man.") In Brooks's earliest account, not only was he told to stay and, as it were, join in but he was also "unconsciously pumped" (to use his own phrase) regarding his opinion of Agassiz:

> The President had never met Agassiz at that time, I believe, and said, "I would like to talk with that man; he is a good man, I do believe; don't you think so?" But one answer could be returned to the query, and soon after the visitors were shown in, the President first whispering, "Now sit still and see what we can pick up that's new."[13]

Whether "Honest Abe" believed Agassiz was entirely "a good man," it is likely he was fishing for Brooks's opinion or predisposing Brooks so he would not be aware of what Lincoln had in mind for this interview. In any case, Brooks seemed amazed by the conversation's blandness, as if he had expected conflict. "To my surprise, however, no questions were asked about the Old Silurian, the Glacial Theory, or the Great Snow-storm." In the later accounts, Brooks replaced that line with this: "The conversation, however, was not very learned. The President and the savant seemed like two boys who wanted to ask questions which appeared commonplace, but were not quite sure of each other. Each man was simplicity itself." Brooks found the mutual wariness puzzling. His earliest account gives a more detailed description of the way the conversation apparently opened:

> [I]ntroductions being over, the President said: "I never knew how to properly pronounce your name; won't you give me a little lesson at that, please?" Then he asked if it were of French or Swiss derivation, to which the Professor replied that it was partly of each. That led to a discussion of different languages, the President speaking of several words in different languages which had the same root as similar words in our own tongue; then he illustrated that by one or two anecdotes, one of which he borrowed from [Thomas] Hood's "Up the Rhine."[14]

While showing an innocent interest in his visitor and offering some humorous entertainment, Lincoln was also demonstrating a powerful memory and surprising interest in foreign languages. He was probably aware, even if Brooks was not, that philological evidence had been used by those wishing to demonstrate a common origin for mankind. Darwin knew the subject well: his cousin Hensleigh Wedgwood had written a book on it. And Agassiz had defended separate creation by attacking "The Reliability of Philological Evidence," the title of his essay for Nott and Gliddon's *Indigenous Races of the Earth* in 1857. Agassiz's philological views were often attacked in reviews Lincoln might have read.

Brooks recollected that the next subject discussed was lecturing. After quoting some humorous verse, the president "soon returned to his gentle cross-examination of Agassiz, and found out how the Professor studied, how he composed, and how he delivered his lectures; how he found different tastes in his audiences in different portions of the country." Although Brooks recognized this as "cross-examination," Lincoln was so indirect—perhaps to lull Agassiz's suspicions—that he lost Brooks's interest: the journalist dropped the last sentence in his later accounts. Yet, Lincoln possibly wished to hear from Agassiz's lips how his theories—especially those touching on the matter of race—had elicited different reactions in the North and in the South.

This point led to the only other topic that Brooks thought worth recording: Lincoln's allusion to his own brief career as a lecturer. Once again, the earliest account is the fullest.

> In passing, the President said that many years ago, when the custom of lecture-going was more common than since, he was induced to try his hand at composing a literary lecture—something which he thought entirely out of his line. The subject, he said, was not defined, but his purpose was to analyze inventions and discoveries—"to get at the bottom of things"—and to show when, where, how, and why such things were invented or discovered; and, so far as possible, to find where the first mention is made of some of our common things. The Bible, he said, he found to be the richest store-house for such knowledge; and he then gave one or two illustrations, which were new to his hearers.

Again, Lincoln demonstrated his amazing memory as well as his seemingly pious ability to quote the Bible at will, but he also revealed that he had thought deeply on the origins of things: whether mankind's origin slipped into the conversation is not recorded. While Brooks's earliest account concluded with the words, "The lecture was never finished, and was left among his loose papers at Springfield when he came to Washington," his second account added some pleasantry from the professor: "Agassiz begged that Lincoln would finish the lecture, sometime. Lincoln replied that he had the manuscript somewhere in his papers, 'and,' said he, 'when I get out of this place, I'll finish it up, perhaps, and get my friend B— to print it somewhere.'" For Brooks, more interested in Lincoln than in Agassiz, this reference to Lincoln's single lecture was fascinating news, but, again, Lincoln may have offered this tidbit mainly to encourage Agassiz to say more about his own lecturing or the concept of origins.[15]

Brooks gave two different versions of the interview's end. The first was written only weeks after Lincoln's death: "When afterward asked why he put such questions to his learned visitor he said, 'Why, what we got from him isn't printed in the books; the other things are.'" This was amplified in the 1878 version:

> When these two visitors had departed, Agassiz and Lincoln shaking hands with great warmth, the latter turned to me with a quizzical smile and said, "Well, I wasn't so badly scared, after all! were you?" He had evidently expected

to be very much oppressed by the great man's learning. He admitted that he had cross-examined him on "things not in the books."

Even after revising it, Brooks did not consider this point—that Lincoln was not overly impressed by Agassiz's learning—worth keeping in any form in the last account written in 1895. To give Brooks his due, he did seem conscious of his own bewilderment but did not appreciate how fully Lincoln was familiar with writings by or about Agassiz, or why Lincoln wished to learn more than those works could tell, or why Agassiz may have been wary of being completely frank with the author of the Emancipation Proclamation. It was Lincoln at his most charming and disarming, no doubt raising many insignificant points to disguise the odd one of consequence. The two protagonists were no doubt more aware of what was happening during this conversation than the friendly journalist.[16]

Brooks did not mention Brazil, and perhaps Agassiz had not yet begun serious planning. However, within a few weeks, Agassiz made up his mind, and the semi-holiday turned into the major expedition Agassiz had always longed to conduct, especially after a philanthropist donated funds and a steamship company put a vessel at Agassiz's disposal. Secretary Gideon Welles provided a letter instructing naval officers to offer every assistance, and Secretary William H. Seward sent a similar message to the American consul in Rio de Janeiro.[17]

Agassiz's expedition left New York on 1 April 1865 and returned in August 1866, just in time for Agassiz to attend another NAS meeting and read a paper on "Traces of Glaciers under the Tropics." This and a new series of lectures promoted Agassiz's supposed discovery of evidence of a glaciation so severe that animals and plants that lived before could have no genetic link to those that came after: evidence that the transmutationists were mistaken.[18] Agassiz dismissed the fact that other researchers had already spent years in the Amazon without seeing any sign of former glaciation. A young geologist who accompanied the expedition, Charles F. Hartt, was troubled by Agassiz's interpretations but waited several years before admitting that the geological finds had never indicated glaciation.[19]

While Agassiz was still planning his journey to slave-ridden Brazil, Lincoln was busy trying to extirpate slavery forever in the United States. Knowing that the Emancipation Proclamation was only partial and, as a wartime measure, might easily be challenged in the courts after the war, Lincoln supported the congressional effort to abolish slavery constitutionally through the Thirteenth Amendment. When Congress approved the amendment on 31 January 1865, Lincoln insisted on signing the document, which required no signature.[20] The subsequent process of state ratification was complicated by controversies over whether states in rebellion could or should be part of the process and, if so, whether ratification would become a condition for their readmission to the Union or whether a speedy "reconstruction" of the Union would make it easier to achieve that ratification. Lincoln did not wish to coerce states, but he did try vaguely to link reconstruction and ratification in the hope they might accelerate each other—in order to end the war more quickly and destroy anyone's hope to preserve slavery. In a month's time, eighteen of the twenty-seven states needed for final ratification (if Southern states were counted) had approved. However, in March, only Vermont added itself to the list. It appeared that the remaining eight ratifications might not occur until the war itself was over.

On their second day out of New York, steaming toward Brazil, members of Agassiz's expedition were glancing westward and saw "a cloud of smoke, in the direction of Petersburg."[21] It was Ulysses S. Grant's final assault on Richmond, Virginia: a week later, Robert E. Lee surrendered at Appomattox. As soon as Darwin read the news, he dashed off a letter to Gray: "I have not written for a long time . . . [and] I have nothing particular to say now, but the grand news of Richmond has stirred me up to write. I congratulate you, & I can do this honestly, as my reason has always urged & ordered me to be a hearty good wisher for the north, though I could not do so enthusiastically, as I felt we were so hated by you." He was glad he and others "who thought that you could not entirely subdue the South" had been proved wrong. Although Darwin had "always thought that the destruction of Slavery would be well worth a dozen years war," he also feared that "it will take many years before your country will shake down to its old routine."[22]

President Lincoln was endeavoring to hasten the time when the country could "shake down to its old routine." The war's end raised new opportunities as well as previously submerged problems. Losing the commander-in-chief's war powers would narrow Lincoln's options, and Congress was keen to assert authority over the process of "reconstruction."

Lincoln favored the most rapid reconstruction possible, on the basis of a plan he announced in December 1863. If the rebel states ended resistance, formed new governments that accepted emancipation, and elected new representatives to Congress, then other issues (punishment of Confederate officials, repudiation of Confederate debts, suffrage for blacks, and whether former rebel states should take part in ratifying the Thirteenth Amendment) could be sorted out later, through collaboration among Lincoln, Congress, and the restored state governments. However, many leading Republicans felt the new "reconstructed" governments must first grant at least some of the emancipated blacks the protection afforded by the right to vote *before* those states could be included in the ratification process or allowed back into the Union. At the time of Lee's surrender, it appeared that those wishing to exclude the rebel states from the ratification process would fail, but those insisting on black suffrage before any particular state was reconstructed were prevailing. A crucial moment had occurred in March, shortly before Lee's surrender, when Congress debated whether to accept Louisiana's new state constitution and to seat her newly elected representatives in Congress.

Louisiana had followed Lincoln's reconstruction plan and had even ratified the Thirteenth Amendment but had not granted voting rights to its black citizens, even though an exceptional proportion of them had been born free, owned property, and served in the Union armies. Lincoln had long urged that some Louisianan blacks, "the very intelligent and those who have fought valiantly in our ranks," ought to be considered for the suffrage, but he was not discouraged or greatly surprised by Louisiana's reluctance: most Northern states had never granted blacks the vote and remained unwilling to do so. However, many influential Republicans in Congress, eager to promote blacks' rights and Congress's control of Reconstruction, made a stand regarding Louisiana's failure. Key senators managed to "talk out" the time allotted for debating a bill for Louisiana's readmission to the Union so that it would have to be reintroduced later, and Congress meanwhile prevented Louisiana's elected representatives from taking their seats in Congress. This naturally cast doubt on the validity of Louisiana's ratification of the Thirteenth Amendment (and likewise on ratifications by Virginia and Arkansas). The whole matter would have to wait until the next session in December 1865. Thus, as of March, the various rebel states could not know for another seven months whether Congress would admit their representatives into the national legislature even if the citizens of those states ceased fighting, took the necessary oaths, and went so far as to approve the Thirteenth Amendment.

Lincoln could not know either, but during those seven months, he could try to move matters forward. In a speech on 11 April, only two days after Lee's surrender, Lincoln forcefully argued why it would be better to accept Louisiana into the Union without first compelling the state to approve black suffrage, and in his conclusion, he said, "What has been said of Louisiana will apply generally to other States."[23] Lincoln hoped to advance his plan for a swift reconstruction, prevent the emergence of guerilla warfare, clear the path for the Thirteenth Amendment, and provide both whites and blacks with ways to work out their problematic relations within the same country. To improve the situation, Lincoln had recently renewed his proposals regarding compensation, and there is even evidence—albeit controversial—that Lincoln also sought to revive interest in colonization.

Proposals for compensation to slave owners had previously faced opposition from both Northerners and Southerners, but Lincoln may have believed the war's end would change that. Allegedly, Lincoln made an offer of compensation for slave owners when he met with Confederate leaders (received only as private individuals) during the Hampton Roads conference in February, but when Lincoln then brought the subject before his cabinet, the idea of broad compensation was promptly rejected. Lincoln dropped the matter but might have brought it up again at a later date.

That Lincoln had "sloughed off" the policy of colonization eight months earlier was something expressed by his secretary John Hay, not by Lincoln himself. Back then, Lincoln had good reasons to ignore a potentially divisive issue during the run-up to his reelection. The earlier colonizing efforts—the Chiriqui project and the Ile à Vache experiment—had, by February 1864, come to naught for reasons that did not necessarily invalidate Lincoln's original purposes. Opponents of colonization felt that the Emancipation Proclamation and blacks' service in the military made colonization even more pointless. When Congress repealed the funds for colonization in July 1864, Hay saw that his boss raised no objection.

Lee's surrender changed the situation. The excellent service rendered by 180,000 black soldiers was about to end, but it was clear that white attitudes toward blacks were still extremely negative. The evidence was in the July 1863 Draft Riots in New York City, which resulted in the savage killing of an unknown number of blacks, in the vicious "miscegenation" campaign during the 1864 election, in the failure of numerous states—south *and* north—to approve black suffrage, and in the stalled effort to ratify the Thirteenth Amendment. If radical Republicans continued to obstruct reconstruction unless the former rebel states granted black suffrage and if those states refused to be blackmailed into doing so after already being defeated in war, then hope of swiftly restoring good relations between the states—and improving those between the races—was indeed faint.

Lincoln's reelection and the end of the war made it possible—and in some ways more pressing—to revive the plans for colonization. The huge blockade fleet could now provide the massive shipping that might be required. With or without the Thirteenth Amendment, emancipation was becoming a practical fact, shifting attention to the underlying problem of how the two races—and especially the defeated former masters and the energized former slaves—were to live together. Lincoln probably felt they would make a better job of it with the "safety valve" of colonization in place, so that blacks who found the continuing prejudice too oppressive could have a means to escape, while those who wished to stay could do so, knowing it was a choice they had made and that some whites might come to respect.

After the Chiriqui project was derailed (largely by opposition from Latin American countries) and even as the Ile à Vache venture was failing through speculators' corruption, Lincoln tried another approach. In June 1863, he discussed with a British official a project to facilitate black colonization to British Honduras, and the planning certainly remained active into 1864 and was perhaps halted only when Congress terminated funds in July. Lincoln asked his attorney general's opinion whether, despite Congress's action, the executive still had authority to pay the Reverend James Mitchell as colonization agent.[24]

The only other direct (but controversial) evidence that Lincoln persisted in contemplating colonization is the testimony of General Benjamin F. Butler, who many years later published two accounts of an interview he had with Lincoln in April 1865.[25] Inconsistencies and contradictions within Butler's two accounts have made historians wary, yet if one accepts that the accounts are not deliberate falsifications and that some interview of this type occurred, then Butler provides possible insights into Lincoln's thinking.

Returned from a visit to captured Richmond and under the spell of victory, Lincoln planned for a postwar future. He worried that rebel troops might carry on guerrilla warfare and also that over a hundred thousand blacks, many only recently freed, now possessed arms and had proved that they knew how to use them: if bitter, defeated, Southern whites tried to enforce their will, these freedmen might demonstrate further that their race was far from "indolent."[26]

Butler's accounts suggest both men saw some value in colonization, although Butler suggested Lincoln had impractical notions that Butler investigated at Lincoln's request, returning with "statistics and calculations" proving it was utterly impossible "to export all of the negroes" because "negro children will be born faster than your whole naval and merchant vessels . . . can carry them from the country."[27] It seems unlikely that Lincoln ever expected to colonize "all of the negroes," knowing well that many had no desire to leave. Perhaps, he gave Butler an improbable plan to mull over so the general could better it with some plan of his own, which was certainly Butler's response. The general's plan concentrated on one group of blacks: soldiers still under Lincoln's command while their enlistments lasted and capable of looking after themselves in a harsh foreign environment. They could even be given something useful to do: dig a canal through the Isthmus of Panama—an idea Lincoln had actually hinted at when he mentioned to the delegation of blacks in 1862 that the location he had in mind "is to be a great highway from the Atlantic or Caribbean Sea to the Pacific Ocean."[28]

Butler's credentials as an abolitionist and a friend to blacks—many of whom he had commanded during the war—made him a good choice politically to fend off opposition to any particular scheme, and the only plan that Butler was not likely to criticize was one he originated himself (or thought he had). Regarding Butler's hastily produced plan, Lincoln made no firmer commitment than to utter a homely phrase: "There is meat in that, General Butler, there is meat in that." He also told Butler to work on the matter further.[29]

For Lincoln, colonization still made some sense. That long history of racial oppression was unlikely to change into one of racial harmony anytime soon. Likewise, it was difficult to imagine how Congress could ever force *any* states to grant blacks suffrage except through some compulsion that would leave deep scars, especially in those recently vanquished. How blacks could be protected without that right to vote was impossible to foresee. Lincoln probably did not believe that blacks were likely soon to "become extinct" as a race or to drift naturally toward the more tropical states, and although he had spoken up for the humanity of blacks and more recently for their possible political rights, he knew that most of his fellow citizens did not share his views. Considering the history of race relations in America in the century that followed, we cannot say that Lincoln's pessimism about the situation was unfounded. The option of a partial colonization, although repulsive to many at the time and to most people today, may have seemed a less harmful course of action than many others then being advocated and later resulting in yet another century of intense suffering for African Americans.

On reading of the Confederacy's surrender, Darwin had written his hearty congratulations to Asa Gray on 19 April 1865, not knowing that Abraham Lincoln had been assassinated five days earlier. The tragic news did not reach London until 26 April. The following day, the London *Times* carried details of the murder, of Britain's shocked reactions, and of the House of Commons' address of sympathy to the American ambassador. Gray, probably in some shock himself, for he had come to adore Lincoln, possibly waited before replying to Darwin's letter until he had received information about the general reaction in Britain.

> I am too much *distracted* with work at this season to write letters on our affairs, and if I once begin, I should not know where to stop. You have always been sympathising and just, and I appreciate your hearty congratulations on the success of our just endeavors. You have since had much more to rejoice over, as well as to sorrow with us. But the noble manner in which our country has borne itself should give you real satisfaction. We appreciate too the good feeling of England in its hearty grief at the murder of Lincoln.[30]

Darwin apparently did not write again until early July, and that letter has not survived. His health had gone into another slump just about the time that Lincoln was killed. Less than a week after learning of Lincoln's death, Darwin received another shock: news that his old commander on the *Beagle*, Robert FitzRoy, who had subsequently denounced Darwin's scientific work as heretical, had slit his own throat. Darwin was "astounded . . . but I ought not to have been," he told Hooker, "for I remember once thinking it likely; poor fellow his mind was quite out of balance once during our voyage. . . . Twice he quarrelled bitterly with me, without any just provocation on my part."[31]

Darwin remembered, though three decades had passed, that the worst of those quarrels had concerned Darwin's antislavery views and had flared up shortly after the *Beagle* carried Darwin to the first slave territory he ever visited, Brazil. Darwin may have recently read in the *Times* some notice picked up from the American press announcing that Brazil was just now enjoying a visit by America's most famous scientist. Searching the interior jungles for nonexisting evidence of glacier action, Louis Agassiz was probably one of the last people from the civilized world to learn of the death of the man who had interrogated him so strangely four months earlier.[32]

The Descent of Man

While Lincoln had few health concerns and should have worried more about other threats to his life, Darwin's ill health caused him, when still in his thirties, to make provisions for an early demise. Yet Darwin died peacefully in his bed seventeen years after Lincoln's violent end at the age of fifty-six. It was six years after Lincoln's death that Darwin finally published the results of his thirty years' investigation into man's origins.

Before his death, Lincoln had given clear indications—albeit in a radically changing environment—of how he would tackle the complex problems of reconstructing the Union politically and working out the new status of freed African Americans, but he died before he could bring his plans to fruition. Lincoln certainly faced massive congressional opposition to his ideas, but he could hardly have botched reconstruction and future race relations as badly as those who took over those difficult challenges.

Lincoln's death probably damaged the effort to improve relations between whites and blacks, and inadvertently and to a lesser degree Darwin's work did the same—not because *The Descent of Man* altered the likely course of racial policies in post–Civil War America but because some of the vocabulary used in arguments about those policies came from *On the Origin of Species*, albeit in a mangled form. Many people extrapolated from *The Origin* what they thought were Darwin's views about the human races and never discovered their error by reading *The Descent* carefully. Throughout the seventeen years separating Lincoln's and Darwin's deaths, the United States developed Reconstruction policies that veered from the former's obvious intentions and ignored the latter's scientific evidence, with results harmful to that cause of mankind's unity and equality that both men had promoted. They would have been appalled that such harm could ever be part of their legacy.

"You see, slavery is *dead*, dead,—an absolute unanimity as to this," Asa Gray wrote to Darwin three months after the Civil War ended. "The Revolted States will behave as badly as they can, but they are so thoroughly whipped that they can't stir, hand or foot." Darwin responded, "We continue to be deeply interested on American affairs; indeed I care for nothing else in the *Times*. . . . How well I remember thinking that Slavery would flourish for centuries in your Southern States!"[1]

However much relief was expressed about slavery's end, it actually sharpened the debate about racial differences. In a short article in May 1865, Thomas Huxley summarized the new situation offhandedly—and insensitively to modern tastes. Employing a slang term for a black slave, Huxley asserted, "Quashie's plaintive inquiry, 'Am I not a man and a brother?' seems at last to have received its final reply." Yet, Huxley argued that the reply—emancipation—still left unanswered the question of racial equality. "It may be quite true that some negroes are better than some white men; but no rational man, cognisant of the facts, believes that the average negro is the equal, still less the superior, of the average white man." Now that the "disability" of slavery was removed and blacks could compete freely, Huxley considered it "incredible" to think "our dusky cousins" would be able "to compete successfully with [their] "bigger-brained" white rivals for "the highest places in the hierarchy of civilisation." While Huxley believed abolition helped both blacks and whites, the "doctrine of equal natural rights may be an illogical delusion; emancipation may convert the slave from a well-fed animal into a pauperised man."[2]

Although Huxley did not seriously think emancipation changed an animal into a man, he did still consider that black man to be a "dusky cousin" rather than a "brother." Huxley was much more willing than Darwin to assume that natural selection led to variations among human races that were not just superficial differences but also, in some vague sense, amounted to serious inequalities in ability. Yet, in a lecture he gave two weeks later, the only specific difference between blacks and whites that Huxley noted was blacks' greater immunity to yellow fever: "the differences between men are . . . so small" that mankind must have arisen from one primitive "stock," the term Huxley used here in preference to species, noting the limits of existing evidence and the fluidity of species under natural selection. However, these "stocks" were also variants that might eventually become separate species. Like Gray and Alfred Russel Wallace before him, Huxley argued that natural selection reconciled and combined "all that is good in the Monogenistic and Polygenistic schools." He rejected the view that hybrids between present-day races were infertile, while accepting that logically that barrier could arise in the future.[3]

Gray, Wallace, and now Huxley had all recognized that the terms of the monogenist-polygenist debate had been made obsolete by natural selection: there was not one creation of mankind or many separate creations of difference races but an ongoing process of change.[4] But for Darwin, the issue was not just about terminology but about *purpose*. It is somewhat ironic that Darwin, who could see no designing role for a creator in natural selection, probably was unable to recognize his own purposeful role in creating the theory of natural selection. However much he merely allowed the evidence to lead him toward the truth, the fact is that it led him where he had always wished to go. Darwin's purpose was still the same as that of the monogenists of his youth: to argue in favor of the unity of man but a unity derived not from God's action in the Garden of Eden but from competition for resources. In that competition, one primate, man, developed a modification toward greater intelligence, which allowed him to outlast less intelligent competitors.

Although Huxley had invoked "Darwinism" in those two 1865 articles, his views did not always represent Darwin's. Frequently corresponding with Huxley at this time, Darwin habitually commented on Huxley's publications, yet found nothing to praise in the first of these two articles, and told Huxley in a postscript that he had read the second "with much interest," adding circumspectly that he could "quite agree on all the points on which I could judge."[5]

The essential problem is that while Gray, Wallace, and now Huxley all suggested that natural selection ended the struggle between monogenism and polygenism, no victor was declared. Polygenists in Britain and America saw no reason to abandon all of their positions. In 1866—five years before Darwin published *The Descent of Man*—the pioneer of American polygenism, Dr. Josiah Nott, declared, "Lamarck, Geoffroy Saint-Hilaire, Darwin and other naturalists, have contended for the gradual change or development of organic forms from physical causes, yet even this school requires millions of years for their theory, and would not controvert the facts and deductions I have laid down." Nott lacked Huxley's satisfaction at slavery's demise but agreed it meant the black and white races might "be left alone face to face" and "soon learn to understand each other, and come to proper terms under the law of necessity." Nott argued against federal interference in those relations, asserting that the two races each had their own "moral and physical laws" and that "all the power of the Freedmen's Bureau or 'gates of hell' cannot prevail against them" because "forms that have been permanent for several thousand years, must remain so at least during the lifetime of a nation." Three years earlier, the American Freedmen's Inquiry Commission, like Huxley and Nott, had decided that once the manmade disabilities were removed, the Negro "will somewhere find, and will maintain, his own appropriate social position."[6]

Although slavery was dead in the United States, Darwin could still become aroused by racial injustice, such as a summary execution approved by the British governor of Jamaica, Edward Eyre, during agitations late in 1865. Huxley, declaring that "English law does not permit good persons, as such, to strangle bad persons, as such," joined the Jamaica Committee created by John Stuart Mill to bring Eyre to justice. Darwin donated £10 to the committee's fighting fund—just as he formerly contributed to abolition societies and cotton famine relief.[7]

Darwin did not need the incident of Governor Eyre to remind him that racism remained a poisonous issue, and he still intended to publish his evidence showing how natural selection applied to the origin of man and human races. However, further experiments, collection of data, revisions of earlier editions of the *Origins*, and especially ill health, caused continual delays. The fact that close colleagues fell short of properly explaining human origins was somewhat irrelevant: Darwin probably always knew he would have to explain the subtle application of sexual selection himself. Of course, *The Origin* did "say a few words" about sexual selection: it "depends, not on a struggle for existence, but on a struggle between the males for possession of the females; the result is not death to the unsuccessful competitor, but few or no offspring" and "that some little light can apparently be thrown on the origin of these [human racial] differences chiefly through sexual selection of a particular kind."[8]

A further, if relatively minor, goad for Darwin to press ahead with his explanation of racial differences was provided by the odious James Hunt. In August 1866, the *Times* reported on a paper delivered by Hunt to the British Association meeting in Nottingham that later appeared in Hunt's *Anthropological Review*. "At present," wrote the defender of Agassiz and more recently of Governor Eyre, " . . . we are quite unable to show the causes which produce the formation of the different races of which the different species of man is composed." Fighting a rearguard action against the surge in favor of the unity of man engendered by Darwinian thinking, Hunt expressed a "wish that, in consideration of the conflicting views held on this subject, Mr. Darwin himself may be induced to come forward, and tell us if the application of this theory leads to unity of origin as contended for by Professor Huxley."[9]

In early 1867, Darwin apologized to his publisher for the delays and the enormous size of the manuscript for what became *The Variation of Animals and Plants under Domestication*, adding that he was writing a concluding chapter on man but was unsure whether to include it. In the end, he decided against, so man did not appear in the two-volume work published in January 1868. However, Darwin mentioned in a footnote on the second page that Georges Pouchet in *The Plurality of the Human Race* (published by Hunt's Anthropological Society in 1864) had "insisted that variation under domestication throws no light on the natural modification of species" and had thus declared impossible what Darwin himself had not yet discussed with regard to man. "I cannot perceive the force of his arguments," Darwin commented, "or, to speak more accurately, of his assertions to this effect."[10]

While correcting the proof sheets of *Variation of Animals and Plants*, Darwin actively pursued another line of inquiry—first conceived nearly thirty years earlier—to argue in favor of the unity of human races. This new effort to support natural selection partly involved obtaining evidence from the same place where Agassiz had just spent over a year seeking evidence *against* natural selection,

Brazil. As usual, Asa Gray kept Darwin informed of some of Agassiz's wilder claims, and Darwin agreed with Lyell "in thinking Agassiz glacier-mad."[11] But Darwin had a different issue in mind as he asked his own Brazilian contact, the brilliant naturalist Fritz Müller, to "make a *few* observations for me, in the course of some months, on Negroes, or possibly on native South Americans, though I care most about Negroes." He enclosed some specific questions, adding, "I am thinking of writing a little essay on the Origin of Mankind, as I have been taunted with concealing my opinions."[12] Darwin's hypothesis was that most expressions of emotion in humans were similar to those found in the higher primates and also common among all human races. Although Darwin did not publish *The Expression of the Emotions in Man and Animals* until 1872, he long believed that this line of research might provide better evidence for the common origin of man than much-disputed fossil skulls or philological ancestry.[13] In 1867, Darwin sent lists of questions about expressions to far-flung contacts in India, China, Borneo, Australia, Africa, South America, and, of course, the United States.

While Agassiz's colleague Benjamin Apthorp Gould was still collating the statistics on the physical measurements of white and black soldiers in America, Darwin was careful to exclude from his study "information in regard to the [former] negro slaves in America" that "would have been comparatively easy to have obtained" but "would have possessed little value" because "they have long associated with white men."[14]

Darwin was laboring over his "little essay on the Origin of Mankind" in 1868 when Agassiz published a book—written mostly by his wife, Elizabeth Cary Agassiz—about their travels in Brazil. Gray referred Darwin to a review that "laughs at [Agassiz] for his iterative refutations of *Darwinism*," but Darwin was not laughing when he told Hooker that anyone could observe "in Prof. & Mrs. Agassiz's Book on Brazil how excessively anxious he is to destroy me."[15]

However little Darwin found to admire in Agassiz's book, it was more than he would have found had he read another book published that year by an admirer of Agassiz. Dr. John Van Evrie's publishing house reissued for the third time his polygenist diatribe—now retitled *White Supremacy and Negro Subordination*. Van Evrie was tapping into a reaction by white Americans against the Radical Republicans' latest step: the Fourteenth Amendment, granting blacks civil rights in all states. This angered even Northerners in ways abolition had not, and the Democrats now assailed Republicans for failing to recognize the blacks' inherent inferiority. Without the "protection" of slavery, Van Evrie wrote, the freedmen's moral and physical deficiencies made it "absolutely certain that, as a class, they will become extinct . . . [in a century] no such social monstrosity as a 'free negro' will be found in America."[16] "Amalgamation," or more recently "miscegenation," remained as central to debates about racial policies as "hybridism" was to controversies over species change, and Darwin had just devoted a long section to it in *Variation of Animals and Plants*.[17] But in the following year, evidence was published supposedly proving that human "hybrids" were in fact so physically weakened (even if not made sterile) by their cross-breeding that perhaps they might become extinct at some future date. And the publisher was not the hate-mongering Van Evrie but the U.S. Sanitary Commission.

In 1869, the commission finally published Gould's 613-page *Investigations in the Military and Anthropological Statistics of American Soldiers*. Appointed in June 1864 to complete the task initiated by Frederick Law Olmsted, Gould had been deeply influenced by his Harvard colleague Louis Agassiz, whose well-known views on the "natural divisions of mankind" had already been pressed on the American Freedmen's Inquiry Commission.[18] Gould believed this was a unique opportunity to determine statistically "the [average or standard] type of human-ity as well as the types of the several classes and races of man"—which made him eager to add as many blacks to the study as possible before they dispersed at the end of the war.[19] Haste added to the difficulty of conducting a study under wartime conditions while using new equipment and new techniques of measure-ment for which the inspectors had received only written instructions. Agassiz's ethnological interests probably influenced Gould's instruction to his inspectors to "state the race, unless Caucasian, (as African, Malay, etc.); or if of mixed races, and what [races]"—as if they would find any "Malays" in the Union army! The inspectors were also to estimate the soldiers' "proportion of black blood, such as Full Black, Mulatto, Quadroon, Octoroon," and somehow assess their levels of in-telligence as compared with "the ordinary white private soldier." Gould regretted that eventually it proved impractical to distinguish between the "three or more distinct races of negroes . . . found in the Southern States"—distinctions about which most Northern whites knew nothing. Perhaps it was that arch taxonomist Agassiz who had asked Gould to collect data on blacks so detailed as to distin-guish them not only by the eighth part of their blood but also by their origins in different regions of Africa. Nevertheless, Gould still assisted the debate about hybridization by tabulating the data in three categories, "whites," "full blacks," and "mixed race" (otherwise ignoring proportions).[20]

Gould had limited access to army records giving rank, nationality, and place and date of birth for over a million soldiers, and he had complete access to Ol-msted's eight thousand records offering physical measurements that were more complex. He now added to the questionnaire six new measurements more likely than hair type and skin color to indicate structural differences between the races and managed to apply the full range of measurements to another 10,876 white soldiers, 1,146 white sailors, 2,020 "full blacks," and 863 "mixed race" (as well as 517 Indians, 291 "students," 3 dwarves, and 2 "Australian children").[21]

Gould clearly hoped to substantiate the polygenists' view that blacks are inferior to whites and that mixed race "hybrids" were *not* intermediate but in-ferior to both. "The curious and important fact that the mulattoes, or men of mixed race, occupy so frequently in the scale of progression a place outside, rather than intermediate between, those races from the combination of which they have sprung, cannot fail to attract attention. The well-known phenomenon of their inferior vitality may stand, possibly, in some connection with the fact thus brought to light." In practice, whenever the statistics did not support this "well-known phenomenon," Gould either stated them without analysis, fudged them, or simply dumped them as flawed by some bias in the examiners.[22]

Although differences in black and white lung capacities were minute, Gould said they could not "fail to attract attention at first glance" but offered no explanation, minimized any "effect of climate and soil upon the blacks," and did not even consider that a background in slavery might play some role. Only one of the six new measurements showed significant differences between the races, the measure of the distance between fingertip and kneecap, employed "to expose, if possible, any ethnological difference or peculiarities in the relative proportions of arms, legs, and body, which might, in their combined influence, be more conspicuous than when severally considered; and the results seem to show its aptitude for this purpose." Gould stressed that this measurement "is, as would be anticipated by ethnologists, one which manifests the most striking contrast with the white race" and interpreted it as showing that the black was closer to "the anthropoid" in development. Because the "mixed races" measurement *was* intermediate and therefore did *not* support the notion of mulatto inferiority, Gould simply obfuscated: "for the mixed races the results . . . are variant and contradictory."[23]

Gould's high standing in the scientific community and the delayed publication of an even larger (and more unwieldy) report by the Provost Marshal-General's Bureau meant that Gould's findings became entrenched, influencing more than a generation of anthropologists, especially in the United States.[24] Gould's results would have become reference points whether or not Darwin gave them a wider publicity in his *Descent of Man*, which would be read by far more people than would ever see Gould's work.[25] Naturally, Darwin could not ignore this important study, but in fact he was extremely cautious about employing Gould's results.

Darwin's "Man book" was finally published in February 1871 as a two-volume work entitled *The Descent of Man and Selection in Relation to Sex*. The second part, on sexual selection, actually dealt mostly with animals and was larger than the first part that applied natural selection to man. Darwin chose to publish even though his important research on the expression of emotions was incomplete and therefore relegated to a later volume. *The Descent of Man* required a full discussion of sexual selection because, as he had told Wallace in 1864, it was "the most powerful means of changing the races of man."[26] Darwin now boldly stated, "We have thus far been baffled in all our attempts to account for the differences between the races of man; but there remains one important agency, namely Sexual Selection, which appears to have acted as powerfully on man, as on many other animals."[27]

Darwin narrowed the assumed gulf between men and animals, showing that "there is no fundamental difference between man and the higher mammals in their mental facilities."[28] After discussing more primitive links between men and animals—rudimentary forms and homologous structures—Darwin sought animal origins for abilities generally considered practically unique to man: memory, imagination, tools, language, sense of beauty, and even spirituality. The final chapter in the first part of *Descent* was "On the Races of Man."

Throughout the entire first edition, Darwin mentioned Gould's *Investigations* seven times (and only twice in the chapter on races). On three occasions, Darwin used Gould's data comparing leg length and arm length of soldiers and sailors to support his own view that the human species is "subject to much variability"—which had nothing to do with race but "proved that local influences of some kind act directly on stature." Darwin noted that Gould "endeavoured" to explain these variations in stature but reached only "negative results, namely, that they did not relate to climate, the elevation of the land, soil, nor even 'in any controlling degree' to the abundance or need of the comforts of life." Darwin thereupon cited four scholars whose studies *did* show that stature was controlled by the abundance or lack of those "comforts." Darwin's next four references did relate to race. Early in his chapter on race, Darwin asserted, "Even the most distinct races of man are much more like each other in form than would at first be supposed," but then conceded, "There is, however, no doubt that the various races, when carefully compared and measured, differ much from each other,—as in the texture of the hair, the relative proportions of all parts of the body, the capacity of the lungs, the form and capacity of the skull, and even in the convolutions of the brain."[29] Regarding "proportions" and "lungs," Darwin cited Gould's "vast number of measurements of Whites, Blacks, and Indians and particularly his chapter 'On the capacity of the lungs.'"

Darwin then raised the important topics of hybrids and the traditional definition of species while addressing Gould's polygenism. "The inferior vitality of mulattoes is spoken of in a trustworthy work [Gould] as a well-known phenomenon; but this is a different consideration from their lessened fertility; and can hardly be advanced as a proof of the specific distinctness of the parent races." Just before this reference, Darwin had already demolished the view that mulattoes were infertile, and right after it Darwin attacked the issue from the other end, pointing out that mules were true hybrids and sterile, yet were "notorious for long life and vigour."[30] Taken out of context, Darwin seemed to accept the "trustworthy" report that people of mixed race were "well-known" to have "inferiority vitality"; read in context, he did no such thing.

The final two references to Gould are in the second part of Darwin's work, on sexual selection, both relating to the variable of hairiness. After citing two

European sources supporting the view that "with negroes the beard is scanty or absent, and they have no whiskers; in both sexes the body is almost destitute of fine down," Darwin cited with surprise Gould's finding that "the pure negroes and their crossed offspring seem to have bodies almost as hairy as Europeans." Darwin used this as a possible example of a principle of reversion, "the truth of which," he asserted in a footnote, "I have elsewhere proved, [that] crossed races would be eminently liable to revert to the primordial hairy character of their early ape-like progenitors." Of course, "eminently liable" is far from a certainty, which is why Darwin expressed frustration that Gould's data did not distinguish between "pure blacks and mulattoes" in this particular measure of "pilosity."[31]

Since Gould was dealing with live soldiers and not dead men's skulls, he did not employ cranial measurements. Darwin raised the issue in chapter 2, accepting there was evidence for "the belief that there exists in man some close relation between the size of the brain and the development of the intellectual faculties." But Darwin deliberately circumscribed that "belief" by asserting in the preceding paragraph that "no one supposes that the intellect of any two animals or of any two men can be accurately gauged by the cubic contents of their skulls."[32] Rather than refer to Dr. Samuel G. Morton's famous collection, Darwin instead cited a very recent study by J. Barnard Davis, who dismissed Morton's work as unreliable, yet still arrived at figures showing that "Europeans" had the largest brains.[33] Davis drew no harsh conclusions about other races' inherent lack of intelligence, but Darwin must have read Davis's brief note in the *Anthropological Review*, pointing out that "Hindostanees" were said to have achieved a high civilization and rational religion *despite* being "a people who are distinguished among human races for the remarkable smallness of their brains."[34] Although Darwin quoted Davis's "careful measurements" of "mean internal capacity" in cubic inches for the skulls of Europeans (92.3), [Native] Americans (87.5), Asiatics (87.1), and [aboriginal] Australians (81.9), it is noteworthy that Davis had in fact also listed "African races" (86), but Darwin himself *chose not to mention that*.[35]

Darwin made use of Gould's and Davis's information without endorsing any racialist bias contained in it, and he was unconvinced by all those extra measurements of blacks added to Gould's study and expected (by consultants such as Agassiz) to prove the primordial and permanent distinctiveness of blacks and the "inferior vitality" supposedly inherited by mulattoes. Naturally, *The Descent of Man* challenged the views of Agassiz himself, though here Darwin's approach took an unexpected turn.

On the first page of *Descent*, Darwin managed to place Agassiz on an endangered-species list without even naming him. Instead, he quoted a recent statement—in French—by Karl Vogt that no one, at least in Europe, maintained any longer that special creation explained species development. Darwin added, "Of the older and honoured chiefs in natural science, many unfortunately are still opposed to evolution in every form."[36] Thus, Darwin used one European to undermine a former European and now famous "American." Quoting "the Darwin of Germany," who had long been a bitter enemy of Agassiz's, was bound to annoy.[37]

Despite such an opening, all of Darwin's further references to Agassiz were positively gentle. He began by citing the work in which Agassiz most recently, if not very prominently, published his arguments against natural selection by inserting them into an 1869 French translation of his earlier *Essay on Classification*.[38] However, Darwin did not then discuss Agassiz's arguments but wrote, "I agree with Agassiz that dogs possess something very like a conscience," while also quoting a passage regarding "les amours des limaçons" and "le double embrassement de ces hermaphrodites"—which may have added some allure to snail reproduction but was hardly controversial. Similarly, there were three pleasant references to Professor and Mrs. Agassiz's *Journey in Brazil* (1868), in one of which Darwin suggested that even Agassiz did not always place Caucasians and Negroes on the extreme ends of the racial hierarchy.[39]

Darwin's chapter on race mentioned Agassiz three times. First, in what seemed to be a concession, Darwin suggested that a hypothetical "naturalist . . . would be deeply impressed with the fact, first noticed by Agassiz, that the different races of man are distributed over the world in the same zoological provinces, as those inhabited by undoubtedly distinct species and genera of mammals." Darwin then gave numerous examples that undermined the very notion of zoological provinces. Next, he countered the polygenist view on hybridity by citing the naturalist John Bachman of South Carolina who "positively asserts that he has known mulatto families which have intermarried for several generations, and have continued on an average as fertile as either pure whites or pure blacks." And, of course, Darwin listed Agassiz among thirteen other naturalists who had individual notions of how many "species or races" mankind could be divided into: for Agassiz it was eight. Darwin also included two innocuous references to sexual selection among fish, Agassiz's specialty, sprinkled with phrases such as: "Professor Agassiz adds," "as I hear from Professor Agassiz," and "as I am informed by the kindness of Professor Agassiz."[40]

Clearly, something had changed in Darwin's view of Agassiz. The latter was mellowing after his return from Brazil where his discoveries, despite the trumpeting, failed to refute natural selection and simply added to his museum more barrels of specimens he would never properly study. The arguments Agassiz expressed in public lectures, popular journals, and a French translation of an older work, seemed increasingly old hat. In October 1866, Agassiz had ended the feud with Asa Gray by formally apologizing for using ungentlemanly language two years earlier.[41] While this did not stop Gray from sending uncomplimentary reports about Agassiz, it did mean that Darwin felt he could again submit technical questions to Agassiz through Gray (as he had done earlier through others).

Darwin must have been surprised in August 1868 when a letter arrived directly from Agassiz, who wrote that although "it is true that I am and have been from the beginning an uncompromising opponent of your views," this was no reason for Darwin to send scientific enquiries to him via Gray. He also acknowledged that he found Darwin's views "mischievous because they lead to a looseness of argumentation which it has been the aim of science to avoid," but he added, "There is nothing in these feelings against yourself, as you have done original researches" of great value. He hoped never to be guilty of "allowing my feeling to be the master of my judgement" and claimed never to have "expressed an unkind word concerning yourself." Whereupon, he provided Darwin with information about fish that Darwin happily included in *The Descent of Man*. In reply, Darwin explained that he had not approached him directly because he thought Agassiz "had formed so low an opinion" of his work. That Agassiz had now sent him valuable information directly was a pleasing sign of regard. "I have never for a moment doubted your kindness and generosity, and I hope you will not think it presumptuous in me to say that when we met many years ago I felt for you the warmest admiration."[42]

Darwin did not write to Asa Gray about this curious exchange because Gray and his wife were just then sailing to Europe for a yearlong tour. No doubt, the two men discussed Agassiz among a million other things when the Grays visited Down for a week in October 1868. Sometime before November 1869, when the Grays sailed for America, they or Darwin received the news that in mid-September Louis Agassiz had suffered a stroke that left him paralyzed and unable to speak.[43] Before departing, Gray mentioned in a brief note to Darwin, "I will hand the slip with question to Agassiz."[44] This "slip," probably combining some professional question with sympathetic sentiment, is not extant, but Darwin apparently asked Gray to use discretion about delivering the slip, depending on Agassiz's condition.

Gray also mentioned to Darwin that Agassiz's son, Alexander, had recently arrived in Europe with his family and was soon to be in London. Before December, Alexander visited Down House, handing Darwin a note of introduction written by his father the previous June: "You will find Alex more ready to accept your views than I shall ever be."[45] Darwin was no doubt moved: before him stood an admirable young naturalist, at odds with his father over Darwin's views, delivering the note from a man who, since writing it, had suffered a paralyzing stroke.

Darwin thought highly of Alexander and his wife and invited them to Down House more than once. Alexander probably passed along news of his father's slow recovery, and Darwin, at Gray's suggestion, subsequently sent questions to Alexander that might otherwise have gone to his father. Gray shared Darwin's high regard: "I knew you would be pleased with young Agassiz and his Yankee wife."[46]

In March 1870, Gray sent Darwin a message from Louis Agassiz's wife, whose ailing husband had dictated an answer to Darwin's query. Gray commented,

"Agassiz evidently regrets having abused you in former times." Darwin responded, "Whenever you have any communication with Agassiz, pray give him my cordial thanks for his kind message & for his information. . . . I wish with all my heart that I could feel that I deserved what Alex. A. says of me."[47] The nature of that praise is unknown, but Darwin's emotional response suggests it was some judgment by Alexander, perhaps comparing his father's harsh attacks on Darwin over the years with Darwin's apparent avoidance of any bitter feelings. If such was Alexander's praise, Darwin knew it fell short of the truth.

In any case, Darwin did not attack Louis Agassiz in *The Descent of Man* since harshness had never been his style, let alone sniping at a man so gravely ill. Moreover, Darwin probably felt that, whatever reception the critics gave to his "man-essay," he had already won the war: even the enemy's son had come over to his side. Repeating the theme played already by Gray, Wallace, and Huxley, Darwin wrote confidently "that when the principles of evolution are generally accepted, as they surely will be before long, the dispute between the monogenists and the polygenists will die a silent and unobserved death."[48]

While Darwin's daughter Henrietta was editing *Descent*, her mother wrote to her that the book "will be very interesting, but that I shall dislike it very much as again putting God further off."[49] Darwin could not be surprised by his wife's reaction but may not have anticipated the mildness of the theological attacks on his latest work. Yet, in the last decade of his life, the issue of religion remained a major topic for Darwin—and for people interested in Darwin. It was simultaneously the cause of angry discussions about Lincoln, who was no longer present to control the debate.

An End to Religion

I n February 1870, William H. Herndon wrote a long letter to *The Index*—not
Henry Hotze's Confederate-funded journal, which had frequently mentioned
Lincoln and sometimes Darwin as well—but to a journal of the same name
newly launched in Ohio as the organ of the recently formed Free Religious Association. Like other association founders, *The Index's* editor, Francis Ellingwood
Abbot, was a Bostonian and a former Unitarian who had found even that liberal
creed too restrictive, especially in its views on the latest scientific advances, such
as natural selection. His search for a sufficiently open-minded Unitarian congregation led him to Ohio, where he founded *The Index*. When his dwindling
congregation stopped paying his salary in 1872, Abbot moved the journal back
to Boston.

Herndon's letter to Abbot concerned Lincoln's religious beliefs and subsequently appeared in *The Index*, in a pamphlet, and in an early biography of
Lincoln.[1] His explanation for writing pointed back to an occurrence shortly
after Lincoln's assassination. Josiah Holland, a Massachusetts newspaper editor
and sometime novelist and lecturer, had delivered a well-received eulogy in his
community emphasizing Lincoln's "simple, honest, Christian heart." Urged to
write a full biography, Holland had swiftly traveled to Illinois, where he found
Lincoln's old law partner extremely helpful. "I freely told him what he asked, and
much more," Herndon told Abbot. "He then asked me what I thought about Mr.
Lincoln's religion, meaning his views of Christianity. I replied, 'The less said, the
better.'" A version of that very phrase appeared as an anonymous quotation in
Holland's book a few months later, but Herndon was disgusted that his opinion
was buried under a load of hagiography. The book's conclusion reprised the
main theme: that "the almost immeasurably great results which [Lincoln] had
the privilege of achieving, were due to the fact that he was a Christian President."
Holland's final prayer-like sentence ended, "[W]e receive thy life and its immeasurably great results, as the choicest gifts that a mortal has ever bestowed upon
us; grateful . . . to God . . . [who] bestowed thee upon the nation and mankind."[2]

To Herndon, this was all "bosh," especially as Holland based much of his account of Lincoln's piety on a single anecdote told by Newton Bateman, Illinois superintendent of public education. Bateman's office was in the State House, and for a few months in 1860, Lincoln used an adjoining office as election headquarters. Bateman wrote for Holland an eight-page account of a conversation that Bateman said "made a vivid impression upon me." Shortly before the election, Lincoln entered Bateman's office, as he did occasionally to escape callers, but this time he locked the door. Referring to results of a recent canvass of Springfield citizens' electoral intentions, Lincoln was exasperated that twenty of the town's twenty-three ministers or church elders intended to vote against him. "Mr. Bateman, I am not a Christian—God knows I would be one—but I have carefully read the Bible, and I do not so understand this book." Lincoln took out a pocket New Testament. "These men well know that I am for freedom . . . and that my opponents are for slavery . . . and yet, with this book in their hands, in the light of which human bondage cannot live a moment, they are going to vote against me. I do not understand it at all." Much verbiage followed—"features surcharged with emotion," "trembling voice," "cheeks wet with tears"—all as untypical as Lincoln's outburst:

> I know there is a God, and that He hates injustice and slavery. . . . I know I am right because I know that liberty is right, for Christ teaches it, and Christ is God. I have told them that a house divided against itself cannot stand, and Christ and reason say the same; and they will find it so. Douglas don't care whether slavery is voted up or voted down, but God cares, and humanity cares, and I care; and with God's help I shall not fail. I may not see the end; but it will come, and I shall be vindicated; and these men will find that they have not read their Bibles aright.[3]

Denying one's Christianity while affirming Christ's divinity is one of many contradictions making Bateman's account dubious, although Allen C. Guelzo has suggested that the conversation may well have "revolved around Lincoln's perceived incongruity between Christian teaching and the reluctance of ministers to criticize slavery."[4] One might add that Lincoln chose his man well: though thirteen years Lincoln's junior, Bateman was an old acquaintance and respected in the community as a strong Christian who had risen from schoolteacher to officeholder. Bateman was clearly surprised by Lincoln's expressions of religious devotion, and he could do more to spread the word to fellow churchmen (hopefully before polling day) than could any of Lincoln's closer associates, who would appear more partisan—and were also less likely to swallow what Lincoln fed Bateman. According to Holland's version of his account, Bateman said to Lincoln, "Certainly your friends are ignorant of the sentiments you have expressed to me." "I know they are," Lincoln replied. "I am obliged to appear different to them; but I think more on these subjects than on all others, and I have done so for years; and I am willing that *you* should know."[5]

This passage, with its echoes of a secretive messiahship, outraged Herndon because it made Lincoln appear duplicitous and somewhat cowardly. After reading Holland's book, Herndon confronted Bateman in his office: "In order to make Lincoln a technical Christian—*you have made him a hypocrite!*" But Bateman, while admitting he had written his account only after Lincoln's death, presumably at Holland's request, backed down only partially.[6]

Whatever the value of Bateman's anecdote, Herndon was alarmed that Holland was making a plaster saint out of Lincoln: the higher Lincoln was raised toward heaven, the farther he would fall whenever the real facts emerged. Herndon decided to forestall Lincoln's "bitter enemies" by writing a biography himself.[7] He began collecting materials and trying them out in some lectures. His investigations led to the surprising conclusion that his former law partner, the cautious politician and rationalist, had not just been aloof from orthodox Christianity in his younger days but openly critical. The story of young Lincoln's "infidel book"—which Sam Hill threw into a stove—came as a shock because Herndon had always perceived Lincoln as far less radical than himself.

Herndon's draft for a December 1865 lecture observed that Lincoln did not believe in miracles, supernatural revelations, or the divinity of Jesus, but he crossed out these passages, saving them for a proper biography. Herndon did tell his audience that Lincoln had been a deeply religious man but added delphically, "If this people—this audience—can make of Mr. Lincoln a technical Christian man as the world—the Christian world—understands it, then this can be done by what is the so-called Christian people."[8]

Herndon neglected his law practice while pursuing his investigations without actually making a start on writing the biography. After 1867, he seemed to give up on the project as well as the law, tried his hand at farming, and failed miserably. In 1869, Herndon sold his notes to another would-be biographer, Ward Hill Lamon, an old acquaintance from the circuit-riding days who had served Lincoln during the White House years as marshal in Washington, D.C., and a sort of personal bodyguard. Herndon told him to "be bold. Tell the truth—that Lincoln was an infidel—a Deist. . . . He held in contempt the Idea of God's Special interferences &c &c." A few months later, Herndon sent the long letter that Abbot printed in *The Index* in April 1870 and then issued as a pamphlet for $3.50 per hundred. And when Lamon, or rather his ghostwriter, Chauncey Black, finally produced a biography, five of the eighteen pages devoted to Lincoln's lack of orthodoxy were filled by "the Abbot letter."[9] The letter ranged widely, but the centerpiece was Herndon's assertion that Lincoln "believed that all things, both matter and mind, were governed by laws, universal, absolute, and eternal." The list of specific doctrines Lincoln did not believe in included the Bible as revelation, miracles, and the divinity of Jesus, but top of the list was "special creation, [Lincoln's] idea being that all creation was an evolution under law."[10]

The Free Religious Association, which Abbot helped to found in 1867, included many figures who had admired Lincoln and were in turn admired by Herndon, such as Robert Dale Owen, Ralph Waldo Emerson, Thomas Wentworth Higginson, Charles Eliot Norton, and Lucretia Mott. Many of these also knew and admired Darwin. Higginson, who had commanded black troops during the Civil War, later corresponded with Darwin and even visited him at Down House, as did Norton. The Free Religious Association generally took an evolutionary view of religion, finding unity amid adaptive theological variation, and Abbot wrote articles for Norton's *North American Review* in praise of Darwin.[11]

Abbot enclosed copies of some of his articles and lectures when he first wrote to Darwin in May 1871 to assure him that, contrary to impressions he might receive otherwise, natural selection was widely accepted by educated Americans. Darwin wrote back immediately, pleased by this news and expressing admiration for Abbot's writings. A few days later he wrote again, praising a particular article by Abbot in *The Index* and enclosing money for a subscription.[12] Abbot was thrilled and sent Darwin a bound edition of the first volume of *The Index*, which included Herndon's letter on Lincoln's religion. Abbot also requested "a little note . . . setting forth your own view of the influence of your theory on religion" that he might quote during an upcoming lecture.[13] After hesitating, Darwin allowed the use of his earlier line of praise for Abbot's work "Truths for the Times": "I admire them from my inmost heart; and I agree to almost every word."[14] When Abbot pleaded that Darwin become a regular contributor, Darwin respectfully declined, citing ill health and asserting disingenuously that he had "never systematically thought much on religion in relation to science, or on morals in relation to society."[15]

In November 1872, Darwin published his most readable and popular book *On the Expression of the Emotions in Man and Animals*, which completed his exposition of natural selection and demonstrated again his commitment to the unity of man. "The theory of expression confirms to a certain limited extent the conclusion that man is derived from some lower animal form, and supports the belief of the specific or subspecific unity of the several races," he wrote on the book's last page, "but as far as my judgment serves, such confirmation was hardly needed." Darwin could even argue magisterially that "blushing" could not have been "*specially* designed by the Creator" because that concept "is opposed to the general theory of evolution, which is now so largely accepted."[16]

Asa Gray's debates with Darwin about design had stalemated when Darwin came up with the analogy of a house built designedly out of stones shaped by pure chance. "I found your stone-house argument unanswerable in substance," admitted Gray, also agreeing with Darwin that one can believe but not know.

Gray also sent Darwin a copy of Gray's review demolishing a book that had equated Darwinism with atheism, saying in the accompanying letter, "You see *what uphill work* I [have] in making a theist of you." Darwin praised the review and then dodged, "The more I reflect on the subject, the more perplexed I grow."[17]

Of those who wrote to Darwin about his religious opinions, Gray and Abbot were among the few who received much response, however indistinct. In 1873, Darwin advised his son George not to publish an essay he had written on religion: "The evils are giving pain to others, & injuring your own power & usefulness."[18] To a young botanist, Darwin commented, "Many years ago when I was collect-ing facts for *The Origin*, my belief in what is called a personal God was as firm as that of Dr Pusey himself, & as to the eternity of matter I have never troubled myself about such insoluble questions."[19] Although he accepted that one reason to believe in God's existence was "the impossibility of conceiving that this grand and wondrous universe . . . arose through chance," he repeatedly stressed that "the mind still craves to know" how even a "first cause" arose and why there is such an "immense amount of suffering through the world." "The safest conclusion," Darwin suggested to another petitioner, "seems to be that the whole subject is beyond the scope of man's intellect, but man can do his duty."[20] When a German student wrote more than once, Darwin testily declared that science had nothing to do with Christ, and "for myself, I do not believe that there has ever been any revelation. As for a future life, every man must judge for himself between con-flicting vague probabilities."[21] To a letter from a law student expressing a desire to read Darwin's books but worried lest they cause him to lose "my faith in the New Testament," Darwin answered, "I am sorry to have to inform you that I do not believe in the Bible as a divine revelation, & therefore not in Jesus Christ as the son of God." As usual, though rarely so ironically, Darwin signed himself, "Yours faithfully."[22]

Darwin dealt extensively with his own religious views in the autobiographi-cal sketch written in 1876 with a few additions made over the next five years. Although writing ostensibly to explain himself posthumously to his own family, he may have assumed eventual publication. In any case, there was a diffidence, even tension, in the presentation. Many of his points have been quoted earlier or echo statements given in the above letters. While expanding on one of the arguments for the existence of God that had "much more weight" than others, Darwin ended one paragraph, "When thus reflecting I feel compelled to look to a First Cause having an intelligent mind in some degree analogous to that of man; and I deserve to be called a Theist." But the next paragraph ended, "The mystery of the beginning of all things is insoluble by us; and I for one must be content to remain an Agnostic." Eventually seeing the awkwardness of claiming to be theistic in one paragraph and agnostic in the next, Darwin later wedged in a clarifying sentence: "This conclusion was strong in my mind about the time, as far as I can remember, when I wrote the *Origin of Species*; and it is since that time that it has very gradually with many fluctuations become weaker."[23] Darwin was reluctant to record that he had entirely lost the status of a "theist," leaving his wife the grain of hope that he had retained a fragment of faith. Darwin told another inquirer in 1879 that "in my most extreme fluctuations I have never been an atheist in the sense of denying the existence of a God."[24] He was conscious, as he wrote in another letter in 1880, of "the pain which it would give some members of my family, if I aided in any way direct attacks on religion."[25]

Avoiding such direct attacks had also become an article of faith for Lincoln the politician, but after his death, his religious views became a political football for Republicans seeking to exalt the martyr and Democrats trying to block this. After Herndon's letter was published, Republican journals led the backlash, and the cause was taken up by the Reverend James A. Reed, who was now pastor at the Springfield church where Lincoln had formerly rented a pew. Reed had not known Lincoln, but he now energetically gathered up testimony from men who had, such as John T. Stuart and James H. Matheny, two of Herndon's best informants, who gave rather different stories to Reed. This material was eventually published in *Scribner's Monthly*, edited by Josiah Holland, the hagiographer who had stirred up Herndon in the first place.[26] Herndon unleashed an aggressive lecture on "Lincoln's Religion," laying into all who disagreed with him, especially those suggesting Lincoln had at some point during his presidency become a true Christian. "He died an unbeliever," Herndon thundered while Republican newspapers condemned, and Democrats made the most of it.[27]

Financial troubles overwhelmed Herndon for a few years, but in 1883, he submitted further articles on Lincoln's lack of religion to the Free Thought tabloid, the *Truth Seeker*.[28] He then read in Isaac N. Arnold's 1884 biography of Lincoln, which otherwise made great use of Herndon's material, that Lincoln was the most "reverent Christian [that] ever sat in the executive chair, not excepting Washington." While not claiming Lincoln was orthodox, Arnold declared, "Belief in the existence of God; in the immortality of the soul; in the Bible as the revelation of God to man; in the efficacy and duty of prayer; in reverence toward the Almighty and in love and charity to man, was the basis of his religion."[29]

Herndon finally produced, with the help of Jesse Weik, his own biography of Lincoln, which appeared in 1889. Weik took the rough edges off some of Herndon's assertions, but the biography retracted nothing significant and provided strong evidence from some of Herndon's best informants. Regarding Lincoln's religious views after he went to Washington and out of Herndon's presence, Herndon offered a letter from Lincoln's secretary John Nicolay, declaring there were no indications that Lincoln's beliefs changed—though Nicolay added, "I do not know just what they were, never having heard him explain them in detail."[30] Herndon relished that letter, having guessed correctly that Lincoln's son Robert had prevented Nicolay and Lincoln's other secretary, John Hay, from discussing

Lincoln's religion in their ten-volume life of Lincoln, which had been serialized in the *Century Magazine* starting in 1886: "they are afraid of Bob; he gives them material and they in turn play *hush*."[31]

Two years after publishing his biography, Herndon died, but the controversy over Lincoln's religion had a life of its own. The subject Lincoln learned to control so carefully causes continual debate and has even turned on itself. The skeptic has become the object of near-idolatrous veneration, as any visitor to various Lincoln pilgrimage sites will notice. In the centenary of his birth, Lincoln's profile replaced that of an American Indian—an earlier symbol for America—on the one-cent coin: the first president to be so honored, with no other U.S. coin series continuing so long. The stirring *Battle Hymn of the Republic*—with verses composed by Julia Ward Howe (Samuel Gridley Howe's wife) to invoke the Messiah's blessing on the North's crusade against slavery—has become the theme tune for every film portrait of Lincoln, who would have been amazed and amused.

By the time Darwin died in 1882, his status as a national institution was so formidable that his plan for a burial in Downe's churchyard was gently swept aside as influential associates arranged for Darwin's remains to be laid in Westminster Abbey beside those of England's greatest leaders and intellects.[32] Yet, before the year ended, a reformist newspaper published two letters Darwin had written about his religious views, causing a Catholic journal to declare him a heretic. This was mentioned the following year in an eight-page pamphlet on Darwin's religion by Edward B. Aveling, a physician, freethinker, socialist, and Karl Marx's son-in-law. Aveling had a brief correspondence with Darwin, and his pamphlet recounts his single visit to Down House, emphasizing a discussion of the terms "atheism" and "agnosticism." Darwin said (in words sounding more Marxian than Darwinian): "It is all very well for educated, cultured, thoughtful people; but are the masses yet ripe for it?"[33]

Just as Robert Todd Lincoln tried to protect his father's reputation by blue-penciling Nicolay and Hay's draft biography (even excising some references to Robert's paternal *grandfather's* religion), Darwin's heirs also took steps to disassociate his name from radical atheism.[34] When Darwin's son Francis produced the usual *Life and Letters* volume, including Darwin's autobiographical sketch, Emma requested that five passages about religion be omitted "to avoid," she said, "giving pain to your father's religious friends who are deeply attached to him, . . . and even the old servants."[35] And just as Herndon had felt compelled to deny that Lincoln had been religiously transformed while president, the Darwin family had to deal with ludicrous claims that Darwin underwent some "death-bed conversion."[36] Such stories have persisted because people who wish to believe them require no evidence. However, Darwin's personal beliefs have had less consequence than the issue that always divided Darwin and Gray: Paley's old argument from design. Unlike Paley, Agassiz, and modern creationists, Gray had never used design in order to demonstrate God's existence but simply suggested that there was more design in nature than "natural selection" could account for, reserving a possible role for God. But both Gray and Darwin, unlike modern creationists, understood that the Prime Mover's existence and the natural selection hypothesis could not prove or disprove each other.

The continuing contest between design and natural selection has a quaint air of futility about it, but far more tragic consequences have attended the continued controversy over the degree of difference among the races of man.

The Dream of Equality

In 1872, *On the Expression of the Emotions in Man and Animals* completed Darwin's work on man. Later works made important contributions to science and sold surprisingly well but related to subjects like "insectivorous plants," "climbing plants," and "the actions of worms." The abolition of slavery in the United States at first seemed to decrease the importance of the issue of mankind's unity, and the growing acceptance of natural selection made the old monogenist-polygenist debate seem obsolete. Also, Darwin felt no further need to counter the influence of Louis Agassiz.

Less than a year after his paralyzing stroke, Agassiz had made a fine recovery, and in early 1870, Asa Gray wrote that Agassiz seemed to have mellowed toward Darwin. But a year later, Agassiz's lectures (according to one student's notes) included references to "the English . . . propensity for fanciful theories."[1] Sometime before June 1871, Darwin must have heard from Alexander Agassiz that his father was not only well but feeling adventurous. "Pray give my most sincere respects to your father," wrote Darwin. "What a wonderful man he is to think of going round Cape Horn; if he does go, I wish he could go through the Strait of Magellan."[2]

During the *Hassler* expedition, named after the ship provided by his friend Benjamin Peirce of the Coastal Survey, Agassiz set out to dredge up seabed specimens along thousands of miles of North and South American coastline. Just before departing, he sent a letter to Darwin through Gray, for which Darwin thanked the latter, not mentioning its contents nor apparently attempting to get a reply to the voyager.[3] Yet Darwin was certainly on Agassiz's mind. "I had a special purpose in this journey," he wrote to a German colleague from aboard ship, " . . . to study the whole Darwinian theory free from all external influences and former prejudices. It was on a similar voyage that Darwin himself came to formulate his theories!" Agassiz mentioned changes in the subject of natural history that "I have pondered over," but (unlike his son) "I have not made any great progress in my conversion to the growing doctrine of evolution." Agassiz now hoped to find "sufficient material to allow thorough comparisons between related living types" that would enable him to test natural selection better than Darwin ever had.[4]

Returning from his journey in October 1872, Agassiz gave a lecture that convinced Gray that he was anything but reformed. "Hasty generalising of observation is Darwin all over," said Agassiz, before offering the bizarre conclusion "The weak may and do survive as well as the strong" based on his observation that large trees appear at the foot of a mountain while at the summit one finds "mere shrubs." Too appalled to write a calm correction, Gray instead wrote a satirical "squib" and sent it to Darwin, explaining that he dare not publish it in America even anonymously: Darwin could either burn it or arrange publication without Gray's name. The piece appeared a month later in *Nature* under the title "Survival of the Fittest."[5]

Agassiz, typically, produced no written report on the *Hassler* expedition, but Mrs. Agassiz produced three popular articles for the *Atlantic Monthly* about the trip. In "A Cruise through the Galapagos," she mentioned, "Here some of the best work of [Darwin's] youth was done; and now, at the close of his life, these very islands connect themselves, by an odd coincidence, with his theory of the origin of species." Clearly reflecting her husband's belief that Darwin's theory lacked substantial evidence, Mrs. Agassiz suggested that these volcanic islands offered too little geologic time for the evolution of "fauna specifically distinct from that of the mainland" and that although "transition types . . . should not elude . . . the watchful spirit of the age," none had yet been found.[6]

Agassiz began a serious effort to write up for the *Atlantic Monthly* the ideas featured in his current lectures. He rewrote it three times, having "too much at stake in this Article," he told the editor, "to be willing to allow it to appear without the severest criticism."[7] When it finally appeared in January 1874, the nine-page article, promised as the first of a series, proved that Agassiz had lost neither his dislike for transmutation nor his affection for special creation. Darwin's work was praised up to a point: "Indeed it might be said that he treated his subject according to the best scientific methods, had he not frequently overstepped the boundaries of actual knowledge and allowed his imagination to supply the links which science does not furnish."[8]

Although Mrs. Agassiz's earlier article had lugubriously referred to Darwin as "now, at the close of his life," in fact, one month before her husband's article appeared, Louis Agassiz died of a cerebral hemorrhage on 14 December 1873. In January, Darwin wrote to Joseph Dalton Hooker, "Many thanks for sending me Gray's interesting letter. What a terrible thing it is about Mrs. Agassiz, & how lost he will be."[9] The "Mrs. Agassiz" referred to was not Louis Agassiz's widow but his daughter-in-law, the wife of Alexander. She had died suddenly only a few days after her father-in-law, and both Gray and Darwin had found her delightful and could well imagine her young husband's grief.[10] Darwin left no record of any reaction to the death of Louis Agassiz himself.

Bostonian Thomas Wentworth Higginson (who mentioned both his friends Agassiz and Francis E. Abbot in other correspondence with Darwin) received in 1873 a letter from Darwin praising his book *Life with a Black Regiment*: "You must allow me to thank you heartily for the very great pleasure which it has in many ways given us. I always thought well of the negroes, from the little which I have seen of them; and I have been delighted to have my vague impressions confirmed, and their character and mental powers so ably discussed."[11] A decade earlier, Higginson had testified to the American Freedmen's Inquiry Commission about his experience commanding the first black regiment in the Union army, and his memoir gave Darwin additional anecdotal evidence not available when Darwin had been writing about blacks in *Descent of Man* and cautiously using of Benjamin Apthorp Gould's tainted statistical evidence.[12] Darwin was currently busy producing a second edition of *Descent*, making many corrections and additions. One of particular relevance is in a section headed "Natural Selection as affecting Civilised Nations."

In *Descent*, Darwin never used the terms "superior race" or "inferior race."[13] He usually characterized human groups as being in a "savage," "barbarian," or "civilised" condition (often qualified as "more civilised," "less civilised," or "semi-civilised"). One addition to the second edition emphasized that whether civilized or not, a group could experience competition within itself as well as with other groups: "Nevertheless the more intelligent members within the same community will succeed better in the long run than the inferior, and leave a more numerous progeny, and this is a form of natural selection." A group's level of "intelligence" was not an inherited condition but a social development: "The more efficient causes of progress seem to consist of a good education during youth whilst the brain is impressible, and of a high standard of excellence, inculcated by the ablest and best men, embodied in the laws, customs and traditions of the nation, and enforced by public opinion." This brought Darwin back to the type of "social instinct" that he felt arose early in man's development and was, therefore, common to all races: "The enforcement of public opinion depends on our appreciation of the approbation and disapprobation of others; and this appreciation is founded on our sympathy, which it can hardly be doubted was originally developed through natural selection as one of the most important elements of the social instincts."[14]

Natural selection has less effect on "highly civilised nations" because they "do not supplant and exterminate one another as do savage tribes"; nevertheless, a "civilised" condition, being an attainment rather than an inherited trait, can also be reversed: "we see, for instance, in parts of S. America, that a people which may be called civilised, such as the Spanish settlers, is liable to become indolent and to retrograde, when the conditions of life are very easy."[15]

In 1876, a two-volume report, *Statistics, Medical and Anthropological, of the Provost Marshal-General's Bureau*, was sent to Darwin by the author, Jedediah Hyde Baxter, an army surgeon during the Civil War. Baxter's remit when organizing examinations of black (as well as white) recruits had been merely to certify the men fit for service. He had a much larger statistical sample than Gould but was not doing an anthropological study for the likes of Louis Agassiz. Baxter felt that the term "Colored Men" ought not to "be admitted in scientific terminology on account of its obvious lack of precision," and his basic questionnaires made no attempt to distinguish "full black" and "mixed race," simply asking examiners to report on "the physical qualifications of the colored race for military service." While some army doctors submitted no reports because they had no black recruits or were too busy, many others offered a wide range of judgments reflecting their own biases. Unlike Gould, Baxter did not find racial differences in chest dimensions and, if anything, found proportionally fewer cases of pulmonary diseases among blacks than whites. Overall, according to one recent study, "Whereas Gould's statistics erased the humanity of the people being measured, the army surgeons cast black recruits as human beings who could participate as active agents in their struggle for freedom."[16]

Had Baxter's evidence of racial similarity been published before 1870, Darwin undoubtedly would have used it to counter Gould's half-baked evidence of racial difference. But Darwin was now sixty-seven years old, preferred dabbling with experiments in which he controlled the sampling procedures, and could have safely predicted that most "observers" would find what they wished to find in Gould's and Baxter's studies. "No longer would attitudes of racial inferiority have to employ those pre-war measurements and conclusions which had been tainted with proslavery arguments," comments historian John S. Haller, referring to the works of Dr. Samuel G. Morton, George Robins Gliddon, Dr. Josiah Nott, and Louis Agassiz. The first two died before outbreak of the Civil War that destroyed slavery, and the latter two within a decade of the war's end. But scientific racism survived. "Perhaps the greatest irony of the Civil War," concludes Haller, "was that its anthropometric investigations [particularly Gould's] were used in the late nineteenth century to support institutional racism."[17]

Darwin wrote about the nature of man for the last time a few months before his death. To his detriment, Darwin's critics have quoted only brief excerpts of the 1881 letter, such as:

> I could show fight on natural selection having done and doing more for the progress of civilisation than you seem inclined to admit. Remember what risk the nations of Europe ran, not so many centuries ago of being overwhelmed by the Turks, and how ridiculous such an idea now is! The more civilised so-called Caucasian races have beaten the Turkish hollow in the struggle for existence.

Looking to the world at no very distant date, what an endless number of the lower races will have been eliminated by the higher civilised races throughout the world.[18]

Gertrude Himmelfarb prefaced her quotation of this passage by declaring "proponents of the doctrine 'might is right' could find ample justification in his theory" and followed it immediately with references to "social Darwinism," "the hero, superman, or Führer," and a quotation from a German general.[19] But we should not ignore the original context of this private letter written to William Graham, a Belfast professor of law and political economy, who had sent Darwin his book *The Creed of Science: Religious, Moral, and Social*. With his usual courtesy, Darwin at first praised the work heartily but then proceeded to argue against some points "which I cannot digest." Graham asserted that "the development of the human species, the civilizations of humanity, have not been accomplished by natural selection, [but] . . . through great individuals, men of higher, deeper, finer, nobler natures, in mind, or soul, or moral purpose."[20] Darwin wished to "make somewhat of a case against the enormous importance which you attribute to our greatest men," for Darwin had never cared for Thomas Carlyle's "great men" theories. Darwin's "case" consisted of two points, the first a personal impression: "I have been accustomed to think, second, third, and fourth rate men of very high importance, at least in the case of Science." His second point—the much quoted passage—suggested Graham had attributed too much to "great individuals" and too little to natural selection as an agent "for the progress of civilization."[21]

Darwin's example of a conflict "not so many centuries ago" between "the nations of Europe" and "the Turks" was probably influenced by the recent Russo-Turkish War. Appalled by Turkish atrocities, Darwin had contributed £50 to a relief fund, but his argument to Graham referred to an earlier period when Europe was threatened by Suleiman the Magnificent—the only "great individual" most people could probably name from that conflict—who hardly represented progress and whose side lost. For Darwin, a higher level of "civilisation"—not great individuals or racial superiority—caused the "so-called Caucasian races" to gain advantage over the Turks (also a nonracial term).

Graham asserted, rather sarcastically, that the "universal medicine of 'natural selection' . . . , applied to human societies, virtually recommends that the present state of things should continue."[22] This provoked Darwin's seemingly harsh response about "an endless number of the lower races" likely "at no very distant date" to be "eliminated by the higher civilized races." This did not endorse the destruction of nonwhite races but pointed out that societies *do* change through causes broader than "great individuals" and that natural selection "recommends" neither change nor continuity. Having witnessed atrocities in South America and Australia, Darwin acknowledged that "civilised" societies possessed the means to destroy less organized peoples, but he never suggested this advantage bestowed any right, let alone any obligation to destroy the weak. "Civilised" is a relative term: if the "higher civilised races" were even *more* "civilised," they would not develop deliberate policies to "eliminate" lower (i.e., less civilised) races, and if the latter *became* more civilised, they might yet avoid the more likely types of "elimination."

A more recent critic, Richard Weikart, followed Himmelfarb in blaming Darwin for later social ills, quoting—in even more abbreviated form—the same passage from the letter to Graham.[23] However, Weikart also showed that a decade before that letter, Darwin had used a similar phrase in a passage in *Descent of Man*: "At some future period, not very distant as measured by centuries, the civilised races of man will almost certainly exterminate and replace throughout the world the savage races."[24] Again, the context shows that Darwin was not endorsing such a development but was explaining how "breaks" or "gaps" between related varieties and species had been created in the past (and would be in the future) as "co-descendants of the same species" developed at different rates and gained advantages over one another.[25] Darwin gave two examples, the first (quoted above) being that "the civilised races of man will almost certainly exterminate and replace throughout the world the savage races." Again, far from endorsing this development, Darwin had personally witnessed and condemned "civilised" people who perpetrated such actions; yet, having no reason to believe they would soon stop, it was a viable example of an action that could widen the "breaks" between co-descendants by causing the extinction of some human groups that happen to have developed less civilized organization. Darwin's second example was that "anthropomorphous apes, as Professor Herman Schaaffhausen has remarked, will no doubt be exterminated" by man but perhaps as much by the "savage races" as by the "civilised" ones.[26] The extinctions would destroy the evidence not only of man's most immediate ancestor but also of various anthropomorphous cousins that had descended alongside man (though with fewer modifications).

"The break will then be rendered wider," Darwin projected, "for it will intervene between man in *a more civilised state*, as we may hope, than the Caucasian, and some ape as low as a baboon, instead of as at present between the negro or Australian and the gorilla" (emphasis added). Darwin accepted that the species of man include various races (e.g., Caucasians, Negroes, Aborigines) and does not include gorillas; and none of the nonwhite races are "intermediate" between apes and white men. Darwin linked blacks, Aborigines, and gorillas *only* by a single factor: their vulnerability in any competition with groups (such as most Caucasians) who possessed a "more civilised" social organization. But, crucially, Darwin actually declared Caucasians themselves to be vulnerable to competition with some "more civilised" group still to develop. In some distant future, *none* of the *existing* human races may survive, any more than the doomed gorillas, and on either side of a widened gap will be the more civilized humans of the future and their nearest, still-existing "co-descendants," some sort of baboon. None of this amounted to an endorsement for any deliberate policy of exterminating "less civilised" races (which could eventually include the present "Caucasian" race).[27]

The letter to Graham was not actually published until 1909. And long before that time, the idea of "the survival of the fittest"—coined by Herbert Spencer before *The Origin* was published—was already being misused to justify European acts of imperialism, a revival of laissez-faire economic policies, and the continuing oppression of blacks in the United States.

The Civil War had allowed Lincoln to free blacks from slavery (partly so they could help fight the war) and to take early steps to accord them political equality. Natural selection allowed Darwin to free blacks from the slur that they were not fully human by showing that *all* humans as a group were related to animals while the only advantageous differences within the group were derived from *social* developments. However, long before Lincoln and Darwin were born, *their* race—the white race—had generally developed social organizations that were more complex than those of other races and was *also* successful in appropriating other races' resources. To many whites, those two facts indicated that it was God's design and therefore "natural." And yet, Lincoln and Darwin both dissented from this prevailing attitude because of that combination of rationality and compassion that was so well blended in both men, enabling them also to recognize the unfortunate depth of their societies' prejudices. This is why Darwin predicted that less "civilised" races would remain under threat and why Lincoln thought the tremendous expense and pain involved in returning at least some blacks to Africa could perhaps be less than the suffering that free blacks might endure if they remained in America. A glance at the history of Spanish, Dutch, French, British, Belgian, and American rule over native populations indicates that Lincoln's and Darwin's worst anticipations were all too realistic and nearly came true.

In America, the Civil War resulted in a victory for the North's political principles but also, paradoxically, for the South's racial ideology. This is partly because plenty of Southerners had always agreed it was better to be in the Union than out of it, and plenty of Northerners shared the view that blacks were inherently inferior. Racism had existed before receiving any veneer of scientific justification and continued after scientific racism shed simple polygenism and donned a misshapen version of natural selection. Polygenists such as Nott (who died in 1873) had already realized that they could employ "Darwinism" by declaring that even if blacks and whites had common origins, they were effectively permanent "variants" of some kind. The phrase "struggle for survival" preceded Darwin's adoption of it, but the concept was also readily accepted by former polygenists forced to abandon separate creations and yet eager to stress the inferiority of nonwhites. There had long been those who predicted blacks in America were destined to decline. Louis Agassiz had told Samuel Gridley Howe that both the black and white races would be weakened by amalgamation and that blacks who had previously fled to the North would have to retreat to more tropical areas. Others concluded that slavery had "protected" blacks from the "struggle for survival": as Van Evrie wrote in 1868, the black's tendency to race extinction "accelerated or diminished in exact proportion as 'impartial freedom' [was] thrust upon him." Gould's data was manipulated to reinforce the notion that weaknesses made blacks less "fit" to compete. For those who wished to believe it, the new solution to the "black problem" did not require slavery, or granting the blacks the protection of equal rights, or attempting colonization: given time and no new black immigration, the existing group would simply disappear.[28]

Two years after Gould's report, the 1870 U.S. census supposedly showed that the population growth among blacks since 1860 was not only less than that of whites but also far below the blacks' growth averages between 1790 and 1850, which, according to one southern journal, proved that blacks had been better off under slavery and that the slowing growth rate would soon become a net fall in black population.[29]

The 1880 census, however, indicated that since 1870, despite substantial white immigration and hardly any black immigration, the black population increased by nearly 35 percent while the white population increased by 29 percent.[30] Rather than reaching the correct conclusion—that undercounting blacks in 1870 had skewed growth rates in both censuses—some people panicked, like the author of an article in *Popular Science Monthly* who now projected that in a century, blacks would number 190 million. Suddenly, instead of seeing blacks as probable losers in some race between races, many whites now blamed the blacks for their "remarkable fecundity."[31]

The situation reverted after the 1890 census showed black population growth of 14 percent compared with 25 percent for whites. This coincided with the period, nearly a decade after Darwin's death, when "Darwinism" was being misapplied as "Social Darwinism" in order to argue that all forms of competition—whether social, political, or economic and whether among individuals, classes, nations, or races—were necessary and beneficial overall and that it was "unnatural" to try to prevent it and positively harmful to society to help the "losers."[32]

A Darwin quotation occasionally cited as providing a basis for Social Darwinism was, again, excerpted by Himmelfarb, this time from *Descent of Man*:

> With savages, the weak in body or mind are soon eliminated; and those that survive commonly exhibit a vigorous state of health. We civilised men, on the other hand, do our utmost to check the process of elimination; we build asylums for the imbecile, the maimed, and the sick; we institute poor-laws; and our medical men exert their utmost skill to save the life of every one to the last moment. There is reason to believe that vaccination has preserved thousands, who from a weak constitution would formerly have succumbed to

small-pox. Thus the weak members of civilised societies propagate their kind. No one who has attended to the breeding of domestic animals will doubt that this must be highly injurious to the race of man.[33]

Himmelfarb prefaced this by asserting that Darwin's view represented a return to "laissez-faire—the free, unrestrained competition of individuals," reversing a more recent trend in which "social legislation" had begun to ameliorate factory conditions: a serious misinterpretation by Himmelfarb. Darwin himself had preceded the passage with references to three authorities who took a far harsher stance than he did, and Himmelfarb curtailed Darwin's argument before it reached a three-way comparison among how "savages" deal with weaker members of their societies, how "civilised men" deal with weakness when breeding animals, and how "civilised men" *should* deal with weakness among their fellow men. Darwin pointed out that

the aid which we feel impelled to give to the helpless [results from] the instinct of sympathy, which was originally acquired as part of the social instincts, but subsequently rendered, in the manner previously indicated, more tender and more widely diffused. *Nor could we check our sympathy, if so urged by hard reason, without deterioration in the noblest part of our nature.* . . . [I]f we were intentionally to neglect the weak and helpless, it could only be for a contingent benefit, with a certain and great present evil [emphasis added].[34]

Darwin can hardly be blamed because Americans (not to mention Germans) misapplied his ideas to nonbiological subjects and by doing so gave support to entirely different views. In America in the 1890s, diverse writers produced influential works all reaching the conclusion that the black race would fairly rapidly become extinct in America. They described no real mechanism for this view, which was based on poor statistics, a misapplication of Darwinian concepts, and, above all, desire. Those believing blacks would soon disappear saw no reason to prepare them to be citizens or to bestow any social rights upon them. "The new prognosis," as historian George M. Fredrickson explains, "pointed rather to the need to segregate or quarantine a race liable to be a source of contamination and social danger to the white community."[35] This attitude sustained the segregation laws that were not only tolerated by the rest of the nation but upheld by the Supreme Court in *Plessy v. Ferguson* in 1896.

Had Lincoln lived to witness such developments or learned for how many more decades blacks would suffer harsh discrimination, he would have been saddened but unsurprised, and he might have concluded that much misery and hypocrisy could have been avoided if white America had either adopted a plan for colonization or made up its collective mind to treat blacks as equals. Legalized segregation was simply a more cruel form of "internal" colonization.

In 1909, the centenaries of Lincoln and Darwin were commemorated on both sides of the Atlantic Ocean, and a century later, numerous well-organized committees prepared larger celebrations for the 2009 bicentenaries. Lincoln and Darwin would have been pleased at being remembered after their deaths, the only immortality they could possibly anticipate, and more pleased by the general success of their viewpoints. Centenaries often foster reassessments, which seem superfluous for two lives that have undergone continuous scrutiny. The now customary attacks will continue—that Lincoln was a racist forced into the role of emancipator and that Darwin's ideas led the world straight to Auschwitz—but their reputations will easily survive such taunts.[36] Both men would be appalled if idolaters prevented intelligent discussion of their lives or, more important, of the complex issues each man had wrestled with. Neither man would accept that any issues have been finally settled.

Abraham Lincoln and Charles Darwin, justly revered for their willingness to challenge existing beliefs through a rational pursuit of truth and justice, have been celebrated in two centenaries. A third centenary may not take place, however, unless leaders with similar qualities—especially a serious regard for science and a concern that human beings cooperate rather than compete—attain influence and the political power that can effect necessary changes in the way their fellow human beings meet the new and dangerous challenges facing mankind.

Notes
Bibliography
Index

Notes

Abbreviations

ALP Abraham Lincoln Papers, Library of Congress, Washington, DC. Available at http://memory.loc.gov/ammem/alhtml/malhome.html.

CCD Frederick Burkhardt and Sydney Smith, eds. *The Correspondence of Charles Darwin*. 17 vols. Cambridge: Cambridge University Press, 1985–. Available at http://www.darwinproject.ac.uk.

CW Roy P. Basler, Marion Dolores Pratt, and Lloyd A. Dunlap, eds. *Collected Works of Abraham Lincoln*. 8 vols. New Brunswick, NJ: Rutgers University Press, 1953–55. Available at http://quod.lib.umich.edu/l/lincoln/.

DAR Charles Darwin Papers. Manuscripts Room, Cambridge University Library, Cambridge, UK.

HI Douglas L. Wilson and Rodney O. Davis, eds. *Herndon's Informants: Letters, Interviews, and Statements about Abraham Lincoln*. Urbana: University of Illinois Press, 1998.

JALA *Journal of the Abraham Lincoln Association*

Preface

1. The phrase comes from a 1969 article by Robert M. Young, updated by his important 1985 article "Darwinism *Is* Social."

2. Miller, Scott, and Okamoto, "Public Acceptance of Evolution," 765–66. In Iceland, Denmark, Sweden, and France, 80 percent or more of adults accepted the concept of evolution. Ibid., 765.

3. Hameed, "Bracing for Islamic Creationism," 1637–38.

4. Desmond and Moore's 1991 biography, *Darwin: The Life of a Tormented Evolutionist*, touched on similar themes, their introduction to the 2004 edition of Darwin's *Descent of Man* developed them further, and both works influenced my research, which was largely completed before their *Darwin's Sacred Cause* was available to me.

Introduction

1. The spelling of the village's name was originally "Down" like Darwin's home but was later changed to "Downe."

2. Wyhe, "Mind the Gap," 195–98.

3. Darwin to W. D. Fox, 12 February 1859, in Burkhardt and Smith, *Correspondence of Charles Darwin* (hereinafter referred to as *CCD*), 7:247–48.

4. "Journal," 19 and 31 March, 14 and 18 May 1859, *CCD* 7:273, 295, 299–300, 504.

5. Darwin, *On the Origin of Species*, 459.

6. J. Browne, *Charles Darwin: The Power of Place*, 59.

7. Darwin to Alfred Russel Wallace, 22 December 1857, *CCD* 6:515.

8. See Livingstone, *Adam's Ancestors*, on nineteenth-century views about Adam, including the "pre-Adamic" rationalizations.

9. Darwin, *On the Origin of Species*, 199.

10. Frederick Smith to Darwin, 26 February 1858 and 30 April 1859, *CCD* 6:481 and 7:287; Darwin to Frederick Smith, before 9 March 1858, *CCD* 7:44–45; Darwin to Emma Darwin, 25 April 1858, *CCD* 7:80; Darwin to W. E. Darwin, 26 April 1858, *CCD* 7:81; Darwin to J. D.

Hooker, 6 May and 13 July 1858, *CCD* 7:89, 129; "Collection of Notes on Instinct, Change in Habit," 17 June–23 July 1858 and 23 July–1 August 1859, 205.11, Charles Darwin Papers (hereafter referred to as DAR); Stauffer, *Charles Darwin's Natural Selection*, 511–12 (in chap. 10 about instincts, which Darwin wrote before 9 March 1858); Darwin, *On the Origin of Species*, 219–24; Desmond and Moore, *Darwin's Sacred Cause*, 222–25, 301–4, 321–22.

11. J. Browne, *Charles Darwin: The Power of Place*, 66.

12. Darwin, *On the Origin of Species*, 223–24.

13. This is discussed further in chapter 3; see also discussions in Gruber, *Darwin on Man*; Herbert, "Place of Man in the Development of Darwin's Theory of Transmutation"; Alter, "Race, Language, and Mental Evolution in Darwin's Descent of Man"; and Desmond and Moore, *Darwin's Sacred Cause*.

14. Frederick Smith to Darwin, 30 April 1859, *CCD* 7:287.

15. Darwin to A. G. Henry, 19 November 1858, Basler, Pratt, and Dunlap, *Collected Works of Abraham Lincoln* (hereinafter referred to as *CW*), 3:339–40.

16. Darwin to A. Sympson, 12 December 1858, *CW* 3:346.

17. Briggs describes the lecture as "a substantial statement about human nature and human progress, one that resonated with, and elaborated, his philosophical and political views." *Lincoln's Speeches Reconsidered*, 192.

18. Temple, "Lincoln the Lecturer, Part 1," 105n58. Most of my details regarding the lecture manuscript and presentations come from this work, supplemented by new evidence in Emerson, *Lincoln the Inventor*, 35–53.

19. Temple, "Lincoln the Lecturer, Part 2," 153.

20. William H. Herndon to Jesse Weik, 21 February 1891, in Hertz, *Hidden Lincoln*, 262.

21. Lincoln to J. M. Carson and F. C. Herbruger, 7 April 1860, *CW* 4:39.

22. Lincoln quoted in Brooks, *Washington in Lincoln's Time*, 306.

23. The manuscript's two portions, tied together with a ribbon, became separated and remain separately owned, and what later was known as "The First Lecture" was published in 1915 (see Lincoln, *Discoveries and Inventions*), while the "second" had already been published in Nicolay and Hay, *Complete Works of Abraham Lincoln*, 1:522–28. The Basler *Collected Works* (1953) continues the presentation as two separate lectures (*CW* 2:437–42 and 3:356–63). Wayne C. Temple's view that the two lectures were really one is accepted by Wills (*Lincoln at Gettysburg*, 103–6), Donald (*Lincoln*, 624n), E. Miller ("Democratic Statecraft and Technological Advance," 485–515), and Briggs (*Lincoln's Speeches Reconsidered*, 190); however, Guelzo (*Abraham Lincoln: Redeemer President*, 173–74) assumes two separate lectures.

24. Temple, "Lincoln the Lecturer, Part 1," 100.

25. Lincoln's invention is discussed in chapter 6.

26. Emerson, *Lincoln the Inventor*, 43–50.

27. Whitney, *Life on the Circuit with Lincoln*, 215. In an earlier account, Whitney relates, "Lincoln then told us . . . that he had thought much of the subject & believed he would write a lecture on Man and his progress." Wilson and Davis, *Herndon's Informants* (hereafter referred to as *HI*), 631, 633.

28. Temple, "Lincoln the Lecturer, Part 1," 97. I am grateful to Dr. Temple for this and other information, including a copy of a broadside "Sale of Herndon's Books in Cincinnati" (cited hereafter as "Herndon's Auction List") mentioning approximately a thousand books auctioned by Herndon, many of which had either belonged or been available to Lincoln.

29. Wills, *Lincoln at Gettysburg*, 46. On Lincoln's opposition to Bancroft's views, see E. Miller, "Democratic Statecraft and Technological Advance," passim.

30. Brooks, "Personal Recollections of Abraham Lincoln," 224, and "Personal Reminiscences of Lincoln," 678.

31. Oldroyd, *Lincoln Memorial*, 522–23.

32. *CW* 2:437.

33. Lincoln quoted in Brooks, *Washington in Lincoln's Time*, 306; Bancroft, "Necessity, the Reality and the Promise of the Progress of the Human Race."

34. *CW* 3:360.

35. *(Bloomington, Illinois) Daily Pantograph*, 9 April 1858, in Temple, "Lincoln the Lecturer, Part 2," 161–62. This "letter to the editor" (possibly written by the editor himself, Jesse Fell, a great supporter of Lincoln) helpfully stressed that Lincoln's "great research and . . . careful study of the Bible" demonstrated that "the lawyer is not by any means unfamiliar with the Book of the Great Law-Giver."

36. *HI*, 167.

37. *CW* 2:438.

38. *CW* 2:440.

39. Swett is quoted as saying, "[Lincoln] was wise as a serpent in the trial of a cause but I have too many scars from his blows to certify that he was harmless as a dove. . . . What he was so blandly giving away was simply what he couldn't get & Keep. By giving away 6 points and carrying the 7th he carried his case. . . . Any man who took Lincoln for a simple minded man would very soon wake [up] with his back in a ditch." *HI*, 636.

40. Burlingame, *Abraham Lincoln*, 1:443–45.

41. *CW* 3:358.

42. *CW* 3:361.

43. *CW* 3:363.

44. *CW* 3:362.

45. Bancroft, "Necessity, the Reality, and the Promise of the Progress of the Human Race," 8–9.

46. *Encyclopaedia Americana*, 1851 ed., s.v. "Slavery"; Temple, "Lincoln the Lecturer," 98. Lincoln probably owned the 1851 edition of *Encyclopaedia Americana*, which duplicated the "Slavery" and "Negro" articles (including page numbers) published in the first edition in 1832. On Lincoln's reading, see also Temple, "Herndon on Lincoln," 34–50, and Bray, "What Abraham Lincoln Read," 28–81. See also Bray, *Reading with Lincoln*.

47. *Encyclopaedia Americana*, 1851 ed., s.v. "Negro." Lincoln probably owned the 1851 edition, which duplicated the "Slavery" and "Negro" articles (including page numbers) published in the first edition in 1832.

1. Origins and Education

1. Verduin, "Brief Outline of the Joseph Hanks Family," 780.

2. Lincoln to Albert G. Hodges, 4 April 1864, *CW* 7:281.

3. Herndon and Weik, *Herndon's Life of Lincoln*, 3.

4. Darwin, *Autobiographies*, 7.

5. Ibid., 19.

6. Donald, *Lincoln*, 605n32.

7. "Autobiography Written for John L. Scripps," June 1860, *CW* 4:61.

8. Darwin, *Autobiographies*, 3, 10, 19–22.

9. Ibid., 21–22.

10. Ibid., 29–31.

11. Ibid., 32–36.

12. Ibid., 48, 64, 72, 84–85.

13. Bray, "What Abraham Lincoln Read."

14. *(Springfield) Illinois State Journal*, 27 January 1859; D. L. Wilson, *Honor's Voice*, 60, 61, 73–76, 310; Milton Hay quoted in Wilson, *Honor's Voice*, 74.

15. *HI*, 577.

16. "Autobiography Written for John L. Scripps," June 1860, *CW* 4:62.

17. Lincoln to Jesse Fell, 20 December 1859, *CW* 3:511.

18. Ibid.; W. L. Miller, *Lincoln's Virtues*, 43–44.

19. *HI*, 132.

20. *HI*, 41; W. L. Miller, *Lincoln's Virtues*, 49.

21. *HI*, 41, 142, 407, 430, 512; D. L. Wilson, *Honor's Voice*, 59–60; W. L. Miller, *Lincoln's Virtues*, 48–49.

22. Beveridge, *Abraham Lincoln*, 1:70, 73–77; F. B. Carpenter, *Six Months at the White House with Abraham Lincoln*, 115; *HI*, 171; Bray, "What Abraham Lincoln Read," 73, 76.

23. John L. Scripps to Lincoln, 17 July 1860, ALP. Scripps informed Lincoln that he "took the liberty of adding Plutarch's *Lives*," assuming Lincoln had read it. "If you have not, then you must read it at once to make my statement good."

24. D. L. Wilson, *Honor's Voice*, 67; Mearns, *Lincoln Papers*, 1:152–53.

25. *HI*, 92, 66, 426.

26. "Autobiography Written for John L. Scripps," June 1860, *CW* 4:64; Donald, *Lincoln*, 51.

27. Maltby, *Life and Public Services of Abraham Lincoln*, 31.

28. Donald, *Lincoln*, 99.

29. W. L. Miller, *Lincoln's Virtues*, 52–53.

30. "Autobiography Written for John L. Scripps," June 1860, *CW* 4:62.

31. *HI*, 499.

2. Voyages and the Experience of Slavery

1. Darwin, *Autobiographies*, 42.

2. R. D. Keynes, *Charles Darwin's* Beagle *Diary*, 23, 42.

3. Donald, *Lincoln*, 35.

4. "Autobiography Written for John L. Scripps," June 1860, *CW* 4:63–64.

5. D. L. Wilson, *Honor's Voice*, 87.

6. *HI*, 26, 114, 118, 131.

7. *HI*, 457.

8. *HI*, 44–45, 615.

9. Herndon and Weik, *Herndon's Life of Lincoln*, 63–64.

10. Lincoln to Joshua Speed, 24 August 1855, *CW* 2:320.

11. Darwin, *Autobiographies*, 41.

12. R. D. Keynes, *Charles Darwin's* Beagle *Diary*, 23.

13. Darwin, *Voyage of the Beagle*, 18, 23, 23.

14. R. D. Keynes, *Charles Darwin's* Beagle *Diary*, 21.

15. Reilly, *Josiah Wedgwood 1730–1795*, 287.

16. E. Darwin, *Botanic Garden*, part 1, *Economy of Vegetation* (1791), canto 2, verses 425–28.

17. Gerzina, *Black England*, 171, 181–85.

18. Hollander, *Slavery in America*, 18–19.

19. Sherwood, "Formation of the American Colonization Society," 209–28.

20. Midgley, *Women against Slavery*, 56, 76–77, 103, 223. See Desmond and Moore, *Darwin's Sacred Cause*, especially 13, 61, 82, 117–18, 134, 261, on "Aunt Sarah's" large donations to antislavery committees and the antislavery activities of several other close relatives of Darwin.

21. On the many reformers who at first supported gradualism and colonization but later turned against both, see Goodman, *Of One Blood*, 20–21, 55–57, 62, 77–78, 86, 106–7.

22. Hart, "Springfield's African Americans as a Part of the Lincoln Community," 34–57. Like many African Americans, those living in Lincoln's Springfield held annual celebrations on August 1.

23. Woodward, *Age of Reform, 1815–1870*, 373; Darwin to E. C. Darwin, 22 May [–14 July] 1833, *CCD* 1:311; Darwin to J. M. Herbert, 2 June 1833, *CCD* 1:319.

24. A. G. Freehling, *Drift toward Dissolution*, 162.

25. Darwin to Gray, 15 August 1865, *CCD* 13:223.

26. Darwin, *Voyage of the Beagle*, 480.

3. The Racial Background, Personal Encounters, and Turning Points in 1837

1. Jordan, *Black over White*, 219.

2. Pope, *Essay on Man*, 2.7–8.

3. Jordan, *Black over White*, 217, 220–22, 241; S. J. Gould, *I Have Landed*, 356–66, and *Mismeasure of Man*, 40.

4. S. J. Gould, *Mismeasure of Man*, 39–41.

5. Jordan, *Black over White*, 247, 251–55, 538–39.

6. Ibid., 225–26, 231–3, 304–9, 496–97, 522.

7. Ibid., 230–236; Wills, *Inventing America*, 220–22.

8. Jordan, *Black over White*, 257, 515–16; Wills, *Inventing America*, 218–23.

9. S. J. Gould, *Mismeasure of Man*, 36.

10. Lincoln to Jesse Fell, 20 December 1859, *CW* 3:512.

11. Lincoln, "Speech in U. S. House of Representatives on the Presidential Question," 27 July 1848, *CW* 1:510.

12. *HI*, 18.

13. *HI*, 372–73.

14. R. D. Keynes, *Charles Darwin's* Beagle *Diary*, 7 September 1832, 101.

15. Darwin, *Voyage of the Beagle*, 96–98.

16. Ibid., 203.

17. Darwin, *Descent of Man*, 2:404.

18. Darwin, *Voyage of the Beagle*, 206, 219.

19. Darwin, *Autobiographies*, 25.

20. Darwin, *Descent of Man*, 1:232.

21. R. D. Keynes, *Charles Darwin's* Beagle *Diary*, 20 January 1832, 26.

22. Darwin, *Voyage of the Beagle*, 219, 263, 388–89, 404, 412, 414, 417–19, 434.

23. R. D. Keynes, *Charles Darwin's* Beagle *Diary*, 444.

24. Lincoln to Joshua F. Speed, 24 August 1855, *CW* 2:323.

25. Arnold, *Life of Abraham Lincoln*, 359.

26. W. L. Miller, *Lincoln's Virtues*, 123, 126. The following discussion relies heavily on Miller's excellent analysis on 116–29.

27. Dan Stone quoted in *CW* 1:74–75.

28. W. L. Miller, *Lincoln's Virtues*, 129.

29. Donald, *Lincoln*, 134.

30. Lincoln to Williamson Durley, 3 October 1845, *CW* 1:348. Lincoln also commented, "[We should not] prevent . . . slavery from dying a natural death [by instead finding] new places for it to live in, when it can no longer exist in the old."

31. *Register of Debates*, 24th Cong., 2nd sess., February 6, 1837, app., 2184–87.

32. Darwin quoted in J. Browne, *Charles Darwin: Voyaging*, 360–61.

33. Hodge, "Notebook Programmes and Projects of Darwin's London Years," 41–42.

34. Darwin, *Autobiographies*, 59.

35. Charles Lyell quoted in Rudwick, introduction, *Principles of Geology*, xiii–xiv.

36. Hodge, "Darwin as a Lifelong Generation Theorist," 211.

37. Rudwick, introduction, *Principles of Geology*, xxiii–xxiv.

38. Darwin to Charles Lyell, March 1841, *CCD* 2:283.

39. R. D. Keynes, *Charles Darwin's* Beagle *Diary*, 403.

40. Darwin, "Ornithological Notes," DAR 29.2:73–74 quoted in J. Browne, *Charles Darwin: Voyaging*, 339.

41. Sulloway, "Darwin and His Finches," 11–12.

42. Darwin, *Autobiographies*, 72.

43. Darwin, *Notebook B*, quoted in Desmond and Moore, *Darwin's Sacred Cause*, 231–32.

44. Darwin, *Notebook C*, quoted in Desmond and Moore, *Darwin's Sacred Cause*, 154–55. See also, for example, *Notebook B*, 244, and *Notebook C*, 53, 138, 204, and 217, cited and discussed in Desmond and Moore, *Darwin's Sacred Cause*, 112–16.

45. Darwin, *Notebook M*, quoted in Desmond and Moore, *Darwin's Sacred Cause*, 84.

4. Religious Reformation

1. Darwin, *Autobiographies*, 8, 10.

2. *HI*, 107, 102, 110.

3. Burlingame, *Abraham Lincoln*, 1:41.

4. Darwin, *Autobiographies*, 29.

5. Brooke, "Darwin and Victorian Christianity," 197–98. "Twiners entwining twiners, tresses like hair—beautiful lepidoptera—Silence, hosannah" (Darwin, *Beagle Field Notebook*, 17 April 1832, EH1.10:27b, Wyhe, *Complete Work of Charles Darwin Online*) and "the Creator creates by laws" (*Notebook B*, 98 [1837]). Quoted in Brooke, "Darwin and Victorian Christianity," 197–98.

6. John Maurice Herbert to Francis Darwin, 2 June 1882, DAR 112, ser. 2.63–64; F. Darwin, *Life and Letters of Charles Darwin*, 1:171.

7. *HI*, 24, 61–62, 172, 179, 210, 251, 513. At least eight of Herndon's informants mentioned Lincoln's early love of Burns's poetry.

8. *HI*, 167–68, 432, 441, 458, 464, 545, 547, 576–77, 579, 588.

9. Darwin, *Autobiographies*, 52, 49.

10. George Darwin and Robert Hamond quoted in J. Browne, *Charles Darwin: Voyaging*, 130, 326.

11. D. L. Wilson, "Most Abandoned Hypocrite," 36–49, 48–49.

12. *HI*, 24, 61–62, 156, 432, 545, 577, 450, 432, 577, 545.

13. Stevens, *Reporter's Lincoln*, 12.

14. Bledsoe, review, "Ward Hill Lamon's *Life of Abraham Lincoln*," 354.

15. *CW* 8:433. Edwards's gift is inscribed: "A. Lincoln—Presented by his friend, N. W. Edwards," 1836[?].

16. Lincoln to Mary Owen, 7 May 1837, *CW* 1:78.

17. *HI*, 576.

18. Guelzo, *Abraham Lincoln: Redeemer President*, 108. Maclure was one of the scientists who established a colony at New Harmony, Indiana, in the mid-1820s, when Lincoln lived fifty miles away.

19. Erasmus Darwin to Darwin, 18 August 1832, *CCD* 1:259.

20. Darwin quoted in J. Browne, *Charles Darwin: Voyaging*, 366.

21. Darwin, *Autobiographies*, 47; *Notebook B*, DAR 121, 101.

22. Darwin, *Notebook C*, DAR 122, 166.

23. Darwin, *Autobiographies*, 49.

24. Ibid., 55.

25. Ibid.

26. Emma Wedgwood to Darwin, 21–22 November 1838, *CCD* 2:123.

27. Desmond and Moore, *Darwin*, 287, and Guelzo, *Abraham Lincoln*, 113. Temple states that Tad was baptized in 1855 but mentions no earlier baptisms. *Abraham Lincoln*, 378.

28. "Second Reply to James Adams," 18 October 1837, *CW* 1:106.

29. *HI*, 576.

30. D. L. Wilson, *Honor's Voice*, 186–87.

31. Joshua Speed quoted in *HI*, 156.

32. *HI*, 158, 342, 500.

33. Lincoln to Mary Speed, 27 September 1841, *CW* 1:261.

34. Darwin to Lyell, 14 September 1838, *CCD* 2:107.

35. Emma Darwin to Darwin, ca. February 1839, *CCD* 2:171–72.

36. Lincoln to Joshua Speed, 4 July 1842, *CW* 1:289.

37. See especially Guelzo, *Abraham Lincoln*, with annotated bibliography.

38. W. L. Miller, *Lincoln's Virtues*, 56.

39. "Temperance Address," 22 February 1842, *CW* 1:279; Lincoln to Joshua Speed, 5 October 1842, *CW* 1:303.

40. F. Darwin, *Foundations of The Origin of Species*, 52.

41. Lincoln to Martin S. Morris, 26 March 1843, *CW* 1:320.

42. Darwin to George Waterhouse, 26 July 1843, *CCD* 2:373.

43. Darwin to Joseph Dalton Hooker, 11 January 1844, *CCD* 3:2.

44. Joseph Dalton Hooker to Darwin, 29 January 1844, *CCD* 3:5.

45. Donald, *Lincoln's Herndon*, 18–20; William H. Herndon to Jesse Weik, 24 February 1887, Herndon-Weik Collection.

46. Donald, *Lincoln's Herndon*, 53; Rankin, *Personal Recollections of Abraham Lincoln*, 120.

47. Townsend, *Real Life of Abraham Lincoln*, 4–5; "Herndon's Auction List"; Donald, *Lincoln's Herndon*, 286.

48. William H. Herndon to John E. Remsburg, before 1893, in Remsburg, *Abraham Lincoln*, 114–15.

49. The latest and most valuable study is Bray, "What Abraham Lincoln Read."

50. Jesse Fell to Ward Hill Lamon, 22 September 1870, in *HI*, 579; Donald, *Lincoln's Herndon* 54–55. On the ideas shared by Parker and Lincoln, see Wills, *Lincoln at Gettysburg*, 106–26. Fell confirms that Lincoln received a copy of Parker's works from Herndon and that Lincoln read and was in accord with Parker.

51. Rankin, *Personal Recollections of Abraham Lincoln*, 123; J. F. Newton, *Lincoln and Herndon*, 254.

52. Darwin to Charles Lyell, 8 June 1850, *CCD* 4:341.

53. Donald, *Lincoln's Herndon*, 54.

54. Herndon and Weik, *Herndon's Life of Lincoln*, 477, 293.

55. Secord, *Victorian Sensation*, 3; "Herndon's Auction List."

56. Herndon and Weik, *Herndon's Life of Lincoln*, 353–54; William H. Herndon to John E. Remsburg, before 1893, in Remsburg, *Abraham Lincoln*, 135.

57. *HI*, 464.

58. Herndon to Remsburg, before 1893, in Remsburg, *Abraham Lincoln*, 135. Herndon, while not quoting, closely echoed a phrase in Lincoln's lecture on "Inventions": "observation, reflection and experiment."

59. Tarbell, *In the Footsteps of the Lincolns*, 270–71.

60. Lincoln to Allen Wood, 11 August 1846, *CW* 1:383.

61. Lincoln, "To the Voters of the Seventh Congressional District," handbill, 31 July 1846, *CW* 1:382.

62. Pratt, "Abraham Lincoln's Religion," 1–4. For the former view, for example, Trueblood, *Abraham Lincoln*, 16–20, 98–99; for the latter view, for example, W. L. Miller, *Lincoln's Virtues*, 56, and Guelzo, *Abraham Lincoln*, 318–28.

63. Lincoln to Allen Wood, 11 August 1846, *CW* 1:384.

64. Darwin to Emma Darwin, 5 July 1844, *CCD* 3:45.

65. Desmond and Moore, *Darwin*, 319.

66. Ibid., 429.

67. Darwin to Joseph Dalton Hooker, 7 January 1845, *CCD* 3:108.

68. Darwin to W. D. Fox, 24 April 1845, *CCD* 3:181.

69. Secord, *Victorian Sensation*, 431, 434–35, 491.

70. Di Gregorio, *Charles Darwin's Marginalia*, 163–65.71. Chambers, *Vestiges of the Natural History of Creation*, 152.

72. Darwin to Charles Lyell, 8 October 1845, *CCD* 3:258.

73. Di Gregorio, *Charles Darwin's Marginalia*, 750.

74. Darwin to Joseph Dalton Hooker, 10 September 1845, *CCD* 3:250–52.

5. Career Preparations and Rivals, 1845–49

1. Darwin, *Voyage of the Beagle*, 380, 393.

2. Darwin to Charles Lyell, 30 July–2 August 1845, *CCD* 3:232.

3. Darwin to Charles Lyell, 25 August 1845, *CCD* 3:241.

4. Darwin, *Voyage of the Beagle*, 499–500. Darwin learned in a brief correspondence with William Lloyd Garrison's son that the great American abolitionist, near the end of his life in 1879, read and approved Darwin's denunciations of slavery. Desmond and Moore, *Darwin's Sacred Cause*, xx.

5. Darwin, *Narrative of the Surveying Voyages*, 617–18; Darwin to Louis Agassiz, 1 March 1841, *CCD* 2:284.

6. Darwin to W. D. Fox, 4 September 1843, *CCD* 2:386.

7. Darwin to Joseph Dalton Hooker, 10 November 1844, *CCD* 3:79. Darwin is presumably referring to Agassiz, "On the Succession and Development of Organised Beings."

8. Darwin to Leonard Horner, 17 August–7 September 1846, *CCD* 3:333.

9. Darwin to Louis Agassiz, 22 October 1848, *CCD* 4:178. Cf. Darwin to J. E. Gray, 18 December 1847, *CCD* 4:99.

10. Love, "Darwin and Cirripedia prior to 1846," 269, 284.

11. Darwin to J. E. Gray, 18 December 1847, *CCD* 4:99; Darwin to Augustus Gould, 3 September 1848, *CCD* 4:165. Both letters chronologically link Darwin's barnacle study to Agassiz's lecture. Two weeks after the Southampton conference, Darwin told Hooker, "I am going to begin some papers on the lower marine animals, which will last me some months, perhaps a year and then I shall begin looking over my ten-year-long accumulation of notes on species & varieties." 2 October 1846, *CCD* 3:346.

12. Lurie, *Louis Agassiz*, 90, 115–16.

13. Lincoln to Williamson Durley, 3 October 1845, *CW* 1:347–48.

14. Lincoln to William A. Minshall, 7 December 1837, *CW* 1:107. Douglas later dropped the second *s* from his name.

15. *CW* 1:108–14. Burlingame argues convincingly that Lincoln's audience would have recognized the allusions to Douglas. An earlier view—that Lincoln was referring to himself—seems unlikely, except possibly as a matter of psychological projection. *Inner World of Abraham Lincoln*, 365–68,

16. Burlingame, *Inner World of Abraham Lincoln*, 365–68.

17. *HI*, 507, 643.

18. *HI*, 181.

19. Lincoln to John T. Stuart, 23 December 1839, *CW* 1:158–9; "Speech on the Sub-Treasury," 26 December 1839, *CW* 1:177.

20. Donald, *Lincoln*, 135.

21. "Remarks and Resolution," 10 January 1849, *CW* 2:20–22.

22. James Q. Howard, May 1860, "Biographical Notes," series 1, General Correspondence, ALP, 15.

23. *Congressional Globe*, 28th Cong., 2nd sess., 25 January 1845, 192–93.

24. Burlingame, *Inner World of Abraham Lincoln*, 242.

25. Stott, *Darwin and the Barnacle*, 84–85, 93–102; Darwin to Joseph Dalton Hooker, 12 November 1846, *CCD* 3:365; Darwin to J. S. Henslow, 1 April 1848, *CCD* 4:128; Darwin to Charles Lyell, 2 September 1849, *CCD* 4:271.

26. Darwin to Joseph Dalton Hooker, 13 May 1848, *CCD* 4:140.

27. Porter and Rousseau, *Gout*, 162.

28. Colp, *To Be an Invalid*; Bowlby, *Charles Darwin*.

6. Mortality, Invention, and Geology

1. Litchfield, *Emma Darwin: A Century of Family Letters, 1792–1896*, 2:78.

2. Baker, *Mary Todd Lincoln*, 125–26.

3. R. Keynes, *Annie's Box*, 148–77, 200.

4. Baker, *Mary Todd Lincoln*, 126–28.

5. Emma Darwin to Fanny Wedgwood, 24 April 1851, Wedgwood-Mosley Collection, Wedgwood Museum, Barlaston, Stoke-on-Trent, England.

6. Emma Darwin to Erasmus Darwin, 25 April 1851, *CCD* 5:26.

7. Darwin to Joseph Dalton Hooker, 13 July 1856, *CCD* 6:178.

8. Darwin to John D. Johnston, 23 February 1850, *CW* 2:77; Turner and Turner, *Mary Todd Lincoln*, 567–68. Temple suggests the event "began to change his entire religious thinking." *Abraham Lincoln*, 36,

9. Temple, *Abraham Lincoln*, 47, 57.

10. Guelzo, *Abraham Lincoln*, 148–57.

11. Temple, *Abraham Lincoln*, 56.

12. R. Keynes, *Annie's Box*, 222.

13. The three exceptions are not general biographies: Bruce, *Lincoln and the Tools of War*; Emerson, *Lincoln the Inventor*; and Temple, *Lincoln's Connections*, 53–72.

14. Temple, *Lincoln's Connections*, 35.

15. Ibid., 54–58; Emerson, *Lincoln the Inventor*, 4–7; Hertz, *Hidden Lincoln*, 397.

16. "Application for Patent on an Improved Method of Lifting Vessels over Shoals," 10 March 1849, *CW* 2:32–35; Temple, *Lincoln's Connections*, 59–63; Emerson, *Lincoln the Inventor*, 15–18, 17.

17. Temple, *Lincoln's Connections*, 69–71. Temple suggests Lincoln made two models. Emerson uses sources that leave unclear whether the trial occurred before or after Lincoln submitted his model to the Patent Office. *Lincoln the Inventor*, 14.

18. *Scientific American*, 1 December 1860, 356.

19. Hertz, *Hidden Lincoln*, 104.

20. Donald, *Lincoln*, 154.

21. Darwin and Seward, *More Letters of Charles Darwin*, 1:27.

22. Hertz, *Hidden Lincoln*, 172, 403; Herndon and Weik, *Herndon's Life of Lincoln*, 257.

23. Joseph Gillespie quoted in *HI*, 505–6.

24. John T. Stuart quoted in James Q. Howard, May 1860, "Biographical Notes," ALP.

25. David Davis quoted in *HI*, 350.

26. Donald, *Lincoln's Herndon*, 15; Dall, "Pioneering," 404.

27. Hertz, *Hidden Lincoln*, 113.

28. "Herndon's Auction List" shows only the 1854 volume of the annual, so perhaps Lincoln's own set was not left in the office to become part of Herndon's collection.

29. Hertz, *Hidden Lincoln*, 116; Herndon and Weik, *Herndon's Life of Lincoln*, 353.

30. There exists a copy of Hitchcock, *Religious Truth Illustrated from Science*, inscribed: "WHH to A. Lincoln." Bray, "What Abraham Lincoln Read," 55. Hitchcock also published *Elementary Geology* (3rd ed., 1844), which was not in "Herndon's Auction List," but a journalist copying down titles of books in Herndon's office in 1867 recorded "Hitchcock's Elements of Zoology," which is unidentifiable and probably a note-reading error. See Temple, "Herndon on Lincoln," 34–50.

31. Temple, *Lincoln's Connections*, 73.

32. Hendrickson, "Nineteenth-Century State Geological Surveys," 357–61.

33. McMillan, "First Century," 4; Temple and Temple, *Illinois' Fifth Capitol*, 151.

34. Clarke, *James Hall of Albany*, 280.

35. Ibid., 283–86.

36. R. P. Stevens to Lincoln, 24 June 1858, ALP.

37. Clarke, *James Hall of Albany*, 295. Orville H. Browning's letter of recommendation to Lincoln described McChesney as "our mutual friend." Lincoln to William H. Seward, 9 December 1861, *CW* 5:62. McChesney said he had been able to campaign effectively for Lincoln in 1860 because "I knew him so well personally." McChesney to John G. Nicolay, 13 January 1865, ALP.

38. *Worthing* [sic] *for Use of McCann v. Maus*, April 1841, in Benner, Davis, et al., *Law Practice of Abraham Lincoln*; Temple and Temple, *Illinois' Fifth Capital*, 151–52.

39. Amos H. Worthen to Joseph Leidy, 1871, Collection 1-B, Joseph Leidy Correspondence, Academy of Natural Sciences.

40. Temple, *Lincoln's Connections*, 32. *CW* 2:10–11 assigns the date 1848 based on the appearance of the paper and handwriting and because Lincoln visited Western New York at that time. However, Temple has argued convincingly that Lincoln barely had time to see the falls during that trip but certainly did in 1857.

41. Lincoln, "Fragment: Niagara Falls," *CW* 2:10–11.

42. For a compendium of early sources, see Dow, *Anthology and Bibliography of Niagara Falls*, 1:495–524.

43. Bakewell, "On the Falls of Niagara," 117–30; C. Lyell, *Principles of Geology*, 1st ed., 1:181.

44. Silliman, "Hamlet Affair," 543.

45. Review of *Natural History of New York*, 25.

46. Hall, *Geology of New York*, part 3, 383.

47. C. Lyell, *Travels in North America*, 2nd ed., 1:37. The thirty-five-thousand-year dating also appears in C. Lyell, *Principles of Geology*, 9th ed., 1853.

48. C. Lyell, *Travels in North America*, 2nd ed., 1:34.

49. Burke, *Burke's Descriptive Guide*, 63.

50. Hunter, *Hunter's Panoramic Guide from Niagara to Quebec*, 12.

51. Herndon and Weik, *Herndon's Life of Lincoln*, 238–39.

7. Scientific Racism

1. Humboldt, *Cosmos*, 1:368; Darwin to Joseph Dalton Hooker, 18 September 1845, *CCD* 3:255. The work also appears in "Herndon's Auction List."

2. Darwin to Charles Lyell, 8 October 1845, *CCD* 3:258. Cf. Darwin to J. S. Henslow, 28 October 1845, *CCD* 3:259.

3. Darwin, *Autobiographies*, 25; Freeman, "Darwin's Negro Bird-Stuffer," 83–86; Desmond and Moore, *Darwin's Sacred Cause*, 18–26.

4. Waterton, *Essays on Natural History*, xv–xvi.

5. Darwin to Charles Lyell, 8 October 1845, *CCD* 3:258. Darwin was referring to Long, *History of Jamaica*, 2:336.

6. Darwin, *Descent of Man*, 1:221.

7. L. Agassiz, *Notice sur la Geographie des Animaux*, 31, as translated in Stanton, *Leopard's Spots*, 101. The best discussion of Agassiz's changing view is in Lurie, "Louis Agassiz and the Races of Man," 227–42.

8. L. Agassiz quoted in S. J. Gould, *Mismeasure*, 44–45.

9. Ibid., 44.

10. E. C. Agassiz, *Louis Agassiz*, 2:409–29.

11. S. J. Gould, *Mismeasure*, 43, 50–69. John S. Michael has shown that while Morton's measurements were largely accurate and not demonstrably skewed by a racist bias, his crude sampling procedures and unbalanced sample sizes made his results "scientifically unsound." "A New Look at Morton's Craniological Research," 349–54,

12. Hart, "Springfield's African Americans," 47.

13. L. Agassiz, "Geographical Distribution of Animals," 182.

14. Darwin to Charles Lyell, 30 July–2 August 1845, *CCD* 3:232; Darwin to Lyell, 2 June 1847, *CCD* 4:45; S. G. Morton, "Hybridity in Animals," 39–50, 203–12; Desmond and Moore, *Darwin's Sacred Cause*, 202–4.

15. Darwin to Louis Agassiz, 22 October 1848, *CCD* 4:178.

16. Ibid.

17. Lurie, *Louis Agassiz*, 151; L. Agassiz, *Lake Superior*, 144, 247–48, 377.

18. Darwin to Louis Agassiz, 15 June 1850, *CCD* 4:345.

19. Lurie, *Louis Agassiz*, 151; Darwin to Charles Lyell, 8 June 1850, *CCD* 4:341.

20. *Lake Superior* appeared in Darwin's list of books read on 16 August 1850, DAR 119:22v.

21. Darwin to Louis Agassiz, 15 June 1850, *CCD* 4:345.

22. Lurie, *Louis Agassiz*, 405n16; L. Agassiz, *Introduction to the Study of Natural History*.

23. Darwin to W. D. Fox, 4 September 1850, *CCD* 4:353.

24. Lurie, *Louis Agassiz*, 260.

25. Nott, "Mulatto a Hybrid" and *Two Lectures on the Natural History of the Caucasian and Negro Races*.

26. Josiah Nott quoted in Lurie, *Louis Agassiz*, 261.

27. On Gliddon and Squier, see Stanton, *Leopard's Spots*, 45–50, 82–88, 98–99, 192–93.

28. L. Agassiz, "Geographical Distribution of Animals."

29. S. G. Morton, "Hybridity in Animals," 39–50, 203–12; Nott, "Life Insurance at the South," 357–76, and "Statistics of Southern Slave Population," 275–89. In February 1846, Lyell met Nott, who reported to Morton that Lyell "seemed to be much staggered" by Nott's notions about the human races. C. Lyell, *Second Visit to the United States*, 2:80; Stanton, *Leopard's Spots*, 68, 80.

30. Reviews include: "Notices of New Books: *Two Lectures on the Connection between the Biblical and Physical History of Man*," *U.S. Democratic Review* 25 (August 1849): 192, and 25 (September 1849): 287; "Critical Notices: *Two Lectures on the Connection between the Biblical and Physical History of Man*," *American Whig Review* 10 (October 1849): 439–40. See also "Natural History of Man," *U.S. Democratic Review* 26 (April 1850): 327–45, reviewing at length F. W. Van Amringe, *An Investigation of the Theories of the Natural History of Man* (1848), James C. Prichard, *Researches into the Physical History of Man (New Edition of This Work from 1813)*, as well as Nott, *Two Lectures*.

31. Squier, "American Ethnology," 386.

32. Desmond and Moore, *Darwin's Sacred Cause*, 176; Bachman, "Investigation of the Cases of Hybridity," *Charleston Medical Journal and Review* 5 (1850): 168–97. The debate

between Bachman and Morton raged through letters to the editor in *Charleston Medical Journal and Review* 5 (1850): 328–44, 466–508, 621–60, 755–805, and 6 (1851): 145–52, 301–8, 373–83, 383–96.

33. "Bibliography: *The Doctrine of the Unity of the Human Race Examined*," *American Journal of Science* 11 (1851): 302; Nott, "Diversity of the Human Race." See also the reviews of *Doctrine of the Unity of the Human Race, Southern Quarterly Review* 1 (April 1850): 250; *Princeton Review* 22 (April 1850): 313–21.

34. Stanton, *Leopard's Spots*, 92–98.

35. Ibid., 95.

36. Ibid., 93, 96.

37. Pickering, *Races of Man*, xxvii, xxx. This is the edition owned and annotated by Darwin, who later cited some of Pickering's data without accepting his conclusions.

38. Review of "The Original Unity of the Human Race—Pickering, Bachman, Agassiz," 543, 545, 546, 584.

39. L. Agassiz, "On the Diversity of Human Races," 113, 142–43; S. J. Gould, *Mismeasure of Man*, 46.

40. L. Agassiz, "Contemplations of God in the Cosmos," 1–17; Lurie, *Louis Agassiz*, 263.

41. Charles Lyell to George Ticknor, 9 January 1860, in K. M. Lyell, *Life, Letters, and Journals of Sir Charles Lyell*, 2:331.

42. Josiah Nott to E. G. Squier, 4 May 1850, Squier Papers, cited in Lurie, *Louis Agassiz*, 241n66.

43. Donald, *Lincoln*, 162; Lincoln, "Speech to the Springfield Scott Club," 14 August 1852, *CW* 2:135–38.

44. *(Springfield) Illinois State Journal*, 13 June 1850.

45. Herndon and Weik, *Herndon's Life of Lincoln*, 292–93.

46. Darwin's edition, read in November 1849, lacked Agassiz's memoir. DAR 119:22v.

47. Herndon and Weik, *Herndon's Life of Lincoln*, 293, and Hertz, *Hidden Lincoln*, 97.

48. Fitzhugh, *Sociology for the South*, 83, 204.

49. Ibid., 95, 147–48, 167, 205.

50. Lurie, "Louis Agassiz and the Races of Man," 239n60.

51. Darwin, "Books Read" and "Books to be Read" notebooks, DAR 128:13–14, 165, 167.

52. L. Agassiz, "Sketch of the Natural Provinces of the Animal World and Their Relation to the Different Types of Men," in Nott and Gliddon, *Types of Mankind*, lviii–lxxviii.

8. *The Types of Mankind* and the Kansas-Nebraska Act, 1854–55

1. Darwin to W. D. Fox, 10 October 1850, *CCD* 4:362. Cf. Darwin to Syms Covington, 23 November 1850, *CCD* 4:368, mentioning New South Wales. The imminent birth of the Darwins' eighth child apparently stimulated this vague speculation about greater opportunities for his children outside England.

2. "Herndon's Auction List." Most of the volumes of essays were published from 1856 to 1858, and the list included works by at least twenty other writers for the *Westminster Review*, all familiar to Darwin.

3. Marion Evans (George Eliot) quoted in Secord, *Victorian Sensation*, 486–87.

4. Hughes, *George Eliot*, 208.

5. T. Huxley, "Science," 264–65.

6. Joseph Dalton Hooker to Darwin, 4 November 1853, *CCD* 5:164.

7. Darwin to Charles Lyell, 15 February 1853, *CCD* 5:118. Cf. Darwin's comment on Louis Agassiz to Thomas Huxley, 23 April 1853, *CCD* 5:133.

8. Joseph Dalton Hooker to Asa Gray, 26 January 1854, in L. Huxley, *Life and Letters of Sir Joseph Dalton Hooker*, 1:475.

9. Darwin to Joseph Dalton Hooker, 26 March 1854, *CCD* 5:186.

10. Asa Gray to Joseph Dalton Hooker, 21 February 1854, in Dupree, *Asa Gray*, 228.

11. T. Huxley, "Review of *Vestiges*," 432, and Darwin to Thomas Huxley, 2 September 1854, *CCD* 5:212.

12. Darwin to Joseph Dalton Hooker, 7 September, *CCD* 5:215; Darwin to A. A. Gould, 9 September 1854, *CCD* 5:218.

13. Desmond and Moore, *Darwin*, 423; Stott, *Darwin and the Barnacle*, 249.

14. Darwin to J. S. Henslow, 28 March 1837, *CCD* 2:13; Darwin to John Lindley, 8 April 1843, *CCD* 2:355; Joseph Dalton Hooker to Darwin, 23 February–6 March, *CCD* 3:12; Hooker to Darwin, 12 December 1844, *CCD* 3:90; Darwin to Hooker, 10 December 1845, *CCD* 3:274.

15. Joseph Dalton Hooker to Darwin, 16 June 1847, *CCD* 4:49; Hooker, *Flora Novæ-Zelandiæ*, 1:xix; Darwin to Hooker, 7 April 1855, *CCD* 5:299.

16. Darwin to Hooker, 24 April 1855, *CCD* 5:319. On Darwin's more bizarre experiments, see two entries in his "experimental notebook," 23 September and 19 October 1856, DAR 157a:15; Darwin to Hooker, 19 October 1856, *CCD* 6:248, and 20 January 1857, *CCD* 6:324.

17. Darwin to Hooker, 1 June 1856, *CCD* 6:122.

18. Darwin to *Gardeners Chronicle*, 21 May 1855, *CCD* 5:331.

19. Darwin to Asa Gray, 3 June 1855, *CCD* 5:346; Gray to Darwin, 30 June 1855, *CCD* 5:362.

20. T. Huxley, "Contemporary Literature—Science," *Westminster Review* 62 (1854): 249–53.

21. Darwin, "Books Read" and "Books to Be Read" notebooks, DAR 128:13–14. The preface is both published as L. Agassiz, "Sketch of the Natural Provinces of the Animal World and Their Relation to the Different Types of Men," in *Edinburgh New Philosophical Journal* and Nott and Gliddon, *Types of Mankind*.

22. Darwin to Charles Lyell, 4 November 1855, *CCD* 5:492. See Bachman for his reviews of *Types*; replies from Nott are in *Charleston Medical Journal and Review* 9 (1854): 862–64 and 10 (1855): 753–67.

23. Di Gregorio, *Charles Darwin's Marginalia*, 604.

24. Agassiz, "Sketch," lxxv.

25. Desmond and Moore, *Darwin's Sacred Cause*, 407n84, must be credited with correcting an earlier mistranscription in Di Gregorio, *Charles Darwin's Marginalia*, 604.

26. The journals include *Living Age* 49 (14 June 1856): 688; "Progress of Infidelity," *Richmond Enquirer*, 29 April 1854, cited in Stanton, *Leopard's Spots*, 232n9; Squier, "Notices of New Books"; "Is Man One or Many?" *Putnam's Monthly Magazine* 4 (July 1854): 1–14; *New Englander and Yale Review* 12 (November 1854): 627–63; *Scientific American* 9 (1 July 1854): 333; "The Human Family," *Southern Quarterly Review* (1855): 116–74.

27. According to Desmond and Moore, "Agassiz helped in large part to trigger Darwin's annus mirabilis in 1854–5." *Darwin's Sacred Cause*, 228.

28. Nevins, *Ordeal of the Union*, 2:96.

29. Lincoln, "Speech at Peoria," 16 October 1854, *CW* 2:282.

30. Lincoln to J. W. Fell, 20 December 1859, *CW* 3:512; "Autobiography Written for John L. Scripps," *CW* 4:67. Matthew Pinsker, arguing toward a different conclusion, agrees that Lincoln depicted his "sudden" return to politics for "campaign purposes." "Not Always Such a Whig," 29.

31. Herndon and Weik, *Herndon's Life of Lincoln*, 295, 304.

32. W. L. Miller, *Lincoln's Virtues*, 240. Miller suggests that "you would be right both times" whether you said Lincoln "opportunistically, seized the opening" *or* responded to "a threat to the moral premises of the nation"; however, Miller repeatedly refers to 1854 as the beginning of Lincoln's "marked moral escalation," a "new level of public moral argument,"

a "new intellectual and moral level," and a "new and unwavering moral clarity." 230–40; 233; 327; 239; 233; 230.

33. Ibid., 250.

34. Ibid., 271–72, 246.

35. Lincoln, "Eulogy on Henry Clay," 6 July 1852, *CW* 2:130.

36. Stanton, *Leopard's Spots*, 52–53, 61–65, 77, 80; Lincoln, "Eulogy on Henry Clay," 6 July 1852, *CW* 2:130–31.

37. I disagree with Allen C. Guelzo's recent argument that Lincoln was *primarily* "aroused" by dismay that the Kansas-Nebraska Act embodied "the sacrifice of political integrity to expediency, . . . pragmatism . . . [and] mere majoritarianism." "Lincoln Aroused," 3.

38. W. L. Miller, *Lincoln's Virtues*, 272.

39. Until the Seventeenth Amendment was ratified in 1913, each state's two senators were elected by the state legislature rather than by direct popular vote.

40. *(Springfield) Illinois State Register*, 6 October 1854, quoted in Donald, *Lincoln*, 173.

9. The Politics of Race

1. Stanton, *Leopard's Spots*, 61–62.

2. Lurie, "Louis Agassiz and the Races of Man," 241n66.

3. Stephen A. Douglas, 30th Cong., 1st sess., *Congressional Globe*, 20 April 1848, app., 507.

4. Jaffa, *Crisis of the Divided House*, 54.

5. Van Evrie, introduction to *Negro's Place*, 3.

6. Van Evrie's *Negroes and Negro "Slavery"* (1853) is in a thirty-two-page format; the same title was used for his 339-page book in 1861.

7. Stanton, *Leopard's Spots*, vii; Van Evrie, introduction to *Negro's Place*, 3–4.

8. John H. Van Evrie to John C. Calhoun, 4 March 1846, in C. N. Wilson, *Papers of John C. Calhoun*, 22:660–62; Van Evrie, *Negroes and Negro "Slavery"* (1853), 2, 6, 29.

9. Van Evrie, introduction to *Negro's Place*, 3–4.

10. Jaffa, *Crisis of the Divided House*, 178.

11. Stephen A. Douglas, *Congressional Globe*, 33rd Cong., 1st sess., 279.

12. Ibid., app., 212–13. 214, 215, 219.

13. Ibid., app., 262–70, 310.

14. "Fragment on Slavery," 1 April 1854[?], *CW* 2:222.

15. "Speech at Winchester," 26 August 1854, *CW* 2:226–27; "Speech at Bloomington," 26 September 1854, *CW* 2:234–40.

16. "Speech at Bloomington," 26 September 1854, *CW* 2:237.

17. "Speech at Springfield," 4 October 1854, *CW* 2:240–47; W. L. Miller, *Lincoln's Virtues*, 251.

18. "Speech at Springfield," 4 October 1854, *CW* 2:242–45.

19. "Speech at Peoria," 16 October 1854, *CW* 2:247–83.

20. Ibid., 2:255–56.

21. See the summaries in Zilversmit, "Lincoln and the Problem of Race," 22–29.

22. "Speech at Peoria," 16 October 1854, *CW* 2:255–56.

23. Ibid., 2:262–65.

24. Ibid., 2:265–66.

25. "Speech at Chicago," 27 October 1854, *CW* 2:283–84.

26. Lincoln to Elihu B. Washburne, 9 February 1855, *CW* 2:306.

27. Lincoln to George Robertson, 15 August, *CW* 2:317–18; Lincoln to Joshua Speed, 24 August 1855, *CW* 2:320–23.

28. Some have suggested this 1855 statement indicated a change in Lincoln's views, because he expressed no horror when, shortly after the event, he described this encounter with the shackled slaves in a letter to Speed's sister. However, that nonpolitical letter was expressing thanks for recent hospitality, and Lincoln's point concerned irrational human behavior, contrasting his own recent depression with the slaves' surprising lack of gloom while being sold "down the river."

29. Herndon and Weik, *Herndon's Life of Lincoln*, 297–98. Cf. Herndon to Weik, 21 February 1891, in Hertz, *Hidden Lincoln*, 264–65.

30. "Speech at Kalamazoo," 27 August 1856, *CW* 2:364; "Speech at a Republican Banquet," Chicago, 10 December 1856, *CW* 2:385. The "Fragment: Notes for Speeches," *CW* 2:205, was tentatively dated "October 1, 1858?" but probably dates to 1856. Ironically, Fitzhugh eventually converted to polygenism after reading the expanded version (published in 1861) of the pamphlet Van Evrie had earlier pushed on politicians, including Stephen A. Douglas in 1853. In a ten-page review ("Black and White Races of Men"), Fitzhugh confessed, "Until we read Dr. Van Evrie's book, we had no idea that this assertion ['The negro is not a black-white-man'] carried with it, when proved, expanded, amplified, and applied, a new discovery and a new and important theory in physiological and sociological science."

31. "Speech at Bloomington," 29 May 1856, *CW* 2:341.

32. Perry, *Little Masterpieces*, 141.

33. Ibid., 161.

34. "Fragment on Slavery," 1 April 1854[?], *CW* 2:222–23.

35. William L. Miller regretted having evidence only that Lincoln had read Wayland's *Elements of Political Economy*, not *Elements of Moral Science*, but "Herndon's Auction List" includes both volumes and two others by Wayland. *Lincoln's Virtues*, 277–79.

36. "Speech at Edwardsville," 11 September 1858, *CW* 3:93–94.

10. Campaigning, 1856–58

1. Darwin to J. D. Dana, 29 September 1856, *CCD* 6:215. Darwin owned and cited information from Frémont's *Report of the Exploring Expedition to the Rocky Mountains* (1845). Desmond and Moore, *Darwin's Sacred Cause*, 268, 407n.

2. Darwin to J. D. Dana, 29 September 1856, *CCD* 6:215.

3. Charles Lyell to Charles Bunbury, 13 November 1854, in Bettany, *Life of Charles Darwin*, 74.

4. Wallace's article is "On the Law Which Has Regulated the Introduction of New Species."

5. L. G. Wilson, *Sir Charles Lyell's Scientific Journals*, xli.

6. Annotations quoted in ibid., editor's footnote 1; ibid., 54; Charles Lyell to Darwin, 1–2 May 1856, *CCD* 6:89.

7. Darwin to Charles Lyell, 5 July 1856, *CCD* 6:167.

8. Darwin to Hooker, 5 July 1856, *CCD* 6:166; Darwin to Hooker, 13 July 1856, *CCD* 6:178.

9. S. P. Woodward to Darwin 15 July 1856, *CCD* 6:183; Darwin to S. P. Woodward, 18 July 1856, *CCD* 6:189. Darwin wrote to him again—four years later—presenting a copy of *On the Origin of Species* even though he suspected (wrongly) that Woodward had already written a particularly unpleasant review of it. Darwin to Hooker, 21 November 1859, *CCD* 7:383.

10. J. D. Dana to Darwin, 8 September 1856, *CCD* 6:215; Dana to Darwin, 8 December 1856, *CCD*, 6:299.

11. Darwin to J. D. Dana, 29 September 1856, *CCD* 6:215; Darwin to Asa Gray, 5 September 1857, *CCD* 6:445.

12. Darwin to Asa Gray, 29 November 1857, *CCD* 6:491.

13. Darwin to Asa Gray, 1 January 1857, *CCD* 6:314. For variations on this jest, see Gray to Darwin, 16 February 1857, *CCD* 6:339; Darwin to Gray, [after 15 March] 1857, *CCD* 6:359; Darwin to Joseph Dalton Hooker, 23 March 1857, *CCD* 6:363, and 3 January 1860, *CCD* 6:8:6.

14. Darwin to Huxley, 26 September 1857, *CCD* 6:456.

15. L. Agassiz, preface, *Indigenous Races*, xiii–xv. This book was the first to use the terms *monogenism* and *polygenism*.

16. Darwin to Asa Gray, 23 January, *CCD* 9:17; Darwin to Charles Lyell, 2 February 1861, *CCD* 9:29.

17. Darwin to Louis Agassiz, 21 February 1858, *CCD* 7:26; Lurie, *Louis Agassiz*, 205; L. Agassiz, *Contributions*, 1:8.

18. Darwin to Thomas Huxley, 24 February 1858, *CCD* 7:33; Darwin to Asa Gray, 4 April [1858], *CCD* 7:62; Darwin to Huxley, 13 March 1859, *CCD* 7:261. Agassiz called transitional forms in the fossil record "prophetic types"; these would only become a reality "in a later period," providing "the most unexpected evidence that the plan of the whole creation had been maturely considered long before it was executed." *Contributions*, 1:177–78. Darwin's penciled annotations in his copy of Agassiz's *Contributions* include "botanists far better authority than zoologists" (5), "mere analogy" (117), "all rubbish" (121), and "all this discussion merely shows that no talent can really plainly define principles of classification" (170).

19. Desmond and Moore, *Darwin*, 467–70; Darwin to Joseph Dalton Hooker, 12 October 1858, *CCD* 7:168.

20. Asa Gray to Joseph Dalton Hooker, 13 July 1858, in Dupree, *Asa Gray*, 229, 248.

21. Dupree, *Asa Gray*, 252.

22. Asa Gray to John Torrey, 7 January 1859, in J. L. Gray, *Letters of Asa Gray*, 2:450; Lurie, *Louis Agassiz*, 238–39, 276; Dupree, *Asa Gray*, 256.

23. Asa Gray to John Torrey, 7 January 1859, in J. L. Gray, *Letters of Asa Gray*, 2:450; Gray quoted in "January 11, 1859, Monthly Meeting," 132; Asa Gray to D. C. Eaton, 12 January 1859, in Dupree, *Asa Gray*, 254; Darwin to Hooker, 3 May 1859, *CCD* 7:291.

24. Darwin to Wallace, 25 January 1859, *CCD* 7:240.

25. *(Springfield) Illinois State Register*, 12 June, 19 August, and 4 September 1856, in *CW* 2:344, 359, 368.

26. *Scott v. Sandford*, 60 US 393, 404–5, 410 (1857).

27. Jaffa, *New Birth of Freedom*, 219–20.

28. *Scott*, 60 US 393, 40.

29. Greeley and Cleveland, *Political Text-book for 1860*, 154–58; Johannsen, *Stephen A. Douglas*, 571.

30. Lincoln, "Speech at Springfield," 26 June 1857, *CW* 2:404.

31. Ibid., *CW* 2:405–7.

32. Darwin later cited the identical statistic, quoting Bachman, *Notice of the "Types of Mankind." Descent of Man*, 1:221.

33. Lincoln, "Speech at Springfield," 26 June 1857, *CW* 2:408.

34. *(Jacksonville, Illinois) Sentinel*, 16 October 1857, and *(Chicago) Daily Democratic Press*, 12 November 1857, in *CW* 2:454; "Fragment of a Speech," 28 December 1857, *CW* 2:448–54, editor's notes 6, 7.

35. Lincoln, "'A House Divided': Speech at Springfield," 16 June 1858, *CW* 2:462–68.

36. Stephen A. Douglas, speech, Chicago, 9 July 1858, in Johannsen, *Lincoln-Douglas Debates*, 33–35.

37. "Speech at Chicago," 10 July 1858, *CW* 2:484–502.

38. Lincoln, "Fragment on Pro-Slavery Theology," *CW* 3:204. Like several other fragments, Nicolay and Hay dated this to 1 October 1858 for no obvious compelling reason.

39. Stephen A. Douglas, speech, Springfield, Illinois, 17 July 1858, in Angle, *Created Equal?* 43–66; Lincoln, "Speech at Springfield," 17 July 1858, *CW* 2:504–21.

40. Lincoln to Gustave P. Koerner, 6 August 1858, *CW* 2:537.

41. Lincoln, "Speech at Lewistown," 17 August 1858, and "Fragment: Notes for Speeches," ca. 21 August 1858, *CW* 2:546–53.

42. Johannsen, *Lincoln-Douglas Debates,* 40, 42, 45–46.

43. Ibid., 52–53.

44. Ibid., 92–93.

45. Lincoln, "Speeches at Carlinville, Clinton, Bloomington, and Edwardsville," 31 August and 2, 4 and 11 September 1858, *CW* 3:77–96.

46. *New York Times,* 3 August 1858; Johannsen, *Lincoln-Douglas Debates,* 128, 163, 189–90.

47. Ibid., 212–13, 219–20.

48. Ibid. 262–63, 282.

49. Ibid., 304–8.

50. Lincoln, "Fragment on the Struggle against Slavery," *CW* 2:482. Robert Lincoln described this as "a note made in preparing for one of the speeches" in the campaign against Douglas in 1858, but the information is not in any known speeches.

11. Publications and Crocodiles, 1859–60

1. Darwin, *Descent of Man,* 1:1.

2. Probably three such letters from Lyell arrived before 15 October, though only one has been found: 3 October 1859, *CCD* 7:339. See Darwin to Hooker, 15 October 1859, *CCD* 7:349.

3. Darwin to Charles Lyell, 11 October 1859, *CCD* 7:343, and 25 October, 1859, *CCD* 7:357.

4. Darwin to Louis Agassiz, 11 November 1859, *CCD* 7:366.

5. John R. Leifchild, "Review of *On the Origin of Species,*" 659–60.

6. Darwin to Joseph Dalton Hooker, 22 November 1859, *CCD* 7:387.

7. Robert FitzRoy, *CCD* 7:413n3. The letter is not extant, but FitzRoy recounted a part of it.

8. Adam Sedgwick to Darwin, 24 November 1859, *CCD* 7:396.

9. William B. Carpenter, 4th ed., *Principles of Comparative Physiology* (1854) contains a section on hybridity, monsters, and the origin of variation (632–40). Darwin read it in May 1855 (DAR 128:12) and recommended it to Hooker in July 1855 (*CCD* 5:376). On Darwin's admiration, see Desmond and Moore, *Darwin's Sacred Cause,* 404n36. Carpenter's *Principles* also appeared in "Herndon's Auction List."

10. W. B. Carpenter, "Darwin and the Origin of Species" and "The Theory of Development in Nature"; Darwin to W. B. Carpenter 18 November, *CCD* 7:378, and 3 December 1859, *CCD* 7:412.

11. W. B. Carpenter, "Darwin and the Origin of Species," 193. Without mentioning Agassiz directly, Carpenter "was one immediatist who got Darwin's anti-Agassiz drift." Desmond and Moore, *Darwin's Sacred Cause,* 320.

12. Darwin to John Murray, 24 November 1859, *CCD* 7:395. The initial sale was especially rapid because Mudie's Circulating Library ordered five hundred copies. Mudie placed much larger orders for popular works, and this unusually large purchase of a scientific work undoubtedly brought it to a far wider audience. J. Browne, *Charles Darwin: The Power of Place,* 88–89.

13. N. Brooks, "Personal Recollections," 229.

14. Lincoln to Henry C. Whitney, 30 November, *CW* 3:343, and 25 December 1858, *CW* 3:347.

15. D. L. Wilson, "Unfinished Text," 70–85; James W. Sheahan to Lincoln, 21 January 1860, ALP; Lincoln to Sheahan, 24 January 1860, *CW* 3:515. On Douglas's reactions, see A. A. Couch to Douglas, 6 April 1959, and Douglas to Follett and Foster Company, 9 June 1860, in Johannsen, *Letters of Stephen A. Douglas*, 489–90, 491n3.

16. Harper, "New Light from a Lincoln Letter," 177–87. See Galloway to Lincoln, 1 September 1858, 23 July, 10 August, and 13 October 1859, ALP; Lincoln to Galloway, 28 July 1859, *CW* 3:394–95; W. T. Bascom to Lincoln, 1 and 30 September 1859, ALP; with the Ohio Republican Party to Lincoln, 7 December 1859, ALP.

17. Harper, "New Light from a Lincoln Letter," 183–84.

18. "Douglas at the South," *New York Times*, 6 December 1858, 2, reprinted from the Memphis *Eagle and Enquirer*, 30 November 1858.

19. "Speech of Senator Douglas at Columbus Ohio," *New York Times*, 8 September 1859, 1.

20. Lincoln, "Speech at Columbus," 16 September 1859, *CW* 3:423–25.

21. Lincoln, "Speech at Cincinnati," 17 September 1859, *CW* 3:445.

22. Lincoln, "Speech at Indianapolis," 19 September, 1859, *CW* 3:470; Lincoln, "Speech at Beloit," 1 October 1859, *CW* 3:483–84.

23. Lincoln, "Address at the Cooper Institute," 27 February 1860, *CW* 3:522–50.

24. Lincoln, "Speech at Hartford," 5 March 1860, *CW* 4:2–13.

12. More Debates and New Reviews

1. Asa Gray to Joseph Dalton Hooker, 16 May, 1859, and manuscript reminiscence, both in Lurie, *Louis Agassiz*, 260; Darwin to Hooker, 3 January 1860, *CCD* 8:6.

2. Lurie, *Louis Agassiz*, 237–38.

3. Asa Gray to Joseph Dalton Hooker, 5 January 1860, *CCD* 8:15.

4. Darwin to Asa Gray, 7 January 1860, *CCD* 8:23.

5. Darwin to Charles Lyell, 4 January 1860, *CCD* 8:15.

6. Asa Gray to Darwin, 10 January 1860, *CCD* 8:26; Gray to Francis Boott, 16 January 1860, in Dupree, *Asa Gray*, 270; Darwin to Hooker, 22 January 1860, *CCD* 8:45; Darwin to John Murray, 25 January 1860, *CCD* 8:50.

7. Asa Gray to Darwin, 23 January 1860, *CCD* 8:46.

8. Darwin to Asa Gray, [8–9 February] *CCD* 8:74, and 3 April 1860, *CCD* 8:140. Darwin told Wallace, "Agassiz sends me personal civil messages but incessantly attacks me." 18 May 1860, *CCD* 8:219.

9. A. Gray, "Review of Darwin's Theory," and Darwin to Asa Gray, 18 February 1860, *CCD* 8:91.

10. Francis Boott to Darwin, 29 February 1860, *CCD* 8:113.

11. Darwin to Asa Gray, 24 February, *CCD* 8:106; Darwin to Charles Lyell, 18 May 1860, *CCD* 8:217.

12. Hay, "Life in the White House," 36.

13. Hertz, *Hidden Lincoln*, 407. Cf. Herndon and Weik, *Herndon's Life of Lincoln*, 353–54, and William H. Herndon to John E. Remsburg, before 1893, in Remsburg, *Abraham Lincoln*, 135.

14. Hertz, *Hidden Lincoln*, 409.

15. Donald, *Lincoln's Herndon*, 59n37. Darwin possessed the same edition of the *Principles*, a gift from the author. The copy in Darwin's library is only lightly annotated, and four years after receiving the book, Darwin told Lyell and even Spencer himself that he had never read it. *CCD* 6:56n2, 8:28, 8:65.

16. Darwin to Alfred Russel Wallace, 18 May, *CCD* 8:219; Darwin to Joseph Dalton Hooker, 15 May 1860, *CCD* 8:210.

17. For a useful discussion of the conference, see J. Browne, *Charles Darwin: The Power of Place*, 118–25.

18. Draper's *Human Physiology* (1856) appears in "Herndon's Auction List."

19. J. Browne, *Charles Darwin: The Power of Place*, 122.

20. Darwin to J. S. Henslow, 16 July 1860, *CCD* 8:289.

21. Asa Gray to Joseph Dalton Hooker, 31 March 1860, in Lurie, *Louis Agassiz*, 295.

22. L. Agassiz, "Review of *On the Origin of Species*," passim.

23. A. Gray, "Darwin on the Origin of Species," 116.

24. Ibid., 111.

25. Ibid., 111.

26. Ibid., 113–15.

27. Josiah Nott to E. G. Squier, [22 August 1860], Squier Papers, Library of Congress, quoted in Stanton, *Leopard's Spots*, 183.

28. Darwin to Charles Lyell, 30 July, *CCD* 8:306, and 11 August 1860, *CCD* 8:319.

29. Darwin to Thomas Huxley, 8 August 1860, *CCD* 8:315; Darwin to Charles Lyell, 11 August 1860, *CCD* 8:317; Darwin to Asa Gray, 11 August 1860, *CCD* 8:319.

30. Charles Lyell to Darwin, 18 September 1860, *CCD* 8:366–69; Darwin to Lyell, 23 September 1860, *CCD* 8:377. See also letters exchanged on 25, 26, and 30 September and 3 October 1860, *CCD* 8:383–86, 398–401.

31. Darwin to J. S. Henslow, 28 September 1860, *CCD* 8:394; Darwin to Thomas Huxley, 1 and 18 November 1860, *CCD* 8:406; Charles Lyell to Darwin, after 3 October 1860, *CCD* 8:458; Huxley, "On the Zoological Relations of Man with the Lower Animals," 67.

32. "Scientific Conference . . . Fourth Day," *New York Times*, 8 August 1860, 4.

33. "Scientific Conference . . . Third Day," *New York Times*, 6 August 1860, 5. Probably "philosophy" should have read "philology."

34. "Progress and Prospects of Science," *New York Times*, 25 August 1860, 4.

35. Bruce, *Launching of Modern America Science*, 256–68.

36. "Scientific Conference . . . Fourth Day," *New York Times*, 8 August 1860, 4.

37. Johannsen, *Stephen A. Douglas*, 804.

38. Donald, *Lincoln*, 260.

13. Designers and Inventors

1. Lincoln to Alexander H. Stephens, 30 November 1860, *CW* 4:146.

2. Lincoln to William H. Herndon, 2 February 1848, *CW* 1:448; Johannsen, *Lincoln-Douglas Debates*, 270.

3. "An Influential Voice for the Union: Speech of Hon A. H. Stephens . . . November 14, 1860," *New York Times*, 22 November 1860, 1.

4. "Southern Politics. Speech of the Hon. A. H. Stephens, of Georgia," *New York Times*, 18 July 1859, 2.

5. Van Evrie, introduction to *Negro's Place*, 3–4.

6. Alexander H. Stephens to Lincoln, 14 December 1860, ALP.

7. Lincoln to Stephens, 22 December 1860, *CW* 4:160–61.

8. Avary, *Recollections of Alexander H. Stephens*, 60.

9. Lincoln, "Fragment on the Constitution and the Union," [ca. January 1861], *CW* 4:168–69.

10. Darwin to J. S. Henslow, 10 November 1860, *CCD* 8:470; Darwin to Charles Lyell, 20 November 1860, *CCD* 8:479; Darwin to Lyell, 12 April 1861, *CCD* 9:91.

11. Darwin to Charles Lyell, 20 November 1860, *CCD* 8:479; Darwin to Leonard Horner, 20 March 1861, *CCD* 9:62; Darwin to Quatrefages de Bréau, 25 April 1861, *CCD* 9:102.

12. Darwin to Asa Gray, 26 November 1860, *CCD* 8:496, and 17 February 1861, *CCD* 9:29.

13. Emma Darwin to Darwin, [June 1861], *CCD* 9:155; Darwin to Asa Gray, 5 June 1861, *CCD* 9:162.

14. Darwin to Asa Gray, 26 November 1860, *CCD* 8:496.

15. Olmsted, *Journey in the Seaboard Slave States* and *Journey through Texas*, DAR 128:23, 25. The former (declared "excellent" by Darwin) also graced a bookshelf in Lincoln's law office. Temple, "Herndon on Lincoln," 40.

16. Darwin to Hooker, 15 January 1861, *CCD* 9:8, and 4 February 1861, *CCD* 9:20.

17. Litchfield, *Emma Darwin, A Century of Family Letters*, 2:169; F. Darwin, *Life and Letters*, 3:200.

18. Darwin to Asa Gray, 17 February 1861, *CCD* 9:29; Henry Ravenel to Gray, 11 December 1860, in Dupree, *Asa Gray*, 310.

19. Lincoln, "Farewell Address at Springfield," 11 February 1861, *CW* 4:191.

20. Lincoln, "First Inaugural Address," 4 March 1861, *CW* 4:262–71.

21. Stephens, 21 March 1861, in Cleveland, *Alexander H. Stephens, in Public and Private*, 717–29.

22. "The President Elect's Mode of Buoying Vessels. Patented May 22, 1849," *Scientific American*, 1 December 1860, 356.

23. Lincoln to Lyman Trumbull, 10 December 1860, *CW* 4:149–50.

24. Alexander H. Stephens, speech before Virginia legislature, 23 April 1861, in Cleveland, *Alexander H. Stephens, in Public and Private*, 742.

25. Nicolay and Hay, *Abraham Lincoln*, 4:79; Donald, *Lincoln*, 305.

26. Duff, *A. Lincoln*, 158–59.

27. Duff, *A. Lincoln*, 322–24; Lincoln to Peter Watson, 23 July 1855, *CW* 2:314–15.

28. Bates, *Lincoln in the Telegraph Office*, 4.

29. Lincoln, "Address to the Wisconsin State Agricultural Society," 30 September 1859, *CW* 3:471–82; Briggs, *Lincoln's Speeches Reconsidered*, 221–36.

30. Bruce, *Lincoln and the Tools of War*, 8–10.

31. Wells, "Notes by the Editor on the Progress of Science during the Year 1854," 23–24; Wells, "Improvements in the Fabrication of Arms at the United States Armories," 92.

32. Bruce, *Lincoln and the Tools of War*, 40–41; Sickles, "Military Affairs in New York: 1861–1865," 2:21.

33. Bruce, *Lincoln and the Tools of War*, 75–76. On Lincoln's dealings with inventors, see Hay, "Life in the White House," 34.

34. "Memorandum: Operation of the Chicopee Works," ca. 25 April 1861, *CW* 4:343; Extracts from Dahlgren Diary, John G. Nicolay Papers; Bruce, *Lincoln and the Tools of War*, 119–20, 139–41, 146; "Endorsement: John A. Dahlgren to Lincoln," 10 June 1861, *CW* 4:399; Hay, "Life in the White House," 34.

35. Bruce, *Lincoln and the Tools of War*, 86–88.

36. Ibid., 103, 114–15, 148.

37. Ibid., 103–4; Stoddard, *Abraham Lincoln and Andrew Johnson*, 223–24; Stoddard, *Inside the White House*, 41–44.

38. Hay, "Life in the White House," 34.

39. Bruce, *Lincoln and the Tools of War*, 142–43.

40. Stoddard, *Inside the White House*, 20, 28–29, 39.

41. Hay, "Life in the White House," 34–35.

42. Perret, *Lincoln's War*, 150.

43. Stephen, "Times" *on the American War*, 16; Brogan, Times *Reports the American Civil War*, xiv.

44. Russell, *My Diary North and South*, 36–39.

45. William Howard Russell to Mary Lincoln, 28 March 1861, ALP.

46. Russell, *My Diary North and South*, 136; Monaghan, *Diplomat in Carpet Slippers*, 83.

47. *(London) Times*, 30 May 1861, in Russell, *My Diary North and South*, 265.

48. Joseph Dalton Hooker to Darwin, 19 January 1862, *CCD* 10:28.

49. Darwin to Asa Gray, 5 June 1861, *CCD* 9:162.

50. Asa Gray to Joseph Dalton Hooker, 10 June, and Hooker to Gray, 5 July 1861, in Dupree, *Asa Gray*, 308, 312.

51. Asa Gray to George Engelmann, 25 May 1861, in J. L. Gray, *Letters of Asa Gray*, 2:466–67.

52. Lurie, *Louis Agassiz*, 305.

53. Ibid., 318; Bruce, *Launching of Modern American Science*, 286.

54. Darwin to Asa Gray, 21 July 1861, *CCD* 9:213.

55. Brogan, Times *Reports the American Civil War*, xviii.

56. Lincoln, "Message to Congress in Special Session," 4 July 1861, *CW* 4:421–41.

57. Brogan, Times *Reports the American Civil War*, xv.

14. Inventions for a Long War

1. Lincoln, "Note to General Scott," 25 July 1861, *CW* 4:460; Perret, *Lincoln's War*, 152, and Bruce, *Lincoln and the Tools of War*, 85–88.

2. Brutus de Villeroi to Lincoln, 4 September 1861; Villeroi to Gideon Welles, 26 September 1861; Martin Thomas to Joseph Smith, 5 March 1863, RG71, Misc. Letters Sent and Recd, Bureau of Yards and Docks 1861–63, National Archives and Records Administration; Bruce, *Lincoln and the Tools of War*, 177.

3. "Death of Major Hunt," *New York Times*, 2 October 1863.

4. Darwin to Charles Lyell 14 August 1863, *CCD* 11:590. Hunt's article is "On the Origin, Growth, Substructure and Chronology of the Florida Reef."

5. Bruce, *Lincoln and the Tools of War*, 138.

6. Ibid., 128–29; Lincoln to Simon Cameron, 5 September 1861 *CW* 4:509; "Memorandum: Interview with Philip L. Fox," 7 September 1861, *CW* 4:512–13; Perret, *Lincoln's War*, 146, 314.

7. Dahlgren diary, 15 September 1861, Nicolay Papers.

8. "Sharpshooters," *New York Times*, 21 September 1861.

9. Bruce, *Lincoln and the Tools of War*, 110–13, 285; Perret, *Lincoln's War*, 152, 277.

10. *New York Herald*, 6 and 29 October 1861; Bruce, *Lincoln and the Tools of War*, 52–53, 95–96, 108, 122; Lincoln to George McClellan, 26 October 1861, *CW* 5:4–5.

11. Bruce, *Lincoln and the Tools of War*, 116, 123, 129–30; Lincoln to James W. Ripley, 19 December 1861, *CW* 5:75–76.

12. Perret, *Lincoln's War*, 146.

13. McPherson, *Tried by War*, 191; Bruce, *Lincoln and the Tools of War*, 117, 225.

14. Reingold, "Science in the Civil War," 308.

15. F. F. Browne, *Every-day Life of Abraham Lincoln*, 496.

16. Stephen R. Mallory to Chairman of the House Committee on Naval Affairs, 8 May 1861, *Official Records of the Union and Confederate Navies in the War of the Rebellion*, ser. 2, 1:740–43; Niven, *Gideon Welles*, 364.

17. Bruce, *Lincoln and the Tools of War*, 171.

18. "New War Steamers," *Scientific American*, 12 January 1861, 25.

19. "Revolution in Naval Warfare. Shot-Proof Iron Steamships," *Harper's Weekly*, 9 February 1861, 92–93; John A. Dahlgren to James Grimes, 11 February 1861, Dahlgren Papers.

20. Stoddard, *Inside the White House in War Times*, 38–39.

21. Milligan, "From Theory to Application," 126–32.

22. James B. Eads to Lincoln, 19 September 1863, ALP.

23. Niven, *Gideon Welles*, 365.

24. Roberts, "Name of Ericsson," 827; Cornelius S. Bushnell to Gideon Welles, 2 March 1877, in Johnson and Buel, *Battles and Leaders of the Civil War*, 1:748; Bushnell to John Winslow and John Griswold, 26 August 1861, MS335, USS *Monitor* Design and Construction Collection.

25. John Ericsson to Lincoln, 29 August 1861, Ericsson Papers.

26. Cornelius S. Bushnell to Gideon Welles, 2 March 1877, in Johnson and Buel, *Battles and Leaders of the Civil War*, 1:748.

27. Ibid.

28. Roberts, "'Name of Ericsson,'" 823–43.

29. Asa Gray to Darwin, 2 September 1861, *CCD* 9:240.

30. Darwin to Gray, 17 September 1861, *CCD* 9:266.

31. Morton and Spinelli, *Beaumarchais and the American Revolution*, 33.

32. Amid the considerable literature, one good recent account is Mahin, *One War at a Time*, 44–57.

33. Lincoln to Gideon Welles, 18 March 1861, *CW* 4:293.

34. Lord Richard Lyons to Lord John Russell, 26 March 1861, T. W. L. Newton, *Lord Lyons*, 1:31; Lyons to Russell, 9 and 15 April 1861, Foreign Office (UK), FO 5/762–141, 311–19; 5/762–146, 369–80. On the technical considerations, see Anderson, "1861," 190–95, basing his account on Beale, *Diary of Gideon Welles*, 1:174, 414; Welles, *Lincoln and Seward*, 122–23. See Ferris, "Lincoln and Seward in Civil War Diplomacy," 21–42, for an important corrective on their collaboration.

35. Welles, *Lincoln and Seward*, 124.

36. Lincoln, "Proclamation of a Blockade," 19 April 1861, *CW* 4:338–39.

37. Fehrenbacher and Fehrenbacher, *Recollected Words of Abraham Lincoln*, 423.

38. Anderson, "1861," 192.

39. Owsley, *King Cotton Diplomacy*, 31.

15. The *Trent* Affair: A Chemistry Problem

1. Asa Gray to Darwin, 9 November 1861, *CCD* 9:335; Darwin to Gray, 11 December 1861, *CCD* 9:368.

2. For the *Trent* affair generally, see E. D. Adams, *Great Britain and the American Civil War*, 1:203–42, Ferris, *Trent Affair*, and Mahin, *One War at a Time*, 58–82.

3. Russell, *My Diary North and South*, 576.

4. Henry Adams to Charles Francis Adams Jr., 13 December 1861, in Levenson, Samuels, Vandersee, and Winner, *Letters of Henry Adams, 1858–1892*, 1:265–66.

5. Darwin to Asa Gray, 11 December 1861, *CCD* 9:368.

6. Cohen, "Charles Sumner and the Trent Affair," 205–19; Russell, *My Diary North and South*, 575.

7. Gurowski, *Diary*, 1:135; Lossing, *Pictorial History of the Civil War*, 2:156; Coffey, "Lincoln and the Cabinet," 201; Bates, *Lincoln in the Telegraph Office*, 97–98.

8. C. F. Adams Jr., "Trent Affair," 546–49, 554.

9. Extracts, Dahlgren diary, Nicolay Papers; M. V. Dahlgren, *Memoir of John A. Dahlgren*, 333.

10. Chandler, "Du Pont, Dahlgren, and the Civil War Nitre Shortage," 144; Hancock and Wilkinson, "'Devil to Pay!'" 21.

11. Niven, *Gideon Welles*, 354.

12. Wilkinson, *Lammot du Pont and the American Explosives Industry*, 76.

13. Chandler, "Du Pont, Dahlgren, and the Civil War Nitre Shortage," 144, and Wilkinson, "'Devil to Pay!'" 77.

14. "Wilkes Banquet," *New York Times*, 29 November 1861.

15. Monaghan, *Diplomat in Carpet Slippers*, 171. Welles's account was anti-Seward, but if Welles was correct that at the beginning, while Lincoln "expressed his doubts of the legality of the capture, . . . nearly every member of the administration, like Mr. Seward, rejoiced in the capture," then the lack of favorable pronouncements by *any* cabinet members in the first two weeks after Wilkes's arrival suggests Lincoln had required restraint during that period. *Lincoln and Seward*, 184–88. On 27 November 1861, Seward had already written confidentially in a private letter to Ambassador Adams in London that Wilkes's action had been unauthorized. NA M77.77, National Archives Microfilm Publications.

16. I disagree with Niven, who suggested that "apparently [Welles] did not consult Lincoln" when drafting the letter, which later "gave Seward and Lincoln the clue they needed" for finding a way through the dilemma. *Gideon Welles*, 445–46.

17. F. B. Carpenter, *Six Months at the White House*, 18; *Congressional Globe*, 37th Cong., 2nd sess., 2 December 1861, 5; 4 December 1861, 13; 19 February 1862, 874.

18. *Times* (London), "Effect on the London Stock Exchange," repr., *New York Times*, 13 December 1861.

19. Burlingame attached relatively little importance to the niter problem: "Lincoln may have also feared a gunpowder shortage, if Britain maintained its embargo of saltpeter, and a bombardment of American ports by ironclads invulnerable to America's antiquated shore batteries." *Abraham Lincoln*, 2:227.

20. Chandler, "Du Pont, Dahlgren, and the Civil War Nitre Shortage," 144n18, and 145n21, citing Henry du Pont to Seward, 13 December 1861 in State Department, Miscellaneous Letters, December 1861, "giving news of Lammot's situation."

21. "Preparations of England for War," *New York Times*, 16 December 1861.

22. Pease and Randall, *Diary of Orville Hickman Browning*, 15 December 1861, 1:515.

23. Russell, *My Diary North and South*, 587.

24. Lord Lyons to Lord Russell, 19 December 1861, *Official Records of the Union and Confederate Armies*, ser. 2, 2:1135.

25. Burlingame, *Abraham Lincoln*, 2:224, citing extract of Dahlgren diary, 18 December 1861, John G. Nicolay Papers; John Van Evrie's Copperhead journal, *Old Guard*, 1 July 1863, 167, calling Forney "Lincoln's Dog."

26. Bruce, *Tools of War*, 147.

27. John A. Dahlgren to William H. Seward, 26 December 1861, ALP.

28. Russell, *My Diary North and South*, 588.

29. Pease and Randall, *Diary of Orville Hickman Browning*, 1:516–17.

30. "Draft of a Dispatch in Reply to Lord John Russell, [December 10? 1861]," *CW* 5:62–64. The tentative dating is slightly early.

31. Charles Sumner to Richard Cobden, 31 December 1861, in Pierce, *Memoir and Letters of Charles Sumner*, 4:60; Dawes, *Charles Sumner*, 165.

32. Charles Sumner to John Bright, 23 and 30 December 1861, and Sumner to Francis Lieber, 24 December 1861, in Pierce, *Memoir and Letters of Charles Sumner*, 4:57–59.

33. Lord Lyons to Lord Russell, 23 December 1861, in T. W. L. Newton, *Lord Lyons*, 1:69–70.

34. E. D. Adams, *Great Britain and the American Civil War*, 1:231.

35. F. W. Seward, *Reminiscences of a War-Time Statesman and Diplomat*, 189–90.

36. Beale, *Diary of Gideon Welles*, 14 October 1862, 1:171; Beale, *Diary of Edward Bates*, 25 December 1861 (the next entry dated 28 December 1861), 211–17; Welles, *Lincoln and Seward*, 188–89.

37. Cohen argues that Sumner "proved helpful at the Cabinet meeting in convincing the President and the other secretaries. It is not improbable that Seward wanted him at the meeting for that purpose." But Lincoln had been continuously briefed by Sumner, so it was presumably other cabinet members who needed convincing. "Charles Sumner and the Trent Affair," 212.

38. Charles Sumner to Francis Lieber, 25 December 1861, Sumner Papers, in Cohen, "Charles Sumner and the Trent Affair," 212; Pease and Randall, *Diary of Orville Hickman Browning*, 25 December 1861, 1:518.

39. Diary of Frances Adelaide Seward, 26 December 1861, William H. Seward Papers.

40. Donald, *Inside Lincoln's Cabinet*, 53. Chase, or the copyist who transcribed the first five chapters, labeled the entry "Dec. 25, Wednesday. The 'Trent' Affair. Remarks of Secretary Chase at the Cabinet meeting." But since the next entry is for 1 January , the previous one might have been written any time that week to describe more than one day's events.

41. Beale, *Diary of Edward Bates*, 25 December 1861, 216.

42. These recent works include Chandler, "Du Pont, Dahlgren, and the Civil War Nitre Shortage"; Hancock and Wilkinson, "'Devil to Pay!'" and Wilkinson, *Lammot du Pont and the American Explosives Industry*.

43. Wilkinson, *Lammot du Pont*, 79–81; du Pont, *E. I. du Pont de Nemours and Company*, 90–91; Hancock and Wilkinson, "'Devil to Pay!'" 26–27; Chandler, "Du Pont, Dahlgren, and the Civil War Nitre Shortage," 145.

44. Chandler, "Du Pont, Dahlgren, and the Civil War Nitre Shortage," 145; Hancock and Wilkinson, "'Devil to Pay!'" 32; Wilkinson, *Lammot du Pont*, 83–86.

45. Mrs. Samuel Francis du Pont to Samuel Francis du Pont (29 April 1862), box 61, group 9, Winterthur Manuscripts. On 27 December, after taking Lincoln on a trip on the Potomac, Dahlgren recorded:, "The President looks grave and absorbed, and a little the worse for cares." Dahlgren diary, Nicolay Papers.

46. Wilkinson, *Lammot du Pont*, 86; E. D. Adams, *Great Britain and the American Civil War*, 1:232; William H. Seward to Lord Lyons, 26 December 1861, *Official Records of the Union and Confederate Armies*, ser. 2, 2:1145–54; *State Department, Great Britain, Instructions*, letter no. 149, William H. Seward to C. F. Adams, 26 December 1861, cited in Chandler, "Du Pont, Dahlgren, and the Civil War Nitre Shortage," 145n25.

47. Du Pont, *E. I. du Pont de Nemours and Company*, 90–91; Chandler, "Du Pont, Dahlgren, and the Civil War Nitre Shortage," 146.

48. Bruce, *Lincoln and the Tools of War*, 116.

49. Schneller, *Quest for Glory*, 189; Lincoln to John P. Hale, 28 January 1862, *CW* 5:112–13.

50. Chandler, "Du Pont, Dahlgren, and the Civil War Nitre Shortage," 146–49; Bureau of Ordnance to Messrs. du Pont, 1 August 1862, Bureau of Ordnance Transcripts, Lincoln Collection, Abraham Lincoln Presidential Library, 1–2, quoted in Schwartz, "'About New Powder,'" 120n3.

51. Bruce, *Lincoln an d the Tools of War*, 209–11.

52. Schwartz, "'About New Powder,'" 121.

53. Lincoln to John A. Dahlgren, in Schwartz, "'About New Powder,'" 119; Lincoln to David P. Holloway, 20 August 1862, *CW* 5:385. The note Lincoln gave Diller to take to Dahlgren bears no date but was presumably written shortly before the 20 August note to Holloway.

54. Lincoln to Gideon Welles, 21 August 1862, in Basler and Basler, *Collected Works of Abraham Lincoln: Second Supplement*, 57–58. The same letter, published earlier in *CW* 5:354, was misdated there as 2 August 1862.

55. Isaac R. Diller to Lincoln, 10 September 1862, ALP.

56. Isaac R. Diller and Lincoln, "Letters and Memoranda on the Uses of Isaac Diller's

Powder," November–December 1862–63, ALP; Bruce, *Lincoln and the Tools of War*, 213–14; M. V. Dahlgren, *Memoir of John A. Dahlgren*, 383.

57. Beale, *Diary of Gideon Welles*, 22 February 1863, 1:239–40.

58. Lincoln to Isaac Newton, 4 April 1863, *CW* 6:342; John Nicolay to John A. Dahlgren, 14 May 1863, *CW* 8:516; Lincoln to James W. Ripley, 21 May 1863, *CW* 8:516; Lincoln to Edwin M. Stanton and Gideon Welles, 21 July 1863, *CW* 6:342.

59. Bruce, *Lincoln and the Tools of War*, 225–26.

60. Lincoln to Isaac R. Diller, 27 October 1863, in Basler and Basler, *Collected Works of Abraham Lincoln: Second Supplement*, 207.

61. Ibid., 270; Chandler, "Du Pont, Dahlgren, and the Civil War Nitre Shortage," 147–49.

16. Delegation and Control

1. Asa Gray to Darwin, 31 December 1861, *CCD* 9:383.

2. Darwin to Joseph Dalton Hooker, 16 January 1862, *CCD* 10:25.

3. Joseph Dalton Hooker to Darwin, 19 January 1862, *CCD* 10:28; Darwin to Asa Gray, 22 January 1862, *CCD* 10:40.

4. Asa Gray to Darwin, 18 February 1862, *CCD* 10:86; Darwin to Gray, 15 March 1862, *CCD* 10:117; Gray to Darwin, 31 March 1862, *CCD* 10:140.

5. John Murray to Darwin, 30 January 1862, *CCD* 10:59.

6. Thomas Huxley to Henrietta Huxley, 22 March 1861, in L. Huxley, *Life and Letters of Thomas Henry Huxley*, 1:190.

7. Owen, "Gorilla and the Negro," 395–96; T. Huxley, "Man and the Apes," *Athenaeum* 1744 (30 March 1861): 433; and 1746 (13 April 1861): 498.

8. Darwin to Thomas Huxley, 1 April 1861, *CCD* 9:77; Darwin to Hooker, 23 April 1861, *CCD* 9:98.

9. Thomas Huxley to Darwin, 13 January 1862, *CCD* 10:15; Darwin to Gray, 23 June–4 July 1862, *CCD* 10:330.

10. Darwin to Charles Kingsley, 6 February 1862, *CCD* 10:71.

11. T. Huxley, "A Lecture on the Fossil Remains of Man," *Lancet* (15 February 1862): 166–67, later chapter 3 in T. Huxley, *Evidence as to Man's Place in Nature*, 119–59; Darwin to Huxley, 30 April 1862, *CCD* 10:176; Huxley to Darwin, 6 May 1862, *CCD* 10:183.

12. Joseph Dalton Hooker to Darwin, 20 August 1862, *CCD* 10:368; Darwin to Hooker, 22 August 1862, *CCD* 10:376; Darwin to Charles Lyell, 22 August 1862, *CCD* 10:395.

13. Darwin to Asa Gray, 21 April 1862, *CCD* 10:162.

14. Nicolay and Hay, *Abraham Lincoln*, 5:155–56.

15. Borrowers' Ledger, 1861–63, 114, Archives, Library of Congress, quoted in Miers, *Lincoln Day by Day*, 3:88; Perret, *Lincoln's War*, 183, 186.

16. Henry Wise quoted in Bruce, *Lincoln and the Tools of War*, 161–63.

17. Perret, *Lincoln's War*, 123, McPherson, *Tried by War*, 69–71.

18. Lincoln to Don C. Buell, 13 January 1862, *CW* 5:98.

19. McPherson, *Tried by War*, 73–74.

20. Ibid., 75–77.

21. Donald, *Lincoln*, 350–51.

22. Darwin to Asa Gray, 10–20 June 1862, *CCD* 10:239.

23. Asa Gray to Darwin, 29 July 1862, *CCD* 10:344; Darwin to Gray, 21 August 1862, *CCD* 10:372.

24. Keyes, *Fifty Years' Observation of Men and Events*, 438, 486–87.

25. Darwin to Asa Gray, 21 Apr. 1862, *CCD* 10:162.

26. Desmond and Moore, *Darwin's Sacred Cause*, 45, 50, 383n3.

17. The Rationality of Colonization

1. Vorenberg, "Abraham Lincoln and the Politics of Black Colonization," 22–25, 43; Boritt, "Did He Dream of a Lily-White America?" 8, 15.

2. Vorenberg, "Abraham Lincoln and the Politics of Black Colonization," 43; Boritt, "Did He Dream of a Lily-White America?" 7, 10–11, 13–14, 16–17. Similar phrases can be found in most studies of colonization, but Boritt's essay offers a wide array, including "uncharacteristic sloppiness in his thought," "unconscious avoidance of the realities," "failed to think in terms of 'dollars and cents,'" "the illusion of a future lily-white America," "the fantasy voyage," "unrealistic design," "highly unrealistic solution," "refusal to face the facts," "detour from reality," and "Lincoln's delusion."

3. Donald, *Lincoln*, 166–67.

4. This "heretical" view was already developed in an important essay by W. Freehling, "'Absurd' Issues and the Causes of the Civil War: Colonization as a Test Case."

5. Goodman, *Of One Blood*, 20–21, 37–44, 77–78, 85, 103–7; Bilotta, *Race and the Rise of the Republican Party*, 274–76.

6. Vorenberg, "Abraham Lincoln and the Politics of Black Colonization," 5; Donald, *Lincoln*, 165; Boritt, "Did He Dream of a Lily-White America?" 2; Lincoln, "Eulogy on Henry Clay," 6 July 1852, *CW* 2:121–32.

7. Johnson, *Charles Reynolds Matheny 1786–1839*, 30–33; Angle, *Here I Have Lived*, 52, 78; *Sangamo Journal* (Springfield, IL), 19 April and 18 October 1839.

8. *Sangamo Journal* (Springfield, IL), 23 January 1845; "Items of Intelligence," 94–95.

9. "First Annual Report of the Illinois State Colonization Society; December 8, 1845," 73–80; John Miller, "Evidence before the English Parliament in Favor of Liberia," 83.

10. Miers, *Lincoln Day-by-Day*, 1:113–16.

11. Hart, "Springfield's African Americans as a Part of the Lincoln Community," 48–49, 52.

12. *Sangamo Journal* (Springfield, IL), 18 February 1858.

13. *(Springfield) Illinois State Journal*, 30 August 1853, and 14 January 1854; Temple, *Abraham Lincoln*, 47.

14. Lincoln, "Speech at Peoria," 16 October 1854, *CW* 2:255–56.

15. Lincoln, "Outline for Speech to the Colonization Society, [4 January 1855?]," *CW* 2:298–301.

16. This estimate moderately updated the 1850 census count of 3.04 million.

17. Freehling, "'Absurd' Issues and the Causes of the Civil War," 148.

18. Lincoln, "Outline for Speech to the Colonization Society," [4 January 1855?], *CW* 2:299.

19. Freehling, "'Absurd' Issues and the Causes of the Civil War," 149, 152, 155.

20. Ibid., 148; Staudenraus, *African Colonization Movement*, 251.

21. Some estimates of the numbers of blacks who left (many still enslaved) during or after the Revolution run as high as a hundred thousand, although Quarles suggests fourteen thousand, and Pybus more recently suggests between eight thousand and ten thousand. *Negro in the American Revolution*, 172; "Jefferson's Faulty Math," 243–64.

22. Freehling, "'Absurd' Issues and the Causes of the Civil War," 155.

23. *(Springfield) Illinois State Journal*, 28 January 1857.

24. Lincoln, "Speech at Springfield," 26 June 1857, *CW* 2:409.

25. Ambrose W. Thompson to Lincoln, 11 April 1861, ALP; Scheips, "Buchanan and the Chiriqui Naval Station Sites." Welles recorded on 26 September 1862 in his diary that "as early as May, 1861, a great pressure was made upon me to enter into a coal contract with this [Chiriqui] company." Beale, *Diary of Gideon Welles*, 1:150.

26. Ambrose W. Thompson, "Chiriqui Improvement Co., (Pamphlet)," ALP. This is archived with a memorandum and Edwards's submission (both discussed below), and only the last can rightly be dated 9 August 1861.

27. Quarles, *Lincoln and the Negro*, 69.

28. Edwards lobbied mutual friends to help him obtain a post from Lincoln. David Davis to Lincoln, 26 July 1861, ALP; Orville Browning to Ninian Edwards, 8 August 1861, ALP. The penciled dating of 8 August 1861 for the latter is wrong.

29. Ninian Edwards to Lincoln, 9 August 1861, ALP.

30. Ambrose W. Thompson to Gideon Welles, 8 August 1861, ALP.

31. Scheips, "Buchanan and the Chiriqui Naval Station Sites," 77–79. "Evans' abilities, ethics and financial affairs have been questioned by historians, who have accused him of engaging in at least one geological hoax [apart from the Chiriqui coal affair]." Rothenberg, Dorman, and Millikan, *Papers of Joseph Henry*, 10:281n.

32. "Chiriqui Improvement Co. (Memorandum on proposed contract)," undated (archived as 9 August 1861 to match Edwards's report), ALP.

33. Gideon Welles to Lincoln, 29 August 1861, RG 56, series AB, 1861, Letters from Executive Officers, II, 5a, General Records, Treasury Department, National Archives; Lincoln to Caleb Smith, 24 October 1861, *CW* 5:2–3.

34. Frank Blair Sr. to Lincoln, 16 November 1862, ALP.

35. Ibid.; "Printed Memoranda Regarding Chiriqui Improvement Co.; with Endorsement by Francis P. Blair Sr.," ALP.

36. Francis P. Blair Sr. to Lincoln, 16 November 1861; Ambrose W. Thompson to Francis P. Blair Sr., 17 and 18 November 1861; Francis P. Blair Jr. to Montgomery Blair (archived as "Dec. 1861"), ALP.

37. (Draft of a Letter for Lincoln to Send To Caleb B. Smith Regarding the Chiriqui Improvement Co.), October 1861, *CW* 4:561–62; Francis P. Blair Sr. to Gideon Welles, December 1861 (Draft of a Letter for Lincoln to Send to Welles Regarding the Chiriqui Improvement Co.); Francis P. Blair Sr. to Simon Cameron, December 1861; (Draft of a Letter for Lincoln to Send to Cameron Regarding the Chiriqui Improvement Co.), December 1861, ALP.

38. Salmon P. Chase to Lincoln, 12 November 1861, ALP; Chase to Lincoln, 27 November 1861, ALP.

39. Lincoln, "Annual Message to Congress," 3 December 1861, *CW* 5:48. Vorenberg suggests that Lincoln's inclusion of ordinary freedmen was a call "for a full program of racial separation," but since the scheme was "voluntary," it would be less "full" than a program of deportation. "Abraham Lincoln and the Politics of Black Colonization," 27.

40. Lincoln, "Message to Congress," 16 April 1862, *CW* 5:192.

41. Two months earlier, Lincoln—notorious for granting pardons and commuting sentences—had rejected pleas to commute the death sentence of a slaver trader, the first time since the relevant law was passed forty years earlier that anyone had been executed for its violation.

42. Schoonover, "Misconstrued Mission," 607–20; Scheips, "Lincoln and the Chiriqui Colonization Project," 424–26; "Chiriqui Improvement Co.: Report on Company Organization and Mission," 1862, ALP.

43. "Report on the Transportation, Settlement, and Colonization of Persons of the African Race," Senate Executive Document No. 55, 39th Cong., 1st sess., 9 May 1862, quoted in Scheips, "Lincoln and the Chiriqui Colonization Project," 426.

44. Caleb Smith to Lincoln, 5 May 1862, ALP; Lincoln to William H. Seward, 3 October 1861, *CW* 4:548; James Mitchell to Lincoln (printed letter), 18 May 1862, ALP.

45. Marcelino Hurtado [?] to Lincoln, 4 June, ALP; William H. Seward to Lincoln, 5 June 1862, ALP.

46. Joseph Henry to Alexander Bache, 21 August 1862, and Joseph Henry to J. Peter Lesley, 28 May 1862, in Rothenberg, Dorman, and Millikan, *Papers of Joseph Henry*, 10:279, 268.

47. Joseph Henry to Alexander Bache, 21 August 1862, in Rothenberg, Dorman, and Millikan, *Papers of Joseph Henry*, 10:279.

48. Nicolay and Hay, *Abraham Lincoln*, 6:356–57.

49. John P. Usher to Lincoln, 2 August 1862, ALP.

18. Colonization and Emancipation

1. Vorenberg, "Abraham Lincoln and the Politics of Black Colonization," 26; Quarles, *Lincoln and the Negro*, 110–11.

2. Lincoln, "Address on Colonization," 14 August 1862, *CW* 5:370–75; Scheips, "Lincoln and the Chiriqui Colonization Project," 428–30.

3. Lincoln, "Address on Colonization," 14 August 1862, *CW* 5:371, 372.

4. Ibid., 372–73.

5. Ibid., 371, 373.

6. Ibid., 373–74.

7. Ibid., 374.

8. Boritt suggests that Lincoln "lowered the bidding" when he heard no offers, which wrongly assumes the AP reporter was recording a discussion. "Did He Dream of a Lily-White America?" 10.

9. Lincoln, "Address on Colonization," 14 August 1862, *CW* 5:374–75.

10. Thompson to Lincoln, 19 August 1862, ALP.

11. Joseph Henry to Alexander Bache, 21 August 1862, in Rothenberg, Dorman, and Millikan, *Papers of Joseph Henry*, 10:279.

12. Burlingame, *Abraham Lincoln*, 2:393; [Drafted by Caleb Smith for Lincoln's signature?] to Samuel C. Pomeroy, 10 September 1862, ALP; Scheips, "Lincoln and the Chiriqui Colonization Project," 436–37.

13. Joseph Henry to Frederick W. Seward, 5 September 1862, ALP.

14. Vorenberg, "Abraham Lincoln and the Politics of Black Colonization," 23; Scheips, "Lincoln and the Chiriqui Colonization Project," 433–38; "Approval of Contract with Ambrose W. Thompson," 11 September 1862, *CW* 5:414; Lincoln to Caleb Smith, 12 September 1862, *CW* 5:418–19; *Tribune* (New York), 15 September 1862.

15. Lincoln to McClellan, 12 September 1862, *CW* 5:418.

16. Burlingame, *Abraham Lincoln*, 2:360; Lincoln to Albert G. Hodges, 4 April 1864, *CW* 7:281–82.

17. Beale, *Diary of Edward Bates, 1859–1866*, 262–64, and *Diary of Gideon Welles*, 1:150–53.

18. Scheips, "Lincoln and the Chiriqui Colonization Project," 437; Schoonover, "Misconstrued Mission," 611–19; Nicolay and Hay, *Abraham Lincoln*, 6:357–60.

19. Beale, *Diary of Gideon Welles*, 1:162; Scheips, "Lincoln and the Chiriqui Colonization Project," 438–41.

20. Lincoln, "Annual Message to Congress," 1 December 1862, *CW* 5:520–21.

21. Ibid., 530.

22. Ibid., 534–35.

23. Ibid., 537.

24. Lincoln, "Emancipation Proclamation," 1 January 1863, *CW* 6:29–30.

25. *Tribune* (New York), 5 August 1862; Guelzo, *Lincoln's Emancipation Proclamation*, 140.

26. Lincoln, "Reply to Emancipation Memorial Presented by Chicago Christians of All Denominations," 13 September 1862, *CW* 5:423.

27. Quarles, *Lincoln and the Negro*, 141–42, 155; Pease and Randall, *Diary of Orville Hickman Browning*, 1 and 29 January 1863, 1:609, 671; Lincoln to Andrew Johnson, 26 March 1863, *CW* 6:149–50.

28. Lincoln to General David Hunter, 1 April 1863, *CW* 6:158.

29. Lincoln to James C. Conkling, 26 August 1863, *CW* 6:406–10.

30. Quarles, *Lincoln and the Negro*, 113–14, 191–94.

31. Dennett, *Lincoln and the Civil War in the Diaries and Letters of John Hay*, 203.

32. Frederick Douglass, in Foner, *Frederick Douglass*, 551.

19. Societies

1. Darwin to Charles Lyell, 22 August 1862, *CCD* 10:378; Darwin to John Lubbock, 5 September 1862, *CCD* 10:395.

2. Asa Gray to Darwin, 22 September 1862, *CCD* 10:428.

3. Darwin to Asa Gray, 16 October 1862, *CCD* 10:470.

4. Asa Gray to Darwin, 27 October 1862, *CCD* 10:485; Gray to Darwin, 10 November 1862, *CCD* 10:534; Gray to Darwin, 17 November 1862, *CCD* 10:546; Darwin to Gray, 23 November 1862, *CCD* 10:551.

5. Joseph Dalton Hooker to Darwin, 3 November 1862, *CCD* 10:602; Hooker to Darwin, 24 December 1862, *CCD* 10:618; Darwin to Hooker, 24 December 1862, *CCD* 10:624; Darwin to Asa Gray, 2 January 2 1863, *CCD* 11:1; Darwin to Hooker, 13 January 1863, *CCD* 11:35.

6. Darwin to Gray, 19 January 1863, *CCD* 11:56.

7. Darwin to Thomas Huxley, 18 February, *CCD* 11:148; Joseph Dalton Hooker to Darwin, *CCD* 11:179; Darwin to Huxley, 26 February 1863, *CCD* 11:180.

8. Darwin to Gray, 23 February 1863, *CCD* 11:166; Darwin to Hooker, 24–25 February 1863, *CCD* 11:172.

9. Desmond and Moore, *Darwin's Sacred Cause*, 330; Lyell, *Geological Evidences*, 504–5.

10. Darwin to Charles Lyell, 6 March 1863, *CCD* 11:208–9; Darwin to Lyell, 17 March 1863, *CCD* 11:243.

11. J. Browne, *Charles Darwin: The Power of Place*, 220.

12. J. Hunt, "On Ethno-Climatology," 60, and "Introductory Essay," 3–4.

13. J. Hunt, "On Ethno-Climatology," 75; Blake, "Lyell on the Geological Evidence of the Antiquity of Man," 129–37.

14. Stocking, *Victorian Anthropology*, 247–53; Rainger, "Race, Politics, and Science," 60n29; Darwin to Armand de Quatrefages, 27 March 1863, *CCD* 11:269; Darwin to Thomas Huxley, 27 June 1863, *CCD* 11:508; Huxley to Darwin, 2 July 1863, *CCD* 11:515.

15. Stocking, *Victorian Anthropology*, 251–53; Rainger, "Race, Politics, and Science," 65; Jameson, "London Expenditures of the Confederate Secret Service," 818; Desmond and Moore, *Darwin's Sacred Cause*, 332, 413n37.

16. Bonner, "Slavery, Confederate Diplomacy, and the Racialist Mission of Henry Hotze," 288–316.

17. Roane, "Moral and Intellectual Diversity of Races," *De Bow's Review* 21 (July 1856): 63–70; *Putnam's Monthly* 7 (January 1856): 102–3. George Fitzhugh, whose writings so disgusted Lincoln, later praised Gobineau's work in "Superiority of Southern Races: Review of de Gobineau's Work," *De Bow's Review* 31 (October–November 1861): 369–81.

18. Owsley, *King Cotton Diplomacy*, 154–61; Bonner, "Slavery, Confederate Diplomacy, and the Racialist Mission of Henry Hotze," 290–95.

19. George McHenry, another proslavery American, was elected to the council of Bledsoe on 1 December 1863. "Ordinary Meeting, December 1st, 1863," *Journal of the Anthropology* 2 (1864): xxiii.

20. *(London) Times*, 6 January 1863; Bonner, "Slavery, Confederate Diplomacy, and the Racialist Mission of Henry Hotze," 298–300; Darwin to Asa Gray, 23 February 1863, *CCD* 11:166; *Index*, 18 June 1863; Henry Hotze to Judah Benjamin, 23 July and 27 August 1863, *Official Records of the Union and Confederate Navies in the War of the Rebellion*, ser. 2, 3:849–51, 878.

21. J. Hunt, *Negro's Place in Nature*, v, 28, 31; *Index*, 26 November, 3 December 1863, and 24 March 1864; George Rolleston to Thomas Huxley, 1 January 1865, Huxley Papers, 25:167.

22. Such as, J. Hunt, "President's Address," xcix.

23. Louis Agassiz to Lincoln, 21 March 1862, and Agassiz to Charles Sumner, 21 March 1862, Richards Manuscript Collection.

24. Louis Agassiz to Henry Wilson, 5 February 1863, in Lurie, *Louis Agassiz*, 331.

25. Joseph Henry to Louis Agassiz, 13 August 1864, in Rothenberg, Dorman, and Millikan, *Papers of Joseph Henry*, 392.

26. Lurie, *Louis Agassiz*, 330–31.

27. Reingold, "Science in the Civil War," 309–10.

28. Ibid., 309, 310; Lincoln to Edwin M. Stanton and Gideon Welles, 16 February 1863, *CW* 6:107; Lincoln, "To the Senate," 19 February 1863, *CW* 6:111–12.

29. Dupree, "Founding of the National Academy of Sciences," 435–38; *Congressional Globe*, 37th Cong., 3rd sess., 29 January 1863, 584, 6 February 1863, 762, 20 February 1863, 1131, 21 February 1863, 1121, 23 February 1863, 1181; Bruce, *Launching of Modern American Science*, 302.

30. Joseph Henry to Stephen Alexander, 9 March 1863, in Rothenberg, Dorman, and Millikan, *Papers of Joseph Henry*, 10:296; Henry to Louis Agassiz, 13 August 1864, in Rothenberg, Dorman, and Millikan, *Papers of Joseph Henry*, 10:392.

31. C. H. Davis to Harriette Davis, 27 February 1863, in C. H. Davis, *Life of Charles Henry Davis*, 291. Lincoln's 23 February note—"Will Senator Wilson please call and see me"—may be unrelated or refer to Senator Robert Wilson of Missouri. *CW* 6:115.

32. Asa Gray to Joseph Henry, 18 April 1863, in Dupree, *Asa Gray*, 319; Dahlgren, *Memoirs*, 389, 394; Benjamin Peirce to Alexander D. Bache, 27 May 1863, in Dupree, *Science in the Federal Government*, 144.

33. Asa Gray to Edward Bates, 4 March 1863, *CCD* 11:195; Gray to Darwin, 26 May 1863, *CCD* 11:450; Gray to Joseph Dalton Hooker, 6 July 1863, *CCD* 11:521–23; Gray to Darwin, 21 July 1863, *CCD* 11:547; Lurie, *Louis Agassiz*, 337.

34. Asa Gray to Darwin, 21 July 1863, *CCD* 11:547; Gray to Darwin, 23 November, *CCD* 11:677; Agassiz, *Methods of Study in Natural History*, iii.

35. True, *History of the First Half-Century of the National Academy of Sciences*, 16–23, 27.

36. Welles's diary, 8 January 1864, in Beale, *Diary of Gideon Welles*, 1:507; True, *History of the First Half-Century of the National Academy of Sciences*, 16; Cochrane, *National Academy of Sciences*, 89–90.

37. "No record of that reception has been found." Cochrane, *National Academy of Sciences*, 90. On 9 January, the *New York Times* ran this Associated Press dispatch of 8 January: "To-day the members of the National Academy paid their respects to the President, to whom they were presented by the Secretary of State."

38. Gurowski, *Diary*, 3:75.

39. Joseph Henry, "Locked Book," 16 January 1864, in Rothenberg, Dorman, and Millikan, *Papers of Joseph Henry*, 10:356.

20. Mill Workers and Freedmen

1. Thomas Huxley to Eliza Scott, 4 May 1864, in L. Huxley, *Life and Letters of Thomas Henry Huxley*, 3:362–63.

2. Jameson, "The London Expenditures of the Confederate Secret Service," 811; Henry Hotze to Percy Greg, 18 August 1864, cited in Bonner, "Slavery, Confederate Diplomacy, and the Racialist Mission of Henry Hotze," 293; Hotze to P. Greg, 8 October 1864, in Owsley, *King Cotton Diplomacy* 158; W. R. Greg, "On the Failure of 'Natural Selection' in the Case of Man," 353–62; Darwin, *Descent of Man*, 1:167, 173–74, 178.

3. Classed Accounts, 1861–1864, 14 July, 19 September, and 23 November 1862, DAR 265.10.

4. Asa Gray to Darwin, 10 November 1863, *CCD* 10:511; Darwin to Gray, 2 January 1863, *CCD* 11:1.

5. London *Daily News*, 2 Jan. 1863, quoted in "The Manchester Workmen's Address," *Living Age* 76, 14 February 1863, 328–30.

6. Lincoln, "To the Workingmen of Manchester," 19 January 1863, *CW* 6:64–66.

7. Stillé, *History of the United States Sanitary Commission*, 460, and Rybczynski, *Clearing in the Distance*, 201, 226, 254–55.

8. Stillé, *History of the United States Sanitary Commission*, 460–61; B. A. Gould, *Investigations in the Military and Anthropological Statistics of American Soldiers*, 221.

9. B. A. Gould, *Investigations in the Military and Anthropological Statistics of American Soldiers*, 221.

10. AFIC documents: Stanton's instructions, *Official Records of the Union and Confederate Armies*, ser. 3, 3:73–74; preliminary report (June 1863), *Official Records of the Union and Confederate Armies*, ser. 3, 3:430–54; final report (May 1864), *Official Records of the Union and Confederate Armies*, ser. 3, 4:289–382.

11. Sproat, "Blueprint for Radical Reconstruction," 25–44.

12. Quarles, *Lincoln and the Negro*, 226. On McKaye's possible work for Lincoln, see L. Cox, *Lincoln and Black Freedom*, 30–32. Herndon's library included at least two works by Robert Dale Owen, *Key to the Geology of the Globe* (1857) and a spiritualist investigation *Footfalls on the Boundary of Another World* (1859). Owen's brother, David Dale Owen, was a noted geologist in Indiana, whose work Darwin read with care. See Di Gregorio, *Charles Darwin's Marginalia*, 645.

13. Christoph Irmscher, e-mail message to author, 19 August 2007; E. C. Agassiz, *Louis Agassiz*, 2:591–617. Mrs. Agassiz bowdlerized the Howe/Agassiz correspondence that is in *Louis Agassiz*. I am grateful to Dr. Irmscher for generously providing me with the more complete transcripts he has prepared of the Howe-Agassiz correspondence of 3–18 August 1863, Houghton bMS Am 1419, microfilm 04-266 H-1257, Houghton Library, Harvard University.

14. E. C. Agassiz, *Louis Agassiz*, 2:595–96, 600.

15. Ibid., 595, 604–8, 611.

16. Cf. Lincoln's "Annual Message to Congress," 1 December 1862: "In *giving* freedom to the *slave*, we *assure* freedom to the *free*—honorable alike in what we give, and what we preserve." CW 5:537.

17. Christoph Irmscher, e-mail message to author, 19 August 2007; E. C. Agassiz, *Louis Agassiz*, 2:599–600; S. J. Gould, *Mismeasure of Man*, 49.

18. E. C. Agassiz, *Louis Agassiz*, 2:615.

19. Ibid., 2:615–16; Christoph Irmscher, e-mail message to author, 19 August 2007.

20. "Final Report of the American Freedmen's Inquiry Commission to the Secretary of War," *War of the Rebellion: A Compilation of Official Records of the Union and Confederate Armies*, ser. 3, 4:373–76. For example, "thermal lines" and that "mulattoes, certainly in northern latitudes, are less healthy and prolific than the pure blacks."

21. Ibid., 369, 370, 377, 381.

22. Lincoln to David Hunter, 10 February 1863, *CW* 6:98–99; "Instructions to Tax Commissioners in South Carolina," 16 September 1863, *CW* 6:453–59; Lincoln to Robert Dale Owen and James McKaye, 22 July 1863, *CW* 8:519.

23. *(New Orleans) Times*, 9 February 1864, in L. Cox, *Lincoln and Black Freedom*, 31.

24. L. Cox, *Lincoln and Black Freedom*, 97–98; Lincoln to Michael Hahn, 13 March 1864, *CW* 7:248; James McKaye to Charles Sumner, 5 February 1864, in Sproat, "Blueprint for Radical Reconstruction," 40.

25. First appearing in Raymond, *Life and Public Services of Abraham Lincoln*, 733–34, before Francis B. Carpenter published a nearly identical version, *Six Months at the White House with Abraham Lincoln*, 208–9. The *New York Times* (edited by Raymond) published a simpler version on 19 April 1865, shortly after Lincoln's assassination.

21. Testing Hopes and Hoaxes

1. Lincoln to George G. Meade, 14 July 1863, *CW* 6:327–28, Hay, *Life and Letters of John Hay*, 1:86.

2. Asa Gray to Darwin, 21 July 1863, *CCD* 11:547.

3. Darwin to Asa Gray, 4 August 1863, *CCD* 11:581.

4. Asa Gray to Darwin, 1 September 1863, *CCD* 11:613.

5. Asa Gray to Darwin, 16 February 1864, *CCD* 12:47.

6. [Croly and Wakeman], *Miscegenation*, 3–8, 23–27, 43, 49–50. See also Kaplan, "Miscegenation Issue in the Election of 1864," 278; Bloch, *Miscegenation, Melaleukation, and Mr. Lincoln's Dog*, passim.

7. Kaplan, "Miscegenation Issue in the Election of 1864," 286, 291, 295.

8. Ibid., 294–95.

9. Ibid., 295–301; John H. Van Evrie, *New York Day Book*, 27 February 1864, quoted in Kaplan, "Miscegenation Issue in the Election of 1864," 301n31; S. Cox, *Eight Years in Congress*, 352–59. Bloch asserts that Cox was unaware of the hoax, yet describes him as "a close friend" of one of the authors. *Miscegenation, Melaleukation, and Mr. Lincoln's Dog*, 66.

10. Kaplan, "Miscegenation Issue in the Election of 1864," 284; Bloch, *Miscegenation, Melaleukation, and Mr. Lincoln's Dog*, 62.

11. T. Huxley, "Professor Huxley's Lectures on 'The Structure and Classification of the Mammalia'," *Reader* 3 (27 February 1864), 266–68; (*New York) Tribune*, 18 March 1864.

12. T. Huxley, "Professor Huxley's Lectures on 'The Structure and Classification of the Mammalia'," 267–68.

13. Gurowski, *Diary*, 10 March 1864, 3:139–42; J. Hunt, "Miscegenation," 116–21; T. Huxley, "Professor Huxley's Lectures on 'The Structure and Classification of the Mammalia'," 266–68; T. Huxley, "Mr. Huxley on the Negro Question," 287–88; T. Huxley, "The Negro's Place in Nature," 334–35; James Hunt, "The Negro's Place in Nature," 368.

14. Van Evrie, *New York Day Book*, 16 July 1864, quoted in Kaplan, "Miscegenation Issue in the Election of 1864," 317; Van Evrie, *Subgenation*, 10–16; Kaplan, "Miscegenation Issue in the Election of 1864," 313–21.

15. Kaplan quotes from Croly's letter and cites it as "MS in Library of Congress," but I have been unable to locate it. "Miscegenation Issue in the Election of 1864," 324.

16. Ibid., 299; "Interview with Alexander W. Randall and Joseph T. Mills," 19 August 1864, *CW* 7:508.

17. Kaplan, "Miscegenation Issue in the Election of 1864," 329.

18. Vorenberg, *Final Freedom*, 160–63.

19. Kaplan, "Miscegenation Issue in the Election of 1864," 325.

20. Darwin to Louis Agassiz, 12 April 1864, *CCD* 12:134; B. D. Walsh to Darwin, 7 November 1864, *CCD* 12:401; Darwin to Walsh, 4 December 1864, *CCD* 12:440.

21. Asa Gray to Darwin, 23 November 1863, *CCD* 11:677; Darwin to Alfred Russel Wallace, 1 January 1864, *CCD* 12:2; Wallace to Darwin, 2 January 1864, *CCD* 12:4.

22. Alfred Russel Wallace to Darwin, 10 May 1864, *CCD* 12:173.

23. Wallace, "Origin of Human Races," clviii–clix, clxiv, clxiv–clxv, clxiv, clxix.

24. Darwin to Wallace, 28 May 1864, *CCD* 12:216.

25. Ibid.

26. Alfred Russel Wallace to Darwin, 29 May 1864, *CCD* 12:220; Darwin to Wallace, 15 June 1864, *CCD* 12:248.

27. Di Gregorio, *Charles Darwin's Marginalia*, 824.

22. Spiritual Forces

1. Cross, *Burned-Over District*, 4. For accounts of the Fox sisters, see also R. L. Moore, "Spiritualism and Science," and Weisberg, *Talking to the Dead.*

2. R. L. Moore, "Spiritualism and Science," 485.

3. *(New York) Tribune*, 8 June 1850; Flint, *Rochester Knockings!* passim; Hare, *Experimental Investigation of the Spirit Manifestations*; "Spiritual Manifestations," *Congressional Globe*, 33rd Cong. 1st sess., 17 April 1854, 923–24.

4. R. L. Moore, "Spiritualism and Science," 495; Putnam, *Agassiz and Spiritualism*; Hardinge, *Modern American Spiritualism*, 186–89; *(Boston) Courier*, 1 July 1857.

5. On Lincoln and spiritualism, see Monaghan, "Was Abraham Lincoln Really a Spiritualist?" and Temple, *Abraham Lincoln*, 196–202.

6. For example, "Dr. Bell on the So-called 'Spiritual Phenomena,'" *Annual of Scientific Discovery for 1856*, 154–60; R. L. Moore, "Spiritualism and Science," 475, 496.

7. Pease and Randall, *Diary of Orville Hickman Browning*, 5 June 1855, 1:186; Baker, *Mary Todd Lincoln*, 218.

8. Bray, "What Abraham Lincoln Read." "Herndon's Auction List" includes the following books about spiritualism: A. J. Davis, *Penetralia: Being Harmonial Answers to Important Questions* (1856), *The Magic Staff: An Autobiography* (1857), and *The Great Harmonia* (1859); William C. Taylor, et al., *The Occult Sciences: Sketches of the Traditions and Superstitions of Past Times, and the Marvels of the Present Day* (1855); and Robert Dale Owen, *Footfalls on the Boundary of Another World* (1859). Herndon also owned *Principles of Human Physiology* (1855) by an associate of Darwin, W. B. Carpenter, who argued against any nonmaterial cause for these so-called spiritual phenomena. Responding to an 1885 article suggesting Lincoln had been a spiritualist, Herndon said Lincoln "made no revelations to me on this subject, but I have grounds [for believing] . . . that he did sometimes attend here, in this city, séances. I am told this by Mr. Ordway, a Spiritualist. I know nothing of this fact on my personal knowledge" Herndon, "Letter from Lincoln's Old Partner," quoted in Hertz, *Hidden Lincoln*, 110.

9. There is, sadly, no basis for the tale that Robert Dale Owen, the most prominent and thoughtful spiritualist writer that Lincoln knew well, once read out a long essay on spiritualism to Lincoln, eliciting his superb response: "Well, for those who like that sort of thing, I should think it is just about the sort of thing they would like." See the discussion in Pullen, "Who Wrote 'The World's Best Book Review'?" 252–59.

10. Baker, *Mary Todd Lincoln*, 217–22; Temple, *Abraham Lincoln*, 196–202.

11. Maynard, *Was Abraham Lincoln a Spiritualist?* 82–91.

12. Joshua Speed to Lincoln, 23 October 1863, ALP.

13. Pease and Randall, *Diary of Orville Hickman Browning*, 1 January 1863, 1:608.

14. For example, Baker, *Mary Todd Lincoln*, 220.

15. Brooks, *Washington in Lincoln's Time*, 64–67; Newcomb, "Memoir of Joseph Henry," 31–32, and *Reminiscences of an Astronomer*, 408–10. Newcomb became the first president of the American Association for Psychical Research in 1885, but the rigorous tests he conducted left him "a skeptic as to every branch of 'occult science.'" *Reminiscences*, 416.

16. Joseph Henry to George H. Thomas, 7 March 1865, in Rothenberg, Dorman, and Millikan, *Papers of Joseph Henry*, 10:484. Henry's papers mention no "Colchester."

17. Temple, *Abraham Lincoln*, 202–3.

18. Chapman, *Latest Light on Abraham Lincoln and War-time Memories*, 506.

19. Lincoln, "Reply to Emancipation Memorial Presented by Chicago Christians of All Denominations," 13 September 1862, *CW* 5:419–25.

20. Wallace, *On Miracles and Modern Spiritualism*, 131–32.

21. Joseph Dalton Hooker to Darwin, 3 November 1865, *CCD* 13:293; Emma Darwin, *Diary*, DAR 242; Darwin to Alfred Russel Wallace, 22 January 1866, *CCD* 14:24; Russell to Darwin, 2 July 1866, *CCD* 14:227–29; Darwin to Russel, 5 July 1866, *CCD* 14:235–36.

22. Wallace, *On Miracles and Modern Spiritualism*; Thomas Huxley to Alfred Russel Wallace, before 1 December 1866, Add. Mss. 46439, A. R. Wallace Papers, vol. 46, British Library; Wallace, *My Life*, 2:280. For the original publication of Wallace's articles, see "The Scientific Aspect of the Supernatural," *English Leader* (11 August–29 September 1866): 52–59. A copy of Wallace's pamphlet, never annotated or mentioned in Darwin's correspondence, eventually came to Cambridge University Library among Emma Darwin's books. Desmond and Moore, *Darwin's Sacred Cause*, 417n24.

23. Wallace, "Sir Charles Lyell on Geological Climates and the Origin of Species," 391.

24. Darwin to Alfred Russel Wallace, 27 March 1869 and 14 April 1869, in Marchant, *Letters and Reminiscences of Alfred Russel Wallace*, 1:240–42.

25. Alfred Russel Wallace to Darwin, 18 April 1869, in Marchant, *Letters and Reminiscences of Alfred Russel Wallace*, 1:243.

26. Robert Chambers to Alfred Russel Wallace, 10 February 1867, in Wallace, *My Life*, 2:303; Secord, *Victorian Sensation*, 494–95; Darwin to Charles Lyell, 4 May 1969, in F. Darwin, *Life and Letters*, 3:116; and Lyell to Darwin, 5 May 1869, in K. M. Lyell, *Life, Letters, and Journals of Sir Charles Lyell*, 2:441–44.

27. Darwin to Joseph Dalton Hooker, 7 July 1854, *CCD* 5:201. Other signs of Darwin's negativity in Darwin to J. B. Innes, 6 September 1860, *CCD* 8:347, and Darwin to J. D. Hooker, 7 January 1865, *CCD* 13:17.

28. R. Keynes, *Annie's Box*, 256; Pearson, *Life, Letters, and Labours of Francis Galton*, 2:62–68; Raby, *Alfred Russel Wallace*, 208–9.

29. Francis Galton to Darwin, 28 March 1872, in Pearson, *Life, Letters, and Labours of Francis Galton*, 2:62–63; Darwin to Galton, 21 April 1872, letter no. 8296, *Darwin Correspondence Project Database*.

30. M. C. Stanley to Darwin, DAR 162:163; Darwin to M. C. Stanley, (tentatively dated "1874?" but could be slightly earlier), in F. Darwin and Seward, *More Letters of Charles Darwin*, 2:443. See also letters of 4 and 7 June 1872, in Pearson, *Life, Letters, and Labours of Francis Galton*, 2:65.

31. Wallace, *My Life*, 2:327; J. Browne, *Charles Darwin: The Power of Place*, 404–6.

32. Darwin to Hooker, 18 January 1874, in F. Darwin, *Life and Letters*, 3:187.

33. J. Browne, *Charles Darwin: The Power of Place*, 404; R. Keynes, *Annie's Box*, 257.

34. Thomas Huxley to Darwin, 27 January 1874, in L. Huxley, *Life and Letters of Thomas Henry Huxley*, 1:420; Darwin to Huxley, 29 January 1874, in F. Darwin, *Life and Letters*, 3:187.

35. Darwin to Alfred Russel Wallace, 14 April 1869, and Wallace to Darwin, 18 April 1869 and 20 October 1869, in Marchant, *Letters and Reminiscences of Alfred Russel Wallace*, 1:242–45.

36. Darwin to Alfred Russel Wallace, 26 January 1870, in Marchant, *Letters and Reminiscences of Alfred Russel Wallace*, 1:250–51.

37. Warren, *Lincoln's Youth*, 225.

38. Speed, *Reminiscences of Abraham Lincoln*, 28–33. According to an anonymous sketch on page 14, Speed "often said he believed the Bible, not because he understood it all, but

because he believed it was God's Word; that, if he could understand it, he would not believe it was God's word."

39. Hay, "Life in the White House in the Time of Lincoln," 34.

40. "Second Inaugural Address," 4 March 1865, *CW* 8:332–33.

41. Darwin to Asa Gray, 22 May 1860, *CCD* 8:223.

23. Meeting Agassiz

1. This assumes Brooks's accounts are more reliable on this point than others mentioned earlier.

2. Brooks, "Personal Recollections," 222–30; "Personal Reminiscences," 673–81; *Washington in Lincoln's Time*, 304–6.

3. Winsor, *Reading the Shape of Nature*, 9–12, 28–34; Lurie, *Louis Agassiz*, 339.

4. L. Agassiz, "Ice-Period in America," 93; B. D. Walsh to Darwin, 7 November 1864, *CCD* 12:401; Darwin to Walsh, 4 December 1864, *CCD* 12:440.

5. Lurie, *Louis Agassiz*, 341; Dupree, *Asa Gray*, 323; Cochrane, *National Academy of Sciences*, 93; Louis Agassiz to Joseph Henry, 8 August 1864, and Henry to Agassiz, 13 August 1864, Benjamin Peirce, papers.

6. E. C. Agassiz, *Louis Agassiz*, 2:619–23; Cochrane, *National Academy of Sciences*, 94; Joseph Henry to Alexander Dallas Bache, 17 January 1865, in Rothenberg, Dorman, and Millikan, *Papers of Joseph Henry*, 10:457–58.

7. E. C. Agassiz, *Louis Agassiz*, 2:625–26; Agassiz and Agassiz, *Journey in Brazil*, 33.

8. Asa Gray to Darwin, 5 December 1864, *CCD* 12:442; Charles Sumner to Louis Agassiz, 20 March 1865, in E. C. Agassiz, *Louis Agassiz*, 2:634.

9. Joseph Henry to Alexander Dallas Bache, 17 January 1865, in Rothenberg, Dorman, and Millikan, *Papers of Joseph Henry*, 10:457–58; *Scientific American*, 28 January 1865, 68.

10. Dall, "Pioneering," 404.

11. Brooks, "Personal Recollections of Lincoln," 222–23.

12. Brooks, "Personal Reminiscences of Lincoln," 678; Brooks, *Washington in Lincoln's Time*, 305.

13. Brooks, "Personal Recollections of Lincoln," 223.

14. Ibid., 223–24; Brooks, "Personal Reminiscences of Lincoln," 678; Brooks, *Washington in Lincoln's Time*, 306; Brooks, "Personal Reminiscences of Lincoln," 224.

15. Brooks, "Personal Reminiscences of Lincoln," 678.

16. Brooks, "Personal Recollections of Lincoln," 224, and "Personal Reminiscences of Lincoln," 678.

17. Agassiz and Agassiz, *Journey in Brazil*, 1–2.

18. Lurie, *Louis Agassiz*, 353.

19. Brice and Figueiroa, "Rock Stars," 18–19.

20. Vorenberg, *Final Freedom*, 198–210.

21. Agassiz and Agassiz, *Journey in Brazil*, 1.

22. Darwin to Asa Gray, 19 April 1865, *CCD* 13:126.

23. Lincoln, "Last Public Address," 11 April 1865, *CW* 8:404.

24. Magness, "Benjamin Butler's Colonization Testimony Reevaluated," 20.

25. John Hay [for Lincoln] to Benjamin F. Butler, 10 April 1865, *CW* 8:588. Although many Lincoln scholars have accepted Mark E. Neely's well-argued verdict in "Abraham Lincoln and Black Colonization: Benjamin Butler's Spurious Testimony" that Butler's accounts are "simply not true," there have always been dissenters from Neely's view, and Philip W. Magness's article makes a strong case that despite Butler's flaws of memory, his anecdotes should not be entirely discounted.

26. Rice, *Reminiscences of Abraham Lincoln by Distinguished Men of His Time*, 259; Butler, *Autobiography and Personal Reminiscences of Major General Benjamin F. Butler*, 903.

27. Rice, *Reminiscences of Abraham Lincoln by Distinguished Men of His Time*, 259–60.

28. Lincoln, "Address on Colonization to a Deputation of Negroes," 14 August 1862, *CW* 5:373.

29. Butler, *Autobiography and Personal Reminiscences of Major General Benjamin F. Butler*, 904.

30. Asa Gray to Darwin, 15–17 May 1865, *CCD* 13:144–45.

31. Darwin to Joseph Dalton Hooker, 4 May 1865, *CCD* 13:137.

32. Agassiz and Agassiz, *Journey in Brazil*, 79.

24. The Descent of Man

1. Asa Gray to Darwin, 24 July 1865, *CCD* 13:208; Darwin to Gray, 15 August 1865, *CCD* 13:222.

2. T. Huxley, "Emancipation—Black and White," 561–62. The "black" part, only a fifth the length of the "white," was largely a foil for the main discussion of women's biological "inequality."

3. T. Huxley, "On the Methods and Results of Ethnology," 248. Huxley gave this lecture to the Royal Institution on 2 June 1865.

4. Of course, that "change" might still include the possibility of a "designer" or a "Higher Intelligence" according to Lyell, Gray, and Wallace.

5. Darwin to Thomas Huxley, 12 July 1865, *CCD* 13:196. Darwin also cited Huxley's "On the Methods and Results of Ethnology" equivocally in *Descent* 1:229.

6. Stanton, *Leopard's Spots*, 184–96; Fredrickson, *Black Image in the White Mind*, 165–97; Nott, *Negro Race*, 12–13, 27, and "Instincts of Races," 1–16, 145–56; "Final Report of the American Freedmen's Inquiry Commission to the Secretary of War," *Official Records of the Union and Confederate Armies*, ser. 3, 4:370, 382.

7. Desmond, *Huxley*, 351–53; J. Browne, *Charles Darwin: The Power of Place*, 255–56.

8. Darwin, *On the Origin of Species*, 88, 199. When finally presenting his full arguments in *Descent of Man*, Darwin decided *both* genders took part in the "struggle," with males driving away rival males and females selecting males for their agreeable qualities. As redefined, sexual selection "depends on the advantage which certain individuals have over other individuals of the same sex and species, in exclusive relation to reproduction." 1:256.

9. Desmond and Moore, *Darwin's Sacred Cause*, 353, 417n11; J. Hunt, "On the Application of the Principle of Natural Selection to Anthropology," 339–40.

10. Darwin to John Murray, 3 January 1867, *CCD* 15:9.

11. Asa Gray to Darwin, 27 August 1866, *CCD* 14:302; Darwin to Charles Lyell, 8–9 September 1866, *CCD* 14:311; Darwin to Gray, 10 September 1866, *CCD* 14:313.

12. Darwin to Fritz Müller, 22 February 1867, *CCD* 15:92–94.

13. Darwin, *Expression of the Emotions in Man and Animals*, 12, 17.

14. Ibid., 22.

15. Asa Gray to Darwin, 24 February 1868, 16:168; Darwin to Joseph Dalton Hooker, 28 July 1868, *CCD* 16:644.

16. Van Evrie, *White Supremacy and Negro Subordination*, 315.

17. This is found in *Variation of Animals and Plants*, 2:178–91.

18. B. A. Gould, *Investigations in the Military and Anthropological Statistics of American Soldiers*, 221.

19. Ibid., 221, 246; Braun, "Spirometry, Measurement, and Race in the Nineteenth Century," 151.

20. B. A. Gould, *Investigations in the Military and Anthropological Statistics of American Soldiers*, 226–27, 236–37, 297, 384–97.

21. Ibid., 312–15. The six additional measurements were: distance from tip of finger to patella (while standing at attention), height to knee, distance between perineum to most prominent part of pubes, girth of neck, distance between nipples, and circumference around hips. Ibid., 223, 358.

22. Ibid., 319, 229, 264, 299, 317–19, 383, 393, 397–99, 347, 462–65, 544. See also a letter from Gould's distressed chief tabulator, Braun, 152.

23. Ibid., 291, 471, 153, 252, 298.

24. Haller, *Outcasts from Evolution*, 58, 62, 94.

25. Braun, "Spirometry, Measurement, and Race in the Nineteenth Century," 158. I disagree with Braun.

26. Darwin to Wallace, 28 May 1864, *CCD* 12:216; Darwin to Wallace, 26 February 1867, *CCD* 15:109.

27. Darwin, *Descent of Man*, 1:249.

28. Ibid., 1:35.

29. Ibid., 1:108, 114–15, 288, 216.

30. Ibid., 1:221.

31. Ibid., 2:321, 378. Darwin's reference to "their early ape-like progenitors" related to both of the "crossed races," white and black; and the logical (but unstated) inference is that whites' greater hairiness might indicate a less advanced level of development!

32. Ibid., 1:145–46.

33. Ibid., 1:146; J. B. Davis, "Contributions towards Determining the Weight of the Brain in Different Races of Men," 505–27.

34. J. B. Davis, "On the Weight of the Brain in the Negro," 190–92.

35. Darwin, *Descent of Man*, 1:146; J. B. Davis, "Contributions towards Determining the Weight of the Brain in Different Races of Men," 513.

36. Darwin, *Descent of Man*, 1:1–2.

37. Lurie, *Louis Agassiz*, 110.

38. L. Agassiz, *De l'Espèce et de la Classification en Zoologie*, 97. See Morris, "Louis Agassiz's Additions to the French Translation of His Essay on Classification," 121–34.

39. Darwin, *Descent of Man*, 1:78, 324–25; 2:13, 323, 342.

40. Ibid., 1:218, 221, 226; 2:13, 20–21.

41. Lurie, *Louis Agassiz*, 350; Asa Gray to Darwin, 6 November 1866, *CCD* 14:377.

42. Louis Agassiz to Darwin, 22 July 1868, *CCD* 16:637–38; Darwin to Agassiz, 19 August 1868, *CCD* 16:686. Agassiz's letter must have arrived only a few days after Darwin had written to Hooker the words quoted earlier about Agassiz's Brazil book being an effort "to destroy me."

43. Lurie, *Louis Agassiz*, 368.

44. Asa Gray to Darwin, 26 and 29 October 1869, DAR 165:172.

45. Darwin to J. F. T. Müller, 1 December 1869, in Darwin and Seward, *More Letters of Charles Darwin*, 2:357; G. R. Agassiz, *Letters and Recollections of Alexander Agassiz*, 97.

46. Darwin to Alexander Agassiz, 2 February 1870, DAR 143:7; Asa Gray to Darwin, 14 February 1870, in J. L. Gray, *Letters of Asa Gray*, 2:599.

47. Asa Gray to Darwin, 27 February 1870, and 1 March 1870, DAR 82:B80, and Darwin to Gray, 15 March 1870, Historical Records Survey, 104.

48. Darwin, *Descent of Man*, 1:235.

49. Litchfield, *Emma Darwin, a Century of Family Letters*, 2:196.

25. An End to Religion

1. Herndon, "Abraham Lincoln's Religion," 5–6, Lamon, *Life of Abraham Lincoln*, 492–97.

2. Donald, *Lincoln's Herndon*, 169; Holland, *Life of Abraham Lincoln*, 241, 542, 544.

3. William H. Herndon to Ward Hill Lamon, 25 February 1870, in Hertz, *Hidden Lincoln*, 68; Newton Bateman to Josiah Gilbert Holland, 19 June 1865, in Guelzo, introduction, *Holland's Life of Abraham Lincoln*, xxi.

4. Fehrenbacher and Fehrenbacher, *Recollected Words of Abraham Lincoln*, 26; Guelzo, introduction, *Holland's Life of Abraham Lincoln*, xxii.

5. Holland, *Life of Abraham Lincoln*, 239.

6. Donald, *Lincoln's Herndon*, 215; *HI*, 436–37, 572.

7. William H. Herndon to Mr. Hickman, 6 December 1866, in Donald, *Lincoln's Herndon*, 216.

8. Donald, *Lincoln's Herndon*, 202; Herndon, "Analysis of the Character of Abraham Lincoln," 417.

9. Donald, *Lincoln's Herndon*, 256, 271, 290.

10. Lamon, *Life of Abraham Lincoln*, 494.

11. Abbot, "Genius of Christianity and Free Religion," 224–25; Abbot, "Philosophical Biology," 384.

12. Francis Ellingwood Abbot to Darwin, 11 May 1871, DAR 159:1; Darwin to Abbot, 27 May 1871, in Burkhardt, Smith, and Kohn, *Calendar of the Correspondence of Charles Darwin*, no. 7771; Darwin to Abbot, 6 June 1871, in Barrett, *Collected Papers of Charles Darwin*, 2:167.

13. Francis Ellingwood Abbot to Darwin, 20 August 1871, DAR 159:2.

14. Darwin to Francis Ellingwood Abbot, 6 September 1871, and 16 November 1871, in Burkhardt, Smith, and Kohn, *Calendar of the Correspondence of Charles Darwin*, nos. 7924, 8070. Abbot complied with Darwin's request to insert the word "almost" and to remove the words "I believe that" that had preceded "I agree."

15. Francis Ellingwood Abbot to Darwin, 1 November 1871, DAR 159:3; Darwin to Abbot, 16 November 1871, in F. Darwin, *Life and Letters of Charles Darwin*, 1:305–6.

16. Darwin, *Expression of the Emotions in Man and Animals*, 367, 338. Cf. 187, 269, and 279 for other references to expressions common "to all the races of mankind."

17. Asa Gray to Darwin, 25 May 1868, *CCD* 16:537, and 16 June 1874, in J. L. Gray, *Letters of Asa Gray*, 2:646; Darwin to Gray, 30 June 1874, in Burkhardt, Smith, and Kohn, *Calendar of the Correspondence of Charles Darwin*, no. 9520.

18. Darwin to George Darwin, 21 October 1873, DAR 210.1:14.

19. Darwin to H. N. Ridley, 28 November 1878, in F. Darwin, *Life and Letters of Charles Darwin*, 3:235–36.

20. Darwin to N. D. Doedes, 2 April 1873, in Bettany, *Life of Charles Darwin*, 163.

21. N. A. Mengden to Darwin, 2 April 1879, in Burkhardt, Smith, and Kohn, *Calendar of the Correspondence of Charles Darwin*, no. 11971; Emma Darwin to Mengden, 8 April 1879, in ibid., no. 11981; Mengden to Darwin, 3 June 1879, in ibid., no. 12079; Darwin to Mengden, 5 June 1879, in F. Darwin, *Life and Letters of Charles Darwin*, 1:307.

22. F. A. McDermott to Darwin, 23 November 1880, DAR 201:22; Darwin to McDermott, 24 November 1880, in Burkhardt, Smith, and Kohn, *Calendar of the Correspondence of Charles Darwin*, no. 12851.

23. Darwin, *Autobiographies*, 54.

24. Darwin to John Fordyce, 7 May 1879, in F. Darwin, *Life and Letters of Charles Darwin*, 1:304.

25. Darwin to E. B. Aveling, 13 October 1880, in Feuer, "Is the 'Darwin-Marx Correspondence' Authentic?" 2.

26. Donald, *Lincoln's Herndon*, 266–72; Reed, "Later Life and Religious Sentiments of Abraham Lincoln," 336–38.

27. Donald, *Lincoln's Herndon*, 277–82.

28. Ibid., 290–91; Herndon, "Abraham Lincoln's Religious Belief," 114; Herndon, "Abraham Lincoln's Religion," 148.

29. Arnold, *Life of Abraham Lincoln*, 446–47.

30. Herndon and Weik, *Herndon's Life of Lincoln*, 357.

31. Nicolay and Hay, *Abraham Lincoln*; Herndon to Weik, 22 January 1887, in Hertz, *Hidden Lincoln*, 158.

32. F. Darwin, *Life and Letters of Charles Darwin*, 3:361.

33. Aveling, *Religious Views of Charles Darwin*, 5–7.

34. Burlingame, "Nicolay and Hay," 6–7.

35. Emma Darwin to Francis Darwin, ca. 1885, in Litchfield, *Emma Darwin, Wife of Charles Darwin*, 2:360; Darwin, *Autobiographies*, 87, 93. Darwin's granddaughter Nora Barlow restored the passages in her 1958 edition of *The Autobiography of Charles Darwin*.

36. J. Moore, *Darwin Legend*, 21, 85–90, 167.

26. The Dream of Equality

1. Lurie, *Louis Agassiz*, 382–83.

2. To Alexander Agassiz, 1 June 1871, in G. R. Agassiz, *Letters and Recollections of Alexander Agassiz*, 119.

3. Darwin to Asa Gray, 15 January 1872, no. 65, Historical Records Survey.

4. Louis Agassiz to Carl Gegenbaur, 28 July 1872, in Lurie, *Louis Agassiz*, 373–74.

5. Asa Gray to Darwin, 25 February 1873, DAR 165:183; A. Gray, "Survival of the Fittest," 404.

6. E. C. Agassiz, "Cruise through the Galapagos," 579–84. In addition to prematurely placing Darwin at death's door, the suggestion that no "transition types" had yet been found ignored the fact that Agassiz had for years been labeling as "prophetic types" various features that Darwinians considered transitional.

7. Louis Agassiz to W. D. Howells, 16 November 1873, in Lurie, *Louis Agassiz*, 383.

8. L. Agassiz, "Evolution and Permanence of Type," 94.

9. Darwin to Joseph Dalton Hooker, 8 January 1874, DAR 95:310.

10. Dupree, *Asa Gray*, 353.

11. Darwin to T. W. Higginson, 27 February 1873, in F. Darwin, *Life and Letters of Charles Darwin*, 3:176; Higginson to Darwin, 30 March 1873, DAR 166:198.

12. "Office [of the] American Freedmen's Inquiry Commission to Secretary of War Edwin M. Stanton," 30 June 1863, Correspondence, Orders, Etc., from January 1, 1863, to December 31, 1863, *Official Records of the Union and Confederate Armies*, ser. 3, 3:435, 439.

13. Darwin three times used the phrase "lower races" but not in contrast to "higher races" (which does not appear in *Descent*): instead, one usage was a paraphrase of Schaaffhausen, and the other two were contrasted with "civilised races" and "civilised nation." *Descent of Man*, 2nd ed., 1:131, 169, 173.

14. Darwin, *Descent of Man*, 143.

15. Ibid.

16. M. L. Baxter to Darwin, 28 September 1876, DAR 160:97; Baxter, *Statistics, Medical and Anthropological*, 4; Haller, *Outcasts from Evolution*, 29–30; Braun, "Spirometry, Measurement, and Race in the Nineteenth Century," 155–57.

17. Haller, *Outcasts from Evolution*, 34.

18. Darwin to William Graham, 3 July 1881, in F. Darwin, *Life and Letters of Charles Darwin*, 1:315–17.

19. Himmelfarb, *Darwin and the Darwinian Revolution*, 343, and *Victorian Minds*, 319.

20. Graham, *Creed of Science*, 72–74.

21. The disdain was mutual: Carlyle considered evolution "rather a humiliating discovery and the less said about it the better." David Wilson, *Carlyle in Old Age*, 328.

22. Graham, *Creed of Science*, 255.

23. Weikart, *From Darwin to Hitler*, 186. His provocatively titled *From Darwin to Hitler* refers to Darwin's own writings in only eight endnotes out of over eight hundred (mostly citing German works from the late nineteenth and early twentieth century) and quoted altogether nine sentences written by Darwin.

24. Weikart, *From Darwin to Hitler*, 1861; Darwin, *Descent of Man*, 1:201.

25. Darwin, *Descent of Man*, 1:200.

26. Darwin, *Descent of Man*, 1:201, quoting *Anthropological Review* (April 1867): 236.

27. Darwin expressed to Charles Lyell his "infinite satisfaction to believe that mankind will progress to such a pitch, that we should be looked back at as mere Barbarians." 27 April 1860, *CCD* 8:171.

28. Van Evrie, *White Supremacy and Negro Subordination*, 311–12; Fredrickson, *Black Image in the White Mind*, 235–38; Haller, *Outcasts from Evolution*, 40–42.

29. Fredrickson, *Black Image in the White Mind*, 239; Haller, *Outcasts from Evolution*, 42.

30. Haller, *Outcasts from Evolution*, 43.

31. Fredrickson, *Black Image in the White Mind*, 240.

32. Diane B. Paul notes that the term "Social Darwinism" was not coined until the end of the nineteenth century, was popularized in the 1940s by Richard Hofstadter, a critic of "Social Darwinism," and is never used by people to identify themselves, and the main contribution of Darwinism "to social theory has been to popularise certain catchwords." "Darwin, Social Darwinism, and Eugenics," 224, 237. Robert M. Young notes that "the concept of struggle is very common in [Charles Lyell's] *Principles*" as well as in the writings of Thomas Malthus, whose "sense of pessimism" was contrasted with Darwin's "very optimistic interpretation" of social conflict. "Darwinism *Is* Social," 619–21.

33. Darwin, *Descent of Man*, 1:168; Himmelfarb, *Victorian Minds*, 316.

34. Darwin, *Descent of Man*, 1:168–69. In the second edition, Darwin intensified his point by changing "if so urged by hard reason" to "even at the urging of hard reason" and "a certain and great present evil" to "an overwhelming present evil." 134.

35. Fredrickson, *Black Image in the White Mind*, 245–55.

36. Having noted the attacks on Darwin by Himmelfarb and Weikart, see those on Lincoln by Bennett, *Forced into Glory*, and DiLorenzo, *Real Lincoln*.

Bibliography

Abbot, Francis Ellingwood. "The Genius of Christianity and Free Religion." In *Freedom and Fellowship in Religion: A Collection of Essays and Addresses*, 222–64. Boston: Roberts Brothers, 1875.

———. "Philosophical Biology." *North American Review* 107 (1868): 377–422.

Adams, Charles Francis, Jr. "The Trent Affair." *American Historical Review* 17 (April 1912): 540–62.

Adams, E. D. *Great Britain and the American Civil War*. 2 vols. London: Longmans, 1925.

Agassiz, Elizabeth C. "A Cruise through the Galapagos." *Atlantic Monthly* 31 (May 1873): 579–84.

———, ed. *Louis Agassiz: His Life and Correspondence*. 2 vols. Boston: Houghton Mifflin, 1886.

Agassiz, G. R., ed. *Letters and Recollections of Alexander Agassiz*. Boston: Houghton Mifflin, 1913.

Agassiz, Louis. "Contemplations of God in the Cosmos." *Christian Examiner* 50 (1851): 1–17.

———. *Contributions to the Natural History of the United States of America*. Boston: Little, Brown, 1857–62.

———. *De l'Espèce et de la Classification en Zoologie*. Paris: Balliere, 1869.

———. "Evolution and Permanence of Type." *Atlantic Monthly* 33 (January 1874): 92–101.

———. "Geographical Distribution of Animals." *Christian Examiner* 48 (1850): 181–204.

———. "Ice-Period in America." *Atlantic Monthly* 14 (July 1864): 86–93.

———. *Introduction to the Study of Natural History*. New York: Greeley & McElrath, 1847.

———. *Lake Superior: Its Physical Character, Vegetation, and Animals, Compared with Those of Other and Similar Regions*. Boston: Gould, Kendall, & Lincoln, 1850.

———. *Methods of Study in Natural History*. Boston: Ticknor & Fields, 1863.

———. *Notice sur la Geographie des Animaux*. Neuchatel: Henri Wolfrath, 1845.

———. "On the Diversity of Origin of Human Races." *Christian Examiner* 49 (1850): 110–45.

———. "On the Succession and Development of Organised Beings at the Surface of the Terrestrial Globe." *Edinburgh New Philosophical Journal* 33 (1842): 388–99.

———. Preface. In Nott and Gliddon, *Indigenous Races of the Earth*, xiii–xv.

———. Review of *On the Origin of Species*, by Charles Darwin. *American Journal of Science* 30 (July 1860): 142–54.

———. "Sketch of the Natural Provinces of the Animal World and Their Relation to the Different Types of Men." In Nott and Gliddon, *Types of Mankind*, lviii–lxxviii. Also in *Edinburgh New Philosophical Journal* 57 (October 1854): 347–63.

Agassiz, Louis, and E. C. Agassiz. *A Journey in Brazil*. Boston: Ticknor & Fields, 1868.

Alter, Stephen G. "Race, Language, and Mental Evolution in Darwin's *Descent of Man*." *Journal of the History of the Behavioral Sciences* 43 (Summer 2007): 239–336.

Anderson, Stuart. "1861: Blockade vs. Closing the Confederate Ports." *Military Affairs* 41 (December 1977): 190–95.

Angle, Paul, ed. *Created Equal? The Complete Lincoln-Douglas Debates of 1858*. Chicago: University of Chicago Press, 1958.

———. *Here I Have Lived: A History of Lincoln's Springfield, 1821–1865*. Springfield, IL: Abraham Lincoln Association, 1935.

Arnold, Isaac N. *The Life of Abraham Lincoln*. Chicago: A. C. McClurg, 1885.

Avary, Myrta L., ed. *Recollections of Alexander H. Stephens*. New York: Doubleday, 1910.

Aveling, E. B. *The Religious Views of Charles Darwin*. London: Freethought, 1883.

Bachman, John. *Continuation of the Review of "Nott and Gliddon's Types of Mankind."* Charleston, SC: James, Williams, & Gitsinger, 1855.

———. *The Doctrine of the Unity of the Human Race Examined on the Principles of Science.* Charleston, SC: C. Canning, 1850.

———. "An Examination of a Few of the Statements of Prof. Agassiz in His 'Sketch of the Natural Provinces of the Animal World.'" *Charleston Medical Journal and Review* 9 (November 1854): 790–806.

———. "An Examination of Prof. Agassiz' Sketch of the Natural Provinces of the Animal World." *Charleston Medical Journal and Review* 10 (July 1855): 482–534.

———. *An Examination of the Characteristics of Genera and Species as Applicable to the Doctrine of the Unity of the Human Race.* Charleston, SC: James, Williams, & Gitsinger, 1855.

———. "An Investigation of the Cases of Hybridity in Animals on Record, Considered in Reference to the Unity of the Human Species." *Charleston Medical Journal and Review* 5 (1850): 168–97.

———. *A Notice of the "Types of Mankind."* Charleston, SC: James, Williams, & Gitsinger, 1854.

———. "Types of Mankind." *Charleston Medical Journal and Review* 9 (September 1854): 627–59.

Baker, Jean H. *Mary Todd Lincoln: A Biography.* New York: Norton, 1987.

Bakewell, Robert, Jr. "On the Falls of Niagara." *Loudon's Magazine of Natural History* 3 (January 1830): 117–30.

Bancroft, George. "The Necessity, the Reality, and the Promise of the Progress of the Human Race." In *Literary and Historical Miscellanies*, 2:481–517. New York: Harper Brothers, 1855.

Barrett, Paul H., ed. *The Collected Papers of Charles Darwin.* 2 vols. Chicago: University of Chicago Press, 1977.

Basler, Roy P., and Christian O. Basler, eds. *The Collected Works of Abraham Lincoln: Second Supplement, 1848–1865.* New Brunswick, NJ: Rutgers University Press, 1990. Referred to as *CW*.

Basler, Roy P., Marion Dolores Pratt, and Lloyd A. Dunlap, eds. *Collected Works of Abraham Lincoln.* 8 vols. New Brunswick, NJ: Rutgers University Press, 1953–55. Available at http://quod.lib.umich.edu/l/lincoln/.

Bates, David Homer. *Lincoln in the Telegraph Office: Recollections of the United States Military Telegraph Corps during the Civil War.* New York: Century, 1907.

Baxter, Jedediah Hyde. *Statistics, Medical and Anthropological, of the Provost Marshal-General's Bureau, Derived from Records of the Examination for Military Service in the Armies of the United States during the Late War of the Rebellion.* 2 vols. Washington, DC: GPO, 1875.

Beale, Howard K., ed. *Diary of Edward Bates, 1859–1866.* Washington, DC: GPO, 1933.

———, ed. *Diary of Gideon Welles.* 2 vols. New York: Norton, 1960.

Benner, Martha L., Cullom Davis, et al., eds. *The Law Practice of Abraham Lincoln: Complete Documentary Edition.* 2nd ed. Springfield: Illinois Historic Preservation Agency, 2009. http://www.lawpracticeofabrahamlincoln.org.

Bennett, Lerone. *Forced into Glory: Abraham Lincoln's White Dream.* Chicago: Johnson, 2000.

Bettany, G. T. *Life of Charles Darwin.* London: W. Scott, 1887.

Beveridge, Albert J. *Abraham Lincoln, 1809–1858.* 2 vols. Boston: Houghton Mifflin, 1928.

Bilotta, James D. *Race and the Rise of the Republican Party 1848–1865.* New York: Peter Lang, 1992.

Blake, C. Carter. "Lyell on the Geological Evidence of the Antiquity of Man." *Anthropological Review* 1 (1863): 129–37.

Bledsoe, Albert T. Review. "Ward Hill Lamon's *Life of Abraham Lincoln*," *Southern Review* 12 (1873): 328–68.

Bloch, Julius Marcus. *Miscegenation, Melaleukation, and Mr. Lincoln's Dog*. New York: Schaum, 1958.

Bonner, Robert E. "Slavery, Confederate Diplomacy, and the Racialist Mission of Henry Hotze." *Civil War History* 51 (2005): 288–316.

Boritt, Gabor. "Did He Dream of a Lily-White America? The Voyage to Linconia." In *The Lincoln Enigma: The Changing Faces of an American Icon*, edited by Boritt, 1–19. Oxford: Oxford University Press, 2001.

Bowlby, John. *Charles Darwin: A Biography*. London: Hutchinson, 1990.

Braun, Lundy. "Spirometry, Measurement, and Race in the Nineteenth Century." *Journal of the History of Medicine and Allied Sciences* 60 (2005): 135–69.

Bray, Robert. *Reading with Lincoln*. Carbondale: Southern Illinois University Press, 2010.

———. "What Abraham Lincoln Read—An Evaluative and Annotated List." *JALA* 28 (2007): 28–81.

Brice, William R., and Silvia F. de M. Figueiroa. "Rock Stars: Charles Frederick Hartt—a Pioneer of Brazilian Geology." *GSA Today* 13 (March 2003): 18–19.

Briggs, John Channing. *Lincoln's Speeches Reconsidered*. Baltimore, MD: Johns Hopkins University Press, 2005.

Brogan, Hugh, ed. *The* Times *Reports the American Civil War: Extracts from the* Times *1860–1865*. London: Times Books, 1975.

Brooke, John Hedley. "Darwin and Victorian Christianity." In Hodge and Radick, *Cambridge Companion to Darwin*, 192–213.

Brooks, Noah. "Personal Recollections of Abraham Lincoln." *Harper's Monthly*, July 1865, 222–30.

———. "Personal Reminiscences of Lincoln." *Scribner's Monthly* 15 (March 1878): 673–81.

———. *Washington in Lincoln's Time*. New York: Century, 1895.

Browne, Francis Fisher. *The Every-day Life of Abraham Lincoln: A Narrative and Descriptive Biography with Pen-Pictures and Personal Recollections*. Chicago: Browne & Howell, 1913.

Browne, Janet. *Charles Darwin: The Power of Place*. Princeton, NJ: Princeton University Press, 2002.

———. *Charles Darwin: Voyaging*. Princeton, NJ: Princeton University Press, 1996.

Bruce, Robert V. *The Launching of Modern American Science, 1846–1876*. Ithaca, NY: Cornell University Press, 1987.

———. *Lincoln and the Tools of War*. Indianapolis, IN: Bobbs-Merrill, 1956.

Burke, Andrew. *Burke's Descriptive Guide; or, the Visitors' Companion to Niagara Falls*. Buffalo, NY: Andrew Burke, 1851.

Burkhardt, Frederick, and Sydney Smith, eds. *The Correspondence of Charles Darwin*. 17 vols. Cambridge: Cambridge University Press, 1985–. Available at http://www.darwinproject.ac.uk. Referred to as *CCD*.

Burkhardt, Frederick, Sydney Smith, and David Kohn, eds. *A Calendar of the Correspondence of Charles Darwin, 1821–1882*. 2nd ed. Cambridge: Cambridge University Press, 1994.

Burlingame, Michael. *Abraham Lincoln: A Life*. 2 vols. Baltimore, MD: Johns Hopkins University Press, 2008.

———. *The Inner World of Abraham Lincoln*. Urbana: University of Illinois Press, 1994.

———. "Nicolay and Hay: Court Historians." *JALA* 19 (Winter 1998): 1–20.

Butler, Benjamin F. *Autobiography and Personal Reminiscences of Major General Benjamin F. Butler*. Boston: A. M. Thayer, 1892.

Carpenter, Francis B. *Six Months at the White House with Abraham Lincoln: The Story of a Picture*. New York: Hurd and Houghton, 1866.

Carpenter, William B. "Darwin and the Origin of Species." *National Review* 10 (1860): 188–214.

———. "The Theory of Development in Nature." Review of *Origin* and Others. *British and Foreign Medico-Chirurgical Review* 25 (1860): 367–404.

Chambers, Robert. *Vestiges of the Natural History of Creation*. London: John Churchill, 1844.

Chandler, Alfred D. "Du Pont, Dahlgren, and the Civil War Nitre Shortage." *Military Affairs* 13 (Autumn 1949): 142–49.

Chapman, Ervin. *Latest Light on Abraham Lincoln and War-time Memories*. New York: Revell, 1917.

Clarke, John M. *James Hall of Albany*. New York: Arno, 1978.

Cleveland, Henry. *Alexander H. Stephens, in Public and Private: With Letters and Speeches, before, during, and since the War*. Philadelphia, PA: National, 1866.

Cochrane, Rexmond C. *The National Academy of Sciences: The First Hundred Years, 1863–1963*. Washington, DC: National Academy of Sciences, 1978.

Coffey, Titian J. "Lincoln and the Cabinet." In Rice, *Reminiscences of Abraham Lincoln*, 189–202.

Cohen, Victor H. "Charles Sumner and the Trent Affair." *Journal of Southern History* 22 (May 1956): 205–19.

Colp, Ralph. *To Be an Invalid: The Illness of Charles Darwin*. Chicago: University of Chicago Press, 1977.

Congressional Globe. 46 vols. Washington, DC, 1834–73.

Contosta, David R. *Rebel Giants: The Revolutionary Lives of Abraham Lincoln and Charles Darwin*. Amherst, NY: Prometheus Books, 2008.

Cox, LaWanda. *Lincoln and Black Freedom: A Study in Presidential Leadership*. Columbia: University of South Carolina Press, 1981.

Cox, Samuel S. *Eight Years in Congress, from 1857 to 1865*. New York: Appleton, 1865.

[Croly, David Goodman, and George Wakeman.] *Miscegenation: The Theory of the Blending of the Races, Applied to the American White Man and Negro*. New York: H. Dexter, Hamilton, 1864.

Cross, Whitney R. *The Burned-Over District: The Social and Intellectual History of Enthusiastic Religion in Western New York, 1800–1850*. Ithaca, NY: Cornell University Press, 1950.

Dahlgren, John A. Papers. Manuscript Division, Library of Congress.

Dahlgren, Madeleine V. *Memoir of John A. Dahlgren*. Boston, MA: J. R. Osgood, 1882.

Dall, Catherine H. "Pioneering." *Atlantic Monthly* 19 (April 1867): 403–16.

Darwin, Charles. *Autobiographies*. Edited by Michael Neve and Sharon Messenger. London: Penguin, 2002.

———. *The Autobiography of Charles Darwin 1809–1882. With the Original Omissions Restored*. Edited by Nora Barlow. London: Collins, 1958.

———. *Charles Darwin's Natural Selection: Being the Second Part of His Big Species Book Written from 1856 to 1858*. Edited by R. C. Stauffer. Cambridge: Cambridge University Press, 1975.

———. *The Descent of Man, and Selection in Relation to Sex*. 2 vols. London: John Murray, 1871.

———. *The Descent of Man, and Selection in Relation to Sex*. 2nd ed. London: John Murray, 1874.

———. *The Expression of the Emotions in Man and Animals*. London: John Murray, 1872.

———. *Narrative of the Surveying Voyages of His Majesty's Ships* Adventure *and* Beagle *between the years 1826 and 1836, Describing Their Examination of the Southern Shores of South America, and the Beagle's Circumnavigation of the Globe. Journal and Remarks. 1832–1836*. London: Henry Colburn, 1839.

———. *On the Origin of Species by Means of Natural Selection, or the Preservation of Favoured Races in the Struggle for Life.* London: John Murray, 1859.

———. Papers. Manuscripts Room, Cambridge University Library, Cambridge, United Kingdom. Referred to as DAR.

———. *The Voyage of the Beagle.* London: Everyman's Library, 1959.

Darwin Correspondence Project Database. University of Cambridge, 2010. http://www.darwinproject.ac.uk/entry-8296/.

Darwin, Erasmus. *The Botanic Garden.* London: J. Johnson, 1791.

Darwin, Francis, ed. *The Foundations of* The Origin of Species: *Two Essays Written in 1842 and 1844.* Cambridge: Cambridge University Press, 1909.

———, ed. *The Life and Letters of Charles Darwin.* 3 vols. London: John Murray, 1887.

Darwin, Francis, and A. C. Seward, eds. *More Letters of Charles Darwin: A Record of His Work in a Series of Hitherto Unpublished Letters.* 2 vols. London: John Murray, 1903.

Davis, C. H. *Life of Charles Henry Davis, Rear-Admiral, 1807–1877 by His Son.* New York: Houghton Mifflin, 1899.

Davis, J. Barnard. "Contributions towards Determining the Weight of the Brain in Different Races of Men." *Philosophical Transactions of the Royal Society of London* 158 (1868): 505–27.

———. "On the Weight of the Brain in the Negro." *Anthropological Review* 7 (April 1869): 190–92.

Dawes, Anna Laurens. *Charles Sumner.* New York: Dodd, Mead, 1898.

Dennett, Tyler, ed. *Lincoln and the Civil War in the Diaries and Letters of John Hay.* New York: Dodd, Mead, 1939.

Desmond, Adrian. *Huxley: The Devil's Disciple.* London: Michael Joseph, 1994.

Desmond, Adrian, and James Moore. *Darwin's Sacred Cause: Race, Slavery, and the Quest for Human Origins.* London: Allen Lane, 2009.

———. *Darwin: The Life of a Tormented Evolutionist.* New York: Warner Books, 1991.

———. Introduction to *The Descent of Man, and Selection in Relation to Sex* by Charles Darwin, xi–lviii. London: Penguin, 2004.

Di Gregorio, Mario A. *Charles Darwin's Marginalia.* New York: Garland, 1990.

DiLorenzo, Thomas J. *The Real Lincoln: A New Look at Abraham Lincoln, His Agenda, and an Unnecessary War.* Roseville, CA: Forum/Prima, 2002.

Donald, David Herbert, ed. *Inside Lincoln's Cabinet: The Civil War Diaries of Salmon P. Chase.* New York: Longmans, Green, 1954.

———. *Lincoln.* New York: Simon & Schuster, 1995.

———. *Lincoln's Herndon: A Biography.* New York: Knopf, 1948.

Dow, Charles Mason. *Anthology and Bibliography of Niagara Falls.* 2 vols. Albany, NY: J. B. Lyon, 1921.

Duff, John J. *A. Lincoln: Prairie Lawyer.* New York: Rinehart, 1960.

du Pont, B. G. *E. I. du Pont de Nemours and Company, a History, 1802–1902.* Boston: Houghton Mifflin, 1920.

Dupree, A. Hunter. *Asa Gray: American Botanist, Friend of Darwin.* Baltimore, MD: Johns Hopkins University Press, 1988.

———. "The Founding of the National Academy of Sciences." *Proceedings of the American Philosophical Society* 101 (1957): 434–40.

———. *Science in the Federal Government: A History of Policies and Activities to 1940.* Cambridge, MA: Harvard University Press, 1957.

Emerson, Jason. *Lincoln the Inventor.* Carbondale: Southern Illinois University Press, 2009.

Ericsson, John. Papers. American Swedish Historical Society, Philadelphia, Pennsylvania.

Fehrenbacher, Don E. "Roger B. Taney and the Sectional Crisis." *Journal of Southern History* 43 (November 1977): 555–66.

Fehrenbacher, Don E., and Virginia Fehrenbacher. *Recollected Words of Abraham Lincoln.* Stanford, CA: Stanford University Press, 1996.

Ferris, Norman B. "Lincoln and Seward in Civil War Diplomacy." *JALA* 12 (1991): 21–42.

———. *The Trent Affair: A Diplomatic Crisis.* Knoxville: University of Tennessee Press, 1977.

Feuer, Lewis S. "Is the 'Darwin-Marx Correspondence' Authentic?" *Annals of Science* 32 (1975): 1–12.

"First Annual Report of the Illinois State Colonization Society; December 8, 1845." *African Repository* 22 (1846): 73–80.

Fitzhugh, George. "The Black and White Races of Men." *De Bow's Review* 30 (April 1861): 446–56.

———. *Sociology for the South, or, the Failure of Free Society.* Richmond, VA: A. Morris, 1854.

Flint, Austin, et al. *Rochester Knockings! Discovery and Explanation of the Source of the Phenomena Generally Known as the Rochester Knockings.* Buffalo, NY: George H. Derby, 1851.

Foner, Philip S., ed. *Frederick Douglass: Selected Speeches and Writings.* Chicago: Lawrence Hill Books, 1999.

Foreign Office (UK). General Correspondence before 1906, United States of America, series 2, Political and Other Departments, National Archives, Kew, United Kingdom.

Fredrickson, George M. *The Black Image in the White Mind: The Debate on Afro-American Character and Destiny 1817–1914.* New York: Harper Torchbooks, 1972.

Freehling, Alison Goodyear. *Drift toward Dissolution: The Virginia Slavery Debate of 1831–1832.* Baton Rouge: Louisiana State University Press, 1982.

Freehling, William W. "'Absurd' Issues and the Causes of the Civil War: Colonization as a Test Case." In *The Reintegration of American History: Slavery and the Civil War,* edited by William W. Freehling, 138–57. New York: Oxford University Press, 1994.

Freeman, R. B. "Darwin's Negro Bird-Stuffer." *Notes and Records of the Royal Society of London* 33 (August 1978): 83–86.

Gerzina, Gretchen. *Black England: Life before Emancipation.* London: John Murray, 1995.

Goodman, Paul. *Of One Blood: Abolitionism and the Origins of Racial Equality.* Berkeley: University of California Press, 1998.

Gopnik, Adam. *Angels and Ages: A Short Book about Darwin, Lincoln, and Modern Life.* New York: Knopf, 2009.

Gould, Benjamin A. *Investigations in the Military and Anthropological Statistics of American Soldiers.* Cambridge, MA: Riverside Press, 1869.

Gould, Stephen Jay. *I Have Landed: Splashes and Reflections in Natural History.* London: Vintage, 2003.

———. *The Mismeasure of Man.* Harmondsworth, UK: Penguin, 1981.

Graham, William. *The Creed of Science: Religious, Moral, and Social.* London: Kegan Paul, 1881.

Gray, Asa. "Darwin on the Origin of Species." *Atlantic Monthly* 6 (July and August 1860): 109–16, 229–39.

———. Review of Darwin's Theory on the Origin of Species by Means of Natural Selection. *American Journal of Science* 2nd series, 29 (March 1860): 153–84.

———. "Survival of the Fittest." *Nature* 7 (27 March 1873): 404.

Gray, Jane Loring, ed. *The Letters of Asa Gray.* 2 vols. Boston: Houghton Mifflin, 1893.

Great Britain. Foreign Office. "Political and Other Departments: General Correspondence before 1906, United States of America." Series 2 (1793–1905). Public Record Office, Kew.

Greeley, Horace, and John F. Cleveland, eds. *A Political Text-book for 1860: Comprising a*

Brief View of Presidential Nominations and Elections Including All the National Platforms Ever Yet Adopted. New York: Tribune, 1860.

Greg, William Rathbone. "On the Failure of 'Natural Selection' in the Case of Man." *Fraser's Magazine* 78 (September 1868): 353–62.

Gruber, Howard E. *Darwin on Man: A Psychological Study of Scientific Creativity.* London: Wildwood House, 1974.

Guelzo, Allen C. *Abraham Lincoln: Redeemer President.* Grand Rapids, MI: Eerdmans, 1999.

———. Introduction. *Holland's Life of Abraham Lincoln*, by Josiah Gilbert, vii–xxvi. 1866. Lincoln: University of Nebraska Press, 1998.

———. "Lincoln Aroused: His Outrage over the Kansas-Nebraska Act." *For the People: A Newsletter of the Abraham Lincoln Association* 2 (Summer 2009): 1–3.

———. *Lincoln's Emancipation Proclamation: The End of Slavery in America.* New York: Simon & Schuster, 2004.

Gurowski, Adam von. *Diary.* 3 vols. Vol. 1, Boston: Lee and Shepard, 1862; vol. 2, New York: Carleton, 1864; vol. 3, Washington, DC: Morrison, 1866.

Hall, James. *The Geology of New York, Part III, Survey of the 4th Geological District.* Albany, NY: Carroll & Cook, 1843.

Haller, John S., Jr. *Outcasts from Evolution: Scientific Attitudes of Racial Inferiority, 1859–1900.* Carbondale: Southern Illinois University Press, 1971.

Hameed, Salman. "Bracing for Islamic Creationism." *Science* 322 (12 December 2008): 1637–38.

Hancock, Harold B., and Norman Wilkinson. "'The Devil to Pay!' Saltpeter and the Trent Affair." *Civil War History* 10 (March 1964): 20–32.

Hardinge, Emma. *Modern American Spiritualism.* New York: Self-published, 1870.

Hare, Robert. *Experimental Investigation of the Spirit Manifestations.* New York: Partridge and Brittan, 1855.

Harper, Robert S. "New Light from a Lincoln Letter on the Story of the Publication of the Lincoln-Douglas Debates." *Ohio Historical Quarterly* 68 (April 1959): 177–87.

Hart, Richard E. "Springfield's African Americans as a Part of the Lincoln Community." *JALA* 20 (Winter 1999): 34–57.

Hay, John. *Letters of John Hay and Extracts from Diary.* Washington, DC: "printed but not published," 1908.

———. "Life in the White House in the Time of Lincoln." *Century Magazine* 41 (November 1890): 33–37.

Hendrickson, Walter B. "Nineteenth-Century State Geological Surveys: Early Government Support of Science." *Isis* 52 (September 1961): 357–71.

Herbert, Sandra. "The Place of Man in the Development of Darwin's Theory of Transmutation, Parts I and II." *Journal of the History of Biology* 7 (September 1974): 217–58 and 10 (September 1977): 155–227.

"Herndon's Auction List." See "Sale of Herndon's Books in Cincinnati."

Herndon-Weik Collection, Library of Congress.

Herndon, William H. "Abraham Lincoln's Religion." 18 February 1870. *Index* 1 (2 April 1870): 5–6.

———. "Abraham Lincoln's Religious Belief." *Truth Seeker*, 24 February 1883, 114–15.

———. "Analysis of the Character of Abraham Lincoln." *Abraham Lincoln Quarterly* 1 (1941): 403–41.

———. "Letter from Lincoln's Old Partner." *Religio-Philosophical Journal* (12 December 1885). In Hertz, *Hidden Lincoln*, 110.

———. "Lincoln's Religion." *Truth Seeker*, 10 March 1883, 148–49.

Herndon, William H., and Jesse Weik. *Herndon's Life of Lincoln.* 1889. Edited by Paul M. Angle. Cleveland, OH: World, 1942.

Hertz, Emanuel, ed. *The Hidden Lincoln: From the Letters and Papers of William H. Herndon.* New York: Viking Press, 1938.

Himmelfarb, Gertrude. *Darwin and the Darwinian Revolution.* London: Chatto & Windus, 1959.

———. *Victorian Minds: A Study of Intellectuals in Crisis and Ideologies in Transition.* New York: Knopf, 1968.

Historical Records Survey, Division of Professional and Service Projects. *Calendar of the Letters of Charles Robert Darwin to Asa Gray.* Boston: Works Projects Administration, 1939. Reprinted, Wilmington, DE: Scholarly Resources, 1973.

Hodge, Jonathan. "Darwin as a Lifelong Generation Theorist." In Kohn, *Darwinian Heritage,* 207–44.

———. "The Notebook Programmes and Projects of Darwin's London Years." In Hodge and Radick, *Cambridge Companion to Darwin,* 40–68.

Hodge, Jonathan, and Gregory Radick, eds. *The Cambridge Companion to Darwin.* Cambridge: Cambridge University Press, 2003.

Holland, Josiah Gilbert. *Life of Abraham Lincoln.* Springfield, MA: G. Bill, 1866.

Hollander, Barnett. *Slavery in America: Its Legal History.* London: Bowes & Bowes, 1962.

Hooker, J. D. *Flora Novæ-Zelandiæ.* London: Reeve, 1853–55.

Hughes, Kathryn. *George Eliot: The Last Victorian.* London: Fourth Estate, 1999.

Humboldt, Alexander von. *Cosmos: A Sketch of a Physical Description of the Universe.* Translated by E. C. Otté. 5 vols. London: George Bell, 1893.

Hunt, Edward B. "On the Origin, Growth, Substructure, and Chronology of the Florida Reef." *American Journal of Science* 35 (1863): 197–210.

Hunt, James. "Introductory Essay." *Anthropological Review* 1 (1863): 3–4.

———. "Miscegenation." *Anthropological Review* 20 (May 1864): 116–21.

———. *The Negro's Place in Nature.* London: Trübner, 1863.

———. "The Negro's Place in Nature." *Reader* 3 (19 March 1864): 368.

———. "On Ethno-Climatology; or the Acclimatization of Man." *Transactions of the Ethnological Society of London* 2 (1863): 50–79.

———. "On the Application of the Principle of Natural Selection to Anthropology." *Anthropological Review* 4 (1866): 320–40.

———. "The President's Address." *Journal of the Anthropological Society of London* 3 (1865): lxxxv–cxxxi.

Hunter, William S., Jr. *Hunter's Panoramic Guide from Niagara to Quebec.* Boston: J. P. Jewett, 1857.

Huxley, Leonard, ed. *Life and Letters of Sir Joseph Dalton Hooker.* 2 vols. London: John Murray, 1918.

———. *Life and Letters of Thomas Henry Huxley.* 3 vols. London: Macmillan, 1903.

Huxley, Thomas. "Contemporary Literature—Science," *Westminster Review* 62 (1854): 242–56.

———. "Emancipation—Black and White." *Reader* 5 (20 May 1865): 561–62.

———. *Evidence as to Man's Place in Nature.* London: Williams & Norgate, 1863.

———. "A Lecture on the Fossil Remains of Man." *Lancet* (15 February 1862): 166–67.

———. "Man and the Apes." *Athenaeum* 1744 (30 March 1861): 433; 1746 (13 April 1861): 498.

———. "Mr. Huxley on the Negro Question," *Reader* 3 (5 March 1864): 287–88.

———. "The Negro's Place in Nature." *Reader* 3 (12 March 1864): 334–35.

———. "On the Methods and Results of Ethnology." *Collected Essays,* 7:209–52. London: Macmillan, 1893–94.

————. "On the Zoological Relations of Man with the Lower Animals." *Natural History Review* 1 (1861): 67–84.

————. Papers. Thomas Henry Huxley Collection, Library Archives and Special Collections, Imperial College, London.

————. "Professor Huxley's Lectures 'On the Structure and Classification of the Mammalia.'" *Reader* 3 (27 February 1864): 266–68.

————. Review of *Vestiges of the Natural History of Creation*, by Robert Chambers, 10th edition. *British and Foreign Medico-Chirurgical Review* 13 (1854): 425–39.

————. "Science." *Westminster Review* 61 (1854): 264–65.

"Items of Intelligence." *African Repository* 21 (1845): 94–95.

Jaffa, Harry V. *Crisis of the Divided House: An Interpretation of the Issues of the Lincoln-Douglas Debates.* New York: Doubleday, 1959.

————. *A New Birth of Freedom: Abraham Lincoln and the Coming of the Civil War.* Lanham, MD: Rowman & Littlefield, 2000.

Jameson, J. F. "The London Expenditures of the Confederate Secret Service." *American Historical Review* 35 (1930): 811–24.

"January 11, 1859, Monthly Meeting." *Proceedings of the American Academy of Arts and Sciences* 4 (1857–60): 130–45.

Johannsen, Robert W., ed. *The Letters of Stephen A. Douglas.* Urbana: University of Illinois Press, 1961.

————, ed. *The Lincoln-Douglas Debates.* New York: Oxford University Press, 1965.

————. *Stephen A. Douglas.* New York: Oxford University Press, 1973.

Johnson, Robert Underwood, and Clarence Clough Buel, eds. *Battles and Leaders of the Civil War: Being for the Most Part Contributions by Union and Confederate Officers.* 4 vols. New York: Century, 1884–87.

Johnson, T. Walter. *Charles Reynolds Matheny 1786–1839: An Illinois Pioneer.* Springfield, IL: Privately printed, 1941.

Jordan, Winthrop D. *Black over White: American Attitudes towards the Negro 1550–1812.* Chapel Hill: University of North Carolina Press, 1968.

Kaplan, Sidney. "The Miscegenation Issue in the Election of 1864." *Journal of Negro History* 34 (1949): 274–343.

Keyes, Erasmus D. *Fifty Years' Observation of Men and Events Civil and Military.* New York: Scribner's, 1885.

Keynes, Randall. *Annie's Box: Charles Darwin, His Daughter and Human Evolution.* London: Fourth Estate, 2002.

Keynes, Richard D., ed. *Charles Darwin's* Beagle *Diary.* Cambridge: Cambridge University Press, 1988.

Kohn, David, ed. *The Darwinian Heritage.* Princeton, NJ: Princeton University Press, 1985.

Lamon, Ward Hill. *The Life of Abraham Lincoln: From His Birth to His Inauguration as President.* With Chauncey F. Black. Boston, MA: James R. Osgood, 1872.

Leidy, Joseph. Correspondence. Library, Academy of Natural Sciences, Philadelphia, Pennsylvania.

Leifchild, John R. Review of *On the Origin of Species*, by Charles Darwin. *Athenaeum* 1673 (19 November 1859): 659–60.

Levenson, J. C., Ernest Samuels, Charles Vandersee, and Viola H. Winner, eds. *Letters of Henry Adams, 1858–1892.* 3 vols. Cambridge, MA: Harvard University Press, 1982.

Lincoln, Abraham. *Discoveries and Inventions: A Lecture by Abraham Lincoln delivered in 1860.* San Francisco: John Howell, 1915.

Lincoln, Abraham. Papers. Library of Congress, Washington, D.C. Referred to as ALP.

———. Abraham Lincoln Collection, Abraham Lincoln Presidential Library, Illinois Historic Preservation Agency, Springfield, Illinois.

Litchfield, H. E., ed. *Emma Darwin, A Century of Family Letters, 1792–1896.* 2 vols. London: John Murray, 1915.

———, ed. *Emma Darwin, Wife of Charles Darwin. A Century of Family Letters.* Cambridge, UK: Cambridge University Press, 1904.

Livingstone, David N. *Adam's Ancestors: Race, Religion, and the Politics of Human Origins.* Baltimore, MD: Johns Hopkins University Press, 2008.

Long, Edward. *The History of Jamaica.* 3 vols. London, 1774.

Lossing, Benson J. *The Pictorial History of the Civil War in the United States of America.* 2 vols. Philadelphia, PA: George W. Childs, 1866.

Love, Alan C. "Darwin and Cirripedia prior to 1846: Exploring the Origins of the Barnacle Research." *Journal of the History of Biology* 35 (2002): 251–89.

Lurie, Edward. *Louis Agassiz: A Life in Science.* Baltimore, MD: Johns Hopkins University Press, 1988.

———. "Louis Agassiz and the Races of Man." *Isis* 45 (September 1954): 227–42.

Lyell, Charles. *The Geological Evidences of the Antiquity of Man.* London: John Murray, 1863.

———. *Principles of Geology.* 3 vols. London: John Murray, 1830.

———. *Principles of Geology.* 1830. 9th ed. London: John Murray, 1853.

———. *Second Visit to the United States of North America.* 2 vols. London: John Murray, 1849.

———. *Travels in North America in the Years 1841-2.* 2 vols. London: John Murray, 1845.

———. *Travels in North America in the Years 1841-2.* 2nd ed. 2 vols. London: John Murray, 1855.

Lyell, Katherine M., ed. *Life, Letters, and Journals of Sir Charles Lyell.* 2 vols. London: John Murray, 1881.

Magness, Phillip W. "Benjamin Butler's Colonization Testimony Reevaluated." *JALA* (Winter 2008): 1–28.

Mahin, Dean B. *One War at a Time: The International Dimensions of the American Civil War.* Dulles, VA: Brassey's, 2000.

Maltby, Charles. *The Life and Public Services of Abraham Lincoln.* Stockton, CA: Daily Independent Steam Power Print, 1884.

Marchant, James, ed. *Letters and Reminiscences of Alfred Russel Wallace.* 2 vols. London: Cassell, 1916.

Mariners' Museum Library, Newport News, Virginia.

Maynard, Nettie Colburn. *Was Abraham Lincoln a Spiritualist?* Chicago: Progressive Thinker, 1891.

McMillan, R. Bruce. "The First Century." *Living Museum* 64 (Summer/Fall 2002): 4.

McPherson, James M. *Tried by War: Abraham Lincoln as Commander in Chief.* New York: Penguin Press, 2008.

Mearns, David C. *The Lincoln Papers.* 2 vols. Garden City, NY: Doubleday, 1948.

Michael, John S. "A New Look at Morton's Craniological Research." *Current Anthropology* 29 (1988): 349–54.

Midgley, Clare. *Women against Slavery: British Campaigns, 1780–1870.* London: Routledge, 1992.

Miers, Earl S. ed. *Lincoln Day-by-Day: A Chronology 1809–1865.* 3 vols. Washington, DC: Lincoln Sesquicentennial Commission, 1960.

Miller, Eugene. "Democratic Statecraft and Technological Advance: Abraham Lincoln's Reflections on 'Discoveries and Inventions.'" *Review of Politics* 63 (2001): 485–515.

Miller, Hugh. *Footprints of the Creator. with a Memoir of the Author, by Louis Agassiz.* Boston: Gould, Kendall, & Lincoln, 1850.

Miller, John. "Evidence before the English Parliament in Favor of Liberia." *African Repository* 26 (1850): 83.

Miller, Jon D., Eugenie C. Scott, and Shinji Okamoto. "Public Acceptance of Evolution." *Science* 313 (11 August 2006): 765–66.

Miller, William Lee. *Lincoln's Virtues: An Ethical Biography.* New York: Vintage Books, 2003.

Milligan, John D. "From Theory to Application: The Emergence of the American Ironclad War Vessel." *Military Affairs* 48 (July 1984): 126–32.

Monaghan, Jay. *Diplomat in Carpet Slippers: Abraham Lincoln Deals with Foreign Affairs.* New York: Bobbs-Merrill, 1945.

———. "Was Abraham Lincoln Really a Spiritualist?" *Journal of the Illinois State Historical Society* 34 (June 1941): 209–32.

Moore, James. *The Darwin Legend.* Grand Rapids, MI: Baker Books, 1994.

Moore, R. Laurence. "Spiritualism and Science: Reflections on the First Decade of the Spirit Rappings." *American Quarterly* 24 (October 1972): 474–500.

Morris, P. J. "Louis Agassiz's Additions to the French Translation of His Essay on Classification." *Journal of the History of Biology* 30 (1997): 121–34.

Morton, Brian N., and Donald C. Spinelli. *Beaumarchais and the American Revolution.* Lanham, MD: Rowman & Littlefield, 2003.

Morton, Samuel George. "Hybridity in Animals, Considered in Reference to the Question of the Unity of the Human Species." *American Journal of Science* 3 (1847): 39–50, 203–12.

National Archives and Records Administration. RG56, series AB, Letters from Executive Officers, General Records, Treasury Department, 1861. Washington, D.C.

———. RG71, Miscellaneous Letters Sent and Recd, Bureau of Yards and Docks 1861–63. Washington, DC..

Neely, Mark E. "Abraham Lincoln and Black Colonization: Benjamin Butler's Spurious Testimony." *Civil War History* 25 (1979): 77–83.

Nevins, Allen. *Ordeal of the Union.* 2 vols. New York: Scribner's, 1947.

Newcomb, Simon. "Memoir of Joseph Henry [1880]." In *Biographical Memoirs,* 5:1–35. Washington, DC: National Academy of Sciences, 1905.

———. *Reminiscences of an Astronomer.* Boston: Houghton Mifflin, 1903.

Newton, John Fort. *Lincoln and Herndon.* Cedar Rapids, IA: Torch Press, 1910.

Newton, T. W. L. *Lord Lyons: A Record of British Diplomacy.* 2 vols. London: Edward Arnold, 1913.

"New War Steamers." *Scientific American,* 12 January 1861, 25.

Nicolay, John G. Papers. Library of Congress.

Nicolay, John G., and John Hay. *Abraham Lincoln: A History.* 10 vols. New York: Century, 1890.

———, eds. *The Complete Works of Abraham Lincoln.* 2 vols. New York: Century, 1894.

Niven, John. *Gideon Welles: Lincoln's Secretary of the Navy.* New York: Oxford University Press, 1973.

Nott, Josiah C. "Diversity of the Human Race." *De Bow's Review* 10 (February 1851): 113–32.

———. "Instincts of Races." *New Orleans Medical and Surgical Journal* 19 (1866): 1–16, 145–56.

———. "Life Insurance at the South." *De Bow's Review* 3 (May 1847): 357–76.

———. "The Mulatto a Hybrid—Probable Extermination of the Two Races If the Whites and Blacks Are Allowed to Intermarry." *American Journal of the Medical Sciences* 6 (1843): 252–56.

———. *The Negro Race: Its Ethnology and History.* Mobile, AL: Mobile Daily Times, 1866.

———. "Statistics of Southern Slave Population." *De Bow's Review* 4 (November 1847): 275–89.

———. *Two Lectures on the Connection between the Biblical and Physical History of Man.* New York: Bartlett & Welford, 1849.

———. *Two Lectures on the Natural History of the Caucasian and Negro Races*. Mobile, AL: Dade & Thompson, 1844.

Nott, Josiah C., and George R. Gliddon. *Indigenous Races of the Earth*. Philadelphia, PA: Lippincott, 1857.

———. *Types of Mankind: or, Ethnological Researches, Based upon the Ancient Monuments, Painting, Sculptures, and Crania of Races and upon Their Natural, Geographical, Philological, and Biblical History*. Philadelphia, PA: Lippincott, Grambo, 1854.

Official Records of the Union and Confederate Navies in the War of the Rebellion. Washington, DC: GPO, 1894–1922.

Oldroyd, Osborn H. *The Lincoln Memorial; Album-immortelles*. New York: G. W. Carleton, 1883.

Olmsted, Frederick Law. *A Journey in the Back Country*. London: Sampson, Low, Son, 1860.

———. *A Journey in the Seaboard Slave States, with Remarks on Their Economy*. New York: Dix & Edwards, 1856.

———. *A Journey through Texas; or, a Saddle-trip on the Southwestern Frontier*. New York: Dix & Edwards, 1857.

Owen, Richard. "The Gorilla and the Negro." *Athenaeum* 1743 (23 March 1861): 395–96.

Owsley, Frank L. *King Cotton Diplomacy: Foreign Relations of the Confederate States of America*. Chicago: University of Chicago Press, 1959.

Paul, Diane B. "Darwin, Social Darwinism, and Eugenics." In Hodge and Radick, *Cambridge Companion to Darwin*, 214–37.

Pearson, Karl. *The Life, Letters, and Labours of Francis Galton*. 3 vols. Cambridge, UK: Cambridge University Press, 1914–30.

Pease, Theodore C., and James G. Randall, eds. *The Diary of Orville Hickman Browning*. 3 vols. Springfield: Illinois State Historical Library, 1925–31.

Peirce, Benjamin. Papers. Houghton Library, Harvard College Library, Harvard University, Cambridge, Massachusetts.

Perret, Geoffrey. *Lincoln's War: The Untold Story of America's Greatest President as Commander in Chief*. New York: Random House, 2004.

Perry, Bliss, ed. *Little Masterpieces. Abraham Lincoln: Early Speeches, Springfield Speech, Cooper Union Speech, Inaugural Addresses, Gettysburg Address, Selected Letters, Lincoln's Lost Speech*. New York: Doubleday & McClure, 1898.

Pickering, Charles. *The Races of Man; and their Geographical Distribution. New Edition*. London: Bohn's Illustrated Library, 1850.

Pierce, Edward L. *Memoir and Letters of Charles Sumner*. 4 vols. Boston: Roberts Brothers, 1877–93.

Pinsker, Matthew. "Not Always Such a Whig: Abraham Lincoln's Partisan Realignment in the 1850's." *JALA* 29 (Summer 2008): 27–46.

Porter, Roy, and G. S. Rousseau. *Gout: The Patrician Malady*. New Haven, CT: Yale University Press, 1998.

Pratt, Henry E. "Abraham Lincoln's Religion: His Own Statement." *Abraham Lincoln Quarterly* 2 (March 1942): 1–4.

Pullen, John J. "Who Wrote 'The World's Best Book Review'?" *New England Quarterly* 59 (June 1986): 252–59.

Putnam, Allen. *Agassiz and Spiritualism, Involving the Investigation of Harvard College Professors in 1857*. Boston: Colby and Rich, 1874.

Pybus, Cassandra. "Jefferson's Faulty Math: The Question of Slave Defections in the American Revolution." *William and Mary Quarterly* 62 (April 2005): 243–64.

Quarles, Benjamin. *Lincoln and the Negro*. New York: Oxford University Press, 1962.

———. *The Negro in the American Revolution*. Chapel Hill: University of North Carolina Press, 1961.

Raby, Peter. *Alfred Russel Wallace: A Life*. London: Chatto & Windus, 2001.

Rainger, Ronald. "Race, Politics, and Science: The Anthropological Society of London in the 1860s." *Victorian Studies* 22 (1978): 51–70.

Rankin, Henry B. *Personal Recollections of Abraham Lincoln*. New York: Putnam, 1916.

Raymond, Henry J. *The Life and Public Services of Abraham Lincoln*. New York: Darby and Miller, 1865.

Reed, James A. "The Later Life and Religious Sentiments of Abraham Lincoln." *Scribner's Monthly* 6, July 1873, 333–43.

Register of Debates. 14 vols. Washington, DC: Gales & Seaton, 1824–37.

Reilly, Robin. *Josiah Wedgwood 1730–1795*. London: Macmillan, 1992.

Reingold, Nathan. "Science in the Civil War. The Permanent Commission of the Navy Department." *Isis* 49 (September 1958): 307–18.

Remsburg, John E. *Abraham Lincoln: Was He a Christian?* New York: Truth Seeker, 1893.

Review of *The Natural History of New-York*. *United States Democratic Review* 19 (December 1846): 433–41; 20 (January 1847): 22–26.

Review of "The Original Unity of the Human Race—Pickering, Bachman, Agassiz." *New Englander and Yale Review* 8 (November 1850): 542–85.

"Revolution in Naval Warfare. Shot-Proof Iron Steamships." *Harper's Weekly*, 9 February 1861, 92–93.

Rice, Allen Thorndike, ed. *Reminiscences of Abraham Lincoln by Distinguished Men of His Time*. New York: Harper & Brothers, 1889.

Richards Manuscript Collection. Howard Gottlieb Archival Research Centre, Boston University, Boston.

Roane, A. "Moral and Intellectual Diversity of Races." *De Bow's Review* 21 (July 1856): 63–70.

Roberts, William H. "'The Name of Ericsson': Political Engineering in the Union Ironclad Program, 1861–1863." *Journal of Military History* 63 (October 1999): 823–43.

Rothenberg, Marc, Kathleen W. Dorman and Frank R. Millikan, eds. *The Papers of Joseph Henry. Volume 10: January 1858–December 1865, The Smithsonian Years*. Washington, DC: Smithsonian Institution Press, 2004.

Rudwick, Martin J. S. Introduction. *Principles of Geology* by Charles Lyell, 1:vii–xli. Chicago: University of Chicago Press, 1990–91.

Russell, William Howard. *My Diary North and South*. London: Bradbury and Evans, 1863.

Rybczynski, Witold. *A Clearing in the Distance: Frederick Law Olmsted and America in the Nineteenth Century*. New York: Scribner, 1999.

"Sale of Herndon's Books in Cincinnati" ["Herndon's Auction List"]. Broadside. January 10 and 11, 1873, no. 20, portfolio 345, W. O. Davie. Ephemera Collection, Library of Congress.

Scheips, Paul J. "Buchanan and the Chiriqui Naval Station Sites." *Military Affairs* 18 (Summer 1954): 64–80.

———. "Lincoln and the Chiriqui Colonization Project." *Journal of Negro History* 37 (October 1952): 418–53.

Schneller, Robert J. *A Quest for Glory: A Biography of Rear Admiral John A. Dahlgren*. Annapolis, MD: Naval Institute Press, 1996.

Schoonover, Thomas. "Misconstrued Mission: Expansionism and Black Colonization in Mexico and Central America during the Civil War." *Pacific Historical Review* 49 (November 1980): 607–20.

Schwartz, Thomas F. "'About New Powder': An Unpublished Lincoln Note." *Illinois Historical Journal* 84 (Summer 1991): 119–24.

Secord, James A. *Victorian Sensation: The Extraordinary Publication, Reception, and Secret Authorship of* Vestiges of the Natural History of Creation. Chicago: University of Chicago Press, 2000.

Seward, William H. Papers. Rare Books and Special Collection. University of Rochester, Rochester, New York.

Seward, Frederick William. *Reminiscences of a War-Time Statesman and Diplomat: 1830–1915.* New York: Putnam, 1916.

Sherwood, Henry Noble. "The Formation of the American Colonization Society." *Journal of Negro History* 2 (July 1917): 209–28.

Sickles, Daniel E. "Military Affairs in New York: 1861–1865." In *The Union Army: a History of Military Affairs in the Loyal States, 1861–65,* 2:18–44. Madison, WI: Federal, 1908.

Silliman, Robert H. "The Hamlet Affair: Charles Lyell and the North Americans." *Isis* 86 (December 1995): 541–61.

Speed, Joshua F. *Reminiscences of Abraham Lincoln and Notes of a Visit to California.* Louisville: John P. Morton, 1884.

Sproat, John G. "Blueprint for Radical Reconstruction." *Journal of Southern History* 23 (1957): 25–44.

Squier, E. G. "American Ethnology: Being a Summary of Some of the Results Which Have Followed the Investigation of This Subject." *American Whig Review* 9 (April 1849): 385–99.

———. "Notices of New Books. Science of Man and Nations, Types of Mankind." *New York Herald* (23 April 1854).

Stanton, William. *The Leopard's Spots: Scientific Attitudes toward Race in America, 1815–59.* Chicago: University of Chicago Press, 1960.

Staudenraus, P. J. *The African Colonization Movement, 1816–1865.* New York: Columbia University Press, 1961.

Stauffer, R. C., ed. *Charles Darwin's Natural Selection: Being the Second Part of His Big Species Book Written from 1856 to 1858.* Cambridge, UK: Cambridge University Press, 1975.

Stephen, Leslie. *The "Times" on the American War: A Historical Study.* New York: Abbatt, 1865.

Stevens, Walter B. *A Reporter's Lincoln.* St. Louis: Missouri Historical Society, 1916.

Stillé, Charles J. *History of the United States Sanitary Commission.* Philadelphia, PA: Lippincott, 1866.

Stocking, George W. *Victorian Anthropology.* New York: Free Press, 1987.

Stoddard, William O. *Abraham Lincoln and Andrew Johnson.* New York: F. A. Stokes & Brother, 1888.

———. *Inside the White House in War Times.* New York: Charles L. Webster, 1890.

Stott, Rebecca. *Darwin and the Barnacle: The Story of One Tiny Creature and History's Most Spectacular Breakthrough.* London: Faber and Faber, 2003.

Sulloway, Frank. "Darwin and His Finches: The Evolution of a Legend." *Journal of the History of Biology* 15 (1982): 1–53.

Tarbell, Ida. *In the Footsteps of the Lincolns.* New York: Harper & Brothers, 1924.

Temple, Sunderine, and Wayne C. Temple. *Illinois' Fifth Capitol: the House That Lincoln Built and Caused to Be Re-Built (1837–1865).* Springfield: Phillips Brothers, 1988.

Temple, Wayne C. *Abraham Lincoln: From Skeptic to Prophet.* Mahomet, IL: Mayhaven, 1995.

———. "Herndon on Lincoln: An Unknown Interview with a List of Books in the Lincoln & Herndon Law Office." *Journal of the Illinois State Historical Society* 98 (Spring–Summer 2005): 34–50.

———. *Lincoln's Connections with the Illinois & Michigan Canal, His Return from Congress in '48, and His Invention.* Springfield: Illinois Bell, 1986.

———. "Lincoln the Lecturer. Part 1." *Lincoln Herald* 101, no. 3 (1999): 94–110.

———. "Lincoln the Lecturer. Part 2." *Lincoln Herald* 101, no. 4 (1999): 146–63.

Townsend, George Alfred. *The Real Life of Abraham Lincoln: A Talk with Mr. Herndon.* New York: Publication Office, Bible House, 1867.

Trueblood, Elton. *Abraham Lincoln: Theologian of American Anguish.* New York: Harper & Row, 1973.

True, Frederick W. *A History of the First Half-Century of the National Academy of Sciences: 1863–1913.* Washington, DC: National Academy of Sciences, 1913.

Turner, Justin G., and Linda Levitt Turner. *Mary Todd Lincoln: Her Life and Letters.* New York: Knopf, 1972.

USS *Monitor* Design and Construction Collection. Mariners' Museum Library, Newport News, Virginia.

Van Evrie, John H. Introduction. In *The Negro's Place in Nature: A Paper Read before the London Anthropological Society,* by James Hunt, 3–4. New York: Van Evrie, Horton, 1864.

———. *Negroes and Negro "Slavery": The First an Inferior Race; the Latter Its Normal Condition.* Baltimore, MD: J. D. Toy, 1853.

———. *Negroes and Negro "Slavery": The First an Inferior Race; the Latter Its Normal Condition.* New York: Van Evrie, Horton, 1861.

———. *Subgenation: The Theory of the Normal Relation of the Races; an Answer to "Miscegenation."* New York: Bradburn, 1864.

———. *White Supremacy and Negro Subordination; or, Negroes a Subordinate Race, and So-Called Slavery Its Normal Condition.* New York: Van Evrie, Horton, 1868.

Verduin, Paul H. "Brief Outline of the Joseph Hanks Family." In Wilson and Davis, *Herndon's Informants,* 779–83.

Vogt, Karl. *Lectures on Man: His Place in Creation, and the History of Earth.* Edited by James Hunt. London: Longman, Green, Longman, and Roberts, 1864.

———. *Vorlesungen über den Menschen, seine Stellung in der Schöpfung und in der Geschichte der Erde.* 2 vols. Geissen, Germany: J. Ricker, 1863.

Vorenberg, Michael. "Abraham Lincoln and the Politics of Black Colonization." *JALA* 14 (Summer 1993): 22–45.

———. *Final Freedom: The Civil War, the Abolition of Slavery, and the Thirteenth Amendment.* Cambridge, UK: Cambridge University Press, 2004.

Wallace, Alfred Russel. *My Life: a Record of Events and Opinions.* London: Chapman & Hall, 1905.

———. *On Miracles and Modern Spiritualism: Three Essays.* 1875. 3rd ed. London: James Burns, 1896.

———. "On the Law Which Has Regulated the Introduction of New Species." *Annals and Magazine of Natural History* ser. 2, 16 (September 1855): 184–96.

———. "The Origin of Human Races and the Antiquity of Man Deduced from the Theory of 'Natural Selection.'" *Journal of the Anthropological Society of London* 2 (1864): clviii–clxxxvii.

———. "Sir Charles Lyell on Geological Climates and the Origin of Species." *Quarterly Review* 126 (1869): 359–94.

War of the Rebellion: A Compilation of the Official Records of the Union and Confederate Armies, The. Washington, DC: GPO, 1880–1901.

Warren, Louis A. *Lincoln's Youth: Indiana Years, Seven to Twenty-One.* New York: Appleton-Century-Crofts, 1959.

Waterton, Charles. *Essays on Natural History, Chiefly Ornithology.* London: Longman, 1838.

———. *Wanderings in South America, the North-west of the United States, and the Antilles in the Years 1812, 1820, & 1824.* London: J. Mawman, 1825.

Wedgwood-Mosley Collection. Wedgwood Museum, Barlaston, Stoke-on-Trent, United Kingdom.

Weikart, Richard. *From Darwin to Hitler: Evolutionary Ethics, Eugenics, and Racism in Germany.* New York: Palgrave MacMillan, 2004.

Weisberg, Barbara. *Talking to the Dead: Kate and Maggie Fox and the Rise of Spiritualism.* New York: Harper, 2004.

Welles, Gideon. *Lincoln and Seward.* New York: Sheldon, 1874.

Wells, David A., ed. "Improvements in the Fabrication of Arms at the United States Armories." In *Annual of Scientific Discovery*, 91–92. Boston: Gould and Lincoln, 1856.

———. "Notes by the Editor on the Progress of Science during the Year 1854." In *Annual of Scientific Discovery*, 23–24. Boston: Gould and Lincoln, 1855.

Whitney, Henry C. *Life on the Circuit with Lincoln.* Boston: Estes & Lauriat, 1892.

Wilkinson, Norman B. *Lammot du Pont and the American Explosives Industry 1850–1884.* Charlottesville: University Press of Virginia, 1984.

Wills, Garry. *Inventing America: Jefferson's Declaration of Independence.* New York: Doubleday, 1978.

———. *Lincoln at Gettysburg: The Words That Remade America.* New York: Touchstone, 1992.

Wilson, Clyde N., ed. *The Papers of John C. Calhoun.* 28 vols. Columbia: University of South Carolina Press, 1995.

Wilson, David. *Carlyle in Old Age.* London: K. Paul, Trench, and Trübner, 1934.

Wilson, Douglas L. *Honor's Voice: The Transformation of Abraham Lincoln.* New York: Knopf, 1998.

———. "A Most Abandoned Hypocrite." *American Heritage* 45 (February–March 1994): 36–49.

———. "The Unfinished Text of the Lincoln-Douglas Debates." *JALA* 15 (Winter 1994): 70–85.

Wilson, Douglas L., and Rodney O. Davis, eds. *Herndon's Informants: Letters, Interviews, and Statements about Abraham Lincoln.* Urbana: University of Illinois Press, 1998. Referred to as *HI*.

Wilson, Leonard G., ed. *Sir Charles Lyell's Scientific Journals on the Species Question.* New Haven, CT: Yale University Press, 1970.

Winsor, Mary P. *Reading the Shape of Nature: Comparative Zoology at the Agassiz Museum.* Chicago: University of Chicago Press, 1991.

Winterthur Manuscripts. Hagley Museum and Library, Wilmington, Delaware.

Woodward, Llewellyn. *The Age of Reform: 1815–1870.* Oxford: Clarendon Press, 1962.

Wyhe, John van, dir. *The Complete Work of Charles Darwin Online. Arts and Research Council*, 2002–10. http://darwin-online.org.uk.

———. "Mind the Gap: Did Darwin Avoid Publishing His Theory for Many Years?" *Notes and Records of the Royal Society* 61 (May 2007): 177–205.

Young, Robert M. "Darwinism *Is* Social." In Kohn, *Darwinian Heritage*, 609–38.

Zilversmit, Arthur. "Lincoln and the Problem of Race: A Decade of Interpretations." *JALA* 2 (1980): 21–44.

Index

James Lander was born and raised in California but has spent most of his life in Britain. He holds degrees from American and British universities in history, classics, and archaeology and has taught U.S. history and European history at an American school in England for twenty-five years. He has published works on archaeology and local history, as well as articles in historical journals.